Killarney Bay

Memoirs of the Museum of Anthropology
University of Michigan
Number 62

Killarney Bay

The Archaeology of an Early Middle Woodland Aggregation Site in the Northern Great Lakes

edited by David Brose, Patrick Julig, and John O'Shea

Ann Arbor, Michigan
2021

Printed in the United States of America
ISBN 978-0-915703-97-5 (print)
ISBN 978-0-915703-98-2 (ebook)

Cover design by John Klausmeyer

Buy this book at **www.press.umich.edu/12037795**.
Browse all of our books at **sites.lsa.umich.edu/archaeology-books**.
Visit the Museum website at **lsa.umich.edu/ummaa**.

The University of Michigan Museum of Anthropological Archaeology (UMMAA) publishes books on archaeology and anthropology.
For permissions, questions, or manuscript queries, contact Museum publications in Ann Arbor, Michigan, by email at umma-pubs@umich.edu.

Library of Congress Cataloging-in-Publication data has been applied for.
Library of Congress Control Number (LCCN): 2021041444
LC record available at https://lccn.loc.gov/2021041444

The paper used in this publication meets the requirements of the ANSI Standard Z39.48-1984 (Permanence of Paper).

Table of Contents

Part III. Materials Recovered during Excavations at Killarney Bay

Part IV. Conclusions

Appendices

Bibliography

Foreword

This volume presents detailed description with meticulous attention to context and material nuances, which the Killarney Bay site (also known as KB-1, KB1, BlHl-1, and the Speigel site) richly deserves. The site has long been known in the oral traditions of Great Lakes archaeology, though with only a minimal preliminary publication (Greenman 1966). Without a report, it was difficult to assess claims for the pivotal place of this site in the network of relations between people throughout the vast northeastern portion of North America during the Early Woodland period.

My own interest in the site is rooted in early experiences with the question of the Adena people (Webb and Snow 1945; Webb and Baby 1957), whose homeland was in middle Ohio Valley (today southern Ohio and eastern Kentucky and parts of Indiana and West Virginia). However, far from this central concentration—on the Middle Atlantic Coast, in the far northeast, and in the Great Lakes region—there were finds of distinctive stemmed bifacially flaked points, tubular pipes, geometric polished stone pendants, and other distinctive items that typified the Adena in their heartland. This vast dispersal of characteristic Adena artifacts was initially explained in terms of "trade" (Griffin 1952:358).

Subsequently, a more careful consideration of the seemly ceremonial context of those few items that had been carefully excavated led William Ritchie and Don Dragoo (1959) to elaborate a model of cultic conflict and dispersion. In this proposition, an Adena "cult" was displaced by the newer Hopewell belief systems, and the practitioners of the older cult fled the Ohio Valley with their paraphernalia and joined distant groups, where eventually these paraphernalia were buried by their hosts, who knew not the proper Adena burial rituals.

The 1946 to 1953 and 1981 to 2002 excavations at Site KB-1 near Killarney, east of Manitoulin Island in Ontario, yielded what were then thought to be Adena points and tubular pipes. Thus the site could provide evidence with which to evaluate such propositions and new ones not yet devised. The basis of any such endeavor would be a detailed monographic publication of all work at the site, describing excavations, contexts, and cultural materials from all prior excavations. Fortunately, the diverse field records and most of the excavated materials have been carefully curated in United States and Canadian museums. The materials are therefore available for re-study with methods that earlier twentieth-century archaeologists could hardly have imagined.

When I arrived in Ann Arbor for my freshman year in September 1960, I was put to work as an assistant in what was then the Museum of Anthropology. The director, James B. Griffin, assigned me to work under Lewis Binford, then a lecturer and research associate standing in for his professor, Albert C. Spaulding, who had become head of the anthropology program at the National Science Foundation.

We students wondered about the identity of an elderly white-haired man we occasionally saw, and eventually learned he was Emerson Greenman, one of the first archaeologists to specialize in the prehistory of the Great Lakes region. He was born near Owosso, Michigan, in 1895, and commenced studies at the University of Michigan in 1916. He trained in archaeology with Francis Kelsey, an eminent classical archaeologist. Greenman's studies were interrupted by Army service during WWI, but he returned to complete his AB in 1923. After graduation, Greenman did additional training in anthropology at the University of Oxford, visited Paleolithic sites in France under the auspices of the American School of Prehistoric Research, and returned to his studies in Ann Arbor, where he received a PhD in 1927. In 1928, Greenman took the post of curator of archaeology with the Ohio State Historical Society and did a number of excavations for them. Perhaps most important of these was his excavation of the Coon Mound, in which he demonstrated the existence of the Adena culture.

In 1935, Greenman returned to Ann Arbor, where he focused on the systematic excavation of later Woodland sites and the training of students in the field. "Doc," as he was known, became increasingly aware of the many former beaches of earlier stages of the Great Lakes. Working with Michigan Pleistocene geologist George Stanley, he documented the association of ancient beaches with stone tools (Greenman and Stanley 1941). His trips in the late 1930s with Stanley to examine sites on the Canadian shores of Lake Huron led to a succession of field schools near Killarney.

Binford had never worked with Greenman, but he regaled the students with secondhand stories of the Killarney Bay field schools and of flaked stone knives still in wooden handles, copper celts still wrapped in beaver pelt pouches, and thoughts about the kind of social analyses one might do with material of such extraordinary preservation. I was curious to see these tools.

Eventually, Greenman had finished his many reports on sites of the Middle and Late Woodland periods in Lower Michigan and was teaching his final courses and preparing to retire. There remained only the Killarney Bay collections. He kept these in locked cabinets. The question for him was whether to focus on his excavations at Killarney Bay Site 1 (KB-1), with Early Woodland Adena related artifacts, or Killarney Bay Site 2 (KB-2), a large quartzite quarry articulated with proglacial lake beaches, thought to date to the Archaic period and perhaps earlier. Perhaps his interest in Paleolithic Pleistocene cultures from his travels in Europe outweighed his interest in the Early Woodland Adena culture from his years in Ohio. He chose to start with the KB-2 quarry site. Now Doc faced the task of analyzing and reporting on tens of thousands of white quartzite chunks, flakes, and biface fragments. He would occasionally unlock the cabinets where many of them were stored and puzzle over them.

As fate would have it, Greenman was unable to finish either of his Killarney reports. The material remained locked long after Greenman died in 1973.

One day the cabinet was left unlocked and I had a quick look—not only at the KB-2 flakes, but at the large KB-1 hafted bifaces with lashed wooden handles, the objects wrapped in organic materials, and the tubular pipes. Various of Greenman's successors as curators of the Great Lakes Range considered the idea of writing up one or both of the Killarney Bay sites, but one hesitates to work on sites excavated by people long gone with the methods of years past. It was only when John O'Shea, David Brose, and Patrick Julig conceived of the idea of bringing all the extant data on KB-1 together that there was some hope of learning what happened on Killarney Bay two millennia ago. They planned a volume that would integrate not only the poorly documented late nineteenth-century investigations of Robert Bell and the mid twentieth-century excavations of Emerson F. Greenman's University of Michigan team, but the more precise excavations of the site's occupational area at the end of the twentieth century and the opening of the twenty-first by Laurentian University teams under the direction Helen Devereux, Ken Buchanan, and Patrick Julig. Many of the artifacts recovered from the different excavations would be studied with new methods only recently available.

This monograph is the result of that collaboration. Its composition proved to be more difficult than anyone anticipated, but it has resulted in startling interrelated conclusions about the site. First, a state-of-the-art analysis of a large suite of radiocarbon dates by Julig and O'Shea indicates that the occupational area excavated by the Laurentian University teams and the burial area excavated by the Michigan teams were used during the same 540-year span of time, approximately 330 BC to AD 210. Second, given this span of time and the number of mortuary features, mortuary ceremonies could have happened only occasionally at Killarney Bay. Perhaps some people did not merit the elaborate burial ritual which would create recognizable features, or perhaps some people were buried elsewhere. The simplest explanation, however, is that within these five centuries, the locality was only periodically occupied. This implies that there were other localities within which the earlier Woodland community of the Killarney Bay area moved cyclically.

Alas, the careful study by Julig of what we know about contexts and artifact distribution in the occupational area shows that two millennia of post-depositional disturbance, ending with cultivation as a potato patch, has compromised any hope of recognizing discrete reoccupations. However, the periodicity implies that there must be other similar sites in the area that can be studied with innovative methods in the future.

Some indication of the periodic use of different localities is implied by the results of the preliminary petrographic analyses of eleven sherds by Mathieu, which reveal considerable variability in proportions of locally common tempers, probably indicating different origins of pottery vessels within the area. Only a study of larger samples, and samples from other sites, can confirm this.

The other common form of cultural debris at Killarney Bay—flaked stone raw material, identified by a range of experts using optical microscopy—has been evaluated by Kamber and Long using inductively coupled plasma mass spectroscopy (ICP-MS) analysis of cherts to characterize trace and rare earth (REE) element distributions. Though limited by the availability of source samples, they show that most tools are made from material available within 250 km of Killarney Bay. Many are available from easily exploited beach and river gravel sources. Some tool stones, however, particularly those found in the mortuary area, are made from material found only in distant sources—as far away as 1600 km to the west and 700 to 900 km to the north and south.

The innovative lipid analysis of Malainey compensates for the absence of well-preserved fish or mammal bones or carbonized seeds or nut fragments at Killarney Bay. Malainey used various forms of gas chromatography with mass spectrometry (HT-GC/MS) to document a balance of floral and terrestrial and lacustrine food preparation in ceramic containers. Tucked away in such technical studies are some surprising nuggets of information. For example, Malainey notes the presence of diagnostic acids that indicate the presence of conifer products. Killarney Bay is solidly fringed with spruce (*Picea* sp.), and spruce needle and bark teas are good sources of Vitamin C, the lack of which was often a problem for Great Lakes peoples (Ford 1977; Yarnell 1964).

Beyond the basics of time, ecology, materials, and subsistence, this study has implications for broader cultural questions. The detailed study by David Brose of earlier Woodland ceramic styles in the Upper and Middle Great Lakes embodies the current state of knowledge of the broader stylistic relations of what has sometimes been called the "Lake Forest Middle Woodland"—an area extending more than 2000 km, from Lake Manitoba on the west to Lake Ontario on the east and beyond.

The very success of this monograph raises new questions and suggests new directions for future research. Chronology remains an enduring problem on both the scale of the region and for understanding the dynamics of local site use and reoccupation. The ability to combine early bulk carbon and new AMS-derived radiocarbon dates via Bayesian modeling offers potential, but only methods more precise than those available today will allow us to resolve fine-grained issues such as the periodicity of site occupation.

The characteristic poor preservation of organic remains in forested environments presents a serious challenge to documenting diet and subsistence. Yet the analyses of organic residues presented in this monograph suggest alternative ways to achieve a broad understanding of subsistence economies, particularly as these methods are applied to new samples from sealed contexts. It should be possible to recover phytoliths, pollen, and organic molecular traces from plant foods. It should likewise be possible to recover molecular traces of the fish and mammals hunted and consumed by early Great Lakes peoples, even in archaeological settings where bone is not preserved.

Finally, what we term "stylistic relations," if reconceptualized as products of symbolic processes, may be much more informative than what we now believe possible. We cannot hear long dead speech or decode ancient meanings, but we can use the evidence we have to answer questions, not only about material processes involving technology or diet or the treatment of the dead, but about past migrations, social processes, and symbolic structures.

Henry T. Wright
Ann Arbor, Michigan

Preface

Killarney Bay is one of the most iconic archaeological sites in the Upper Great Lakes. It is also one of the most poorly known. The copper ornaments, exotic tubular pipes, hafted bifaces, and preserved fabrics all add to the site's mystique, which is amplified still further by the absence of any final or authoritative publication of the site and its materials. The very long and discontinuous history of research at the site, along with the involvement of multiple investigators from multiple institutions in both Canada and the United States, have all contributed to the absence of a final report. It is this absence that the present volume strives to correct.

My personal involvement with the Killarney Bay site began, literally, on my first day as curator of Great Lakes Archaeology at the University of Michigan Museum of Anthropological Archaeology (UMMAA). It was a letter addressed to the Curator of Great Lakes Archaeology from James V. Wright, in which he suggested that as Michigan was not interested in the collection, it should be transferred to the National Museum of Man (later to be the Canadian Museum of Civilization, and currently the Canadian Museum of History). The letter elicited a laugh from Richard Ford, then the UMMAA director, who told me not to worry about it, as the Canadians periodically made such demands. Later that same year I received a request from Helen Devereux, a professor and archaeologist at Laurentian University in Ontario, to examine the Killarney Bay collections and records at UMMAA. There clearly was more to the story than I was aware of, as the chapters in this volume illustrate.

The existence of the present volume is due to the diligence and persistence of the two senior editors, David Brose and Patrick Julig. While both had interests in the site, they came to it from different perspectives: Brose with a focus on the Middle Woodland adaptations of the Upper Great Lakes, and Julig with a long-term interest in the regional archaeology of Manitoulin Island and northern Lake Huron. Each also felt a nagging obligation to bring the site to publication: Julig as the director of some of the later excavations in the habitation area of the site, and Brose as a former graduate student at the University of Michigan who had observed firsthand Emerson Greenman's troubled relationship to the site materials and the Museum. Together they brought complementary analytical skills to the project and were able to enlist the range of scholarly and analytical expertise needed to create a comprehensive report on the site in all its manifestations.

The unsung hero of the volume is UMMAA editor, Elizabeth Noll. She inherited the difficult job of melding together manuscripts written by multiple authors from different national and academic traditions that had been accumulated over more than ten years. As the volume began to take shape and chapters were variously split, combined, dropped, and added, she calmly adjusted, queried authors, and essentially ensured that the project stayed on track. It would be dishonest not to admit that at several points, including quite recently, I seriously doubted whether this manuscript would ever be completed.

As is clear in the chapters that follow, research at Killarney Bay spanned multiple eras of archaeological investigation, from treasure hunting to systematic excavation. It has similarly spanned eras of analytical methods, from the original appreciation of changes in Holocene lake levels, to the early application of radiocarbon dating, to contemporary composition and isotopic analysis. The challenge is how to present data collected in very different eras and with very different goals in an integrated and useful way. The organization of chapters is in part our effort to present the excavation and recovery within their respective contexts but also, to as great a degree as possible, integrate the findings into the dating and analysis of recovered materials.

In this volume, the authors first provide descriptions of the environmental and cultural background of the region and accounts of the excavations conducted at the site. These chapters are followed by descriptions of the various categories of materials recovered from the site and a more synthetic evaluation of their cultural and historical significance. The volume ends with a brief summary that attempts to draw together many of the issues raised in the preceding chapters. The reader will notice that there is not always interpretive agreement between the chapters or even between some sections within the same chapter. Such disagreement is common among archaeologists and in this report is inevitable, given the differences in excavation strategy and academic interests. While there has been no effort to smooth over interpretive differences, we have attempted to separate the descriptive and interpretive portions of the discussion so that readers and future researchers may draw their own conclusions and build upon the results presented here.

In reading the completed volume, it is interesting to see how much archaeological approaches to excavation and analysis have changed and how much these old museum collections still have to tell us about the past. In a not altogether ironic way, modern methods of analysis allow these collections to reveal much more about ancient life at Killarney Bay than if they had been analyzed at the time of excavation and then discarded. In a similar vein, many of the present contributions highlight how much is still to be learned and suggest that the collections will continue to be a source of new discoveries into the foreseeable future. As analytical technology develops, we will be in a position to ask new questions from well-curated museum collections. What is irreplaceable is the material record itself. For me, that may be the most important lesson learned from the archaeological investigations at Killarney Bay.

John M. O'Shea
Ann Arbor, Michigan

Collaboration and First Nations Consultation Statement

The local community of Killarney/Shebahonaning has had a long-term involvement/collaboration with archaeology since the initial discovery and excavations at the site by the owner de Lamorandierie, with the family and descendants, and working with Bell and later Greenman. This community welcoming continued with the later salvage and field school Laurentian University (LU) excavations—led by (respectively) Helen Devereux, Ken Buchanan, me (Patrick Julig)—and by the present owner, J. Speigel. The LU focus was to protect the Killarney Bay site (KB1) from destruction and salvage artifacts from the habitation area while avoiding the mound area and any human remains. In addition, Devereux, Buchanan, and I investigated the return to Canada of the Greenman collections from the mound area, including visits to UMMAA, as requested by the local Metis descendant and broader Indigenous community. The curator of Great Lakes Archaeology at UMMAA, John O'Shea, consulted with Whitefish River First Nation and arranged for the repatriation of the nearby Birch Island burial remains excavated by Greenman, showing respect for the First Nation reserve west of Killarney.

There has also been long-term collaboration and consultation by LU archaeologists with Wikwemikong, the nearest First Nation, on heritage issues and on archaeology surveys conducted around Killarney, the adjacent Georgian Bay Islands (Land Claim), and Point Grondine Reserve lands between Killarney and the French River. A large survey was organized and funded by the WHO (Wikwemikong Heritage Organization), which was headed by Doris Peltier at the time. I was contracted to work with band members and the Wiky Lands Department to survey and study the Point Grondine/ Killarney area sites and burial areas. Several additional burial mounds and cemeteries were recorded. At the time, this KB1 site analysis project was being planned, and work on studying the collections was discussed, as well as the prospects for the return of both the Greenman and Bell collections after the analysis. Since the KB1 collections were at Laurentian University and did not involve human remains, no issues were raised. The survey work was with Wiky band members; the crew stayed around the Killarney area, which facilitated meeting and staying with knowledgeable First Nations community members, such as the Pitfields and Burks, and discussing the KB1 site with these families and the direct descendants of the de Lamorandieres.

Additional First Nation consultation was facilitated by a 2010 Ontario Archaeological Society (OAS) annual symposium organized by LU archaeologists and Wikwemikong band members. It was held in Killarney, with the theme of First Nations and Archaeological Collaborations; it was attended by OAS members, regional chiefs, and some locals. There were regular sessions as well as case-study collaborations by Manitowabi, Pittawanikwatt, and me on examples of the Sheguiandah site and the Point Grondine/ Collins Inlet lands survey (Manitowabi and Julig 2010).

A question during consultation is who to consult with. Often there are multiple factions. Recently, a new local group, the Shebahonaning Anishinaabek, with members from multiple other local First Nations living at Killarney/ Shebahonaning, has claimed jurisdiction. They have worked with me on surveys around Killarney and have provided a historical background statement for archaeology reports, showing close collaboration. Several years ago they requested data and photographic records of the KB1 excavations, and they asked to read the introductory chapter of this volume; they were provided with this information. They are helping to arrange the return of the LU KB1 collections to a local Indigenous repository, the Ojibway Cultural Foundation.

There has been considerable close collaboration over the past 15+ years with local First Nations, showing support of this research. Most First Nations colleagues with whom I have discussed this would like to see the current publication, would like to have access to the data, and would like to have the collections returned to a local community repository such as the Ojibway Cultural Foundation.[1]

Patrick Julig
Sheguiandah, Manitoulin Island, Ontario, Canada

1. *Editors' note*: Although there is a history at Killarney Bay of consultation with First Nations, it is also true that scholarly expectations of collaboration have changed since this project began, many years ago. Two of the volume's contributors felt so strongly about aspects of this issue that they withdrew their names from their respective chapters. Dr. Alicia Hawkins, who with her Canadian colleagues prepared portions of Chapters 5, 8, 10, and 11, and approved these chapters, and Dr. Alice Wright, who with Amy Nicodemus prepared and approved Chapter 9, relinquished their authorship while supporting the research and the publication of this volume.

Part I

Background to Excavations at Killarney Bay

Chapter 1

Introduction to the Killarney Bay Site

Patrick Julig and David Brose

The Killarney Bay site (also known as KB-1, KB1, BlHl-1, and the Speigel site) is located on a ridge in a sandy field near the village of Killarney on the northeast side of Georgian Bay, a part of Lake Huron in Canada (Figure 1.1). Approximately 2,000 years old, this burial and habitation site rests atop a raised beach about 8 m above the present level of Lake Huron. The archaeology itself is especially interesting thanks to a number of unusual factors, finds, and research questions that arose in three separate investigations of the site, from 1876 to the twenty-first century. This volume reports on the long history of excavations and the changing objectives of the various researchers, from the early treasure-hunting phase to several long-term field schools held by the University of Michigan (directed by Emerson Greenman) and Laurentian University (Buchanan 2002; Devereaux 1981; Julig 2004). The book includes an analysis of the site's artifacts and human remains and the documentation of site features, including the reported burial mound, artifact spatial distributions, and settlement patterning. The collections are held at three different institutions in two countries: the University of Michigan Museum of Anthropological Archaeology (UMMAA) in the United States, and the Canadian Museum of History (CMH) and Laurentian University in Canada.

The archaeological interpretation of the Killarney Bay site is problematic, because its mortuary ceremonialism and artifacts seem out of place with respect to other Middle Woodland sites and assemblages in the Upper Great Lakes. Due to the mound burials and the exotic mortuary artifacts, some researchers believed it to be similar to Adena or Hopewell. The wide range of artifacts deriving from sources throughout the Great Lakes and beyond indicates that the occupants of Killarney Bay were involved in long-distance trade, not unlike the Odawa, who occupied the same area of the northeastern Georgian Bay when French explorers such as Samuel de Champlain arrived about 400 years ago (Fox 1990).

The part of the site along the crest of the beach ridge, which contained mortuary components, was designated

Figure 1.1. Location of the Killarney Bay site (KB-1) on the Killarney Peninsula, northern shore of Lake Huron.

Killarney Bay 1. This was excavated by Robert Bell in 1896 and Emerson Greenman in the 1930s and 1940s. Greenman was able to date the site occupation to roughly 2,000 years ago, using the then-new radiocarbon technique (see Chapter 7).

In the 1980s–1990s, field school excavations were conducted by Laurentian University in this locality, but at a slightly lower part of the beach terrace, which Devereaux (1981) and Buchanan (2002) designated the "habitation area." To distinguish this area from the burial site, they termed it the Speigel site, after the owners of the property. The habitation area lacked mortuary evidence and had fire-cracked rock hearth features, lithic reduction scatters, and thin-walled tool-impressed pottery. Excavators thought the pottery was from a later date than the thicker-walled ceramics that Greenman recovered in the mortuary area. However, the habitation area was never radiometrically dated, so the idea of an earlier mortuary complex and a later habitation area remained an untested hypothesis. In this work, we present new ^{14}C dates for these two areas of the site (see Chapter 4). The dates demonstrate that the two areas are contemporaneous and represent a single occupation. As such, in the chapters that follow, the name Killarney Bay is used to designate the site area as a whole; the term "habitation area" is the nonfunerary area examined by researchers from Laurentian University; and the "burial mound" or mortuary area is that excavated by Bell and Greenman.

Crossroads for trade

Killarney Bay is strategically located on the ancient trade network system of the Upper Great Lakes (Figure 1.2), which follows to some extent the Canadian–United States boundary. History tells us that Killarney was in fact an important part of the fur trade's east-west canoe travel route. A number of rivers, including the French, the North Spanish, and the Whitefish, empty into Lake Huron to the north and east of the Killarney peninsula. These rivers could be likened to major highways linking the west and the east via Lake Nipissing and the Ottawa River Valley. Travel from either direction (east or west) to southern Ontario or Michigan also passed through the Killarney area, either following the eastern coast of Georgian Bay towards the Huronia region of Ontario or heading southwest via the Mackinac Straits into Michigan. In 1820, Étienne Augustin de la Morandière, a European fur trader formerly settled in the La Cloche area, relocated his trading post to Killarney because Indigenous people more often frequented the area (Derry 2007:49). Similarly, life in Killarney during the Middle Woodland era was a time of widespread social interaction, with trade networks spanning thousands of kilometers. At that time, the higher water levels of Lake Huron meant that the site was located by the water's edge in an area protected from the large open waters of Georgian Bay. Indeed, Killarney's Anishinabek name, Shebaonaning, translates as "clear passage through." Killarney's location and surrounding geography made it a strategic stop and a true crossroads within this trade network.

Figure 1.2 illustrates the most likely travel route through the Killarney region. The large, open waters of Georgian Bay can be very dangerous and pose a threat to any vessel in rough weather. The trade network would not necessarily follow the most direct route between points. Travelers would instead try to navigate the many protected channels and waterways along the coast, making use of such features as Collin's Inlet, the Killarney passage, and the great many small islands that dot the coast. At the time the Killarney Bay site was occupied, water levels were much higher, and a protected (interior) passage was located immediately north of the site (see Chapter 2).

Extraordinary nature

The natural setting of the Killarney Bay site is spectacular. The area falls within an ecotone of considerable complexity, where the intricate shorelines and associated wetlands typical of the Canadian Shield meet the limestone/dolomite outcrops of Manitoulin Island and the 1.2 billion-year-old quartzite of La Cloche Mountains. The region contains a very high level of species diversity: approximately one-third of all the plant species in Canada are present (Morton and Venn 2000:41). Blueberries, which grow well on the acidic soil typical of the Canadian Shield, are abundant in this area. Haw berries, wild grapes, and plums grow on Manitoulin's more basic soils. Fish and other aquatic life are extremely abundant. The bedrock geology is also rather unusual, being near the junction of various rock types (see Chapter 2). A range of lithic materials for stone technologies exists here, including local Bar River quartzite, Gowganda argillite,

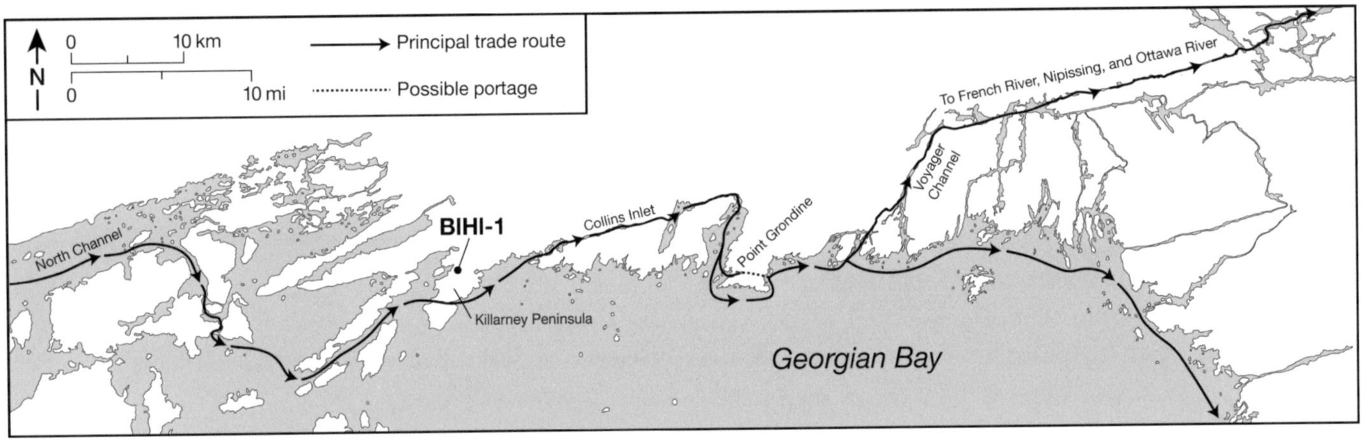

Figure 1.2. Principle trading route from the west passing through the Killarney area and adjacent waterways, heading east by way of the French River, or south by way of Georgian Bay. Note the possible location of the trading route passing by the Killarney Bay site (BlHl-1)when the water levels were higher.

Fossil Hill type chert (on Manitoulin Island), and mylonite. From historical records we know that seasonal Anishinabek subsistence activities took place in the Killarney area, particularly fishing and berry picking.

The current Killarney Provincial Park, part of the Manitoulin Island archipelago, is considered a jewel in the crown of the Ontario Parks system. Earlier in the century, artists known as the Group of Seven (or the Algonquin School) captured its spectacular natural beauty on canvas. The region was also once known as a playground for the rich and famous. President Franklin Delano Roosevelt had a favorite fishing spot there, and Al Capone used to vacation at a cottage on Three Narrows Lake, which was owned by William Hale Thompson, a former mayor of Chicago (Debicki 1982).

Incredible archaeology

The Killarney Bay site is often referred to in the literature (e.g., Ellis and Ferris 1990; Wright 1999), but no detailed report on the site has been published until now.

The recovery of both local and exotic materials throughout the site and the nature of their deposition raises many research questions. A remarkable copper beaver effigy was reportedly found in the burial mound at the site (Greenman 1951). However, its current location is unknown. Grave goods included fur pelts and weavings made from beaver skins, which were used to wrap copper and shell beads and other artifacts. The mortuary complex opens a window into the complex social dynamics of this Great Lakes culture.

Thanks to the presence of copper salts, the Killarney Bay site had unusually good organic preservation when compared to other boreal forest sites. Some of the flint bifaces were still in their wooden hafts, and excavators found animal fur and woven organic fibers in excellent condition in the burial contexts, as noted in later chapters. Artifact types included southern tubular Ohio pipes, a variety of Middle Woodland ceramics, a wide range of copper artifacts, various nonlocal chert bifaces, and exotic shell beads. The human remains and associated mortuary artifacts suggest the site represented a small mortuary complex, either in an intentionally constructed mound or a naturally occurring beach ridge. In later chapters we present the sedimentary evidence for small mound construction and lack of sand dune activity.

Some artifacts recovered from Killarney Bay show connections to southern Middle Woodland cultures. Mound-building Middle Woodland cultures like Adena are typically associated with the rich Carolinian forest zones of the lower Great Lakes, although some are known in southern

Ontario. The fact that the Killarney Bay site lies north of the normal range of these cultures, on edge of the rocky Canadian Shield, prompted some researchers to suggest it represents a movement of southern Adena/Hopewell-like people into the region (Richie and Dragoo 1960; Spence, Pihl, and Murphy 1990:142).

Much time has passed since these materials were first excavated, but their importance has not diminished. The recent analyses and analytical methods applied to the collections have shed new light on the Middle Woodland lifeways and social dynamics in and around Killarney and across the Upper Great Lakes area. In addition, the history of investigations at Killarney Bay is likewise a mirror that reflects the changing face and shifting theoretical perspectives of North American archaeology, from simply digging mounds to using classification and artifact typology to applying archaeometric techniques.

International collaboration

The seeds for this multi-authored volume were sown at the 2009 Canadian Archaeological Association conference symposium. At the time, co-editors Julig and Brose were researching various aspects of the site and collections independently, from different perspectives. Julig, who had been involved in Laurentian University field schools at the site and others in the vicinity (Buchanan 2002; Julig 2004), approached the UMMAA about analyzing the collections excavated by Greenman. Brose had been studying Greenman's collections at UMMAA to analyze the ceramic complex and interpret its relationship to the mortuary complex. He contacted Bill Fox, who suggested further discussion with Julig regarding lithic identifications. Their objective expanded; they decided to create a complete site report. They obtained grants and ultimately the collaboration of colleagues at a number of other institutions. John O'Shea, curator of Great Lakes Archaeology at UMMAA, helped greatly with the project through his contributions and with the final editing and publication of the manuscript.

The completion of the volume now, after a lengthy gestation period, is due to a number of factors. Firstly, it is a testament to the great value of museums and the deep history of Great Lakes archaeology. From as early as the nineteenth century, the Killarney Bay site has sparked the interest of archaeologists and geologists. It has figured in the training of several famous anthropologists, including Marshall Sahlins, Elman Service, Wilfrid Jury, and James V. Wright. The Canadian Museum of History and the University of Michigan Museum of Anthropological Archaeology have preserved and curated these collections for decades—and in the case of Robert Bell's materials, for more than a century and a half.

This work also reflects the history and value of archaeological field schools. The Killarney Bay and Speigel area excavations are mostly the result of two field schools, one run by the University of Michigan in the mid-twentieth century and one by the Laurentian University from the 1980s into the early twenty-first century. As such, the excavations cover a transitional era in North American archaeology: early on, certain data were not collected that would be recorded during excavation today. For example, the first excavators never took flotation samples of soils or features at the site, nor did they use fine screening to find the small bones and seeds suggestive of ancient diets. Lacking such data, we have employed new methods, such as analyzing the residues of ceramics and using other archaeometric analyses to learn more about past economies, technologies, and trade and social interaction patterns around ancient Killarney.

Volume overview

The chapters that follow are grouped into four parts. Part I (Chapters 1 to 3) is a description of the environmental and cultural background of the Killarney Bay site. Part II (Chapters 4 to 8) covers the various investigations that were conducted at the site. Part III (Chapters 9 to 13) is a description of the materials recovered from the site, and Part IV (Chapter 14) is a consideration of the site within its larger cultural and regional context. There are six appendices, which cover lipid residue analysis, shell beads, textiles, geochemistry, pollen analysis, a summary of the Schlegel site (a neighboring archaeological site similar to Killarney Bay), and a selection of field notes.

Chapter 2

The Natural Environment

Patrick Julig and Darrel G. F. Long

In this chapter, we explore the environmental context of the Killarney Bay site. We will focus mostly on the natural environments, viewed within the context of regional prehistoric human ecology. We will include some aspects of geoarchaeology at the Killarney Bay site, including site formation processes and the question of the burial mound on the beach ridge. The spatial perspective will be on several scales or levels, including the broader regional setting of Killarney and Manitoulin Island and details of local site environs. The broader regional perspective will approximate what may have been a seasonal band range of the Middle Woodland cultures represented at Killarney Bay, excluding their widespread trade networks. From the perspective of human ecology, the larger region includes where the majority of the sites of their seasonal round may have occurred, and where most subsistence and raw materials, including local lithic sources, may have been procured. We will describe the floral and faunal communities and the Georgian Bay fishery and other available aquatic resources, including the potential for wild rice. However, we will first review the geological context and Holocene water level changes at Killarney Bay, as these can help provide relative geological dating for this beach ridge site. The local geographic context and beach ridge stratigraphy and sedimentology will also help address the question of whether the Killarney Bay mounds are cultural or natural beach ridge formations.

As mentioned in Chapter 1, the Killarney/Manitoulin region straddles two geological provinces. To the north and east lie the acidic Precambrian rocks of the Canadian Shield, with their thin podzolic soils; to the west, on Manitoulin Island, are the much younger Paleozoic limestone and dolomite bedrock, with more basic soils and somewhat warmer conditions. The Killarney Bay site is located on a raised beach ridge. Indeed, the entire north shore region and larger surrounding islands like Manitoulin have numerous uplifted beaches, since the land has been steadily rising due to isostatic uplift and subsequent changes in Great Lakes water levels. At the time the site was occupied, several

Figure 2.1. Location of the Killarney Bay site (grassy ridge in center of photograph), based on an image from National Air Photo Library, Natural Resources Canada.

millennia ago, it was on an island, separated from the mainland by a narrow inlet that would have provided a protected canoe passage along this northeast coast of Lake Huron (see Figure 1.1). Many sites in the northeast Georgian Bay region are preserved on raised beach terraces. In the context of a dynamic and changing landscape, investigations of the geoarchaeological aspects of the Killarney Bay site, including paleogeography and site formation processes, can help resolve the issue of whether the burial "mounds" were cultural or natural (that is, sand-dune enhanced beach ridges).

The fluctuating water Great Lakes levels, and gradually isostatically rising terrain along the northeastern shores of the Upper Great Lakes, contributed to new and changing coastal shoreline and wetland environments, which may have had high potential for certain subsistence resources. While there are few subsistence indications or faunal remains in the preserved site assemblage, subsistence modeling can be made, based on the primarily littoral resources available within the local environment. As evident in Figure 2.1, the large grassy beach ridge location of Killarney Bay is currently located well back (>150 meters) from the present shoreline. About 2,000 years ago, however, it was located on the water's edge. This shift is due to differential isostatic uplift of the northeastern Great Lakes basin. A close examination of Figure 2.1 shows a mix of vegetation and tree types, with larger bushy deciduous trees (large maples and red oak) evident on the beach ridge site area and adjacent rocky uplands and white cedar, black ash, poplar, and willow adjacent to the shore. This portion

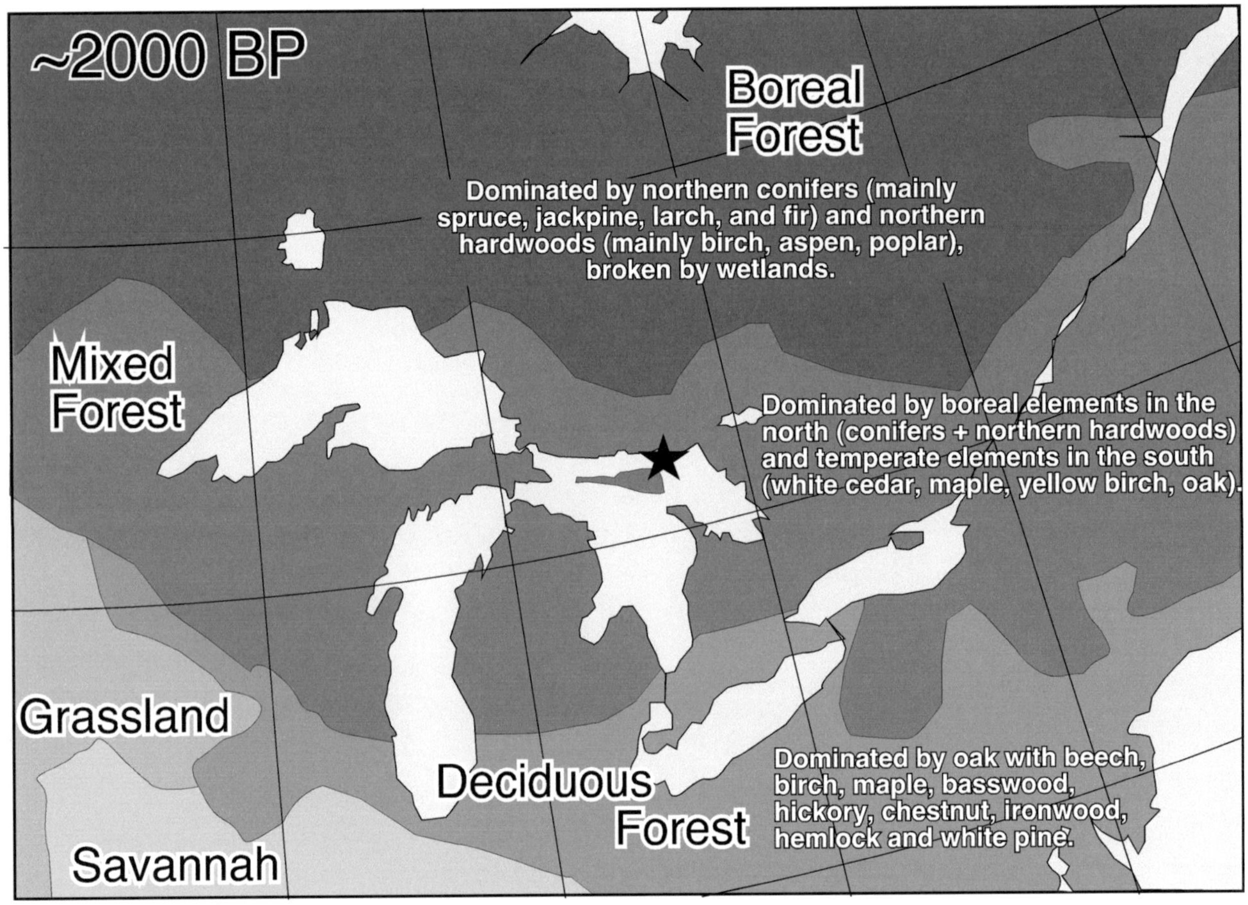

Figure 2.2. Biozones in the Great Lakes Region c. 2000 BP (based on Dyke et al. 2004). Star indicates location of site.

of the Great Lakes region (Figure 2.2) was within the mixed forest biozone 2,000 years ago, and species then included a mixture of boreal conifers and hardwoods in the north and more temperate species (cedar, maple, birch, etc.) in the south (Dyke et al. 2004). As we show in the next sections, the Killarney Bay site is located in an area of considerable environmental variability (which depends on local factors, including geology, soil, slope, and aspect) and considerable species diversity.

Geological background

The bedrock geology of the Killarney/Manitoulin area is illustrated in Figure 2.3, based on Card (1978). The oldest rocks in the area belong to the (2.5–2.2 Ga) Paleoproterozoic Huronian Supergroup. This is made up of a thick sequence (5–12 km) of metamorphosed mudstone, sandstone, and conglomerate, which has been described in detail by Card (1978), Young et al. (2001), and Long (2004), and papers cited therein. Most of the sandstone units within the Huronian Supergroup (including the Matinenda, Mississagi, Serpent formations, and most of the Lorrain Formation) contain significant amounts of feldspar and were unsuitable for production of high-quality stone tools (Julig et al. 1998; Long et al. 2002). Quartz-rich meta-sandstones (quartzites) with more than 95 percent quartz are restricted to the upper part of the Lorrain Formation and the Bar River Formation. The latter, which was exploited at Sheguiandah and George Lake, was preferred by Paleoindian and later groups (Julig 2002), especially where it had been pervasively sheared (Julig and Long 2006). Outcrops of this formation would have been accessible to the occupants of the Killarney Bay site in the hills (Killarney Ridge) and small islands (Sheep and Pine) immediately north of the site; on the crests of small islands (Badgeley, Centre, Partridge, and Heywood

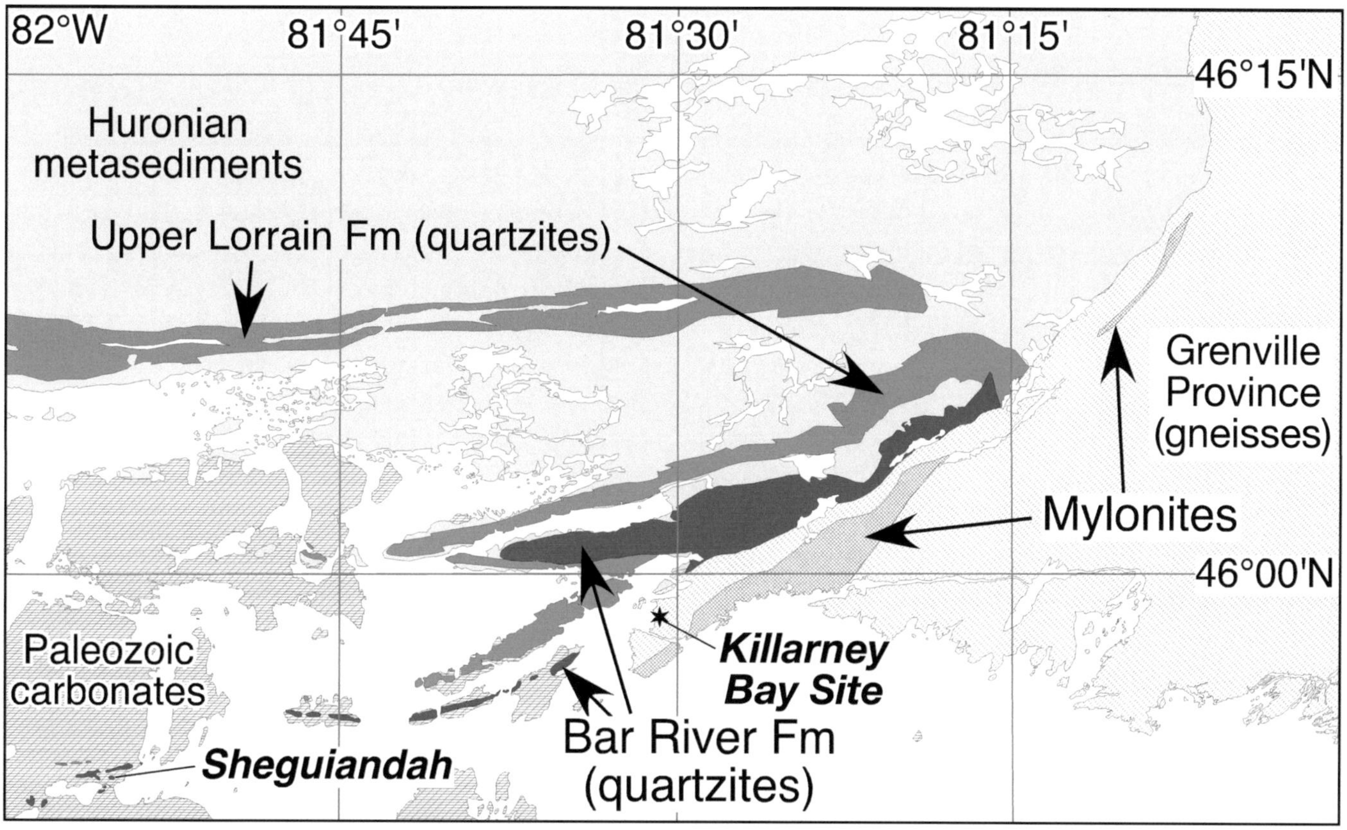

Figure 2.3. Simplified regional geology of the area around the Killarney Bay site (based on Card 1978). Dark shading indicates distribution of siliceous quartz arenites (quartzites) that may have been used for production of artifacts.

Islands) in the north channel of Lake Huron; and at the Sheguiandah site and elsewhere in northeastern Manitoulin Island. Possible sources of siltstone for production of other tools include red and greenish-gray chertlike siliceous mudstone in the Gordon Lake Formation, known as Gordon Lake chert (Fox 2009:358), on Badgeley Island and around Lamorandière Bay. Local toolmakers also used gray laminated mudrocks (argillites) from the upper part of the Gowganda Formation and fine-grained diorite and gabbro from the Nipissing diabase intrusives, which cut through most of the Huronian strata.

The area immediately to the east of the Huronian outcrop belt (and beneath the Killarney Bay site) is underlain by feldspar-rich plutonic intrusives (quartz-monzonite, granodiorite, quartz-diorite, and minor trondhelmite), which are collectively known as the (~1.7 Ga) Grenville Front Plutons (Card 1978). Locally these have been intensively sheared to produce a fine-grained cataclastic rock, which may also have been used for artifact production, as a few artifacts of mylonites have been recorded. East of the belt of Grenville Front Plutons, much of the low-lying terrain is underlain by gneiss and migmatite of the (1.2–1.0 Ga) Grenville Province.

Overlapping the deformed Precambrian bedrocks is a series of gently dipping Paleozoic limestones and dolostones of Ordovician and Silurian age (465–420 Ma). These are best developed on Manitoulin Island (Brunton et al. 2009; Coniglio et al. 2006; Robertson and Card 1972; and references therein), where they are collectively about 300 m thick. Chert has been recorded in the uppermost Ordovician Manitoulin Formation by Brunton et al. (2009) but does not appear to have been used extensively for artifact production. Chert is common in dolostones of the Silurian Fossil Hill Formation and has been used extensively for artifact production (Long et al. 2001). There are several color varieties of Fossil Hill chert, with the gray banded and speckled variety in useable size bands. This is the most commonly used chert at Killarney Bay. The Manitoulin Formation chert is mostly found as small nodules; it fractures easily and was not often used.

Multiple glacial advances during the Pleistocene molded the bedrock of this part of Ontario, producing extensive asymmetric roche moutonnée on Precambrian strata and excavating broad tunnel valleys through carbonates on Manitoulin Island (Barnett 2002). Quaternary glacial deposits are predominantly of Upper Pleistocene (Tarantian) to early Holocene age. They reflect recession and local advance on major ice sheets since the Early Pleistocene (~1.66–0.78 Ma: Dyke 2002), when the area was initially covered by continental ice sheets. The area was essentially covered in ice for most of the Middle (0.78–0.13 Ma) and Late (0.13–0.10 Ma) Pleistocene (Barnett 1992, 2002; Dyke 2002). By 11,000 BP, the ice front had retreated north of the Sudbury Basin, and much of the study area was covered with water (Dyke 2002). Lake levels were controlled by glacioeustatic rebound and the elevation of lake outlets, as detailed below.

Holocene water level changes

The high-water levels of Lake Algonquin, which covered most of Manitoulin Island, fell after about 10,500 years ago, as the glaciers began to recede (Barnett 2002). They gave way to the Lake Stanley low stand in the Huron basin and Lake Chippewa in the Michigan basin (Lewis et al. 2007; McCarthy et al. 2015). During this period, late Paleoindians are thought to have moved into Manitoulin Island (Julig 2002), which was connected to the Bruce Peninsula of south-central Ontario (Janusas et al. 2004). At that time, the Upper Great Lakes drained through the French River outlet and through the Ottawa Valley drainage system via Lake Nipissing. Lake levels fluctuated in direct response to climate changes. There was at least one and possibly two low-water periods, when Georgian Bay was actually a separate lake (Lake Hough: Eschman and Karrow 1985; Lewis et al. 2005; McCarthy et al. 2015). There were also several flood events that occurred from the west into Lake Superior as the glaciers melted. As these floods cascaded into Lake Huron, life would have been unstable, as the beach zones and hunting and fishing areas would have changed regularly.

Larsen (1987) provided a record of relative middle to late Holocene lake-level fluctuations for southern Lake Michigan (Figure 2.4; see also Monaghan and Lovis 2005). Although the absolute lake levels are valid only for the southern part of Lake Michigan, these can be correlated to modern levels near the Killarney Bay site, given that an uplift of ~160 m has been estimated for this area since 10.6 ka BP (12.6 cal ka BP) by Lewis et al. (2005) and only 11 m for the southern part of Lake Michigan. Historical records indicate the current rate of uplift in the vicinity of the Killarney Bay site is between 1 m/century (Larsen 1987) and 0.27 to 0.37 m/century (Mainville and Craymer 2005), relative to southern Michigan. The beach at the habitation area of the Killarney Bay site is located about 7.2 m (24.5 feet) above the current level of Lake Huron. Using the low estimate of relative lake-level change indicated by Mainville and Craymer (2005), the Killarney Bay site would have been flooded at least three times since its formation about 2000 BP (Figure 2.4).

More recent evaluations of paleolake levels in the Michigan and Huron basins by Baedke et al. (2004) indicate a slightly lower amplitude of lake-level change in the past 2,000 years than indicated in Figure 2.4. Baedke et al. (2004) calculated the absolute extent of lake-level change at the outlet of Lake Huron and corrected this for local subsidence. If the curve is adjusted for a relative uplift rate of about 27 cm/century, the projected lake levels at the Killarney Bay site intersect the lake-level curve at 23 to 24 feet above the historic average lake level in the interval around 2000 BP (Figure 2.5). Based on this curve, the secondary beach, at about 12 feet above the survey base, probably developed between 650 and 800 BP.

Local site geography and sedimentology

The paleogeography of the Killarney area between ca. 2000 and 1500 BP is shown in Figure 2.6, with the water level at the 182 to 184 m level, just below the Algoma lake level. This indicates that the Killarney Bay site was on a separate island (Speigel Island) at that time, surrounded by shallow swampy areas and adjacent to an inside passageway.

Using the topographic survey made by Greenman (1959, unpublished data on file at UMMAA), it is possible to reconstruct the paleogeography of the site. Flooding the topography to the 24-foot level (Figure 2.7) suggests that

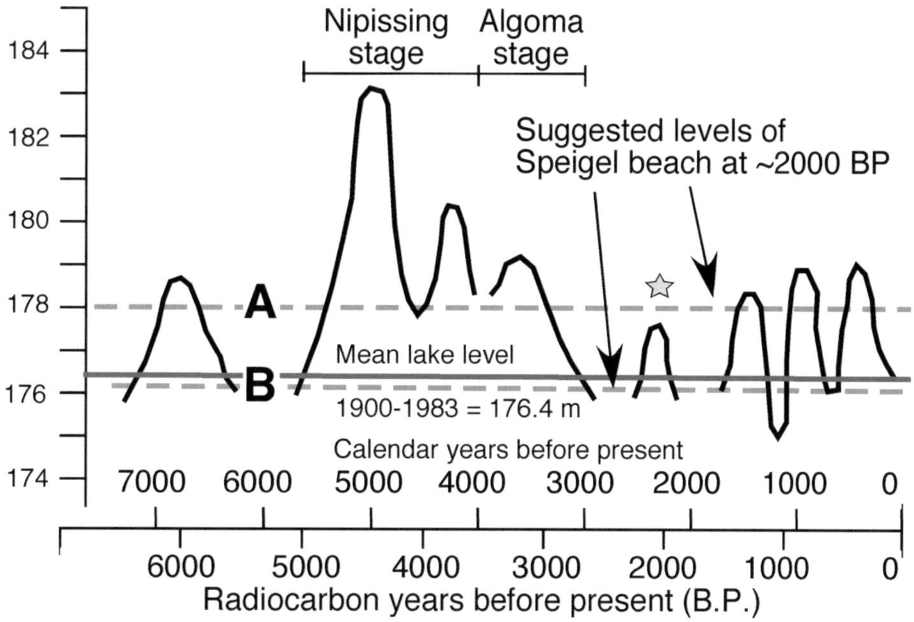

Figure 2.4. Relative lake level fluctuations at the south end of Lake Michigan (from Larsen 1987). Dashed lines indicate uplift corrected level of the lake at the time of occupation of the Killarney Bay site, using the historical lake level data provided by Mainville and Craymer (2005). Level A assumes a subsidence level of 27 cm/century (based on data from Little Current, relative to the modern outlet at Lakeport). Level B is based on the differential uplift rate between Little Current and Milwaukee of about 37 cm/century. The latter appears to have a better fit and provides a base level close to that at the south end of Lake Michigan. Based on this, if the topography of the area is flooded to 7.3 m (approximately 24 feet) above the present lake level, then the Killarney Bay site appears to have occupied a beach with a narrow point (a portage ?) between two islands (see also Figure 2.5).

the main occupation site was on a beach ridge facing Lake Huron. Behind the ridge is a small back-barrier lagoon. A profile of the occupation site (Figure 2.8) supports this model, as does coring in the back-barrier area (Figure 2.9).

The beach face was investigated by trenching in 1984. The results indicated progradational growth, with interbedded small pebble gravels and sands, overlying 30 cm of ripple cross laminated sand (Figure 2.10a). Underneath is a set of sandy gravels, and beneath that are medium-grained lacustrine sands (Figure 2.10b). Details of grain size and site stratigraphy collected in 1984 appear to have been lost. There is fine-grained material at the crest of the beach ridge (Figure 2.10c).

Killarney mounds: cultural or natural?

In 2008, Julig and Long investigated the formation of the so-called Killarney "mounds." Historical records and archaeological opinions are divided on the question of whether these deposits represent a natural beach enhanced by dune activity (J. V. Wright 1995) or a mound that is cultural in origin (Bell 1896; Greenman 1966).

The investigators collected cores across the main beach, just south of the Greenman mound excavations. They did grain-size analysis to assess the amount of aeolean (sand dunes) or normal beach sand. Sand dune deposits (aeolean sand) is typically better sorted into one grade of fine sand, with no mix of medium, coarse, or very coarse size grades, as the wind will not move the larger grains. By contrast, typical beach sands are a mix of various grain sizes, from coarse to very fine silts and clay. Investigators also took a third core in the back-beach swale, east of the beach ridge, as dune sand might have been blown into this area during times of declining water levels. Any dune-forming episodes would be evident in dune sand layers, which should be well sorted and of fine sand grade.

The grain size data are shown in Figure 2.9: there is mostly beach sand, with light gray muds at depth in core

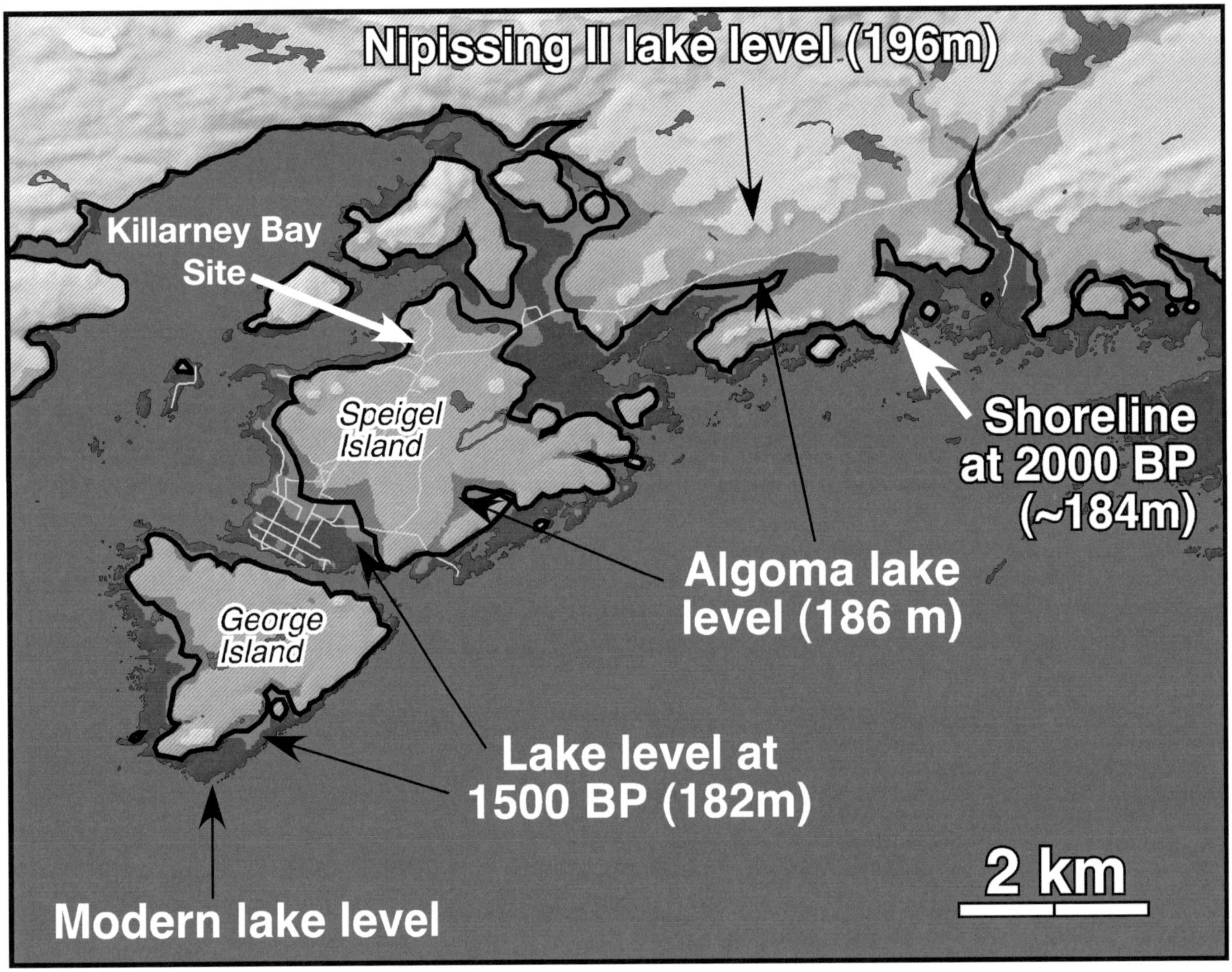

Figure 2.5. Killarney area flooded to 7.3 m (approximately 24 feet) above the modern water level of Lake Huron (Scale 1:40 000). Shallow water-covered areas west of the site show up as swampy areas in Figure 2.1.

2 and through most of core 3. Sand at 1 m in core 2 (25 m east of the beach crest) and at the base of core 3 (45 m east of beach crest) may be aeolian but was formed during an early phase of beach development. The mean grain size (measured in phi; 1.30 ϕ = medium sand grade) of the sand deposits in the upper meter of cores 1 and 2 indicates the dominance of medium sand. This suggests a typical beach rather than dune sand, which would be predominantly fine sand and well sorted (as in Figure 2.10c).

In the back-barrier lagoon, the upper sediments include some medium- and coarse-grained sand above a gray mud. The underlying fine-sand unit at the base is poorly sorted and may represent an earlier phase in the near-shore zone, when the site was underwater and the fine sand was washed off the higher beaches.

Based on our observations, there is no evidence for significant dune formation on the beach ridge at Killarney Bay. Coppice dunes were developed locally (Figure 2.10c) as grasses baffled the fine sand along the beach crest. The absence of clear windblown layers of sand in the back-barrier muds appears to rule out an aeolian origin of the ridge. These results do not, however, demonstrate any intentional construction of the ridge. It appears that the ridge or mound was formed by normal shore processes

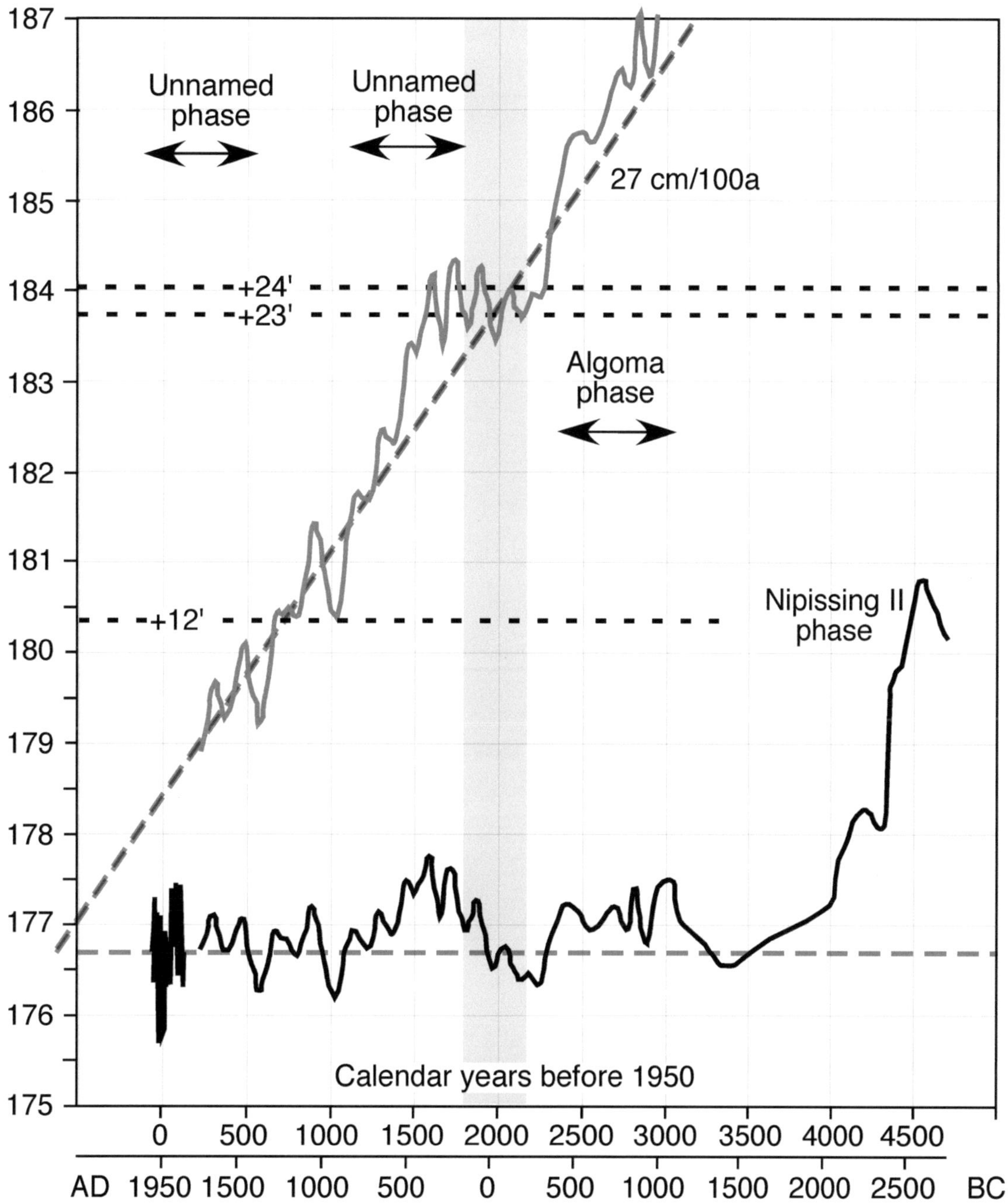

Figure 2.6. Absolute lake levels (dark lines) at the outlet of Lake Huron, corrected for uplift/subsidence (Baedke et al. 2004). Inclined gray lines indicate relative lake levels at the Killarney Bay site, adjusted for an uplift rate of about 27 cm/century. Shaded block indicates possible age of the site.

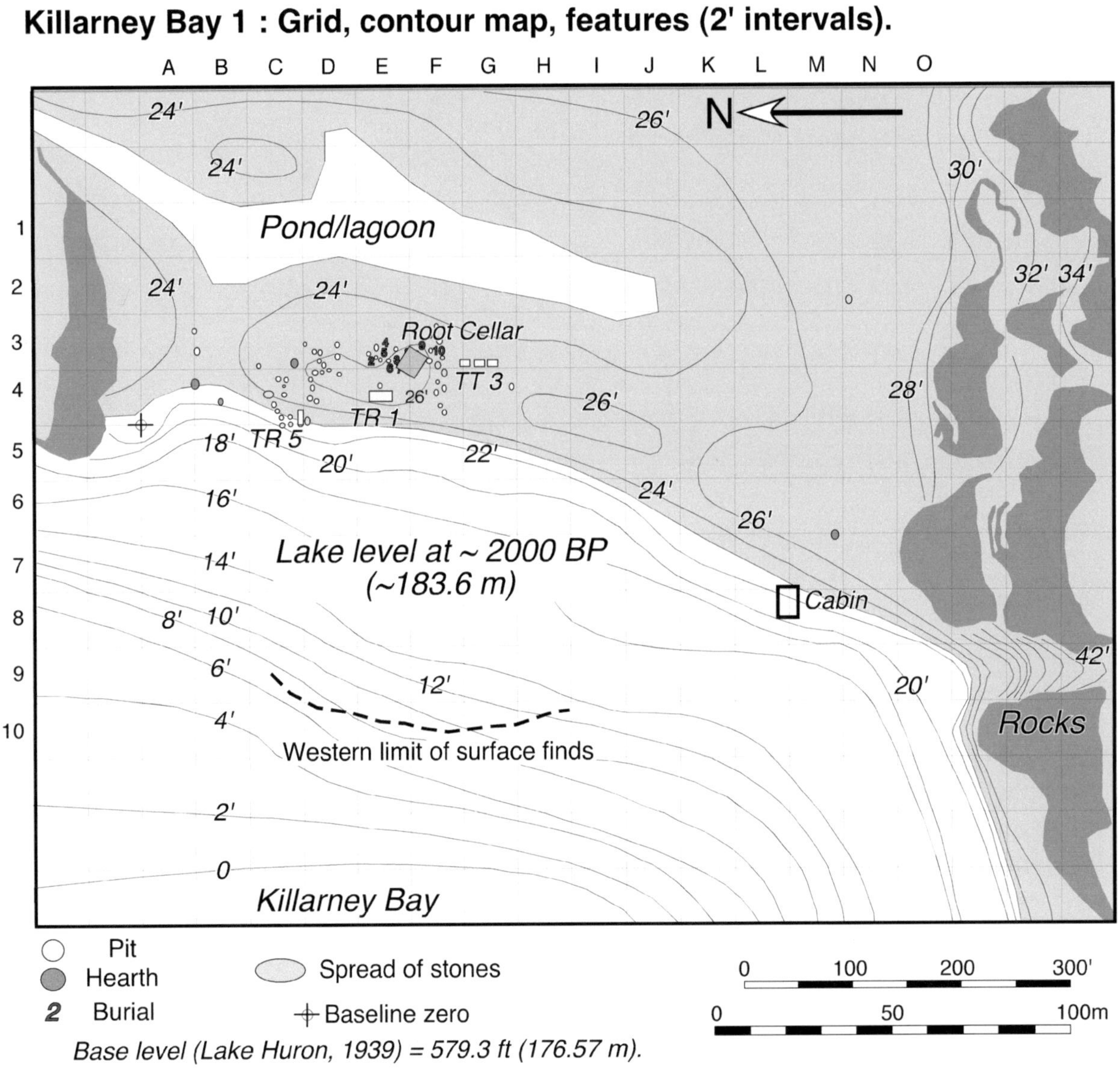

Figure 2.7. Paleogeography of the Killarney Bay site, based on topographic data collected by Greenman prior to 1959. Flooding to a level of about 7 m (23 feet) above the present lake level at Killarney Bay would place most of the recovered stones and hearths and all of the burial structures above lake level and would still allow for a small stream outlet at the north end of the beach. The western limit of surface finds indicated by Greenman (1959, 1960 field notes) is immediately below a second beach ridge formed during a falling stage of the lake.

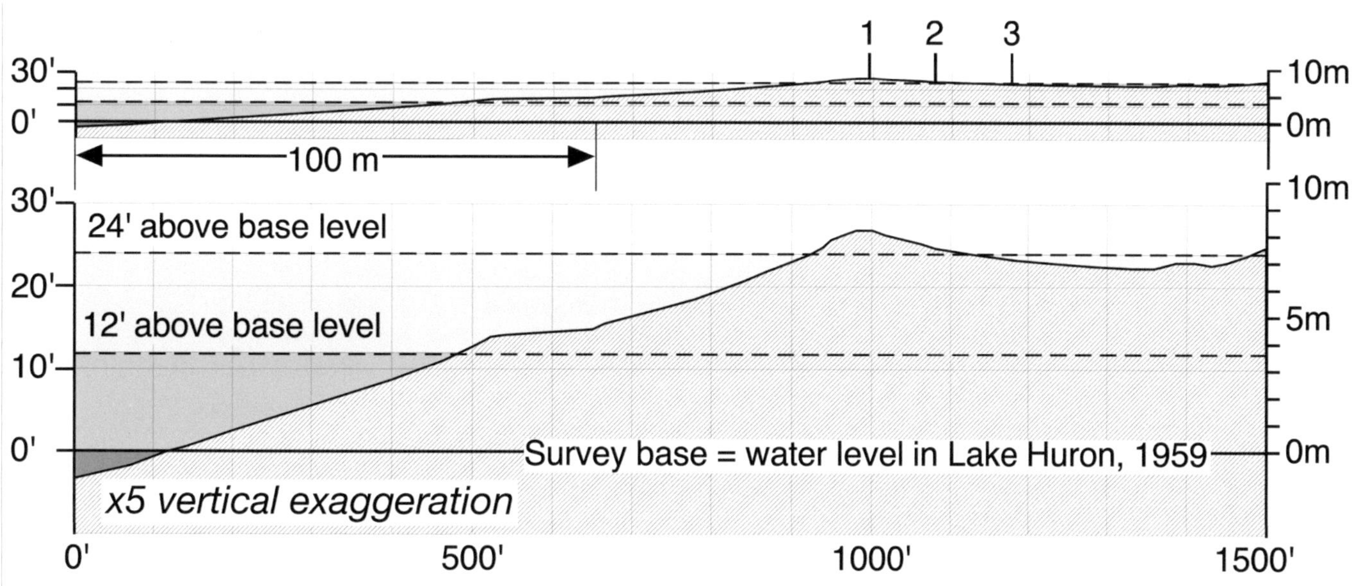

Figure 2.8. Cross-section of beach at the Killarney Bay site, based on topographic information collected by Greenman. Sites 1, 2, and 3 indicate location of cores collected during this study (see also Figure 2.9).

plus culturally purposeful movement or piling of materials during the occupation of the site. There was at least a 2.5-m water-level change during occupation, with ponding occurring in the back-beach area during the higher stands. During the main phase of occupation, the site was on the west side of an island (see Figure 2.5), next to a passageway from the Collins Inlet travel route to the east and points west. This passage allowed travelers to avoid exposure to the rough west and southwest winds of Killarney Point.

Present and past plant and animal communities

The study area appears to have been characterized by a mixed-boreal forest biozone since 7.0 ka BP (Dyke et al. 2004). The current environment is typical of the deciduous-coniferous mixed forests of the Great Lakes-St. Lawrence forest region (Morton and Venn 2000:16; Rowe 1972). These forests are common in areas of good to poor drainage, depending on the local bedrock, and include a variety of tree and plant species that make use of the varying soil types. Historically, the area included tree species typically found in the coniferous forests of northern Ontario, such as the Eastern white pine (*Pinus strobus*), the red pine (*Pinus resinosa*), the Eastern hemlock (*Tsuga canadensis*), and the yellow birch (*Betula allegheniensis*), as well as a mix of broad-leaved trees associated with the deciduous forests of southern Ontario, such as the sugar maple (*Acer saccharum*), the red maple (*Acer rubrum*), the red oak (*Quercus rubra*), the basswood (*Tilia americana*), and the white elm (*Ulmus americana*). In addition to these, the area includes smaller numbers of boreal species, such as the balsam fir (*Abies balsamea*), the white spruce (*Picea glauca*), the black spruce (*Picea mariana*), the jack pine (*Pinus banksiana*), the trembling aspen (*Populus tremuloides*), the balsam poplar (*Populus balsamifera*), and the paper birch (*Betula papyrifera*). The northern white cedar (*Thuja occidentalis*), large-toothed aspen (*Populus grandidentata*), white ash (*Fraxinus americana*), and beech (*Fagus grandifolia*) are also interspersed throughout these forests. Such mature old-growth forests are not as common these days as they once were in the area (Morton and Venn 2000:16). Today, the Killarney Bay site is very lightly vegetated, containing only a few large sugar maples and white ash and a number of ground juniper bushes (*Juniperus communis*) and staghorn sumac (*Rhus typhina*) (Buchanan 2002:8).

The Killarney/Manitoulin region lies at the boundary of two geological zones. A variety of plants take advantage of either the limestone terrain or the more acidic rocks and

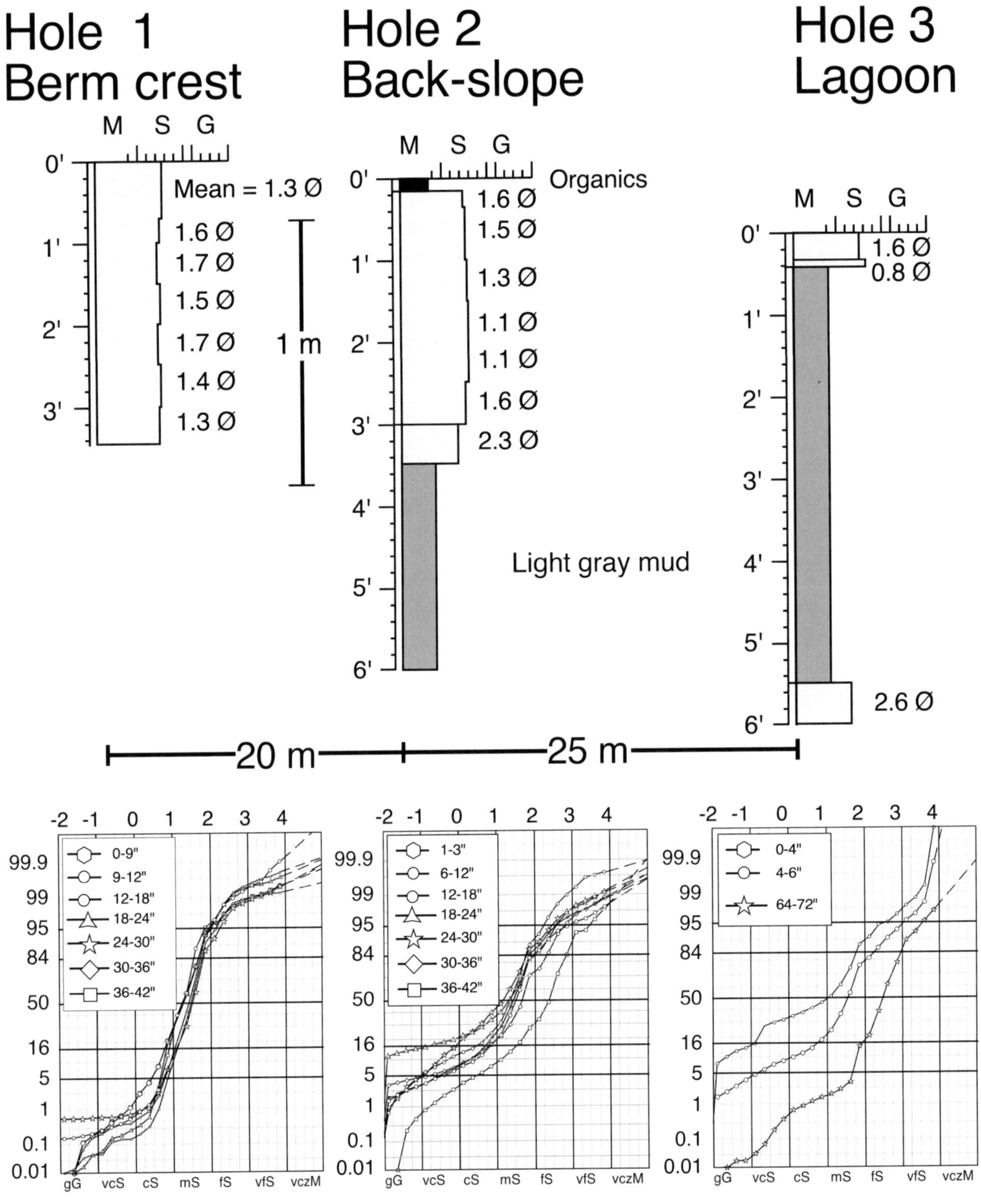

Figure 2.9. Core data, indicating median grain size of sandstones (light gray). See Appendix D for further details of grain size analysis.

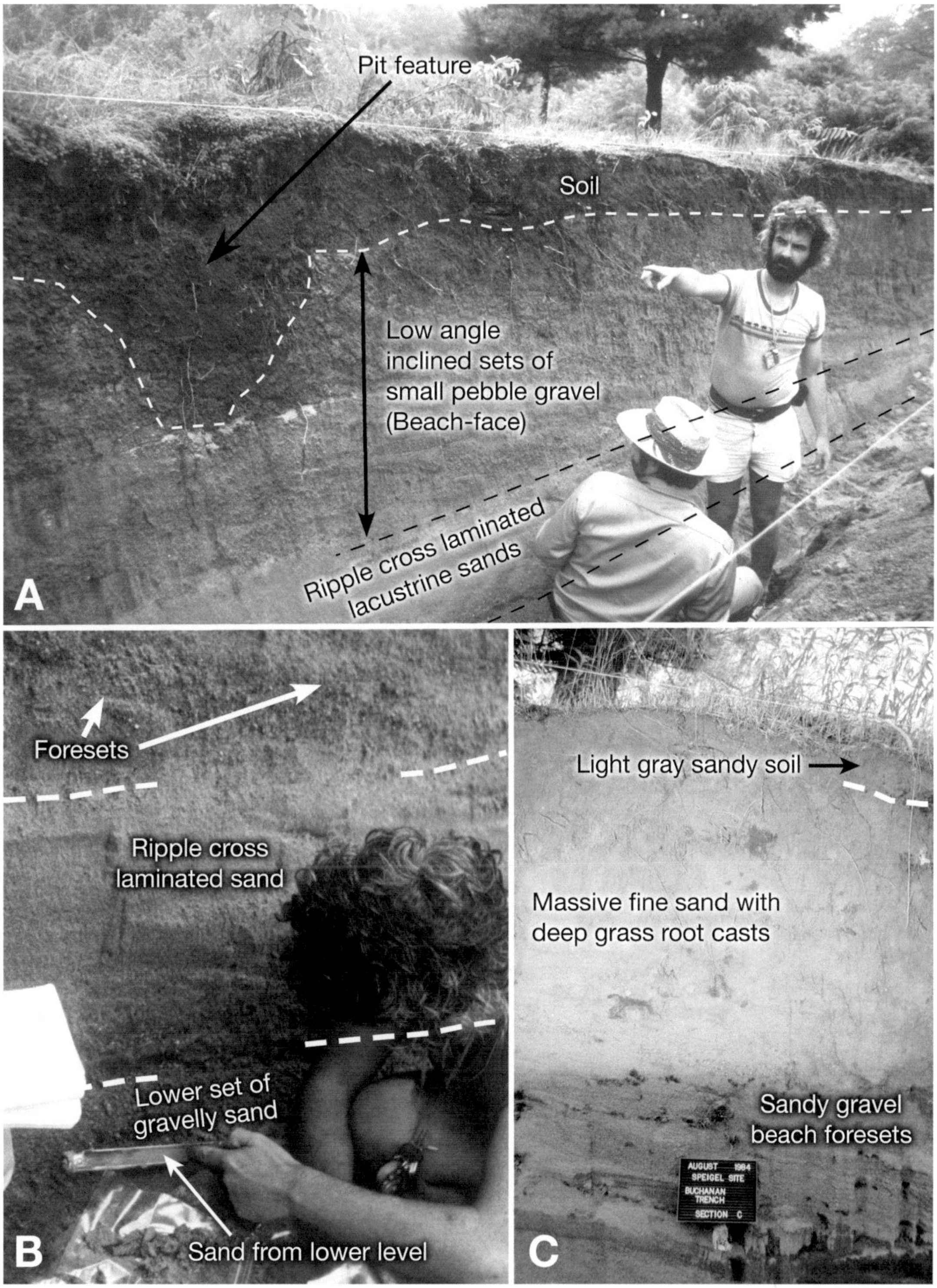

Figure 2.10. A: View of gently dipping progradational beach foresets, overlying ripple cross laminated sands of subaqueous lacustrine origin. Beach strata is overlain by a moderately well-developed soil profile, high in organics (c.f. Greenman 1966). Note the dark organic rich pit area, indicating the location of a hearth, a decayed tree root, or a tree throw. B: Detail of base of trench. Note the sharp contact of gravely sand foresets of the beach with the underlying lacustrine sand. This overlies a second set of (inclined) gravely sands developed as a beach face during a lower stand of the lake. C: Massive fine sand unit at ridge crest. Structure has been obscured by root turbation.

soils typical of the Canadian Shield. The area is also on the boundary between two major climate regions (Morton and Venn 2000:13). The high-pressure systems dominant in northern Ontario often keep away the poor-weather systems prevalent in southern Ontario. Because of the cooling effect of the westerly to southwesterly winds moving along the waters of Lake Huron towards its northern shore, the area often escapes the hot and humid conditions common in the southern part of the province (Morton and Venn 2000:13). The weather conditions allow a variety of floral species to survive in the area: the cool air coming from the water supports the growth of predominantly arctic grass species on the shores of the islands and coasts, whereas prairie species of trees and grasses thrive on the upland limestone alvars, and boreal species thrive in the cool and damp coniferous forests (Morton and Venn 2000:13).

The forests have changed considerably from the Paleoindian period to the present, due to gradual climate change (Dyke et al. 2004). After the waters subsided from Lake Algonquin at about 10,500 BP, it was an open pine woodland with species such as cedar and balsam in the poorly drained areas and some deciduous species in the better-drained areas. There was a cooling event related to the Lake Agassiz flood, and the vegetation changed back to spruce dominance at about 9,500 BP (Julig 2002). About 8,000 years ago, the area warmed up, and white pine again became the dominant species, replacing red pine, jack pine, and spruce (Julig 2002). Forest fires were common, leading to ecological cycles of vegetation succession. Changes in climate, swamp levels, and animal species can all affect local vegetation and land use. For instance, species like beaver are major modifiers of local wetland ecology. They dam up wetlands and change floral species community, cutting and eating the deciduous trees and gradually leading to more coniferous forests. This is all part of the boreal forest succession.

Figure 2.2 shows a reconstruction of biozones in the Great Lakes region at the time of the site's occupation.

Animal species in the Killarney area have likewise changed greatly through time, particularly during the historic period. Woodland caribou (*Rangifer tarandus*) were common on Manitoulin in the early historical and prehistoric times and only became extirpated from the area during the last few centuries (Gilbert 1990; Peterson 1966). This herding species thrives on climax boreal forest; they feed on the lichens in such environments. Caribou were likely a major food source for early populations, particularly the Paleoindians (Julig 2002). The Shawana site, which dates to about 500 years ago, has caribou faunal remains, and is believed to represent a fall butchering site.

White-tailed deer (*Odocoileus virginianus*) are browsing ruminants that prefer secondary growth areas, and their numbers have expanded greatly since farming was introduced. They were not common in prehistoric times in the Killarney region, whereas further south they were exploited by prehistoric populations and later by the Huron and Iroquois. In the winter months, they can be taken in large numbers when they "yard" in conifers. They were an important food and leather source for native populations to the south (Gramly 1977) but were likely rare in the predominant climax white pine forests of the prehistoric past.

Other "big-game" cervid species, such as moose (*Alces alces*) and wapiti or elk (*Cervus canadensis*), were available at various times during the early and middle Holocene, when changing water levels created abundant coastal habitat and land connections from Manitoulin Island to other parts of Ontario. Moose and deer are not compatible due to disease, and Manitoulin was probably more suitable for moose and caribou in prehistoric times than for absent to rare elk and white-tailed deer, which have more limited distributions and traditionally were exploited in restricted areas. Black bear (*Ursus americanus*) was also a traditional economic resource for native populations in some parts of the central subarctic (Rogers and Leacock 1981), but despite widespread distribution, they were never a major food source.

Algonquian tribes in the Upper Great Lakes used smaller species such as beaver (*Castor canadensis*), hare (*Lepus americanus*), woodchuck (*Marmotta monax*), raccoon (*Procyon lotor*), and muskrat (*Ondatra zibithicus*). Beaver was particularly important for boreal forest Algonquian groups such as the Ojibwa and Cree, who prized the fat meat with its high caloric value (Julig 1982). The Ojibwa band who occupied the Killarney area at contact time in the 1600s were the Amikwa, or beaver people, and a beaver copper effigy was reportedly found in the mound. Unfortunately, its location is now lost.

Birds were also an important food source, including both migratory waterfowl and other species, such as the now-extinct passenger pigeon (*Ectopistes migratorus*). The migratory passenger pigeons fed on beech mast and other seeds from deciduous trees, stands of which existed on Manitoulin (Morton and Venn 2000).

Fish were a major food source for the Ojibwa, Odawa, Cree, and other First Nation cultures in this area of the Great Lakes (Cleland 1982). People took large numbers during annual spawning runs in the spring and fall (depending on species), but they also used nets, hooks, and spears to catch fish year-round. Species common to the study area and Georgian Bay include lake trout (*Salveninus namarycush*), lake white fish (*Coregonus upeaformus*), lake herring (*Coregonus artedi*), yellow perch (*Perca flavescens*), walleye (*Stizosedion vitreum*), northern pike (*Esox lucius*), muskellunge (*Esox masquinongy*), lake sturgeon (*Asipenser fulvescens*), brown bullhead (*Ameiurus nebulosus*), and many others (Mandrak and Crossman 1992; Scott and Crossman 1973). Those species that were naturally fatty, such as whitefish and lake trout, were preferred because of their higher caloric content; however, both large (i.e. sturgeon and lake trout) and small species (i.e. whitefish, suckers, and bullheads) would have provided valuable food resources in the area of east Manitoulin Island (Cleland 1982).

Indigenous people used a variety of plants for foods, medicines, crafts, and buildings. The Manitoulin district contains over one-third of all plant species found in Canada, making this area one of the most diverse floral regions in the country (Morton and Venn 2000). Many of the species currently found in the area, such as sweet flag (*Acorus americanus*), are known ingredients in traditional native herbal medicines. Plants such as the velvetleaf blueberry (*Vaccinium myrtilloides*), American cranberry (*Vaccinium macrocarpon*), and riverbank grape (*Vitis riparia*) are prized for their edible berries.

Wild rice (*Zizania palustrus*) is native to the area and stands of it can be seen today in the waters of nearby Lamorandière Bay. Native populations heavily exploited wild rice in the Great Lakes area for hundreds of years, and archaeological evidence has been recovered from periods as early as the Late Archaic and Middle Woodland in the Great Lakes region (Arzigian 2000; Benn 1980; Ford and Brose 1975a, b; Lopinot 1987; Munson et al. 1971). Two varieties of wild rice are known to exist in the northern Great Lakes area of Ontario: an interior variety and a northern variety. The latter is more common in the Manitoulin area and tends to grow in extensive beds in areas of shallow brown waters. Today large amounts are commercially harvested (Dore 1969). This annual plant is highly sensitive to the environment in which grows. It must take root in the muddy bottoms of gentle but steady streams and rivers and does not respond well to rapidly fluctuating water levels.

The question of whether wild rice was harvested and used to any great extent at the Middle Woodland Killarney Bay site was an open one throughout this reinvestigation process. Various indirect lines of evidence for wild rice use included numerous pit features recorded across the beach ridge by Greenman. Although Greenman interpreted them as (sweat) bath features, such pit features have been interpreted elsewhere as ricing pits used to process the grain. Because we lacked both flotation samples for floral recovery and organic (midden) soil samples for analysis, we could not search for direct evidence of preserved rice, or rice phytoliths.

The presence and importance of wild rice at other Middle Woodland mound sites across the Upper Great Lakes is well documented. Examples include the Rainey River mound complex at the border of Minnesota and northwestern Ontario and the Rice Lake mounds near Peterborough, Ontario (Hamilton 2013). As noted above, there is currently wild rice growing in smaller patches in the nearby shallow bays around the Killarney Bay site and elsewhere along Collins Inlet towards the French River. Because of this, we decided to look for rice pollen in the sediments of adjacent bogs that were part of the shallow embayments around Killarney Bay about 2,000 years ago. Specifically, we cored the Ministry of Transport Ontario bog, about 1 km east of the site, in the inlet embayment that existed between Speigel Island and the mainland (see Figure 2.5). Several cores were taken to a depth of nearly 2 m, and the sediment samples were analyzed for fossil pollen by John McAndrews.

Despite the importance of wild rice regionally, pollen analysis undertaken by McAndrews and Julig (see Appendix E, this volume) found no evidence that wild rice occurred within or near Killarney Bay during the time of site occupation. The cores from the nearby swamp contained no evidence of prehistoric wild rice growth. As expected, pine dominated the well-preserved pollen flora. The four regional pollen zones correlate with the profile from Fawn Lake, but the subzones cannot be distinguished. There may be a hiatus between zones 2 and 3. Three radiocarbon dates anchor the Fawn Lake calibrated-year chronology. The small Poaceae (grass) peak at 142–150 cm has a pollen-grain size distribution too small to be wild rice.

Conclusions

The Killarney Bay site is in an ecotone area of the Great Lakes. In prehistoric times, it was on an island within an archipelago with shallow water and lagoons, surrounded by thousands of islands of variable size. Manitoulin, the largest island within a freshwater lake in the world, is a short paddle away. The bedrock geology is highly varied, with Precambrian Canadian Shield white quartzites forming the bedrock of the La Cloche Mountains to the north, and limestones and dolomite alvar islands like Manitoulin to the south and west, all favoring different floral and faunal species. This area hosts more than a third of all known Canadian plant species, ranging from Arctic to Carolinian (southern deciduous) forest species. Coastal wetlands and newly emerging landscapes are among the most ecologically productive, and with the vast extent of coastal area (shorelines), this was truly a land of plentiful resources. Floral resources included wild fruits (hawberries, plums, blueberries, cranberries) and nuts; available fish included whitefish, lake trout, and sturgeon; fauna included both wetland species such as turtles, waterfowl, beaver, and larger terrestrial species such as deer, caribou, and moose. Despite the lack of direct evidence for local wild rice procurement, this was a land of relative plenty, and possibly a good example of the "original affluent society." It appears that a relative sedentism may have occurred and allowed time for the creation of larger features such as the mortuary mound complex (as covered in subsequent chapters).

Chapter 3

The Culture History of the Upper Great Lakes: An Overview

David Brose, William Fox, and Patrick Julig

The Killarney Bay and Manitoulin Island region has a rich archaeological record, extending from the Paleoindian period more than 10,000 years ago to the arrival of the first Europeans 400 years ago. The productive Lake Huron north shore environments, including terrestrial game and a rich freshwater fishery, made the region an important focal point for prehistoric occupation, while the large island known as Manitoulin was part of a traditional canoe travel route across northern Lake Huron. In this chapter, the prehistoric cultural periods represented in this region are summarized, with an emphasis on what is known to archaeologists as the Middle Woodland period, dating to between a little over 2,000 years ago to more than 1,000 years ago.

The Earliest Peoples

The prehistory of the region dates to the end of the Pleistocene some 12,000 years ago, with the first people, known as Paleoindians, moving into the Great Lakes from the south and west as the glaciers receded to the north. The "Eastern Plano" population occupied northeastern Manitoulin Island at sites such as Sheguiandah by 10,000 years ago (Julig 2002; Lee 2013) and spread as far east as southern Quebec (Chapdelaine and Graillon 2020) and the Maritimes, likely with the aid of watercraft (Fox 1975 and Jodry 2005). They were contemporary and interacted with groups to the south who followed a different lifestyle and practiced a different technology for toolmaking (Pilon and Fox 2015). Next came the Woodland period (c. 3000 before present to European contact). Archaeological sites from all these periods are known around the Killarney mainland and on Manitoulin Island. It appears that some of the same locations were used for quarry, habitation, and other purposes (for example, fishing) over extended periods.

Paleoindian populations were mobile hunter-gatherers who relied mainly on large and medium-size game species. The pioneering peoples (Deller et al. 2018) who moved northward lived and traveled along the shorelines of early Great Lakes such as Lake Algonquin, a high-water stand of Lake Huron (Ellis 2000 and Storck et al. 1997). Glacial ice was still present along the north shores of the Great Lakes, and taiga and a tundra-like environment continued to be present until around 10,000 years ago (Dyke et al. 2004). There is limited direct evidence for the Paleoindian way of life in the north. Few artifacts other than stone tools have survived; however, we can make inferences from site locations, size, and context. Their chipped stone tools include materials from distant geological sources, indicating considerable mobility and interaction with other bands (Buckmaster and Paquette 2018; Julig et al. 1989; Julig and Beaton 2015a, Fox et al. 2015, O'Shea et al. 2021). Their tool forms include lanceolate-shaped points, large bifaces used as knives and cores, and many unifacial tools made from flakes, such as scrapers and engraving tools. Paleoindians preferred to obtain these stone tool materials from bedrock outcrops rather than from secondary deposits such as tills and gravels, and local populations focused on re-crystalized quartzite bands with few joint planes (Julig and Long 2010). Northeast of Killarney, around George and Lumsden Lakes, there are similar indications of Paleoindian quartzite quarrying activity (Greenman 1966). These early inhabitants also used small amounts of local flints, such as Wiki chert from eastern Manitoulin (Fox 2009). The small mobile bands are assumed to have depended on herd animals such as caribou, as well as elk and moose, small game, and fish. However, archaeologists have not recovered many bones of the food sources they used, nor evidence of their house forms, so archaeologists do not have detailed information on their lifeways, subsistence, and settlement patterns. One exception is a complex of hunting sites and other features located on the Alpena-Amberley Ridge beneath modern Lake Huron (Lemke and O'Shea 2019; Sonnenburg et al. 2015). The submerged sites are associated with the Lake Stanley low stand in the Huron basin and date to around 9000 before present, when lake levels were up to 100 meters lower than those at present (Janusas et al. 2004; Lewis et al. 2007; McCarthy and McAndrews 2012). These hunters employed stone drive lanes to exploit caribou during the annual migrations. The stone assemblages associated with these hunters differ significantly from the Plano tradition hunters; they made use of small flake tools as well as composite tools fashioned on bone and antler.

The lengthy Archaic era as defined by archaeologists, beginning over 8,000 years ago (Hanks 1988) in the northern Great Lakes region and lasting until almost 3,000 years ago, was similar in many ways to the late Paleo period (Storck 1974). In the boreal forest, the culture is referred to as the Shield Archaic (Wright 1995). The hunting-gathering-fishing way of life continued, with some evidence that larger macro-bands assembled at larger lakes and rivers throughout the region, with a greater focus on specific resources such as fish. Archaic people used local chert, quartz, quartzite, and poorer-quality materials such as greywacke and argillite for producing lithic (stone) tools. The working of native copper from Lake Superior basin sources also began early during this period (Beukens et al. 1992; Pompeani et al. 2021). New hunting technology is evident in the Archaic era, with the recovery of side-notched early Archaic dart points and knives (Pilon and Fox 2015). In addition, other new tool forms appear, such as ground stone gouges and trihedral chipped adzes (Fox 1980), which indicate a variety of woodworking activities. Archaic people evidently used watercraft such as dugout canoes or hide-covered boats to travel throughout the Canadian Shield during the warm season.

Studies indicate repeat occupation of shoreline and lithic acquisition sites along the north shore of the Great Lakes, from Paleo through Archaic times (Julig 2002; Julig and Beaton 2015a). Since water levels during the 5,000 years of Archaic occupation fluctuated to points that are both lower and higher than the modern Great Lakes, many coastal sites in the Huron basin dating to the early and middle Archaic periods are now underwater (Janusas et al. 2004; McCarthy et al 2015; Sonnenburg et al. 2015). However, numerous aceramic sites directly associated with Nipissing high-stand beach terraces dating to 5,000 years ago most probably represent Middle Archaic occupations (e.g. Julig and Beaton 2015a:Figure 5.2). These strandlines, which average from six to thirty meters above present water levels from south to north in the Lake Huron basin due to post-glacial isostatic rebound, flooded late Paleo and early Archaic occupation sites in the southern basin, evidenced by water-rolled bifaces (Deller 1976). Lake levels receded to modern elevations over the centuries, as represented by a succession of lower strandline terraces occupied by late Archaic peoples until shortly after 3,000 years ago. Their campsites, characterised by changing biface projectile point styles, have been recorded around the Lake Huron basin

(Lovis and Robertson 1989; Ramsden 1975; Wright 1972a). Throughout the Archaic era, archaeology has evidenced a continued east-west interface between peoples of differing cultural traditions occupying the shores of the northern and southern Lake Huron basin (Ellis et al. 2015).

During the final centuries of the Archaic era, cemeteries were established at strategic points within macro-band homelands (Conolly 2018), and mortuary ritual became elaborated through the use of red ochre paint and exotic marine shell and stone artifact inclusions in burials (Abel et al. 2001). Archaeologists have applied names to these mortuary complexes, such as Glacial Kame (Converse 1979; Donaldson and Wortner 1995; Spence and Fox 1986) in the eastern lower Great Lakes region and Red Ochre to the west (Pleger 2000). Distinctive marine shell gorgets and bar-style birdstones characterize assemblages from cemeteries scattered across the Carolinian biotic province of southern Ontario, while Onondaga chert Hind bifaces anticipate the slightly later forms of the Meadowood Early Woodland culture (Spence and Fox 1986).

The Woodland Era Peoples

The single defining attribute used by archaeologists to signal the beginning of the Woodland era is the adoption of ceramic technology—the construction and use of clay pots, as opposed to bark or wooden containers for liquid food preparation—some 3,000 years ago (Taché and Hart 2013). Otherwise, the day-to-day life of Indigenous peoples throughout the Great Lakes region changed little in terms of terminal Archaic lifestyle. Southern populations continued to subsist on hunting, fishing, and gathering, including the growth of domesticated wild seed plants and the addition of an exotic cultigen: squash or gourds (Otto and Redmond 2008; Ozker 1982). Subsistence activities changed little for more northerly populations occupying the Canadian biotic province, with the possible exception of more intense harvesting of wild rice. Mortuary ceremonialism continued to elaborate, particularly at warm season macro-band gatherings. Mound building was initiated by the western Adena populations (Fitting and Brose 1971), but was not practiced by eastern bands participating in the Meadowood interaction sphere (Taché 2011). Neither Vinette 1 ceramics nor the Onondaga chert biface cache blades characteristic of Meadowood have been recovered from the Killarney Bay area, although Vinette 1 sherds were identified on a Lake Nipissing campsite (Spence et al. 1990) and a nearly complete vessel was recovered on the upper Ottawa River to the east (Mitchell 1963).

By approximately 2,300 years ago, the Meadowood interaction sphere had disappeared, to be replaced by a Middle Woodland mortuary complex characterized by large bifaces of chert from south of the Great Lakes (Fox 2010). Societies in this region, referred to as Hopewell, established one of the largest North American interaction spheres on record, with materials used in ritual activities acquired from the Rocky Mountains to the Atlantic seaboard and northern Ontario to the Gulf coast (Struever 1963; Struever and Houart 1972). The construction of massive mortuary and geometric earthworks (Redmond et al. 2019; Romain 2015) did not generate large-scale towns, as local populations continued to occupy scattered extended family domestic units (Brose and Greber 1979; Redmond et al. 2020). Hunting, fishing, and gathering subsistence activities continued with little change, except for the addition of a new exotic cultigen, which would increase in importance as the centuries passed: maize (Hart et al. 2021). The Killarney Bay archaeology—including a material culture record of local domestic activities and participation in exchange networks for exotic native copper, marine shell, the first tobacco smoking pipes, and chert bifaces—documents local Indigenous activities spanning some 600 years.

The Hopewell interaction sphere, with all of its social implications, disappeared by 1,500 years ago, and the archaeological record throughout the Great Lakes region evidences considerably less long-distance interaction until European contact (Fox 2008). There were exceptions to this trend. In the Midwest, the rise of the town of Cahokia impacted populations to the north a little less than 1,000 years ago, particularly in the Lake Michigan basin. There are tantalizing pieces of organic evidence reflecting some long-distance contacts, such as cotton fibers from an Erie lakeshore site dating to a little more than 1,000 years ago (Blatt et al. 2011), and the identification of caffeine residue in a 1,200-year-old ceramic vessel recovered from the bottom of Lake Ontario (Poulin 2014). The only North American plant containing caffeine is yaupon, a Southeastern ivy used in the famous "black drink" of Mississippian populations to the south. Ancestral Huron–Wendat agriculturalists moved into Odawa territory along the south shore of Georgian Bay more than 700 years ago (Fox and Garrad

2004), establishing a close relationship with Algonquian populations in the Upper Great Lakes, particularly the Odawa and Nipissings, as evidenced by the distribution of Iroquoian ceramics throughout the Upper Great Lakes and north into the Canadian Shield (Guindon 2009). By the early seventeenth century, the French documented a series of Anishinaabe bands occupying river drainages along the north Huron shore, including the Amikwa or beaver people situated in the Killarney vicinity (Heidenreich 1988; Steckley 1990). Anishinaabe people continue to reside at Killarney and on First Nation reserve lands a short distance to the west, south, and east.

The Middle Woodland Period in the Great Lakes

The Killarney Bay site belongs chronologically to the Middle Woodland period. This is the time of the iconic Adena and Hopewell complexes in the Midwest, with their elaborate earthworks and burial mounds filled with ornate ceramics and exotic materials acquired from across the continent. Among these latter exotics, artifacts fashioned from copper figure prominently, which immediately turned archaeologists' eyes northward for possible copper sources and interacting trade partners. Yet even as elaborate models of the Hopewell Interaction Sphere (Struever and Houart 1972) and the Adena burial cult (Wright 1987: Plate 14) were invoked to link sites like Killarney Bay to a Hopewell world system, it was clear to some scholars that the more northerly Middle Woodland sites represented a very different kind of cultural and economic adaptation, one often subsumed under the term Laurel or Lake Forest, and Point Peninsula in the northeast (Mason 1981). Yet even this does not do justice to the variation in form and adaptation observed among Middle Woodland groups in the Upper Great Lakes. Ceramic vessels are the hallmark of the arrival of the Woodland period across the Great Lakes region, but this class of artifacts is much more common in the south than north. Ceramic sherds may be sparse to absent on many northern Middle Woodland sites (Wright 1987). Likewise, the mortuary mound complexes common for southern Middle Woodland are clearly represented only in parts of the north, such as the large Laurel burial mounds in the boundary waters of Minnesota and northwestern Ontario, and Point Peninsula mounds in eastern Ontario, both around large wild rice producing lakes. On the Canadian Shield area across the vast northern coasts of Lake Superior and Lake Huron, mound ceremonialism is largely absent, except for some small mounds such as those at Killarney Bay (which is near the boundary of northern and southern regions—the French River, just south of Killarney).

The archaeological record for Middle Woodland on the edge of the Canadian Shield, including the Killarney region, is rather different than that for southern Ontario and much of the lower Great Lakes region. There is more agricultural activity in the south, and surface survey there has revealed many more sites. By contrast, researchers in northeastern Ontario have located relatively fewer Middle Woodland sites. Those recorded are mostly from shoreline surveys of rivers and lakes and tested with few major excavations. Few sites with large mounds or earthworks—comparable to Laurel sites in the west and Point Peninsula sites to the southeast—have been recorded. Such Middle Woodland mound and earthwork sites are typically associated with wild rice lakes and harvesting. In the northeast, the Canadian Shield terrain is very rugged, with few clay-bottomed lakes suitable for rice habitat. As noted by Wright (1999), small Middle Woodland campsites often resemble Archaic lithic scatters and have few ceramic sherds. Further, he noted, "a scattering of southern "diagnostics" is not a sufficient basis for reconstructing culture histories" (ibid. p. 704).

As discussed in Chapter 2, the northeast region of the Great Lakes is an ecotone—a cool humid forest with a mixture of deciduous and conifer species and a high diversity of prey species as well. The archaeological assemblages recovered are a mixture of Laurel, Point Peninsula, and some southern influences (Figure 3.1).

Wright (1967) originally referred to Middle Woodland sites from this area as "Eastern Laurel." Some influences of Hopewell combine with Laurel, as seen in ceramic assemblages with the combination of Pseudo-Scallop Shell and Rocker Stamping techniques on the same vessels. Pollock (1976) used Wright's model to outline the boundaries of this tradition to include Manitoulin Island and Killarney; the French, Mattawa, and Ottawa River systems and Lake Abitibi to the north; and the Moose River drainage even further north. Julig (1982) recorded a Laurel site on the Albany River, even further north. Conway (1980, 1981) echoed the impression of Wright that a somewhat distinct regional prehistoric cultural complex, combining some

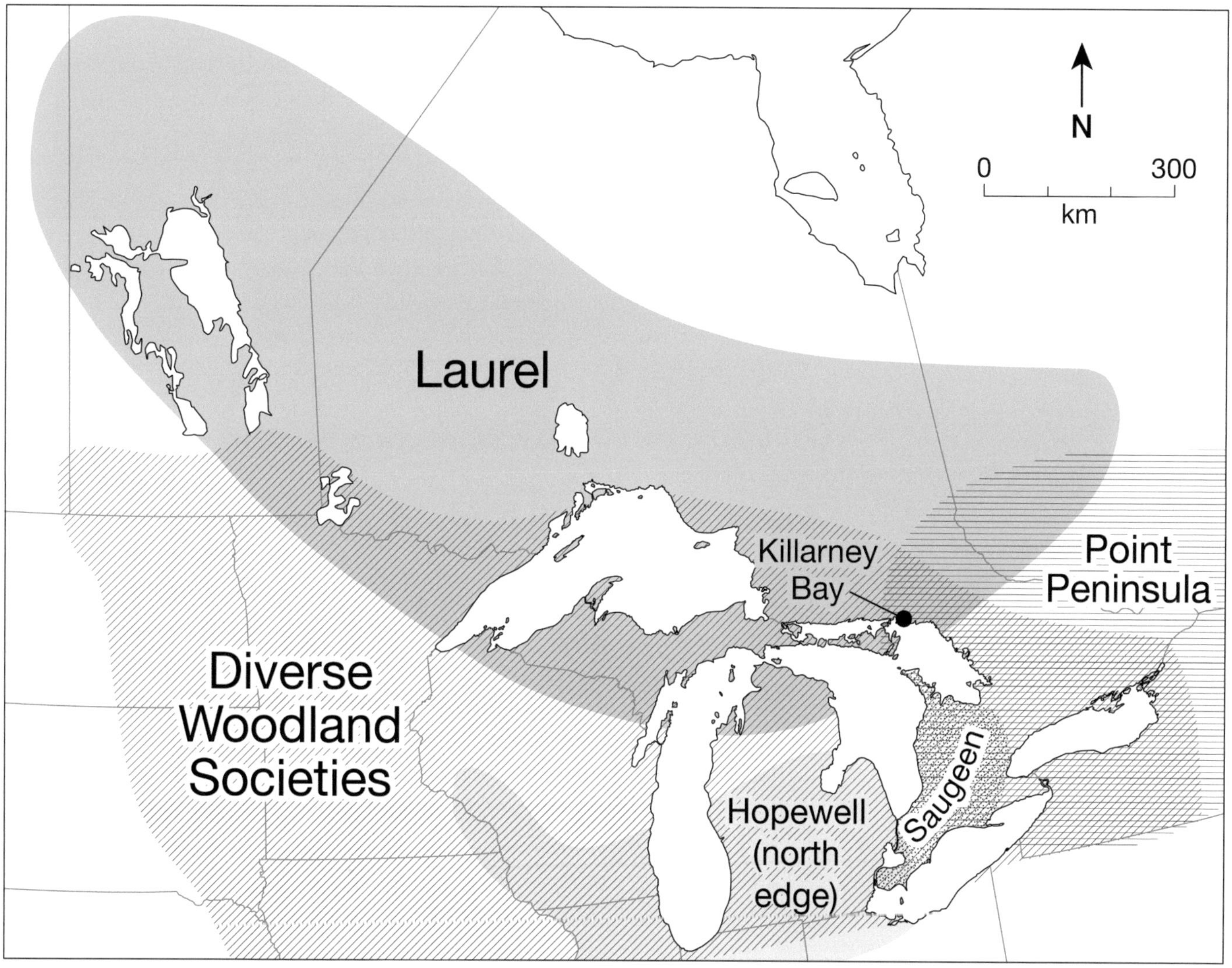

Figure 3.1. The Killarney Bay site in the context of the approximate distribution of major Woodland cultures in the Upper Great Lakes. (Map by John Klausmeyer, after Hamilton 2013: Figure 5.9.)

Laurel and Hopewell influences, existed, and outlined the area of this proposed "La Cloche Complex" to include the north shore of Lake Huron and the La Cloche Mountains near Killarney. Conway said that Eastern Laurel was present around Sault Ste. Marie, including the eastern Canadian shore of Lake Superior from Michipicoten River to the Straits of Mackinac in upper Michigan (see Figure 3.1).

Later, Wright (1999) refined and greatly changed his Middle Woodland interpretation of the region and dropped the Eastern Laurel designation in favor of Late Eastern Shield culture. He preferred to interpret sites from this region based on lithic technology rather than ceramic traits, since the sparse pottery with its mixture of traits was difficult to interpret. Also of note for this region was the relatively high percentage of end scrapers in the lithic assemblage, as we see at the Killarney Bay site. Wright thought the trait mixtures were likely rooted in marriage patterns and felt that they made the creation of a sharp cultural boundary nearly impossible, particularly without the excavation and analysis of more complete assemblages. He considered portions of northeastern Ontario to represent an eastern regional variant of Late Western Shield culture but dropped the Eastern Laurel designation.

Other proposed models include Mason's (1981) synthesis of Great Lakes archaeology, which sees the Middle Woodland as three latitudinal tiers: the southern

Hopewellian; a middle tier, including Point Peninsula and Saugeen; and towards the west, the Nokomis and North Bay. In this model, Laurel remained the sole Middle Woodland culture of the northern tier. The area around Killarney would be on the boundary of Laurel and Point Peninsula. However, Mason also notes that this situation was likely much more complex; he recognized "the certainty that other regional and local Middle Woodland cultures remain undiscovered or unrecognized" (1981:260). Since Mason's work, our understanding of this region's prehistoric culture has been refined, particularly in southern Ontario. While some may disagree with Mason's three-tier approach, ceramic traditions suggest interaction spheres of fairly discreet cultural groups to the south in Ontario, including the Point Peninsula, Saugeen, and Couture. Work is still needed in the Shield region, particularly in the northeast. Ceramics frequencies are low on most sites, and ceramic traditions, while evident, are not grouped discreetly. Consequently, some archaeologists (e.g. Wright 1999) have suggested this class of artifacts is not useful in defining cultural affinity in the northeast. The fact that senior archaeologists have regularly changed their minds and revised their own (conventional) interpretations of the Middle Woodland in the northeast shows the complexity of the situation (Gordon 2013).

What is clear is that this area of the Great Lakes was a dynamic region influenced by a variety of people during the Middle Woodland time period. Intermarriage would have affected the cultures of northeastern Ontario, as would the influx of new ideas, exotic goods, and cultural constructs through established trade networks with distant cultural centers. Certain raw materials like copper, silver, argillite, and exotic chert, as well as abundant beaver furs and other resources, may have contributed to the trade networks that are evident in the archaeological assemblages. As noted, southern exotics were certainly traded into the Shield regional sites, including marine whelk shells, Ohio Valley flints, tubular pipes, and galena (lead ore). Also present throughout the entire Middle Woodland region are Lake Superior copper, Hudson Bay Lowland chert, and small amounts of Knife River flint, western obsidian, Mistassini, Ramah, and Albanel (Labrador) chert (quartzite), Gowganda argillite, Cobalt (northern Ontario) silver, red ochre, and other minerals and ores. Most of these minerals, metals, and lithics are of northern sources, showing the importance of northern exotics to the lower Great Lakes Middle Woodland cultures (Wright 1987:Plate 14). Indeed, several sources of red ochre (ancient mines), are located in the region fairly nearby, one east on the Mattawa River and another near Sault Ste. Marie, west of Killarney (MacDonald et al. 2018). These moved to Middle Woodland sites through various interaction spheres. For the northern Middle Woodland (or Laurel), including Mason's (1981) northern tier, the sites spread from Manitoba and Saskatchewan in the west across all of north central Ontario and through Quebec, encompassing much of the Canadian Shield. This is an area of several thousand square miles.

The Middlesex Mortuary Complex

The Middlesex Focus was first defined based on sites such as the Palatine Bridge site in New York State (Ritchie 1944:186–202, Plate 90). Middlesex Focus components are distributed from the Killarney Bay site in the west to the Augustine and Skora mounds in eastern Canada (Bourque 1994:33; Turnbull 1976:50–62). The manifestation in the Maritime Peninsula has since been named the Northeastern Middlesex Tradition (Deal 2001). In a 1960 volume co-authored with Dragoo concerning the eastern dispersal of the Ohio Valley Adena culture, Ritchie writes "the chief coincidences of Middlesex and Adena were stated to be... the blocked-end tubular pipe; leaf-shaped knife; discoidal shell bead; copper bead; copper awl, rectangular in section; and boatstone" (Ritchie and Dragoo 1960:27). Ritchie and Dragoo present the number of "Middlesex traits not reported for Adena" found at nineteen northeast United States sites (Ritchie and Dragoo 1960:Figure 2). Forty-one traits are so identified (Ibid.:77–80, Table 5), and the number of strictly Middlesex traits at the nineteen sites increases as one proceeds northward. Many such sites have been equated with a movement of Adena people (Ritchie and Dragoo 1960:61) or as a "communication of ideas" (Turnbull 1976:60) from the Ohio Valley to points north and east.

Spence et al. (1990:138–142) have continued to use the term Middlesex Complex in regards to north central Ontario sites such as Killarney Bay and Morrison Island 2. They considered this mortuary complex to be Early Woodland in age (this does not, however, agree with the ^{14}C dates reported in this volume). Consistent with Turnbull's perspective, they note "a good deal of localized variation...Incoming goods and ideas were screened, selected and adapted to fit local systems of ritual and social expression" (Spence et al. 1990:142).

Other Middlesex sites in southern Ontario include Schlegel (Thor 2008), See mound (Boyle 1888:9–11, 46–47; Spence 1967:3–7, Plates I–III), Pike farm (Boyle 1889:11, 41, 44; Spence 1967:7–10, Plates IV and V), Grenadier Island (Wintemberg 1928:178), Morrison Island (Spence et al. 1990:140), and Long Sault Island (Ritchie and Dragoo 1960:39–56). All are or were situated on islands some two millennia ago. They are sited at strategic points on major waterways on or adjacent to the Canadian Shield. The fact that they are not distributed to the west of the Shield may be significant from a cultural standpoint—that is, all are located within the historically documented homeland of northern Algonquian peoples. All are co-terminous with or at least peripheral to the distribution of the Point Peninsula culture region. The latter is also true for New York State Middlesex sites. However, as noted by Spence et al. (1990:138), "The Middlesex complex is known almost exclusively from burial components, most of which are in New York and New England states," with a few components and some isolated finds along the St. Lawrence River, and to the east as far as Labrador. Only a few components are located on the Canadian Shield, such as Killarney, Schlegel, and Morrison Island 2. Nearly all southern Middlesex complex sites have not been found associated with habitations and/or workshop activities, while the northern examples—such as Killarney Bay, Schlegel, and Morrison Island—have habitation and workshop activities directly associated. In this sense, those northern examples stand apart from the southern Middlesex model.

The Killarney Bay site conforms to this model in the sense that several of the burials represent a unique site-specific expression of multiple interaction spheres, based on a variety of artifact classes and mortuary program characteristics ("traits" as articulated by Webb and Snow (1945) for Adena). One of the more illuminating artifact classes in this regard is the lithic bifaces recovered from these specific mortuary contexts. The range of chert materials reflects connections with Shield regions to the northwest and northeast of the site as well as the Mississippi Valley to the southwest and Ohio Valley to the south. Local quartzites and cherts (Wiki and Detour) are also represented, but the majority of the chert and quartzite bifaces from mortuary contexts are northern in origin.

The context of the sites and burial places across the region is variable north to south, with southern Middlesex mortuary components found isolated from living habitation sites. In the north, burials are often found right in habitation workshop areas or directly adjacent, as with Archaic to Middle Woodland sites along the Ottawa River, such as Morrison and Allumette Island, the Killarney Bay and Schlegel sites, and other examples mentioned.

A tradition of small burial mounds is observed in the Early and Middle Maritime Archaic of northeastern Canada going back 7,500 years, so we need not look south of the Great Lakes for early burial mounds. The L'Anse Amour burial mound in southern Labrador is the earliest elaborate mortuary structure in Canada, with a one-meter-high mound with a subadult of between 11–13 years, abundant bone and stone artifacts, and abundant red ochre (McGhee and Tuck 1975). This pattern of occasional small mound burials with grave goods and red ochre is found in adjacent Quebec, at Tumulus II near Blanc-Sablon, dating to ca. 3500 before present, and elsewhere across the region north of the St. Lawrence over a considerable time span (Wright 1995:87). These mound mortuary features are likely of special ceremonial significance, and not the normal burial methods, as burial pits with grave offerings are also found. Most dating to this Archaic era are lacking bones, having been dissolved by soil acids. These occasional burial mounds may have functioned as sacred territorial markers to the Archaic populations along the St. Lawrence, to mark special places or summer camps along the coast. Similar patterns may have existed for Killarney and elsewhere in the uppermost regions of the St. Lawrence river system, into the late Archaic and Middle Woodland. Indeed, we have evidence of such small traditional burial mounds being built and maintained in the Killarney, French River/Point Grondine, and Beaverstone river area into the current century (Julig et al. 2006).

There are numerous small mounds at other sites around the Killarney/French River and along the shores of many larger lakes and rivers, as reported in regional survey over the past half-century. However, due to the moratorium on Indigenous burial site excavations since the Ontario Heritage Act (1974), it is not normally possible to investigate such mounds, unless they are eroding away or being destroyed. For example, surveys in 2003 and 2004 of Point Grondine Reserve Number 3 and Collins inlet (Julig et al. 2006; Pitawanakwat et al. 2004), directly south of Killarney, recorded five mounds associated with sites. The largest, Beaverstone River #2 at Beaverstone Bay village, was built in shape of a beaver—about 1.5 m in height, 6 m long, oval in shape with a depression on the top, with a tail.

Most of the other mounds along the Beaverstone River and nearby Chichanishing Creek are relatively small, fairly near the water, and could almost be mistaken for large beaver houses except that they are constructed from river bank alluvial sediments and some have drainage ditches around the edges, which lead to the river. None of the mounds recorded around the region since the 1970s have been excavated, so artifact associations are unknown.

Several of the mounds reported in the 2003/04 Point Grondine survey (Julig et al. 2006) are at fairly low elevations above Lake Huron lake levels, suggesting late Woodland to historic era construction. One was still being tended (brush removed), and there was traditional effigy replacement (fresh bear totem), showing ritual activities and use of small mounds up to the present era. The larger beaver-shaped mound is further back at higher elevation. We therefore suggest this small to medium-sized multiple mound cluster mortuary practice is a "tradition" of several millennia in the Killarney and surrounding region.

Local and Regional Exchange

The Killarney Bay site existed during a dynamic time period. Across 1000 km, from the prairies to the Appalachians, hundreds of ceremonial and mortuary sites and scores of archaeological complexes dating from 450 BCE to 450 CE have been assigned to these Woodland cultures. As we have seen, there is a lack of congruence between the social organization of mortuary ritual and the potential settlement and economic systems of those who occupied the Killarney Bay site (however ephemerally) and the ceremonialism and inferred economies of any one of the archaeological cultures of the Upper Great Lakes (such as Meadowood, Adena, Hopewell, Middlesex, Laurel, or Point Peninsula).

Yet the site contains a range of exotic materials known from these contemporary archaeological cultures, including cold-hammered copper celts and beads, drilled shell beads, cut and polished metamorphic stone, and oddly patterned or colored chipped sedimentary rock. These materials were used in socially reintegrative mortuary ceremonies across the mid-continent for a millennium (Baby and Snow 1957; Brose 1994a; Brose and Greber 1979; Fitting 1972, 1978; Fitting and Brose 1971; Fox and Spence 1990; Greenman 1932; Griffin 1967; Mason 1981; McManamon et al. 2009; Otto and Redmond 2008; Struever and Houart 1972; Taché 2011; Willey and Sabloff 1980; Winters 1968). They are thought to have tied disparate groups across patchy ecosystems into some sort of systematic relationships, but whether economic or social or ritual or merely iconographic (or all of those potential connections) is as yet undetermined (Brose 1979, 2005; Carr and Case 2005; Greber 2005; Lynott 2009; Penney 1985).

The emergence of long-distance exchange networks and elaborate funerary ceremonialism associated with the Early and Middle Woodland periods in the Midwest is conventionally attributed to climatic shifts that necessitated changes in subsistence activities and associated social interaction. Where dense populations strained seasonal subsistence resources, intergroup collaboration became structured by individual and family ritual exchange. Native copper tools and ornaments, large ornaments of marine shell, and large caches of exotic chert and flint blades, along with tubular and effigy pipes of exotic material all played a role in this social intensification, with elite lineage burials and constructed ceremonial structures. Through time there was an increase in the number and size of circular earthworks and burial mounds, and their distribution tended to become more centralized and discontinuous. Mortuary offerings included shell, mica, and pipestone from Mid-Atlantic and Appalachian groups and geometric objects, ornaments, or small tools of Great Lakes copper, hematite, or central Mississippi Valley galena.

By the Early Woodland Period, a localized pattern of diffuse hunting, fishing, and gathering had become established throughout the Midwest. In broad river valleys, residents encouraged or deliberately cultivated the growth of sunflower, chenopods (including goosefoot), and marsh elder in order to obtain starchy and oily seeds. By the beginning of a warmer climatic period, ca 500 BCE, people were growing cucurbits in the Great Lakes river valleys (Lovis and MacDonald 1999). During the following centuries, they cultivated large-seeded native grasses on the terraces of the major river valleys to the south (Cowan 1977, 1978; Smith 1992; Struever and Houart 1972; Yarnell 1964). Sometime during this early era (ca. 200 BCE–200 CE), wild rice had appeared in the archaeological record of Ontario Point Peninsula sites in the Trent/Severn region of Ontario (Spence et al. 1990) and at Laurel and Laurel-like sites in Minnesota. Features from Manitoba/Ontario waterside Middle Woodland sites were interpreted as wild rice jigging or stomping pits.

By 500 BCE, these Midwestern patterns of local exchange coalesced in two regional traditions. Morton complexes in Illinois had group burials in log crypts within groups of mounds at seasonally reoccupied sites on major river terraces. Ochre was liberally used, and several individuals display cranial deformation. Ceramics showed local technology and morphology but carried decorative motifs from the Lower Mississippi Valley. The few goods with individuals or in isolated caches included copper beads, Illinois and Indiana flint blades, gorgets of marine shell, and fragments of hematite and galena.

At the same time, in the discontinuous concentrations of Adena ritual sites along the Scioto and Ohio River valleys, a few related individuals were cremated and placed in log- or clay-lined pits below small mounds, all within a circular house. These in turn were burned and mounded over with earth. Some sites, such as the Adena and Miamisburg Mounds in Ohio, the Anderson Earthworks in Indiana, Grave Creek Mound in West Virgina, and the Robbins and Mt. Horeb Mounds in Kentucky, showed several styles of grave and mortuary treatment and numerous episodes of accretion. Grave goods, generally with only a few individuals in any mound, included cut animal teeth and jaws (some as masks); gorgets of polished Appalachian slate or native copper; occasionally fully carved tubular pipes of stone from Ohio, Ontario, or the mid-Atlantic; and caches of points and blades of Ohio Flint Ridge flint or Pennsylvania jasper.

From centers in the southern Indiana/southwestern Ohio region and along the north-flowing Kentucky/West Virginia watersheds, one vector of exchange ran north to Ontario and Quebec, where Adena-like mortuary artifacts such as projectile points and stone tubular pipes appeared at sites along lakes Huron and Ontario and the lower St. Lawrence.

By 200 BCE, Early Woodland ceramic innovations had spread across the northern Great Lakes from both east and west. The consistent exchange of local materials over time and the broad participation in similar social rituals at many sites suggests these connections were more than occasional southern excursions.

Yet throughout this region in the Early Woodland, there were distinctions between societies that participated in long distance exchange and a larger number of societies that did not. There were also status distinctions among and within the involved groups, marked by material goods and by regionally restricted rituals—quite different from the more uniform occurrences of the Late Archaic.

The Middle Woodland social relations of the Midwest and the Great Lakes were variable. Though the Midwest had long, warm, moist summers with short mild winters from 300 BCE to 536 CE, no Middle Woodland economy was committed to agriculture. The rare cobs or kernels recovered from a few ceremonial and domestic sites in Ohio and Illinois represent occasional gardening at best. People continued to intensively harvest several native and tropical seed plants. Collecting acorns, nuts, and shellfish; fishing; and hunting deer and turkey structured the seasonal locations of most Middle Woodland sites. Their overall material culture and domestic architecture seem to have changed little over the millennium between 250 BCE and 650 CE. Raw materials and the styles of domestic artifacts were also regional, although exotic materials from the Upper Great Lakes, the Gulf and south Atlantic coasts, the farthest Missouri Valley, and the south Appalachian piedmont occurred in mortuary rituals, along with new, pan-regional icons. The regional foci for these cultural patterns were the Havana complex of central Illinois and, somewhat later and far more spectacular, the Hopewell complex of southern Ohio.

In Illinois and Indiana, incised Havana and Crab Orchard pottery became common in small river terrace villages. It occurred in the few associated early Havana mortuary mounds, which were constructed in stages over structures containing platforms with fires. Family groups in subfloor tombs had personal possessions and a few exotic goods or iconographic ceramics. More plentiful, if smaller and less complex, Middle Havana tradition mounds served several larger villages on bluffs and terraces. Most mounds contained a few reburials with few grave goods, including Classic Hopewellian pottery vessels. Smaller and later mounds were constructed over single subfloor pit cremations or burials with few status distinctions or individual accumulations of goods. At many mounds, one or two individuals had a mica mirror or an Ohio-style effigy pipe. There were cut carnivore or human teeth and jaws, a few copper or exotic stone ornaments, many rubbed fragments of Missouri galena, and numerous bracelets or necklaces of local and/or marine shell beads and pearls. Caches of local chert points were frequent. Sites also yielded a few points of obsidian or Knife River chalcedony from the upper Missouri River, and a few points of Ohio Flint Ridge. In many respects, it appears that some of the more iconic exotic goods found in surprising quantities within certain Ohio Hopewell burial mounds are also present in association with a number of Illinois Havana mound burials, albeit in far lower frequencies.

In regions beyond the core Illinois Havana Hopewell area, such as southern Michigan and Wisconsin, there are sites that, to some extent, replicate the Havana ritual patterns. Havana ceramics and a few objects occurred in the Trempealeau Mound group in Wisconsin, at related sites in southeast Minnesota, and at sites in eastern Iowa and Missouri and along the Missouri River to the Renner site at Kansas City. Havana styles and rituals were adopted at a few sites up the Illinois and Kankakee rivers to the Lake Michigan shore and to the Muskegon and Grand River Norton Mounds in western Michigan, and thence to the small mounds at the large reoccupied Schultz fishing site near Saginaw Bay. Most Havana individuals received mound burials and burial goods. However, the ritual patterns found at these peripheral Havana sites (from Kansas to Michigan), differed in frequency from those in Illinois. And all of these related sites, including Havana Hopewell, differed substantially from core Ohio Hopewell manifestations.

The most well-known Ohio Hopewell sites are the large ceremonial mound and earthwork complexes of the Miami, Scioto, and Muskingum river valleys. In Ohio, these large and complex earthwork centers are nestled amidst arrays of domestic architecture and activities, only some of which appear to be seasonally or ritually restricted. Recent excavations continue to reveal a surprising number of adjacent small domestic camps and hamlets, as well as a few similar domestic and/or workshop sites in nearby drainages (Nolan et al. 2016; Pacheco 1996; Redmond et al. 2020). The sites, usually on river floodplains, consist of a few subrectangular single post houses for minimally extended families practicing general hunting and gathering, with some limited gardening of local seed plants. They contain little of the exotic material and few of the artifacts or elaborate ceramics found with burials.

In the Upper Great Lakes generally—east from Manitoba and northern Minnesota, around Lake Huron, to the St. Lawrence Valley of southern Ontario and New York—small Northern Tier Middle Woodland camps and large mounds spanned the period 250 BCE to 500 CE. The populations of the northern lakes were more dispersed and mobile than their southern contemporaries. Nevertheless, they did participate in the Middle Woodland exchange networks to varying degrees. Despite economic and social differences, these exchange networks tied them to the Havana and Hopewell systems. However, these ties or links were not expressed in a uniform manner; we can discern several distinct temporal and geographic patterns. Only in some regions were the exotic artifacts accompanying burials related to age or sex. Few mounds or even mound groups contained all potential status classes. While great concentrations exist, they are not restricted to specific sources or artifact types, nor were they associated with the same types of social groupings.

Despite the similarity of exotic goods, as ritual objects they were often used in distinctive ways among the various groups, suggesting there was no single ideological system structuring their use and occurrence. During the millennium between the end of the Late Archaic and the last of the Middle Woodland Period (450 BCE to 450 CE), mortuary behavior and ceramic technology and decoration (and likely, ceramic functions) showed changes across the vast northwest to southeast drainage of the Great Lakes. It is equally apparent that lithic sources, functions, styles, and ritual disposal systems developed and changed at different rates in different parts of this region. And, perhaps more importantly, all of these phenomena showed differing relationships to zones beyond the drainage basin, and no single Middle Woodland exchange network operated across 1500 km and 750 years.

This is the "global" context within which the Killarney Bay site was inhabited and in which the exotic goods recovered from the site must be understood. The site existed in a nodal geographic location for the acquisition of copper and for the movement of more distant exotic goods from the west, north, and east. It also existed on an ecological frontier between the more sedentary and horticultural societies to the south and the more mobile hunting-fishing-gathering adaptations of the Upper Great Lakes, as well as on the periphery of the more formalized ritual and symbolic system represented by Ohio and Illinois Hopewell. All of these factors will come into play in the chapters that follow, as we seek an archaeological and anthropological understanding of the Killarney Bay site.

Part II

Archaeological Investigations at Killarney Bay

Chapter 4

Dates and Chronology of the Killarney Bay Site

Patrick Julig and John O'Shea

The attribution of Killarney Bay to a specific cultural and chronological context has been a central question in its long history of investigation; from its potential very early date and its connection with early Holocene changes in lake levels, to its possible association with the Meadowood Complex with its cache blades and red ochre, and potential ties to Adena/Hopewell seen in copper artifacts and exotic tubular pipes. These disparate finds tended to confound traditional methods of dating based on diagnostic artifact types. As luck would have it, technology, in the form of Libby's newly discovered method of dating via ^{14}C, had the potential to resolve these questions (Libby et al. 1949). Equally fortuitously, Greenman had access to the technique via the early establishment of a carbon dating lab at the University of Michigan.

The first date run for the Killarney Bay site appeared in the first list of dates published by the Michigan lab in 1956. The sample derived from a deep stone feature in the burial area that Greenman expected to reflect a very early occupation of the region. It did not and, as Brose notes in Chapter 5, this had a major impact on Greenman's approach to the site. Subsequently, two additional dates were run by the Michigan lab that supported the original determination (Table 4.1).

As discussed in earlier chapters, several factors provide a reasonable temporal placement for the mortuary area of the Killarney Bay site: the geological position of the site on a ca. 2,000-year-old Algoma-age beach; the recovery of Middle Woodland ceramics and lithic artifacts of possible Middlesex complex affinity; and three ^{14}C dates done by Greenman (1966). These dates, including one from Burial 8 (beaver fur), range from 2180 to 1930 years BP, with a mean of 2040, but with large standard deviations, as they were done using the gas sample technique.

While the three ^{14}C dates were useful for dating the mound complex and one burial (Burial 8), the large standard deviations associated with the early gas method and limited counting time left unresolved many questions regarding the

Table 4.1. University of Michigan carbon dates for the Killarney Bay site.

Lab Number	Age BP	Standard Deviation	Context	Reference
M-194	2180	150*	Lower stone feature	Michigan List I, Crane 1956
M-428	2040	100*	Burial 8	Michigan List IV, Crane and Griffin 1959
M-1482	1930	130	Higher stone feature	Michigan List XI, Crane and Griffin 1966

*The originally published figure was in error: it was double the statistical standard deviation (Crane and Griffin 1966:256). Here we correct the published values to reflect the actual standard deviation for the sample.

regional cultural association of the site. They also failed to address a series of important questions relating to the site itself, including:

- What is the date of the habitation area at the slightly lower beach terraces?
- Are the burials contemporary with the habitation area occupation?
- What is the chronological span of the burial activity?
- What is the chronological relationship between the two main varieties of ceramics?

AMS (accelerator mass spectrometry) ^{14}C dating, now common, can utilize small samples of only a few milligrams. With this method, it is possible to address these questions using samples from existing museum collections (Hart and Lovis 2014). The dating of food residues on ceramics is one popular application. Since charred food remnants on pottery have indisputable chronological association to artifact use (Fischer and Heinemeier 2003), this is a powerful new chronological tool for archaeological interpretation. However, it has been argued that some food residue dates on ceramics are typically several centuries too old, due to the freshwater reservoir effect (cf. Roper 2013; Hart and Lovis 2014). This effect is similar to the marine reservoir effect and occurs when fish and mollusks from freshwater ecosystems are cooked in the pots, and the residues dated. This effect has also been observed in Arctic marine ecosystems, where marine mammals and fish remains date older by at least several hundred years in comparison to terrestrial carbon samples with different ^{14}C fractionation effects. The relative amount of ^{14}C and other carbon isotopes (^{13}C) in different ecosystems is variable, so animals living and growing in fresh water or marine water will take in slightly different amounts of the various carbon isotopes compared to those living in terrestrial environments (cf. Schulting et al. 2015). As a result, fish fat carbon residue on a ceramic sherd from a fish soup may date several hundred years older than a piece of charcoal from the fire where the soup was cooked.

Recently, residues from Middle Woodland vessels recovered underwater—some with motifs similar to those from Killarney Bay—have been dated. Some of these reported dates appear to have a fairly wide range: e.g. from 639 BC to AD 240, calibrated (Fox et al. 2016). The freshwater reservoir effect may be an issue with such variable dates, if the food residues and carbon contain fish oils that derive from freshwater ecosystems. As reported in the European studies, such aquatic-derived food residues may date 100 to 500 ^{14}C years older than their archaeological contexts (Fischer and Heinemeier 2003). A more likely situation may be that food residues contain ^{14}C from several sources (both terrestrial and aquatic ecosystems).

Radiocarbon dates from textiles and bark from mortuary contexts in museum collections have also recently been used to re-date Middle Woodland sites such as the central grave at the Adena Mound in Chillicothe, Ohio (Lepper et al. 2014). The use of short-lived terrestrial materials such as bark and twigs or small branches may help to more accurately date such sites and associated cultural activities; we know that charcoal and wood samples from logs and old trees may give anomalously older dates. The Adena central grave organics dates were found to be more recent than previously suspected, based on older solid sample ^{14}C dates.

In order to address the chronological questions described above, we selected eight new samples for AMS ^{14}C dating: four from organics associated with the mortuary complex and four ceramic carbon residue dates, including some of the thinner walled tool-impressed variety from the habitation area. One of the ceramic residue samples (# 1264) was analyzed twice with different treatments. These samples were analyzed by the new A.E. Lalonde AMS facility at the University of Ottawa. These new AMS ^{14}C dates are shown in Table 4.2 and Table 4.3.

In Table 4.2, sample OUC-1923 (Catalog number 1264-D) was a duplicate run of 1922, with a solvent extraction to test to see if preservatives had been used on the ceramic sherds, in addition to the acid rinse. The other samples were too small for a full AAA pretreatment, so they only underwent an acid wash. The A.E. Lalonde AMS Laboratory stated that there were "no issues with the (ceramic organic) samples to report of." None of the sherds excavated by Laurentian University field schools were treated with preservatives (Julig, personal communication).

In Table 4.3, the four new dates on copper-preserved materials (hide and bark) were from samples associated with four of the burials, provided by UMMAA. The new uncalibrated values ranged from 1886 to 2149 BP, with a mean of 2003 BP. The values for the uncalibrated ceramic samples had a similar range: 1875 to 2254 BP, with a mean of 2040 BP. These samples are from the habitation area excavations, and are in reasonable agreement with the dates run by Greenman on organics from the burial area.

All of the carbon dates were calibrated using the Oxcal v4.41 program (Bronk Ramsey 2020). The dates were then incorporated into Bayesian models (Bayliss and Bronk Ramsey 2004; Bronk Ramsey 2009) to investigate the underlying structure of the groups of dates, and specifically to determine the use spans of the burial and habitation areas, and the relative chronological association of the ceramics, and to assess the likelihood that the burial and habitation areas were used at differing times. The Bayesian modeling also allowed the earlier Michigan dates to be combined with the newer AMS dates run by the Lalonde AMS facility.

As a start for the modeling, all of the radiocarbon dates were combined with the assumption that they derived from a single phase of occupation. These results are presented in Table 4.4 and Figure 4.1. The model has a high agreement index, indicating a good fit between the model and raw data. The model also estimates the likely starting and ending

Table 4.2. Radiocarbon results for cooking residues from Laurentian University's Killarney Bay collection.

Lab number	Catalog number	Material samples	wt./gm.	^{14}C yr BP	Standard deviation
OUC-1922	1264	KB smooth sherd	5.0	1875	33
OUC-1923	1264-D*	KB smooth sherd	5.0	1926	29
OUC-1924	1628	KB smooth sherd	2.1	2147	27
OUC-1925	1652	KB thick sherd	1.0	2254	24
OUC-1926	1371	KB smooth sherd	2.0	1999	26

*This sample was a duplicate run of 1922.

Table 4.3. Radiocarbon results for samples from Killarney Bay burials, UMMAA collection.

Lab number	Catalog number	Material samples	wt./gm.	^{14}C yr BP	Standard deviation
OUC-1927	30293-B2	Hide	2.4	1986	24
OUC-1928	38501-B6	Bark	2.2	2149	26
OUC-1929	39518-B8	Hide	2.3	1985	29
OUC-1930	39684-B10	Hide	2.4	1894	29

Table 4.4. One phase model for the Killarney Bay site occupation.

Name Show all Show structure	Unmodelled (BC/AD)			Modelled (BC/AD)			Indices A_{model}=100.8 $A_{overall}$=101.3					Select All Visible	Page break
	from	to	%	from	to	%	A_{comb}	A	L	P	C		
▼ Sequence												☑ 2	☐
Boundary Start				-464	-207	95.4					98	☑ 3	☐
▼ Phase												☑ 4	☐
R_Date UOC-1922	79	240	95.4	62	225	95.4		86.9			99.7	☑ 5	☐
R_Date UOC-1923	26	206	95.4	21	200	95.4		105			99.8	☑ 6	☐
R_Date UOC-1926	-47	108	95.4	-48	108	95.4		99.8			99.8	☑ 7	☐
R_Date UOC-1924	-351	-54	95.4	-347	-53	95.4		100.4			99.8	☑ 8	☐
R_Date UOC-1925	-391	-207	95.4	-381	-201	95.4		89.1			99.7	☑ 9	☐
R_Date UOC-1928	-351	-56	95.4	-347	-54	95.4		99.8			99.8	☑ 10	☐
R_Date UOC-1927	-43	115	95.4	-43	114	95.4		99.9			99.9	☑ 11	☐
R_Date UOC-1929	-43	117	95.4	-43	116	95.4		100.2			99.8	☑ 12	☐
R_Date Mich-194	-749	201	95.4	-359	123	95.4		109.9			99.6	☑ 13	☐
R_Date Mich-428	-356	212	95.4	-339	190	95.4		107.5			99.7	☑ 14	☐
R_Date Mich-1482	-348	410	95.4	-210	238	95.4		108.5			99.6	☑ 15	☐
Boundary End				80	337	95.4					96.4	☑ 16	☐

dates for the occupation (labeled Boundary start and end on the table). These dates represent a two standard deviation (95%) age range. If we take the median values for the two phase boundaries, it would suggest the Killarney Bay site use began around 289 BC and that its final use occurred around AD 201, representing a span of 490 years. This span of use is somewhat longer than some earlier archaeological estimates, but is wholly consistent with the site materials as a whole and are in good agreement with geological estimates of the locality's exposure for occupation.

To determine whether the larger standard deviations from the early Michigan dates might be responsible for this age spread, the analysis was run a second time, excluding the three initial Michigan dates. Interestingly, this run resulted in a slightly longer span of use and a lower index of agreement.

Next, and with the Michigan dates excluded, the Bayesian analysis was run with the assumption that the habitation and burial areas were chronologically separate. This produced a model with unacceptably low indices of agreement between the model and raw data. This result further underlined the significant overlap in the use span of the two areas of the site.

To look more closely at the internal chronologies of the two areas, each was analyzed independently, with the assumption that they each, internally, represented a single phase of use. For the burial area, interest was specifically in the timing and frequency of interments, and for the habitation area, we again looked for evidence of continuous use and for potential insight into the chronological association of the two ceramics wares.

The model for the burial area (Table 4.5 and Figure 4.2), which excluded the early Michigan dates, had acceptable indices of agreement, which suggest a reasonable fit between the single phase model and the raw data. The two standard deviation span represented for the burials is longer than for the site as a whole, which reflects the smaller number of samples. Taking the midpoints of the starting and ending boundaries, these four dates suggest a span of 762 years of use. The indices may also hint that the deposition of burials at the site, or at least of those that are directly dated, was more sporadic and less continuous than anticipated.

These dates are in good general agreement with the relative ordering of graves outlined by Brose in Chapter 7. Grave 10, which appears to be the last interment placed at

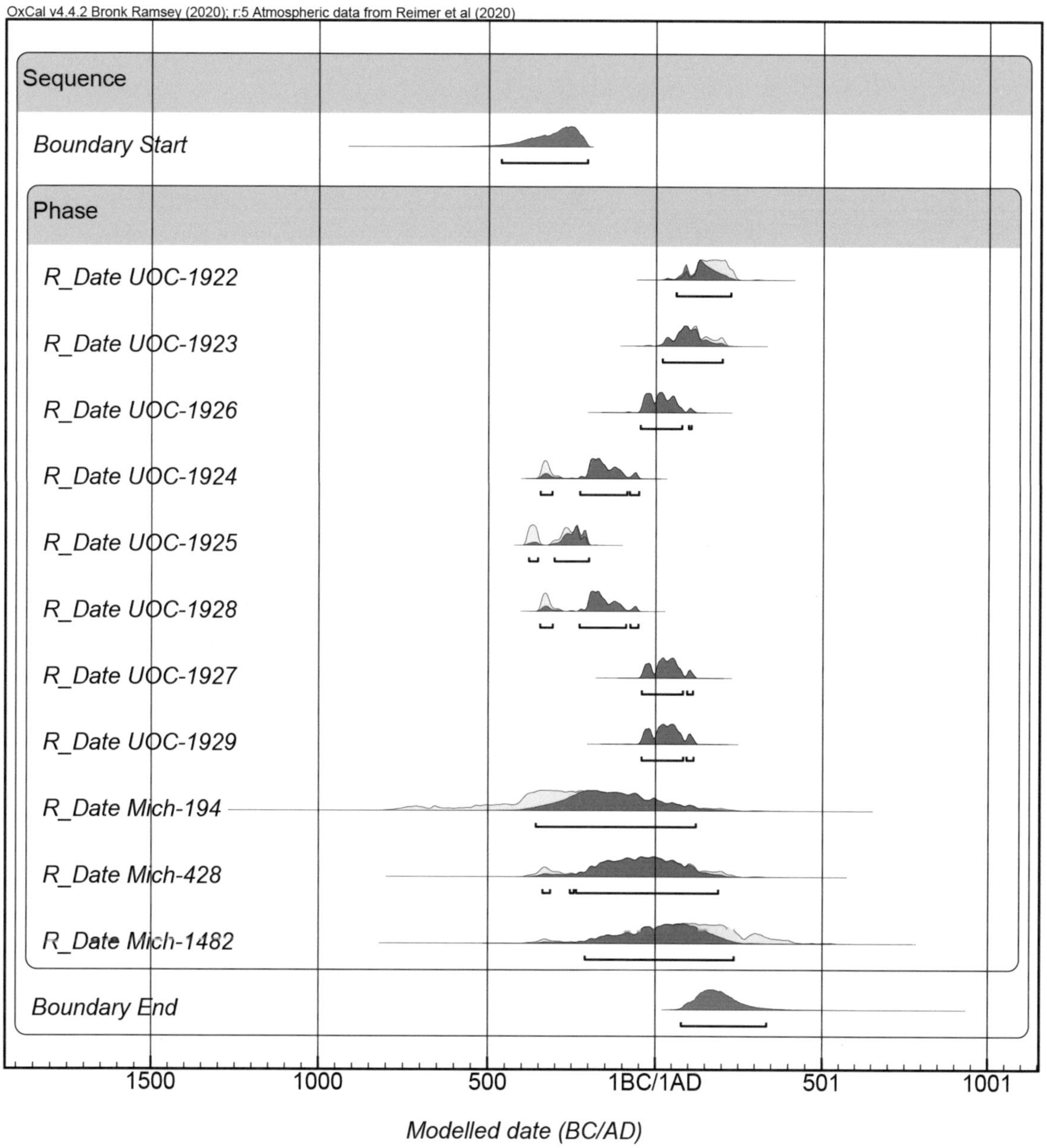

Figure 4.1. Distribution of modeled one phase Killarney Bay dates.

the site, has the youngest ^{14}C date (UOC-1930), while Grave 6, described as one of the deepest pits, had the earliest ^{14}C date (UOC-1928). Burials 2 and 8 have nearly identical middling ^{14}C dates (UOC-1927, UOC-1929). Unfortunately, Burial 9, which on stratigraphic evidence might be the earliest interment at the site, was not dated.

The model for the habitation area (Table 4.6 and Figure 4.3) produced higher indices of agreement, but an even longer time span of use, estimating some 871 years. As was seen in the combined model (see Figure 4.1) there is a relatively even spread of dates covering the occupation of the habitation area. It is also interesting to note that the date for sample UOC-1925, which is the earliest recovered from the habitation area, is the sample associated with the Killarney Bay Thick ware ceramic. While a single determination is insufficient for a conclusive demonstration,

Table 4.5. Dated Killarney Bay interments in single phase model.

Name Show all Show structure		Unmodelled (BC/AD)			Modelled (BC/AD)			Indices A_{model}=87.3 $A_{overall}$=87					Select All Visible	Page break
		from	to	%	from	to	%	A_{comb}	A	L	P	C		
▼ Sequence													☑ 2	☐
Boundary Start 1					-742	-53	95.4					95.8	☑ 3	☐
▼ Phase 1													☑ 4	☐
R_Date UOC-1928		-351	-56	95.4	-344	-50	95.4		84			98.9	☑ 5	☐
R_Date UOC-1927		-43	115	95.4	-43	113	95.4		100.2			99.7	☑ 6	☐
R_Date UOC-1929		-43	117	95.4	-43	115	95.4		100.4			99.7	☑ 7	☐
R_Date UOC-1930		70	225	95.4	28	215	95.4		89.7			99.5	☑ 8	☐
Boundary End 1					33	695	95.4					97	☑ 9	☐

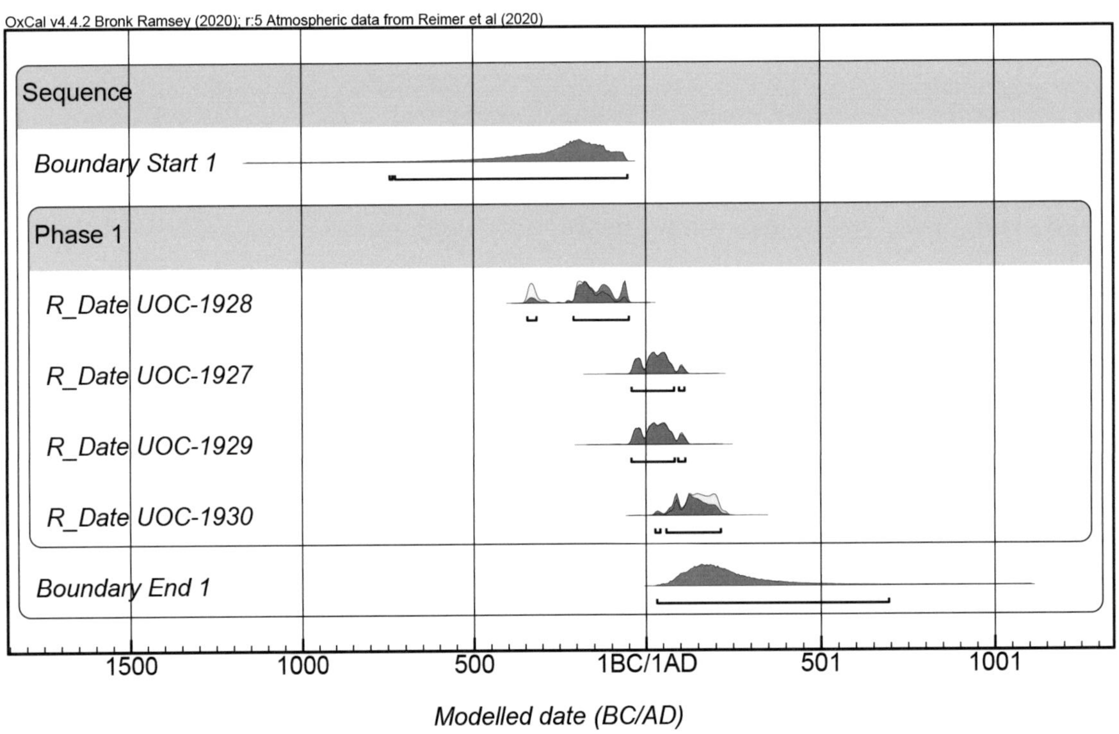

Figure 4.2. Distribution of modeled one phase burial dates.

Table 4.6. Dates from Killarney Bay habitation area modeled as a single phase.

Name Show all Show structure	Unmodelled (BC/AD)			Modelled (BC/AD)			Indices A_{model}=95.8 $A_{overall}$=95.9					Select All Visible	Page break
	from	to	%	from	to	%	A_{comb}	A	L	P	C		
▼ Sequence												☑ 2	☐
Boundary Start 1				-780	-206	95.4					96.4	☑ 3	☐
▼ Phase Settlement												☑ 4	☐
R_Date UOC-1922	79	240	95.4	72	233	95.4		95.2			99.2	☑ 5	☐
R_Date UOC-1923	26	206	95.4	25	201	95.4		102.5			99.7	☑ 6	☐
R_Date UOC-1926	-47	108	95.4	-48	108	95.4		99.5			99.5	☑ 7	☐
R_Date UOC-1924	-351	-54	95.4	-350	-53	95.4		99.9			99.6	☑ 8	☐
R_Date UOC-1925	-391	-207	95.4	-388	-203	95.4		94			99.7	☑ 9	☐
Boundary End				77	679	95.4					97.3	☑ 10	☐

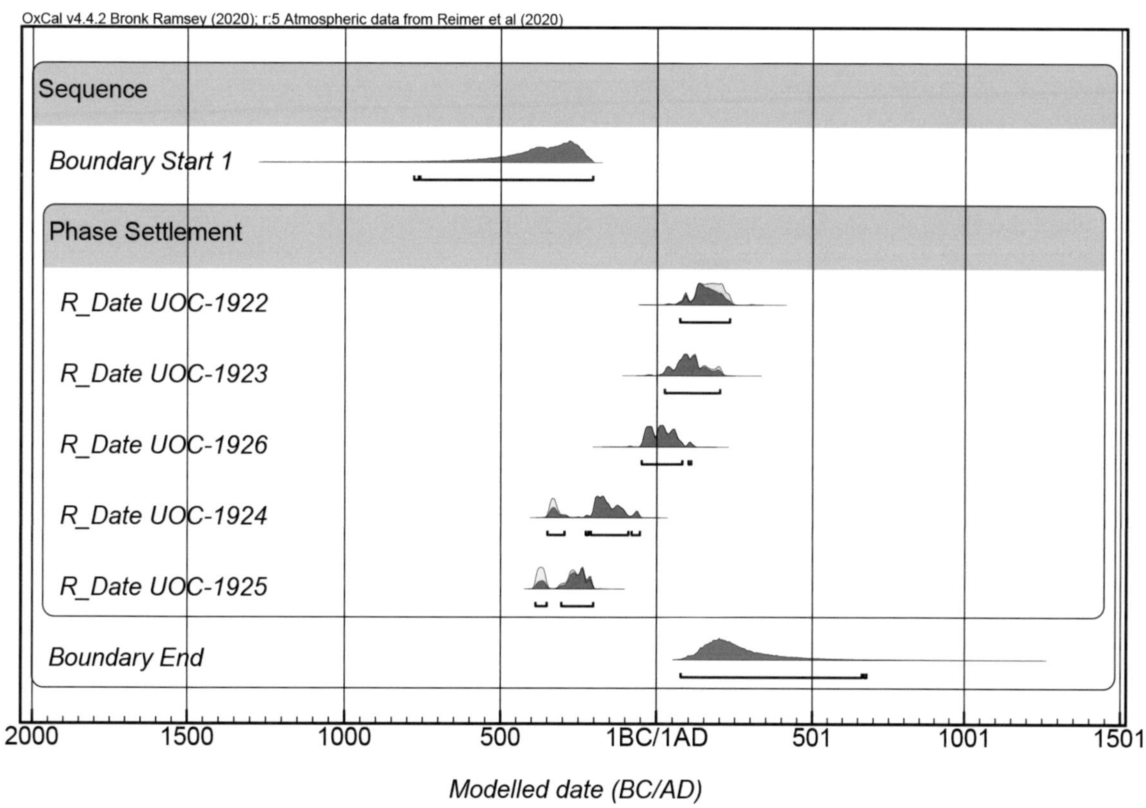

Figure 4.3. Distribution of dates from Killarney Bay habitation area.

this date does lend support to the belief that the Thick ware ceramics were chronologically earlier. It is also interesting to note in this regard, that the Thick ware date is very close in age to the earliest of the dated burials, Burial 6.

Taken together, the new AMS dates and the Bayesian modeling allow us to provide plausible answers to the questions posed at the beginning of this chapter. The habitation area on the lower beach at Killarney Bay was, in all probability, occupied over the same duration of time as the burial area was used, which, for the site as a whole, lasted nearly 490 years, from roughly 289 BC to AD 201. Both the habitation and burial areas appear to have been used more or less continuously over this time span. For the 16 burial features reported from the site, this would be the equivalent of one burial every 34 years! While there were other interments known from the general area of the site, these dates do not suggest that the burials were accumulated evenly over this span of time, but rather appear to be scattered across the period of site use from very early to quite late. The fact that burial events may be occurring over spans of time equivalent to once every generation or two makes it clear that the Killarney Bay site was not simply a cemetery or a location that was opportunistically used when a death happened to occur there.

The ^{14}C AMS dates on ceramics produce results that are more suggestive than conclusive. The sample from the single Killarney Bay Thick sherd did produce the earliest date from the habitation area, but there also appears to be overlap between this date and the earliest of the thin-walled ceramic sherds dated. Unfortunately, some of the better Killarney Bay Thick organic samples were used up in the residue analysis (see Appendix A), which precluded a more definitive test of the chronological overlap of the two wares. It is possible that functional differences between the vessel types might be responsible for the differences in date. If the thick ceramic pots were used for cooking fish (thus containing aquatic residues, which date older due to freshwater reservoir effects), and the thinner pots were used for tea, medicine, or other substances, this might produce artificially earlier dates for the thicker vessels. However, the hide dates from the burials seem to be in agreement with the range of ceramic dates from the habitation area, and do not suggest a significant reservoir effect on the ceramic residues.

Chapter 5

A History of Investigations and Collections

David Brose and Patrick Julig

The history of investigations at the Killarney Bay site is a long and complicated one, spanning more than a century and half. Various archaeologists associated with different institutions worked at Killarney Bay between 1876 and 2009, and the circumstances that led to the site being excavated and the artifacts preserved and curated were often a result of serendipity. Remarkably, much of what was recovered during this period exists today: the artifacts and associated documentation appear to be mainly extant. This chapter describes the broad outlines of those investigations and some relevant aspects of the excavators' histories as they affect the interpretation of the site.

In the nineteenth century, the Killarney Bay site was owned by Etienne Augustin de la Morandière, the first European fur trader to establish a post in Killarney (Derry 2007). In the 1820s, he built a maple sugar-shack on the highest part of a sandy ridge we now know to be a burial area and possibly a constructed mound. In the 1850s, during excavations for a root cellar, he unearthed a copper effigy beaver from the mound, along with other grave goods and a number of human burials. The whereabouts of these artifacts is no longer known, but knowledge of this remarkable find persisted in local folklore (Greenman: journal notes for 1938).

In 1876, the site came to the attention of Robert Bell, a geologist working for the Canadian Geological Survey (CGS). As a Victorian-era scientist, Bell's interests were broad, encompassing ethnology and archaeology as well as geology. In that year, de la Morandière sold Bell the rights to dig the mound for a price of sixteen dollars (Bell 1876). Bell hired de la Morandière's sons to help excavate the main mound and two smaller ones nearby. The property remained in the de la Morandière family, and in 1939 they gave permission for a second set of major excavations at the site, this time by University of Michigan archaeologist Emerson Greenman. He held a field school at the site for many years, bringing in money to the remote community and providing summer jobs to an area dependent on the fishing and tourism industries.

Joshua Speigel, an American neurosurgeon from the Chicago area, purchased the property in the 1950s. The Speigel family built a summer home there, and, happily, they were willing to allow archaeological investigations to continue. Greenman held his last field school at Killarney Bay in 1953.

In 1980, as the site was eroding, Laurentian University archaeology professor Helen Devereux did an initial site survey and some salvage excavations. A few years later, Devereux, Ken Buchanan, and later Patrick Julig, all from the Laurentian University Anthropology Department in Sudbury, directed a series of field schools focused on the possible habitation area of the site, which lay on a slightly lower beach terrace southwest of the main mound. This area was renamed the Speigel site.

In addition to gracious landowners, archaeologists at Killarney Bay have had the advantage of an interested and supportive community, which is linked to adjacent Manitoulin Island. Local people (French, Métis, and First Nations) have had firsthand involvement in all archaeological investigations held at the site. Currently, the Wikwemikong First Nation is researching the archaeological history of the area as part of their land claims on the islands in Georgian Bay and nearby Point Grondine Reserve, which is a part of Wikwemikong unceded Indian reserve (Julig et al. 2006). The Indigenous name for the settlement is Shebahonaning, and both names were used at the time Robert Bell's investigations began in the 1870s.

The Killarney Bay collection is divided among three different institutions in two countries, rendering a complete analysis of the material challenging. Materials excavated by Bell and Greenman were recovered at a time when precise and detailed cataloging standards and preservation techniques were not as common as they are today, further complicating matters for those seeking a record of items collected at the site. Greenman's collection was curated at the University of Michigan Museum of Anthropological Archaeology (UMMAA; formerly the Museum of Anthropology or UMMA), where the organic artifacts were held under variable storage conditions. The archaeological remains recovered from more than two decades of Laurentian University field schools have only recently been fully analyzed. Finally, some of the Bell collection initially housed at the Geological Survey of Canada (and later transferred to the Canadian Museum of History) was not at first identified as originating from the Killarney Bay site. One of this project's goals is to present a detailed analysis of the entire extant collection from the site.

Robert Bell

Robert Bell figures among the most important of the early geologists of Canada. He was born the son of a Church of Scotland clergyman in Toronto in 1841 (Ami 1927:19). His father, Reverend Andrew Bell, was a well-known amateur geologist who made significant and systematic geological collections in the Ottawa Valley (Ami 1927:19). Biographers attribute the development of Robert Bell's taste for the natural sciences to the early expeditions Bell made with his father (Ami 1927).

Bell's first association with the Geological Survey of Canada (GSC) was in 1856. At age 15, he joined a GSC field party and was appointed to the staff. Bell earned a degree in civil engineering from McGill in 1861, and he followed this with a year's study in Edinburgh (MacDonald 1995:38). During his undergraduate years, Bell worked for the GSC in the summer, heading his own expedition at the age of 18 in 1859 (MacDonald 1995:38). Following his return from Edinburgh, he took up a post at Queen's University in Kingston, teaching chemistry and natural history (MacDonald 1995:38). He left this position in 1867 and became a permanent officer of the GSC in 1869. Bell had a long career with the GSC, rising through the ranks to become assistant director (1877), chief geologist (1890), and finally acting director (1901) (Waiser 2000). During his long career he received many accolades, honorary degrees, and society memberships.

Bell could be described as a typical Victorian man of science: his interests were not limited to geology. His many publications include papers on forests, the porcupine, the red squirrel, and birds, in addition to many wide-ranging geological topics (Ami 1927:27–34). According to Ami, Bell's principal interests outside of geology were in the fields of folklore and forestry. During his early tenure at the GSC, the survey was located in Montréal, and during this time Bell managed to obtain a medical degree from McGill while still working at the GSC (MacDonald 1995:386–387). An account of his career shows that Bell was clearly a field geologist: nearly every summer in his early career was spent exploring and mapping various parts of Canada. Even after he was appointed to more senior posts at the

GSC, Bell continued to carry out fieldwork in remote parts of Canada. He retired in 1906 and passed away on June 17, 1917, in Rathwell, Manitoba, leaving a son and three daughters (Ami 1927).

Bell's field surveys were remarkably broad. Zaslow, in his history of the GSC, describes Bell's work as follows: "In a 50-year period, Bell ranged as far afield as the prairies of Saskatchewan, the oil sands of the Athabasca, and north to Great Slave Lake and Baffin Island. But mainly his work was concentrated in what is now northern Ontario and Quebec, in an arc extending from the Saguenay to Lake Winnipeg and from these points north to the shores of Hudson and James Bays." The field seasons of 1865, 1876, and 1887 to 1892 saw Bell in the Manitoulin, northern Georgian Bay, and Sudbury area. However, it is only during 1876 that his biographers specifically record a visit to She-ba-o-na-ning, which is the Indigenous name for the settlement of Killarney, and more specifically the waterway or inlet passing between George Island and the mainland, which functions as Killarney's harbor (Ami 1927:22).

Letters from Bell to his wife confirm that during the summer of 1876, someone brought the Killarney Bay site to Bell's attention. On June 27, 1876, Bell wrote to his wife Agnes from Byng Inlet as follows:

> [...]At She-ba-o-na-ning (or Killarney) which you may remember is about 25 miles east of Little Current, I was fortunate enough to get a stone spearhead, three interesting arrowheads and a small native copper axe which had all been dug from an ancient Indian mound nearby. I hear there are two more mounds there which I propose digging out on our return. [...]

The fact that Bell describes these objects before he excavated the mound suggests that they may have been obtained from the de la Morandière family. On August 10, 1876, Bell again wrote to Agnes, this time from Sault Ste. Marie:

> [...] I wrote to you last from (Shibaouanning) (Killarney P.O.). I staid there four days doing geology of the neighborhood and digging out the Indian Mounds I spoke of in my letter. There [were] three of them—all very ancient—probably 1000 years old. I found a lot of treasures...bones ec ec. [...]

We can only speculate on Bell's specific motivation for excavating the mounds. His use of the word "treasures" may suggest that Bell's interests were largely antiquarian. This is perhaps supported by the fact that the archaeological material was not placed at the GSC, but rather maintained in his private collection. In 1876, archaeology was in its infancy in Ontario: the first archaeologist, David Boyle, was not appointed to the Provincial Museum until 1887 (Killan 1988).

Bell's excavations should probably be best viewed as a general scientific curiosity about the region's history and aboriginal people. One example of this is the question of the source of the "flints" used by the site's occupants. For example, Bell records the occurrence of

> [...] a band only a few feet in thickness, of dark smoke-coloured chert –rock, ribboned with streaks of dull red colour. It breaks easily with a fine conchoidal fracture and appears to identical with a rock which was used by the "mound builders" for making some of their arrowheads. [...]. (Annual Reports of GSC, Explorations and Surveys, 1876–1877:209)

This outcrop occurs on the north side of Lamorandière Bay, about two kilometers north of the site. Bell also speculates on the source of copper found at Killarney Bay (Bell 1876).

Julig and students surveyed this area and the location of possible brown chert reported by Bell during the Killarney Bay field schools. They located a band of light brown mylonite, a fine recrystallized quartz sandstone (see Figure 2.3). However, no true chert was in evidence. Some artifacts from Killarney Bay are made of mylonite, a local material, so Bell appears correct on this point.

Nearly fifty years later, Bell's reports of the excavation at the site were confirmed in a newspaper article by Pierre Regis deLamorandière, one of E. A. de la Morandière's sons (deLamorandière 1922). Pierre, who had excavated for Bell, recalled various aspects of the dig:

> Sheba[h]onaning, now Killarney, must have been a paradise, and greatly frequented by the Indians centuries before the whites discovered the Georgian Bay (Mer Douce). In 1826, a large mound was chosen by Mr. E. A. deLamorandière, the first settler of that village as a suitable place to build a sugar camp, a short distance from the water of the beautiful Killarney bay. On this mound stood at that time two very large trees, a white birch and a white pine. These were chopped down as level with the ground as possible and a sugar camp built on it then, which was used for many years and no one ever thought for a moment that this mound was the last sleeping place for four tall Indian warriors until Professor Bell, of Ottawa, bought the mound from Mr. Charles deLamorandière for $16.00 [sixteen dollars] and employed the writer of this article and two of his brothers to dig it when it was discovered that four Indian warriors had

> been buried there no less than three hundred years before. Each warrior had his own hunting or fighting apparatuses, consisting of several flint arrow heads of different size and shapes, two copper hatchets, copper necklaces, and each had a beautiful gray stone pipe. All these articles had been wrapped in beaver skin as there was still part of the skin and hair on them.
>
> Further up the hill, two more mounds were dug, containing one body each with flint arrow heads, hatchet, copper necklace and stone pipe. On one of these mounds had stood a large white pine, which someone had chopped down about the year 1852 for barrel staves. The Professor managed to count 250 rings on the stump of this large pine tree, and he said that this pine had not grown on the mound till fifty years after these warriors had been buried and gone to the happy hunting ground. These warriors must have been at least six feet tall as the thigh bones and arms were very long, what was very remarkable, not a single decayed tooth was found in any of the six heads.

In sum, based on the accounts in letters to his wife and the account of Pierre Regis deLamorandière, Bell and his local helpers excavated three mounds in the space of four days. From the largest—the main mound at Killarney Bay—they excavated four skeletons and associated burial goods, and from each of the other two mounds they excavated one skeleton and associated grave goods.

The Killarney Bay site collections at the Canadian Museum of History

The Canadian Museum of History holds human skeletal material, copper, organics, shell, and a small amount of lithic material and pottery from the Killarney Bay site. Collections from the Geological Survey of Canada eventually moved to the National Museum of Man, which was later renamed the Canadian Museum of Civilization (CMCC) and is now the Canadian Museum of History. However, Bell's collections from Killarney Bay were not among them. All of the accession numbers associated with the Killarney Bay (KB-1) material indicate that the museum acquired the skeletal remains and artifacts at a later date.

As described above, Bell had a long career, traveled widely in Canada, and had disparate interests. MacDonald, in his history of the Robert Bell library, described Bell and his collecting habits as follows: "Bell was an inveterate packrat .... He saved scraps of paper on which he had scribbled notes, catalogs from booksellers and publishers, receipts for a wide assortment of purchases, and more" (MacDonald 1995:389). Given these habits, and the fact that the Geological Survey of Canada did not have collections relating to the site, it is reasonable to assume that Bell kept the material he recovered in his private collection. Bell had two residences: one in Ottawa and one in Rathwell, Manitoba (MacDonald 1995). His library was housed in Ottawa (MacDonald 1995:399), and it is likely that his collection of geological, ethnological, and archaeological specimens was housed in the same location. On his death in 1917, the Ottawa materials were passed on to his daughter Olga and son-in-law, John Outram (MacDonald 1995:399).

The registry at the Canadian Museum of History indicates that the KB-1 collections were all acquired in 1961. One set of material is associated with a date of April 1960, but there is reason to believe that the year was written incorrectly. There are three lots of material: a) human skeletal remains, b) artifacts likely associated with a burial context (copper, shell beads, large stone tools, and organics), and c) artifacts more typical of the area described as the "habitation area." However, the amount of material in the Canadian Museum of History is less than what would be expected if Bell had brought back to Ottawa everything he recovered. There are several possible explanations, each of which may be partially correct:

1. The amount of material recovered is exaggerated, particularly in the de Lamorandière report; or
2. Bell left some material in Killarney; or
3. Some of it was sent to a museum in a nearby town to the south.

John and Olga Outram died in a house fire in 1962, leaving behind the Bell library and collection (MacDonald 1995:385). Robert Bell Douglas, Robert Bell's grandson, later described this collection as follows: "twenty six tons of scientific papers, note-books, geological specimens, skeletons, skins of animals & birds, Indian & Eskimo tools, games, toys, etc. a mind-boggling collection" (quoted in MacDonald 1995:399). MacDonald documents the history of the library, but the histories of the collections are not as clear. It is possible that some Killarney Bay artifacts and skeletal material were part of the collection in the Outram home and have not been re-identified as coming from Killarney Bay.

Emerson Greenman

Emerson Greenman was born in 1895 in central Michigan and matriculated in the University of Michigan's College of Engineering from 1916 to 1918. After serving with the US Army in Europe, he entered the College of Literature, Science, and the Arts in 1920 to study archaeology with W. B. Hinsdale, the emeritus dean of the Homeopathic Hospital and "custodian-in-charge" of the new Museum of Anthropology's Great Lakes division. Greenman also studied zoology with university president, Alexander Ruthven. After receiving his AB in 1923, Greenman earned an Oxford University diploma in prehistoric archaeology. While abroad, he worked with the American School of Prehistoric Research at Paleolithic sites in England and visited ongoing excavations at many of the well-known Paleolithic sites in France. He returned to Michigan in 1924 and, again working closely with Hinsdale, received a PhD in archaeology from Carl Guthe, director of the museum.

In his 1927 doctoral dissertation, The Earthwork Enclosures of Michigan, Greenman noted the non-Iroquoian and non-Mississippian nature of the few recovered ceramics. However, ignoring coeval enthusiasm for what would come to be called the direct historic approach (Brose 1971, 1973, 2005), he proposed no ethnic affiliations in placing this concatenation of minimally occupied ditch-and-embankment features (now known to date to the Late Woodland Period [Fitting 1964; Fitting and Zurel 1976; Halsey 1976; Howey and O'Shea 2006; Mason 1981]) into the still fluid cultural classificatory schemes then promulgated for eastern North America.

Although offered an appointment as Great Lakes curator by Guthe, Greenman seized the chance to follow Henry C. Shetrone as curator of archaeology at the Ohio State Archaeological and Historical Society. In his "Report on Michigan Archaeology," Greenman (1926) attributed the lack of systematic study in the state to the academic anthropology community's belief that Michigan's archaeology was uninteresting, thereby leaving to the ravages of pot-hunting tourists Michigan's aboriginal copper mines, trephined skulls, geometric garden beds, and earthen "forts." The situation was not significantly changed throughout the era of Works Progress Administration archaeology (Guthe 1939).

Shetrone, then one of the nation's exemplary field archaeologists, had become director of the Ohio State Museum, and from 1929 to 1934 Greenman joined him excavating and reporting on some of central and southern Ohio's most important Adena and Hopewell sites, now dated to the Early and Middle Woodland periods. Greenman also excavated, and several years later reported on, a series of sites across northern Ohio that had mounds and/or ditch-and-embankment walls. Some of these sites are now known to date to the early Middle Woodland period, but most are assigned to the Late Woodland Whittlesey Tradition (Brose 1973, 1994a, 2002; Fitting 1964; Morgan 1952). In the ceramics from these village sites, Greenman recognized the mixture of Iroquoian and Peninsular Woodland (presumably "Algonquian") traits but again did not propose any ethnic identity (Greenman 1937a, 1937b).

During this period of intense field activity, Greenman wrote the first drafts of what would be several highly regarded synthetic papers, placing Adena and Hopewell in broad taxonomic and cultural contexts on the basis of a series of specific traits (Greenman 1932, 1938). (However, in 1940, Greenman was chagrined to have to publicly acknowledge and apologize for a 1938 Michigan Academy paper describing the aboriginal cultures of the Great Lakes, in which he presented McKern's Lake Michigan Phase and Oneota pattern as if they were his own concepts.) Then, as Griffin (1974) wrote later:

> After Hinsdale became quite ill during the winter of 1934-35 Carl Guthe was notified by President Ruthven that Greenman would return to the Museum of Anthropology for 1935–36 on Graduate School research funds [as a Research Associate] and then on the regular museum budget beginning in July, 1937.

As a member of the National Resource Council in the 1930s, Guthe had promoted federal archaeology, soliciting additional support from Eli Lilly to start the new Ethnobotanical Laboratory and Ceramic Repository. He also raised federal relief funds for graduate students to work with the new material being collected. In 1933, James Bennett Griffin, who had a degree in sociology and anthropology and a year working with the University of Chicago field program, had come to Ann Arbor to be the anthropology museum's fellow in aboriginal ceramics. By 1936, he had received his PhD from Guthe and accepted a research position as director of the ceramic repository. Griffin wrote ceramic analyses for major mid-continent federal archaeology projects and co-authored monographs and syntheses. These became instant classics, although many of them were not formally published for years (Griffin 1943,

1946, 1952; Parsons 1972). In addition to his acknowledged expertise in the most arcane details of prehistoric ceramics, Griffin was increasingly involved in the creation of the modern schemata of American archaeology.

Greenman's Canadian research

Once back at the University of Michigan, Greenman, now assistant curator, befriended amateur archaeologists, editing their journals and monitoring their meetings. He also worked on national archaeological projects, helping establish what would become the Society for American Archaeology. Greenman spent the 1935, 1936, and 1937 field seasons excavating, analyzing, and publishing reports on a series of Late Woodland cemeteries and campsites in southeast Michigan. He noted the mortuary patterns were akin to Canadian Iroquoian historic reports, while the ceramics were proto-Iroquoian but seemingly also related to later Peninsular Woodland materials (Greenman 1937b, 1939a). Becoming increasingly interested in the ethnohistoric connections of these aboriginal inhabitants of this region of the Great Lakes, Greenman took the spring and summer of 1938 to visit native communities of the Georgian Bay who had maintained their language and cultural practices since European contact. He apparently hoped to discover the degree to which the earliest historical examples of their culture could be linked to the kinds of materials he had excavated farther south.

Greenman and his small survey crew of Michigan students began systematically examining potential beach sites along Lake Huron's northern shore. Over the course of this multi-year effort, he visited members of the Whitefish River Band of the Ojibway tribe living on La Cloche Island, just to the northeast of Manitoulin Island, at the east end of the North Channel.

Elder members of the band showed Greenman a number of abandoned village locations and burial sites on then-unoccupied Old Birch Island. Working with members of the community, he excavated a number of Middle Historic period burials from Old Birch Island. (Many years later, John O'Shea, the Great Lakes curator at the University of Michigan Museum of Anthropological Archaeology, negotiated the repatriation of these excavated remains in a spirit of international cultural empathy (Kan 2005).) Greenman reported on the material evidence of acculturation among aboriginal groups in the Upper Great Lakes, but was unable to find any artifacts or patterns ("traits") that would link these Algonquian-speaking peoples directly with the prehistoric potters of southeastern Michigan (Greenman 1950). What he did find would change the direction of his research for the next quarter century.

In his field journal for 1938, Greenman wrote that, many years before, a copper effigy beaver had been unearthed during the excavation for a root cellar that also contained a human burial. Visiting the site on the mainland, Greenman was struck by the dense scatter of crude quartzite bifaces on the series of low beaches rising from the shoreline along Killarney Bay into the fields to the northwest. In the few test units he dug through sand and gravel lenses, his excavations encountered not only tantalizing quartzite preforms, rejects, and debitage, but the scattered and tumbled remnants of ephemeral hearths. These features Greenman later interpreted as sweat-lodge "baths" because of their numerous, heat-shattered cobbles. All of these cultural remains lay on what had been the accreting surfaces of storm beaches deposited during the rise from the Lake Stanley low stand to the higher Algoma Lake levels.

Greenman immediately realized that the sequences of proglacial Lake Huron stages provided a way to date what seemed to him a newly discovered North American Paleolithic industry. It was an idea almost certainly based on his knowledge of the Somme River terraces and Clactonian gravels (at which he had worked), which were used to date the European Paleolithic hand-axe sequences. Later in 1939, back in Michigan, he initiated a collaborative effort with the geologist George Stanley. They published a series of short papers outlining the importance of the discovery, the research strategy they planned to take, and the results they achieved (Greenman 1940, 1948; Greenman and Stanley 1941). Greenman (1943b:262) related the scrapers from the George Lake I site to those Frank Roberts had found with extinct fauna at Lindenmeier. (The George Lake sites I and II were found northwest of the Killarney Bay site, at a much higher elevation.) Greenman called the quartzite cores Levallois flakes, citing local experts who found them comparable to European industries (Greenman 1943b:264). He identified the site as having two Woodland occupations: one in the waterlaid gravels, presumably postdating the quartzite lithic assemblage, and the other, presumably still later, in the topsoil.

From 1939 through 1943, Greenman's strategy for the excavation of Killarney Bay was based on his assumption that he was dealing with a series of Paleolithic beds, naturally stratified by changing levels of Lake Huron. His field experiences in England and Ohio had taught him the importance of a detailed record of artifacts, cultural features, and their spatial and sedimentary contexts to reveal what were considered coeval occupational surfaces. He was determined to instill these practices, rarely used in the Great Lakes, in his few chosen students. In Chapter 6, we describe the sequences of those trench excavations, indicating the cultural and stratigraphic contexts and the significance of the recovered artifacts and features the work revealed. We also remark on the questions these raised, which Greenman alluded to in his private journal entries.

Following a two-year hiatus due to World War II, Greenman returned to Killarney Bay determined to continue the excavations.

Shortly after the 1947 season ended, Greenman learned from the first ^{14}C trials the relatively recent age of the presumed Paleolithic tools and their sedimentary matrices. He abandoned much of the field provenance control he had once insisted upon and extended a trial excavation into the knoll along whose southern edges his previous years' excavations had been concentrated. As detailed in the description of the mortuary complex, once Greenman had determined to explore the burial mound from which the Woodland copper artifacts had been taken in previous decades, he altered his excavation methods to copy those he had used in the excavation of Adena and Hopewell mounds in Ohio.

The excavations of the knoll soon revealed the extent of earlier disturbances: subsequent aboriginal occupation, Bell's digging, and LaMorandière's adaptive reuse of the open excavation pit for a log crib root cellar. With declining student assistance and his own loss of interest on the taxonomic details of the unusual mortuary complex, Greenman engaged in a number of expedient methods for recovery. These methods left the finer chronological and spatial relationships among the burials open to interpretation. We explore Greenman's work and its regional implications further in our discussion of the Killarney Bay mortuary complex.

The fate of the excavated Killarney Bay collections

Between 1954 and 1956, Greenman oversaw various graduate students' production of post-field typescript notes, numerous set-ups for photographic plates, and many composite maps and drawings (now archived in the University of Michigan Bentley Historical Library collections). By 1957, however, he had lost his enthusiasm for detailed artifact analysis and the interpretation of northern Lake Huron sites that he no longer believed were among the earliest in America. He wrote a series of papers on his own and with others, briefly describing the Georgian Bay quartzite industry and noting the relative (and now radiometrically dated) sequencing of the beaches on which occupations had occurred (Greenman 1966). In these papers he described the Killarney Bay mortuary complex and summarily assigned it to an ill-defined Adena category with New York additives. Greenman's sometime student, Tom Lee, continued to argue for a Pleistocene age for the nearby site of Sheguiandah (Julig 2002).

In understanding why the Killarney Bay site remained unwritten for the next half-century, it is important to recognize that some of Greenman's analytical desuetude was due to the disdain in which some of his colleagues held his "provincial" research. And despite the suspicions of some of his colleagues that he was no longer engaged, Greenman was allowed the traditional academic privilege of controlling the investigation of the site he had excavated. By the late 1960s, Greenman had virtually ceased fieldwork, analysis, and writing. He retired in 1970 and died in Ann Arbor in 1973.

From our present perspective, there must always remain some question as to why Griffin (1967) referred to Killarney Bay as a significant Middle Woodland site, while Greenman, after having to acknowledge the site was not Paleolithic, never accorded it the same import. Greenman tended to interpret cultural artifacts as potential examples of generalized traits whose compilation would allow him to assign the sites to the correct existing taxonomic unit or historical ethnic group (e.g. Greenman 1932, 1940). In contrast, Griffin broke assigned cultural traits of groups of sites into exquisitely detailed artifact types in order to reconfigure classifications so they could reveal often surprising new cultural relationships among the peoples who had occupied the sites that had yielded the artifacts, regardless of presumed historic cultural affiliations or lack thereof (e.g. Griffin 1943).

This is not to say that either Greenman or Griffin could entirely avoid the need to group archaeological objects and sites into industries and cultural categories.

Indeed, Griffin, in his 1943 work with such late prehistoric phenomena as Fort Ancient, was prepared to advance plausible ethno-linguistic connections and he was prepared to offer speculative assignments even for Hopewellian material. Greenman, however, tried to resolve only his latest sites into Iroquoian or non-Iroquoian complexes, being perfectly willing to deal with earlier materials in terms of larger and more theoretical constructions, largely based on evolutionary stages that were akin to the models of European prehistory.

Greenman may have considered some of the Killarney Bay pottery, points, and pipes to be Adena-like, but he could not overlook the fact that in no way did the site exhibit the use of space or orientation that marked Adena and Point Peninsula sites. Although there was iconography and a considerable number of grave offerings, he did not analyze these or publish reports on them. For Greenman, Adena (or its New York equivalent, Vinette I) *was* Early Woodland. Hopewell (or its New York companion, Point Peninsula) *was* Middle Woodland. As the Killarney Bay burial site was neither Adena nor Point Peninsula, the site would have been considered an aberrant site to one who had come to understand the evolution of Archaic or Woodland based on familiarity with these archetypes. As a result, in Greenman's archaeological schemata, Killarney Bay could only be a site of limited importance (cf., Brown 1997:475–479).

It was not until the 1980s, more than a decade after Greenman's death, that archaeologists Helen Devereux and Ken Buchanan from Laurentian University came to the University of Michigan to inspect and photograph the collections and to make copies of Greenman's field notes to help orient their field school excavations on unexcavated portions of the Killarney Bay site. They and other Canadian archaeologists, particularly James V. Wright, asked for the return of the collections to Canada for analysis.

James V. Wright

For about three decades after Greenman's departure in 1953, one archaeologist was particularly interested in Killarney Bay: James V. Wright. Wright visited Ann Arbor in 1961, during Greenman's lifetime. The Canadian Museum of History records indicate accession of the skeletal material and grave goods in April 1961, suggesting that Wright had succeeded in recovering Bell's collection. Wright also visited the archaeological site itself in 1961. A small collection of surface material, similar to that later excavated by teams from Laurentian University, is attributed to him.

Wright believed that the mound at Killarney Bay was a sand dune rather than something of human construction (Wright 1967:110). Given that the mound had been entirely excavated by the time he visited the site—and he did not excavate—the basis of his assertions is unclear. However, his conclusions based on examination of the artifact assemblage have proven reliable. He correctly inferred that the artifacts represented a Middle Woodland Point Peninsula culture rather than a Hopewellian assemblage, and he identified the thicker pottery as Havana-like. He also identified a habitation component and suggested that the site inhabitants had an industry producing gorget preforms from local slate (Wright 1999:667).

Helen Devereux and Ken Buchanan

Killarney Bay once again became the focus of archaeological investigations in 1980, with work initially led by Helen Devereux from Laurentian University (LU) in Sudbury (Figure 5.1).

When Devereux began research at the site, archaeology in northeastern Ontario was in the midst of a period of heightened interest. The Ontario Department of Lands and Forests had conducted underwater archaeology along the French River in the early to mid-1960s (known as the Royal Ontario Museum, River Archaeological Prospecting Expedition) (Kenyon 1975:51–54), and a Provincial government program was initiated in 1972 (MacLeod 1973). Many papers (Bertulli 1981; Bertulli and Kilpatrick 1977; Brizinski 1975, 1977; Brizinski and Savage 1983; Buchanan 1979a, 1979b; Conway 1979, 1989a, 1989b; Conway and Conway 1989; Devereux 1982; Pollock 1975, 1976; Pollock et al. 1977; Tyyska and Burns 1973) document surveys throughout the northeast and attest to that era's vibrant Ontario Ministry of Natural Resources (later Ministry of Culture and Recreation) archaeological program, which was based out of regional offices in Sault Ste. Marie and Cochrane. John Pollock conducted numerous regional surveys in the north and Thor Conway did surveys throughout northeastern Ontario. They published their findings in an extensive series of government reports. Academic interest in the region from the late 1960s to the early 1980s included a limited number of survey and excavation projects undertaken by graduate students from the University of Toronto (Knight on the Montreal River) and McMaster University (Brizinski on Lake Nipissing). However, the major regional archaeology program was based out of the new Laurentian University in Sudbury and directed by Professor Helen Devereux and her assistant, Ken Buchanan (Figures 5.2 and 5.3). Devereux (1982) described the Killarney Bay work as "salvage" archaeology, because the sandy surface of the ridge was eroding and artifacts were being damaged or removed from their contexts. However, it is clear that during the first few seasons, the goals of the LU investigation were broader than simply collecting artifacts from the eroding ridge.

In 1980, Devereux and Buchanan made a surface collection and carried out a radial test-pit survey aimed at determining the site's extent (Devereux 1982). Recognizing the importance of determining whether the mound was natural or artificial, Devereux had a stratigraphic trench excavated across the ridge. Laurentian University sedimentologist Darrel Long assisted in its interpretation. Long also sampled a 2-m-deep Algoma Phase beach deposit in order to study the site formation processes at the site. This work led Devereux to conclude that the main beach ridge—although not necessarily the mound—was formed naturally (Devereux 1982). Further, she found that the habitation area of the site was still intact because it was only partly located on the eroding edge of the ridge. Devereux appears to have focused on investigating two aspects of the site that Wright questioned: whether the mound was natural or cultural, and whether there was a habitation component associated with the mound.

With time, the implementation and reporting of the Laurentian University excavations increasingly fell to Ken Buchanan (Figure 5.4). Devereux worked with many local students and avocational archaeologists, and Buchanan, a craft potter and retired schoolteacher, was one of these. He enrolled in the master's program at Trent and later became a permanent instructor at Laurentian University, responsible primarily for teaching the second-year archaeology course.

The proximity of the field school site to the university and the sandy nature of the sediment allowed students to get a taste of archaeological fieldwork on a weekend. During the same fall term, students cataloged the artifacts recovered and frequently wrote short reports about the specific unit where they worked. The weekend field schools carried out in the context of a second-year archaeology class served a mainly pedagogical function. Laurentian University teams carried out these weekend excavations every fall from 1981 through to 2002, excluding the years 1987 and 1988. There were two extended seasons in 1982 and 1984, the more extensive of which occurred in 1984 in order to "re-assess" the site (Buchanan 1992:3). Julig joined the Department of Anthropology in 1990 and assisted Buchanan on many of the later excavations. In the autumn of 2002, Julig directed the most recent field school to be held there (Julig 2004). Subsequent work at Killarney Bay has been limited to monitoring the site and coring for sediment samples and pollen, and, more recently, cultural resource management (CRM) survey work at the southwestern edge of the site, as part of property development activities (Julig and Beaton 2015b).

Figure 5.1. Helen Devereux in 1983, at the Killarney Bay site. Devereux was a professor of anthropology and archaeology at Laurentian University for many years. She restarted the Killarney Bay investigations in 1980, initially as a salvage excavation and later as an annual Laurentian University field school, which was continued by Ken Buchanan and Patrick Julig until 2002.

With the exception of the work in the first season, the Laurentian University teams used essentially the same methodology every season. The excavation grid was laid out in 1 m squares. Each season began with a survey of surface

Figure 5.2. Helen Devereux (left) discusses the site with a student (seated) and Ken Buchanan (right)during a season of the Laurentian University field school excavations at Killarney Bay.

finds followed by excavations on the 1 x 1 m grid (Buchanan 1995a:5). Units were excavated following a checkerboard pattern, and all sediment was screened through 1/8-inch mesh. The Killarney Bay site was registered by Buchanan with the Ontario Ministry of Culture, Archaeology branch, assigned a Borden number BlHl-1 and called the Speigel site, after the property owners.

In 1982, Devereux and Buchanan traveled to the University of Michigan Museum of Anthropology in Ann Arbor to examine the artifacts and notes from Greenman's excavations (Buchanan 1990). Although the survey that Buchanan made in the same year recovered only a small amount of diagnostic material, the information obtained from these pieces and his analysis of the Greenman collection led Buchanan to conclude that the site was occupied by two different cultural groups. In his words: "…it seems safe to state that the Speigel Site was occupied by both Initial Woodland Laurel/Point Peninsula indigenes and by Adena Culture people" (Buchanan 1992:118–119). Buchanan further suggested that the groups may have jointly occupied the site. Some of Buchanan's later conclusions were also surprising. For example, in his 1992 site report, he stated that "it is becoming increasingly evident that the Adena presence at [BlHl-1] was probably male only" as it was represented only by lithic artifacts and lacked ceramics typical of that tradition (Buchanan 1992:32). He identified the ceramics as belonging solely to the Laurel Culture Tradition (Buchanan 1992:33).

Having not involved any mortuary components with organic preservation, the collections obtained through the Laurentian University field school excavations are fundamentally different from those obtained by Bell and Greenman. Consisting mainly of lithic debitage and small pottery sherds from a disturbed, plow zone context, and siltstone/argilitte manufacturing debris in gorget production, this collection has not received the same type of attention as the University of Michigan material. In fact, it was not until 2008 that this collection was fully cataloged. While a number of reports describing the field school excavations exist (Buchanan 1992, 1995a, 1995b, 1996, 1997, 1998, 1999, 2000, 2001, 2002), and some students have examined the material for their honors theses, to date details of the work have not been published, except for conference presentations.

The question of a full KB-1/Speigel site report and analysis was discussed between Julig and Buchanan, but Buchanan felt it would require the involvement of University of Michigan, which held the Greenman collection. On several occasions in the early 1990s, Julig discussed the importance of a comprehensive analysis of the KB-1 artifacts with the directors of the UMMA (initially Wright and later O'Shea). They agreed it would be desirable under the right conditions, but that the collections should remain at the University of Michigan.

David Brose and Patrick Julig

In 2006, David Brose visited the Killarney Bay collection at the University of Michigan Museum of Anthropology to ascertain whether the patterning of ritual object and human skeletal internment could shed light on a somewhat later ritual re-interment from the Dunn Farm site in northwest Michigan. Recognizing the chronological value of the recovered spectrum of Early/Middle Woodland ceramics in the Killarney Bay collection, he agreed to Great Lakes curator John O'Shea's suggestion that he prepare a brief report on the entire collection. Encouraged by Bill Fox, he enlisted Pat Julig's expertise in identifying the sources of cherts in the Great Lakes region and cache blades from several of the burials. Julig, a professor at Laurentian

University who had excavated at Killarney Bay, studied the Bell collection, and curated the Laurentian University collection, suggested embarking on a study of all aspects of the site, including the analysis of Killarney Bay collections in the three institutions. Julig and Brose then requested contributions from colleagues; the result is the present international multidisciplinary study.

Conclusion

We are fortunate that the Killarney Bay site lay on a property owned by families who recognized the value of archaeology. They allowed professionals to dig there and they likely protected it as best they could from the hands of looters and pot hunters.

Nonetheless, destructive activities continue to occur in the area. The series of field schools held by Laurentian University initially served as "rescue" excavations, but the elevated Algoma-age extinct beach is continuously eroding and is modified by nesting turtles and burrowing foxes. An ATV/snowmobile/pedestrian trail crosses the southwest quadrant of the site. All of these activities cause damage to unexcavated areas of the site.

It is not uncommon for mound sites in eastern North America to have storied excavation histories, where different people at different times excavated them for various reasons. Some mounds were first explored for the purposes of treasure hunting; later they were dug under the aegis of academic research. The usual fate of all but the most spectacular collections is to undergo quiet cultural erosion: objects and provenance data often end up at understaffed borrowing institutions or with curatorially careless researchers far afield. The Killarney Bay site has been the happy exception. Ironically, this may be partly attributed to the many factors that delayed or impeded the full analysis of the separate collections. The separate housing of the collections in the US and Canada added a logistical and financial challenge to researchers interested in viewing them, and because of this, they were to some degree protected from potentially ambitious scholars who might have further splintered the collections. The different excavation and recovery techniques employed by the various excavators make comparison of the assemblages difficult. None of the principal excavators published in detail, yet the literature is replete with casual referents, creating an added and continuing challenge for comparative research interests.

This research project is truly a testament to the value of artifacts and materials excavated many years ago, the value of maintaining and preserving collections in museums such as UMMAA, and the power of international collaboration among researchers. The analysis of these collections was delayed for many decades, which is unfortunate; however, we now have more powerful methodologies and more comparative data sets to assist in their interpretation.

Chapter 6

Features, Stratigraphy, and Spatial Distribution

Patrick Julig and Darrel G. F. Long

This chapter describes Killarney Bay's features and the spatial and stratigraphic aspects of early field investigations. Subsequent chapters discuss work by researchers from the University of Michigan (Chapter 7) and Laurentian University (Chapter 8), as well as the results of new radiocarbon dates for the site.

As discussed in previous chapters, the Killarney Bay site is large and complex, with both mortuary and habitation area components. The actual boundaries of the site are uncertain. Three mounds were excavated in the early years of investigations by Robert Bell and by local Killarney excavators, but as with many early digs, they are poorly documented with respect to spatial and stratigraphic context. About all that is known about the original stratigraphic and spatial context comes from historical reports written by crew members many years later, as noted in Chapter 5. It was thought that the area with the two (missing) mounds was excavated as part of a gravel pit adjacent to the east of the Killarney Bay site (Ken Buchanan, personal communication).

John de la Morandière, the local landowner, actually found and reported the Killarney Bay site. In the late 1870s, geologist Robert Bell excavated three separate mounds at Killarney Bay. However, all three were only partly excavated. Locals from Killarney, who helped with the Bell excavations, mention human bones being found at the main mound, and copper artifacts found at all three.

In 1939, about 60 years after Bell, Emerson Greenman began excavations. The only presumed mound remaining at Killarney Bay by that time had been modified by construction of a root cellar, with log cribbing placed around the old Bell excavation unit in the original mound (Figure 6.1). Greenman tested various locations, and in his work, he paid closer attention to stratigraphic and spatial context. He also mentions in his early notes (Greenman 1939, Field Notes, July 30) some critical information about Bell's early mound diggings. He noted that two of the Bell mounds were located 300 yards east of the main mound, at a slightly higher elevation.

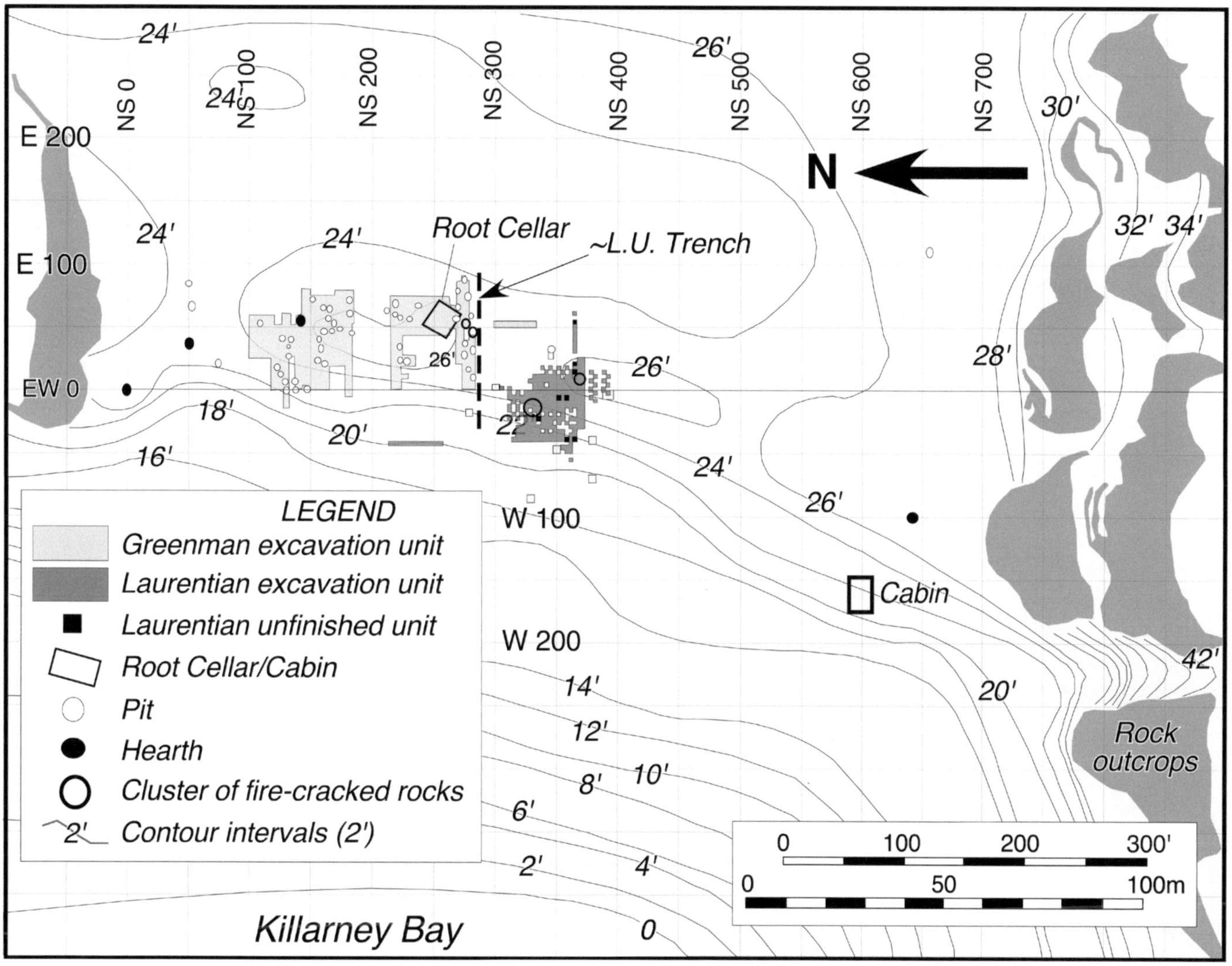

Figure 6.1. Map of excavations at Killarney Bay based on Greenman's topographic surveys and grid system. Note Laurentian excavations located southwest of Greenman excavations and having fewer features.

> To the east of this site (KB1) some 300 yards are two large holes in the ground which, according to John Lamorandiere, are the sites of excavated mounds. They were excavated some years ago by a man named Bell. A few copper axes were found, and they were taken to Owen Sound.

Greenman (1939, Field Notes, August 16) comments on material found by Bell in the main mound, where the root cellar was excavated:

> John Lamorandiere brought an elderly man to the site who described the material found when the rise of ground where the root cellar is was excavated. He said a tubular pipe in effigy of a mink or similar animal, was found. The description was quite accurately that of a large zoomorphic effigy pipe with the bowel somewhat forward of center, and the curved head of the animal at the end … He also said some chisels of brass were found, but on questioning, he admitted they might have been copper.

Julig (personal communication, 2010) suspects that this elderly man may have been one of the original excavators; possibly the great uncle or grandfather of the settler John de la Morandière.

In 2021, a partly excavated mound was rediscovered by Julig and S. Proulx while doing CRM survey on private property adjacent to the Killarney Bay site. This mound was located near the de la Morandière farm house, about 300 meters south of the main mound, and appears to be one of the mounds that Bell excavated in 1876. It is large, built up with fine beach sand, and is mostly intact. It has two

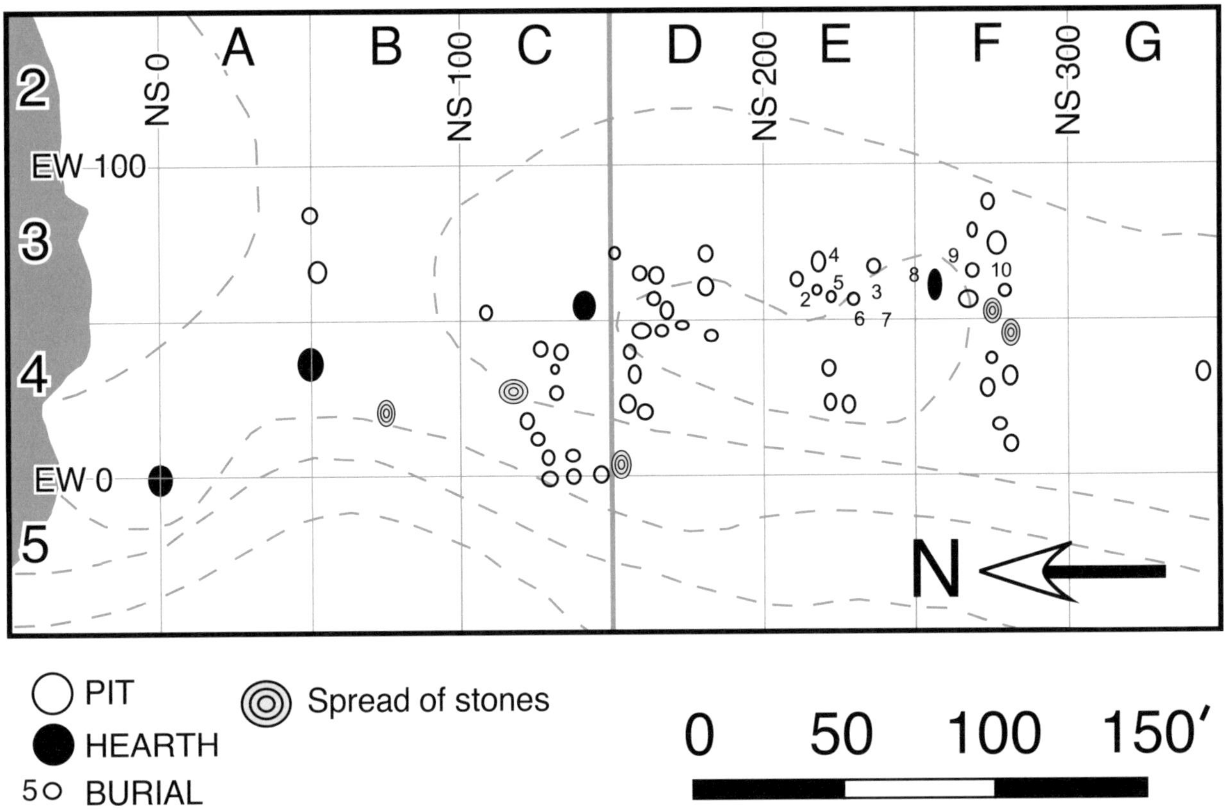

Figure 6.2. Location of features recorded during Greenman excavations and survey of main beach ridge.

trenchings into it, the most recent from about 70–80 years ago. Possibly the elder who guided Greenman was being protective of this remaining mound, which was in the forest, adjacent to the original 1800s farmhouse.

By the late 1960s, when the talk in the UMMA coffee room came around to the Great Lakes work being done by graduate students, Greenman's recollections about Killarney Bay would frequently include reference to a beaver effigy of copper. It is possible he was conflating the reports of copper chisels and a mammalian effigy pipe. In any case, by the early 1950s, there was enough federal archaeology from the mid-south for Greenman to have known that his informant's pipe may have been like one of the massive tubular effigy pipes from the Ohio Hopewell Seip mound (Mills 1909; Shetrone and Greenman 1931) and thus far more similar to the great majority of animal or bird-headed effigy tubular pipes from well-dated Middle Woodland Copena sites in Alabama and Tennessee (Brose 1985: plates 60–63; Webb 1942) than to the well-known Adena animal effigy pipes from Ohio or West Virginia sites (Dragoo 1963: Fig. 17; Fitting 1978). He included no mention of this effigy pipe in his 1966 *American Antiquity* report, in which he argued for Killarney Bay's Adena connections.

While certainly interested in the remains of the larger mound, Greenman saved that until his last years of work at Killarney. Between 1939 and 1953 Greenman surveyed the site, developing a detailed topographic map, with elevations to nearest tenth of a foot. From this he established a grid, as shown in Figures 6.1 and 6.2, with 50-foot grid excavation blocks surveyed along the top of the beach ridge. His excavations proceeded mostly from north to south. The mode of excavation involved using 5-foot squares (as a moving trench) to expose vertical stratigraphy, as his objective included determining the site chronology. As a result, the records include reasonable stratigraphic profiles every 5 feet from 135 to 180 feet (Figure 6.3).

By the early 1950s, the Greenman excavations were approaching the root cellar (old mound) and were winding

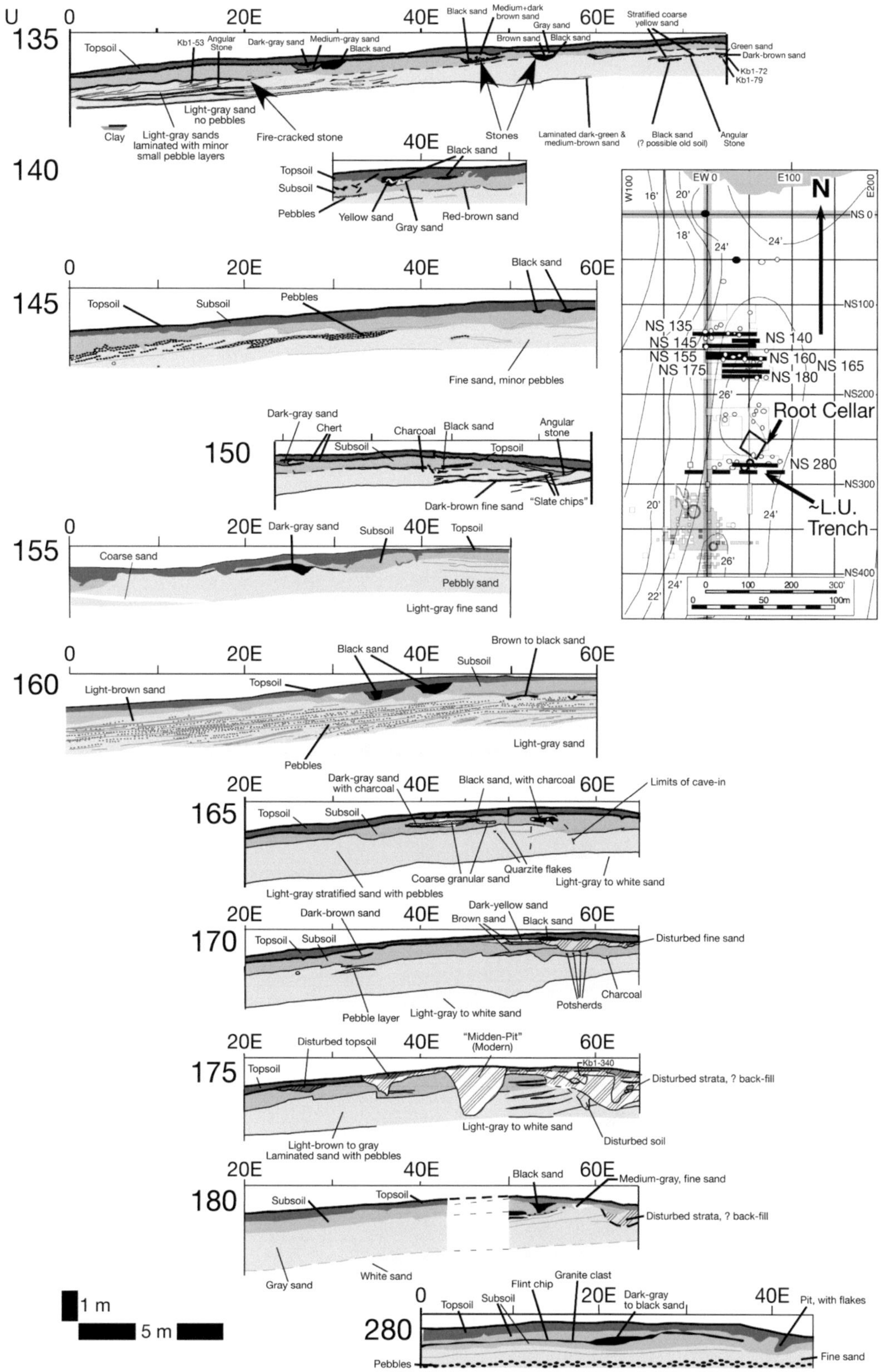

Figure 6.3. Trench profiles, redrafted from Greenman's unpublished field notes, illustrate the profile across the site. Sections have been redrawn to show the appearance of each trench from the south. Dark layers at the top of each profile are typically humus-rich topsoils. These are typically underlain by a layer of gray subsoil, then layers of mixed sand and gravel. Organic rich zones (buried soils, hearths, and pits) are shown in black where they had a high organic content, including charcoal.

down. The field notes and maps of Greenman's excavations are detailed for the individual burials (see Chapter 7), but there was no complete summary of the main mound stratigraphy. It was described as quite disturbed—the sand of the mound (root cellar) was supported by log cribbing. In 1953, according to Greenman's field notes: "between June 24th and 26th the later most [sic] of the mound fill of the root cellar was bulldozed off, leaving a flat platform at the top of the unmoved light brown beach sand." Excavations of the remaining mortuary assemblages under the mound were accomplished. These excavations and context are covered in Chapter 7.

The stratigraphic context and features outside of the mound area are covered below.

Spatial distribution of features near the main mound

Greenman reported four main kinds of features: pits, hearths, burials, and stone concentrations (Figures 6.1 and 6.2). Greenman called some of these stone concentrations "baths." However, since the functional interpretation of this kind of feature is uncertain (baths, ricing pits, ritual, or other uses), here we refer to these types of features as a "spread of stones." The specific features recorded in the Greenman excavations are shown relative to the beach topography in Figure 6.2. Some are outside his excavated areas found with test pits. Some clustering of burials is evident, but other features (pits, hearths, and spreads of stones) appear randomly located along the beach ridge.

Greenman also reported some features called "streamers" in the subsoil, some of which contained faunal remains (Table 6.1). These may have been natural features that happened to contain some faunal remains and other artifacts. Also, some of the pit features may have been natural tree throws, which may also contain some artifacts. It is not always easy to determine cultural from natural pit features, and example of both types are evident in the stratigraphic sections shown in Figure 6.3.

Although Greenman recorded many pits, Laurentian University researchers found none. This could be due to agricultural disturbance in the intervening years or to differing methodologies. Although the field school excavations did uncover some rock features just below the plough zone, the students covered these in plastic instead of excavating them, because there was a moratorium on burial excavations in Ontario at that time. In addition, the LU field school dig grid was intentionally located below and to the west of the crest of the main ridge, in an assumed habitation area—one that would be less likely to contain burials and features (Julig, personal communication).

Stratigraphic context of features

The whole area around the original mound has been disturbed for thousands of years, beginning with the mound fill that was first brought in around 2,000 years ago by Middle Woodland people. In the historical era, the mound was found and partly excavated by Lamorandière and then by Bell. It was plowed for many years and then excavated by Greenman. Then it was leveled by bulldozing. It is also likely that there has been unrecorded digging; burials and grave goods are said to have been recovered by locals. The scale of disturbance makes interpretation of the stratigraphy difficult.

In most of the trench profiles shown in Figure 6.3, a deep buried layer of pebbly sand (an older beach face) is capped by a layer of light gray to white sand and then a sequence of varicolored sand with local inclined stratification, reflecting progradation of the beach profile. In some sections, this is succeeded by an organic rich zone, possibly representing a buried soil (locally disturbed by pits and "hearths" containing concentrations of charcoal). These are typically capped by gray, mottled subsoil and dark gray topsoil, much of which may have been modified by tilling in the European interval. (Around 1850, de la Morandière began using the area as a sugar maple bush, and later owners farmed it and then established a golf course.) This upper unit may contain some aeolian sand (trapped in vegetation along the beach ridge), but this cannot be clearly demonstrated from Greenman's observations.

Many of the pits with deeper organic layers that Greenman recorded in his profiles (e.g. profiles 135, 140, 155, 160 in Figure 6.3) could have been produced when trees toppled over after wind events. These are known as tree throws. This beach ridge was somewhat exposed to the prevailing western winds, and storm events off Georgian Bay could lead to such natural site disturbance. This is common on other regional Great Lakes beach sites (Julig 2002). It is also possible that tree stumps may have been

Table 6.1. Faunal remains from nonmortuary features—including hearths, pits, and "streamers"—from Greenman excavations.

KB number	Trench	Section	Feature	Layer	Other context	Taxon	Element	Portion	N (Total=123)	Alteration	Notes
233	4D	C9	"streamer"	subsoil	"streamer"/burned area from C10 hearth	cf. *Rangifer/Odocoileus*	longbone	shaft fragment	3	calcined	class IV mammal
250	4D	D8-9	"streamer"	subsoil		Mammalia Class III	rib	fragment	1	calcined	
250	4D	D8-9	"streamer"	subsoil		Mammalia	longbone	shaft fragment	1	calcined	
1466	4D	G9	hearth			*Rangifer/Odocoileus*	tooth	enamel fragment	1	calcined	premolar/molar fragment
1466	4D	G9	hearth			*Rangifer/Odocoileus*	vertebra	articular facet	2	calcined	
1466	4D	G9	hearth			*Rangifer/Odocoileus*	vertebra	neural arch fragment	1	calcined	
1466	4D	G9	hearth			*Rangifer/Odocoileus*	femur	distal epiphysis fragment	3	calcined	may be same bone
1466	4D	G9	hearth			cf. *Rangifer/Odocoileus*	longbone	shaft fragment	11	calcined	class IV mammal
1466	4D	G9	hearth			Mammalia Class III	longbone	shaft fragment	11	calcined	
1466	4D	G9	hearth			Mammalia Class III	longbone	epiphysis fragment	3	calcined	
1466	4D	G9	hearth			cf. *Lepus americanus*	lumbar vertebra	neural arch fragment	1	calcined	class II mammal, hare sized
1466	4D	G9	hearth			Mammalia	NID	fragment	72	calcined	
1466	4D	G9	hearth			Testudines	plastron	fragment	1	calcined	
1466	4D	G9	hearth			Testudines	carapace	fragment	1	calcined	
160	4D	B9	pit			Large mammal	longbone	epiphysis fragment	1	calcined	
1154	3E	E2	pit	topsoil	"pit over Burial 2," SW corner of section	Testudines	carapace	fragment	8	calcined	
1154	3E	E2	pit	topsoil	"pit over Burial 2," SW corner of section	Testudines	carapace	margin fragment	2	calcined	

removed or "pulled," as this was common practice while clearing fields. Other pits and burned areas with charcoal and stone concentrations are probably various ancient cultural features, such as baths or sweat lodges, storage pits, wild-rice processing areas (jigging pits), or mortuary features.

In addition, there are several examples of more recent features caused by historic-era disturbance and digging. The historical pit features are the easiest to define, as they often contain relatively recent artifacts and may lack organic horizons. Major pits seen in profiles along the 165, 175, and 180 survey lines in Figure 6.3 probably reflect relatively modern excavations (one reportedly contained broken china) and could have initially been excavated for fill to pile around the root cellar. The complex stratigraphy seen in the profile at 280, with a distinct buried subsoil and soil profile, may reflect burial of the original land surface during construction of the root cellar. Alternatively, it may represent aspects of the mound-building as burials were added to the mound. As shown in Figure 6.1, the large Laurentian University trench was located at around NS 290 and represents fairly normal beach ridge stratigraphy, with no evidence of anthropomorphically induced layering. The other major recent historic disturbance is the result of plowing at the site. This is evident in some areas with plow marks, as seen in the LU excavations. We discuss this further in Chapter 7. However, there may not have been plowing all along the ridge top, as there are some very large trees shown in early photos, and some of the ridge topography does not suggest tilling. This may be the reason the features along the crest of the ridge tend to be more intact. As mentioned, there is some "modern" pit fill in line 175–180. This may be the result of fairly recent land leveling related to the use of the area as a "bush" golf course. Ceramics from the 1960s are preserved in the backfill.

Unfortunately, Greenman's notes do not contain any stratigraphic records for the mound area. As described in Chapter 2, Julig and Long collected core samples and analyzed the size of sand grains in an attempt to determine if the original mound represented natural features (beach ridge and dunes) or was wholly cultural in origin. They found no evidence for aeolian size grains or for natural dune building activity, leading them to conclude that the ridge or mound was formed by a combination of normal shore processes and human construction. However, it is possible that aeolian features were present prior to agricultural modification by early European settlers. The presence of a thin layer of fine sand on the beach crest in the Laurentian trench lends some support to the argument for prior natural dune features, but it is clear that aeolian dunes were not evident to Bell (a trained geological observer) at the time of initial discoveries in the area. Unfortunately, Bell's notes on the early excavations are very sparse.

Feature origins and function

There are many pits, hearths, and clusters of rocks at Killarney Bay (see Figure 6.1). Pits are the most numerous. Hearths and clusters of possible fire-cracked rocks are also common, as are rock-lined pits, all of which may contain charcoal. Since the beach ridge is composed of medium- to coarse-grained sand, with some small to medium pebbles (maximum size about 3 cm), any concentrations of larger rocks were probably brought in by human activity. Such rocks have been called "site furniture" (Binford 1980) and are common in hearth construction.

There are numerous sketch maps of features in Greenman's field notes, but not all features were recorded in a standard way, due partly to the way the site was excavated and the input of many different students over the years. Some of the features were relatively large (Figure 6.4) while others are small (Figure 6.5). Greenman indicates that many of the rocks are rather angular, suggesting fire-cracked rocks. However, it is clear that not many were cracked in situ. These features are certainly rock-lined but may not necessarily be large fire-pits or hearths. They are not typical of more recent sweat baths, where rocks tend to be more concentrated and show signs of in situ fracturing. The faunal remains found in certain nonmortuary features provide some evidence of function (see Table 6.1; see also Chapter 13). All of the faunal bone recovered from hearths, pits, and subsoil streamer contexts was calcined and most was large mammal. However, turtle shell was found in a pit feature overlying Burial 2 and in hearth features. It appears these features were for cooking and possibly, in the case of some turtle remains, grave offerings.

Unfortunately, it may not be possible to interpret many of these circular features with certainty, as they were not excavated and recorded with much consistency. We don't know what size rocks were recorded, and what size

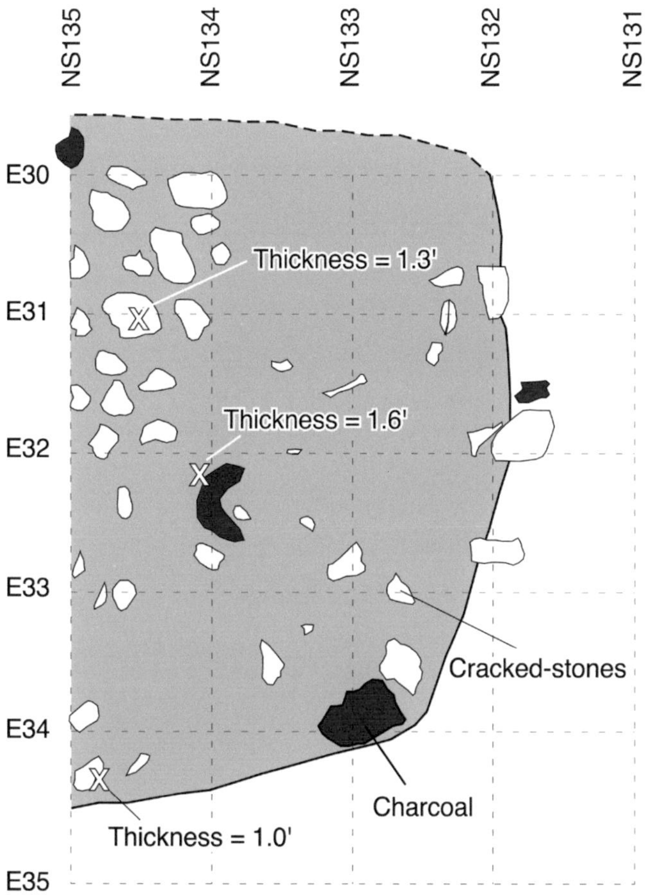

Figure 6.4. Sketch map of part of a rock-lined pit with large charcoal chunks (from Greenman map 10, 1955). Note: the average thickness of the deposit was recorded as 0.9 feet (27.4 cm). Stones lie in sand colored by charcoal. About fifteen stones were removed before the map was drawn.

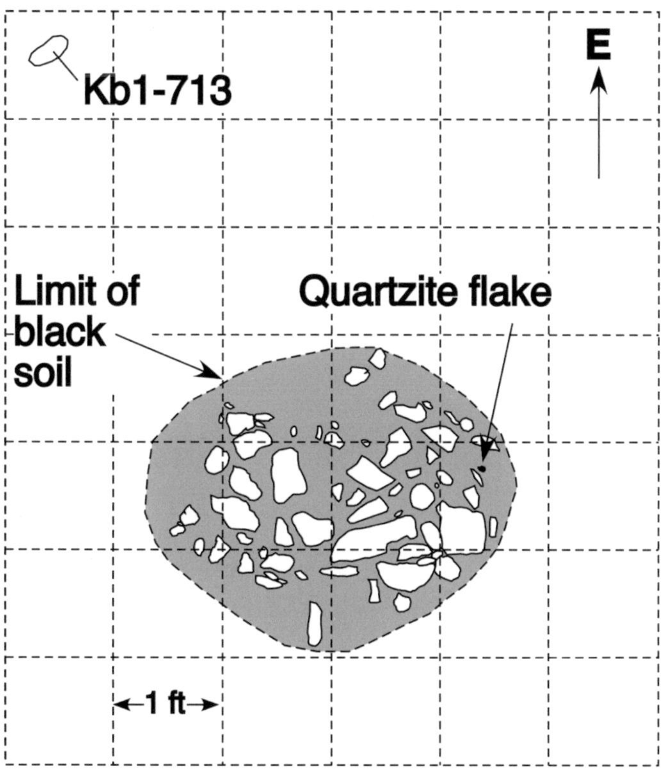

Figure 6.5. Sketch map of small rock-lined pit exposed in topsoil, about 0.6 feet (18 cm) below the surface in test trench No. 6 and area to the west (from Greenman map 61, 1946).

omitted, as clearly many were removed before researchers recorded the features (see Figure 6.4). At Squawkie Hill and many other mound sites around Lake Ontario (Fox 2004:51), there is well-documented stone architecture: stone slabs and boulder features in the mound areas; water-worn pebbles and rock fragments placed in a circle; and stone-lined cists.

Conclusions

The Greenman excavations were done as a field school project, as were the later Laurentian excavations (Chapter 8), indicating the value of such activities for research purposes, despite some methodological limitations. Due to the excavation methods used by Greenman (known as moving profile), the stratigraphic profiles recorded across the beach ridge at Killarney Bay are quite detailed. In contrast, the many stone scatters and other recorded features are more difficult to interpret. Further sampling may resolve the question of dune activity (aeolian sands), although sediment analysis by coring in 2010 and a deep test trench by Laurentian University in the 1980s indicated no significant dune deposits or other evidence of aeolian activity in the Killarney Bay site.

Greenman's many profiles and detailed sketches and field notes are curated at the University of Michigan Museum of Anthropological Archaeology. Unfortunately, the photographic record is quite sparse, as are the field notes (which were retyped). The original field notes and photographs seem to be missing from the archives. This limits the interpretive value of the surviving excavation records. The Greenman records are a good source of stratigraphic and feature data, but not as good for spatial data. The Laurentian Field school excavations provided more spatial data on activity areas, as reported in subsequent chapters.

Chapter 7

The University of Michigan Excavations (1939–1953)

David Brose

In this chapter we summarize the excavations conducted at Killarney Bay by the University of Michigan between 1939 and 1953. The descriptions of excavation units, procedures, and strategies derive from Emerson Greenman's notes and plans and from participants in the excavations. Because methods changed over the course of the investigation (see Chapters 5 and 6), we present the description as a chronological narrative. The sources for most of this chapter are the Greenman archive at the University of Michigan's Bentley Historical Library and the archive at the UMMAA Great Lakes Range (see references).

During his short 1938 reconnaissance trip and again in the summers of 1939 and 1940, Greenman excavated a few small test pits across the upper portions of the site area (Figure 7.1). But with its plow-disturbed soils, shallower lacustrine strata, and few quartzite artifacts, he must have thought there would be little left undisturbed on the knoll near the old root cellar that had been built into the then 60-year-old pothole. The quartzite debitage and preforms that Greenman recovered were cataloged and are discussed in the lithic chapter (Chapter 10). These small test units were not part of any later plan, although their apparent stratigraphic location vis-a-vis the levels of Lake Huron appear to have given Greenman the idea that he would be able to tie the artifacts into the developing Great Lakes geochronology.

Historical documents indicate that Robert Bell dug three mounds at Killarney Bay: the main one at KB-1 and two smaller ones "up the hill." The location of these small mounds does not show on any of Greenman's Killarney Bay maps, but Greenman reported being taken to see their pitted remains 300 yards east of his own excavations. Julig et al. (2009) noted that this would place the small mounds either under a former gravel ridge or, more likely, in the area of the current "old gravel pit" just east of Speigel's property line. Unfortunately, this area is now excavated to bedrock. Julig has suggested that since the two smaller Bell mounds were at a higher elevation, they may have been a bit earlier in

Figure 7.1. This field photograph from the University of Michigan excavations shows a view of the main mound at the Killarney Bay site. Between Bell's excavations in the 1870s and Greenman's work sixty years later, a root cellar had been built on the main mound and Bell's excavation unit surrounded by log cribbing.

Figure 7.2. Students working on Greenman's crew at Killarney Bay in 1947.

time. He notes that there are local reports of other burials on beach ridges. At Chickinishing Creek, for example, several burials were found by the former mayor while digging gravel for the new bridge. They were covered back up and left. These too may have been earlier than KB-1, as they sit on the lower Nipissing ridge.

Greenman began his excavation by laying out a Cartesian grid. He set numbered stakes along a baseline between large granite outcrops, 600 feet from west to east, and 200 feet from the baseline to the north end of the property (see Figure 6.1). A west to east series of potential trenches, each 50 feet wide, was laid out on this grid. He gave each trench an alphabetic designation (i.e. Trench C). Within each potential trench, 50-foot "sections" were laid out to the south from the northern rock outcrop. He gave each of these sections a numeric designation (i.e. Trench 3C). Then, within each of these 50 x 50 foot sections, 1000 5 x 5 foot squares were laid out, each designated by a number (from 1 at the south to 10 at the north) and a letter (from "a" at the west end to "j" on the east). Every possible five-foot square could thus be identified (e.g. Trench 3D section 7c).

Greenman's crews also scattered a number of 5 x 5 foot and 5 x 10 foot excavation units (called "test trenches") across the fields during the first few years of work. No extant documentation indicates the specific logic behind their placement. The larger excavations did not proceed in a systematic trench-by-trench fashion. Not all surveyed trenches were excavated. Sometimes work in adjacent or separated trenches occurred concurrently and not always under Greenman's personal supervision. After 1946, he occasionally left a student in charge of the always-small crew while he boated off to find other sites in the region (Figure 7.2).

In each trench, work began by digging a number of 5 x 5 foot numbered section squares on the north-south baseline in the southern end of a subsection of the trench (i.e. Trench 3E section 2e). After the first *tranche* or cut in each trench had reached a depth Greenman considered to

Figure 7.3. Stratigraphy in a profile of Trench 4E at Killarney Bay (Negative 7290).

represent the pre-occupation surface, the northern vertical face of the next subsection was dug away to that depth, often in stepwise fashion and occasionally as a whole unit. With this system (used for the first decade), excavation seldom exposed paleo-surfaces or living floors. Most features, such as hearths and pits (and later, the first burials), were initially exposed in vertical cross-section, with no knowledge of their shape or extent. Think of a layer cake. Cutting off an end slice would make the stratigraphy (layering) very clear but would leave the extent and overall configuration of each layer unknown (Figure 7.3).

Greenman used the same recording techniques he had learned in Europe and practiced while excavating Adena and Hopewell sites in Ohio. These techniques were unusual for the generally shallow sites then being dug in the Great Lakes region (Brose 1973; O'Brien and Lyman 2001; Wright 1974). He made sure that all hearths, pits, artifacts, fire-cracked rock concentrations, and features he encountered were measured in place. If warranted, his students took photographs and drew each feature or artifact on a sequentially numbered drawing, called a "map" in the field notes (Figure 7.4). Each student also wrote a journal with daily entries describing the course of excavation and noting any unusual strata, feature, or artifact. Greenman collated and corrected these "notes" daily and, at the end of each field season from 1946 through 1952, he typed

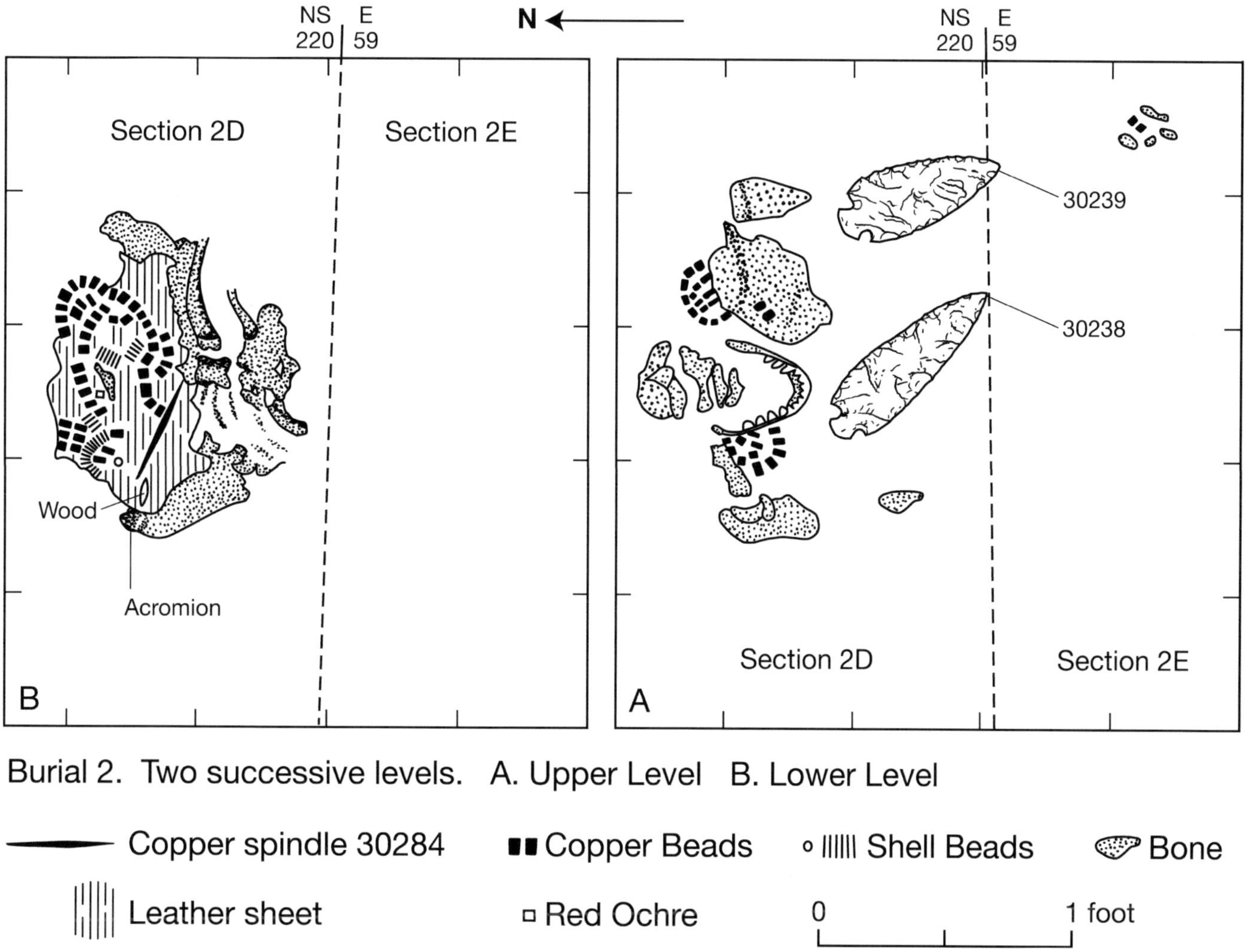

Figure 7.4. A field map of Burial 2 at Killarney Bay, excavated by Greenman's crew in 1949.

up an edited summary of each day's work, which was later hand corrected. Nearly all of these documents have been preserved, and they reveal Greenman's efforts to bring uniformity to often unclear field observations and conflicting interpretations. Most artifacts, including large debitage pieces, were given a field catalog number while in situ, and many of the maps and field notes reference these by number. With a plethora of old engineers' tapes on hand, all measurements were in feet and tenths of feet: a bizarre blend of English and metric systems. All depth measurements were taken in feet and tenths of feet from a datum set each year as a specific elevation above the surface level of Lake Huron. Because of this, it requires considerable effort to determine the relative stratigraphic positioning of paleo-beaches, features, and artifacts encountered in different years (Figure 7.5).

Excavation of the burial area: 1947–1953

The University of Michigan Museum of Anthropological Archaeology files contain few general stratigraphic drawings of Greenman's last few years of work, no doubt because the excavation strategy had radically changed after Greenman decided that little stratigraphic data was to be found within the knoll area. The exceptions are the drawings

Figure 7.5. Stones in a hearth feature found in Test Trench 6 at Killarney Bay (Negative 7229). Despite Greenman's efforts to bring consistency and uniformity to the process of excavation, it is often difficult to determine, more than seventy years later, the relative stratigraphic positioning of features and artifacts at the site.

and photographs of the burial features that were encountered in those years. There are also drawings of pits and "baths" like those encountered in the trenches between 1940 and 1950. Among the features Greenman recorded, it is possible to tentatively identify those from which the radiocarbon dates were taken. Nonetheless, there will always be some uncertainties regarding the provenience of any material that did not come from a burial encountered in the final years of work on the root-cellar area of Killarney Bay. A number of finished bifaces and sherds have been given a provenience indicating they were picked up from the surface of what Greenman termed the old "throw-out pile," but there is no indication in any extant notes that disturbed or excavated mound sediments were screened. This includes the sediments from the final excavations, when the uppermost remnants of the mound were scraped off.

At the start of the 1947 season, Greenman noted that planned excavation in Trenches 4F and 3F (NS 270, E20–90) would partially intrude into

> …a mound, which until recently was a fruit cellar…there is a dug out area besides the mount [sic] beginning in Trench 3F from E 55 to E 65. There have been many cave-ins of the vertical face along the NS 270 line due to the weight of the earth being piled on top of the mound.

Greenman began with a wide frontal approach to the mound, using the north end wall of Trench 4D as a starting face. During the second week of that season, after having determined what he called the "old land surface," Greenman ran into pits filled with fire-cracked rocks, charcoal, and a number of sherds of what are now called the Killarney Bay Thick variety Plain (Figure 7.6). Despite his statement

Figure 7.6. During the second week of the 1947 season, trenching into the main mound, Greenman's crew began to find pits filled with fire-cracked rocks, charcoal, and a number of sherds of what are now called the Killarney Bay Thick variety Plain. The trowel points to one such sherd (KB1100) in the vertical face of the north wall of Trench 4E, Section E6 (Negative 7288).

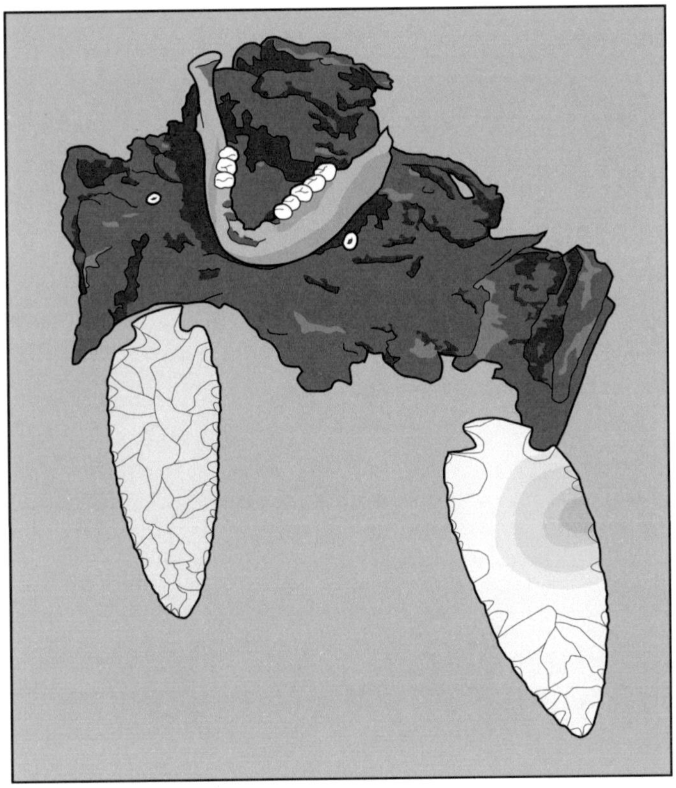

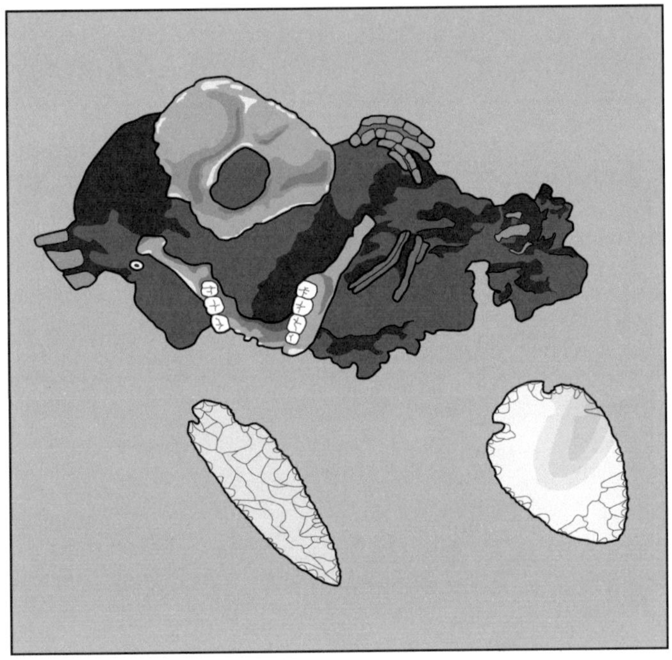

Figures 7.7 (left) and 7.8. Drawings of field photographs of Burial 2 at Killarney Bay, which Greenman's crew found in 1949. Drawings by John Klausmeyer.

that there was no indication of in situ burning, his notes indicated this was the remains of a fire that had taken place at the hearth encountered a few feet to the north. There, among large fire-cracked rocks, excavators found a sherd of Killarney Bay Thick variety Pseudo Scallop Shell. Greenman noted a nearby cluster of another 45 sherds, now assigned to Killarney Bay Thick variety Plain, which he believed represented three different vessels (see Chapter 11, this volume).

Burial 1

Greenman devoted the 1948 summer to extending trench excavation into older beach formations and investigating nearby sites. The 1949 season began in Trenches 3E and 4E from Section D1 to Section D10. The northern edge of this area was at the base of the former mound. While excavating in the topsoil near the mound, Greenman encountered a highly fragmented section of a blackish-brown tubular pipe. Soon after, the crew ran into the remains of Burial 1 in the subsoil. The burial appeared as a disturbed oval pit, with a sheet of bark laid over the bones of a child and a single finished biface.

Burial 2

Moving north, into the mound, excavators encountered Burial 2 to the northeast of the previously excavated central mound area. They first noticed the burial when they found several pieces of a brown tubular stone pipe at the base of the overlying disturbed topsoil, along with five Killarney Bay Smoothed sherds. Over the next two weeks, they excavated Burial 2 and its plentiful caches of grave goods (Figures 7.7, 7.8, 7.9). The upper levels of the Burial 2 pit contained some calcined bone and fire-cracked rock, below which lay a copper-stained skull and a large quartzite blade. This upper level also contained fragments of "baked clay," suggesting a prepared crematory basin or a hearth.

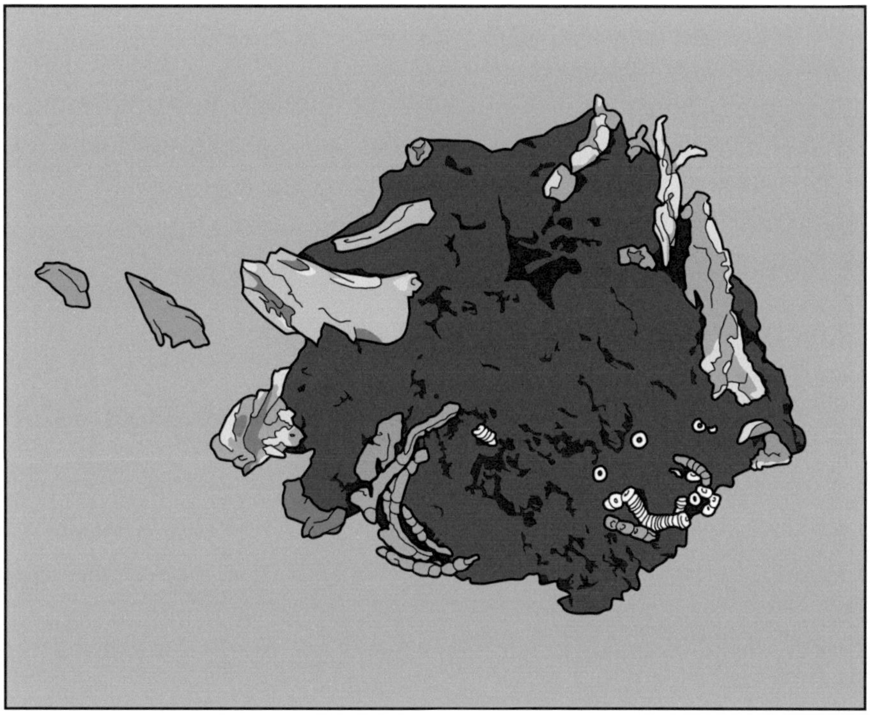

Figure 7.9. Another view of Burial 2 at Killarney Bay, drawn from a field photograph. Among the grave goods were more than 100 copper beads on seven necklace strands, a strand of drilled shell beads, and a copper spindle with a wooden handle. Drawing by John Klausmeyer.

Researchers encountered a half-oval zone of dark organic staining and several lumps of charcoal along edge of this area, which contained a large projectile point that Greenman called "Bayport nodular flint."

The field notes say excavators believed Burial 2 was originally fully extended and supine, with both legs and at least one arm outstretched to the southeast. However, only the copper-associated bones survived to be discovered. The skull and cervical vertebrae appeared to be separated from upper body bones, with the skull and mandible to the north and facing south. These were thought to have been contained or wrapped in a leather bag or a leather cape-like garment with leather-wrapped fiber thongs. More than 100 tubular copper beads were counted in seven necklace strands, including three very large folded copper beads. A single strand of drilled shell beads was around the back of this possible garment or bag. There were also additional bones, which Greenman thought might have been from a second individual. These bones lay on top of the leather. A number of large chipped stone bifaces were placed on the chest and shoulders of the first individual. Below the first set of bones in Burial 2, there lay a long copper spindle with a leather-tied short wooden handle.

A radiocarbon sample is linked to this feature. Greenman noted on August 8 that he was collecting charcoal "...for analysis by carbon 14..." However, there is some question as to whether the charcoal derived from the burial feature proper or an abutting charcoal-filled pit.

Burial 3

Excavators first observed Burial 3 as a circular area of copper-stained skeletal material in a disturbed condition near the central mound area. Ed Norbeck, a graduate student working with Greenman, first encountered and described these materials. There were a few historic materials in and even possibly underlying some layers, representing a possible remnant of Bell's 1870 excavation. The field notes suggest there was a pelt or hide wrapping around some of the individual bones. It appeared as if skull fragments, the mandible, and the maxillary bone were entirely enclosed in leather (Field Notes 1949:19). The only artifacts that might have been associated with this burial were a finished chert scraper, two rough unused scrapers, three long, narrow copper beads, a fragment of sheet copper, and small lumps of red ochre.

The 1950 field season began on the same subsoil level at which Burial 3 was encountered. In the subsoil between disturbed Burial 3 and undisturbed Burial 4, the excavators ran into shallow lenses and pockets of ochre-stained and charcoal-stained earth as well as areas of charcoal and fire-cracked rock (Field Notes 1950:20–25; Comments p63; Map 138). In a shallow depression that appeared to have been the base of a pit with mottled lenses of very dark charcoal-stained soils, they recovered a small sherd of Killarney Bay Smoothed and an ochre-stained fragment of a perforated gorget. They also found a complete 2-hole quadrilateral gorget of Gowganda slate overlying two sherds of Killarney Bay Thick in what they called "a pocket of black earth." Subsequent and more extensive excavation (after removal of Burial 4) revealed that this dark lens occurred within a larger shallow pit with red ochre. About 5 cm below the gorget in this lens of ochre, there was a copper bead and fragments of bone and leather.

Working across this ill-defined surface, the field crews also recovered additional Killarney Bay Smoothed ceramics, another triangular cache blade, several scrapers, and a stemmed projectile point of local chert. Along with red ochre in a shallow pit or dip in the ground surface were several chipped and partially ground unfinished preforms of Gowganda slate and below that a conical copper bead with fragments of leather and bone (Field Notes 1950:24).

Burial 4

Excavators first saw Burial 4 as a well-defined pit lined with and capped by red ochre. The upper north edge contained a dark lens with three copper beads, fragments of copper-stained calcined bone and leather, and flint projectile points. Nearby were two strands of leather-covered copper beads along with a maxilla and mandible with deciduous teeth lying on the left side facing northeast, toward a large cache of rough side-struck quartzite and flint cache blades. Most of the specimens appeared covered with a thin wash of ochre (Field Notes 1950:22–25; Maps 138–142). A sherd of Killarney Bay Smoothed and a small flint scraper appeared to overlay the burial pit. The field drawings by Ken Wittick and Marshall Sahlins clearly reveal a pit filled with and capped by red ochre, in which was placed the leather bundle of bones and copper, lying on top of most of the cache blades and in turn capped by about 10 other cache blades.

Burial 5

Burial 5 is nearby. Field crew first saw it as a pit-like area of dark soil with spots of red ochre (Field Notes 1950:25). It contained two groups of teeth, organic bits of leather, and fragments of bark and charcoal. Three fused copper beads were found in the soil immediately above this pit, and nearby lay a piece of Gowganda slate, possibly part of a ground stone pendant preform.

Burial 6

The first sign of Burial 6 was a copper-stained disc shell bead just below the topsoil in the wall of Trench 3E, Sections G1 and G2. Further excavation into the vertical face of the trench revealed a deposit of copper beads in darker soil, which was soon exposed as a pit. In the top of the pit were "badly worn" sherds (KB2140), small flint chips, and lumps of dark heavy soil (Greenman's rewritten field notes suggest that the dark areas of soil were more compact than much of the matrix for the upper part of the pit fill). The pit had been dug down into the underlying water-laid gravels, possibly representing one of the earliest interments at the site. Excavators found several copper-stained countersunk drilled disc shell beads at the base of topsoil at the edge of Section H1, where they exposed a deposit of copper beads in the face of the excavation unit. The crew took a sample from the burial pit, which was filled with "dark heavy soil." There were "few" badly weathered Killarney Bay Smoothed ceramic fragments in the upper fill of the pit, below which lay a circular sheet of birch bark that was 1.3 feet in diameter. Underneath this was a piece of leather outlined with an embedded strand of copper beads. Below this leather lay more bark, and below that, portions of a woven net-like basket or bag. This fabric appeared to have contained one long bone, a mostly complete skull, mandible fragments, and

Figure 7.10. The field crew at Killarney Bay found Burial 6 by investigating a copper-stained disc shell bead in the wall of Trench 3E, Sections G1 and G2. This woven basket or bag was in the lower part of the burial pit (Negative 8628).

part of the pelvis, which had been placed atop 38 "grayish blue" flint cache blades. Below this was more of the basket or bag (Figure 7.10; see also Appendix C).

In 1951, a short field season, Greenman's field crew continued excavations into the faces of several previously excavated trenches in the area of the root cellar. Greenman opened the field season by removing earth along the north-south 180 line in hopes of finding a vertical face of earth that had not been excavated previously. The stratigraphic wall profiles drawn for the 1951 trenches far exceed the number of wall profiles compiled in the first 12 years' work. They provide a clear picture of the water-laid gravels and sands underlying the culturally attributed lenses of clean sand and the basket loads of culturally enriched soils that capped the knoll. By this point, Bell and Greenman had excavated at least eight burials from the knoll. But although the 1951 trench excavations were carried into the disturbed center of the knoll, the crew recovered no burials that year.

In 1952, a small crew returned and focused their work on the west ends of the trenches that had been excavated

Figure 7.11. In 1952, the Killarney Bay field crew found Burial 7 in the northeastern part of the mound (Negative 8636).

the previous year. The goal was to reach the highest central portion of the knoll. There they abutted the Lamorandiere log-crib root cellar, two sides of which had been removed the previous year. Continuing to dig eastward, the crew found a black lens of soil with small fire-cracked rock fragments below the root cellar. This appeared to be the original ground surface on which the mound had been built. Below this surface, excavators found a large projectile point of white chert at the edge of the disturbed area. It was two feet above the underlying water-laid gravels.

As has been discussed in Chapter 2, it appears that the original burials were placed in a naturally wave-laid stretch of higher ground, and successive fire hearths, rock alignments, and covered burials created the higher central elevation that Bell and Greenman called a mound.

Burial 7

The summer of 1952 was bedeviled by rain and the disturbance resulting from Bell's Victorian excavation techniques (he essentially pot-hunted the mound). At the beginning of that season, the field crew continued to excavate, following the 1951 surface across the northeastern portions of the mound. They found Burial 7 in a wide, broadly sloping pit with indistinct edges and mottled fill (Figure 7.11). The stratigraphic profile of this burial shows that below the plow-disturbed upper topsoil, the upper part of the fill in the burial pit was a zone of differentially colored fill soils. This is typically seen in mounds constructed by dumping basket after basket of soils from different sources.

This pit was cut by a smaller pit of darker mottled soils extending down into the light subsoil. Field notes suggest that the inner pit had been dug down to the surface of gravel through the center of the earlier, wider, sloping shallow pit. At the base of this deeper pit was a hide or leather bag containing the disarticulated vertebrae, ribs, scapula, and part of the humerus of an infant lying atop a flint blade. This mass of organic fur and matting was sewn over with or wrapped in knotted-spacer, double-twisted and sheathed leather or sinew thongs, forming strands of 27 drilled, copper-stained Marginella shell beads. A copper celt and a copper chisel were also in the pit, which was filled with basket loads of organically stained dark soils with copper-stained wood and fire-cracked rock, possibly from a ritual fire (Field Notes 1952:J. Oliver 3-8, Maps 162,164; Field Notes 1952:R. S. Hall 1-8, Maps 163, 165, 166).

Burial 8

The field crew first noted nearby Burial 8 as a black deposit extending 4.5 feet below the surface. The deposit was thought to be backfill from earlier excavations (Figure 7.12a-c). The notes described it as the central mound burial, below but partially disturbed by the root cellar and "... excavation of the mound some 75 years ago" (Field Notes 1952: R.S. Hall 1). Burial 8 appeared to be in its original position below another flint blade covered in leather, lying adjacent to what was first thought to be pieces of large animal rib but which further excavation revealed to be a copper spindle lying on another piece of leather along with a human cervical vertebrae. The main trunk of the body was said to have been disturbed by the root cellar, with neither skull nor leg bones present.

Other skeletal elements were on a circular piece of leather or hide or within a hide bag that had several folds or a doubled thickness at the bottom of bag. A copper axe wrapped in deer skin with fur was associated with the upper end of a leg bone, below which lay a large hafted knife. Other notched knives lay on and under a band of leather sewn over with strands of twisted fiber, containing more than 100 small copper beads, which were wrapped around three long bones. Below this were two copper celts wrapped in long-haired deer hide (probably winter-killed, according to Dr. Phillip Meyers, University of Michigan Museum of Zoology), beside or between which was another hafted knife.

Toward the west lay a human scapula, vertebrae, and ribs, below which lay a hairy deer hide and one Killarney Bay Smoothed sherd. The sherd was described as a "... piece of pottery, body sherd, thick, lay below the sacrum with some sand between it and the sacrum. This looks like pottery from the water-laid component and may have been in its original position or it may have been accidentally or otherwise on the bottom of the grave" (Field Notes 1952:5).

It appeared to the excavators that the entire skeleton of Burial 8 had been enclosed in another, larger skin bag (Field Notes 1952:16; map 165 shows leather knot tying bag closed), and that the group of artifacts on the east side,

Figure 7.12, a-c (above and facing page). The field crew at Killarney Bay found Burial 8 in 1952. This primary burial of an adult male contained numerous grave goods, including leather and beaver fur, shell beads, large flint bifaces, and several copper items (Negatives 10702, 10704, 10705).

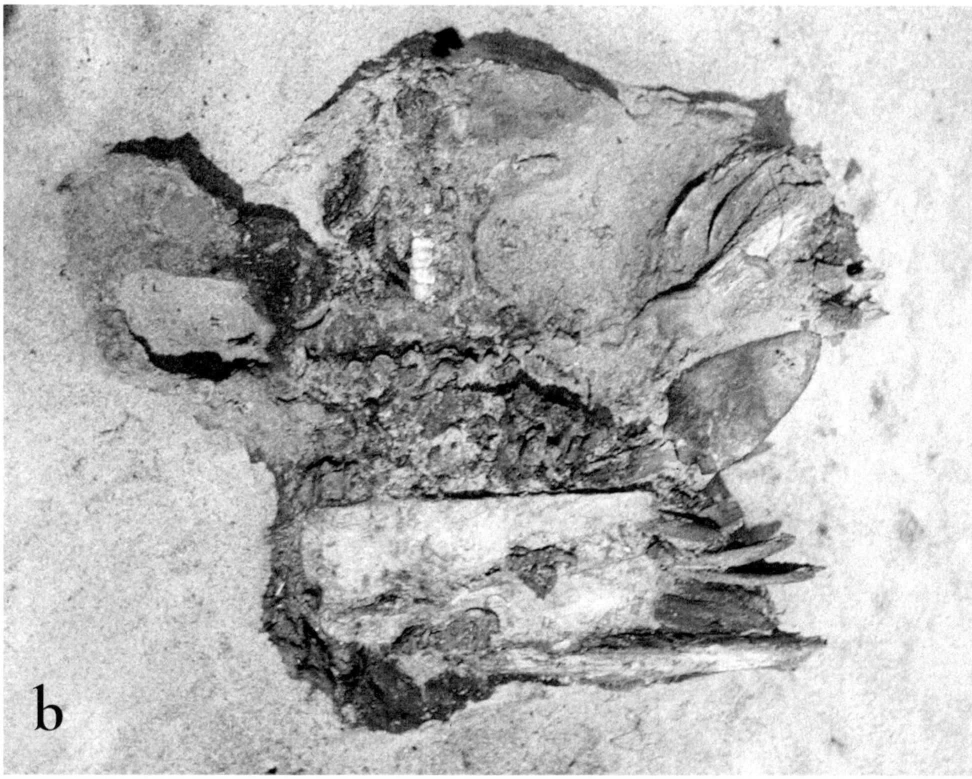
b

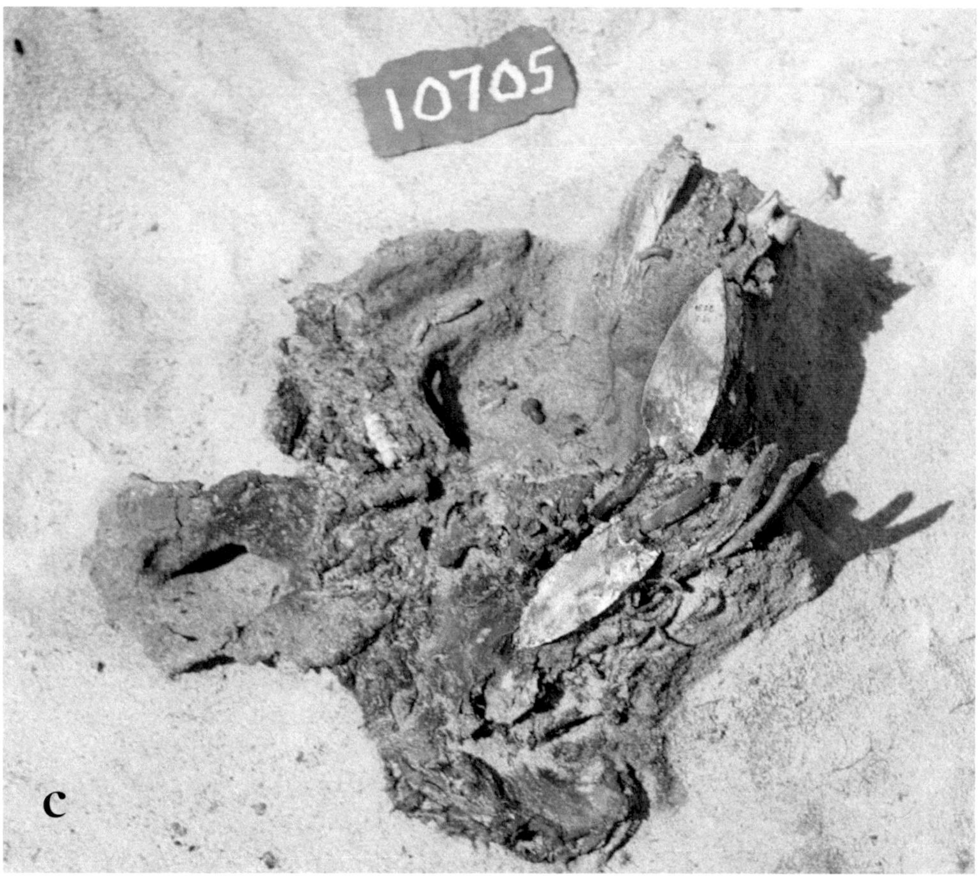
10705
c

including two copper celts and three hafted knives, were enclosed in separate folds of deerskin with the hair on it. After this had been placed with the burial, the pit had been refilled with soils containing charcoal, fragments of fire-cracked rock, and a single sherd of Speigel Tool-Impressed, variety Linear Dentate. Then a fire had been burned over the pit, leaving a number of large fire-cracked rocks that were not charred (indicating that the rocks were not in direct contact with the burning fuel; possibly they were in some boiling liquid). Finally, basket loads of altered soils were built up to create a mound over the entire area. Unfortunately, during the last full week of the 1952 season, it rained heavily. Because the root-cellar log cribbing over the Burial 8 pit had been removed, portions of the wall profile and pit (shown in Field Notes 1952: Map 162) collapsed into the previously excavated trench.

Burial 9

Returning to Killarney Bay in 1953, Greenman was dismayed that the previous year's fieldwork had revealed little more than Burial 8 and large areas of loose sand, which had been picked over by Bell and then shoveled into the crib over the root-cellar. During most of the time he worked in Ohio, Greenman's archaeological experience on Adena and Hopewell burial mounds involved the use of scrapers (often pulled by mules) to remove "disturbed overburden" and quickly reach some suspected stratum that would yield what could be the remains of a single behavioral event. So Greenman decided to push the upper disturbed "mound" off with a bulldozer, rather than merely continue with the process of moving the excavation face of a trench southward through the undisturbed lower parts of the features of the central knoll area. From his notes of July 1, 1953:

> The first actual work on the site was between June 24 and 26th, and later most of the mound fill of the root cellar was bulldozed off, leaving a flat platform at the top of the unmoved light brown beach sand. The section lines were set up and excavations begun at the north edge of this platform, beginning where last years trench ended.

Robert Ackerman, a student on the crew, recorded in his student journal that he had picked up a complete stemmed projectile point on ground the bulldozer had cleared to the east of the cabin. This might have been the area Greenman initially called KB-2.

Excavation by hand then began on the surface of light brown subsoil sands that were left at the base of the root cellar.

Greenman opened TR3 from what he took to be the center of mound, digging from where Burial 8 had been excavated at the end of the 1952 season toward the eastern edge of the higher knoll along north-south Line 260 E65–E90. Burial 9 showed up as a pit filled with black earth, dug into beach sands and the coarse gravels below. Excavators found a chipped, flat, tabular brown/gray quartzite blade tip or adze-like preform in the surface of this pit. Below this lay a 2 x 3 foot layer of red ochre, fire-cracked rock fragments, and charcoal. In the center of this layer was a one-inch thick mass containing the calcined bones of a juvenile and adult embedded in red ochre (Field Notes 1953a:2,15; 1953EFG: 1–44; Maps 167, 168, 173). Additionally, there were two nondescript body sherds on the east side of the pit, below the level at which B8 originated. From the upper outer levels of this pit, the excavators recovered a rough, partially grooved, oval stone hammer. Greenman's notes suggest the possibility that these may have been accidental inclusions in the earlier sands into which this cremation was placed.

Burial 10

Running east for 10 feet from Burial 9 was a circular line of fire-cracked rock and charcoal on top of burned beach sands. These sands were the level at which all pits on the site originated. Many of the large boulders had been fire-cracked in situ. It is possible they formed a hearth for a steam bath that was built on the sandy floor of the mound into which B9 had been dug. Excavators first noted Burial 10 while clearing a spread zone of red ochre (Field Notes for 1953: 6, 10, 14; Maps 174, 175). The pit cut down through the western edge of the possible steam bath rocks and burned sands that overlay Burial 9 in the vicinity of the north-south Line 260 E65–E90. Reading two slightly differing field journals from graduate students in reverse stratigraphic order, it seems clear that in the Burial 10 pit there were two double caches. One possible leather bag (Field Notes 1953:7) contained 20 unnotched ovate blades, 4 leaf-shaped blades, 4 lanceolate blades, 2 hafted spear points and hafting, and 7 other distinctly differing stemmed points. About half a foot away, a possible twined and twilled basket held a reddish-brown tubular pipe with a carbonaceous internal crust. A constricted-end bluish-gray tubular pipe with a pebble and charred organic mass lay nearby at about the same level (Figure 7.13).

Overlying these artifacts, the copper-stained bones and teeth of the tightly flexed (possibly tied into a bundle) Burial 10 had been placed in a basket of woven string or fiber. All of this seemed to have been placed inside another bag, this one of leather—or perhaps it was merely covered by a folded hide, which was in turn covered by more than an inch of red ochre. Below, within another fiber bag, lay the bones mixed with leather strips sewn over with (or entwined with) strands of 25 small rolled copper beads and coils of 100 disc copper beads on 2-ply cordage. These had been placed atop an organic (possibly burned) mat, on which were also placed a copper celt in layers of a worked leather or rawhide bag or fabric with babiche ties. Two fused copper spindles were lying diagonally across it. One of these spindles may have had a wooden handle, and they, in turn, overlay more strands of copper beads. Two large dark bluish flint blades were excavated nearby at the same level.

Again that year, continual midsummer rains hampered careful fieldwork on the exposed surfaces. The slumping of several portions of the excavations into the lower mound ended Greenman's effort to determine the extent of the mound and expose any remaining burials.

Table 7.1 provides catalog numbers assigned by Greenman (where available) for some of the burial artifacts from Killarney Bay.

For the author's notes on the journals and drawings of students who worked with Greenman at Killarney Bay, see Appendix G.

Figure 7.13. Burial 10, found in 1953, is a young woman. This is the most complete skeleton in the Killarney Bay assemblage. Copper beads and blades, baskets, fur, decorated leather, and two pipes accompanied this burial, which was topped with ochre (Negative 10772).

Table 7.1 (page 1). Artifacts from burials with catalog numbers assigned by Greenman.

Burial number	Item description	Greenman number
2	copper-stained skull and large quartzite blade	
2	three very large folded copper beads	KB1 1171
2	long copper spindle	KB1 1188
2	leather-tied short wooden handle	KB1 1187, 1186
3	a finished chert scraper	KB1 2046
3	two rough unused scrapers	KB1 2036, 2049
3	a fragment of sheet copper	KB1 2031
3	a small sherd of Killarney Bay Smoothed	KB1 2035
3	an ochre-stained fragment of a perforated gorget	KB1 2047
3	complete 2-hole quadrilateral gorget of Gowganda slate	KB1 2069
3	two sherds of Killarney Bay Thick	KB1 2058, 2056
3	a copper bead	KB1 2121P
3	additional Killarney Bay Smoothed ceramics	KB1 2051, 2067, 2059
3	another triangular cache blade	KB1 2045
3	several scrapers	KB1 2053, 2060
3	a stemmed projectile point of local chert	KB1 2057
3	several chipped and partially ground unfinished preforms of Gowganda slate	KB1 2054, 2050, see Field Notes 1950:21–22
4	two strands of leather-covered copper beads	KB1 2075, 2118
4	a maxilla and mandible with deciduous teeth (?) or a large cache of rough side-struck quartzite and flint cache blades	KB1/2077–2115
4	a sherd of Killarney Bay Smoothed	KB1 2126
4	a small flint scraper	KB1 2072
5	two groups of teeth	KB1 2122, 2123
5	small bits of leather	KB1 2124
5	fragments of bark	KB1 2125
5	fragments of charcoal	KB1 2131
5	a piece of Gowganda slate, possibly part of a ground stone pendant preform	KB1 2128
6	badly worn sherds	KB1 2140
6	a deposit of copper beads exposed in the face of the excavation unit	KB1 2139
6	a soil sample from the burial pit	KB1 2142
6	badly weathered Killarney Bay Smoothed ceramic fragments	KB1 2140
6	a piece of leather	KB1 2146
6	an embedded strand of copper beads, associated with KB1 2146	KB1 2137, 2144, 2145
6	bark	KB1 2147
6	a woven net-like basket or bag	KB1 2148
6	38 grayish-blue flint cache blades	KB1 2154-2192

Table 7.1 (page 2). Artifacts from burials with catalog numbers assigned by Greenman.

Burial number	Item description	Greenman number
7	a hide or leather bag	KB1 2203
7	infant bones atop a flint blade	KB1 2198
7	mass of organic fur and matting	KB1 2210
7	knotted-spacer, double-twisted and sheathed leather or sinew thongs	KB1 2209
7	strands of 27 drilled, copper-stained Marginella shell beads	KB1 2202
7	a copper celt	KB1 2200
7	a copper chisel	KB1 2201
8	a copper spindle found on a piece of leather with a human cervical vertebrae	KB1 2230
8	a copper axe	KB1 2232
8	a large hafted knife	KB1 2238
8	notched knives found on and under a band of leather sewn over with strands of twisted fiber	KB1 2233
8	more than 100 small copper beads	KB1 2239, 2240
8	three long bones, wrapped by the small copper beads	KB1 2237
8	two copper celts	KB1 2241, 2242
8	a hafted knife	KB1 2245
8	one Killarney Bay Smoothed sherd	KB1 2251
8	single sherd of Speigel Tool-Impressed, variety Linear Dentate	
9	chipped, flat, tabular brown/gray quartzite blade tip or adze-like preform	KB1 2295
9	rough, partially grooved, oval stone hammer	KB1 2296
10	possible leather bag with 28 blades, 2 spear points and hafting, and 7 other stemmed points	KB1 2364
10	2 hafted spear points and hafting	KB1 2331, 2319
10	7 stemmed points	KB1 2309, 2311, 2353, 2333, 2312, 2320, 2317
10	possible twined and twilled basket	KB1 2326
10	reddish-brown tubular pipe from the possible basket	KB1 2321
10	carbonaceous internal crust from the pipe	KB1 2322
10	constricted-end bluish-gray tubular pipe	KB1 2323
10	pebble associated with the pipe	KB1 2324
10	charred organic mass associated with the pipe	KB1 2325
10	copper celt	KB1 2352
10	two fused copper spindles	KB1 2319, 2351
10	possible wooden handle for a copper spindle	KB1 2331
10	two large dark-bluish flint blades	KB1 2309, 2310

Chapter 8

The Laurentian University Excavations (1981–2002)

Patrick Julig, Andrew Meehan, and Kristin Thor

The Killarney Bay site represents one of numerous Middle Woodland sites in Ontario that contain both a mortuary and a habitation component. However, the association between the two areas at Killarney Bay was not clear to Greenman (1966) or to some other archaeologists (Spence et al. 1990), who had not visited or studied the entire Killarney Bay site assemblages. The mortuary component, which Greenman dated to 90 BC based on the early ^{14}C dates on beaver fur from one of the mound burials (Greenman 1966), includes artifacts that had been assigned to the Early Woodland Middlesex component (Spence et al. 1990:126). This date was used as the "mound date" in later publications (e.g. Spence et al. 1990:140). By contrast, the most diagnostic artifacts from the "habitation area" (so designated by Laurentian University) are the ceramics bearing pseudo-scallop shell or dentate stamp decoration, which have been assigned to a Laurel or Point Peninsula component (Spence et al. 1990:140); the tool-impressed decoration suggests a later Middle Woodland component. After the Laurentian excavations of the habitation area, analysis of the assemblages, and further ^{14}C dating of the ceramic carbon residues, the temporal association of the two components was revealed (see Chapter 4, this volume).

In this chapter, we present the results from years of work at the Laurentian University excavation area. Between 1981 and 2002, students who participated in the university's field school mapped the distribution of the artifacts they found. They also washed, labeled, and cataloged thousands of these frequently very small artifacts. The analysis presented here is based on a complete re-cataloging of the field school material in order to minimize issues related to observer variation. Kristin Thor, with the guidance of Patrick Julig and Darrel Long, classified and cataloged the lithic materials. Similarly, with the assistance of Alicia Hawkins, Elaine Cheng sorted and cataloged the pottery. Excavators did not retain the fire-cracked rock discussed in this paper. Andrew Meehan compiled the locations of fire-cracked rock on a single map using available information from original field notes.

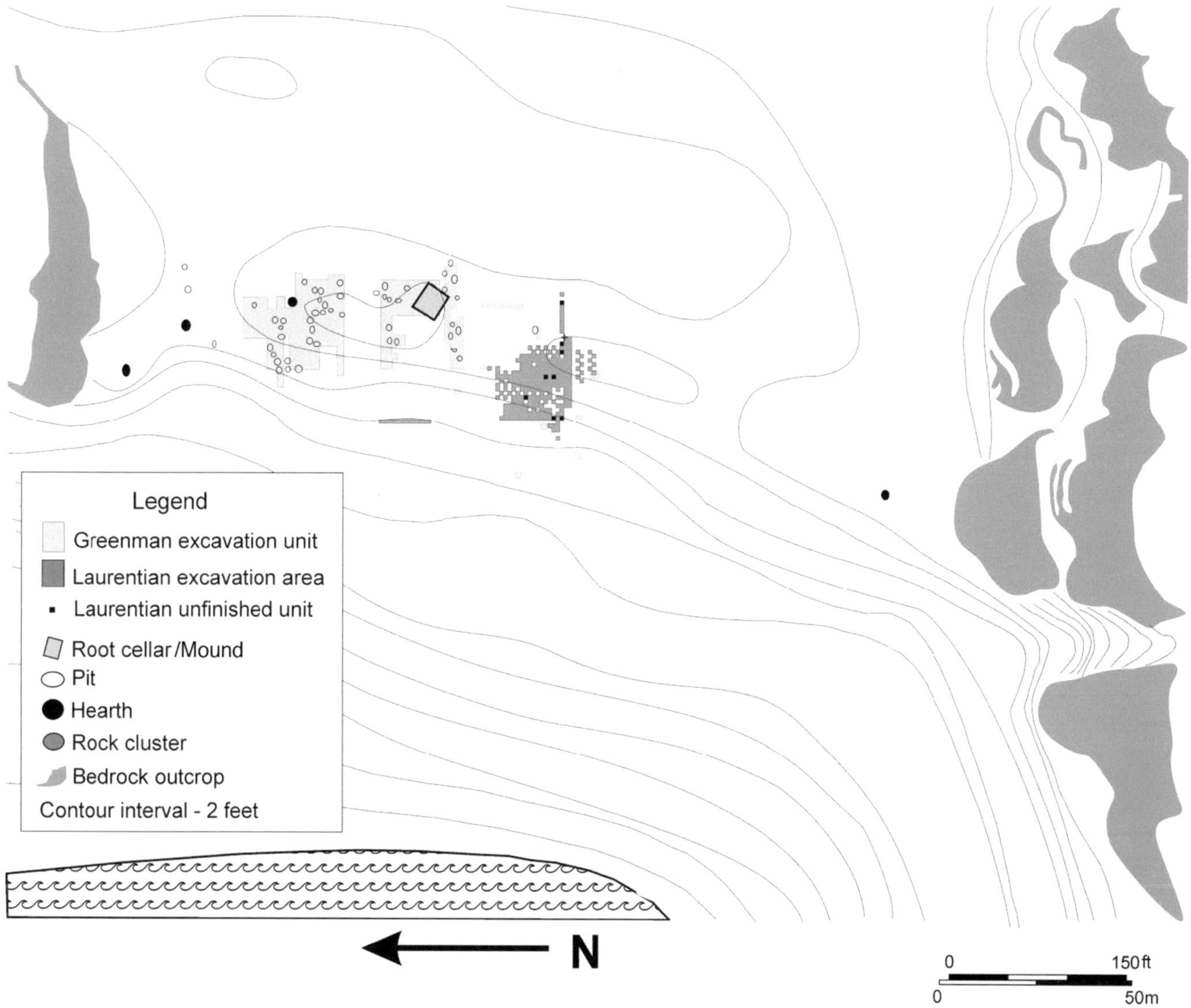

Figure 8.1. Location of the Laurentian University excavations with respect to the Greenman excavations at the Killarney Bay site. Compiled from original maps by Emerson Greenman and LU field notes.

Helen Devereux, Ken Buchanan, Patrick Julig, and students from Laurentian University field courses worked mostly in a location south and somewhat west of the burial mound (Figure 8.1) (Buchanan 1990, 1992, 1995a, 1995b, 2002; Devereux 1982; Julig 2004). The initial work by Devereux (1982) included a radial survey covering the entire site area from a central datum, test pitting until artifacts were no longer present.

The excavation area encompassed both an area on the same beach terrace as the mound and a slightly lower, more recent terrace (Julig et al. 2009). It is clear that the material found in direct association with the burials (mostly complete artifacts) bears little resemblance to the artifacts (mostly fragmentary; mostly derived from the plow zone) recovered by the Laurentian teams. For example, among the more than 24,000 items recovered by Laurentian staff and students, there exists neither copper artifacts nor human bone fragments. (Some small bone fragments were found in surface sediments but were not retained; it is possible that some were human. In addition, some calcined bone was evident during excavation of a square, but it was abandoned and covered, as it may possibly have been human and from a cremation.) At the same time, materials from the upper layers of both areas—for example, gorgets, scrapers, pot sherds and concentrations of fire-cracked rock—are similar. What is the relationship between the two areas?

Buchanan (1992, 1995a, 1995b) speculated that the habitation area was mainly occupied subsequent to the use of the area for mound building and interments. Alternatively, it could be that people camped in the habitation area for relatively short periods, during which they engaged in or prepared for mortuary ceremony. In order to answer these questions, researchers analyzed the material for an indication of the types of activities they represented; they also studied whether the debris and its distribution suggested day-to-day camping activities related to subsistence or certain stone tool manufacturing practices.

The lower terrace habitation area was not carefully examined or excavated by Greenman. Rather, he focused on the main beach ridge terrace, where he recorded rock-lined pits in addition to burials. He interpreted some of these rock-lined features as baths. However, rock-lined pits have been associated with a number of differing uses and were initially interpreted here as areas for the processing of wild rice.

Yet, as pollen analysis of a core nearby showed no wild rice pollen (McAndrews, n.d.; and see Appendix E) and because environmental conditions at the site are not ideal for large stands, the hypothesis concerning wild rice was subsequently discarded. Since then it has been reported to Julig by a local Killarney resident (Sarah Proux) that the small wild rice stands evident in some local bays were planted in the last decades by a local citizen, and not originally present.

Excavation methodology, formation processes, and limitations of the data

The fieldwork strategies employed by Laurentian students and faculty between 1981 and 2002 include surface collection, test pitting, and hand excavation of 1 x 1 m units (Buchanan 1990, 1992, 1995a, 1995b, 2002; Devereux 1982; Julig 2004). In most cases, field school students worked during the fall for a short period—normally these were only a weekend. In considering the data presented below, it is important to note that the skills of the excavators were variable, as were excavation conditions. This may explain some of the inconsistencies in the numbers of artifacts per unit that are noticeable in some areas of the grid. On one occasion, excavators had difficulty re-establishing the grid in precisely the same location as in previous years, as can happen when excavations are carried out over multiple seasons. The error was found to be caused by tree growth obscuring the datum mark on the bedrock knob at the south end of the site, and corrected in the following field season.

The standard methodology for most of the field schools entailed excavations in arbitrary 4-cm levels, screening of all sediment through ¼-inch mesh screen, and plotting artifact locations on level forms projected to the base of each level (Buchanan 1990, 1992, 1995a, 1995b, 2002; Devereux 1982; Julig 2004).

Plowing

Helen Devereux initiated and supervised the initial Laurentian excavation in 1981. During that season she took soil samples and described the sections. She recognized four levels: sterile sod; an artifact-bearing gray humus; and two levels of sterile sand. Grain-size analysis led her to conclude that "all soils can be classified as coarse sand" (Devereux 1982:20). However, Julig and Long's analysis (this volume) indicates that most sediments are "medium sand." Students were trained in the screening and identification of artifacts in the screens and were helped by supervisors at the screening stations. Supervisors instructed students to retain all objects that could be artifactual. Students later sorted artifacts from natural objects in the laboratory after all objects had been washed.

Devereux (1982) noted the presence of undulations in the interface between the cultural layer and the sand below. Figure 8.2 shows that these are almost certainly plow scars, being linear in form and running parallel to one another. According to Greenman (Field Notes 1939), the area was used for potato and general garden farming; this was such a regular activity that the owners built a root cellar for the produce into the mound. The depth of the plow zone, which in general correlates with the cultural level in this part of the site, is not great (ca. 20 cm). This suggests that plowing activity was limited: deep and prolonged plowing would lead to a thicker layer of artifact-bearing sediment. In some areas, excavators encountered features below the upper soil horizon that were undisturbed by plowing. Clearly, agricultural activities would have altered the original locations of artifact deposition, and for this reason, there is little point in examining the vertical distribution of

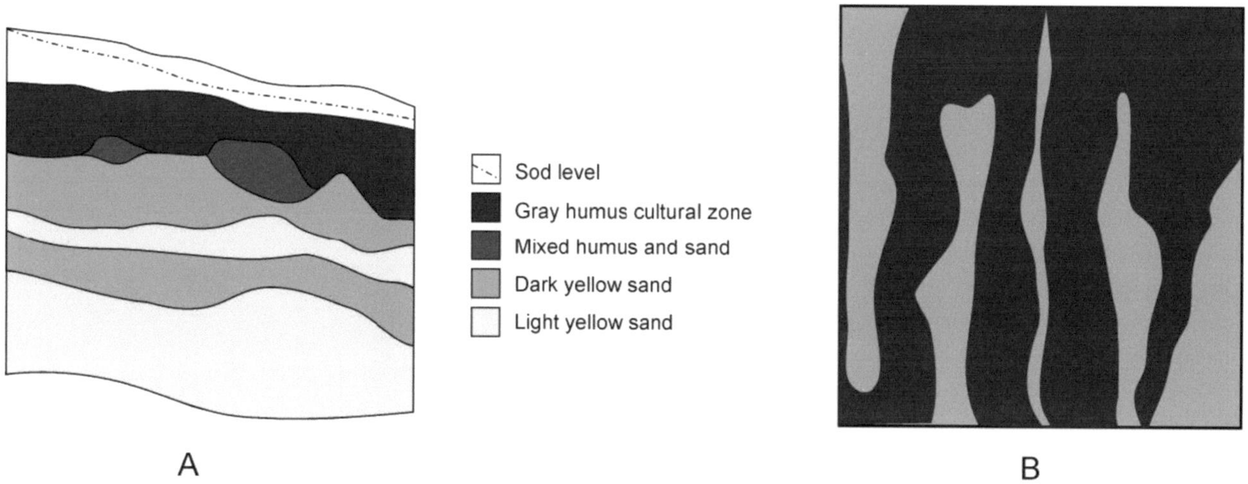

Figure 8.2. A. North profile of N1E3, and B. plan drawing of interface between humus and sand zones of unit N1E1. After Devereux (1982:24, 26).

artifacts. However, it is possible that general trends in the horizontal distribution are still discernable. Figure 8.3 shows the location of matching pottery sherds and sherds that are believed to derive from the same pot but do not actually mend. While in places there is a significant distance between mends, in general the distances are short. This suggests that horizontal displacement was not great.

Other limitations

Other limitations in this study include the fact that at least one unit, N1W6, had been previously excavated, possibly by Greenman's group, and was mistakenly re-excavated during the field school. This could explain depressed artifact counts in some specific areas of the Laurentian excavations, specifically one year when the grid was slightly misaligned.

The natural topography of the site, and specifically the presence of several beach ridges, is such that some areas have a moderate slope. It is clear that some degree of erosion has occurred in these areas and that areas of higher and lower artifact density relate in part to this process. This natural process may be accelerated by activities that disturbed the thin grass cover. Indeed, it was the displacement of artifacts caused by the playing of "bush golf" that prompted Devereux's salvage excavations in 1981. The fire department at Killarney had a short golf course laid out on the property, as it was relatively open area. There were some large maple trees and patches of small shrubs, but it was clear enough for bush (or back country) golf.

Time constraints and the limited experience of the students meant that some of the deeper units with features were never completely excavated. The possibility that features contained human remains was also of concern to the field school. These units were covered with plastic, backfilled, and left for possible completion later. The counts for those units are considered partial. They are included in some plots, but the values are excluded for the purposes of contour mapping. Partially excavated units are shown in Figure 8.3, indicated by the blackened squares.

The majority of excavators at the field school were second- and third-year university students who were archaeological neophytes. However, some crew members were more experienced: former students and other volunteers returned for multiple years to excavate, as this was an annual autumn weekend dig. The difference in the abundance of fire-cracked rock from unit to unit may reflect significant variability in the students' ability to identify this class of artifact. In some cases, students appear to have recorded every small cracked rock fragment, while excavators in neighboring units observed or mapped no fire-cracked rock at all. Further, prioritizing the mapping

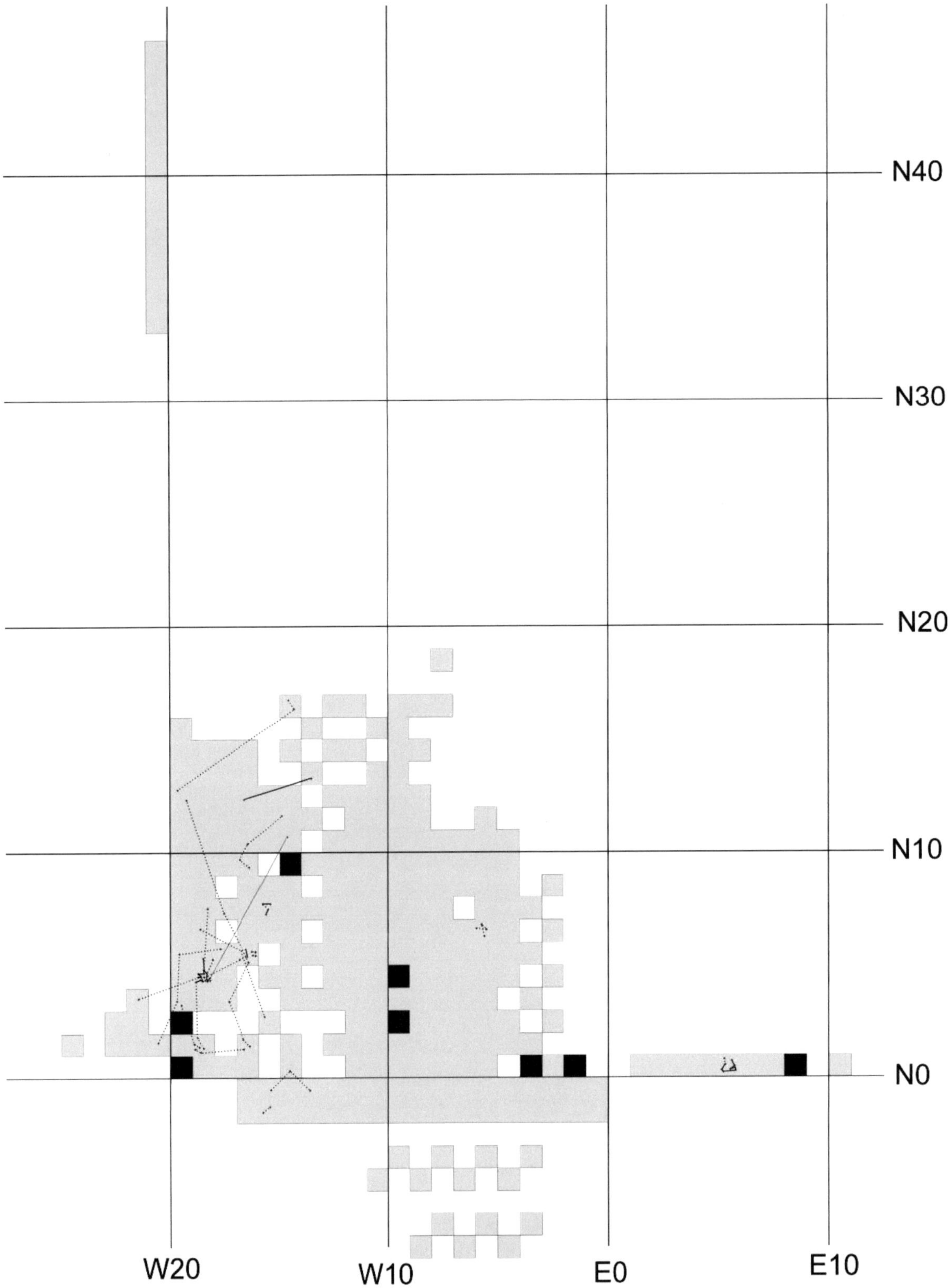

Figure 8.3. Laurentian excavation areas showing the location of cross-mending sherds (solid lines) and sherds that likely derive from the same pot but do not actually mend (dotted lines). Blackened units indicate squares that were not completely excavated.

of artifact distributions appears to have varied from year to year. As a result, the plotted distribution of fire-cracked rock may demonstrate a general pattern—and it must be remembered that fire-cracked rock is generally concentrated in features rather than scattered evenly across sites, which could account for most of the variability—but the record should be considered neither complete nor totally accurate.

Overall, the large, mainly contiguous area excavated using similar methodologies makes this a reasonable dataset for examination of spatial data. There are a few further limitations: several unexcavated units exist within the area, and the locations of fire-cracked rock were recorded by piece plotting while those of other artifact types are assigned only to 1 x 1 m units.

Evaluating expectation of long- or short-term use of the area

In the absence of undisturbed sediments with associated floral and faunal remains, it is challenging to interpret the full range of activities that the materials from the Laurentian University excavations reflect. The quantity of material recovered from this area is not insignificant, and therefore, interpretations of the area's use must include at least one of the following propositions: use by a large number of people, use for an extended period of time, or use on many occasions separated in time. Similar interpretations exist for other Middle Woodland sites in Ontario. Finlayson (1977) argues for repeated use of the Saugeen site because of the rich resources available there. Wilson (1990) suggests prolonged use of the Boresma site as a base camp. Spence et al. (1984) propose that Middle Woodland peoples used some sites on multiple occasions through the year, sometimes as part of a macroband pattern.

If individuals used the location regularly or seasonally, there may have been reuse of the same hearth areas, the same disposal areas, and so forth. By contrast, if use was very sporadic, it is possible that the feature distributions would vary between usages, with landscape features and topography structuring the location of archaeological deposits.

The settlement pattern resulting from a long-term occupation of the site would be evident in post mold distributions. While excavators recorded some posts molds at Killarney Bay, the recent use of the location as a golf course makes interpretation of their distribution impractical. Further, some of the stains encountered were animal burrows or roots. Posts that were noted do not appear to form any type of pattern. For this reason, and because the resources at the site were only available seasonally, it is likely that debris at the habitation area relates to short-term occupations either closely or widely spaced in time. By short-term occupations, we refer to periods from a few days to perhaps months.

If the area was used over shorter periods, widely separated in time, it would be expected that disposal areas would vary from occupation to occupation, and for this reason there would not be concentrated midden deposits. We would also expect clusters of like artifact types, particularly pottery, representing deposition at one time in one place. Each occupation would have different disposal locations.

By contrast, if the area was used consistently by people who held memories of the previous usages, we would expect clear disposal areas, showing elevated proportions of artifacts compared with those found elsewhere (this is clearly evident at the adjacent mound/mortuary). Also, there would be an intermingling of artifact types, as those disposed of on different occasions all form part of the same deposition unit. Finally, there would be work areas or places where the same type of activity was carried out from year to year (i.e., argillite manufacturing areas).

It is also envisioned that there would be differences related to the duration of use. Long-term occupations would feature

- debris concentrated on the margins of the area, away from features indicative of structures
- intermingling of different debris types
- debris from a living area that would tend to be smaller sized than that from middens or concentrations, as the larger objects are cleaned away from spaces used on a daily basis
- a higher proportion of used tools, including utilized pieces

Clearly, even in short-term occupations there is likely to be spatial patterning in the discard of artifacts. If there were

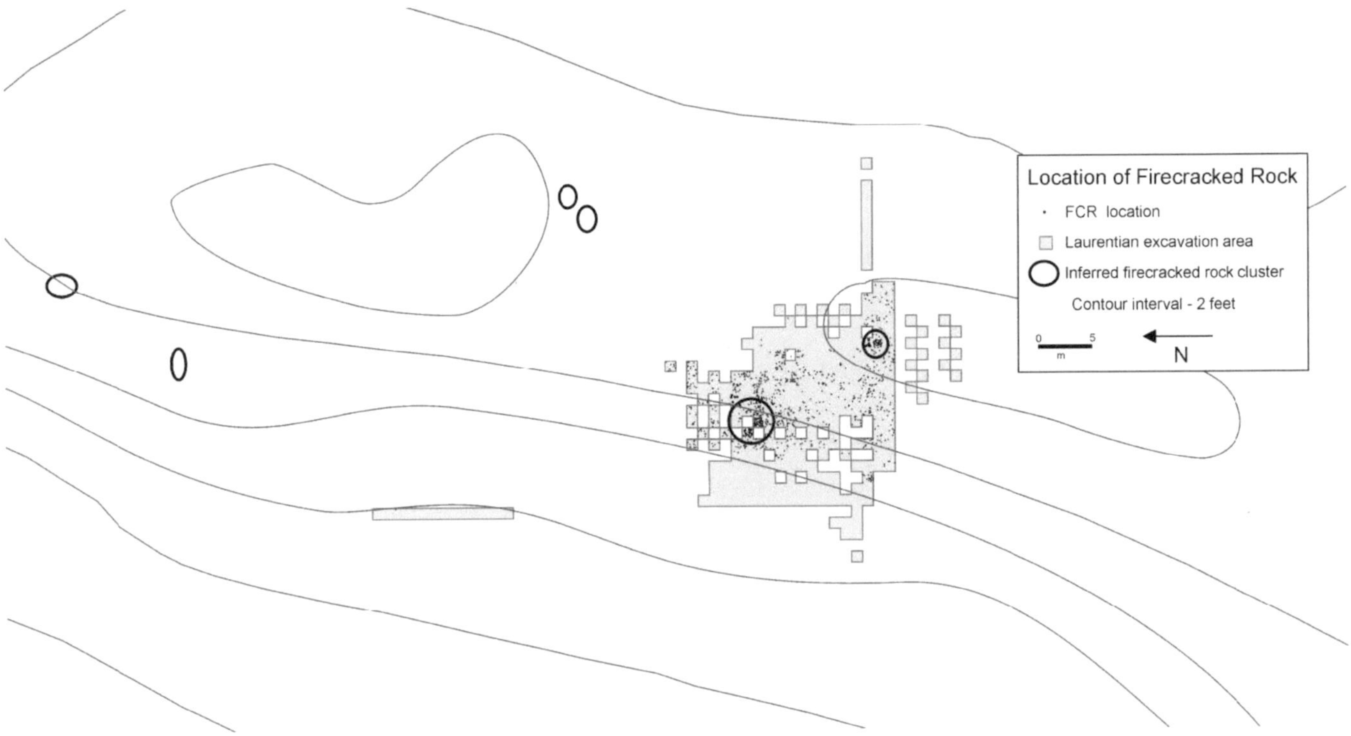

Figure 8.4. Clusters of fire-cracked rock (FCR) noted by Greenman and inferred based on mapping by Laurentian University field school students.

multiple short occupations, and camp locations were placed in similar locations from year to year, it would be expected that similar patterns to those described above would occur. If camps were in slightly different locations, there should be a lower concentration of artifacts and potentially more spatial segregation of artifact types.

Artifact distributions

Fire-cracked rock

As indicated, students drew square plans at the bottom of each 4-cm arbitrary level. Many, but not all, of these drawings recorded the locations of artifacts, including fire-cracked rock. To determine if clusters of fire-cracked rock existed, we examined all of the level forms on file at Laurentian University and plotted the location of fire-cracked rock on a single map (Figure 8.4).

This clearly shows that some excavators probably hyper-recorded rocks that they identified as fire-cracked rock. For example, unit S1W6 shows a high density of fire-cracked rock and is surrounded by units that are virtually empty. The area around N11/12 and W13/14 also have a high density of these types of artifacts, but in this case the surrounding units are not completely devoid of fire-cracked rock, leading us to suggest that this is more likely to represent the location of a true cluster.

Although initially we attempted to discern clusters using statistical means (Meehan 2008), this effort was abandoned because of inconsistency in student recording. Greenman mapped the general location of rock clusters, and we combined our data with his to show some general areas where fire-cracked rock density appears higher. These areas may represent fire-cracked rock dumps, the remains of hearths or sweat lodges (possibly "baths" in Greenman's terms (Field Notes 1939), or wild rice roasting pits (Vennum

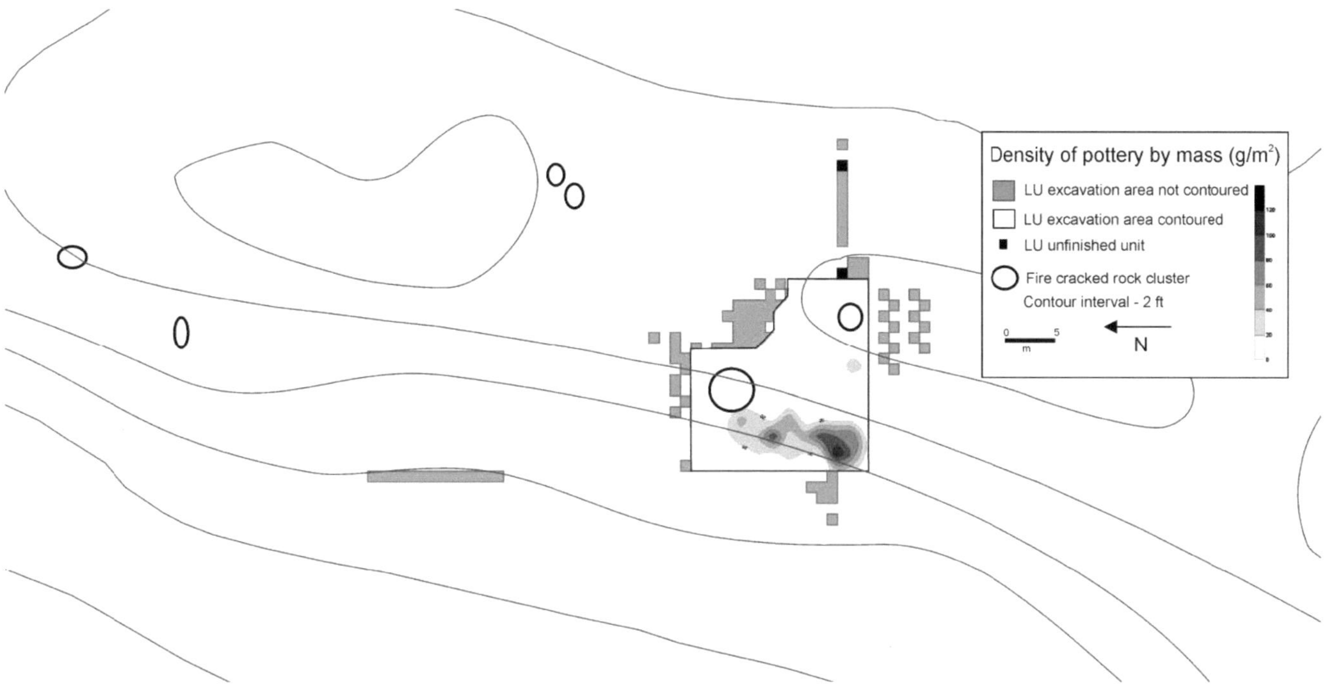

Figure 8.5. Variation in pottery by mass within the Laurentian University excavation area (g/m2).

1988:118). To evaluate this, we examined the distribution of other artifact types.

Pottery

Both Greenman (1966) and Brose (Chapter 11, this volume) indicate that the pottery from Killarney Bay can be attributed to different periods. Brose's generalized classification ascribes pottery that has thick walls, little decoration, and coarse temper to the Early Middle Woodland. Later Middle Woodland pottery has thin walls, fine sand temper, and is variably decorated. Finally, there is a small component of Late Woodland pottery, which has medium-thick walls and is tempered with crushed grit or limestone.

Much of the pottery recovered from the habitation area is extremely fragmentary, possibly due to long-term plowing and cultivation, and cannot for that reason be ascribed to any one of these three groups. Figure 8.5 shows variation in density of pottery recovered by mass. In general, the Laurentian University excavation area shows only a thin spread of pottery. The highest density is found around the W16 location and in a somewhat linear spread northwards. The linear spread corresponds with a slope and is also the location of elevated numbers of other artifact types.

When the pottery that can be typed is mapped according to the typological classification as Early Middle Woodland, Late Middle Woodland (Figure 8.6), and Late Woodland, a slightly different distribution is apparent. The Early Middle Woodland material clusters in the southwest corner, the Late Woodland (not included in figure) is spread very thinly across the entire area, and the Late Middle Woodland follows approximately the same distribution as the original plot. However, as new the ^{14}C dates on the carbonized ceramic residues indicate (see Chapter 4, this volume), the Middle Woodland types all date to about the same time period, and possibly even the same occupations, as would be expected if several bands met for ceremonial feasting or trade.

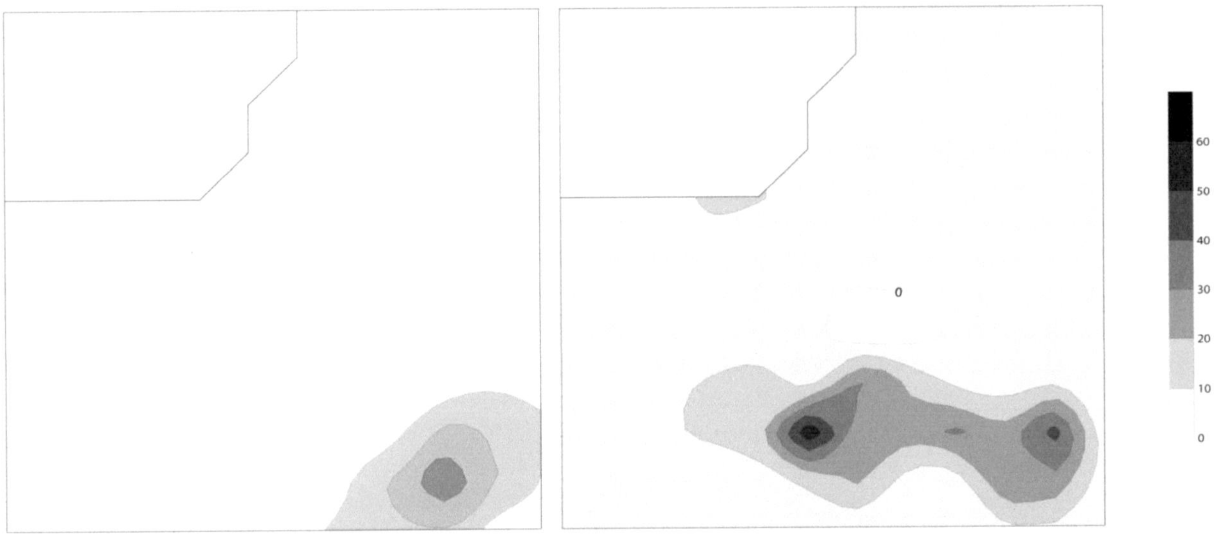

Figure 8.6. Distribution of Early Middle Woodland pottery (l) and Late Middle Woodland pottery (r) by mass per unit (g/m2). See Figure 7.5 for the location of the area contoured.

It is noteworthy that the main concentration of pottery does not fall in the same location as the highest concentration of fire-cracked rock, which occurs in the N10W12 area.

Quartzite and mylonite

Quartzite and mylonite are both coarser-grained and silica rich. Quartzite outcrops in the Bar River Formation near the site. Mylonite occurs in an adjacent formation to the south (see Chapter 2, this volume). They are grouped together for the purposes of this study. They account for the bulk of the material recovered, both by count (n=9894) and by mass (ca. 23 kg). The vast majority of this material is chipping detritus and cores, although it also includes bifaces, biface preforms, scrapers, and utilized pieces.

Figure 8.7 shows that, by count, quartzite occurs in two general areas. One is in approximately the same location as the pottery fragments, although the highest density occurs in the northern part of the grid. The second is in the N8W8 area. The distribution maps by mass show essentially the same pattern.

Chert

Several types of cherts are represented in the habitation area collections. These include Fossil Hill, Hudson Bay Lowland (HBL), Gordon Lake, and distant exotics such as Knife River Flint. The Fossil Hill chert includes the Wiki variant, obtained from Manitoulin Island (Julig et al. 2009). Most of the chert artifacts are Fossil Hill formation (84 percent), which outcrops closer to the site than the other raw materials. HBL also makes up a significant portion of the assemblage (12 percent). Gordon Lake and Knife River are represented by only a few pieces. Again, chert artifacts are mainly flaking debris, but tools and utilized pieces are also represented, including a variety of scraper forms.

Examination of the distribution of all chert artifacts (Figure 8.8) shows that the bulk of material is found in approximately the same linear distribution as the pottery. This is the case if the material is plotted either in terms of count or mass. The distribution of the two main raw materials, Fossil Hill and HBL, shows that there are two concentrations of HBL, while the Fossil Hill chert

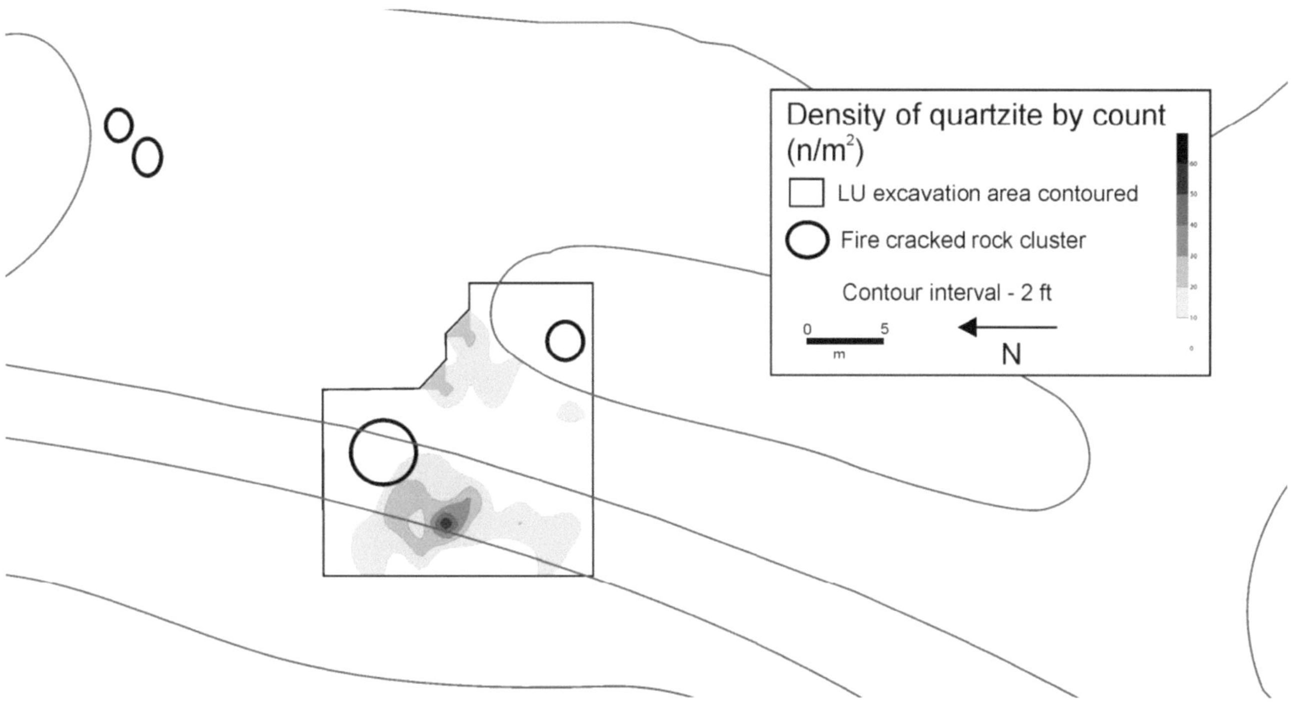

Figure 8.7. Quartzite and mylonite artifacts by count.

distribution is essentially the same as that of the general distribution pattern of chert (Figures 8.9 and 8.10). However, the total number of HBL artifacts is much lower than the total number of Fossil Hill artifacts, which includes much debitage. This is as expected, because the source region for HBL is much more distant, to the north (see Appendix D). However, there are many HBL scrapers, and both the HBL and Fossil Hill chert scrapers are distributed across the overall site (Figures 8.9 and 8.10); many are along the upper beach terrace excavated by Greenman.

The density of debitage on its own is compared with the locations of scrapers made from these two raw materials (Figures 8.9 and 8.10). In both cases, most debitage occurs in concentrations in the west part of the excavation area. Scrapers are found in two locations. A number of them are found in the high concentration area. However, for both HBL and Fossil Hill scrapers, there are a number of examples found in the eastern portion of the grid. It is worth noting that the number of HBL scrapers is higher than that of the Fossil Hill scrapers, despite the fact that Fossil Hill chert artifacts far outnumber those made from HBL, and the HBL is from a much more distant source.

Siltstone and argillite

We combine siltstone and argillite for this analysis—siltstone accounts for the majority of this artifact group. Students recovered slightly more than 2,000 siltstone artifacts. These are mainly flaked items, which we believe to be debris from the early stages of gorget manufacturing (Wright 1999:667). There are relatively few actual gorgets among the materials recovered from the Laurentian excavations: only four gorget preforms and two fragmentary gorget preforms. Greenman's group also recovered gorget preforms, but they are not included in this map. Other tools produced from siltstone and argillite include a projectile point preform, the base of an Adena-like point, scrapers, and a number of utilized pieces.

The distribution of siltstone by count is similar to the distribution of quartzite (Figure 8.11). However, unlike the situation for other stone materials, the distribution by count

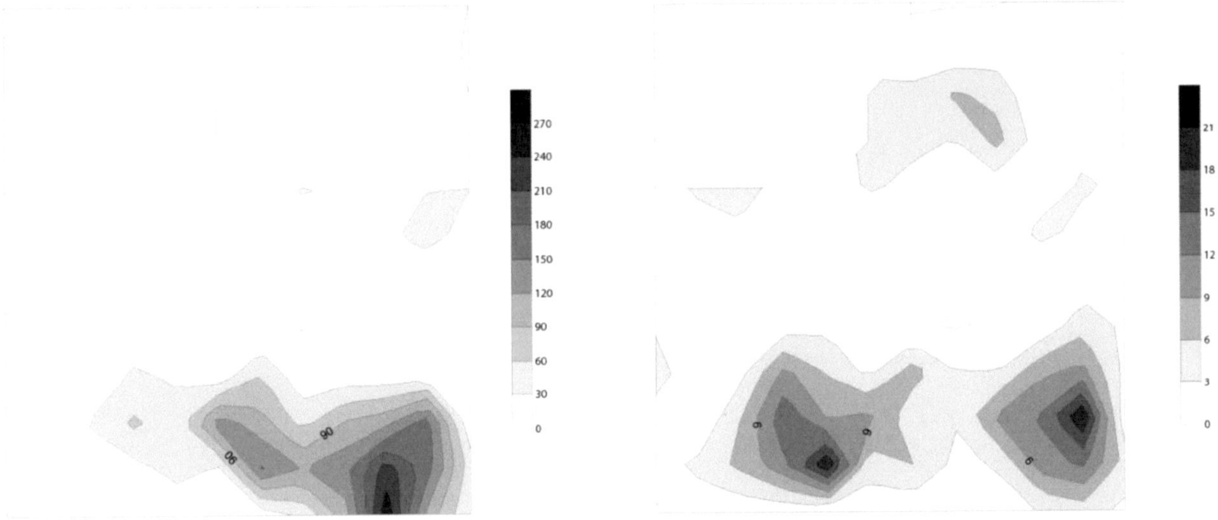

Figure 8.8. Density of Fossil Hill (l) and Hudson Bay Lowland (r) chert by count per meter square, all artifact types included.

and mass are not the same. The highest siltstone/argillite mass is in the W8N6 area, and the linear area of siltstone debitage is not evident in the distribution map for mass, indicating that this area was a location of discard of several large pieces (rough preforms) of siltstone. On other Middle Woodland sites in the region, clusters of flaked siltstone/argillite and failed early stage preforms indicate gorget manufacturing. We suggest that is the case here, particularly as the raw material, Gowganda Formation banded argillite, is located nearby.

Discussion and interpretation

How can we interpret the distribution of materials at the habitation area at Killarney Bay? The following points can be noted:

1. Fire-cracked rock clusters occur in a different location than other debris clusters. The average size of artifacts found in this area is not particularly high.

2. Pottery, chert, siltstone, and quartzite are all found in high concentrations on the west side of the grid. This linear distribution occurs at the bottom of a slight slope, interpreted as the western edge of a beach terrace (Julig et al. 2009). The artifacts are well intermingled, suggesting a long-term disposal area or an area used on many occasions.

3. The small amount of pottery that can be generally assigned to a time period (or presumed cultural group) has slightly different distributions. The Late Middle Woodland pottery that is tool impressed and thin walled is generally concentrated in the area where other artifact types are also concentrated. The Early Middle Woodland pottery is concentrated in one location. This potentially reflects a lesser degree of use of the area during this time. The small amount of Late Woodland pottery occurs in a thin veneer over the entire area, suggesting an ephemeral later occupation. Overall, there is a relatively small amount of pottery recovered on this site, similar to many other Middle Woodland sites in the northeast region. Wright (1999) suggested that pottery is not a very useful indicator of Middle Woodland cultural affinity, as many small Middle Woodland sites have no ceramics.

4. The proportion of scrapers on the eastern part of the grid is relatively high when compared with the amount of debitage in this area. This is particularly true for HBL scrapers. While the scrapers on the west side of the grid are likely to have been disposed of with other debris, those on the east side of the grid may reflect abandonment with the intent to use them again at a later date. This may be considered a type of "provisioning of place" (Kuhn 1992).

An alternative explanation may be suggested by tool (scraper) recoveries across the site. The area excavated by

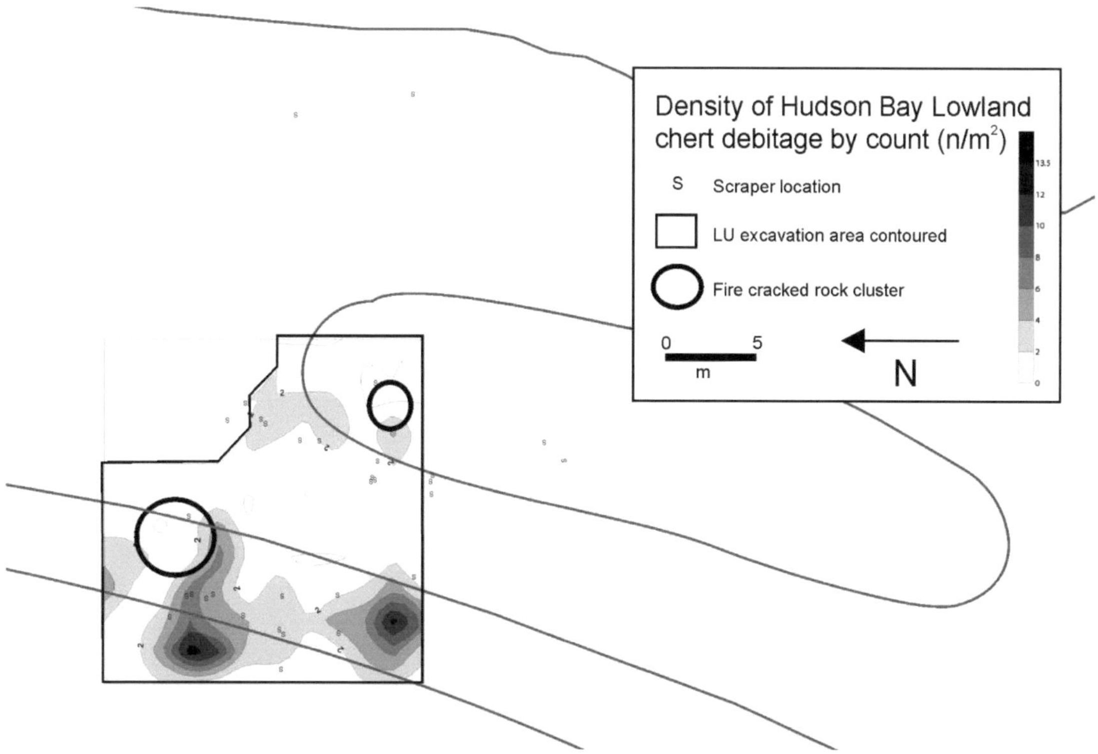

Figure 8.9. Fossil Hill scraper locations compared with the density of Fossil Hill chert debitage in the Laurentian University excavation area.

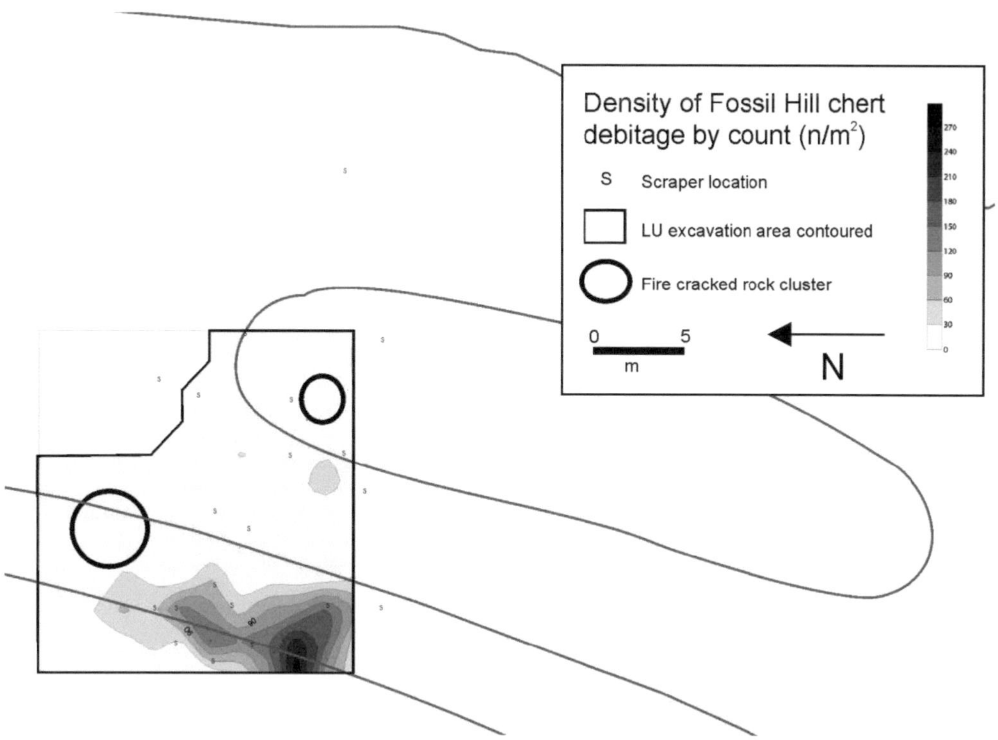

Figure 8.10. Hudson Bay Lowland scraper locations compared with the density of Hudson Bay Lowland chert debitage in the Laurentian University excavation area.

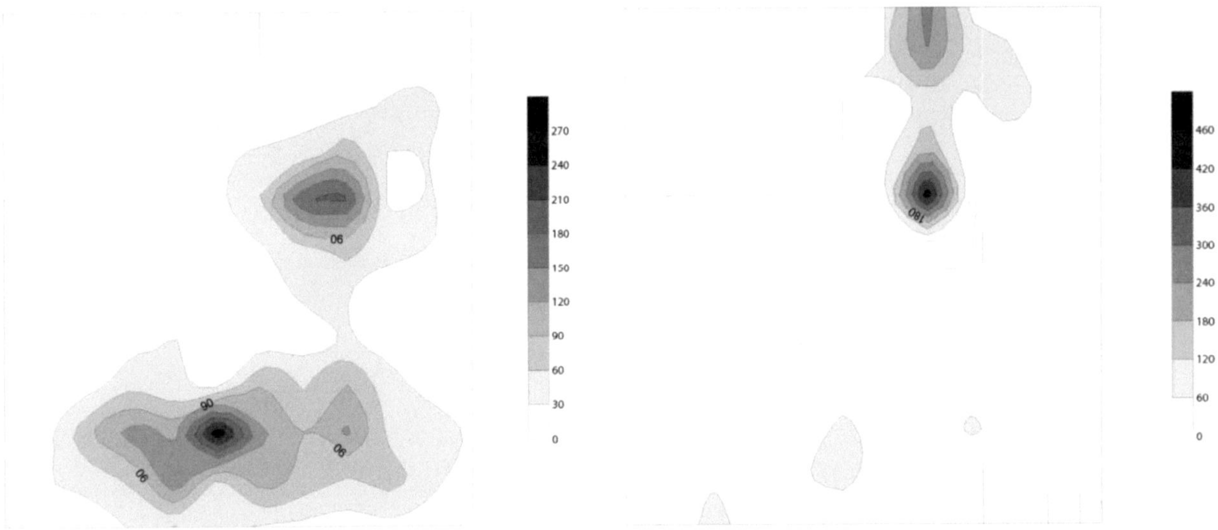

Figure 8.11. Distribution of siltstone and argillite artifacts by count per meter (l) and grams per meter (r).

Greenman, adjacent to the eastern portion of the Laurentian grid, also had numerous HBL scrapers. Many of these scrapers are heavily used, and worn, with steep bit angles, suggesting discard after hide processing (see Chapter 10 on lithic analysis). The relatively large numbers of semi-exotic distant chert (HBL) scrapers may also suggest a special demand for this particular material for specific tool types. Lithic caches of manufactured and unused HBL chert artifacts along northern waterways, as with the Spanish River cache (Julig and Long 2013), suggest specialized procurement and exchange of this lithic material.

5. A possible lithic manufacturing area occurs in the W4N4 to W8N6 area, where siltstone and quartzite are concentrated but chert and pottery are not found in high concentrations. This potentially relates to gorget preform manufacturing. A number of large pieces of siltstone were recovered from this area. Their occurrence together with quartzite hints at the possibility that the latter was used in grinding activities. The gorget preforms are roughed out and then ground smoothly, and the flat joint planes of quartzite blocks are useful for the final stage of processing such siltstone artifacts (gorgets, pins, etc).

Middle Woodland site structure

There are numerous large Ontario Middle Woodland sites that contain both mortuary and habitation components at the same location. The Middlesex complex is the only exception, known almost completely from mortuary contexts (Ferris and Spence 1995; Spence et al. 1990; Wright 1999). Point Peninsula and Laurel sites are better known (Ferris and Spence 1995; Spence et al. 1990), and in both cases mortuary ceremonialism and subsistence activities appear to have been carried out in the same locations. A similar pattern is evident at Saugeen complex Middle Woodland sites such as Donaldson (Finlayson 1977; Spence et al. 1990:150; Wright and Anderson 1963)—further south along the Lake Huron shore—where mortuary and living activities occurred, possibly over several centuries.

The Point Peninsula Rice Lake sites, such as Serpent Mounds and Cameron's Point, have shell midden deposits, indicating some duration of occupation. Spence et al. (1990:164) suggest a macroband-microband pattern, with groups coalescing near lakes to exploit aquatic resources in the warm months. These are also the locations of burial mounds (Spence et al. 1990:158).

In the Rainy River area, there are burial mounds associated with a habitation component (Wright 1999). These include the MacGillivray site, where the habitation component is later than the burial component (Dawson 1980), and the multicomponent Long Sault site (Arthurs 1986; Kenyon 1971), both of which indicate extended periods of occupation and the exploitation of aquatic resources such as wild rice and fish (Wright 1999:762). These sites and other Middle Woodland habitation sites on the Canadian Shield include features such as pits, hearths, and/or post molds, which could be used in the interpretation of settlement patterns (e.g., Reid and Rajnovich 1991). Wright (1999:753) argues for the importance of wild rice harvesting in some Middle Woodland Shield sites, and notes that rice parching pits are filled with fire-cracked rock, such as were found at the Big Rice site in Minnesota.

Conclusions

These conclusions include the Laurentian University excavations and analysis and the ^{14}C chronology of the overall site, including the Greenman excavations and recoveries. The earlier Greenman excavations were along the top of the beach, including the disturbed mound area (considered the mortuary area), and the later Laurentian excavations were field school excavations on a slightly lower Algoma age beach terrace. The Laurentian excavations were outside the mortuary area, in what was considered a habitation area.

Considerable lithic debitage was recovered from the habitation area, including all three of the lithic artifact classes (chert, quartzite, and siltstone/argillite). Most of the material was available locally. Many tools were also recovered, including objects broken in manufacture and pieces that show evidence of use and resharpening, including many end scrapers. The end scrapers include many heavily resharpened Hudson Bay Lowland specimens, a material not available locally. In addition, clusters of fire-cracked rocks were recorded. The intermingling of debris in an area slightly separated from clusters of fire-cracked rock suggests that the site was used as a habitation area either for periods of some duration or in the same way on many sequential visits, probably by people who had memory of how the area was used previously. This is also suggested by the ^{14}C dating. Gorget artifacts and preforms and argillite debitage indicate onsite manufacture of these artifacts in a part of the habitation area. However, Greenman also recovered gorget preforms and manufacturing debris along the top of the beach ridge, so this manufacturing pattern appears to be across the site. Much of the area on the site's lower terraces has not been excavated.

Based on ceramic recoveries and other data, the mound and habitation areas were previously considered to be two separate sites, called the Killarney Bay and Speigel sites. The redating of the site reported here indicates that the two ceramic types and the mortuary area are roughly contemporaneous. It is evident that there is one large site—Killarney Bay—which saw multiple uses (habitation, manufacturing, mortuary) over an extended period.

The locational context of Killarney Bay in the northeast corner of Georgian Bay, Lake Huron, in an ecotonal area with many resources and on a major canoe travel route (Chapters 1 and 2) helps explain this unique site with such high artifact raw material diversity. Initially, researchers interpreted it as one of many similar presumed warm-season Middle Woodland sites with possible local wild rice use. However, the modern wild rice stand nearby was found to be recently planted, and there is no pollen evidence for ancient wild rice presence or use onsite.

Other resources include beaver, other small and larger game, and certainly fish. Being on an island 2,000 years ago, with a narrow passage between it and the mainland, residents may have used a fish weir. The many cache pits reported by Greenman may have been used to dry and/or store smoked fish (possibly fall spawners such as lake trout and whitefish). The large numbers of end scrapers suggest hide processing and possibly a fall occupation. Canoe building and maintenance may also be considered, as birch are large and plentiful on such sandy beach ridge areas.

Killarney Bay was ideally situated to participate in and control trade, being situated at the entrance to a sheltered inside canoe route passage (currently Collins Inlet to the south and east leading to the French and Ottawa rivers, and the North Channel to the west between the North Shore and Manitoulin Island). Goods such as copper and Hudson Bay Lowland chert would have come from the northwest, and beaver furs, hides, gorgets, and red ochre from the west and east. Other valuable trade goods from southern Middle Woodland groups moving north would have passed through this travel route, including shell, tobacco, clay pipes, and southern flints. This strategic location is evident in the exotic cherts with mortuary contexts discussed in other chapters. This location is similar to that of the island sites on the Ottawa River—Morrison and Allumette islands—where many similar patterns of trade and site use are evident. At Killarney Bay, the mound construction suggests a concept of ownership and long-term use and investment. It is possible that a complex hunter-gatherer pattern was emerging, as suggested in the mortuary pattern.

Part III

Materials Recovered during Excavations at Killarney Bay

Chapter 9

Osteology and Burial Practices at Killarney Bay

Amy Nicodemus

The Killarney Bay site includes a series of burials dating to the early Middle Woodland. During his 1876 excavation, Robert Bell unearthed at least four individuals from the main mound, as well as single burials from two smaller mounds to the east. Emerson Greenman continued excavations at the site from 1939 through 1953, recovering an additional 11 individuals from the principal mound. These burials were provided with a diversity of grave goods. Among these were numerous copper artifacts, which preserved portions of the human remains that otherwise would not have withstood the degrading effects of the region's acidic soils. While the population is relatively small and incompletely preserved, the available osteological data provide a preliminary look into the general health and demography of the Killarney Bay people. This information, combined with burial treatment data, allows an initial assessment of their mortuary program and general comparison with other regional traditions. The analysis of the human remains was undertaken as part of the broader Killarney Bay research collaboration (see collaboration statement, page xii, this volume). Basic nondestructive documentation was conducted in accordance with U.S. NAGPRA guidelines for culturally unidentified collections.

Methodology

There is a scarcity of preserved (and published) osteological material from the early Middle Woodland period in the Upper Great Lakes region. Consequently, thorough data collection and presentation is a primary goal of this chapter. The Killarney Bay assemblage was documented following Buikstra and Ubelaker's (1994) standards, including collection of age, sex, metric, nonmetric, and pathology information. Additional references for supplemental data collection and analyses are provided within their respective appendices. The complete skeletal inventory is listed in Appendix 9.1, and demographic, morphologic, and health data are presented in appendices 9.2 through 9.11 (included at the end of this chapter). Individual burials are described below and summarized in Table 9.1.

Table 9.1. Killarney Bay burial summary.

Collection	Burial	Individual	Sex	Age in Years: Infant	Child	Adolescent	Adult	Burial Type: Extended	Flexed	Secondary	Indet. Inhumation	Cremation	Position: Supine	Left Side	Orientation: N-S	E-W	W-E	SW-NE
Greenman	1			?	?						X							
Greenman	2		F				16-22	X					X		X			
Greenman	3				5-6						X							
Greenman	4				~6						X			?		?		
Greenman	5				X					?								
Greenman	6		M				20-30			X								
Greenman	7			2-3							X						?	
Greenman	8		M				X		X				X					X
Greenman	9	1				14-18						X						
Greenman	9	2	M?				X					X						
Greenman	10		F				16-22		X				X					X
Bell		A	?				35-40				X							
Bell		B	M?				20-24?				X							
Bell		C			6-7						X							
Bell		D	F				24-35				X							
Bell		E	M?				X				X							
Bell		F	?				>35					X						

X = present
? = uncertain attribution

Burial descriptions

Greenman Collection

Materials from Emerson Greenman's expedition, including Burials 2 through 10, are housed at the University of Michigan Museum of Anthropological Archaeology (UMMAA). Greenman's excavation notes, drawings, and photographs (1949–1953) provide general information about the burials and associated artifacts that he recovered from the principal mound. Burial practices are described below to the most thorough degree possible, given the level of detail in field documentation and the preservation of human remains. Maps of burial locations as well as additional information on excavation history, stratigraphy, grave goods, and the mortuary program can be found in other chapters in this volume.

Burial 1

Burial 1, excavated in 1949, was found in a disturbed pit in Trench 3A, Section 6E. The remains are not in UMMAA collections, but basic information can be derived from Greenman's field notes. According to Greenman, this burial is an inhumation of a juvenile of undetermined age (infant or child). Minimally, a maxilla with deciduous dentition was preserved. There was a bark sheet placed over the body and a spear point to the southwest, as well as copper beads and a celt or spindle.

Burial 2

Burial 2, also recovered in 1949, lay in a pit located in the northeast portion of a previously excavated section of the central mound (Trench 3E, Sections 2D/2E). It contained a young adult female in an extended supine position, with the skull to the north and body to the south. Judging from the position of the hand, at least one arm was outstretched along the body. It is the only extended inhumation currently known in the Killarney assemblage.

The skeleton is in relatively good condition where mineral salts from copper beads (around the neck and left hand) and a copper spindle (on the chest) preserved both tissue and bone. This includes the base of the skull, several teeth from the upper and lower dentition, cervical and thoracic vertebrae (some still articulated), ribs, right clavicle, both scapulae, left radius, and a left metacarpal. The remainder of the body is not preserved. The adult dentition is fully erupted, and the composite wear stage of the preserved teeth suggests an age of 16–22 years. The postcranial skeleton agrees with this estimate. All of the present epiphyses are fused except for the ribs, vertebral pads, and acromion processes (scapula), which are partially fused. Sexually dimorphic cranial features score within the female range (1–2) and the general build is very gracile. The molars have light to moderate calculus formation and the lower left first molar has two small occlusal caries. The upper third molars are asymmetric. There is no evidence of postcranial pathology.

This individual appears to have been clothed in a hide garment with beaver fur and cordage around the collar, portions of which are preserved. Field notes suggest that it was cape-like and tied around the neck. In addition to the aforementioned copper artifacts, the burial also included shell bead strands, two large chipped stone spear points, fragments of a tubular pipe, cedar bark, and red ochre. The upper levels of the pit contained calcined animal bone.

Burial 3

Burial 3 was found disturbed in the central mound area (Trench 3E, Sections H2–H3) in 1950, associated with modern refuse. This may represent remnants from Bell's excavations in 1876. The child's skeleton was partially scattered, displaying varying degrees of weathering from exposure. Because of this disturbance, it is not possible to specify burial treatment beyond some form of inhumation (as opposed to cremation), although the presence of several articulated ribs suggests that the individual was not entirely disarticulated when interred.

Despite being disturbed, much of the axial skeleton is well preserved, being among the most intensely copper-stained remains in the assemblage. The basal cranium, vertebral column (through the first lumbar vertebra), associated ribs, scapula, and indeterminate long bone fragments are present. The deciduous dentition is fully erupted and in wear, the adult first molars are erupted, and the second molars are in their crypts. The lateral/basilar-occipital and all of the postcrania elements are unfused, except for the neural arches of the thoracic vertebrae. This places the age between five and six years. There are no indications of pathology other than light calculus deposits on the right deciduous second molar and first adult molar.

The strong copper staining of the skeleton indicates that this burial was initially interred with more copper artifacts than the three beads and small sheet copper fragment that Greenman recovered. Other items found in the vicinity include a finished scraper, two rough scrapers, birch bark, red ochre, and an ochre-stained ground slate pendant, though their exact association cannot be confirmed. Calcined turtle bone was also collected around the burial. Greenman notes that several of the human bones appeared to be wrapped in leather, although this is not visible in the current collection. While it is possible that individual bones were wrapped, the partial articulation of the body and the presence of preserved tissue suggest that this leather may have been part of the body tissue, clothing, or larger hide encasing the body. Several possible sheet leather fragments were recovered from the neck and chest areas.

Burial 4

Burial 4 was found in a pit lined with and capped by red ochre in Trench 3E, Sections F3–F4. Poor preservation of the body obscured its exact orientation and placement. However, from field drawings it is apparent that at least the skull (with articulated cranium and mandible) was laid on its left side facing southwest (field notes describe the skull as facing to the northeast, but the north arrow on the plan map indicates that it was drawn "upside down," making the orientation to the southwest). Postcranial elements, including thoracic vertebrae, ribs, a humerus, a femur, and indeterminate long bone fragments, were to the west of the skull in unknown positions. While some tissue is preserved, particularly around the ribs, no bones are currently articulated. Excavation notes suggest that this may have been a bundle burial wrapped in leather, but this cannot be confirmed with available data.

Only a small portion of the body is present, and it is highly friable, with little to no copper staining. The most complete elements are the mandible and maxilla—preserved by copper bead strands near or around the neck—containing the full deciduous and adult dentition except for one upper premolar. The permanent first molars are in wear and the other adult teeth are in their crypts (the third molar is not yet formed). The adult teeth are slightly more developed and/or worn than in Burial 3, suggesting that this child is closer to six years of age. There is light calculus formation on the right deciduous molars and a small occlusal carie on the lower left deciduous second molar. Postcranial pathologies are not evident.

This child burial was provided with two caches of blades, placed above and below the body. Ground slate and a scraper are also present. The copper bead necklace preserved beaver fur and sheet leather fragments, which may have been part of a garment or burial wrapping/bag.

Burial 5

Burial 5 was recovered in 1950 from a dark "pit-like area" in Trench 3E, Section F2. The body is in very poor condition, with only the dentition preserved. Field drawings indicate that the mandible and maxilla were separated from one another and not in anatomical position, suggesting that this was not a primary inhumation. It appears that the teeth were in situ within the upper and lower jaws respectively when buried. The teeth show no copper staining and are extremely fragile. They are now fragmented into more than 150 enamel pieces, few of which are identifiable. There are portions of unworn adult premolars and an upper molar, both of uncertain position within the arcade. Given the lack of wear on these teeth, this individual is a child of indeterminate age. No additional data could be collected.

Most of the probable grave goods were found above or nearby the burial itself. These include three copper beads, a ground stone pendant, and a slate fragment. Red ochre, birch bark, and copper-stained leather and beaver fur were in the burial pit.

Burial 6

Burial 6 was placed within a small burial pit, just over 1 foot in diameter, which cuts into the gravels underlying the mound. It is situated in Trench 3E, Sections G1 and 2, and was recovered during the 1950 campaign. This is the best-preserved secondary burial, with the body placed inside a cedar bark basket, covered by layers of birch bark, hide, and hemlock bark. Copper beads sewn around the basket preserved skeletal elements near its rim, including portions of the skull, vertebrae, ribs, right scapula, left radius, pelvis, and either femur or tibia fragments. The bones appear to be mixed, highly fragmented, and only lightly stained with copper. The mandible may have been articulated with the cranium, which is crushed. The top of the cranium is to the south and the mandible to the north, both along the west edge of the bundle. The pelvis is at the east edge of the basket with various long bones and axial elements in between. There is tissue preserved, indicating that the individual was not completely disarticulated when placed within the basket. Given the ambiguity in the field drawing and notes, it is possible that the individual could be tightly flexed on his left side within a basket. However, it is unlikely that a fully articulated adult male would fit into a basket with an approximate diameter of 1 foot, 4 inches.

Few of the teeth are preserved, but the alveoli show that all of the adult dentition was erupted. Wear on a lower canine and premolar corresponds to a rough age estimate of between 20 and 30 years. All of the postcranial epiphyses are fused and there is no evidence of degenerative arthritis, also suggesting that this individual is a younger adult. While the pelvis is too fragmented for sexing, the mandible is very robust, consistent with male morphology. The only observable pathology is a broken crown with abnormal wear on the lower left fourth premolar.

In addition to the materials associated with the beaded basket and its leather/bark coverings, Burial 6 included a cache of 38 flint blades, which was placed under the body.

Burial 7

Burial 7 was placed in a deep pit that cut through a larger, shallow pit originating immediately below the topsoil in Trench 3E, Section H1. The northeastern portion of this feature was removed with the Burial 6 excavations earlier in the 1950 season. Much of the burial was a dense mass of bone, tissue, leather, fur, and other copper-stained organics, part of which was removed in bulk and further excavated in the UMMAA lab. It is not possible to discern details of burial position from available field maps and notes, except that the cranium appears to be to the west with copper artifacts and the arm/hand to the east. The bones display strong copper staining and there is a large amount of tissue preserved. Portions of the neck vertebrae are articulated. Given the large amount of tissue, semi-articulation, and presence of small/fragile elements, this is more likely to be a primary rather than secondary burial, although it is possible that the individual could have been bundled while substantially intact.

Skeletal material includes the basal cranium, mandible, hyoid, cervical and thoracic vertebrae, ribs, the right shoulder girdle (including clavicle, scapula, and proximal humerus), and an indeterminate carpal. The deciduous teeth are fully erupted, the permanent incisors and first molars are visible in their crypts, and the second molars are only small buds. This development stage indicates a child two to three years old. The two neural arch halves are unfused in the atlas and axis but fused in the remaining cervical vertebrae, indicative of an individual two to four years old. The size of the basilar occipital corresponds to three years of age. There is no evidence of pathology.

As mentioned above, there was a great deal of beaver fur associated with the burial. Greenman notes that the grave goods (flint blade, copper chisel and celt) appear to have been placed within a "leather bag" under the body, near the neck and right shoulder area. This is consistent with the celt impressions left on the interior surfaces of the beaver pelts. A number of shell beads were also found within the organic mass, at least some of which were around the neck.

Burial 8

Burial 8 was removed in 1952 from a pit near the original mound center and was partially disturbed by a root cellar and perhaps also by Bell's nineteenth-century mound excavations. There is some discrepancy between the notes and the labeled field drawings of the burial as to its orientation. Given the position of the copper artifacts, the specific elements present in the osteological collection, and direct identification of bones numbered on the plan map, it appears that the individual was laid with the head to the southwest and body towards the northeast, which is consistent with Greenman's notes. The skull and cervical vertebrae are not present, but a single tooth was recovered in the area where the head would have been situated, suggesting that it was likely removed during prior excavations.

Among the numerous grave goods were two copper celts placed on the right shoulder and chest, which preserved the vertebrae, ribs, the right scapula, clavicle, and humerus. The right hand, including several still-articulated elements, was laid over the celts. The right lower arm, also articulated, was wrapped in copper bead strands. Several left-shoulder elements are present, overlying a copper spindle, but are not as well preserved as the right side of the body. Fragments of the left lower arm appear to have been outstretched along the torso. From the orientation of the upper body, it appears that the individual was laid on his back. The only portion of the lower body present is a left femur shaft, which appears to have been folded on top of the body, indicating a flexed supine burial. There is a large amount of leather and beaver fur in the burial, some of which may be artifact bags and others of which may have been wrappings around or underneath the body, or even a single large hide bag in which the body was placed, as suggested by Greenman. Given the clear anatomical position, number of articulated elements, and high degree of tissue preservation, this is a primary burial.

While much of the torso is well preserved, the lack of the skull prevents more precise aging. However, all of the postcranial elements are fully fused, indicating adult age. The skeleton is extremely robust, with long bones nearly 50 percent thicker than the Burial 10 individual. This is consistent with male morphology. There is degenerative arthritis present in three of the four vertebrae (both body and articular facets), the right scapula (glenoid), and the right hand (intermediate and distal phalanx joints), suggesting an older adult.

This older male was placed with many and diverse grave goods, including the copper and fur items discussed above, shell beads, and a number of large flint bifaces, three of which were hafted. A layer of fire-cracked rock overlaid the pit, which was then covered with basket loads of soil.

Burial 9

Burial 9, which was excavated in 1953, is unique because it is the only cremation and the only multiple burial in the UMMAA collection. The remains were placed in a pit in Trench 3F near the mound center. Since the pit originated in the sands underlying the mound and cut into the deeper gravels, it is possible that Burial 9 represents the earliest interment in the mound and may have served as a founding burial.

The cremated bone is highly fragmented and distorted. Relatively few pieces could be confidently identified to element or individual. However, it is clear that there are at least two people present: one adolescent and one older adult. The adolescent bones tend to be burned to a greater degree than the older adult, being highly cracked, deformed, and uniformly white in color. The vertebral pads and at least two indeterminate long bone shafts are unfused, but near adult size, placing this individual between 14 and 18 years old. Elements likely belonging to the adolescent include lumbar and other indeterminate vertebrae, the right humerus, radius, femur, tibia, and calcaneus, the left talus, and the unsided fibula and metapodial shaft fragments. Both left and right elements are probably represented for most long bones, given variability in surface color and texture and the quantity of shaft fragments. No sexable elements are present and there is no evidence of pathology.

The adult bones are large and robust, more complete, and generally gray-black in color, indicating burning at a lower temperature. These represent the bones to the southeast noted in the field as being "larger and less completely calcined than the others" (Greenman 1949–1953:6). Identifiable elements are similar to those of the adolescent and include thoracic, lumbar, sacral, and indeterminate vertebrae, a humerus, left radius and ulna, a femur and tibia, the right fibula and calcaneus, left and right tali, and metapodials. Again, both left and right long bone elements are likely present. All of the epiphyses are fused, indicative of an adult, and the vertebrae show light to moderate arthritic growths on the centra and articular facets, suggesting an age greater than 30 years. Although no sexable elements are present, the size and robusticity of this skeleton are consistent with other males in this collection.

A large number of small bone fragments were not attributable to either individual, including more than 1,300 vertebral, rib, pelvic, long bone shaft, and cancellous bone fragments. Conspicuously absent are any cranial elements or dentition. Given that teeth are usually the best-preserved elements because of enamel's high density, and that even very small cranial fragments are readily identifiable in other contexts, it appears that the heads are not present in the burial. Additionally, there are no cervical vertebrae apparent. These individuals may have had their heads removed prior to cremation and/or they were simply not interred with the rest of the cremated body. Ribs are also underrepresented, and no hand elements were identified. The unspecified metapodials are likely metatarsals, given the presence of tarsals from both individuals. Overall, it appears that only selected skeletal elements were included in these burials. It seems that the bodies were partially disarticulated but not completely dry prior to cremation, since the burning pattern is consistent with wet bone. The cremations were not performed in situ, as there is no evidence of extreme burning within the pit itself.

The only possible grave goods in Burial 9 are a quartzite blade fragment, a grooved ground stone, and a point tip found in the surface of and adjacent to the burial pit. The pit itself was covered with a thick layer of red ochre. Fire-cracked rocks and charcoal overlay the burial as well and are cut by the Burial 10 pit. The intrusive burned bone from Burial 10 was refitted with the Burial 9 material.

Burial 10

Burial 10 is the most complete skeleton in the Killarney Bay assemblage. The burial pit, excavated in 1953, cut though part of the Burial 9 cremations and the associated fire-cracked rock feature. The body was lying on its back with legs folded over the chest. The poorly preserved head lay at the southwest side of the pit, and although the direction it was facing was indeterminate, the body was oriented to the northeast. Both arms were bent across the abdomen and the right hand rested on the left hip. Two copper spindles and a copper celt on the abdomen preserved most of the thoracic and lumbar vertebrae, ribs (partially articulated), and left arm. Field notes state that part of the pelvis was present during excavations, though it is not in the current UMMAA collection. Portions of the legs, which were folded over this cache, were also preserved, including both femurs and possibly a fibula, as described in the field. The right wrist was wrapped in copper beads, preserving much of the lower arm and hand, including several still-articulated digits. There is also an imprint from the femur on which the hand rested. As there were no copper beads around the neck, the head is not preserved except for a few loose teeth. This is a primary burial since the elements are in anatomical position, often still articulated, and much tissue is present.

This individual appears to be close in biological age to Burial 2. The ribs and vertebral pads are in the processes of fusing, which is associated with an age of 17–23. However, the few teeth present show slightly more attrition, likely falling into the latter portion of the age estimate. The body is quite gracile, also similar to the Burial 2 female. The small estimated humerus length also points to female sex. The relative completeness of the long bones allows a rough stature estimate of between 5 feet and 5 feet 4 inches tall (156–159 ±4.5 cm).

A lower left canine and lower right first molar both have small calculus deposits. The mid-thoracic vertebrae show interesting pathology and provide the only clear evidence of postcranial trauma in either the Greenman or Bell collections. The anterior centrum of the seventh thoracic vertebra displays a compression fracture. A portion of the vertebral body is displaced and healed asymmetrically. There are extensive reactive osteophytic growths on the central and especially articular facets. The adjacent vertebrae (T5–8) have moderate lipping and spicules on their facets and the fifth and sixth thoracic vertebrae also have medio-laterally compressed bodies that mirror the morphology of the damaged seventh thoracic vertebra. The remaining vertebrae are not affected. Given the young age of this individual and the localized nature of the pathology, the fracture and resulting growths are likely the result of trauma rather than age-related degeneration. This type of fracture is commonly associated with falls (Aufderheide and Rodriguez-Martin 1998).

Like Burial 8, this young woman was richly endowed with grave goods. There are two caches: one contains the copper artifacts and blades (one hafted) on the abdomen and the other two tubular pipes and additional blades on the right shoulder. There were numerous organic artifacts preserved as well, including bags that appear to have contained the caches. Cedar bark basketry and fur is associated with the copper items, and the celt was found with remnants of pointelle-decorated leather. Other leather pieces, including some with cordage, may be garment or lined bag fragments, while a coarse winter deer hide, preserved with the copper beads, may underlie the body. The burial was topped with ochre.

Bell Collection

A portion of Robert Bell's collection from Killarney Bay is curated at the Canadian Museum of History. Unfortunately, there is only limited contextual information for this assemblage. The remains were co-mingled after excavation and stored by element rather than discrete individuals. Jillian Fraser (2005), an Algonquin College museum studies undergraduate, researched the collection history as part of a student project and conducted a preliminary sort and identification of the skeletal remains. She separated the elements into four individuals: three adults and one child.

For this publication, the assemblages produced by Fraser's work were arbitrarily labeled A through D. At the time of the data collection, the material was cataloged as if these four groups represented the original, discrete burials from the site; the authors only learned of the 2005 sorting afterwards. With this in mind, it is likely that not all of the bones within Groups A through D necessarily belong to the same individuals, thus complicating age and sex attribution, which often produced contradictory results. Moreover, during this current study, an extra mastoid was found, representing a fourth adult inhumation (E). The cremated remains of a fifth adult (F) were located within a collection of burned animal bone. There was also an unburned sacrum fragment with this cremation, which may or may not belong with the other inhumations.

The data are presented in this chapter's appendices according to Fraser's initial groupings. They appear to be largely correct for the axial portions, which are often articulated or able to be reconstructed. However, other portions must be discussed by individual element without making assumptions as to origin. In this review, only the crania and axial elements directly associated through refitting and taphonomic criteria are considered discrete individuals according to the original bone group designations, A through F. The other postcranial material will be described by element.

At present, there is a minimum of six individuals in the Bell collection. Importantly, descriptions of the burials from a newspaper publication on Bell's excavations suggest the presence of six noncremated adults (de Lamorandière 1922). This does not correspond to the museum's assemblage, which includes a child and a cremation, in addition to at least four adult inhumations. Further, it is unclear whether the current collection derives from only the main Killarney Bay mound or from the smaller two mounds as well. Due to the uncertain number and origin of these individuals, and the minimal details on burial orientation and contents from field notes, the Bell assemblage cannot be assessed in the same manner or level of detail as the Greenman collection.

Burial A

Burial A includes the well-known "Greenman" cranium and mandible. The cranium was labeled "Killarney Ont Greenman 200 B.C." in marker on the right parietal/frontal. This is thought to refer to Dr. Emerson Greenman, who may have examined or borrowed it. A hyoid and partially ossified laryngeal and cricoid cartilages from the throat are likely associated with this burial, given the similarly high level of preservation and age. Fraser (2005) appears to have refit a complete cervical series with the cranium as well. It is not possible to ascertain the burial type other than inhumation, but the pattern of preserved elements and the presence of tissue suggest a primary, or at least partially articulated, burial. In addition, this individual probably had significant copper bead necklaces and/or other large copper item(s) near the head and neck, based on their exceptional condition.

The skull is nearly complete, allowing detailed data collection. Cranial and palatine suture fusion indicates that this individual is a middle adult, probably around 35–40 years old. The wear stage of the fully erupted adult dentition supports this age estimate. Epiphyseal fusion of the postcrania and ossification of the laryngeal and cricoid cartilages also demonstrate adult status. Many researchers have assumed the skull to be male (e.g., the "green man"), but its sexually dimorphic attributes are ambiguous. The important glabella area (supra-orbital ridge) is damaged, and other traits show a mixture of relatively gracile (mandible, occipital) to more robust aspects (mastoid, supra-orbital margin) (Appendix 9.3). While clearly not displaying the great robusticity of many males at contemporary Great Lakes sites (Anderson 1968; Ritchie and Dragoo 1960; Spence and Harper 1968; Wright and Anderson 1963), the Burial A skull does fall within the range of variation of gracile males. However, female cranial morphology can become increasingly robust with age (Buikstra and Ubelaker 1994), so it is possible that this cranium may be from a female who was older and more robust than the younger, gracile females in Burials 2 and 10. Without additional sexable elements, a conservative attribution of ambiguous sex is preferred.

This individual suffered from a number of age-related pathologies, nutritional stress, and possibly trauma. Most of the well-worn teeth have calculus deposits, with the third molar severely affected. Four teeth show hypoplasia, corresponding to dietary stress at 2–2.5 and 4–4.5 years of age. There are no caries or abscesses visible. All of the present vertebrae have slight osteophytic growths, representing early stages of degenerative arthritis, again consistent with the cranial/dental age estimate. There is also a depression on the top of the skull (left superior parietal), which may be a fracture associated with blunt force trauma. However, portions of the cranium are eroded and display postmortem damage, some of which has been reconstructed or covered with a preservative, making more precise identification impossible.

Burial B

Burial B contains a basal cranium with portions of the temporals (including mastoids), occiput, and sphenoid preserved. The mastoids are large, falling within the male size range.

Burial C

Burial C is the least ambiguous assemblage. The preserved elements include portions of the basal cranium, mandible, first through sixth cervical vertebrae, a first rib, and the left clavicle and humerus. The heaviest copper staining and tissue are found on the mandible and cervical vertebrae, suggesting the presence of a copper bead necklace. This was an inhumation of uncertain type, but the individual was at least partially articulated.

It is a child burial, similar in age to the individuals in Burials 3 and 4 in the Greenman collection. The deciduous teeth and first permanent molars are fully erupted and in wear, the second permanent molar crowns are fully formed in their crypts, and the permanent second incisors are beginning to erupt through the jaw, corresponding to a developmental stage of 6–7 years. Unlike in Burials 3 and 4, the neural arches are fused to the bodies in the third through sixth vertebrae. However, the atlas and axis are incompletely fused. The postcranial skeleton suggests a slightly younger age than the teeth, between approximately 5 and 6 years. There is no evidence of dental or skeletal pathology.

Burial D

Burial D is the most complete skeleton in the Bell collection. The basal cranium is still articulated with the first three cervical vertebrae. The rest of the vertebral column, with the exclusion of several lumbars, is also present. The pelvis and sacrum cannot be directly refit with the spinal column, given the missing lumbar vertebrae. However, only this individual has portions of the lower axial skeleton preserved, so they are likely from the same individual. The mandible fragments display the same high degree of copper staining and extensive tissue preservation. This individual was likely endowed with many copper grave goods that were placed near the neck and abdomen, as in Burial 8. This is a probable primary burial, given its completeness and partial articulation.

Dentition and skeletal traits indicate a young to middle aged adult. Of the teeth, only the upper left third molar is well preserved, showing a wear stage of 24–30 years. Palate suture fusion points to a slightly older age of 30–35 years. All of the spinal elements are fused, including the sacral vertebra, supporting the palate age estimation. Portions of the pelvis have two sexable features preserved, both consistent with female morphology. The mastoids are the most gracile in the burial assemblage, scoring as probable female.

The vertebral column shows extensive osteophytic growths. All of the vertebrae from the fifth cervical to the twelfth thoracic have spicule development on the articular facets and/or elevated rings on the centra. This is most severe on seventh and eighth thoracic vertebrae, combined with deformation of the vertebral bodies. The fifth through tenth thoracic vertebrae also exhibit arthritic growths on the rib articular facets and their associated rib heads. This degree of vertebral pathology is unexpected for an individual this age (around 30) and may be in part trauma related. There is no indication of dental problems, although little is preserved for evaluation.

Burial E

Burial E is represented by a single left mastoid from a fourth adult inhumation. It is robust, falling in the male range, and is similar in morphology to those on the Group B cranium.

Burial F

Burial F contains cremated human remains that were found co-mingled in a box of burned animal bone. It is not known whether these derive from the same archaeological deposit or if they were stored together as a general collection of calcined material. These 155 small bone fragments represent the cranium (unlike Burial 9) and most of the long bones, including metapodials and/or phalanges. There is no indication of rib or vertebral fragments, also in contrast to Burial 9. It is possible that only select elements were chosen for cremation or deposition in this burial as well. There is at least one individual represented. Only a few ageable or sexable elements are present, all of which are adult sized. There is a fused proximal radius, and the suture closure stage of the occipital fragment indicates a middle-aged to older adult. A right orbit fragment scores ambiguously for sex. There is no pathology evident.

Other remains

Other postcranial remains cannot be conclusively attributed to the above individuals. They all derive from adult inhumations. A complete list of these elements is presented in Appendix 9.1, marked with asterisks. Several of the elements warrant further discussion.

A left half of a mandible may belong with either Burial B or E (it was originally grouped with B, but there is no reason to assume association). The M3 is only lightly worn, consistent with an age of 20–24 years. The mental eminence is damaged and scores ambiguously for sex, but appears to be slightly more robust than the mandible associated with Burial A.

Cervical vertebrae, also originally grouped with Burial B, are very gracile, more so than the vertebrae associated with Burials A or D, the latter of which is a probable female. If the male sex attributions of Burial B and E mastoids are correct, they are unlikely to belong with these individuals either. This raises the possibility that there is an additional burial represented—a gracile adult female. Alternatively, mastoid size may be a poor indicator of sex within the Killarney population. Note that Rogers (2005) found that mastoids are less reliable sex indicators than cranial traits like the supraorbital ridge and nuchal crest.

Two sets of shoulder elements, including the scapulae, clavicles, and humeri, are present. One right set, originally sorted with the gracile vertebrae in Burial B and later boxed with Burial A, is smaller. The clavicle falls intermediate in size range to the Burial 2 female and Burial 8 large male, while the humerus is similar to the Burial 10 gracile female. The other set, originally sorted with Burial D, includes both left and right elements. These are more robust qualitatively, but no measurements could be taken for comparison. However, they are not as large as Burial 8. Portions of a right radius and ulna, also initially grouped with Burial D, are gracile, being the same size as Burial 10, and more likely belong with the smaller right shoulder elements. If cranial completeness is an indicator of postcranial preservation, then the gracile right arm may be associated with the Burial D probable female and the more robust shoulders with Burial A. Preservation of these elements is consistent with the placement of copper grave goods in the neck and shoulder regions, as seen in the Greenman collection.

In summary, the number of individuals and age/sex attribution for the Bell collection should be treated with caution, given the questionable association of some of the cranial, axial, and appendicular elements. This assemblage contains minimally six individuals. There is a child 6–7 years old (Burial C), a cremated middle-age to older adult of uncertain sex (Burial F), and at least four adult inhumations, based on the left mastoid counts. There appears to be one young adult female (Burial D), two adult males (Burials B and D), one of which is 20–24 years old, and a middle-aged adult of ambiguous sex (Burial A). There is the possibility of an additional female, given an unattributed gracile vertebral column. Additional analysis of the Bell collection could better assign elements to individuals and refine age and sex attribution.

It should also be noted that nothing in the Bell collection definitively matches the missing skull and neck from Burial 8, which was disturbed by a historic root cellar. It had been suggested that the most likely candidate for such a match would be the "Greenman" cranium (and spinal column) from Group A, if the limbs in that assemblage are not actually associated with it. While the Group A vertebrae do not duplicate the Burial 8 series, and both have arthritis, the "Greenman" skull does not display the high level of robusticity expected, given the great size and strongly developed muscle attachments in the Burial 8 postcrania, which clearly represent a large male. Nonetheless, it cannot be excluded that this or one of the other probable male crania originated with Burial 8.

Discussion

The Killarney Bay site existed in a dynamic Great Lakes region where early Middle Woodland groups interacted regularly with each other, predominately along an east-west axis, and to varying degrees with Adena and later Hopewellian societies to the south. Shared aspects of material culture and social organization have often blurred the geographic and temporal boundaries between Great Lakes archaeological cultures, since at least the Late Archaic (Brose 1968, 1970a; Brose and Hambacher 1999; Ferris and Spence 1995; Fitting 1970; Fitting and Brose 1971; Heckenberger et al. 1990a, b; Janzen 1968b; Mason 1969, 1991; Pleger 2000; Ritchie 1955; Spence 1986; Spence and Fox 1986; Taché 2011b; Versaggi 1999; Wright 1995). In part, these similarities derive from common ancestry, similar ecological adaptations, relatively high mobility, and fluid group membership in many Great Lakes groups. However, increased regional interaction during the Woodland period, manifesting from intensified exchange and social networks, was also an important factor. Despite a number of common features, there is a high level of archaeologically visible variability present (Brose 1994a; Ferris and Spence 1995; Garland and Beld 1999; Heckenberger et al. 1990a, b; Janzen 1968b; Spence 1986; Spence et al. 1979; Spence et al. 1990; Stoltman 1973; Versaggi 1999), which further complicates our understanding of regional development. This variability extends to mortuary ritual as well, creating a mosaic of shared and unique burial practices throughout the Great Lakes region.

Killarney Bay, located on the northern shore of Georgian Bay, is situated at the geographic and temporal interface of several major Woodland cultures. The burials date to the final centuries BC and into the first centuries AD, an important transitional phase between the Early and Middle Woodland in the Great Lakes region that is not well understood (Loring 1985; Spence and Fox 1986; Spence et al. 1990). Killarney Bay is also located in an area that is at a nexus of east-west and north-south trade routes for various raw materials and finished goods, including socially important items often used in mortuary contexts. Indeed, it appears that the production of argillite gorgets and perhaps hides and furs may have been important activities at the site, in addition to its use as a burial station (see other chapters in this volume). Not surprisingly, Killarney Bay funerary practices share many traits with other regional traditions, particularly those to the east and south, while exhibiting its own specific combination of features.

This discussion first addresses the biological aspects of the burial assemblage— specifically the demography, health, and populational affinities of the Killarney Bay people as compared to neighboring groups. Several aspects of the Killarney funerary program are then briefly examined in a regional context, with particular attention given to body treatment and placement. Regional analyses utilize sites

Table 9.2. Select Great Lakes Early/Middle Woodland mortuary sites with demographic and/or osteological information, MNI >10 individuals.

Site	Culture	Location	MNI	% Infant	% Subadult	% Male	Reference
Killarney Bay	Omiquan	Ontario	17	5.9	35.3	55-63	(this volume chapter)
Boucher	Middlesex	Vermont	72	20.3	39.1	54.2	Heckenberger et al. 1990
Smith Mound 3	Laurel	Minnesota	13	0.0	0.0	50.0	Torbenson et al. 1994
Smith Mound 4	Laurel	Minnesota	189	20.1	41.0	61.5	Torbenson et al. 1992, 1994
Serpent Mounds	Point Peninsula	Ontario	73	16.4	45.2	75.0	Anderson 1968, Johnston 1968, Wilkinson 1971
Cameron's Point	Point Peninsula	Ontario	64	18.8	59.4	83.3	Spence and Harper 1968
LeVesconte	Point Peninsula	Ontario	43	20.9	27.9	66.7	Molto 1983, Patterson 1984, Ritchie 1980
Sea Breeze	Point Peninsula	New York	13	0.0	15.4	62.5	Ritchie 1944
Donaldson Cemetery I	Saugeen	Ontario	12	50.0	75.0	40.0	Molto 1979, Wright and Anderson 1963
Donaldson Cemetery II	Saugeen	Ontario	11	18.2	36.4	71.4	Finlayson 1977, Molto 1979
Norton Mounds	Michigan Hopewell	Michigan	33	15.2	48.5	80.0	Griffin et al. 1970, Wilkinson 1971

from roughly contemporaneous Woodland groups, including Middlesex/Adena and early components of Laurel, Point Peninsula, Saugeen, and Hopewellian groups in the Upper Great Lakes area.

Unfortunately, there are relatively few publications with detailed information on burial treatment, demography, and especially osteology. This is due in part to taphonomic issues such as poor skeletal preservation and use of cremation, but also to infrequent biological data collection and the lack of systematic excavation at many of the sites. This situation is particularly acute for the earlier Woodland material (Heckenberger et al. 1990a, b; Ritchie and Dragoo 1960; Spence and Fox 1986; Taché 2011b). Comparative analyses are restricted to assemblages with at least ten well-documented individuals, a sample that is skewed towards eastern Middle Woodland occupations from the first several centuries AD, postdating the Killarney burials to some degree. Discussions of mortuary goods and a comprehensive overview of the funerary program can be found in other chapters in this volume. Sites mentioned in this chapter, including their location, cultural affiliation, basic demographics, and respective references, are provided in Table 9.2.

Demography

Given the very small size of the sample, little can be said regarding the demographic characteristics of the Killarney Bay population. As paralleled in other aspects of Great Lakes funerary programs, burial site demography varies within and between culture areas, particularly in sex composition. Sex distribution generally falls along a continuum between roughly equal male-female ratios to strongly male-biased populations. Killarney Bay lies closer to the first end of the spectrum, with at least five adult males and three or four adult females (Appendix 9.2). More strongly male-biased populations are generally found in later Middle Woodland groups thought to have increased social inequality and/ or status marking, particularly among Rice Lake Point

Peninsula (Spence 1986; Spence and Harper 1968) and Hopewellian-related populations in Michigan (Griffin et al. 1970) (Table 9.2).

Few funerary sites contain sufficient sample sizes to produce detailed age profiles. The Killarney Bay population is extremely small, which limits the conclusions that can be drawn (Appendix 9.3). What is clear, however, is that the individuals recovered from the site do not represent a "natural" death population. Compared to such a natural population distribution, the Killarney Bay interments contain too few infants and too many older subadults (adolescents) and young adults. Individuals of these latter age classes have the lowest expected age-specific mortality rates and would not be expected to occur in the proportions observed at the site. This indicates that the individuals interred at Killarney Bay are not representative of a natural population but rather represent a specially selected portion of the deaths experienced by the living population.

Health

The Killarney Bay assemblage is incomplete and variably preserved, so only a limited amount of health-related data could be collected. Nonetheless, what is present suggests that the Killarney population was relatively healthy. The teeth show few serious dental pathologies other than high levels of attrition, which is typical for pre-agricultural populations (Patterson 1984; Pfeiffer 1977) (Appendix 9.4). Caries occur at a low to moderate frequency, present in 3.3 percent of deciduous teeth and 9.3 percent of permanent dentition. These are found only in Burials 2 and 4, and all are the size of pin-pricks. This rate is well under most agricultural populations but higher than many hunting and gathering groups globally, which have rates typically less than 2 percent (Patterson 1984). Killarney Bay is similar to LeVesconte Mound (6.5 percent), Donaldson II (7.7 percent), and Norton Mounds (11.8 percent), falling within ranges for horticultural or mixed subsistence populations (Griffin et al. 1970; Molto 1979; Patterson 1984). This indicates a relatively high proportion of carbohydrates in the diet, perhaps related to wild rice utilization. Note, however, that this rate is far less than that seen at Hungry Hall Mound 1 (Late Woodland) where the population is thought to be wild rice reliant (Spence et al. 1984). At Hungry Hall, 25.8 percent of the deciduous and 52.8 percent of the permanent dentition is carious, a rate much higher than seen in most horticultural groups (Patterson 1984).

Calculus deposits are common. Except for the infant, all individuals with well-preserved dentition show some level of calculus formation, concentrated on the molars. The calculus deposits are more pervasive and severe with increasing age; 14 percent of the deciduous and 51 percent of the adult teeth are affected. This dental pathology is rarely recorded in osteological reports, so it is difficult to make regional comparisons. However, the rates at Killarney are less than those found at LeVesconte Mound, where 52 percent and 85 percent of deciduous and permanent teeth have accumulations, respectively (Patterson 1984). Severe calculus deposits, which can lead to periodontal disease, are only present on the third molars of Burial A, where there is also evidence of mild alveolar blunting resorption. Unfortunately, most of the burials have poor preservation of the alveoli, so researchers could not assess periodontal disease systematically. Where observable, no abscesses are visible, nor is there evidence of premortem tooth loss.

Hypoplasias occur at a low rate at Killarney Bay. They are present in none of the deciduous and only 8 percent of the adult teeth, all of which were found in a single individual, Burial A. These correspond to metabolic disruption around two and four years old, perhaps related to weaning stress. Much higher incidences of hypoplasia are found at LeVesconte Mound (19.6 percent), Donaldson Cemetery I (20.3 percent), and Donaldson Cemetery II (63 percent) (Molto 1979; Patterson 1984). Burial A is also the only individual with evidence of dental crowding. This trait appears to be more common in females and may be partly related to size (Pfeiffer 1977). Tooth trauma, particularly molar chipping, is common for this time period (Patterson 1984). The majority of the Killarney Bay teeth have significant postmortem enamel spalling, so trauma generally was not able to be evaluated. However, Burial 6 has a premolar that was fractured premortem with subsequent wear. There are no congenitally absent or supernumerary teeth apparent in this population.

Most of the observable skeletal pathology is age-related degenerative arthritis (Appendix 9.11). Every adult over thirty has osteophytic growths to some degree on the vertebrae, associated with load-bearing activities. The asymmetric vertebral growths seen in Burial 8 are not uncommon and can be related to handedness (Bridges 1994). This individual also suffered from arthritis in his right shoulder and fingers. The severe vertebral arthritis seen in Burial 10 and Burial D may be associated with trauma. In Burial 10, there is a healed compression fracture in the seventh thoracic vertebra, perhaps from a fall, which spurred reactive osteophytic growths. In Burial D, the arthritis is most prominent in the ribs and their corresponding thoracic vertebrae, but of unknown etiology. Such high levels of arthritis, particularly on the spinal column, are typical in prehistoric populations throughout the region (Mason 1981; Patterson 1984; Spence and Harper 1968; Torbenson et al. 1994; Varney and Pfeiffer 1995). At Serpent Mound, 80 percent of the adults had afflicted vertebrae (Anderson 1968). In contrast, only 33 percent and 35 percent of the Donaldson II and Norton Mounds burials, respectively, displayed vertebral lipping. However, the low values for Donaldson are related to the disproportionate number of younger versus older adults (Griffin et al. 1970; Molto 1979).

Skeletal trauma, particularly healed fractures, is frequently observed elsewhere (Anderson 1968; Mason 1981; Torbenson et al. 1994). In addition to the fractured vertebra in Burial 10, there is also a possible depression fracture in the Burial A cranium, but surface erosion and heavy preservative obscures observation. Other cases may be underrepresented, given the low number of well-preserved long bones. For the same reason, the lack of evidence for metabolic, dietary, or infectious disorders may be spurious, as these commonly are found, albeit in low numbers, at contemporary sites. Cranial deformation and plaque removal, respectively documented in more than 40 percent and 73 percent of the individuals at Norton Mounds (Griffin et al. 1970), is not present in Burial A, the only individual in the Killarney population sufficiently preserved for evaluation.

Biological affinities

Little can be said about the biological relationships between the Killarney Bay people and their neighbors. This is due to both the limited information available from the present assemblage and the paucity of publications with relevant systematic data from contemporary Great Lakes sites. For the Middle Woodland, notable exceptions include Serpent Mounds (Anderson 1968), Cameron's Point (Spence and Harper 1968), LeVesconte Mound (Molto 1983), Donaldson I and II (Anderson 1963; Molto 1979), and Norton Mounds (Griffin et al. 1970; Wilkinson 1971). Wilkinson (1971) also includes data from several Late Woodland sites in Michigan and Wisconsin as part of his regional assessment of biological affinities. Reports with basic metrics do exist for several other sites (Ritchie 1944; Ritchie and Dragoo 1960; Torbenson et al. 1994), and systematic data from earlier Woodland populations are available for the Meadowood sites of Bruce Boyd (Spence 1986; Spence and Fox 1986) and Liahn II (Pfeiffer 1978a). There are a number of publications with Archaic period data (Pfeiffer 1977, 1978b, 1979; Varney 1994; Varney and Pfeiffer 1995), but since these populations significantly predate Killarney Bay, they are not included regional comparisons.

Table 9.3. Average female height for contemporary Great Lakes populations in comparative samples.

Site	Average F stature (cm)	n	References
Smith Mound 4	160	9	Torbenson et al. 1994
Cameron's Point	163	1	Spence and Harper 1968
Norton Mounds	164	1	Wilkinson 1971
Serpent Mounds	166	9	Anderson 1968
Donaldson 1/2	172	3	Anderson 1963, Molto 1979

Standard anatomical measurements and nonmetric traits of Killarney Bay dentition and skeletons are presented in appendices 9.4 through 9.10. Only a single individual had elements preserved sufficiently for stature estimation—the young adult female in Burial 10 stood around 155–160 cm in height (Appendix 9.9). This individual is not representative of the entire population, but it is noteworthy that she is considerably shorter than the average female stature of 172 cm for the Saugeen occupants at Donaldson (Anderson 1963; Molto 1979). Smaller statures are found among Laurel, Point Peninsula, and Michigan Hopewell populations, with site averages ranging from 160 to 166 cm (Table 9.3). Larger sample sizes are required to better establish regional patterns.

Of the standard nonmetric traits documented for the site (Buikstra and Ubelaker 1994), most could only be assessed in a single individual, restricting comparative analyses (Table 9.4, Appendix 9.10). The following considers traits

Table 9.4. Comparison of nonmetric traits with > 5 observations.

	Killarney Bay 1		Serpent Mounds		Cameron's Point		LeVesconte		Donaldson 1/2		Norton Mounds		Bruce Boyd	
	cases	%	cases	%	cases	%	cases	%	cases	%	cases	%	cases	%
Mylohyoid arch/spur	1/13	7.7%	29/98	29.6%	9/20	45.0%			5/16	31.3%			3/9	33.3%
Divided hypoglossal canal	1/12	8.3%	37/141	26.2%	6/17	35.3%	4/27	14.8%					1/10	10.0%
Multiple mental foramina	0/10	0.0%	1/80	1.3%	1/16	6.3%			1/22	4.5%			0/8	0.0%
Mandibular torus	1/7	14.3%	1/42	2.4%					0/16	0.0%				
Auditory exostoses*	0/11	0.0%									7/18	38.9%	4/10	40.0%

*The frequency of auditory exostoses are statistically signifcant at the α=0.05 level using Fisher's Exact Test: KB1-Norton p=0.026, KB1-Bruce Boyd p=0.035.

observable in at least five burials. Only one individual, Burial 2, has a divided hypoglossal canal (1/6 individuals, 1/11 observations). All seven of the burials with significantly preserved mandibles show a single mental foramen (10/10 observations). Burial 7 has a mylohyoid bridge (1/8 individuals, 1/12 observations) and Burial 4 presents a mandibular torus (1/6 individuals). Using Fisher's Exact Test, none of these traits differs statistically at the α= 0.05 significance level from other Woodland groups in this study. However, the lack of auditory exostoses in the Killarney burials (0/6 individuals, 0/11 observations) does differ statistically from populations at Norton Mounds (Griffin et al. 1970) and Bruce Boyd (Spence and Fox 1986).

Other studies of biological affinities have found some general geographic patterning. Wilkinson (1971) was able differentiate populations in the Great Lakes region from those elsewhere in the Midwest. Molto (1983) noted differences between Saugeen and Point Peninsula groups on either side of the Niagara escarpment. At Cameron's Point, Spence (1986) identified possible evidence of separate lineages in the subfloor and mound-fill burials, perhaps related to status. Nonetheless, there is considerable intrapopulational variability, and high levels of gene flow appear to characterize Woodland populations (Spence 1986; Spence and Fox 1986; Spence et al. 1984). While small and incomplete, the Killarney Bay sample seems to support this idea, as it does not demonstrate any striking differences from neighboring groups.

Burial practices

Diversity in, and elaboration of, interment practices characterizes much of Eastern North America since at least the Late Archaic. In the Upper Great Lakes region, Middle Woodland sites typically show a mixture of burial treatments, with variability in number (single versus multiple), type (primary, secondary, cremation), placement, orientation, and grave offerings (Allen 1980; Anderson 1968; Barondess 1994; Clermont 1990; Davis 1991; Dawson 1980; Emerson 1955; Finlayson 1977; Ford and Brose 1975b; Garland and Beld 1999; Gifford 1948; Griffin et al. 1970; Hayes 1963; Heckenberger et al. 1990a, b; Janzen 1968a; Johnston 1958a, b, 1960, 1968b; Kenyon 1971; Kenyon and Cameron 1960; Kingsley 1984; Loring 1985; McPherron 1967; Molto 1979, 1983; Moorehead 1922; Perkins 1873; Perry 1868; Ritchie 1944, 1955, 1980; Ritchie and Dragoo 1960; Ritchie and Funk 1973; Robertson 2001; Ross 1935; Spence 1967, 1986; Stothers 1974; Sundick 1978; Torbenson et al. 1994; Turnbull 1986; Willoughby 1935; Wintemberg 1928; Wright 1967; Wright and Anderson 1963). This variability extends to larger scales as well—although there are shared elements within (and between) archaeological culture areas, there is not a highly standardized program that defines any region. Killarney Bay and the greater Georgian Bay area are no exceptions.

It should first be noted that Killarney Bay uses mound burials. In the Great Lakes region, mound building is common to a number of traditions, although their size, form, and construction techniques vary considerably and not all communities within an archaeological culture area engaged in this practice. Burial mounds are significant features among some Middlesex, Laurel (Boundary Waters area), Point Peninsula (Rice Lake region), Michigan Woodland, and perhaps Couture groups, but notably absent in Saugeen sites. Mound use is spatially discontinuous. It appears that local groups variably participated in Adena and later Hopewellian-related mortuary systems, which influenced the adoption of mound construction (Brose 1994a; Spence and Fox 1986; Versaggi 1999).

The early date and presence of tubular stone pipes appears to link Killarney Bay with Middlesex and other Adena-influenced sites. Middlesex mound burials are typically found in the far eastern range of this complex, distant to Georgian Bay (Davis 1991; Spence 1967; Turnbull 1986). However, there is at least one other burial in the Georgian Bay region with Adena-related mortuary goods ascribed to a Middlesex tradition. To the south, Wright (1995:667–668) describes a single child burial with tubular pipes near Honey Harbor, Ontario. Single burials are common within regional practices and it is possible that this site should be included within the Killarney Bay tradition. Adena-related sites, including burial mounds, have also been found to the south in Michigan (Fitting 1974, 1975; Ford and Brose 1975b; Garland and Beld 1999), but have an uncertain relationship to other regional traditions.

Like most Woodland sites, the Killarney mounds are earthen. The Killarney mounds lack evidence of central burial facilities (log-lined or stone-slab crypts, etc.) that are occasionally found elsewhere (Dawson 1980; Griffin et al. 1970; Kenyon 1971; Robertson 2001).

At Killarney Bay, despite incomplete body preservation, uneven quality of field documentation, and—for the Bell collection—co-mingled remains, it is apparent that burials were conducted in a variety of ways (see Table 9.1). Single burials are the dominant mode of interment, at least as described by Greenman for the principal mound. The sole multiple interment is potentially the first burial: Burial 9, a double cremation with the mixed remains of an adult male and an adolescent. Single burials are typically more common than multiple burials in the region. However, ossuary pits appear to characterize Saugeen burials at Donaldson I and II (Finlayson 1977; Wright and Anderson 1963) and Michigan Laurel sites (McPherron 1967; Sundick 1978), while large collections of secondary burials, with up to 84 individuals, were interred as groups in Laurel mounds along the Rainy River (Torbenson et al. 1994).

Killarney Bay, like most Great Lakes mortuary sites, contains a mixture of primary burials, secondary burials, and cremations. The majority of interments are inhumations; only three of the estimated seventeen individuals analyzed were cremated, and none of these are children or infants. Fracture patterning at Killarney Bay indicates that the bones were burned before they were completely dry, and all three cremations are missing significant portions of the body. In Burial 9, the skulls and perhaps the hands are missing, while the Burial F cremation (unsexed adult) seems to contain only cranial and long bone fragments. It is likely that partially defleshed burials were cremated, with perhaps selection of certain elements to be burned and/or incomplete recovery of remains.

None of the Killarney cremations was burned in situ, although this is seen at some other sites, including Ault Park (Wright 1995), Donaldson (Finlayson 1977), LeVesconte mound (Patterson 1984; Ritchie 1980), Serpent Mounds (Johnston 1968b), and Cameron's Point (Spence and Harper 1968). Note that in situ cremations are common at earlier Woodland Meadowood sites (Loring 1985; Mason 1981; Ritchie 1944, 1955), and also occur regularly but in a minority of burials at most Middlesex, Saugeen, and Point Peninsula sites. They do not occur in Laurel burials or at Norton Mounds (Michigan Hopewell).

Cremation is practiced more commonly in eastern traditions, and there is a trend for cremations to decrease in frequency through time from the Late Archaic throughout the Woodland period (Clermont 1990; Davis 1991; Finlayson 1977; Ritchie 1953a; Spence 1986; Spence and Fox 1986; Spence et al. 1990).

The Killarney Bay inhumations are a mix of primary extended, primary flexed, and secondary burials. There are two flexed individuals, Burial 8 (older adult male) and Burial 10 (young adult female), both with legs folded onto their chests. This supine position, while far less common than flexed to the side, has been documented at a number of sites, including Arrowhead Drive (McPherron 1967), Donaldson (Finlayson 1977; Wright and Anderson 1963), Brock Street (Kenyon and Cameron 1960), Kant (Emerson 1955), Cameron's Point (Spence and Harper 1968) and Serpent Mounds (Johnston 1968b). Burial 2 (young adult female) is the sole extended burial. This burial type also occurs in low frequencies regionally, but is more common at Hopewellian-related sites and is usually associated with mound floor or crypt burials (Griffin et al. 1970). Extended burials appear not be used in the preceding Meadowood period (Ritchie and Funk 1973).

Burial 6 (young adult male) and Burial 5 (child) are clearly secondary burials in various states of disarticulation, and at least the former was bundled in a decorated basket. It appears that most, if not all, of the body was present with some preserved tissue. Note that the Killarney assemblage lacks the completely defleshed skull/long bone piles that characterize Laurel mounds in the Boundary Waters region (Stoltman 1973; Torbenson et al. 1994). The remaining inhumations are of indeterminate type. Field notes and drawings are unclear about body position for these burials, but the range of elements preserved, presence of tissue, and often articulated vertebrae and ribs suggests that they were predominantly primary or at least partially articulated secondary burials.

There is a high level of variability in the proportion of primary versus secondary burials within all regional traditions, but higher frequencies of secondary burials are more commonly found in mounds, especially those interred within the fill. Secondary burials of various forms are the most common burial mode at Vine Valley (Ritchie 1944), Norton Mounds (Griffin et al. 1970), Cameron's Point (Spence and Harper 1968), Serpent Mounds G and I (Johnston 1968b), and Smith Mounds 3 and 4 (Torbenson et al. 1994). Primary burials are the dominant mode of interment at Boucher (Heckenberger et al. 1990a), McKinlay (Turnbull 1986), Donaldson (Finlayson 1977; Wright and Anderson 1963), Kant (Emerson 1955), and Serpent Mound E (Emerson 1955; Finlayson 1977; Johnston 1968b).

There is not a standard burial orientation overall at Killarney Bay, but both flexed burials are aligned SW-NE, and the single extended burial lay N-S. Unfortunately, there is relatively little comparative information available on burial orientation. At Donaldson Cemetery I (Wright and Anderson 1963) and Brock Street (Kenyon and Cameron 1960), primary burials were laid N-S, and at Donaldson II they lay NE-SW (Finlayson 1977; Molto 1979). At many mound groups, burials tend to be oriented along the long axis of the mound or central burial facilities, often NE-SW or E-W (Griffin et al. 1970; Johnston 1968b; Spence and Harper 1968). In the earlier Meadowood period, burials often are found in groups in the east-facing side of natural ridges (Ritchie 1955, 1980). An unusual radiating pattern has been reported for burials within the Middlesex See Mound (Boyle 1887). However, at most sites, there is rarely a uniform burial orientation (Heckenberger et al. 1990a; Ritchie 1944).

At Killarney, there does not appear to be any correlation of burial type or position and age or sex in this small sample. While there are no infant/child cremations, this may be spurious due to the small population interred at this site and the general infrequency of cremation as a funerary practice. Other regional studies have also noted this lack of standardized burial type with demographic variables (Donaldson and Wortner 1995; Heckenberger et al. 1990a; Stothers and Abel 1993; Taché 2011b). It has been suggested that body treatment is more likely to be related to temporal issues rather than status (Heckenberger et al. 1990a; Spence 1986; Spence and Fox 1986; Stothers and Abel 1993). Individuals who died during periods away from burial stations may have been temporarily buried, exposed, or cremated, and later transported to the central burial facilities. However, it should also be noted that, given general bias towards adult males at most sites, inclusion within larger and/or more formalized cemeteries likely reflects status differences based at least in part on age/sex and perhaps achieved status.

Although incompletely preserved, the Killarney burials lack evidence for extensive postmortem manipulation seen in some other traditions, particularly at the Boundary Waters Laurel mounds. For example, the Smith Mounds remains show defleshing cut marks, occipital removal, and long bone puncturing, the latter two of which have been argued to be ritual extraction of marrow and brains (Mason 1981; Stoltman 1973) or spirit release (Torbenson et al. 1992). Defleshing/dismemberment marks and occipital removal was also found at the Donaldson Cemetery II (Finlayson 1977), the latter of which has been linked to Hopewellian influence (Wright 1995). However, Hopewellian burials in Michigan tend to have the parietal, not the occiput, removed (Wilkinson 1971). A parietal plaque, drilled and polished, was included as a grave good at the Laurel Gyftakis Site in northern Michigan (Sundick 1978). Individual curated, but apparently unaltered, crania are occasionally found at other Middle Woodland sites, but are generally not common. For example, they have been recovered from burials at Naomikong Point (Janzen 1968b), Kant (Emerson 1955), and Serpent Mound G (Johnston 1968b).

Grave goods

All of the graves excavated by Greenman contained burial goods and were generally associated with red ochre, chipped stone points/cache blades, and copper beads. Most also had some form of organic material covering or containing the body, including leather, fur, sheet bark, and basketry.

Ground stone tubular pipes and pendants, shell beads, animal bone, and copper celts, spindles, chisels, and sheets were also found in several burials. The presence of tubular stone pipes would appear to link Killarney with Middlesex/Adena. Note also the pipes are found exclusively with females, a pattern documented at other sites (Heckenberger et al. 1990a, b; Taché 2011b).

More detailed discussions of these items are presented in other chapters in this volume, but some basic patterns will be noted here. For primary inhumations, the grave offerings tended to be placed on the right shoulder and abdomen, sometimes in bags, and the beads were wrapped around the neck and/or wrists. The bundle burials were placed on top of their grave goods and the cremations had few to no items. A sharp contrast in the number and type of grave goods between individuals is not apparent in Greenman assemblage, except for the cremations, but there does seem to be some correlation of grave good quantity and age. In this period, it is common for cremations to have few or no grave goods associated with them (Heckenberger 1990a, b; Johnston 1968b; Spence and Harper 1968). This may be due to the goods being consumed in the funeral pyre or, as suggested by Heckenberger and colleagues (1990a:211), being considered less relevant for secondarily interred burials.

While the distribution of grave goods does not indicate strong social differentiation, some level of achieved status marking may have been present. This is in contrast to some later Middle Woodland groups—namely Rice Lake Point Peninsula and Hopewellian-related sites—where grave goods are more numerous, unequally distributed, and largely correlated with initial mound burials, suggesting that social differentiation was more strongly marked in these societies (Griffin et al. 1970; Johnston 1968b; Kingsley 1984; Mason 1981; Spence et al. 1990; Wright 1995). The abundance and ubiquity of grave goods at Killarney also differs from Laurel sites, where they are generally infrequent or absent (Janzen 1968b; McPherron 1967; Sundick 1978; Torbenson et al. 1994). However, in Boundary Waters Laurel mounds, there do appear to be offerings on the original ground surface and in the fill (Torbenson et al. 1994).

Conclusion

At Killarney Bay, excavations unearthed at least seventeen individuals, and likely more were originally placed within the three documented mounds. Overall, the population was in relatively good health, discounting degenerative pathologies and minor dental issues common to pre-agricultural populations. Because of the small assemblage size and variable preservation, only limited measurements and nonmetric data could be collected. As a consequence, detailed biological comparisons to other populations are not possible currently, but there do not appear to be any major differences. No age or sex classes were excluded from mound. Age distribution roughly parallels contemporary sites in the region, but sex ratios are not as strongly male-biased as at some other cemeteries, particularly those with more status marking.

Considered together, burial practices at Killarney Bay share many features with neighboring Great Lakes groups, particularly those to the east like Middlesex and Point Peninsula. The greatest divergence appears to be with Laurel burial practices. While both groups share mound construction (at least in the Boundary Waters area), Killarney lacks the great use of secondary and multiple burials, extensive postmortem manipulation, and paucity of grave goods. Killarney Bay also uses cremation.

Funerary treatment mirrors the high level of variability seen within most Woodland period sites in the region. The Killarney people buried their dead using a combination of cremation, secondary, and primary flexed and extended interments, with single inhumations predominating. There is no overall preference for orientation, but the two flexed burials had their heads to the southwest. There does not appear to be any correlation between age or sex and burial treatment except for the lack of infant/child cremations, which may be spurious. Aside from the cremations, the burials were provided with a variety of grave goods, including (often substantial) amounts of copper, and there appears to be some correspondence between age and burial offerings. Overall, mortuary practices do not indicate high levels of social differentiation within the individuals interred within these mounds. Yet, given that the burials at Killarney Bay represent a special sample of the dead, the potential status or social significance of these individuals cannot be discounted.

Appendix 9.1 (page 1). Killarney Bay 1 skeletal inventory.

Burial	Ind.	Field #	UMMA/ CMCC #	Element	Portion	Qnt	Side	Fusion**	Condition	Comments
2	1	1169	30301	cranium	temporal and occipital fragments, 15 pieces	1			mod. Cu, tissue	w/ 30303 and 30304
2	1	1173	30304	temporal	mastoid and auditory meatus	1	R		mod. Cu, tissue	articulates with 30303
2	1	1172	30303	occipital	foramen magnum, 19 pieces	1			mod. Cu, tissue	thin walled (gracile)
2	1	1165	30299	UI?	enamel fragment	1			mod. Cu, consolidant	upper incisor 1/2?
2	1	1165	30299	UM1	crown	1	L		mod. Cu, consolidant	possibly asymmetric M2
2	1	1165	30299	UM2	crown	1	R		mod. Cu, consolidant	
2	1	1165	30299	UM3	complete	1	L		mod. Cu, consolidant	R/L asymmetric
2	1	1165	30299	UM3	complete	1	R		mod. Cu, consolidant	R/L asymmetric
2	1	1174	30305	mandible	near complete, LP3-M3, RM1-3, 6 Non ID enamel fragments	1			light Cu, tissue, consolidant	ochre staining on right teeth, R/L M3 asymmetric
2	1	1165	30299	LC1	crown	1	L		heavy consolidant	with 30305 mandible
2	1	1165	30299	LP3	crown	1	R		mod. Cu, consolidant	
2	1	1165	30299	LP4	crown	1	R		mod. Cu, consolidant	
2	1	1165	30299	tooth	root	1			mod. Cu, consolidant	
2	1	1165	30299	tooth	enamel fragments	32			mod. Cu, consolidant	mostly incisor fragments?
2	1	1174	30305	cervical vertebra	C1-5	5		Fsg	mod. Cu, tissue	with 30309 C6-T7, articulated
2	1	1191	30309	cervical vertebra	C6-7	2		Fsg	mod. Cu, tissue	articulated C6-T7
2	1	1191	30309	thoracic vertebra	T1-7	7		Fsg	mod. Cu, tissue	articulated C6-T7, with ribs, T7 fragmentary
2	1	1191	30309	1st rib	complete	1	R	Fsg	mod. Cu, tissue	with T1-7
2	1	1191	30309	rib	head/neck	6	R	Fsg	mod. Cu, tissue	with T1-7
2	1	1191	30309	rib	head/neck	7	L	Fsg	mod. Cu, tissue	with T1-7
2	1	1191	30309	rib	fragment	10			mod. Cu, tissue	with T1-7
2	1	1190	30311	clavicle	near complete	1	R	Fsg	mod. Cu, tissue	gracile
2	1	1184	30306	scapula	blade fragments, 102 pieces	1	L		light Cu and tissue, friable	highly fragmented, may be some small rib or vertebral fragments mixed in
2	1	1189	30308	scapula	glenoid fragment	1	R	F	no Cu	w/ 30309?
2	1	1191	30309	scapula	acromion process, 6 blade fragments	1	R	Fsg	mod. Cu, tissue	
2	1	1170	30302	scapula	blade fragment, 2 pieces	1			mod. Cu, tissue, heavy consolidant	likely with 30309 scapula fragment
2	1	1168	30300	radius?	distal shaft fragment	1	L?		mod. Cu, tissue	side based on map position
2	1	1170	30302	metacarpal III/IV	shaft	1	L?		mod. Cu, tissue, heavy consolidant	side based on map position
2	1	1191	30309	indeterminate	fragments	75			mod. Cu, tissue	small vertebra/rib/scapula fragments with tissue
3	1	2041	38479	cranium	L palatine, L maxilla, *in situ* : Ldm1-2, LI2	1	L		heavy Cu	in poor condition
3	1	2041	38479	ethmoid	sinus fragment	1			heavy Cu	
3	1	2041	38479	sphenoid	body fragments, 2 pieces	1			heavy Cu	
3	1	2042	38480	sphenoid	pterygoid plate and process	1	R		heavy Cu	
3	1	2041	38479	temporal	petrosal, anterior squama	1	R		heavy Cu	
3	1	2041	38479	temporal	petrosal and mastoid, 3 pieces	1	L		heavy Cu	
3	1	2041	38479	occipital	occipital condyles and pars basilaris	1			heavy Cu	anterior intra-occipitalis suture unfused
3	1	2041	38479	incus	complete	1			mod. Cu	
3	1	2041	38479	cranial	vault fragments	11			heavy Cu	very thin
3	1	2042	38480	cranial	vault fragment	1			heavy Cu	very thin
3	1	2041	38479	mandible	L/R condyle; *in situ* : Ldm1-2, LM2; loose Ldc1, 4 enamel fragments, 7 ramus fragments	1			heavy Cu	with 38480 mandible, left portion more weathered, from disturbed context w/ 1950s refuse
3	1	2042	38480	mandible	*in situ* : Ldi2, Rdc1, Rdm1-2, LI2, RM2; loose: LM1	1			heavy Cu	with 38479 mandible
3	1	2024	38478	atlas	posterior arch	1	L	U	mod. Cu	refits with 2042 fragment
3	1	2042	38480	atlas	anterior arch	1		U	heavy Cu	anterior synchondroses fused, unfused neuralcentral junctures

Appendix 9.1 (page 2). Killarney Bay 1 skeletal inventory.

Burial	Ind.	Field #	UMMA/ CMCC #	Element	Portion	Qnt	Side	Fusion**	Condition	Comments
3	1	2042	38480	axis	complete	1		(2)	heavy Cu	odontoid fusion level 2, unusual fusion
3	1	2042	38480	cervical vertebra	C3 or C4	1		PU	heavy Cu	
3	1	2041	38479	cervical vertebra	C5-7	3		PU	heavy Cu	
3	1	2042	38480	cervical vertebra	centrum	1		U	heavy Cu	centrum/arch unfused
3	1	2042	38480	lumbar vertebra	transverse process	1			heavy Cu	very thin, small
3	1	2041	38479	thoracic vertebra	T1-3, arches only	3		U	heavy Cu	arches unfused to centrum (not present)
3	1	2041	38479	thoracic vertebra	arch fragments	5		U	heavy Cu	arches unfused to centrum (not present), MNE=?
3	1	2024	38478	thoracic vertebra	arch fragments	2		U	mod. Cu	arches unfused to centrum, MNE=2
3	1	2041	38479	vertebra	articular facet	1			mod. Cu, tissue	
3	1	2041	38479	rib	head	2	L	U	heavy Cu	small, thin
3	1	2024	38478	rib	neck/body fragments	4	L		mod. Cu, tissue	small, may include rib 1 or 2, MNE=4
3	1	2041	38479	rib	head	2	R	U	heavy Cu	small, thin
3	1	2042	38480	rib	head	4	R	U	heavy Cu, tissue	some rib shafts connected by tissue, MNE=4
3	1	2042	38480	rib	fragment	3	R		heavy Cu, tissue	some rib shafts connected by tissue
3	1	2042	38480	scapula	blade fragment, 3 pieces	1			heavy Cu	very thin
3	1	2041	38479	longbone	shaft fragment	3			heavy Cu	radius/ulna/fibula size
3	1	2041	38479	indeterminate	fragment	10			heavy Cu	
4	1	2119	38481	maxilla	R/L di1-dm2, R/L I1-M2 (complete dentition), 13 bone fragments	1			light Cu, friable	no teeth *in situ*
4	1	2119	38481	mandible	*in situ* : Rdi1-dc1, Ldm2, R/L I1-P3. loose: Ldi1-dc1, Rdm1-2, R/LP4-M2	1			light Cu, friable	deciduous dentition in wear, permanent dentition in crypts, missing only LUP4
4	1	2119	38481	thoracic vertebra	neural arch fragment	2			light Cu, friable	
4	1	2119	38481	vertebra	arch fragments	2			light Cu, friable	small fragments
4	1	2119	38481	rib	body fragments, 90 pieces	4			light Cu and tissue, friable	4 ribs originally identified, now highly fragmented
4	1	2119	38481	radius?	shaft, 3 pieces	1			highly friable	fragmented medium-sized longbone shaft fragment, ID as radius in field
4	1	2120	38482	femur	shaft fragment, foramen, 24 pieces	1			highly friable	
4	1	2119	38481	indeterminate	fragments	42			light Cu and tissue, friable	small bone and tissue fragments
5	1	2122		premolar	enamel fragment	2			highly friable	indeterminate, no wear
5	1	2122		UM1/2	enamel fragment	1	R		highly friable	central crown fragment, not in wear
5	1	2122		tooth	enamel fragment	150			highly friable	indeterminate
6	1	2149	38484	occipital	foramen magnum and 16 vault fragments	1			light Cu and tissue, friable	
6	1	2193	38488	maxilla	R nasal aperture, R/L canine/incisor alveoli	1		F	mod. Cu, consolidant	
6	1	2152	38487	mandible	L ascending ramus, LI2, P3-M3, RI1, C1-P3	1		F	light Cu, tissue, consolidant	tooth crowns broken except RC1, P3
6	1	2149	38484	cervical vertebra	centrum/arch fragment	1		F	light Cu, tissue	
6	1	2149	38484	vertebra	centrum fragment	2		F	light Cu, tissue	
6	1	2149	38484	rib	fragments	106			light Cu and tissue, friable	highly fragmented, MNE=?
6	1	2149	38484	scapula	coracoid process and blade fragment	1	R		light Cu	
6	1	2150	38485	radius	shaft	1	L		light Cu, tissue	not humerus as identified in field
6	1	2193	38488	pelvis	acetabulum and misc. fragments, 94 pieces	1		F	light Cu and tissue, friable	highly fragmented, MNE=1
6	1	2151	38486	longbone	shaft, 112 pieces	1			highly friable	highly fragmented, non ID large longbone, femur or tibia, possibly switched with 2150 radius
6	1	2149	38484	indeterminate	fragments	67			light Cu and tissue, friable	highly fragmented
7	1	2211	38491	temporal	auditory meatus	1	L		mod. Cu	
7	1	2211	38491	occipital	pars basilaris and L partes lateralis	1		U	mod. Cu	
7	1	2199	38489	maxilla	near complete	1	L			
7	1	2199	38489	maxilla	near complete	1	R			
7	1	2211	38491	Udc1	crown	1	L		mod. Cu	with 38489 maxilla

Appendix 9.1 (page 3). Killarney Bay 1 skeletal inventory.

Burial	Ind.	Field #	UMMA/ CMCC #	Element	Portion	Qnt	Side	Fusion**	Condition	Comments
7	1	2199	38489	mandible	near complete, *in situ*: L/Rdm1, LI1, L/RM1; loose: Ldi2, Rdc1, L/R dm2	1			light Cu	lacks R ascending ramus
7	1	2199	38489	hyoid	greater horns	1			heavy Cu	
7	1	2211	38491	cervical vertebra	C1-2, 2 half neural arches	2		U	Cu strained, heavy tissue	articulated
7	1	2211	38491	cervical vertebra	4 centra, 8 arch fragments	4		U	mod. Cu	arches and centra unfused
7	1	2211	38491	1st rib	complete	1	R	U	mod. Cu	very small
7	1	2211	38491	rib	head/neck, second rib?	1	R	U	mod. Cu	very small
7	1	2211	38491	rib	near complete, third rib?	1	R	U	mod. Cu	very small
7	1	2211	38491	rib	fragment	1			mod. Cu, tissue	very small
7	1	2211	38491	clavicle	complete	1	R		mod. Cu, tissue	very small
7	1	2211	38491	scapula	coracoid, glenoid, and partial blade	1	R	U	mod. Cu, tissue	
7	1	2211	38491	humerus	proximal epiphysis and shaft	1	R	U	mod. Cu, tissue	
7	1	2199	38490	carpal?	complete	1				sesamoid bone is likely carpal found near phalanx
8	1	2248	39515	thoracic vertebra	T9-T11, arches only	3		F	heavy Cu, tissue	arthritis, assemetrical L/R facets
8	1	2254	39519	thoracic vertebra	arch fragments, 23 pieces	2		F	heavy Cu, tissue	arthritis, assemetrical L/R facets
8	1	2257	39520	lumbar vertebra	L2-L5, arches only	4		F	light to heavy Cu, tissue	arthritis, assemetrical L/R facets
8	1	2244	39512	lumbar vertebra	centrum fragment	1		F	light Cu	
8	1	2230	39510	1st rib	proximal fragment	1	L	F	mod. Cu, some tissue	
8	1	2250	39517	rib	2 heads and 4 necks	4	R	F	mod. Cu, some tissue	
8	1	2230	39510	rib	body	1	R		mod. Cu, some tissue	
8	1	2230	39510	rib	fragment	2			mod. Cu, tissue	
8	1		39498	clavicle	lateral shaft	1	L		light Cu, tissue	robust
8	1	2249	39516	clavicle	shaft	1	R		heavy Cu, tissue	robust
8	1	2253	39518	scapula	near complete	1	R	F	heavy Cu, heavy tissue	robust/large, athritic lipping on glenoid
8	1	2244	39512	humerus	shaft	1	R		heavy Cu, tissue	extremely large and robust, probably male
8	1	2239	39496	radius	shaft	1	R		mod. Cu, heavy tissue	robust, articulated with ulna, wrapped in copper beads
8	1	2230	39510	ulna	proximal epiphysis/olecranon	1	L	F	mod. Cu, some tissue	
8	1	2239	39496	ulna	shaft	1	R		mod. Cu, heavy tissue	robust, articulated with radius, wrapped in copper beads
8	1	2247	39514	ulna	olecranon fragment	1			light Cu	
8	1	2247	39514	metacarpal I	distal epiphysis fragment	1		F	light Cu, tissue	
8	1	2247	39514	metacarpal II	distal epiphysis and shaft	1		F	light Cu, tissue	
8	1	2247	39514	metacarpal III	shaft	1			light Cu, tissue	
8	1	2247	39514	metacarpal IV/V	shaft fragment	1			light Cu, tissue	
8	1	2247	39514	metacarpal	distal epiphysis fragment	1			light Cu, tissue	
8	1	2247	39514	proximal phalanx	hand, digit II-IV, proximal epiphysis and shaft	1		F	light Cu, tissue	
8	1	2246	39513	intermed. phalanx	hand, digit II?, complete	1		F	light Cu, tissue	articulated w/ distal phalanx, robust, arthritic
8	1	2247	39514	intermed. phalanx	hand, digit III-IV, complete	1		F	light Cu, tissue	arthritic lipping lateral distal epiphysis
8	1	2247	39514	intermed. phalanx	hand, digit V?, near complete	1		F	light Cu, tissue	
8	1	2246	39513	distal phalanx	hand, digit II?, complete	1		F	light Cu, tissue	articulated w/ int. phalanx, robust, pathological, arthritic
8	1	2247	39514	distal phalanx	hand, digit III-IV, complete	1		F	light Cu, tissue	pathological, same lipping as int. phalanx
8	1	2244	39512	femur	near complete	1	L	F	mod. Cu, tissue	large bone, hide stuck to dorsal femur
8	1	2247	39514	indeterminate	cancellous bone fragment	1			light Cu	
9	1	2306	39669	lumbar vertebra	centrum/arch fragment	5		U	cremated, white/cracked	unfused pads, small
9	1	2306	39669	vertebra	centrum fragment	5		U	cremated	
9	1	2306	39669	humerus	proximal shaft, deltoid tuberosity	1	R		cremated	
9	1?	2306	39669	humerus	head fragment	1			cremated, white/cracked	small
9	1?	2306	39669	humerus	shaft fragment	5			cremated	gracile
9	1	2306	39669	radius	bicipital tuberosity	1	R		cremated	gracile
9	1?	2306	39669	radius	shaft fragment	6			cremated	gracile

Appendix 9.1 (page 4). Killarney Bay 1 skeletal inventory.

Burial	Ind.	Field #	UMMA/ CMCC #	Element	Portion	Qnt	Side	Fusion**	Condition	Comments
9	1	2306	39669	femur	shaft fragment, foramen, 2 pieces	1	R		cremated, white/cracked	small
9	1?	2306	39669	femur	patellar groove fragment	1	R		cremated, white/cracked	
9	1?	2306	39669	femur	patellar groove fragment	3			cremated, white/cracked	
9	1?	2306	39669	femur	condyle fragment	6			cremated, white/cracked	
9	1?	2306	39669	tibia	proximal epiphysis fragment	1	R		cremated	
9	1	2306	39669	tibia	tuberosity fragment	1			cremated	
9	1	2306	39669	tibia	shaft fragment	6			cremated, white/cracked	gracile, may be L and R
9	1	2306	39669	fibula	shaft fragment	4			cremated, white/cracked	gracile
9	1	2306	39669	talus	trochlea	1	L		cremated, white/cracked	small
9	1?	2306	39669	calcaneus	medial/posterior talar articular facet	1	R		cremated	
9	1	2306	39669	metapodial?	shaft fragment	4			cremated	gracile
9	1?	2306	39669	longbone	epiphysis fragment	7			cremated, white/cracked	humerus/femur epiphysis fragments
9	1	2306	39669	longbone	shaft fragment	2		U	cremated, white/cracked	tibia/femur unfused shaft fragments
9	1	2306	39669	longbone	shaft fragment	10			cremated, white/cracked	gracile, humerus/femur/tibia size
9	1	2306	39669	longbone	epiphysis fragment	1		U	cremated	radius/ulna/fibula size
9	1?	2306	39669	indeterminate	articular facet	13			cremated, white/cracked	
9	2	2306	39669	thoracic vertebra	centrum	4		F	cremated	misshapen bodies, slight osteoarthritis
9	2	2306	39669	thoracic vertebra	neural arch fragment	1			cremated	
9	2	2306	39669	thoracic vertebra	articular facet	1			cremated	
9	2	2306	39669	lumbar vertebra	centrum	4		F	cremated	slight osteoarthritis
9	2	2306	39669	sacrum	partial articular surface	1			cremated	osteoarthritis
9	2	2306	39669	sacrum	fragment	2			cremated	large
9	2	2306	39669	vertebra	centrum fragment	5			cremated	slight osteoarthritis
9	2	2306	39669	vertebra	articular facet	2			cremated	osteoarthritis
9	2?	2306	39669	humerus	shaft fragment	3			cremated	robust
9	2?	2306	39669	humerus	trochlea fragment	1			cremated, gray	
9	2?	2306	39669	humerus	distal epiphysis fragment	1			cremated	
9	2?	2306	39669	radius	shaft fragment, bicipital tuberosity	1	L		cremated	robust
9	2	2306	39669	radius	shaft fragment, foramen, 212 pieces	1			cremated, gray/brown	highly fragmented, distinctive color
9	2	2306	39669	radius?	shaft fragment, foramen	2			cremated	L and R?, may also be clavicle, small fragments
9	2?	2306	39669	radius	shaft fragment	36			cremated	robust, L and R?
9	2?	2306	39669	ulna	distal shaft fragment	1	L		cremated	
9	2	2306	39669	femur	head fragment	1			cremated, gray/black	large
9	2	2306	39669	femur	condyle fragment	1			cremated, gray/black	
9	2	2306	39669	femur	shaft fragment, 53 pieces	1			cremated, gray/black	robust, with epiphyses
9	2?	2306	39669	tibia	proximal epiphysis fragment	3			cremated, gray	
9	2	2306	39669	fibula	shaft fragment, 8 pieces	1	R		cremated, gray	
9	2	2306	39669	talus	trochlea	1	L		cremated	large
9	2?	2306	39669	talus	posterior	1	R?		cremated	
9	2	2306	39669	calcaneus	tuber	1	R	F	cremated, gray	
9	2	2306	39669	calcaneus	anterior talar articular facet	1	R		cremated, gray	
9	2	2306	39669	metapodial?	shaft fragment	5			cremated	robust
9	2	2306	39669	longbone	shaft fragment	61			cremated	robust, femur/tibia
9	2?	2306	39669	longbone	epiphysis fragment, 5 pieces	1			cremated, gray	1 bone?
9	2?	2306	39669	indeterminate	articular facet	17			cremated, gray	
9	-	2306	39669	vertebra	centrum fragment	60			cremated	
9	-	2306	39669	vertebra	articular facet	11			cremated	
9	-	2306	39669	vertebra	fragment	10			cremated	Non ID
9	-	2306	39669	rib	fragment	9			cremated	

Appendix 9.1 (page 5). Killarney Bay 1 skeletal inventory.

Burial	Ind.	Field #	UMMA/ CMCC #	Element	Portion	Qnt	Side	Fusion**	Condition	Comments
9	-	2306	39669	pelvis	acetabulum fragment	1	R		cremated	
9	-	2306	39669	pelvis	fragment	39			cremated	MNE=?
9	-	2306	39669	femur	distal epiphysis fragment	1			cremated	
9	-	2306	39669	femur	epiphysis fragment	1			cremated	
9	-	2306	39669	longbone	shaft fragment	486			cremated	humerus/femur/tibia size
9	-	2306	39669	longbone	shaft fragment	499			cremated	highly fragmented
9	-	2306	39669	indeterminate	fragments	250			cremated	
10	1	2305	39668	UI2	crown	1	L		light Cu	
10	1	2305	39668	UC1	crown	1	L		light Cu	
10	1	2305	39668	UP4	crown	1	R		light Cu	
10	1	2305	39668	LC1	crown	1	L		light Cu	
10	1	2305	39668	LM1?	crown fragment	1	L		light Cu	crown broken
10	1	2304	39667	thoracic vertebra	T5-6	2		Fsg	mod. Cu, tissue	T5-T7 center deformed, assymetric
10	1	2357	39671	thoracic vertebra	T7-12	6		Fsg	mod. Cu, tissue	T7 pathology distorted anterior centrum, spondylitis on facets
10	1	2357	39671	lumbar vertebra	L1-4	4		Fsg	mod. Cu, tissue	
10	1	2357	39671	vertebra	fragments	6			mod. Cu, tissue	with T7-L4
10	1	2359	39672	rib	near complete	6	L	Fsg	heavy Cu, tissue	reconstructed, not 7 ribs as originally recorded
10	1	2357	39671	rib	head/neck and 3 fragments	2	L	Fsg	mod. Cu, tissue	MNE=2
10	1	2361	39673	humerus	distal epiphysis and shaft	1	L	F	mod. Cu, tissue	perforated olecranon fossa, gracile
10	1	2361	39673	radius	proximal epiphysis and shaft	1	L	F	mod. Cu	
10	1	2365	39675	radius	shaft	1	R		light Cu, tissue	
10	1	2361	39673	ulna	proximal epiphysis and shaft	1	L	F	mod. Cu, tissue	
10	1	2365	39675	ulna	shaft	1	R		light Cu, tissue	
10	1	2263	39674	metacarpal I	distal epiphysis and shaft	1	R	F	light Cu	
10	1	2363	39674	metacarpal II	complete	1	R	F	mod. Cu	with phalanges 39670?, gracile
10	1	2363	39674	metacarpal III	complete	1	R	F	mod. Cu	with phalanges 39670?, gracile
10	1	2363	39674	proximal phalanx	hand, digit I, complete	1	R	F	mod. Cu	
10	1	2308	39670	proximal phalanx	hand, digit II-III, complete	1	R?	F	mod. Cu, a lot of tissue	tissue imprint from articulation with femur(?)
10	1	2308	39670	proximal phalanx	hand, digit II-III, complete	1	R?	F	mod. Cu, a lot of tissue	tissue imprint from articulation with femur(?), articulated digit
10	1	2308	39670	intermed. phalanx	hand, digit II-III, complete	1	R?	F	mod. Cu, a lot of tissue	tissue imprint from articulation with femur(?), articulated digit
10	1	2308	39670	intermed. phalanx	hand, digit II-III, complete	1	R?	F	mod. Cu, a lot of tissue	with non-articulated proximal phalanx?
10	1	2308	39670	distal phalanx	hand, digit II-III, complete	1	R?	F	mod. Cu, a lot of tissue	tissue imprint from articulation with femur(?), articulated digit
10	1	2308	39670	femur	shaft	1	L		light Cu, tissue	strongly curved shaft, pre vs post-mortem?
10	1	2361	39673	femur?	shaft	1	R		light Cu and tissue, friable	very poor condition, disintegrating, probable femur
10	1	2308	39670	longbone	fragments	10			light Cu, friable	Non ID, highly fragmented, with femur?
	A		669	cranium	near complete	1			sup light Cu, inf heavy Cu	left half calvarium partially reconstructed, arches broken, labelled "Killarney Ont Greenman 200 BC"
	A		669	mandible	complete	1			heavy Cu	
	A		669	hyoid	complete	1		U	heavy Cu	body and horns present
	A		669	laryngeal cartilage	near complete	1	R			"windows" present, mostly ossified
	A		669	cricoid cartilage	near complete	1	L			no anterior arch
	A		669	cricoid cartilage	near complete	1	R			no anterior arch
	A		669	atlas	complete	1		F	heavy Cu	osteoarthritis
	A		669	axis	complete	1		F	heavy Cu	osteoarthritis

Appendix 9.1 (page 6). Killarney Bay 1 skeletal inventory.

Burial	Ind.	Field #	UMMA/ CMCC #	Element	Portion	Qnt	Side	Fusion**	Condition	Comments
	A		669	C3-7	near complete	5		F	heavy Cu, tissue	slightly damaged, some osteoarthirtis, copper beads fused to C4
	A		669	thoracic vertebra*	complete	1		F	heavy Cu, tissue	osteoarthritis, connective tissue present, not T1-- does not appear to articulate with C7
	A		669	rib*	shaft fragment	5			mod. Cu	
	A		669	scapula*	acromion and superior blade fragment	1	R	F	heavy Cu	
	A		669	clavicle*	lateral half	1	R		mod. Cu	lateral end damaged, gracile
	A		669	humerus*	proximal and shaft	1		F	mod. Cu	surface eroded, head damaged, gracile
	B		669	cranium	occipital, L/R temporal fragments, R sphenoid	1			mod. Cu	
	B		669	mandible*	left half	1	L		mod. Cu	I2, C1 root fragment only, M1-3 present, surface enamel fractured.
	B		669	atlas*	complete	1		F	heavy Cu	
	B		669	axis*	complete	1		F	heavy Cu	
	B		669	C3-4*	complete	2		F	heavy Cu	very gracile, small centra
	B		669	cervical vertebra*	centrum	1		F	mod. Cu	probably C5, very gracile, small
	B		669	1st rib*	head/neck	1	R	F	heavy to mod. Cu, tissue	Cu stain stongly only heads
	B		669	1st rib*	head/neck	1	L	F	heavy to mod. Cu, tissue	Cu stain stongly only heads
	B		669	rib*	head/neck	6	R	F	heavy to mod. Cu, tissue	Cu stain stongly only heads
	B		669	rib*	head/neck	2	L	F	heavy to mod. Cu, tissue	Cu stain stongly only heads
	C		669	cranium	occpitial, L/R temporal fragments	1			mod. Cu	L/R parts occipital w/ condyles unfused to basioccipital (not present), R petrosal, L petrosal/meatus, basal arch frag, L sphenoid
	C		669	mandible	L/Rdm2-angle	1			mod. Cu, tissue	
	C		669	mandible	LM1-RI1	1			heavy Cu	
	C		669	atlas	complete	1		U	heavy Cu, tissue	articulated with tissue, 2 halves arch and centrum unfused
	C		669	axis	near complete	1		U	heavy Cu	2 halves fused, centrum missing, unfused
	C		669	C3-6	near complete	4		PU	heavy Cu, tissue	3 parts fused, pads unfused, small
	C		669	1st rib	head/neck	1	R	U	heavy Cu	
	C		669	clavicle	shaft	1	L		heavy Cu	
	C		669	humerus	proximal shaft fragment	1	L	U	mod. Cu	
	D		669	cranium	maxilla, temporal, occipital, sphenoid fragments	1			heavy Cu, tissue	heavy Cu around base of skull, C1-3 articulated with occiptial, most of maxilla is broken, alveolus for LM1, L/RM2, RM3, LM3 present
	D		669	mandible	R/L P4-angle	1			heavy Cu, tissue	only M1 present
	D		669	atlas	complete	1		F	heavy Cu, heavy tissue	encased in tissue, articulates with cranium, C1-3
	D		669	axis	complete	1		F	heavy Cu, heavy tissue	encased in tissue, articulates with cranium, C1-3
	D		669	C3	complete	1		F	heavy Cu, heavy tissue	encased in tissue, articulates with cranium, C1-3
	D		669	C4-7	near complete	4		F	heavy Cu, tissue	osteoarthritis
	D		669	T1-12	near complete	12		F	mod. Cu, tissue	osteoarthritis
	D		669	lumbar vertebra	neural arch fragment	1			light Cu	may be L4
	D		669	L5	near complete	1		F	mod. Cu	
	D		669	sacrum	near complete	1		F	tissue	only 4 vertebral sections present (fused)-- S5 unfused and not present
	D		669	pelvis	ilum fragments	1		F	mod. Cu	3 pieces, L ilium with auricular and acetabulum fragment, R auricular and sciatic notch fragment, Cu strongest in sacral area.
	D		669	1st rib	head/neck	1	R	F	heavy Cu	
	D		669	rib	head/neck	9	R	F	heavy to mod. Cu	more copper on upper ribs in sequence, two osteoarthritis
	D		669	rib	head/neck	6	L	F	heavy to mod. Cu	one osteoarthritis

Appendix 9.1 (page 7). Killarney Bay 1 skeletal inventory.

Burial	Ind.	Field #	UMMA/ CMCC #	Element	Portion	Qnt	Side	Fusion**	Condition	Comments
	D		669	rib	body fragment	2			light Cu	
	D		669	clavicle*	near complete	1	R	F	mod. Cu	2 pieces, broken midshaft, robust
	D		669	clavicle*	near complete	1	L	F	mod. Cu	2 pieces, broken midshaft, robust
	D		669	scapula*	near complete	1	L	F	heavy Cu	Cu heavier on medial blade
	D		669	scapula*	near complete	1	R	F	heavy Cu	
	D		669	humerus*	proximal half	1	R	F	mod. Cu	robust, proximal epiphysis broken
	D		669	humerus*	distal shaft fragment	1	R		mod. Cu	
	D		669	radius*	distal half	1	R	F	mod. Cu	
	D		669	ulna*	shaft fragment	1	R		light Cu	
	E			cranial	mastoid and auditory meatus	1	L		light Cu	"extra" left adult mastoid
	F			cranial	frontal, orbit w/ zygomatic suture	1	R		cremated	
	F			cranial	frontal, temporal line	2			cremated	
	F			cranial	parietal, squamosal suture	1			cremated	
	F			cranial	occipital, sulcus	1			cremated	
	F			cranial	occipital, lamboid suture	1			cremated	
	F			cranial	occipital	1			cremated	
	F			cranial	vault fragment	19			cremated	
	F			ulna	proximal shaft fragment	1			cremated	
	F			ulna	distal shaft fragment	1			cremated	3 pieces, interosseous groove
	F			radius	proximal epipysis fragment	1		F	cremated	
	F			tibia	distal shaft fragment	1			cremated	
	F			longbone	shaft fragment	49			cremated	humerus/femur/tibia size
	F			longbone	shaft fragment	26			cremated	radius/ulna/fibula size
	F			longbone	shaft fragment	7			cremated	metapodial/phalanx size
	F			longbone	shaft fragment	27			cremated	very small fragments
	F			longbone	articular surface fragment	1			cremated	
	F			cancellous bone	fragment	15			cremated	
				sacrum	proximal S1 fragment	1		F	light Cu	in burial "F" collection, different individual
						2616				

*May not be associated with cranial elements in group

**F=fused, U=unfused, Fsg=fusing, PU=vertebral pads unfused (see Appendix 2 for suture scores)

Appendix 9.2. Age determination.

	Burial/ Elements	1	2	3	4	5	6	7	8	9-1	9-2	10	A	"A" arms*	B	"B" mandible	C	D	"D" arms*	E	F	"F" sacrum*	gracile vertebrae*
Suture Fusion	(1) Midlamboid																				1		
	(9) Inf. Sphenotemporal		0												0		0	2					
	(16) Endocranial Lambdoid																				3		
	Vault Score (1-7)												12/S4										
	Lat-Ant Score (6-10)												8/S5										
	Maxilla Score (11-14)			0-1									7-9					6-7					
	Est. Vault Age												30-60										
	Est. Lat-Ant Age												35-55										
	Est. Maxilla Age			<12									35-40					30-35					
	Estimated Age			<12									35-40					30-35			>35		
Dental Development (Upper/Lower)	dm1	+?		≥10/11.5	≥7/14			10/10									-/14						
	dm2	+?		≥10/11.5	≥7/14			11/10									-/14						
	M1			-/7.5	≥6/≥10	+?		5/≥6									-/14						
	M2			-/6	5/6	+?											-/7.5						
	M3																						
	Estimated Age	juv		5-6	~6	4-12		2-3									6-7						
Dental Attrition (Upper/Lower)	M1		-/17			0?							22/20										
	M2		10/15			0?							15/19										
	M3		5/4-6										10/14			-/8		*-/14*					
	Comp. Wear Stage**		B1-C				D-E					B2-C	F-G			D		E					
	Estimated Age		16-22			juv	20-30					16-22	30-40			20-24		24-30					
Post-Cranial Fusion	0-2		F	F	F		F	F	F	F	F	F	F		F		F	F					
	2-6		F	U			F	U	F	F	F	F	F		F		U/F	F					
	5-7		F	U			F	U					F		F		U	F					
	11-13			U										F			U		F				
	12-15						F					F							F		F		
	15-18		F/Fsg					U	F	U	F			F			U				?		
	17-23		Fsg	U			F	U	F	U	F	Fsg	F	F	F		U	F	F			F	F
	17-30		Fsg															F					
	Estimated Age		17-23	2-6	≥2		≥17-23	2-4	≥17-23	≥6	≥17-23	17-23	≥17-23	≥17-23	≥17-23		5-6	≥17-30			≥12	≥17-23	≥17-23
Measurements	Basilar Occipital Length							14.7															
	Basilar Occipital Width							26.1															
	Estimated Age							~3															
Arthritis***									+		+		+					+					
General Size			adult	yg. child	yg. child		adult	infant	adult	adult/ adol	adult	adult	adult	adult	adult	adult	yg. child	adult	adult	adult	adult	adult	adult
Composite Age Estimate		**juv**	**16-22**	**5-6**	**~6**	**child**	**20-30**	**2-3**	**M/O adult**	**14-18**	**M/O adult**	**16-22**	**35-40**	**adult**	**adult**	**20-24**	**6-7**	**24-35**	**adult**	**adult**	**M/O adult**	**adult**	**Y adult**

\+ = present, *italics* = estimated, ? = uncertain, U = unfused, F = fused, Fsg = fusing, blank = no data

*Reassigned elements: "A" arms=more robust series, "D" arms=more gracile series, "F" sacrum=unburned element mixed with F cremations, "gracile vertebrae"= unattributed to individual

**From Lovejoy (1985) in White and Folkins (1991)

***Degenerative arthritis versus trauma-related osteophtic growth

Notes:

Suture scoring and general age estimates: Buikstra and Uberlaker (1994), except where noted

Maxillary suture scoring: Mann et al. (1991) and Beathier et al. (2010)

Juvenile measurment based age estimates: Scheuer and Black (2004)

Y= young, M/O= middle to older

Appendix 9.3. Sex determination.

Burial	Skull: Nuchal Crest	Skull: Mastoid Process	Skull: Supra-orbital Margin	Skull: Supra-orbital Ridge	Skull: Mental Eminence	Pelvis: Grater Sciatic Notch	Pelvis: Preauricular Sulcus	Limbs: Humerus Length	Limbs: Humerus Septal Aperture	Post-cranial Morphology	Estimated Sex	Comments
2	1-2	2			1-2					gracile	female	
6					4-5						male	
8										very large, robust	male	
9-2										robust	male	
10								293	2	gracile	female	
A	2-3	3-4	4	3	2					intermediate	ambiguous	limbs tentatively associated
B		4			3?						male?	mental eminence damaged, may belong with E
D		2-3				2-3	4			gracile	female	limbs tentatively associated
E		4									male?	
F			3								ambiguous	

Long bone sexing from Trotter and Gleser (1952)

Appendix 9.4 (page 1). Dental inventory and pathology.

Burial	Upper/ Lower	Side	Tooth	Presence	Develop.	Wear	Caries	Abscess	Calculus[a]	Hypoplasia Location[b]	Hypoplasia Age Develop.	Comments
2	Upper	R	M3	2		5	0	9	1/BL	0		loose tooth
			M2	2		10	0	9	1/L	0		loose tooth
			I1	2			9	9	0	0		loose tooth, side/position indet.
		L	M1	2		5	0	9	0	0		loose tooth, asymmetric wear
			M3	2		5	0	9	9	0		loose tooth
	Lower	L	M3	2		4	0	0	1/BL	0		
			M2	7			0	0	1/B	0		
			M1	2		17	1/1	0	1/B	0		
			P4	2		2	0	0	0	0		
			P3	7			9	0	0	9		
			C1	2		4	1	0	9	0		loose tooth
			I2	5				9				
	R		I1	5				9				
		L	I1	5				9				
			I2	5				9				
			C1	5				9				
			P3	2		2	9	9	9	0		loose tooth
			P4	2		2	0	9	1/L	0		loose tooth
			M1	7			9	0	9	0		
			M2	2		15	0	0	2/B	0		
			M3	2		6	0	0	1/B	9		
3	Upper	L	di1	5				0				
			di2	5				0				
			dc1	5				0				
			dm1	2	≥10		0	0	9	9		
			dm2	2	≥10		0	0	9	9		
		L	I2	8	6			0		9		
	Lower	L	dm2	2	11-12		9	0	9	9		
			dm1	2	11-12		9	0	9	9		
			dc1	2	14		9	9	9	9		loose tooth
			di2	5				9				
			di1	5				9				
		R	di1	5				9				
			di2	2	12		0	0	9	9		
			dc1	2	12		0	0	9	9		
			dm1	2	12		9	0	9	9		
			dm2	2	11		0	0	1/B	0		
		L	M2	8	6			0		9		
			M1	1	7	0	0	0		9		loose tooth
			I2	8				0		9		
		R	M1	1	8	0	0	0	1/B	0		
			M2	8	6			0		9		
4	Upper	R	dm2	2	≥7		0	9	1/B	0		loose tooth
			dm1	2	≥7		0	9	1/BL	0		loose tooth
			dc1	2	≥7		0	9	0	9		loose tooth
			di2	7			9	9	9	9		loose tooth
			di1	2	≥11		9	9	0	0		loose tooth
		L	di1	2	≥7		9	9	0	0		loose tooth
			di2	7			9	9	9	9		loose tooth
			dc1	7			9	9	0	0		loose tooth
			dm1	2	≥7		0	9	0	0		loose tooth
			dm2	2	≥7		0	9	0	0		loose tooth
		R	M2	1	5			0		0		loose tooth
			M1	2	≥6	3	0	0	0	0		loose tooth
			P4	1	≥6					0		loose tooth
			P3	1	≥6					0		loose tooth
			C1	1	≥6					0		loose tooth
			I2	1	≥6					0		loose tooth
			I1	1	≥6					0		loose tooth
		L	I1	1	≥6					0		loose tooth
			I2	1	≥6					0		loose tooth
			C1	1	≥6					0		loose tooth
			P3	1	≥6					0		loose tooth
			M1	2	≥6	3	0	0	0	0		loose tooth
			M2	1	5			0		0		loose tooth
	Lower	L	dm2	2	14		1/1	9	0	0		
			dm1	2	14		0	0	0	0		
			dc1	2	14		0	0	0	0		loose tooth
			di2	2	14		0	0	0	0		loose tooth
			di1	7			9	0	9	9		loose tooth
		R	di1	7			9	0	9	9		
			di2	2	14		0	0	0	0		
			dc1	2	14		0	0	0	0		

Appendix 9.4 (page 2). Dental inventory and pathology.

Burial	Upper/ Lower	Side	Tooth	Presence	Develop.	Wear	Caries	Abscess	Calculus[a]	Hypoplasia Location[b]	Hypoplasia Age Develop.	Comments
			dm1	2	14		0	0	0	0		loose tooth
			dm2	2	14		0	9	1/BL	0		loose tooth
		L	M2	1	6			9		0		loose tooth
			M1	2	≥8	2	2	9	0	0		loose tooth
			P4	1	6					0		loose tooth
			P3	1	≥7					0		
			C1	7								
			I2	7								
			I1	7								
		R	I1	7								
			I2	7								
			C1	7								
			P3	1	≥7					0		
			P4	1	6					0		loose tooth
			M1	2	≥10	3	2	9	0	0		loose tooth
			M2	1	6			9		0		loose tooth
6	Upper	R	C1	5				0				
			I2	5				0				
			I1	5				0				
		L	I1	5				0				
			I2	5				0				
	Lower	L	M3	5				0				
			M2	5				0				
			M1	5				0				
			P4	7		*	0	0	0	0		*pathological wear, broken crown
			P3	7			0	0	0	0		
			C1	5				0				
			I2	7			9	0	9			
			I1	5				0				
		R	I1	7			9	0	9			
			I2	5				0				
			C1	2		5	0	0	0	0		
			P3	2		5	0	0	0	0		
7	Upper	R	dm2	2	10		0	0	0	0		loose tooth
			dm1	2	11		0	0	0	0		loose tooth
			dc1	5				0				
			di2	5				0				
			di1	5				0				
		L	di1	5				0				
			di2	5				0				
			dc1	2	≥10		0	0	0	0		loose tooth
			dm1	2	11		0	0	0	0		loose tooth
			dm2	2	10		0	0	0	0		loose tooth
		R	M1	1	5			0		0		loose tooth
		L	M1	1	5			0		9		loose tooth
	Lower	L	dm2	2	10		0	0	0	0		loose tooth
			dm1	2	≥10		0	0	0	0		
			dc1	5				0				
			di2	2	13		0	0	0	0		loose tooth
			di1	5				0				
		R	di1	5				0				
			di2	5				0				
			dc1	2	≥11		0	0	0	0		loose tooth
			dm1	2	≥10		0	0	0	0		
			dm2	2	10		0	0	0	0		loose tooth
		L	M1	8				0		9		
			I2	8	≥6			0		9		
			I1	8				0		9		
		R	M1	8	≥6			0		9		
10	Upper	R	P4	7		1-2	0		0	0		loose tooth, lingual cusp only
		L	I2	2		3	0		0	0		loose tooth
	Lower	L	C1	2		2	0		1/BL	0		loose tooth
		R	M1	7			0		1/BL	0		loose tooth, broken, tentative ID
A[c]	Upper	R	M3	2				0				
			M2	2				0				
			M1	2				0				
			P4	2				0				
			P3	2				0				
			C1	2				0				
			I2	5				0				
			I1	2				0				
		L	I1	2		5	0	0	1/BL	0		

Appendix 9.4 (page 3). Dental inventory and pathology.

Burial	Upper/ Lower	Side	Tooth	Presence	Develop.	Wear	Caries	Abscess	Calculus[a]	Hypoplasia Location[b]	Hypoplasia Age Develop.	Comments
			I2	2		5	0	0	0	1/6.7, 2.9?	2, 3.5 yrs	
			C1	2		4	0	0	0	1/2.9	4-4.5 yrs	
			P3	2		3	0	0	0	1/3.1	4 yrs	
			P4	2		3	0	0	2/BL	0		
			M1	2		22	0	0	1/BL	1/3.5?	2-2.25	
			M2	2		15	0	0	2/BL	0		
			M3	2		10	0	0	3/BL	0		
	Lower[d]	L	M3	2		14	0	0	3/BL	9		
			M2	2		19	0	0	9	9		
			M1	2		20	0	0	2/BL	9		
			P4	2		3	0	0	2/BL	9		
			P3	2		4	0	0	1/BL	9		
			C1	2		4	0	0	0	9		
			I2	2		5	0	0	0	9		
			I1	2		5	0	0	0	9		
		R	I1	2				0				
			I2	2				0				
			C1	2				0				
			P3	2				0				
			P4	2				0				
			M1	2				0				
			M2	2				0				
			M3	2				0				
B*	Lower	L	M3	7		8	0	0	1/BL	9		
			M2	7			9	0	9	9		
			M1	7			9	0	9	9		
			P4	5				0				
			P3	7			9	0	9	9		root only
			C1	5				0				
			I2	7			9	0	9	9		root only
			I1	5				9				
		R	I1	5				9				
			I2	5				9				
C	Lower	L	dm2	2	14		0	0	0	0		
			dm1	2	14		9	0	9	9		
			dc1	5				0				
			di2	5				0				
			di1	5				0				
		R	di1	5				0				
		L	M2	5				0				
			M1	5				0				
			I2	1	≥10			0		0		
			I1	5				0				
		R	M1	7	14		9	0	9	9		root only, in or near full eruption
			M2	1	7-8			0				
D	Upper	R	M3	5				0				
			M2	5				0				
		L	M1	5				0				
			M2	5				0				
			M3	7		~14	9	0	9	9		
	Lower	L	M3	5				0				
			M2	5				0				
			M1	7			9	0	9	9		
			P4	5				0				
		R	P4	5				0				
			M1	7			9	0	9	9		root only
			M2	5				0				
			M3	5				0				

*May belong with E

[a] type/position

[b] type/mm from cingulum

[c] Only the left half of the dental arcade was recorded (there were no significant differences in the right arcade)

[d] heavy calculus deposits and preservative prevent observation of hypoplasias

Notes:
Follows coding guidelines from Buikstra and Uberlaker (1994)
When deciduous dentition is in wear, only observable adult teeth are recorded
Wear, caries, calculus not recorded for teeth in crypts
Missing teeth with no associated alveolar bone are omitted (presence score 3)

Appendix 9.5. Dental measurements.

Burial	Upper/ Lower	I1 Mesiodistal	I1 Labiolingual	I1 Crown Height	I2 Mesiodistal	I2 Labiolingual	I2 Crown Height	C1 Mesiodistal	C1 Labiolingual	C1 Crown Height	P3 Mesiodistal	P3 Buccolingual	P3 Crown Height	P4 Mesiodistal	P4 Buccolingual	P4 Crown Height	M1 Mesiodistal	M1 Buccolingual	M1 Crown Height	M2 Mesiodistal	M2 Buccolingual	M2 Crown Height	M3 Mesiodistal	M3 Buccolingual	M3 Crown Height
2	Upper																11.8	10.3		10.5*	11.6*		7.8	9.5	6.7*
4	Upper	9.2	7.3	12.6	7.0	6.5	10.6	8.2	9.3	9.8	7.4*	9.3*		7.8	10.3	8.6	11.1	11.9	8.2	9.4	10.7	6.2	11.4*		
7	Upper																10.4*	11.0*	6.2*						
10	Upper				7.4	5.5	8.3	8.9	8.9	10.9															
A	Upper	9.6	11.2	9.6	7.0	7.0	9.8	9.2	9.0	11.4	7.4	10.2	8.6	7.0		7.3	11.0	12.9	7.0	10.2	12.7	*6.3*	9.5	11.3	*6.7*
D	Upper																							*10.6*	*5.9*
2	Lower							6.6	7.1	10.2	7.1*			7.1	7.0	7.4	10.5	10.5	5.9	10.7*	10.4*	*6.9*	9.4	10.1	*6.4*
3	Lower																11.7*	10.7*	7.5*						
4	Lower										7.8*	8.4*	*9.0**	7.6	7.9	7.0	12.6	10.7	9.0	12.6	10.2	*6.9*			6.8
6	Lower							8.0	8.8	10.5*	7.6*	8.7	6.6												
10	Lower							7.5	7.4	10.8															
A	Lower	6.0	6.1	7.5	6.8	6.5	7.5	7.3	9.5	11.7	8.1	9.2	9.3	7.3	9.4	8.7	11.8	12.0	6.2	12.0		6.9	11.9	11.9	6.6
B**	Lower																		6.7			7.0		10.0	10.6
D	Lower																		5.7						

*Right antimere, *italics* are approximate

**May belong with E

Notes:

Dental measurements in mm, left arcade

Appendix 9.6. Dental non-metric traits.

		Burial	2		3	4		6	7		10	A	B**	D	
	Tooth	Trait	L	R	R	L	R	L	L	R	L	L	L	L	R
Maxilla	I1	Winging										3			
		Shoveling				6	5				1	3			
		Double-shoveling				0	0				0	0			
	I2	Shoveling				4	4				0	5			
		Double-shoveling				0	0					0			
		Peg-shaped Incisor		0		0	0					0			
	C1	DAR*									4				
	P3	Root Number													
	M1	Hypocone	0			5	4					3.5			
		Metaconule	0			1	1								
		Carabelli's Trait	0			1	1								
		Enamel Extensions													
	M2	Hypocone		2								3			
		Metaconule		0											
		Carabelli's Trait		0											
		Enamel Extensions													
	M3	Hypocone	0	0						3		2			
		Metaconule	0	0						0					
		Carabelli's Trait	0	0						0					
		Enamel Extensions		0						0					
	di1	Shoveling*				2	2								
	dm1	Crown Pattern*				4-	4-								
	dm2	Crown Pattern*				4	4								
		Carabelli's Trait*				1	1		0	0					
Mandible	C1	DAR*						*4-5*			4				
	P3	Root Number													
		Cusp Pattern*				9	9								
	P4	Cusp Pattern*		0		0	0								
	M1	Groove Pattern	Y		Y	X	X					*Y*			
		Cusp Number	5		5	6	6					*4*	5		
		Protostylid	2		0	0	0								
		Cusp 5	3		3	3	3								
		Cusp 6	0		0	2	2								
		Cusp 7	0		0	0	0								
		Root Number													
	M2	Groove Pattern	+	+		X	X					*Y*			
		Cusp Number	4	4		6	6					*4*	5		
		Protostylid	0	0		0	0								
		Cusp 5	0	0		2	2								
		Cusp 6	0	0		2	2								
		Cusp 7	0	0		0	0								
		Root Number						*3*						*2*	*2*
	M3	Groove Pattern										*X*	+		
		Cusp Number	4	5								*4*	4		
		Protostylid	0	0											
		Cusp 5	0	0											
		Cusp 6	0	0											
		Cusp 7	0	0											
		Root Number						2						*1*	*1*
	dc1	Shoveling*				2	2		2						
	dm2	Central Ridge Metaconid*				2	2		2	2					
		Trigonid Crest*				*0*	*0*								
		Cusp 7*				0	0		0	0					

*Turner series, not recorded for CMCC material

**May belong with E

Notes:

Coding follows Buikstra and Uberlaker (1994) series, except where noted

Unobservable traits not recorded (see App 4 for complete dental inventory)

Observations in *italics* are approximate (e.g., severe attrition, pathology, preservative, etc.)

Appendix 9.7. Cranial measurements.

	Name	Abv.	2	6	7	A	B*	D
Cranium	Bizygomatic Diameter (3)	zy-zy				*>116*		
	Basion-Prosthion Length (6)	ba-pr				102.9		
	Maxillo-Alveolar Breadth (7)	ecm-ecm				67.8		*66.7*
	Maxillo-Alveolar Length (8)	pr-alv				54.9		
	Biauricular Breadth (9)	au-au				128.4		
	Upper Facial Height (10)	n-pr				71.7		
	Minimum Frontal Breadth (11)	ft-ft				100.9		
	Upper Facial Breadth (12)	fmt-fmt				117.0		
	Nasal Height (13)	n-ns				60.3		
	Nasal Breadth (14)	al-al		*19.0*		21.1		
	Orbital Breadth (15)	d-ec				40.0		
	Orbital Height (16)					31.4		
	Biorbital Breadth (17)	ec-ec				96.3		
	Interorbital Breadth (18)	d-d				18.0		
	Frontal Chord (19)	n-b				109.8		
	Parietal Chord (20)	b-l				116.9		
	Occipital Chord (21)	l-o				95.7		
	Foramen Magnum Length (22)	ba-o	34.1			35.3	*39.0*	
	Foramen Magnum Breadth (23)					30.4	32.1	
	Mastoid Length (24)					*28.8*	32.6	*31.0*
	Basilar Occipital Length (inf 5a)				14.7			
	Basilar Occipital Width (inf 5b)				26.1			
Mandible	Chin Height (25)	id-gn				32.3		
	Height Mandibular Body (26)		28.1			31.7	27.3	
	Breadth Mandibular Body (27)		15.7			14.8	12.3	
	Bigonial Width (28)	go-go	99.4			114.7		
	Bicondylar Breadth (29)	cdl-cdl				133.1		
	Minimum Ramus Breadth (30)					44.0	35.5	35.2
	Maximum Ramus Breadth (31)					48.5	40.3	
	Maximum Ramus Height (32)					76.2	69.8	
	Mandibular Length (33)		90.3			116.1	103.1	
	Mandibular Angle (34)		125°	90°		*105°*	*110°*	*115°*
	Length of Body (inf 8a)				57.6			

*B mandible may belong with E

Notes:

Measurements in italics are approximate

Numbers in parentheses (XX) refer to Buikstra and Uberlaker (1994) series

All measurements in mm exept where noted

Bilaterial measurements are taken on the left side where possible

Appendix 9.8. Vertebral measurements.

Burial	Vertebra	Ant. Body Ht	Post. Body Ht	Vert. Index	Pathology*
2	cervical 5	10.5	10.4	99.0	
	cervical 6	10.0	11.4	113.5	
	cervical 7	10.0	12.4	124.0	
	thoracic 2	13.1			
	thoracic 3	12.7			
	thoracic 4	13.1			
	thoracic 5	15.0			
	thoracic 6	14.8			
9-2	thoracic indet.	*18.6*	16.0	85.6	degenertive arthritis
	thoracic indet.	15.0			degenertive arthritis
10	thoracic 5	*16.1*			reactive osteophytes
	thoracic 6	17.3			reactive osteophytes
	thoracic 7	18.3			compression fracture
	thoracic 8	20.0			reactive osteophytes
	thoracic 9	*18.6*			
	thoracic 10	*20.0*			

*See Appendix 9.11 for detailed pathology inventory

Notes:

Measurements in *italics* are approximate

Appendix 9.9. Post-cranial measurements.

		2	8		9-2	10		A*		D*	
		R	L	R	L	L	R	L	R	L	R
Scapula	Breadth (39)							103.1			
Clavicle	Maximum Length (35)	138									
	Anterior Diameter Midshaft (36)	8.3	*15.2*						11.1		
	Superior Diameter Midshaft (37)	8.1	*9.7*						8.8		
Humerus	Segment 3 Length					18.8					
	Segment 4 Length					17.0					
	Maximum Length (estimated from seg. 3/4)					293 ± 11					
	Max. Diameter Midshaft (43)			*27.1*		*20.0*				*20.8*	
	Min. Diameter Midshaft (44)			*19.5*		*14.7*				*16.3*	
	Minimum Circumference			68		57					
	Stature Estimate (cm)					156.4 ± 4.5					
Radius	A-P Diameter (46)					*11.6*	*10.5*				*11.4*
	M-L Diameter (47)					*13.8*	*14.5*				*14.4*
	Midshaft Circumference					39	40				
Ulna	A-P Diameter (49)			*19.8*		15.7	15.8				
	M-L Diameter (50)			*16.1*		11.5	12.4				
	Min. Circumference (52)					44	43				
Hand	Metacarpal II Length						63.1				
	Metacarpal III Length						59.7				
	Stature Estimate Metacarpal II (cm)						159.3 ± 4.3				
	Stature Estimate Metacarpal III (cm)						157.3 ± 4.3				
	Proximal Phalanx I Length						29.9				
	Intermediate Phalanx II Length		23.4								
	Distal Phalanx II Length		17.9								
Pelvis	Os Coxae Height (56)							*199*			
Femur	A-P Midshaft Diameter (66)					*23.9*					
	M-L Midshaft Diameter (67)					*22.8*					
	Midshaft Circumference (68)					*73*					
	Pliastric Index					104.8					
Talus	Max. Width Trochlea				*27.7*						

*Reassigned elements: "A" elements=more robust series, "D" elements=more gracile series

Notes:
Measurements in *italics* are approximate
Numbers in parentheses (XX) refer to Buikstra and Uberlaker (1994) series
Stature estimation from Trotter (1970)
All measurements in mm exept where noted

Appendix 9.10. Cranial and post-cranial non-metric traits.

	#	Name	2		3		4		6		7		10	A			B*		C		D	
			L	R	L	R	L	R	L	R	L	R	L	L	M	R	L	R	L	R	L	R
Cranium	2a	Supraorbital Notch												0		1						
	2b	Supraorbital Foramen												0		0						
	3	Infraorbital Suture												0								
	4	Multiple Infraorbital Foramina												0		0						
	5	Zygomatico-facial Foramina														1						
	6	Parietal Foramen														0						
	7a	Epipteric Bone												0		0						
	7b	Coronal Ossicle												*0*		*0*						
	7c	Bregmatic Bone													*0*							
	7d	Sagittal Ossicle													0							
	7e	Apical Bone													0							
	7f	Lamboid Ossicle												0		0						
	7g	Asterionic Bone												0		0					0	0
	7h	Ossicle in Occipito-matoid Suture												0		0						
	7i	Parietal Notch Bone												0		0						
	8	Inca Bone												0		0						
	9	Condylar Canal	1	1	1	1								0		0			0	0		
	10	Divided Hypoglossal Canal		1	0	0					0	0		0		0	0	0	0	0		
	12	Foramen Ovale Incomplete												0		0			0	0		
	13	Foramen Spinosum Incomplete												0		0						
	14	Pterygo-spinous Bridge														2						
	15	Pterygo-alar Bridge												0		0						
	16	Tympanic Dihiscence												0		0						
	17	Auditory Exostosis			0	0					0			0		0	0	0	0	0	0	0
	18a	Mastoid Foramen Location												2		2					1	
	18b	Mastoid Foramen Number												1		1					2	
Mandible	19	Mental Foramen	1	1		1	1**		1		1	1		1		1	1					
	20	Madibular Torus			0	0	2	2	0	0	0	0		0		0	0					
	21a	Mylohyoid Bridge Location	0		0	0			0		2			0		0	0		0	0	0	0
	21b	Mylohyoid Bridge Degree	0		0	0			0		1			0		0	0		0	0	0	0
Atlas	22a	Atlas Bridging Lateral	0	0	0	0								0		0	0	0				
	22b	Atlas Bridging Posterior	0	0	0	0								0		0	0	0				
C7 vertebra	23	Accessory Transverse Foramina	0	0	0	0																
Humerus	24	Septal Aperture											2									

*May belong with E

**1 large foramen with 2 smaller foramina

Notes:

refers to Buikstra and Uberlaker (1994) series

Blank=unobservable, 0=absent

Observations in *italics* are approximate (e.g., damaged or partial element)

Appendix 9.11. Post-cranial pathology.

Burial	Element	#	Portion 1	Observation	Degree	Code*	Comments
8	thoracic 9	1	articular facet	lipping	sharp ridge/spicules	8.1.2	asymmetric, right facets more severe
	thoracic 10	1	articular facet	lipping	sharp ridge/spicules	8.1.2	asymmetric, right facets more severe
	thoracic 11	1	articular facet	lipping	sharp ridge/spicules	8.1.2	asymmetric, right facets more severe
	thoracic vertebra	2	articular facet	lipping	extensive spicules	8.1.3	asymmetric, right facets more severe
	lumbar 2	1	articular facet	lipping	extensive spicules	8.1.3	asymmetric, left facets more severe
	lumbar 3	1	articular facet	lipping	sharp ridge/spicules	8.1.2	asymmetric
	lumbar 4	1	articular facet	lipping	sharp ridge/spicules	8.1.2	asymmetric
	lumbar 5	1	articular facet	lipping	sharp ridge/spicules	8.1.2	asymmetric
	lumbar vertebra	1	body	osteophytes	elevated ring	7.2.2	
	scapula	1	glenoid	lipping	sharp ridge/spicules	8.1.2	right
	intermediate phalanx	1	distal	lipping	slight ridge	8.1.1	
	intermediate phalanx	1	distal	lipping	sharp ridge	8.1.2	
	distal phalanx	2	proximal	lipping	slight ridge	8.1.1	
9-2	thoracic vertebra	4	body	osteophytes	elevated ring	7.2.2	
				form	angular	1.8.1	centra asymmetric
	lumbar vertebra	4	body	osteophytes	curved spicules	7.2.3	2 of 4 have less elevated ring
	sacral vertebra	1	body	osteophytes	curved spicules	7.2.3	
	indet. vertebra	5	body	osteophytes	elevated ring	7.2.2	
	indet. vertebra	2	articular facet	lipping	extensive spicules	8.1.3	
10	thoracic 5	1	body	form	angular	1.8.1	centra asymmetric
			articular facet	lipping	some spicules	8.1.2	reactive osteophytes
	thoracic 6	1	body	form	angular	1.8.1	centra asymmetric
			articular facet	lipping	spicules	8.1.3	reactive osteophytes
	thoracic 7	1	body	fracture	compression	5.1.6	dislocated sup/ant fragment, callus formation
			articular facet	lipping	extensive spicules	8.1.3	severe reactive osteophytic growths on facets
	thoracic 8	1	body	form	angular	1.8.1	centra asymmetric
			articular facet	lipping	spicules	8.1.3	reactive osteophytes
A	cranium	1	parietal	fracture?	depression outer table	5.1.7	depression left superior surface, possible trauma?
	atlas	1	articular facet	lipping	slight ridge	8.1.1	
	axis	1	body	osteophytes	barely discernable	7.2.1	
			articular facet	lipping	slight ridge	8.1.1	
	cervical 3	1	body	osteophytes	barely discernable	7.2.1	
	cervical 4	1	body	osteophytes	barely discernable	7.2.1	
	cervical 5	1	body	osteophytes	barely discernable	7.2.1	
	cervical 6	1	body	osteophytes	barely discernable	7.2.1	
	cervical 7	1	body	osteophytes	barely discernable	7.2.1	
	thoracic vertebra	1	body	osteophytes	elevated ring	7.2.2	
D	cervical 5	1	body	osteophytes	elevated ring	7.2.2	
	cervical 6	1	body	osteophytes	elevated ring	7.2.2	
	thoracic 3	1	articular facet	lipping	sharp ridge/spicules	8.1.2	
	thoracic 4	1	articular facet	lipping	sharp ridge/spicules	8.1.2	
	thoracic 5	1	rib facet	lipping	sharp ridge/spicules	8.1.2	left
	thoracic 6	1	articular facet	lipping	sharp ridge/spicules	8.1.2	
			rib facet	lipping	barely discernable	8.1.1	
	thoracic 7	1	body	osteophytes	elevated ring	7.2.2	
			body	form	angular	1.8.1	centra asymmetric
			articular facet	lipping	extensive spicules	8.1.3	
			rib facet	lipping	barely discernable	8.1.1	left
	thoracic 8	1	body	osteophytes	elevated ring	7.2.2	
			body	form	angular	1.8.1	centra asymmetric
			articular facet	lipping	extensive spicules	8.1.3	
			rib facet	lipping	barely discernable	8.1.1	left
	thoracic 9	1	body	osteophytes	elevated ring	7.2.2	right
			articular facet	lipping	sharp ridge/spicules	8.1.2	
			rib facet	lipping	barely discernable	8.1.1	right
	thoracic 10	1	body	osteophytes	barely discernable	7.2.1	
			rib facet	lipping	sharp ridge/spicules	8.1.2	right
	thoracic 11	1	articular facet	lipping	sharp ridge/spicules	8.1.2	
	thoracic 12	1	articular facet	lipping	sharp ridge/spicules	8.1.2	
	rib	2	head	lipping	extensive spicules	8.1.3	left, likely with T7 and T8
		1	head	lipping	sharp ridge/spicules	8.1.2	right, likely with T9 or T10

*Coding follows Buikstra and Uberlaker 1994

Chapter 10

The Stone Industries

David Brose, William Fox, Patrick Julig,
Darrel G. F. Long, and Kristin Thor

The lithic assemblage associated with the Killarney Bay mortuary complex has acquired almost legendary status since the site was initially excavated. Yet it was the potential of correlating primitive-seeming argillite and meta-quartzite bifaces and preforms with the Lake Huron beaches in which they occurred that first brought the site professional archaeological attention; a potential that radiometric chronology failed to verify. More recently, the variety of lithic sources and techniques in the mortuary contexts and adjacent areas has again attracted archaeological attention. However, with the exception of the relatively few bifacial knives whose hafting and handles had been preserved by copper salts, there has been little actual study of stone tools recovered from the various areas that comprise the Killarney Bay site.

This chapter presents an analysis of the chipped, polished, and ground stone industries and a description of minimally modified coarse stone artifacts such as hammerstones. We include both technological and typological analyses of the chipped stone material. The latter allows for integration of the Killarney Bay material into the existing literature on the Great Lakes Middle Woodland.

The site is characterized by a very wide range of lithic materials, some of which come from very far away, including some from distant southern sources (Figure 10.1). Killarney Bay has been reported to have more chert raw material types represented than other Middle Woodland burial sites in Ontario (Spence et al. 1990). This is to be expected, since the other mortuary artifacts, including shell beads and copper, are also imports from as far as western Lake Superior and southern marine sources (see Chapter 12 and Appendix B). In this chapter we confirm that many of the bifaces in mortuary context are from distant geological sources. However, the vast majority of lithic artifacts from the habitation and manufacturing parts of the site are locally derived quartz and siltstone/argillite, in addition to chert varieties from northern sources (Hudson Bay Lowland) and local materials such as Fossil Hill formation chert, which is very widely distributed.

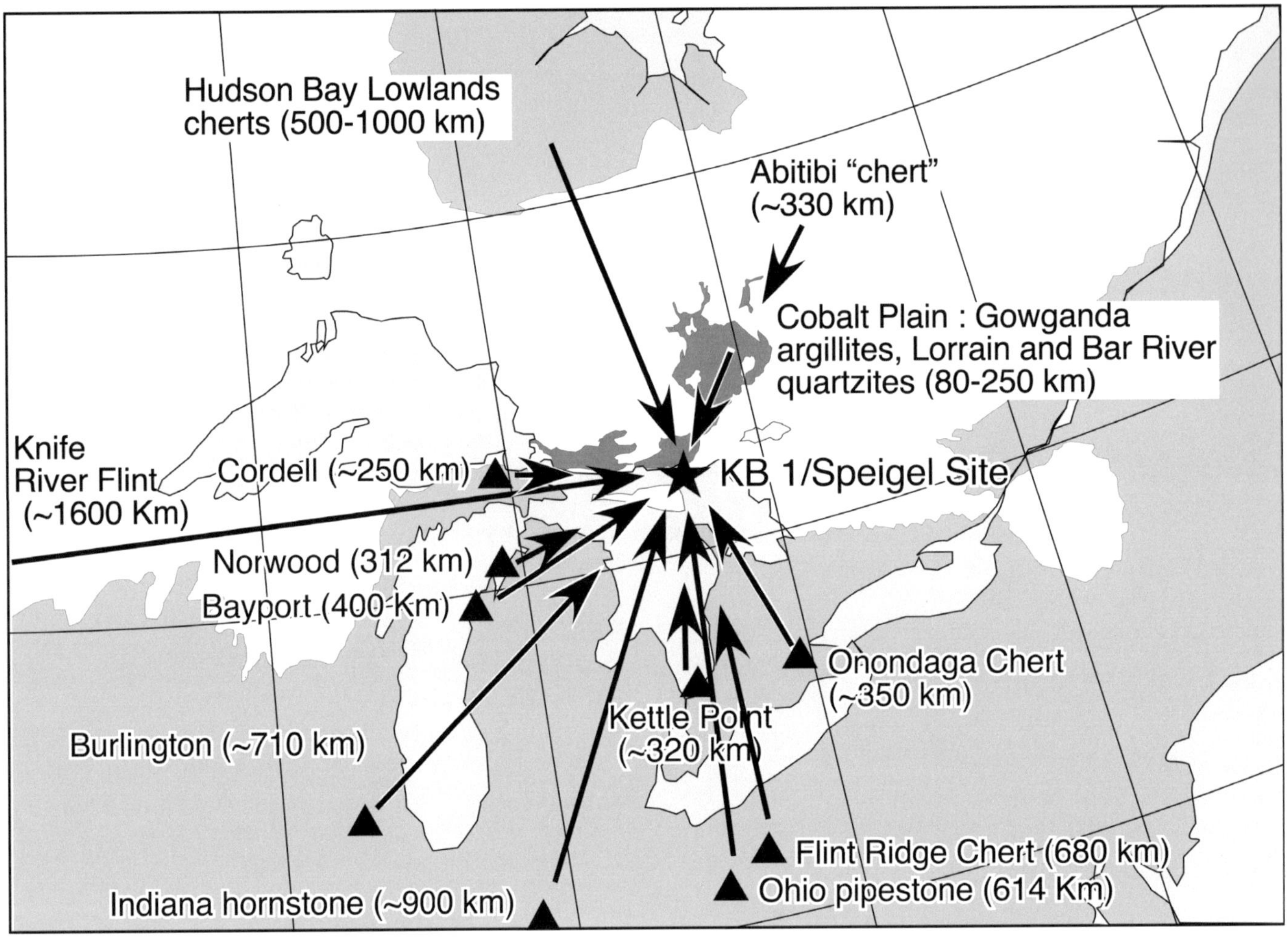

Figure 10.1. Sources for some of the lithic materials found at Killarney Bay.

Context and collections

The lithic material described in this chapter includes artifacts collected by Robert Bell; the University of Michigan team directed by Emerson Greenman; and the Laurentian University field schools. These are referred to below as the Bell, UMMAA, and LU collections, respectively. The excavation techniques and research priorities of the three groups differed, and as a result, collections from each team have been used in different ways. The Bell collections reportedly include debitage, pipes and points, and copper and shell beads (de Lamorandière 1922), but the pipes and points have not been relocated. The remaining Bell material is discussed briefly, but interpretations are limited by a lack of contextual information. The UMMAA materials include formal chipped and ground stone tools and debitage. Until 1949, Greenman's team collected and piece-plotted quartzite flakes and cores, but it is not clear if they collected all debitage or whether they used screens throughout the excavations (Greenman 1953). Greenman's team collected formal tools found in surface context, but not in a systematic fashion. Greenman's tool collection, including bifaces, formal unifaces, pipes, gorgets, and gorget preforms, remains intact. The debitage and utilized flakes from the UMMAA collection have not been analyzed. The Laurentian teams piece-plotted all artifacts, including fire-cracked rock, and screened soil through ¼-inch mesh (some feature soils were screened through 1/8-inch mesh).

The excavators collected all material encountered, making the LU collections appropriate for debitage analysis, in addition to analysis of formal and informal tools.

Ceramic analysis (Chapter 11) and ^{14}C dates (Chapter 4) indicate that the mound area excavated by UMMAA and the habitation area excavated by Laurentian University are essentially contemporary. In this analysis, the datasets from the two areas are examined separately because they likely derive from different activities and differ in the nature of the deposits and recovery. Unprovenienced materials, such as the Bell collection and the UMMAA tools from surface context, are discussed, although their contextual uncertainty is noted.

Sources and qualities of the lithic raw materials

The residents of Killarney Bay used three types of raw material for their stone tools: 1) chert and cryptocrystalline materials; 2) quartz, quartzite, and mylonite; and 3) siltstone, argillite, and other softer sedimentary rocks suitable for manufacture of ground stone tools and ornaments. In some cases, these materials were used to manufacture items locally; in other cases, it appears that the inhabitants of Killarney Bay brought finished or nearly finished objects to the site. In addition, some coarse stone artifacts such as hammerstones and grinding stones were used and discarded in the onsite manufacturing.

The methodology employed for raw material identification varied slightly depending on the collection, although in all cases it was first identified by visual examination and comparison to geological samples from known locations. The raw materials in the Laurentian collection are mainly local. Kristin Thor identified these, in consultation with Patrick Julig and Darrel Long. The Bell collection and the UMMAA collection include exotic raw materials. In order to identify the exotic cherts, a number of experts were consulted, including Jack Holland, Jeff Bursey, William Fox, Pat Julig, and Darrel Long. The geochemical ICP-MS (inductively coupled plasma mass spectrometry) analysis of geological and archaeological cherts was used to confirm visual identifications (Julig et al. 2009; see also Appendix D, this volume). The major types of chert represented—such as Fossil Hill varieties, Hudson Bay Lowland, and other regional and northern cherts—were tested by ICP-MS and other methods in previous studies (Julig and Long 2013). Southern exotics and chert from the mortuary contexts were identified by visual examination but not tested; such analysis was beyond the scope of the present investigation. It is hoped that such testing will be conducted in the future, as the results would be of great significance.

Chert and cryptocrystalline materials

Fine-grained siliceous chert and other cryptocrystalline materials form the second largest fraction of the lithic assemblage by count. They include chert that could be obtained from relatively local sources, as well as a number of cherts from distant sources, both northern and southern. Flaked chert objects are associated with burials but also found in large numbers in the habitation area, specifically certain artifact classes such scraping tools.

Local sources

We consider local chert sources to be those within a distance of about 150 km of the Killarney Bay site. These include bedrock sources of Fossil Hill Formation chert on Manitoulin Island and Gordon Lake "chert." Hudson's Bay Lowland (HBL) chert and possibly Abitibi "chert" (silicified metavolcanic material) may have been obtained from secondary sources, such as glacial outwash deposits, rather than from more distant bedrock sources (see Figure 10.1).

Fossil Hill. The Middle Silurian Fossil Hill Formation includes several chert facies (nodular and bedded), all of which are gray to cream in color and blocky with abundant microfossils. The type locality for the formation is on Manitoulin Island, within 50 km of Killarney Bay (Eley and Von Bitter 1989; and see Figure 10.1). Major used geological outcrops on eastern shores of Manitoulin (Wiki Fossil Hill) are within 25 km. The formation extends along the Niagara Escarpment from just south of the Blue Mountain area to the Bruce Peninsula, then across Manitoulin Island and through the straits of Mackinac, following the north shore of Lake Michigan towards Green Bay as part of the Clinton-Cataract Group.

Several varieties of Fossil Hill chert occur in the archaeological assemblage, including Collingwood, which is found in large, high-quality blocks; Wiki, which is chalkier (porcelainous) and found in medium-size blocks in the main quarry area; and Detour, which is darker in color with patches (Fox 2009). These three variants can be chemically distinguished, as there is a chemical difference with respect to rare-earth elements (Julig et al. 2009; see also Appendix D, this volume). All have characteristic Middle Silurian (llandovery) fossil fauna. Collingwood chert is a cream-colored variety found in the Beaver Valley and as clasts (pebbles, cobbles) in more southern glacial deposits (Eley and Von Bitter 1989; Fox 2009). Wiki chert is a white- to cream-colored variety with occasional banding and common vugs, typically with chalcedonic crystal infill (Fox 2009). It outcrops along the southeastern and western bluffs of Wikwemikong Unceded Indian Reserve on Manitoulin Island. Detour chert is a glossy gray-green to brown variety, found in stratigraphically equivalent strata of the Cordell Formation on the Detour Islands, as pebbles on the shores of Detour Strait, and in outcrops on the northeastern part of Michigan's Lower Peninsula. It may be mottled and can contain distinctive circular white inclusions (Fox 2009).

Hudson Bay Lowland (HBL). Cherts have been identified from a variety of Paleozoic formations in the Hudson Basin, including the early Devonian Stooping River and Kwataboahegan formations, the mid-Silurian Severn River and Ekwan Formation, the late Silurian Kenogami Formation, and the Ordovician Bad Cache Rapids Formation (Figure 10.1). Hudson Bay Lowland chert is a catch-all term established by Fox (1975:34) to describe pebble and cobble cherts glacially transported south from Hudson Basin formations. It is found extensively in secondary deposits in and south of the Hudson Basin, occurring in glacial outwash gravels as far south as the south shore of Lake Superior (Julig et al. 1992). Indigenous people in the Killarney Bay area obtained this material from these local secondary deposits (Fox 2009:355–357).

Bipolar reduction of this chert can result in flakes suitable for small scrapers. The average size of chert nodules decreases from north to the south. HBL chert is highly siliceous and waxy in appearance: it is typically brown or gray and the deep brown color varieties may be confused with Knife River chert (see below) and Lake Superior agate (Julig et al. 1991). As reported initially by Sir Daniel Wilson (1890:85), chert is found on a branch of the Kenogami River. Rudkin (personal communication, 1989) has documented outcrops of the Kenogami Formation on the Kabinakagami River, which contain nodules of black to gray high-quality chert, closely resembling these color variants of HBL chert. In a large sample of high-quality HBL biface preforms on the Spanish River cache, near Killarney, the color varieties ranged from gray to dark brown and blackish, with toffee brown the most common (Julig and Long 2013). In a survey of the lower Albany River within the Stooping River Formation, high quality HBL was fairly common in larger river gravels and cobbles and in biface preform production with massive amounts of debitage on a Middle Woodland (Laurel) site (Julig 1982, 1988).

Gordon Lake. Gordon Lake chert is a metasandstone (a metamorphosed, very fine-grained sandstone: silicified quartz arenite) and is Paleoproterozoic in age. It includes both green and brown varieties. It appears that the preferred material was massive and green, possibly coming from the north-northwest: from the Welcome Lake (~145 km from Killarney Bay) or Smoothwater Lake (~170 km) areas of the Cobalt Plain (see Figure 10.1; Ayer et al. 2010; Card et al. 1973; Long and Colvine 1986). The Gordon Lake Formation is also exposed north of Elliot Lake (~ 106 km; around Flack Lake) and east of Sault Ste. Marie, between Echo Lake (~ 200 km) and Ottertail Lake (180 km: Frarey 1977). Gordon Lake greenish color chert artifacts are fairly common in lithic debitage assemblages from interior sites around Sudbury (based on CRM survey data, Julig, pers. comm), where neither local chert nor quartzite are available, including some examples of very large (ceremonial) bifaces.

Abitibi. Abitibi "chert" consists of fine-grained grayish-green silicified metavolcanic material (probably a metarhyolite, silicified andesitic tuff, or dacite) from the northern part of the Abitibi Greenstone belt, near Lake Abitibi, Quebec. Fox (2009) suggests that this material may have been quarried along the northern margin of Lake Abitibi and was probably extracted from rocks of the Kinojevis Group, following the work of Kritsch-Armstrong (1982) and Pollock (1984). Given that this group occurs in a broad band across the northern margin of the Abitibi belt, extending north of Lake Superior, it may also be a component of glacial outwash to the south. Geochemical analyses of rhyolites from this unit are provided by Kerrich et al. (2008).

Intermediate and distant sources

Other exotic chert types occur at Killarney Bay in small quantities, mostly as mortuary items. Some of these come from southern Ontario and Michigan (see Figure 10.1). Some come from even further away: Indiana, Pennsylvania,

North Dakota, and elsewhere. Full descriptions of cherts from some of these locations can be found in papers by Eley and von Bitter (1989), Fox (2009), and Holland (2005, 2008a, 2008b). Brief descriptions are provided below, but readers must be aware that geochemical testing is often necessary to resolve "look-alike" problems. The fossils and inclusions in lower grade chert are useful for geological identification, but higher quality, knappable varieties of artifacts are often rather different.

South Central Great Lakes basin cherts. Chert in the upper member of the Middle Ordovician Bobcaygeon Formation has been referred to as Balsam Lake chert by Fox (2009). This chert is typically light bluish-gray, with a light yellow weathering patina, a waxy lustre, a well-developed conchoidal fracture, and a highly distinctive pelloidal texture, with lighter colored silicified fossil fragments (Eley and von Bitter 1989; von Bitter and Eley 1984).

Chert from the Middle Devonian (Eifelian to Givetian) Onondaga Formation occurs as nodules of dark gray to light gray mottled material in outcrops distributed along the north shore of Lake Erie, east of the Grand River (Fox 2009; and see Figure 10.1). Chert is also present in the Middle Devonian Dundee Formation, along the shore of Lake Erie between Pelee Island and the mouth of the Grand River (Telford and Tarrant 1975). This microcrystalline chert, also known as Selkirk chert (Fox 2009), may be white mottled with gray-brown inclusions; dark gray to gray-brown with lighter and darker inclusions; black mottled with white inclusions; or light brown mottled with white and brown inclusions (Eley and von Bitter 1989). It is typically dull to waxy or lustreless, with an irregular or subconchoidal fracture, and may contain fossils, including crinoid fragments. Key features are mottling, a light-colored patina, and the presence of styolites.

Chert found at the contact between the Late Devonian Kettle Point and underlying Ipperwash formations is a waxy, dense, nonporous, dark microcrystalline chert. It may be brown to bluish-gray to black and may be mottled with minor lamination (Eley and von Bitter 1989; Fox 2009; Janusas 1984). It is characterized by rusty staining, related to the presence of ferruginous inclusions.

Other source material represented in the site's assemblages may have come from several locations in Michigan. Yellowish-gray chert may have come from the Late Mississippian Bayport limestone. Bayport chert occurs in Huron and Arenac counties in the Saginaw Bay area. Samples collected from the Charity Islands include a nodular replacement chert with a sugary texture (recrystallized medium sand grade pelloids) and an irregular cleavage. Porcellanite layers in these samples are spherical to subspherical, with gray well-crystallized material encompassed by spherical layers of light gray to white porcellanite. The samples examined also contained abundant dark grains, representing carbonaceous or phosphatic fossil material.

White to light gray chert with moderately well-developed planar to wavy lamination, a dull lustre, and a subconchoidal fracture may come from the Norwood limestone of northwest Michigan (see Figure 10.1). This material appears granular under the binocular microscope (possibly representing silicified pelloids of very coarse silt to very fine sand grade) and appears to be a bedded replacement chert with minor black grains and where preserved, a pale yellow weathering patina.

Material identified as Mackinac chert may have been derived from the Devonian Bois Blanc Formation, exposed on Mackinac Island, Michigan, beneath the bridge. Equivalent cherty dolostones are also present in southern Ontario.

Beyond the southern Great Lakes basin. Chert possibly derived from the Middle Pennsylvanian Allegheny Formation in Ohio (~770 km south of Killarney Bay) and adjacent parts of Pennsylvania has been characterized as Vanport chert by Holland (2005) and Flint Ridge chert by Mullet (2009) and others. It is typically a black to medium gray silicified mudstone, with a waxy lustre and subconchoidal fracture. It may contain sponge spicules and small multilayered spherules that have a light-yellow weathering patina. Cherts from the late Early Mississippian (Tournasian) Burlington Limestone in Illinois (William et al. 1975) are typically waxy and moderately translucent. They are white to light gray to cream-colored when fresh but take on pink, red, or orange colors when heat-treated (Holland 2008a; Morrow 1995).

Chert from Indiana present in Killarney Bay assemblages (based on visual characteristics) includes material from the Muldraugh member of the Mississippian Borden Formation (Holland 2008b; Smith 1965) as well as blue-gray chert in the upper part of the Fredona member of the Mississippian Ste. Genevieve limestone (~860 km south-southwest of the site). This has been referred to as Indiana hornstone by Luedtke (1978, 1979) and Wyandotte chert by Smith (1990) and Morrow et al. (1992). Chemical characteristics of the Wyandotte chert have been examined by Glascock (2004) but were not geochemically tested in this study. It is typically opaque, gray, cryptocrystalline material, with a glassy lustre; it may have dusty or light gray patination with hints of yellow or tan (Mullet 2009).

North Dakota material, tentatively identified in the Killarney Bay assemblages, includes examples of Knife River chert (KRF). This occurs in a primary context in the Eocene-aged Golden Valley Formation, which is now completely eroded. Today, KRF is found only in a secondary context in western North Dakota, in Dunn and Mercer Counties, in gravels along the Missouri River about 1,600 km west of Killarney Bay (see Figure 10.1; Clayton et al. 1970). This raw material was widely traded throughout the Midwest and Northeast since Paleoindian times (Julig et al. 1991). KRF is semi-translucent brown to golden brown in color and contains fossil algae fragments. It can be visually misidentified with some translucent varies of brown semi-translucent HBL chert.

Quartz, quartzite, and mylonite (QQM)

Two quartzite-bearing formations (silicified quartz arenite) occur locally: the Paleoproterozoic Lorrain and Bar River formations (see Figure 2.3, this volume). The Lorrain Formation is older and occurs in a lower stratigraphic position and is separated from strata of the Bar River Formation by mudstones of the Bar River Formation. The upper part of the Lorrain Formation is medium to coarse sand grade and is white to light greenish white. In comparison, the Bar River Formation is of medium to fine sand grade and can be white or pink and tan in color. Within both formations, local cataclastic metamorphism (dynamic grinding) has altered the structure, resulting in a glassier texture, which was preferred by flintknappers (Julig and Long 2010; Long, Julig, and Hancock 2002). Similar Precambrian quartzites occur in a broad belt from Michigan to Quebec. These can be distinguished from quartzite occurring in Killarney using petrographic analysis of grain size (Julig, Long, and Hancock 1998).

Mylonite in the vicinity of Killarney Bay is a dynamically metamorphosed, stress-recrystallised metasandstone or feldspathic gneiss that is found in narrow bands within the La Cloche range along the contact between the Southern and Grenville geological provinces. It is present locally in a belt passing through Lamorandière Bay (see Figure 2.3). Robert Bell, the geologist who first investigated and excavated at Killarney Bay, reported a local brown chert, which may have been the mylonite. It is typically grayish-brown in color and finer grained than the local Proterozoic quartzites.

Vein quartz is ubiquitous in the Canadian Shield and occurs in small amounts in this assemblage. No clear source location(s) can be identified.

Siltstone and argillite

Argillite is a fine-grained metamorphosed mudstone that may appear banded due to preservation of original bedding features. It is typically dark green in color due to the presence of reduced iron or, more commonly, of abundant chlorite. The upper part of the Paleoproterozoic Gowganda Formation (Firstbrook member) represents a potential source for most of these artifacts, which are chlorite rich. The formation is exposed locally to the northwest of the site (5 to 10 km), and more extensively to the north and north-northeast, where it extends from just north of the Killarney region to Cobalt and Rouyn-Noranda (see Figure 10.1). It is also glacially transported and can be scavenged widely. A key identification feature is the presence of thin-graded laminae (1 to 3 mm thick). This raw material can be both flaked and easily ground. It is also found as cobble- to boulder-sized clasts in secondary glacial and beach deposits close to the site. Several beach boulders of argillite with cores removed were observed during survey along Collins Inlet a few kilometers south of Killarney Bay (Julig et al. 2006; Pitawanakwat, Peltier, and Julig 2004).

Other raw materials

Ohio firestone

Another fine-grained mudstone that may have been used is Ohio firestone, also known as Ohio pipestone (Wisseman et al. 2002). This is a Phaneozoic (Carboniferous) "flint-clay" or hard kaolinite that developed as a seat earth (an old soil) beneath coal seams. It is now exposed near Portsmouth, Ohio, some 614 km south of Killarney Bay (see Figure 10.1).

Granite

Granite is a coarse-grained igneous rock, consisting predominantly of coarse-grained quartz and feldspar, with or without micas or hornblende. Along with associated granodiorite, syenite, and quartz monzonite, it makes up almost half of the Superior Geological Province of the Canadian Shield (shown in white on Figure 10.1), so it is not source specific. Granite-like rocks with a strong planar fabric (gneisses) are also common in the Grenville Geological Province, which lies beneath Killarney Bay and extends from central southern Ontario to eastern Quebec and Labrador. These materials, which were probably used as a raw material for hammerstones, are also a common component of glacial outwash. They were most likely recovered from secondary sources rather than primary bedrock.

Lithic materials from mortuary contexts

The UMMAA collections include clusters of artifacts found in association with the Killarney Bay burials. In general, these are chert biface preforms or finished objects, intentionally interred with the individuals buried. Most of the stone burial objects are chert bifaces, but flaked quartzite and ground stone artifacts also occur. Occasionally Greenman's team recovered objects from disturbed contexts associated with burials.

Many of the items in the Bell collection probably derived from mortuary context, but we have no way to determine which of the several burials they are associated with. As is evident from the descriptions of the UMMAA collections, the items in each burial are distinctive. Some suggest northern connections while others reflect southern ones. For this reason, we list the materials in the Bell collection, but interpretation is limited by the lack of provenience information.

Lithic materials from burials

Burial 1

This child was interred with three bifaces: one of HBL chert found at the edge of the pit, one of local quartzite, and the third of an unidentified Paleozoic chert, similar to Selkirk chert from southern Ontario (Fox 2009:362). In general, there is a northern Ontario cast to these offerings. However, the biface made of Paleozoic chert is an expanding stem form reminiscent of Etley points, which are common in Illinois and Missouri (Justice 1987:146–148).

Burial 2

Two large exotic chert bifaces are among the offerings associated with this adolescent female. One biface is of Bayport chert from Saginaw Bay, Michigan (Ozker 1982:83–86) and the other is manufactured from Muldraugh chert from southern Indiana (Cantin 2008:56–60; Holland 2008a:21). Consequently, there is a southern origin for these items, with both notched bifaces conforming to the "Snyders Cluster" (Justice 1987:201–204) in form. According to Justice, Snyders points may be attributed to the early Middle Woodland and are widely distributed in the northeast, with a few examples known from New York and the upper peninsula of Michigan (Justice 1987:203).

Burial 4

This adult male was accompanied by 28 ovate to leaf-shaped biface preforms, all of north Lake Huron shore materials (Figures 10.2, 10.3). The majority (21, plus a possible Lake Manitou variant) are the Wiki variant of Fossil Hill Formation chert available from the east end of Manitoulin Island (Fox 2009:360). Two (and possibly two more) are of the Detour variant from the same formation. The final two bifaces are of local quartzite or mylonite. The forms of the bifaces are described as ovate, leaf-shaped, or trianguloid. The latter may have affinities to the Pomranky points, which are similar to Meadowood cache blades (Justice 1987:145). The distribution of this point form is restricted compared to that of Snyders, but includes Michigan, southern Ontario and Quebec, and parts of New York and Pennsylvania (Justice 1987:145). The majority of the bifaces in this group have red ochre staining. This is a strongly local assemblage.

Burial 6

All 39 biface preforms associated with this young adult male are of HBL chert (Fox 2009:355–357, Fig. 2), available in secondary deposits to the north and east of Lake Superior and possibly acquired from "a branch of the Kinogami River, ...called by the Indians Flint River (*Pewona sipi*) from the abundance of the favorite material they find in the river gravel and shingle." (Wilson 1890:85). The forms of the bifaces in this group are similar to those in Burial 4: they are ovate, trianguloid, and leaf shaped (Figures 10.4, 10.5). This offering also has a strong northern flavor, but it clearly differs from Burials 1 and 4 in that the raw

Figure 10.2. Biface preforms from Burial 4 at Killarney Bay, all from north Lake Huron shore materials. Most of the 28 biface preforms found with this burial have red ochre staining.

material is not strictly local. HBL chert can be considered an intermediate material (not too distant), as it is common at sites along Lake Huron's north shore area, such as along the Spanish River (Julig and Long 2013). At Killarney Bay, many of the scrapers are from HBL glacial cobbles and beach pebbles. One is struck by the uniformity in the raw material at this burial.

Burial 7

Two bifaces were recovered with this infant burial: one is a lobate stemmed form of Bayport chert and the other a leaf-shaped preform of Gordon Lake/Abitibi chert from northeastern Ontario (Fox 2009:358). The stemmed point may be an Adena or Kramer point. These offerings resemble those in Burial 1, in that there is a mix of local and distant raw materials and forms.

Burial 8

All nine bifaces included with this older adult male are exotic, and seven exceed 100 mm in length (Figure 10.6). Three are of Vanport formation ("Flint Ridge") chert (Kagelmacher 2001:95–105) from central Ohio, and at least two, and possibly as many as four, are of Burlington formation chert (Holland 2008a:4) from the Mississippi Valley to the southeast. The final two, which are less than 100 mm in length, are manufactured from Bayport and Norwood chert (Stafford 1998). The two possible

Figure 10.3. Three biface preforms from Burial 4 at Killarney Bay.

Burlington chert bifaces are of Snyders form, as are two of the Vanport chert specimens and the Bayport chert biface. The third Vanport chert biface is a Robbins blade, while the two Burlington chert bifaces are Little Bear Creek variants of the "Dickson Cluster" (Justice 1987:196–197). Justice (1987:188) considers Robbins blades to be an Early Woodland type centered south of the Great Lakes. This offering is strongly southern in origin.

Several objects from the disturbed edge of Burial 8 include both local and exotic materials. A stemmed point from Wiki chert bears similarity to Kramer points. Two preforms are made from local materials: Detour chert and quartzite. Exotics include a biface tip of Burlington chert and a side-struck flake of Bayport chert. There are at least three hafted Snyders blades (Figures 10.7, 10.8, 10.9) that display small-diameter hafts and minimal binding, suggesting their use for display as opposed to a cutting or projectile point function (Fox 2010:10).

Burial 9

Two large Vanport chert biface preforms and two smaller Bayport chert leaf-shaped biface preforms were interred with a cremated adolescent and an older adult male. One of the Vanport chert preforms is of an unusual rectangular or quadrilateral form. These offerings also have a southern origin.

Figure 10.4. The young adult male in Burial 6 was accompanied by 39 biface preforms, all made of Hudson Bay Lowland chert.

Burial 10

The offerings associated with this young female included 37 bifaces, two pipes, and a catlinite groover (Figure 10.10). Of the bifaces, 14 or perhaps 15 are of local Wiki, Providence Bay (a visually distinctive variant of Fossil Hill chert), and Detour chert (Fox 2009: Fig. 3). Ten or eleven are of northeastern Ontario HBL and Gordon Lake/Abitibi chert. Seven to ten are exotic materials from southern sources, including Bayport, Kettle Point, Vanport, Wyandotte, and possibly Onondaga cherts, and one biface is of an unidentified material. The Wyandotte chert biface is of classic Adena-stemmed "Dickson Cluster" form (Justice 1987:191–196). Two of the Vanport (Flint Ridge) chert specimens are of Snyders form and two are Robbins blades. Two Little Bear Creek style Bayport chert bifaces were discovered in wood hafts, and one of the Snyders style Vanport chert bifaces exceeds 100 mm in length.

The two Bayport chert specimens were bound to small wooden hafts with split bark binding. Given the size and weight of these bifaces, such hafts are unlikely to have served as knife handles but may have functioned as inserts for display of the items. Display of these exotics in the context of a mortuary ceremony is consistent with the hypothesized emic quality of such

Figure 10.5. Biface preforms from Burial 6, all crafted from Hudson Bay Lowland chert.

items within a major social gathering, as discussed by Abel et al. (2001) at the Williams site on the Maumee River in northern Ohio.

This burial included two tubular pipes (see description below). One is likely made of reddish Feurt Hill pipestone, and the other is probably from gray Feurt Hill pipestone, both from Ohio. The first is described as tapered, the second as blocked end (Figure 10.11).

A grooved punch, likely made of catlinite, completes the assemblage from this burial, which is the only burial that has local, northern, and southern materials and forms represented in significant quantities.

Other tools and ornaments in the UMMAA collections, not assigned to specific burials

There are 37 other chipped stone objects in the UMMAA collections that were not recovered from clear mortuary contexts, but rather from around the site in mostly surface contexts. The provenience of these objects ranges from "on road, 50 ft from farm gate" to "surface of upper terrace."

Table 10.1 lists the raw material of bifaces from nonmortuary contexts. This shows that most of the bifaces are produced from local chert, and that other raw materials

Figure 10.6. In Burial 8, archaeologists found nine bifaces: all were crafted of materials from distant sources.

Figures 10.7 (above left), 10.8 (above right), and 10.9 (left). Hafted blades from Burial 8.

Figure 10.10. Many of the 37 bifaces found with the young woman in Burial 10 are of local materials.

from Ontario the U.S. are present in limited numbers by comparison to the mortuary cache blades.

A range of notched and stemmed biface forms are represented in this assemblage, including a number of types encountered in the burials, such as Snyders and Kramer points. In some cases, these forms occur on points made of exotic raw materials, such as Burlington, and in other cases, they occur on points made from local Wiki chert. There are also several examples of preforms or blanks from Wiki chert and Gowganda argillite.

The quartzite pieces in the UMMAA collections that have no burial provenience are relatively evenly split between finished objects and preforms. The bifaces include one identified as a stemmed Lowe point, one unnotched biface, and one narrow-waisted biface.

A number of siltstone and argillite objects in the UMMAA collections have no mound provenience. The majority of these are preforms or rough-outs and are discussed below; manufacturing of gorgets and other ground stone argillite was evident in the habitation area.

Tools and ornaments in the Bell collection

The Bell collection includes two chert bifacial pieces. One is a biface tip from Flint Ridge chert and the other is a leaf-shaped biface from Detour chert. The Detour chert biface has a width to thickness ratio of 3.6 and is flaked alternately.

One quartzite biface tip and one broken mylonite biface are extant in the Bell collection. The mylonite biface has a relatively thick width to thickness ratio (2.4) and may have been used as a sidescraper. The biface tip has some cortex on it and is only flaked unifacially. It may have been discarded onsite during manufacture.

Finally, the collection includes one backed biface made of mudstone. The width to thickness ratio is 2.3 and the nature of flaking could not be determined.

Lithic materials from nonmortuary contexts

This section presents the analysis of the lithic materials in the Laurentian University collections, with comparisons to select items in the Bell and UMMAA collections. We begin with a discussion of the chert artifacts, follow with a description of the quartzite material, and conclude with the siltstone and argillite pieces.

Chert artifacts

The following raw materials are represented in the Laurentian collection: Fossil Hill (variant not determined), Fossil Hill (Wiki), low-grade chert (possibly Fossil Hill), Gordon Lake, HBL, Knife River, and Muldraugh. The vast majority of the chert from nonmortuary contexts may be classified as Fossil Hill, both by count and by mass (Table 10.2). HBL chert is also well represented in the assemblage but makes up only about 10 percent of the total material, both by count and by mass. Gordon Lake chert is uncommon, and Knife River flint and possible Muldraugh chert are only represented by single examples.

The chert materials from the habitation area can be further sorted. Table 10.3 presents the tools recovered during the Laurentian field schools, classified by tool category. Utilized pieces comprise almost half of the tools from the habitation area. Utilized pieces are defined as those that are "lightly retouched pieces with less than 1.5 mm vertical retouch" (Julig 1994:101).

Approximately 40 percent of the tools are scrapers of various kinds. Three types of scrapers are recognized: endscrapers, in which the modified edge is opposite to the striking platform; sidescrapers, in which the modified edge is perpendicular to the striking platform; and other scrapers. Other scrapers are random pieces with retouch that is greater than 1.5 mm vertically (Julig 1994). Thumbnail scrapers are considered a type of endscraper.

The remainder of the tools consist of bifacial types, including finished tools such as projectile points, broken tools, and preforms. The assemblage includes approximately equal numbers of Fossil Hill and HBL tools, despite the fact that Fossil Hill chert is much more common in general. Apparently more finished HBL tools were brought to Killarney Bay, while more Fossil Hill chert tools were produced onsite when needed. This is supported by examination of the tool types. There are more utilized pieces of Fossil Hill chert, and the proportion of scrapers of HBL is disproportionately high. This difference is significant at the 0.05 level (Fisher's exact test). It is interesting to note that the raw materials from distant or intermediate sources are not always represented by formed tools. There are no tools of Knife River flint in this sample, and the Gordon Lake tool is a utilized piece. The example of Muldraugh chert is a broken biface, perhaps intended for or disturbed from a mortuary context. (A Muldraugh chert biface was also recovered from Burial 2.)

Chert debitage

Table 10.4 shows the debitage categories for chert artifacts from the habitation area by count and mass. Clearly, the vast majority of chert lithic material from this part of the site is debitage, indicating a significant amount of knapping was carried out at the site. This involved mainly Fossil Hill chert, but also a significant quantity of HBL chert.

In all debitage categories, the average size of HBL fragments is smaller than that of the Fossil Hill (Table 10.5). Over one-third of the HBL debitage is extremely small (less than 0.2 g), whereas only 12 percent of the Fossil Hill debitage is this small. The difference in the size of Fossil Hill versus HBL debitage is significant (Kolmogorov-Smirnov, $\alpha = 0.01$).

Several factors probably account for this: HBL chert occurs in smaller nodules in secondary deposits such as glacial gravels and beaches (Julig et al. 1991). By contrast, Fossil Hill chert (Wiki variety) is quarried from primary outcrops, about 20 km across the water on Manitoulin Island. Secondly, HBL chert (in its core area) is found at a greater distance from Killarney Bay than Fossil Hill chert (see Figure 10.1), but smaller cobbles and pebbles of HBL chert are available in beach and river gravels within less than 150 kilometers. Finally, as discussed above, a high proportion of the HBL sample is represented by formed

Figure 10.11. Archaeologists found two tubular pipes in Burial 10: both are probably of Feurt Hill pipestone from Ohio.

Table 10.1. Raw material of bifaces recovered in nonmortuary contexts by University of Michigan teams, in descending order of abundance.

Raw material	Number of bifaces
Wiki	11
Lorrain quartzite	3
Gordon Lake/Abitibi	3
Onondaga	3
Gowganda argillite	2
Detour	2
Bayport	2
Norwood	2
Hudson Bay Lowland	1
Kettle Point	1
Burlington	1
Unidentified	6

Table 10.2. Chert raw material by count and mass from the habitation area at Killarney Bay.

	Fossil Hill	Fossil Hill Wiki variant	Low grade	Hudson Bay Lowland	Gordon Lake	Knife River	Muldraugh	Indeterminate	Total
n	7441	7	342	1027	13	1	1	2	8834
Mass (g)	8325	17	327	993	24	< 1	29	5	9721

Table 10.3. Formed and informal chert tools from the habitation area by raw material type (n).

	Fossil Hill	Fossil Hill Wiki variant	Low grade	Hudson Bay Lowland	Gordon Lake	Knife River	Muldraugh	Indeterminate	Total
Bifacial tools									
Backed biface				1					1
Biface	1			1					2
Biface drill	1								1
Biface preform	1								1
Bifacial knife				1					1
Projectile point				1					1
Projectile point preform	1								1
Fragmentary biface	4	2		2			1		9
Fragmentary projectile point	1								1
Graver	2			1					3
Scrapers									
Endscraper	18			31					49
Scraper	3			4					7
Sidescraper	4			4					8
Thumbnail scraper	1			5					6
Informal tools									
Utilized piece	51		2	37	1			1	92
Total tools	88	2	2	88	1	0	1	1	183

Note: In the more detailed analysis of scrapers represented in Tables 10.7 to 10.11, some scraper categories were combined. Several artifacts were reclassified in the final analysis, as these plow-zone battered artifacts were occasionally ambiguous.

Table 10.4. Debitage categories for chert artifacts recovered from the habitation area. Top number is number of artifacts; bottom number is mass in grams.

	Fossil Hill	Fossil Hill Wiki variant	Low grade	Hudson Bay Lowland	Gordon Lake	Knife River	Indeterminate	Total
Complete flake	1733 1715.5	1 1.8	79 89.9	275 168.0	4 9.5			2092 1984.6
Broken flake	603 544.4		57 72.5	69 41.5	1 1.4			730 659.9
Flake fragment	2619 1438.2	1 2.9	139 83.6	478 201.7	7 12.4	1 0.5		3245 1739.2
Debris	2385 4002.7	3 2.3	65 70.1	114 133.2			1 4.5	2568 4212.8
Total	7340 7700.8	5 7.0	656.1 316.1	936 544.4	12 23.2	1 0.5	1 4.5	8635 8596.5

Table 10.5. Average mass of debitage categories by raw material.

	Fossil Hill	Fossil Hill Wiki variant	Low grade	Hudson Bay Lowland	Gordon Lake	Knife River	Indeterminate
Complete flake	0.99	1.76	1.14	0.61	2.38		
Broken flake	0.90		1.27	0.60	1.39		
Flake fragment	0.55	2.92	0.60	0.42			
Debris	1.68	.76	1.08	1.17	1.76	0.48	4.51

Table 10.6. Chert cores recovered from the habitation area of Killarney Bay by raw material. Numbers in parentheses indicate average mass in grams.

	Fossil Hill	Fossil Hill Wiki variant	Low grade	Hudson Bay Lowland	Gordon Lake	Knife River	Indeterminate	Total
Core	8 (20.3)							8
Bipolar core	2 (10.8)			2 (5.62)				4
Biface core	1 (36.5)							1
Total	11	0	0	2	0	0	0	13

tools such as scrapers. These appear to have been curated, and the very small size (<= 1 g) of about 85 percent of the HBL debitage suggests that a significant portion were derived from resharpening these tools. Many of the small HBL flakes are resharpening flakes.

Chert cores

The data from cores support those from other artifact types. In general, very few chert artifacts are classified as cores. Of these, only two raw materials are represented: Fossil Hill and HBL (Table 10.6). Fossil Hill cores are much more common than HBL cores. All of the cores are small in size, but the HBL cores are particularly small. This suggests that ancient knappers worked this raw material more intensively before considering the cores exhausted. It is noteworthy that both cores classified as HBL are bipolar cores. Bipolar reduction is frequently a strategy for reducing raw material nodules that are small in size (Andrefsky 1994). Small size HBL pebble chert from the south shore of Lake Superior was utilized for flake tools, using bipolar reduction (Julig et al. 1992).

The Fossil Hill cores range from pieces with more than two-thirds of the surface flaked to pieces with less than a third flaked. Almost all cores have some cortex remaining on the surface. The cores that are not classified as bipolar are described as irregular and polyhedral, most having multiple parallel flake scars. This suggests production of flakes for informal tools, perhaps for immediate uses, in which the form of the blank may have been less important than the form of the edge (Andrefsky 2005:227).

Chert tools

In addition to the basic debitage analysis and categorization of tools described above, our work included metric analysis of tools from all the excavations. The materials in the Laurentian collections are considered representative of the nature of objects in the habitation area but are compared with selected tools from the Bell collection and UMMAA collections.

A range of different scraper types occur. These include endscrapers, sidescrapers, and other scrapers, as defined above.

Endscrapers. In the Laurentian collections, endscrapers occur in a wide range of sizes. There are more HBL endscrapers, but the number of Fossil Hill examples is not insubstantial. Both types of raw materials show a large range in size, and the HBL scrapers are slightly smaller than the Fossil Hill ones (Table 10.7). However, this difference is not significant.

The UMMAA and Bell collections also contained endscrapers. Table 10.8 shows a summary of the dimensions of Fossil Hill and HBL endscrapers from the UMMAA collection. There are many more scrapers in this collection than in the Laurentian collection, suggesting that scraping activities occurred over much of the site, including around the upper terrace and mortuary area. In the UMMAA collection, there are an additional five endscrapers that are tentatively identified as Balsam Lake chert. These are not included in this comparison. As was the case in the Laurentian collection, there is little difference in the average dimensions of the two main raw material types. The dimensions of the Fossil Hill scrapers from the two collections are similar in size and there is no significant difference in their lengths. However, there is a statistically significant difference in the size of the HBL scrapers from the two collections—those from the Laurentian excavations are smaller. This may arise from the fact that the Laurentian crews screened for artifacts, while the Michigan crews did not always do so. The Bell collection only contains three endscrapers: two of HBL and one of Fossil Hill. Their sizes are comparable to those in the other two collections.

A second difference that we observed between the two collections was in bit height, or the vertical height of edge retouch from ventral surface of flake tool in millimeters. This difference occurs for both raw materials. The bit heights in the UMMAA collection endscrapers are approximately 2 mm greater than those in the Laurentian collection. For both raw materials this is a statistically significant difference. Given that the scrapers were measured twice by the same person (Julig), we argue that the difference is real and not an artifact of the analysis. For this reason, it is important to suggest some potential reasons for the difference. This may suggest that the scrapers in the UMMAA collections were more heavily used and resharpened than the ones in the Laurentian collection. If the area of the UMMAA collection was a center of activity for a long period of time, while that of the Laurentian excavation was used relatively lightly, this could explain the difference: scrapers left at the end of one visit may have been relocated, rehafted, and reused on subsequent visits. Alternatively, the nature of scraping activities may have been different in the two locations.

Table 10.7. Comparison of dimensions of Fossil Hill and HBL endscrapers from the Laurentian excavations.

	Fossil Hill, n = 19				Hudson Bay Lowland, n = 35			
	Max	Min	Mean	St dev	Max	Min	Mean	St dev
Mass (g)	55.6	1.2	9.1	12.4	46.2	0.5	6.6	8.4
Length (mm)	57.2	17.1	30.8	10.1	49.0	11.4	26.8	8.5
Width (mm)	43.6	15.1	24.5	8.0	41.5	10.6	21.8	6.4
Thickness (mm)	26.5	3.8	10.1	6.3	25.4	2.2	8.5	4.6
Bit height (mm)	9.2	2.1	4.5	1.6	9.4	1.8	4.5	1.8

Table 10.8. Comparison of the dimensions of endscrapers in the UMMAA collections by raw material.

	Fossil Hill, n = 47				Hudson Bay Lowland, n = 44			
	Max	Min	Mean	St dev	Max	Min	Mean	St dev
Length (mm)	67.4	15.2	35.9	9.6	64.1	16.8	31.9	9.8
Width (mm)	44.5	16.4	28.3	6.3	40.3	13.5	26.1	6.6
Thickness (mm)	20.2	4.3	10.6	3.5	19.6	2.8	9.6	3.5
Bit height (mm)	11.2	1.8	6.5	2.5	12.8	1.9	6.3	2.5

A further explanation may be that by screening, the LU excavators may have found smaller scraper tool fragments with smaller bit heights. As noted above, the LU excavations recovered more small HBL scrapers.

A further consideration with respect to the mortuary area scrapers may merit investigation: were they being used in mortuary activities, possibly defleshing? This type of activity has been suggested for similar tools at Middle Woodland Laurel mounds in northwestern Ontario/Minnesota boundary.

Sidescrapers. The number of recovered sidescrapers in the Laurentian collections is quite low, comprising only eight chert tools (Table 10.9). Once again, we find that the average dimensions of HBL tools are slightly less than those of Fossil Hill tools, but that the difference is not significant.

The sample of sidescrapers from the Michigan excavations is larger than that in the Laurentian collection, but once again, it is substantially smaller than the sample of endscrapers. There appears to be little difference in the average dimensions by raw materials. Although at first glance there do appear to be differences in the overall dimensions of scrapers in the two collections, these are insignificant because the sample sizes are so small and because there is significant variation in size within the samples (Table 10.10).

Once again, we observe a difference in bit height and once again, despite the very small number of objects involved, this difference is statistically significant. This is the case for sidescrapers of both raw materials. The Bell collection contains no chert sidescrapers.

Other scrapers. Tools described simply as scrapers are found only in the Laurentian collections (Table 10.11). Because these pieces may have relatively small amounts of retouch on pieces which may not be flakes, this is not surprising. (We defined scrapers based on a continuously unifacially retouched edge of >1.5 mm vertical height, and these can be on chert fragments and tabular pieces, not only formally shaped flakes.) The analysed objects

Table 10.9. Comparison of the dimensions of Fossil Hill and HBL sidescrapers in the Laurentian University collections.

	Fossil Hill, n = 4				Hudson Bay Lowland, n = 4			
	Max	Min	Mean	St dev	Max	Min	Mean	St dev
Mass (g)	5.0	0.8	3.3	1.8	3.4	1.6	2.4	0.7
Length (mm)	37.5	17.2	28.6	9.2	32.7	21.5	25.8	4.8
Width (mm)	21.5	13.7	17.8	3.4	19.4	15.0	17.0	1.9
Thickness (mm)	11.1	3.7	6.3	3.3	9.2	4.3	6.1	2.2
Bit height (mm)	2.6	1.6	2.1	0.5	3.4	1.2	2.3	0.9
Bit length (mm)	17.3	17.0	17.1	0.2	24.8	15.3	20.5	4.9

Table 10.10. Comparison of the dimensions of sidescrapers in the UMMAA collections.

	Fossil Hill, n = 12				Hudson Bay Lowland, n = 8			
	Max	Min	Mean	St dev	Max	Min	Mean	St dev
Length (mm)	49.5	19.3	34.7	7.8	72.5	18.3	38.6	20.9
Width (mm)	33.0	14.9	27.0	5.5	34.0	13.5	24.3	7.3
Thickness (mm)	11.9	5.3	8.5	2.2	13.6	3.0	8.5	3.7
Bit height (mm)	7.9	2.0	4.7	2.3	7.3	2.5	4.9	1.8

from the UMMAA collections favor formed tools, possibly because objects with only a small amount of retouch were not separated from debitage, or possibly because of selection priorities of field workers. The other scrapers in the Laurentian collection are mainly HBL chert and they are relatively small. The single example of Fossil Hill chert is similar in dimensions to the HBL examples.

Chert bifaces from nonmortuary contexts. By comparison with scrapers, chert bifaces are relatively uncommon in nonmortuary contexts (Table 10.12). The Laurentian field school excavations recovered only 14 chert bifaces, bifacial tools, and biface fragments. This comprises less than 0.1 percent of the chert objects recovered and only about 7 percent of the tools. Half of these bifacial tools are broken.

The very low number of bifaces in the Laurentian collections precludes meaningful statistical analysis of metrics. Nonetheless, some trends are observable. Table 10.13 shows a number of measurements that pertain to the degree of knapping of a piece: the higher the width to thickness ratio, the thinner the biface and presumably the closer it is to a finished product. Stage 4 bifaces may have ratios of 4–5, while Stage 2 bifaces will have ratios of 2–3 (Callahan 1979:30). Cortex and medial ridges are not expected to exist on finished pieces (Callahan 1979). By contrast, fine edge retouch is expected. The HBL and Muldraugh bifaces and fragments all appear to be finished or close to finished. The Fossil Hill examples are mixed, with some appearing finished and others appearing less finished. This suggests that some knapping of bifaces, particularly of those made from Fossil Hill chert, may have occurred at the site. Some bifaces from other raw materials (quartzites and argillite) were also produced onsite, showing examples of unfinished rejects.

The complete finished bifaces and biface fragments may be related to the mortuary material in that they may have been intended for use in mortuary context. Indeed, they may once have been in mortuary context but were displaced at a later time. Some small biface (points?) may have also been intended for projectiles or spear points for

Table 10.11. Dimensions of scrapers of Fossil Hill and HBL in the Laurentian University collections.

	Fossil Hill, n = 1	Hudson Bay Lowland, n = 5			
	Value	Max	Min	Mean	St dev
Mass (g)	5.9	13.3	2.1	5.8	4.5
Length (mm)	26.1	42.5	21.4	30.3	8.2
Width (mm)	23.6	28.3	17.7	21.5	4.2
Thickness (mm)	12.5	17.5	4.3	9.5	5.6
Bit height (mm)		5.8	2.5	3.4	1.4
Bit length (mm)		42.4	16.5	24.2	12.34

Table 10.12. Chert bifaces recovered from by the Laurentian University field schools by raw material.

Raw material	Fossil Hill	Hudson Bay Lowland	Muldraugh
Biface	1	1	
Fragmentary biface	4	1	1
Biface preform	1		
Bifacial knife	1		
Bifacial drill	1	1	
Fragmentary bifacial drill		1	
Backed biface		1	
Total	8	5	1

Table 10.13. Attributes of bifaces and biface fragments found by the Laurentian excavations.

Raw material	Width to thickness ratio		Cortex present	Order of flake removal	Biface form	Medial ridge	Fine edge retouch
	Average	St dev					
Fossil Hill	3.7	0.4	1 of 4	3 of 5 alternating, 2 of 5 unifacial	small, oval	2 of 5 yes	3 of 5
Hudson Bay Lowland	3.9	0.1	0 of 2	1 of 2 alternating	small, oval	no	2 of 2
Muldraugh	5.1		0 of 1	1 of 1 alternating	indeterminate	no	1 of 1

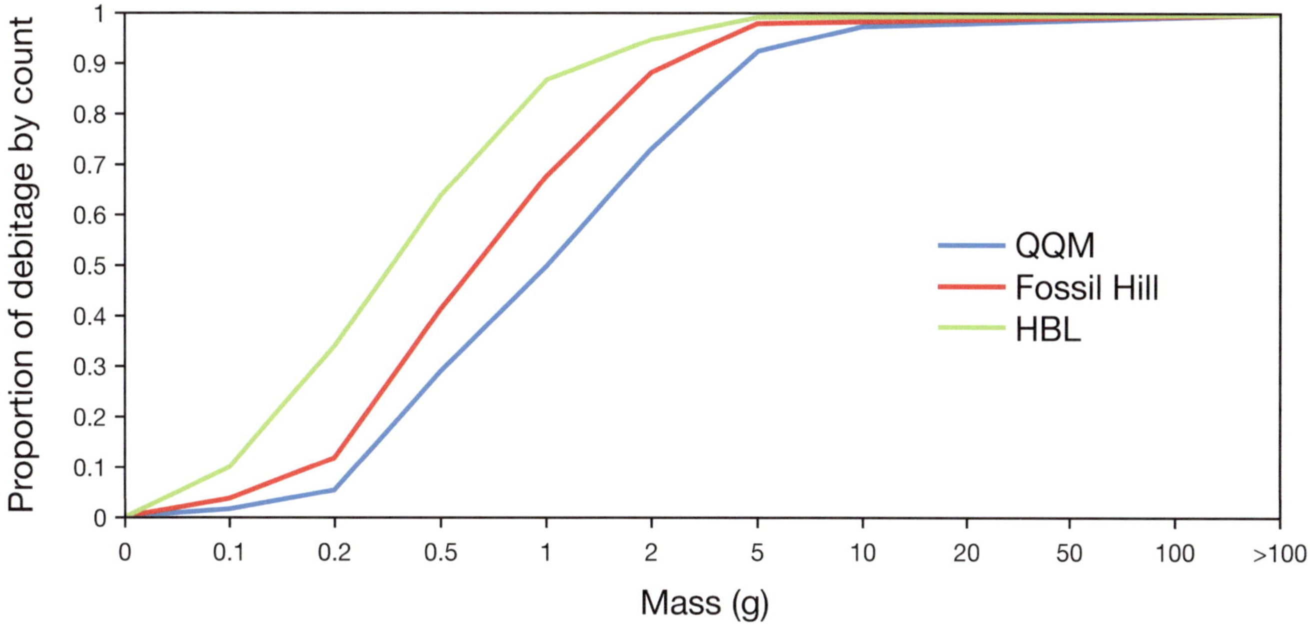

Figure 10.12. Comparison of Fossil Hill, Hudson Bay Lowland, and quartz-quartzite-mylonite debitage by count and mass at Killarney Bay.

resource acquisition, and a few appear to have been poorly knapped and discarded.

In addition to the bifaces and biface fragments, there are a small number of other bifacial tools. These include a biface preform made from Fossil Hill chert, which may suggest that bifaces from this chert were being produced at this location. Knives (including a backed biface) and drills are the other bifacial forms in the collection. These too may have been intended for or disturbed from mortuary contexts, or they may have been used for regular habitation, manufacturing, or maintenance activities. There are faunal and floral remains, ceramic cooking vessels, beaver fur, and ash wood (potentially related to baskets) at Killarney Bay, all of which suggest the inhabitants were engaged in many activities at the site in addition to mortuary activities.

Summary of the chert assemblage from nonmortuary contexts

The chert assemblages from nonmortuary contexts indicate two primary activities in the habitation area: scraping and the knapping of raw materials transported to the site from elsewhere. The debitage analysis used in Sullivan and Rozen's (1985) system did not include quantification of the amount of cortex on fragments, nor categorization of flakes as primary knapping flakes, secondary flakes, or biface thinning flakes (Andrefsky 2005). However, it would appear that people brought both Fossil Hill chert and HBL chert to Killarney Bay in partially roughed out or fully knapped forms. There is a great deal of Fossil Hill chert debitage and it is larger than the HBL debitage (Figure 10.12). This suggests that more Fossil Hill chert was brought to the site, and possibly that it was in larger pieces, which could mean that there was a relatively low degree of preliminary knapping at the source location. Both Fossil Hill and HBL chert were knapped onsite to produce scrapers and tools that were used in an expedient fashion (Julig 1994; Nelson 1991:64), but there was more early-stage knapping of Fossil Hill chert.

A small amount of the knapping activity in the habitation area involved biface production. While chert bifaces make up a substantial portion of the knapped stone from mortuary contexts, they are a minor component of the material from the habitation area. Differences also exist between the habitation area and mortuary area in terms

Table 10.14. Breakdown of the QQM group by count and mass.

	Mylonite	Quartz	Quartzite	Total
n	5	26	9889	9920
Mass (g)	16.4	159.0	22,877.2	23,052.6

Table 10.15. QQM debitage recovered from the habitation area by count (n) and mass (g).

Debitage category	Quartz		Quartzite		Total	
	n	Mass	n	Mass	n	Mass
Complete flake	2	0.79	2240	4349.3	2242	4350.1
Broken flake	1	6.36	1158	1962.1	1159	1968.5
Flake fragment	3	3.61	4184	4850.6	4187	4854.2
Debris	19	145.3	2228	9736.9	2247	9882.2
Total	25	156.1	9810	20,898.9	9835	21,055.0

of the scrapers. The raw materials are similar, but the bit height of the scrapers from the UMMAA collections, which we believe to be predominantly associated with the mortuary area, is much greater than that of the habitation area scrapers.

Quartz, quartzite, and mylonite artifacts

By both count and mass, the most important lithic raw material at the habitation area is the group consisting of quartz, quartzite, and mylonite (QQM). Quartzite is the most common of these raw materials (Table 10.14). Given its local availability, this is not surprising.

Quartz, quartzite, and mylonite debitage

The vast majority of the QQM group may be considered debitage (Tables 10.14 and 10.15). By count, debitage accounts for 99 percent of the sample—by mass it makes up 92 percent of the sample. It is interesting to note that none of the pieces classified as mylonite is debitage. However, mylonite flakes are difficult to distinguish from iron-stained or oxidized quartzite flakes. Mylonite occurs in narrow bands within the local quartzite bedrock several kilometers north and east of Killarney Bay (see Figure 2.3; Julig, personal communication). It breaks out in flat tabular pieces, which can be retouched into scraping tools. It is not easily formed into flakes, as normal cores cannot easily be extracted from the bedrock deposits.

Table 10.16 shows the average mass of the quartz and quartzite debitage. The number of quartz items is quite low, but there are many quartzite items, so this average should be a relatively accurate descriptor of the size of quartzite debitage. Compared with both of the common chert types (Fossil Hill and HBL), quartzite debitage of all categories is larger. Examination of Figure 10.12 shows that there is proportionately more large-sized QQM debitage than there is of Fossil Hill chert. This difference is significant (Kolgomorov-Smirnov, $\alpha = 0.01$). While two-thirds of the Fossil Hill debitage is less than 1 g in mass, only about half of the pieces of QQM debitage are this small. Furthermore, there are a number of large pieces of QQM, whereas pieces of Fossil Hill chert heavier than 10 g are nearly nonexistent.

Again, without having classified the debitage by the stage in which it was produced, we can only suggest the type of knapping of QQM that was carried out at Killarney Bay. The difference in size is probably related to several things. First, quartzite is one of the raw materials found closest to the site (roughly the same distance as mylonite; some blocks of argillite may be even closer). If quartzite blocks were brought to the site for knapping without initial working at a quarry or with only minimal knapping, the flakes from initial working would likely be larger. Secondly, if the intended end products were different, the size of debitage may have been different. The blocks and larger tabular pieces of quartzite with flat surfaces may have been used as grinding surfaces for production of the gorgets and other argillite ground stone artifacts, and not intended for further reduction into quartzite tools. Finally, the knapping properties of the raw materials may contribute, with quartzite blocks breaking along joint plains.

Quartz, quartzite, and mylonite cores

We recovered only five QQM cores in the habitation area (Table 10.17). All of these cores are quartzite. Given that the QQM debitage is larger than the chert debitage, it is not surprising that the average mass of quartzite cores is also larger. One of these shows only a single flake scar, another has multiple parallel flake scars, and the other three have multiple nonparallel scars and are reminiscent of the Fossil Hill chert cores.

Quartz, quartzite, and mylonite tools

The tools made of QQM bear some resemblance to those of chert, but it should be noted at the outset that the number of QQM tools is less than half the number of chert tools, despite the higher number of QQM objects and the much greater mass of QQM material. This may relate to the difficulty with which retouch and utilization are identified on quartz and quartzite tools. As was the case for chert tools, about half of the QQM tools are classified as utilized flakes. The remainder of the tools consists mainly of bifacial forms and scrapers (Table 10.18). While scrapers account for about 40 percent of the chert tools, they only amount to slightly more than 20 percent of the QQM tools. No thumbnail scrapers are represented. Bifacial forms are more common in the QQM sample. As is the case for chert, the bifacial tools include some complete forms, but also a number of preforms and fragmentary bifaces, as would be expected given the amount of knapping of QQM that occurred at the site. The mylonite artifacts include one complete and four fragmentary objects. The complete lack of mylonite debitage suggests either that catalogers did not recognize this raw material or that fragmentary objects were discards that had been produced elsewhere and were exchanged at Killarney Bay. The most likely explanation is that since mylonite occurs in tabular form, tools could be produced with a minimal amount of knapping, which would produce little debitage.

Quartz, quartzite, and mylonite scrapers. The number of QQM scrapers is low compared with chert, and there is a difference in the distribution of scraper types. The Laurentian collection includes only seventeen QQM scrapers, all but one of which are classified as quartzite. The single exception is quartz. There are two QQM scrapers identified in the UMMAA collections, and both of these are described as mylonite. Other scrapers from QQM may exist in the UMMAA collections; the debitage has not been analyzed. As discussed above, these scrapers exist in a range of forms, and the retouch on them may be relatively minimal.

The dimensions of the quartzite scrapers are shown in Table 10.19. This raw material clearly differs from chert in that the majority of quartzite scrapers are classified as "other scrapers." This suggests that this raw material may have been used for production of tools as needed in an expedient framework: both the quartzite and the time needed to prepare it for a task were predictable and available (Nelson 1991). Other scrapers occur in a wide range of sizes, which supports the idea that what was of interest was the production of a

Table 10.16. Average mass (g) of debitage categories of quartz and quartzite.

Debitage category	Quartz	Quartzite
Complete flake	0.4	1.94
Broken flake	6.4	1.7
Flake fragment	1.2	1.2
Debris	7.64	4.4

Table 10.17. Quartzite cores by type. The number in parentheses indicates the average mass.

Nature of object	n	Mass (g)
Biface core	1	50.6
Core	4	317.1 (79.3)

Table 10.18. QQM tools from the habitation area at Killarney Bay.

Nature of object	Mylonite	Quartz	Quartzite	Total
Bifacial tools				
Backed biface	1		1	2
Biface			2	2
Biface preform			2	2
Fragmentary biface	3		6	9
Fragmentary biface preform			3	3
Fragmentary projectile point	1			1
Unifacial tools				
Uniface knife			1	1
Scrapers				
Endscraper			1	1
Scraper			9	9
Sidescraper		1	6	7
Informal or other tools				
Fragmentary chipped stone tool			1	1
Utilized piece			42	42
Total tools	5	1	74	80

Table 10.19. Summary dimensions of quartzite scrapers in the Laurentian University collection.

	Endscraper, n = 1	Sidescrapers, n = 6				Scrapers, n = 8			
		Max	Min	Mean	St dev	Max	Min	Mean	St dev
Max (g)	20.23	65.0	13.2	31.1	19.5	141.1	4.0	44.7	57.3
Length (mm)	44.8	78.3	41.2	58.5	13.7	90.1	32.5	51.3	21.6
Width (mm)	43.24	48.8	27.5	37.7	10.1	67.2	24.5	42.6	18.0
Thickness (mm)	15.45	19.8	8.3	15.1	4.4	22.1	5.8	13.4	6.0
Bit height (mm)	3.34	3.8	1.1	2.5	1.0	14.5	1.9	5.5	4.6
Bit length (mm)	37.51	77.6	18.8	45.5	21.8	53.4	53.4	32.5	13.8

useable edge, regardless of the form of the initial piece. Sidescrapers also occur in a wide range of sizes, but not to the same extent as other scrapers. The single endscraper is significantly larger than the average dimensions of chert endscrapers. Analysis of quartzite quarry workshop activity and tool production at the nearby Sheguiandah site indicates that the Bar River Formation quartzite (same as at Killarney Bay) knaps very well, and a full range of well-formed formal scraper types were produced and used (Julig 2002). The main difference observed for the "expedient quartzite tools" at Killarney Bay is that at Sheguiandah the specific quartzite quarried is more recrystallized and glassey and knaps easier (Julig and Long 2010).

Both of the QQM scrapers at the UMMAA are described as thumbnail scrapers made from mylonite. Their sizes are smaller than the average dimensions of chert scrapers in the UMMAA collections but fall within the range of chert scrapers. The dimensions of mylonite scrapers may relate to the way in which the raw material fractures—it occurs in thin bands that fracture into plate-like pieces.

Quartz, quartzite, and mylonite bifaces. In contrast to chert, the QQM tool assemblage from the Laurentian field school excavations contains slightly more bifacial tools than scrapers. Nevertheless, the number of bifacial objects is quite low, comprising only nineteen bifaces, bifacial tools, and biface fragments. Of the fourteen analyzed objects, most are broken or classified as preforms.

Summary of the quartz, quartzite, and mylonite assemblage from nonmortuary contexts

The quartz, quartzite, and mylonite industries from the habitation area show that considerable knapping of this raw material occurred at Killarney Bay. Some of this activity may have been oriented towards production of tools for immediate use, but some was clearly directed at production of formed tools such as bifaces. The size of the quartzite debitage, when compared with that of Fossil Hill chert and HBL chert, suggests that more early-stage knapping of this raw material was carried out onsite. While some chert formed tools appear to have been brought to Killarney Bay, where they were subsequently modified, it seems likely that people transported QQM material mainly in rough-outs or tested blocks.

As was the case with chert, artisans at Killarney Bay considered QQM flakes to be suitable for expedient or opportunistic use (Nelson 1991). The high proportion of utilized flakes suggests that when the past inhabitants of the site were in need of a sharp edge, they produced one from a nearby core or selected a flake from those left at the site from previous knapping activities. There was also ground stone artifact production: the quartzite blocky fragments made suitable grinding stones for argillite and other softer sedimentary lithics.

Table 10.20. Breakdown of siltstone and argillite artifacts by number and mass (g).

	Argillite	Siltstone	Total
n	7	2174	2181
Mass (g)	929.3	7420.3	8349.6

Production of formal tools from QQM is directed more towards bifaces than scrapers. This is interesting in the context of the nature of the bifaces found in mortuary context. The overwhelming majority of these are chert bifaces. As discussed above, some burials are dominated by imported cherts and others by local cherts. Even the burials with mostly local chert show little quartzite. For example, Burial 4 contains 3 quartzite bifaces and 21 Fossil Hill chert bifaces. Artisans may have produced QQM bifaces at Killarney Bay for creating points or knives to be used in daily activities, including resource procurement and maintenance, rather than for interment.

Siltstone and argillite artifacts

Siltstone and argillite comprise the smallest portion of the major lithic materials recovered by the Laurentian team from the habitation area. Nevertheless, the number of pieces collected and their mass is not insubstantial (Table 10.20). A very small portion of the sample is argillite, and all of it is recorded as banded Gowganda argillite. In addition, approximately 14 percent of the siltstone artifacts (n = 305) are recorded as banded. Both the siltstones and the argillites may be sourced in the Gowganda Formation.

Wright (1999:667) noted that Killarney Bay was one of the Middle Woodland production areas for siltstone ornaments such as gorgets. As such, we should expect knapping debris from roughing out preforms, portions of partially made tools, and potentially also tools broken in production.

Siltstone and argillite debitage

As is the case for chert and QQM, the vast majority of the material is comprised of debitage, both by count and by mass. The proportion by mass (0.72) is somewhat lower than the proportion by count (0.98), indicating that some of the nondebitage items are quite large. Table 10.21 shows the breakdown by debitage category.

The average mass of siltstone debitage is similar to that of QQM and is larger than that of chert, suggesting that early-stage knapping of siltstone occurred at the site (Table 10.22).

The Bell collection includes a small amount of debitage classified as Gowganda argillite.

Siltstone and argillite cores

The Laurentian excavations recovered a single siltstone core. It is quite large, having a mass of 614 g. It is a thick flake core with multiple removals in different directions. Less than one-third of its surface is flaked.

Siltstone and argillite tools and ornaments

The worked siltstone from the Laurentian excavation includes similar types to those made from other raw materials, with the additional categories of gorgets and preforms (Table 10.23). As is the case for chert and QQM, more than half of the tools are informal varieties that are classified as utilized pieces. Scrapers account for a very small portion of the overall siltstone tool assemblage (6 percent). There are a number of bifaces and fragmentary bifaces, and it is interesting to note that these are twice as common as gorgets and gorget preforms.

Siltstone and argillite scrapers. Two tools in the Laurentian collections are classified as siltstone scrapers. These are both large, having masses of 87 and 61 g. The smaller one is a sidescraper and the larger one an "other scraper." The Bell collection contains an additional four sidescrapers, all of which are described as Gowganda argillite. These pieces are mainly unifacial, but one is described as flaked on both sides. The Bell collection sidescrapers are also large, ranging from 109 to 141 mm in length. There are no argillite or siltstone scrapers in the UMMAA collections. Large unifacial tools flaked from siltstone or similar materials are known from Archaic occupations throughout the northern US and southern Canada (Gordon in press/pers comm). These sidescrapers

Table 10.21. Debitage categories for siltstone and argillite, by count and mass (g).

Nature of object	Argillite		Siltstone		Total	
	Count	Mass	Count	Mass	Count	Mass
Complete flake			267	492.5	267	492.5
Broken flake			98	176.6	98	176.6
Flake fragment	1	18.2	687	829.6	688	847.8
Debris	1	24.4	1092	4466.4	1093	4490.9
Total	2	42.6	2144	5965.1	2146	6007.8

Table 10.22. Average mass (g) of debitage categories of siltstone and argillite.

Nature of object	Argillite	Siltstone
Complete flake		1.8
Broken flake		1.8
Flake fragment	18.2	1.2
Debris	24.4	4.1

appear to bear greater resemblance to large Archaic scrapers or knives than to the smaller sidescrapers of quartzite and chert in the Killarney Bay collections.

Siltstone and argillite points and bifaces. The Laurentian University collection includes two siltstone bifaces, one backed biface, and five fragmentary bifaces. These vary considerably in dimensions, having lengths ranging from 38 mm to 81 mm. The width to thickness ratio of several pieces is quite high (over 4.0), indicating late-stage manufacture (Callahan 1979). However, the two complete bifaces both have relatively low width to thickness ratios (3.3 and 2.2). If they were produced onsite, they may have been abandoned while partially flaked because of flaws in the raw material or irreparable knapping errors. None of the objects has medial ridges and all but one have fine-edge retouch. The order of flake removal appears quite variable, with alternate, unifacial, and random flaking being represented equally.

Three fragmentary projectile points include two made of siltstone and one of argillite. It was not possible to measure lengths on any of the specimens. Width to thickness ratios are low for the two that could be measured (2.9 and 3.5). The argillite example is described as having an Adena-like base and the other two are lanceolate in form, with one having side- or corner-notching.

Greenman's team also collected a number of siltstone or argillite pieces. Table 10.24 shows that these are predominantly preforms or rough-outs. In some cases, it is possible to suggest the type of intended object (e.g., gorget or axe), but in others the knapping ended at a very early stage. Gorget preforms are more common than other types of argillite preforms. This supports Wright's (1999:667) contention that Killarney Bay functioned in part as a gorget-manufacturing site. There are Middle Woodland sites to the south of Killarney Bay, Baxter and Bressette (Dodd 1996; Lennox et al. 1994), which also have banded argillite

Table 10.23. Argillite and siltstone tools at Killarney Bay.

Nature of object	Argillite	Siltstone	Total
Bifacial tools			
Biface		2	2
Fragmentary biface		6	6
Fragmentary projectile point	1	1	2
Gorgets and preforms			
Fragmentary gorget preform	2	1	3
Gorget preform	2		2
Scrapers			
Scraper		1	1
Sidescraper		1	1
Informal tools			
Utilized piece		17	17
Total	5	29	34

Table 10.24. Number of argillite objects (n) in the UMMAA collections without mound associations.

Object type	n
Adze roughout	1
Axe preform	5
Gorget preform	13
Axe or broad gorget preform	4
Block preform	2
Bifacial preform	6
Projectile point	1
Flake	4

preforms indicating manufacturing of this specialized artifact, the gorget.

Siltstone and argillite ground tools. The Bell collection includes a celt and a broken celt. The complete one measures 146 mm x 65 mm x 21 mm. It is described as banded and chipped around the perimeter. The fact that there is red ochre on one side strongly suggests that it originally was interred with a burial. Only the proximal end of the broken celt is present. Its thickness suggests it may have originally been similar in size to the complete celt.

Re-examination of select lithics from the Greenman excavations

In this section we re-examine select chipped and ground stone artifacts from the Greenman (UMMAA) and Bell collections from a typological perspective, to help integrate this information into the previous lithic technological analysis. The UMMAA artifact collections were only partly analyzed (most complete bifaces, scrapers, and other formal artifacts, but no debitage analysis), and some classes of materials, such as argillite and quartzite preforms, require additional consideration regarding lithic production at the site. The Greenman field notes are also consulted regarding artifact and feature context, as their excavations were much deeper than the Laurentian field school excavations, which were mostly within the plow zone. It appears that Killarney Bay was not only a mortuary and habitation site, but also a manufacturing site for the production of certain lithic tools and ornaments, possibly for export and trade to other Middle Woodland sites as part of the interregional exchange system.

Ground stone artifacts and preforms

At Killarney Bay, ground and polished artifacts include at least three kinds of lithic material: coarse stone (granitic), sedimentary (including argillite and siltstone), and several kinds of pipestone. The sedimentary stones would have first been shaped by flaking and then ground and polished, while the coarse stone artifacts would have been hammered and pecked into the desired shape.

As with the chert sources, an approach to describing the numerous ground stone artifacts from the Killarney Bay site begins by indicating the range of lithic sources represented, as these to a significant degree correlate with the nature of the artifact. Local, intermediate, and distant raw materials are represented in the collections. Many of the larger chipped stone artifacts recovered from Greenman's excavations were initial "preforms" or quarry blanks and rejects for what would have been finished as ground stone artifacts, such as gorgets.

The Bell collection includes a mano or pounder and a metate, both of granite and well formed. Interestingly, the mano bears what is described as a red ochre sheen, indicating at least one of its functions. Other coarse stone industry artifacts are minimally modified, including hammerstones.

Excavations across the stratified beach levels of the site yielded over 70 whole and broken bifaces chipped into rough, rectangular Gowganda Formation argillite blocks approximately 15 cm by 75 mm by 45 mm in size. While most of the larger ones were more or less rectangular, several dozen showed rounded ends and slightly concave long sides, which was apparently an early reduction stage in the shaping of gorgets such as the finished one (Figure 10.13). Approximately 180 bifacial thinning flakes and block chips of Gowganda argillite of many sizes, all larger than 1 mm x 1 mm, were found at most subsoil levels in many of the excavation trenches, with a total weight over 1250 grams. (Smaller crumbs and unmarked chips abound, but they are without provenience.)

The argillite debitage was far exceeded in volume and weight by the more than 2,300 bifacial flakes and 390 cores (weighing more than 18.8 kilograms) of Lorrain Formation quartzite (an older quartzite with a greenish tinge) and mylonite (a very fine-grained stone that breaks naturally into tan-colored tabular pieces) of every size and degree of processed workmanship. Greenman's crews carefully recorded this debitage, which they collected from every trench and level excavated from 1940 through 1949. Based on inspection of wear and striation, several of the larger rosy-tinted sections of the Bar River Formation quartzite were chipped into large chopper-like biface-blades, which were heavily used, at least in part, in a sawing motion. The much harder quartzite biface edges functioned as a grindstone or saw to shape the argillite blanks prior to finishing by grinding flat and drilling the holes. Given his expectation that these were extremely early, Greenman (1940) initially described these quartzite preforms in terms borrowed from

Figure 10.13. A gorget with two drilled suspension holes made of argillite (lower left) and other ground stone pieces from Killarney Bay suggest that people there manufactured argillite artifacts onsite.

Western European Lower and Middle Paleolithic studies. By the time he wrote his last Killarney Bay report (Greenman 1966), however, his awareness of their true age (as being much more recent) left him taxonomically adrift. This illustrates the problems with typological classification being used as index fossils.

On a sand floor of the mound, between Burial 3 and Burial 4 excavations, was one complete finished flat quadrilateral gorget made of the locally available argillite with two conically drilled suspension holes. Excavators in nonmound or knoll trenches below the topsoil recovered one other broken, narrow argillite bar gorget with a partially drilled suspension hole. Such completed and partly finished failures point to the onsite manufacturing of argillite ground stone artifacts.

Also recovered were two flat argillite triangular pieces—one with a single suspension hole drilled in the broader end—that would be considered pendants, as well as a small block of black soapstone, in one face of which shallow drill marks could be observed.

Two of the more unusual ground stone artifacts were picked up during Greenman's first season of excavation. A thick and slightly convex disc of micaceous schist (KB1-61/UMMAA 22525) was apparently used as a palette. The dished surface of this 5.5 cm thick artifact measures 22 cm by 17 cm (Figure 10.14). It appears that the first artifact Greenman entered in the Killarney Bay catalog (KB1-1/UMMAA 22442) was a small polished cone of plagioclase feldspar. This hemispherical cone measured 669 mm in height and between 76 and 78 mm in diameter. The lower

Figure 10.14. Unusual stone artifacts found at Killarney Bay during Greenman's first season of excavation include a thick disc of micaceous schist (left), a polished cone of plagioclase feldspar (top right), and a heavily battered rhyolitic cobble (bottom right).

edges of the longer ends of the base showed small step fractures that had been initiated from the outer circumference. There were faint striations along the longer axis of the base. Inspection at 30 magnifications did not encounter any traces of foreign material within those shallow striae, but decades of casual handling may have removed any that once existed. It is possible that this cone was used in some sort of ceremony; more widely reported hematite cones are believed to have been used in ceremonies at relatively late Adena sites in the Ohio River Valley (Dragoo 1976). It is also possible that such stones were used as a dye. At the nearby Middle Woodland site Sheguiandah East, nodules of galena (lead) ore were recovered, which may have been used for a darker pigment. A purple stone mined at the adjacent Strawberry Island was used to color materials.

Tubular stone pipes

There are three tubular stone pipes in the UMMAA collection, at least one of which meets the definition of having a blocked proximal end. The crew removed two relatively complete pipes, one red (UMMAA 39631) and one very dark gray (UMMAA 39632), from Burial 10 during the final, rainy days of Greenman's last (1953) field season at Killarney Bay. These pipes were apparently found wrapped together in deerskin, perhaps some form of pouch, near the top of the burial pit. The skin was folded on or partially wrapped by a bag or net made of 3-ply twisted bast fiber, lying beneath the very richly accompanied remains of an adult female (see Chapter 9, this volume). Regarding the manufacturing techniques and functions of this and all

Figure 10.15. The fragment of a black tubular stone pipe (left) and argillite pins from Killarney Bay.

other vegetal artifacts, certainty is severely limited due to the fact that only those portions preserved by copper salts remained. The third, quite fragmentary black tubular pipe from the site (Figure 10.15) had been recovered many years earlier, not from the burial mound but during Greenman's excavations into the stratified beach deposits on the lower terrace. It was located in a small gravel lens. Within that same lens, the field crew recovered what was described as a "blocking pebble" along with "an organic bolus," which, unfortunately, was never analyzed.

Perhaps due to his belief that these were physical relics of an Ohio Adena presence, Greenman's brief notes and his summary publications implied that all three of these should be considered as "blocked end" tubular pipes (with one end deliberately constricted or blocked by a thickened section of the cylinder). It is true that in all three cases the opening at one end is somewhat smaller than the opening at the other end of the cylinder. However, only the fragmentary black pipe shows evidence of the artisan deliberately leaving a "block" in one end of the cylinder during manufacture.

Both pipes from Burial 10 taper slightly to a smaller end that is somewhat thinner (Table 10.25). The dark gray tubular pipe from Burial 10 is somewhat flattened, giving it a somewhat elliptical cross-section. The red tubular pipe from Burial 10 is quite circular in cross-section and is noteworthy for the worn chip in one end. Apparently, a spall was removed as the result of some sharp trauma from the end, and then the edges of the break were smoothed by nonabrasive means—possibly by constant rubbing.

Almost every author commenting on Archaic, Woodland, or even Mississippian ground stone artifacts has suggested that the interior of such artifacts had been bored out by some form of helical or rotary abrasion. The broken black pipe from the beach gravels did show both a structural blocked end and clear helical striae from the manufacturing process. In distinction, the red and very dark gray pipes from Burial 10 had no structural blocked end and their internal striae were parallel with each other and with the long axis of the pipe.

Thor (2006; and Appendix F, this volume) noted that three similar "structurally unblocked" pipes from the Schlegel site (about 100 kilometers south of Killarney Bay along Georgian Bay) also had relatively parallel internal surface striae that ran from one end of the pipe to the other. There would seem to be considerable merit in Thor's hypothesis of initial circular drilling with subsequent

Table 10.25. Comparison of three stone pipes found at Killarney Bay.

UMMAA number	Field number	Description	Length	External diameter		Internal diameter		Block depth	Provenience
				Large end	Small end	Large end	Small end		
39631	KB-2322	Red pipe with smoothed chip	133.5	35.1	33.1	29.7	23.6	NA	Burial 10
39632	KB-2323	Dark gray/green "flattened"pipe	113.7	28.7/27.6	27.2/26.8	19.1	17.4	NA	Burial 10
30280	KB-1131	Black blocked-end broken pipe	46.2x	23.5	11.2	18.5	9.5	5.2	Trench 4, Section B -2.1', in gravel lens

longitudinal smoothing (rather than the "reaming" other scholars had suggested) for those pipes without a true structural blocked end.

It had initially been assumed (Brose 2006) that the red tubular pipe was made of catlinite, as it appeared visually similar to samples of red pipestone taken from the seam that for millennia had been quarried at the Pipestone National Monument in southwest Minnesota. Also, the raw material for the very dark gray was described as Ohio pipestone, similar to samples acquired from the Feurt Hill quarry just east of the junction of the Scioto River and Ohio River. This metamorphosed material had been called Ohio fireclay in the earliest state geological reports. Those assumptions were only partially correct.

In November 2006, Thomas Emerson and Kenneth Farnsworth of the Illinois Transportation Archaeological Research Program submitted these three pipes for PIMA (portable infared mineral analyzer) scans. Subsequently, Emerson reported that comparative analyses by Randy Hughes and Sarah Wisseman of the Illinois Program on Ancient Technologies and Archaeological Materials revealed that UMMAA 39631, the large dark red intact tubular pipe from Burial 10, and UMMAA 30280, the fragmentary black blocked-end pipe from the beach gravels, were similar.

Hughes also noted that UMMAA 39632, the large intact grayish-green tubular pipe also from Burial 10, appeared distinct. All three of the Killarney Bay pipes had mineralogical signatures closely resembling control samples from Ohio's Feurt Hill "flintclay" quarry, some two miles upstream from the Portsmouth Earthworks, which occupies both banks of the Ohio River (Squier and Davis 1848; Emerson, personal communication 2007). The Feurt Hill quarry is also about 30 miles south of the eponymous Adena Mound, where there were a number of Middle Woodland mounds, within which there were many burials accompanied by copper celts and Flint Ridge chert corner-notched blades similar to those at Killarney Bay.

Similar analyses on the two large caches of effigy platform pipes from Mound City and the Hopewell site itself had demonstrated that these Hopewell effigy pipes were not made from Ohio fireclay but rather from sources in the north-central portions of the Mississippi River basin (Farnsworth et al. 2004). However, the effigy platform pipes from coeval Havana burial mounds in that region were made from the Ohio sources.

Conclusions

Our conclusions of the lithic analysis will follow the order of the chapter, based on lithic artifact sourcing, technology of the industries, and artifact typology. As described above, the provenience of some of the lithic artifacts at Killarney Bay remains unclear, and while some visual identifications of presumed distant exotics may be in error, the overall pattern of exotic lithic acquisition and the widespread trade networks and interaction spheres it suggests fits with other patterns for the Middle Woodland era in North America.

The lithic artifact sources are highly varied and from a broad region, specifically those associated with the mortuary area. However, the vast majority are from within the Great Lakes drainage basin. The small percentage from beyond include some southern cherts from Indiana and Illinois and some from western sources, such as Knife River Flint (North Dakota). The cherts from the northern Great Lakes basin and beyond, including HBL and Abitibi, have primary geological (bedrock) sources in the Hudson Bay basin and were transported far to the south by glaciation. Lacking evidence of direct human acquisition from Hudson Bay, we must assume Hudson Bay Lowland artifacts found at Killarney Bay were knapped from HBL found in these secondary glacial gravels. These HBL cobbles and pebbles may have been collected for knapping within about 150 miles of the Killarney Bay site, around the drainage divide between the Great Lakes and Hudson Bay to the north.

The mortuary lithics differ from the habitation area lithics in a number of respects. Firstly, the objects are mainly lithic finished artifacts, formed bifaces, or biface preforms. Burial offerings do not include scrapers, and few gorgets, in contrast to Middle Woodland sites to the south. As described above, the bifaces associated with each burial vary in terms of raw material and the form of the biface. In some cases, the offerings are strongly local and the raw materials parallel those found in the habitation area. In other cases, the raw materials and form of the bifaces indicate southern connections, and in still others, northern connections. One individual (Burial 10) shows a mix of materials and forms from all three areas. Since the treatment after death, including mortuary assemblage, reflects the status during life, the lithics might indicate social status and possibly regional connections. Burial 1, that of an infant, contained HBL, local quartzite, and Selkirk. The offerings had a "northern cast," as noted earlier. Burial 7, also an infant, contained Abitibi and Bayport chert lithics.

Certain male burial assemblages at Killarney Bay (Burial 4 and 6) show strong northern connections with predominately northern cherts. However, adult male burials 8 and 9 have mostly southern exotic lithics. Clearly some of the female burials, such as 10 and 2, indicate high status, and mostly southern (but some northern) lithics. The stone pipes (southern, Ohio area) are associated with the female burials as well. Is there a pattern of females showing southern connections in mortuary lithics, and infants showing more northern cast, while the adult males show a mixture? The samples are small but suggestive. Future elemental analysis of the skeletal materials may make it possible to determine where these individuals spent their lives, and whether the lithic sources were intentionally used to demarcate individual origins.

The Killarney Bay lithic assemblage is rich and varied and reveals much about the site and its occupants. The assemblage demonstrates wide trading connections to the south, north, and west. The onsite manufacturing of gorgets and other artifacts, along with rich trade goods, including copper and exotic flints, stresses the active participation in the trade of exotic materials and suggests continuity with a pattern for earlier populations in this region. In particular, it is similar to late Archaic sites on Morrison and Allumette islands to the east on the Ottawa River. As discussed in Chapter 12, northern copper was exchanged with southern cultures. Killarney Bay was also involved in the manufacture and exchange of other (lithic) artifacts, including ground and polished stone gorgets and pendants, and likely other artifacts such as birdstones and banner stones. These were destined as grave offerings in southern Great Lakes St. Lawrence, Adena, Meadowood, and related Middle Woodland cultures.

Chapter 11

Ceramics from the Killarney Bay Site

David Brose and Jordan Mathieu

Archaeologists have long recognized that ceramics are among the most culturally and chronologically sensitive artifacts. During the past half-century, fine-scale spatial and stylistic analyses have wrung a surprising level of sociological information from these humble vessels, and new physical methods have revealed economic details of their manufacture, use, and disposal. The aboriginal pottery recovered from the various areas that comprise the Killarney Bay site have been the focus of all of these approaches in the fifty years since they were first excavated.

In this chapter, we present a general description of the ceramic assemblage and a definition of the ceramic types present at Killarney Bay. This is followed by a discussion of the character and distribution of ceramics recovered from the habitation area by Laurentian University and by a consideration of how the Killarney Bay ceramics fit into the larger region and time period. Co-author Brose describes the ceramic types, explains the distribution and provenience for materials recovered during the University of Michigan excavations, and compares the ceramic assemblage with other Middle Woodland sites across the Upper Great Lakes region. Co-author Mathieu analyzed the temper and mineralogy of the sherds. Alicia Hawkins analyzed the ceramics recovered during the Laurentian University excavations and compared them to Ontario and New York Point Peninsula ceramics.

Archaeologists often find it advantageous to create highly detailed stylistic categories for specific interpretations of ceramic ecology (e.g. Brose 1968; Deetz 1965). Nonetheless, it is not generally productive to create provisional types for new occurrences of well-described prehistoric ceramics. Indeed, nearly all archaeologists heed the seventeenth-century scientific adage known as Occam's razor, that entities should not be multiplied unnecessarily.[1] In that spirit, we have refrained from creating a plethora of new types for the Killarney Bay site ceramics, as these would have to be mostly based on minor variations in decorative styles or early radiometric dates from limited sampling of partially altered site contexts (contra Finlayson 1977). It is our contention that all of the ceramics recovered from Killarney Bay comfortably relate to described single prehistoric cultures or traditions, such as the early Middle Woodland from the Saginaw and Kalamazoo River valleys across central lower Michigan (Garland and Beld 1999); the Middle Tier North Bay complex and/or Laurel sites (Birnbaum 2009; Brose 1968; Mason 1981, 1991) in the northern Lake Michigan basin, the range of what has been called Middle Woodland in northern Michigan (Brose and Hambacher 1999; Janzen 1968b); or the amorphous Early and Middle Woodland continuum of southern Ontario (Spence et al. 1990).

Based on morphological analysis and a review of the distribution of ceramics from the Killarney Bay site, it is possible to technically segregate the limited sample into three types, each of which has within it several provisional types and/or decorative varieties. It is not yet possible to assign an absolute date to each type (although see discussion of ^{14}C dates below), but stratigraphic and surface proveniences do indicate their relative temporal position.

The provisional Killarney Bay Smoothed type appears to span the end of the Early Woodland and the beginning of the Middle Woodland period, between the third and second centuries BCE and the second century of the common era. The provisional Killarney Bay Thick type begins with the early Middle Woodland and persists into the early phases of the Middle Woodland period, but in very different functional and/or social settings than its thinner companion. It is during these latter subperiods, between the first century BCE and the second century CE, that the provisional Speigel Tool-Impressed type and its North Bay/Laurel/Point Peninsula congeners dominate the region's ceramic assemblages.

While not wholly chronologically equivalent, the three ceramic types described above were almost certainly in contemporaneous use at the site over an archaeologically indeterminate period of time between the end of the second century BCE and the end of the third century CE. In addition, at what must be the very end of the stratigraphic deposits, there is a late scatter of sherds representing a few limited short-term early Late Woodland visits to the site sometime after the fifth or sixth century CE. Each of these ceramic categories is discussed below.

Analysis of ceramics from the mortuary area

The limits of the sample

Based on thorough inspection of the UMMAA catalogs and cabinets and Greenman's 1938–1953 field catalogs and excavation notes in the University of Michigan Bentley Historical Library[2], it appears that what are now available for study from those field seasons are approximately 602 ceramic sherds that were larger than 1 cm and that could be assigned to some type and had recorded proveniences. In addition, from disturbed or mixed or missing proveniences, there were at the time of these analyses another 220 smaller spalled or fragmented body sherds that could be assigned to a ceramic ware, and some 95 crumbs, which could be assigned to neither type nor ware. Of the typed sherds from known proveniences, there are 92 rim sherds and reconstructed rim-sherd combinations (here termed rim sections), 117 neck/shoulder sherds, 381 body sherds, and 6 undecorated, plain-surfaced basal sherds, including 2 partial and 1 nearly complete conical vessel base (Figure 11.1).

Some sherds had split so that the former exterior surface was not present, and therefore no applied decoration was discernible. Of those that did have an intact exterior surface, most had been smoothed, and some of these were decorated. More specifically, 584 of the 718 rim, neck/shoulder, and body sherds with intact exterior surfaces, and the 195 (of the 220) untyped body sherds from uncertain provenience, had smoothed exterior surfaces. Eighty-one others appear to have been "dry-wiped" or lightly brushed, and 53 others show evidence that such smoothing had taken place over a fabric or cord-wrapped paddle-impressed surface. Of the entire UMMAA ceramic assemblage of 822 sherds, interior surfaces are identifiable on 751 sherds, and 698 of these are smooth. The remaining 53 sherd interiors show extremely faint cord or fabric impressions. If they were more distinct, these might be akin to what has been called channeling. The frequencies of ceramics, by type and variety, are shown in Table 11.1 from the mortuary complex (the University of Michigan excavations) and in Table 11.2 for those from the habitation area (the Laurentian University excavations).

Figure 11.1. Semi-conoidal vessel bases from Killarney Bay: Killarney Bay Smoothed (left) and Killarney Bay Thick (right).

According to Greenman's field catalogs and excavation notes, all of these ceramic fragments came from one of four rather general provenience sets.

1. All 220 untyped sherds and some 232 of the 387 (59 percent) typed but undecorated body sherds and basal sherds with intact surfaces, along with 98 of the 209 (47 percent) typed rim sherds and decorated neck and shoulder or body sherds, are described as being from the surface, or back-dirt piles, or the "topsoil" from an excavation unit of some depth, or from areas designated "disturbed subsoil." (Included here are the 5 surface-recovered sherds without visible inclusions, probably from 2 miniature pinch pots, and the 4 rims, along with 4 body and basal sherds from perhaps 5 other grit and limestone-tempered cord-marked, nondescript, but typologically Late Woodland vessels, the limestone temper in which is from a nonlocal calcareous rock.)
2. Another 105 undecorated but typed body sherds and basal sherds (28 percent) and 52 of the rims and decorated neck and shoulder sherds (30 percent), were encountered with no discernable cultural associations in one of two areas. Most of these came from one of the many superimposed sand or gravel levels that made up the arbitrary upper and lower lacustrine strata of the trenches excavated across the rising beaches toward the area later identified (and excavated) as a mound.
3. A few of these sherds came from below the topsoil in one of the small scattered test squares excavated farther from the bay. (These units did not appear to Greenman and/or his students to have any subsoil stratigraphy.) These units are in the terrace area that was later called the Speigel site (BlHl-1), which in this volume is called the habitation area. For a decade, this area had been archaeologically sampled by students under the direction of Devereaux (1982), Buchanan (1992), and Julig (2004). In 2007, Alicia Hawkins performed a detailed thin-section analysis of the 50 rim sets and 86 intact body sherds (representing some 44 distinct vessels) recovered from those excavations.

Table 11.1. Killarney Bay ceramics by type and variety in UMMAA collections.

Type and Variety	Rim sets	Neck/Sh	Body	Base	Sherds	Vessels	Holotype	Additional Sherd Catalogue Numbers
KB Thick v. Plain Lip	9	0	15	2	26	4	30250	21164; 22664; 22716; 22717; 22740; 22779; 22805; 22832; 22850; 30245; 30250; 38915; 38924; 38933; 39489+39661*
KB Thick v. Flat Lip	9	4	3	0	16	7	22849	22761;22833; 22860; 222890; 23698; 23262; 22494; 30250
KB Thick v. PSS-stamp	3	3	0	0	6	2	38447	28851; 28995
KB Smoothed v Plain Lip	7	37	120	0	165	3	29274	22306; 22454; 22514; 22674; 22832; 22840; 22842; 22854; 38251
KB Smoothed v Glittery	1	0	4		5	1	38897	N/A
KB Smoothed v Rolled lip	5	2	43	0	50	3	22674	22818; 38251; 38444; 38445; 38446
KB Smoothed v Flat lip	28	25	103	3	159	9	22550	22494; 22698; 22702; 22717; 22746; 22766; 22805; 22809; 22820; 22832; 22849; 22860; 22974; 23262; 23306; 23344; 28991; 29000; 29017; 29025; 29274; 38443; 38897; 38924; 39487
KB Smoothed v Lip Impressed	2	2	0	0	4	4	27862	22501; 28550; 28990
KB SERIES TOTALS	**64**	**73**	**288**	**5**	**431**	**33**		
Speigel Tool-Imp v Linear PSS	4	3	0	0	7	3	22783	22350; 22498; 228322; 22851; 22850; 28522; 22888
Speigel Tool-Imp v Narrow Tool	5	7	50	0	62	2	23267	22737; 28522
Speigel Tool-Imp v Square Dent	2	10	33	0	45	3	29273	22770; 28550
Speigel Tool-Imp v Alternate Bands	3	3	0	0	6	2	28551	23267; 22498*; 39000
Speigel Tool-Imp v Zoned Punct	2	3	7	0	12	1	22805	22688
Speigel Tool-Imp v LS Vinette II	1	2	0	0	3	1	39490*	39489; 39664
Speigel Tool-Imp v Dragged Dent	2	1	0	0	3	1	23306	22808
Speigel Tool-Imp v Banked Dent	4	11	0	0	15	2	22768	22493; 22764; 22770; 22784; 22805; 23267; 38447
Speigel Tool-Imp v Pronged	1	1	0	0	2	1	22752	23307
Speigel Tool-Imp v Blurred Knot	2	1	0	0	3	1	23362	0
SPEIGEL SERIES TOTAL	**26**	**42**	**90**	**0**	**158**	**17**		
Plain LS-T Notched Lip	2	0	1	0	3	2	N/A	22717; 22776; 27867
Collarless G-T Corded	2	1	1	1	5	3	N/A	23362; 29002; 23286; 23598
Temperless Toy Pinch Pot	4	1	1	0	5	2	20263	22635; 22540; 28526; 38467
MISC WARES TOTALS	**8**	**2**	**3**	**1**	**13**	**7**		
UMMA COLLECTION TOTALS	***92***	***117***	***381***	**6**	***602***	***57***		
								Another 173 KBT/KBS series and 47 ST-I series spalled or split bodysherds, unidentified as to type; and an additional 95 ceramic crumbs unidentified as to series, were also recovered from mixed provenances

Table 11.2. Speigel ceramics identified to type and variety.

Type and Variety	Rim sets	Body-sherds	Vessels	LU Illustrated Vessel No.	Excavation Unit Occurences
KB Thick v. Plain Lip/Nail Impressed	3	7	1	2	1
KB Thick v. Flat Lip	4	8	1	7	2
KB Thick v. PSS-stamp	2		1	16	Smoothed-over frabric impressions noted in laboratory (Brose and Julig: 2006)
KB Smoothed v Plain Lip	1		1	6	1
KB Smoothed v Lip Impressed	3	10	2	3,8	2
KB SERIES TOTALS	13	25	6		
Speigel Tool-Imp v Linear PSS	9	38	10	1,6,14,15,16,17,20,22,30,34	17
Speigel Tool-Imp v Narrow Tool	3		2	9, 40	3
Speigel Tool-Imp v Square Dent	2	2	2	10,12	4
Speigel Tool-Imp v Alternate Bands	1		1	39	1
Speigel Tool-Imp v Zoned Punct	4		3	35,38,41	4
Speigel Tool-Imp v LS Vinette II	2	4	2	19,37	4
Speigel Tool-Imp v Dragged Dent	1		1	29	1
Speigel Tool-Imp v Banked Dent	7	6	8	24,25,26,28,30,31,32,33	10
Speigel Tool-Imp v Pronged	1		1	11	1
Speigel Tool-Imp v Blurred Knot	3	6	3	4,13,36	5
Speigel Tool-Impressed v Indet	3	3	4	44a, 44b, 44c,44d	
SPEIGEL SERIES TOTAL	36	59	37		
Temperless Toy Pinch Pot	1	1	1	27	1
MISC WARES TOTALS	1	1	1		
LU Totals	*50*	*86*	*44*		57 excavation units yielded ceramics
	In the LU collections, made from 1981 - 2004, there are 393 small undecorated body-sherds and another 2679 spalled or split sherds that are unidentifiable to type. Of these, 81 are from now unknown contexts.				

All of these ceramics came from what appeared to be plow-disturbed upper soil levels in an alternating series of 1 m squares located about 150 m east of the knoll in which Robert Bell and Emerson Greenman found at least 10 copper-accompanied burials (Hawkins 2008; Chapter 12, this volume).

4. Some 36 typed but undecorated body sherds (9 percent of the UMMAA sample) and some 18 typed rims, decorated neck and shoulder sherds (11 percent of the UMMAA sample) were recovered from one of the cultural features that the field crews recognized, excavated, and recorded as a pit or a hearth or a "sweat bath."

The remaining handful of typed sherds in the UMMAA collection were recovered on what appears to have been one of the several (and sequential) prepared floor areas within the burial mound. Or they were recovered from the sand underlying the bones of Burial 8 within the mound, like the one Speigel Tool-Impressed variety Linear Stamped a la Vinette rim and the one Killarney Bay Smoothed variety Plain neck/shoulder sherd.

Analytical methods

Given the small number of sherds that could be connected, rim diameters and vessel capacity could not be estimated with any degree of precision. Ranges for dimensions given in the following discussions are based on vernier caliper measurements of rim sets (groups of two or more sherds that fit together as a portion of the same rim) and body sherds. These measurements confirm earlier observations (Brose 1970a) that there was as great a range for measurements on a single vessel as there was between several vessels of the same type. Evidence suggests that the Speigel Tool-Impressed vessels were significantly smaller than the Killarney Bay Smoothed vessels. It appears that the positive correlation between vessel thickness and estimated rim diameter for all vessels is due to stylistic and functional reasons rather than mechanical covariables. That is, the larger pots tended to be thicker, but there was no mechanical or technological need for that to have been the case.

Researchers measured all sherds for hardness and conducted scratch tests on exterior and interior surfaces and on the edges of fresh breaks. Since hardness varied considerably among several vessels assigned to a single type or variety, it seems doubtful that more refined techniques of testing would yield statistically significant results. This had been implied previously (Brose 1968). Paste texture was classified as compact, laminar, or friable. The thinner upper shoulder and neck portion of most vessels was more compact than other areas. Shoulders tended to display a higher frequency of laminar fracturing, while the conical vessel bases were all compact.

We examined colors under a 3200 degrees Kelvin daylight-type light and compared them to hue/chroma values from the book of Munsell Soil Color Charts (Munsell 1954). Most color changes are due to firing conditions, but some are certainly due to differential weathering and post-depositional organic and mineral staining.

We did not undertake microscopic or refractive mineralogical analyses of the tempering particles for the UMMAA collection, as the level of analysis described here provided the details needed to address the questions of ceramic ecology. The mineral identifications given are based on visual examination with 10x and 30x hand lenses and treatment with 20 percent solution of hydrochloric acid. Following the initial identifications by Darrel Long during the winter of 2007/2008, David Brose undertook hand lens and binocular microscopic analyses of the edges and spalled surfaces of sherds from the UMMAA collection. The implications of those studies confirm Long's initial observations and offer evidence of the changing ceramic material sources and manufacturing processes that occurred during the use of the site. There is almost certainly overlap among the three most common ceramic types and varieties under investigation. There is a paucity of evidence for the other (almost certainly much later) ceramic series. That said, we offer a tentative picture of what Matson (1951) called the ceramic ecology of the Middle Woodland (and later Late Woodland) occupants of the Killarney Bay site.

Minimal vessel reconstruction

Researchers sorted the prehistoric ceramic sherds recovered from Killarney Bay into what have traditionally been called types. This sorting was based primarily on characteristics of paste, manufacturing technology, morphology, size and shape, firing conditions, nonstructural differences in orifice treatment, and the presence or absence of particular classes of decoration. All vessels displaying similar manufacturing technology, surface treatment, rim/lip treatment, and presence or absence of additional decoration were considered to represent a single type. Where decorative motif or decorative technique or application of design elements differed, varieties of this type were established.

Occasionally, sherds of the same ceramic type and variety fit together as portions of individual vessels. For a few varieties, it was possible to identify vessel portions representing lip to base, or sections representing enough of the circumference at shoulder, neck, and rim, to virtually reconstruct their vessels' form and capacity. In many such cases, it was possible to reconstruct the vessel's overall decorative pattern or lack thereof, making only minimal assumptions of continuity and symmetry. We determined rim diameters for these vessels by comparing rim sherds and restored rim sections to semicircles of known diameter. The estimated range of rim diameters for any ceramic type or variety is largely based on the degree of curvature for individual rim sherds.

To determine if they could have been a physical portion of an existing reconstructed vessel, we compared remaining sherds having similar paste and temper, shape and size, and surface finish and decoration to reconstructed vessels of each type and variety. When they could not be so assigned, they were considered a different vessel. This resulted in an estimate of the minimum number of ceramic vessels present at the site. It is possible that there was a greater number of vessels, since some of the sherds assigned to one or another of the virtually reconstructed vessels may have been part of a separate vessel of identical size, shape, and appearance.

Ceramic types and varieties at Killarney Bay

From the University of Michigan and the Laurentian University excavations combined, there were several hundred sherds representing more than a dozen vessels of Killarney Bay Smoothed variety Plain—a relatively thin and compact, flat-lipped, smooth-surfaced, and undecorated variety. It may be that some unknown proportion of those body sherds represent the half-dozen vessels of the companion type, Killarney Bay Smoothed variety Lip-impressed, which displayed a band of oblique simple tool or nail impressions along the lip.

On the other hand, there are fewer than 70 sherds that represent what may have been only six vessels of the low-fired, coiled, and friable Killarney Thick ceramic type: nearly each vessel represents a different but indistinct provisional variety.

A very different situation occurs with the Speigel Tool-Impressed ceramics, likely due to the differing sizes and differing functions for which these vessels were used. There are 253 sherds that represent as many as 54 vessels and at least 7 different thin and compact dentate and complex tool-impressed Speigel Tool-Impressed varieties. Only one or two sherds represent the decorative motifs that comprised each of these decorative varieties. A few cord-marked body sherds represent perhaps two or three thin, limestone-tempered, nondescript but typologically Late Woodland vessels of uncertain site provenience. The heteroskedastic type and variety frequencies in this ceramic assemblage argue for extraordinary statistical caution, if not skepticism, as does their curatorial history.

During the years that Killarney Bay materials were curated at the UMMAA, numerous curators, visiting scholars, and students illustrated, compared, and even studied portions of the collection. Unfortunately, this led to considerable damage of the fragile and poorly conserved organic materials. Various artifact classes, especially the copper grave goods and ceramics, were resorted and dislocated. In some instances, boxes of labeled ceramics from other sites were mixed in with drawers of Killarney Bay materials and given new UMMAA catalog numbers. Fortunately, the assignment of new numbers was based on, but did not obliterate, Greenman's original field catalog numbers. Thus we have been able to assign sherds to the correct site and/or provenience over the course of our current investigation. However, many scholars' comparative statements regarding the ceramic affiliations of the Killarney Bay site appear to have been based on cursory inspection of the materials, which in some cases included ceramics from other sites.

At Laurentian University, the curatorial responsibilities occasionally languished with the changing investigators. For all save the latest of these, the disjunctive excavations at Killarney Bay were a short-term field exercise for untrained students, not a significant research project. Pat Julig, assisted by Kristen Thor, completed cataloging the recovered materials in 2007.

Any interpretations of Killarney Bay must be cautious, given the very scanty ceramic sample recovered with secure stratigraphic provenience. A tabulation of the distribution of the ceramic types and varieties from concatenated stratigraphic zones on the site (Table 11.3) documents the wholly unsurprising relative chronological sequence of the Killarney Bay Smoothed and the Speigel Tool-Impressed types. What does appear startling at first glance is the ambiguous chronological position of the Killarney Bay Thick vessels. Prior to the initiation of the mortuary excavations (Greenman 1966), these were thought to represent the earliest occupation of the site. On reflection, we should always have questioned the simplistic logic that thick=crude=old. The residue analysis (Appendix A) reveals the rather specialized, ritual uses these vessels served during those years when the mound was used and quotidian culinary and storage needs were served by vessels of other types. Details of the provenience of Killarney Bay sherds is found in Table 11.4.

Killarney Bay Thick

The ceramic type Killarney Bay Thick is represented by thick, poorly fired, yet thoroughly oxidized sherds with thick, contorted, and very friable paste, sparsely tempered with large angular fragments. Temper particles often protrude from vessel surfaces and occasionally obtrude onto both the vessel exterior and interior. Broken sherds reveal manufacture by poorly welded clay coils averaging nearly 14 mm in diameter. Each clay coil was slightly flattened side-to-side and each was poorly welded to the coil above and below. Artisans smoothed a thin layer of clay over the vessel exterior prior to firing. Due to post-depositional weathering, this clay slip tends to spall off sherds.

Surprisingly, fewer than half of the Killarney Bay Thick sherds of any variety are tempered with fragments from the ubiquitous local quartzite outcrops. Furthermore, very little olivine or hornblende occur as tempering in these vessels. Most of them are sparsely tempered with large and coarse biotite or orthoclase feldspar and angular quartz fragments, apparently selected from thermally degraded fine granitic pegmatites. Although such pegmatite cobbles are rare along the Killarney beaches today, similar glacial erratics can be found inland on the higher terraces of more ancient lake levels. This should not be taken to suggest that the Killarney Bay Thick vessels were made at some other location, however. As Long noted, several of the Killarney Bay Thick sherds that had coarse biotite and plagioclase fragments as predominant tempering also incorporated limited areas of subangular and lightly frosted quartzite fragments, as if one or several of the still-wet clay coils had been laid on the beach sands during construction of the vessel. In light of the nonquotidian early Middle Woodland use of the site, perhaps nonfunctional considerations were operating. As Greenman's students noted (Field Notes 1942, 1950), nonlocal coarse-grained igneous rocks were common among the stones selected for ritual fires near early internments in several of the submound areas. Perhaps some of the lighter-colored broken fragments or those heat-stressed cobbles were selected and then crushed to become temper in pottery made on the site for ritual uses, albeit not for mortuary accompaniment.

Killarney Bay Thick vessel shapes are unknown, but the few sherd combinations that can be reconstituted suggest simple, open, cylindrical jars with rounded, slightly conoidal bases, slightly restricted necks, and nearly vertical rims. Body sherds average 16.3 mm in thickness, and rims average 14.5 mm in thickness. Bases approach subconoidal, and vessel walls range from 17.3 to 21.5 mm thick, some 20 mm above the curve to their apparent apex. Hardness ranges from 3.0 to 3.5 on the Mohs scale and sherd colors are occasionally dark on exterior surfaces but more often are buff to salmon on both surfaces and throughout the sherd core. This suggests that the vessels were fired in an oxidizing atmosphere, likely in open wood fires of no great heat.

Unlike the technologically similar, strongly cord-marked Couture ceramics (Spence et al. 1990), Killarney Bay Thick exterior surfaces are smoothed with few faint impressions of stiff grasses or fabric. (One area of a Killarney Bay Thick vessel in the UMMAA collection shows the blurred impression of simple two-ply cordage, and one vessel recovered by the Laurentian University excavations shows faint fabric impressions.) Interior rim to neck areas also show discontinuous impressions of apparently identical "stiff grass wiping," which approximates faint channeling as described in the Saugeen and early Point Peninsula 1 ceramics (Emerson 1955; Wright and Anderson 1963).

The few sherds of Killarney Bay Thick may represent only a dozen vessels of three variants. From the UMMAA collections, we assigned seven vessels to Killarney Bay Thick variety Flat Lip, four vessels to Killarney Bay Thick variety Plain Lip, and two vessels to Killarney Bay Thick variety Pseudo-Scallop Shell Impressed (Figure 11.2). The

Figure 11.2. Killarney Bay Thick variety Pseudo-Scallop Shell Stamp (UMMAA 38447).

Laurentian University excavations on the habitation area of this site yielded fourteen sherds of two vessels assigned to Killarney Bay Thick variety Flat Lip. Also, a rim and neck sherd combination from at least one vessel of Killarney Bay Thick, variety Fabric Impressed, with traces of an overlying pseudo-scallop shell impression was located in the Laurentian University collections. The sherds came from the upper soil of a test excavation on the upper terrace just southeast of the recovered burial area (Julig, personal communication 2006). Decoration on those two joined sherds consists of faint, mostly parallel zones of thin pseudo-scallop shell impressions over some previously partially smoothed surface on the upper rim. This vessel might easily have been assigned to a single vessel of Killarney Bay Thick variety Pseudo-Scallop Shell Impressed (Hawkins 2008), but it conforms in many technical respects to what has been called Saugeen Pseudo-Scallop Shell Impressed (Finlayson 1977; Wright and Anderson 1963).

The Killarney Bay Thick type appears to have led several earlier scholars to their claims of early Adena site unit intrusion. However, to a far greater extent than either the earlier Morton or Marion ceramics of the Illinois or Ohio valley ceramic wares, the Killarney Bay Thick resembles the rather crude technology and imprecise decorative applications of the much later Saugeen ceramics of the Bruce Peninsula or the Late Marion-like thick ceramics found around the southern end of Lake Michigan and in the Saginaw River Valley of central lower Michigan, which persist well into the second century AD (Fitting 1972, 1978; Garland and Beld 1999). All of the Laurentian University specimens came from either late or unknown contexts. Those very few Killarney Bay Thick specimens in the UMMAA collection that come from controlled contexts largely occurred in those water-laid strata exposed during the first seasons of excavation, which appear relatively coterminous with early exposure of the knoll on which the mortuary activities occurred as the area was raised by post-glacial uplift. Some of these cultural contexts may predate the construction of the burial mound, but at least one sherd of Killarney Bay Thick variety Plain Lip did occur in what stratigraphy suggests was one of the earlier burials. Certainly the most interesting aspect of these few Killarney Bay Thick vessels is the amino acid residue study, which indicates their restricted culinary use. People used these vessels only to cook fish and nonstarchy vegetation such as spruce buds, as opposed to the seeds and general large game cooked in other types of vessels (Appendix A).

Killarney Bay Smoothed

The Killarney Bay Smoothed type, which has basal and body sherds approaching the average thicknesses of Killarney Bay Thick, forms the largest part of the site's ceramic assemblage. It is characterized by its dense and coarsely tempered, slab-made, smoothed-over malleated surfaces. Killarney Bay Smoothed sherds have a rather compact paste, abundantly tempered with very coarse to medium-coarse angular fragments, occasionally mixed with crushed fragments of light-colored granitic minerals including quartz, plagioclase, and biotite. Most Killarney Bay Smoothed sherds are heavily tempered with rather

Table 11.3 (page 1). Killarney Bay Thick ceramic spatial stratigraphic distributions.

UMMA#	Type	Variety	Grid Location	Depth	Stratigraphy	Cultural Assn or notes	Strat Group
22501	Killarney Bay Smoothed	rolled lip	TT 7	*no data*	in water-laid strata		1
22664	Killarney Bay Thick	plain lip	Tr 4 Sec BB-3	22.9' above lake	water-laid strata		1
22716	Killarney Bay Thick	plain lip	Tr 4D Sec D-5	2.4' below datum	flat in water-laid strata	24' above lake level	1
22818	Killarney Bay Smoothed	rolled lip	Tr 3D Sec C-2	*no data*	disturbed	deep as water-laid strata	1
23262	Killarney Bay Smoothed	flat lip	Tr 4C Sec I-1	2.5' below datum	sub-soil gravel lens		1
23267	Speigel Tool-Impressed	narrow tool	Tr 4C SecI-2`	2.3' below datum	waterlaid pebbles		1
29274	Killarney Bay Smoothed	flat lip	Tr 6-5 Sec 7F	3.4' below datum			1
38924	Killarney Bay Smoothed	flat lip	Tr 3D Sec G1	4.2' below surface	in water laid gravels		1
22454	Killarney Bay Smoothed	plain lip	Tr 2	2.0' below surface	below stratified pebbles		2
22550	Killarney Bay Smoothed	flat lip	C-9	2.0' below datum	in water-laid sands	above white sands	2
22860	Killarney Bay Smoothed	flat lip	Tr 3B Sec F-1	2.1' below datum		Map 32	2
23344	Killarney Bay Smoothed	plain lip	Tr 4C Sec I-1	2.6' below datum	in waterlaid strata		2
38933	Killarney Bay Thick	plain lip	Tr 4D Sec G-9 &10	*no data*	from hearth		2
22766	Killarney Bay Smoothed	flat lip	Tr 4D Sec F9	24.3' above lake			2
29000	Killarney Bay thick	*variety indeterminate*	Tr 3F	24" above lake			2
23286	Collarless Cord-Marked	Grit-tempered	Tr 4C Sec I-2	2.0' below datum	in water-laid pebbles		3
22833	Killarney Bay thick	*variety indeterminate*	Tr 3D Sec E1	2.1' below datum		Map 32	3
30250	Killarney Bay Smoothed	flat lip	Tr 3E Sec D-5	*no data*	sandy subsoil		3
38443	Killarney Bay Smoothed	flat lip	Tr 3E Sec E4	1.8' below datum	in subsoil		3
38445	Killarney Bay Smoothed	rolled lip	Tr 3F Sec E-4	1.8' below datum			3
38447	Killarney Bay Thick	pseudo scallop shell	Tr 3F Sec E-4	1.8' below datum	top of sub-soil		3
38447	Speigel Tool-Impressed	Banked dentate	Tr 3E Sec E-4	1.8' below subsoil			3
39489	Killarney Bay Thick	plain lip	*mound stripping*		in sands below Burial 8		3
39490	Speigel Tool-Impressed	linear stamp Vinette II	*mound stripping*		below sacrum in Burial 8	Map 167	3
38463	Killarney Bay Smoothed	*variety indeterminate*	Tr 3E Sec G-5	23.2' above lake			3
38447	Killarney Bay thick	pseudo scallop shell	Tr 3E Sec E4	1.8' below surface	in subsoil		4
22498	Speigel Tool-Impressed	linear pss				overlying Burial 1	4
22698	Killarney Bay Smoothed	flat lip	Tr 4D Sec C-10	1.5' below datum			4
22761	Killarney Bay Thick	flat lip	Tr E8 Sec F7		subsoil		4
22846	Killarney Bay Smoothed	*variety indeterminate*	Tr 3D Sec E3		from pit in subsoil	Map 29	4
22849	Killarney Bay Smoothed	flat lip	Tr 3D Sec E3		bottom of pit	Map 29	4
28550	Speigel Tool-Impressed	square dentate	Tr 4C Sec 6J	1.65' below datum			4
29017	Killarney Bay Smoothed	flat lip	Tr 3F		subsoil		4
30245	Killarney Bay Thick	plain lip	*no data*	*no data*			4
38897	Killarney Bay Smoothed	Glittery	Tr 4D Sec G-8	1.7' below datum	subsoil		4
22779	Killarney Bay Thick	plain lip	Tr 3D Sec B1		subsoil		4
38915	Killarney Bay Thick	plain lip	Tr 3D Sec G-4		upper subsoil		4
22688	Speigel Tool-Impressed	zoned punctate	Tr 4D Sec C8		near fp in subsoil		4
39661	Killarney Bay Smoothed	*variety indeterminate*	*mound stripping*		over Burial 8 @ pit edge		4
22702	Killarney Bay Smoothed	flat lip	Tr 4D Sec D5	1.3' below datum	in pit from topsoil		5
38900	Speigel Tool-Impressed	Alternate Bands	Tr 4D Sec D-9	0.75' below surface	topsoil		5
23307	Speigel Tool-Impressed	pronged	Tr 4C Sec I-3		pit in topsoil		5
28551	Speigel Tool-Impressed	alternate bands	Test Trench 10			Map 63 & 64	5
28551	Killarney Bay thick	pseudo scallop shell	Test Trench 10			Map 63 & 64	5
28991	Killarney Bay thick	*variety indeterminate*	Tr 4F		top soil		5
29273	Speigel Tool-Impressed	square dentate	Tr 3F		bottom of pit		5
38467	Toy pinch pot	*no varieties assigned*	Tr 3E Sec G2	24.2' above lake	*no data*		5
38251	Killarney Bay Smoothed	rolled lip	*mound stripping*	*no data*	*no data*		5

Table 11.3 (page 2). Killarney Bay Thick ceramic spatial stratigraphic distributions.

UMMA#	Type	Variety	Grid Location	Depth	Stratigraphy	Cultural Assn or notes	Strat Group
22832	Killarney Bay Smoothed	flat lip	Tr 3D Sec E-1		pit or topsoil		5
39664	Killarney Bay Smoothed	*variety indeterminate*	*mound stripping*	on throw-out pile	Final 1952 stripping		5
22350	Speigel Tool-Impressed	linear pseudo scallop	Tr 3D Sec E34		top soil		6
22674	Killarney Bay Smoothed	rolled lip	Tr 4D Sec B10		top soil		6
22717	Plain limestone temper	*no varieties assigned*	Tr 4D Sec D10		top soil		6
22752	Speigel Tool-Impressed	pronged	Tr 4D Sec F-5		topsoil		6
22768	Speigel Tool-Impressed	banked dentate	Tr 4D Sec F-9		topsoil		6
22783	Speigel Tool-Impressed	linear pseudo scallop	Tr 3D Sec B-2		topsoil		6
22805	Killarney Bay Thick	plain lip	Tr 3B Sec C-2		topsoil		6
22850	Plain limestone temper	*no varieties assigned*	Tr 3D Sec E3		top soil		6
22868	Killarney Bay Smoothed	flat lip	Tr 3D Sec E2		top soil		6
23306	Killarney Bay Smoothed	flat lip	Tr 4C		top soil		6
23598	Speigel Tool-Iimpressed	*variety indeterminate*	Tr 4C Sec I 10		top soil		6
28674	Killarney Bay Smoothed	rolled lip	*no data*		plowed up	.	6
30253	Killarney Bay Smoothed	*variety indeterminate*	Tr 3F SecD-4		topsoil		6
20263	Temperless toy pinch pot	*no varieties assigned*	Tr 4E Sec E2		disturbed top soil		7
22770	Speigel Tool-Impressed	banked dentate	Tr 4D		general surface		7
23306	Killarney Bay Smoothed	plain lip	Tr 4C Sec 6J		disturbed top soil		7
28522	Speigel Tool-Impressed	linear pseudo scallop	Test Trench 7		*no data*		7
39487	Killarney Bay Smoothed	flat lip	*mound salvage*	final work	root cellar fill		7
23362	Collarless Cord-Marked	*no varieties assigned*	Tr 4C		washed from throw out pile		7
28526	Toy pot	*no varieties assigned*	Test Trench 7		surface		7
28550	Killarney Bay Smoothed	lip-impressed	*no data*		*no data*		x
22820	Killarney Bay Smoothed	flat lip	Tr 3D Sec I2		*no data*	Map 29	x

small angular orthoclase and plagioclase crystal fragments, many with intact facets. These tempering particles (lightly crushed if at all) are likely to have been thermally freed (loosened from their rock matrix under direct exposure to fire) from granitic cobbles that litter the shores of the Killarney Peninsula and nearby islands. Similar granitic cobbles also predominate among the rocks collected from what Greenman's crews called "baths," several of which occurred in the early subsoil gravel and sand lenses of the beach excavations.

The vessels of Killarney Bay Smoothed variety Glittery are tempered solely with crushed micaceous schist or gneiss fragments, rich in hornblende and muscovite. This variety is further decorated by floating, or lightly smoothing the surface with a damp or wet skin or fabric, so that the mica and quartz crystal surfaces parallel the exterior ceramic surfaces, giving the dark vessels considerable reflective sparkle. Suites of metamorphic gneiss and schist occur in nearly every outcrop of the folded belts of the Laurentian Shield, which begins some 20 km to the north of the site. Water-worn cobbles of schist and gneiss are common in fluvial gravels of the lower Spanish and French rivers, some 25 km to the east and the west of the Killarney Peninsula, and pebbles of these rocks occur on nearly every local beach. However, there are so few sherds of this type and variety that they may represent an idiosyncratic rather than a community endeavor.

Among the Killarney Bay Smoothed variety Glittery sherds, hardness ranged from 3.0 to 3.5 on the Mohs scale, with most measured sherds approaching 3.5. Sherd colors tend to be dark black on upper vessel exterior and interior surfaces and sherd cores. Shoulder and lower body sherds have dark exterior surfaces and salmon-colored interior surfaces, and cores and basal sherds show dark salmon to buff exteriors and light gray to buff-colored interior surfaces and cores. It is likely these vessels were fired with the rims

Table 11.4 (page 1). Provenience for Killarney Bay typed ceramics.

UMMA#	Type	Variety	Grid Location	Depth	Stratigraphy	Cultural Assn or notes
22454	Killarney Bay Smoothed	plain lip	Tr 2	2.0' below surface	below stratified pebbles	
20263	Temperless toy pinch pot	NV	Tr 4E Sec E2		disturbed top soil	
22350	Speigel Tool-Impressed	linear pseudo scallop	Tr 3D Sec E34		top soil	
22498	Speigel Tool-Impressed	linear pss				overlying Burial 1
22501	Killarney Bay Smoothed	rolled lip	TT 7		in water-laid strata	
22533			Tr 2 Sec B5			Map 12A
22550	Killarney Bay Smoothed	flat lip	C-9	2.0' below datum	in water-laid sands	above white sands
22664	Killarney Bay Thick	plain lip	Tr 4 Sec BB-3	22.9' above lake	water-laid strata	
22674	Killarney Bay Smoothed	rolled lip	Tr 4D Sec B10		top soil	
22688	Speigel Tool-Impressed	zoned punctate	Tr 4D Sec C8		near fp in subsoil	
22698	Killarney Bay Smoothed	flat lip	Tr 4D Sec C-10	1.5' below datum		
22702	Killarney Bay Smoothed	flat lip	Tr 4D Sec D5	1.3' below datum	in pit from topsoil	
22716	Killarney Bay Thick	plain lip	Tr 4D Sec D-5	2.4' below datum	lying flat in water-laid strata	24' above lake level
22717	Plain limestone temper	NV	Tr 4D Sec D10		top soil	
22752	Speigel Tool-Impressed	pronged	Tr 4D Sec F-5		topsoil	
22761	Killarney Bay Thick	flat lip	Tr E8 Sec F7		subsoil	
22766	Killarney Bay Smoothed	flat lip	Tr 4D Sec F9	24.3' above lake		
22768	Speigel Tool-Impressed	banked dentate	Tr 4D Sec F-9		topsoil	
22770	Speigel Tool-Impressed	banked dentate	Tr 4D		general surface	
22779	Killarney Bay Thick	plain lip	Tr 3D Sec B1		subsoil	
22783	Speigel Tool-Impressed	linear pseudo scallop	Tr 3D Sec B-2		topsoil	
22805	Killarney Bay Thick	plain lip	Tr 3B Sec C-2		topsoil	
22818	Killarney Bay Smoothed	rolled lip	Tr 3D Sec C-2		disturbed	deep as water-laid strata
22820	Killarney Bay Smoothed	flat lip	Tr 3D Sec I2			Map 29
22832	Killarney Bay Smoothed	flat lip	Tr 3D Sec E-1		pit or topsoil	
UMMA#	Type	Variety	Grid Location	Depth	Stratigraphy	Cultural Assn or notes
22833	Killarney Bay thick	NV	Tr 3D Sec E1	2.1' below datum		Map 32
22846	Killarney Bay Smoothed		Tr 3D Sec E3		from pit in subsoil	Map 29
22849	Killarney Bay Smoothed	flat lip	Tr 3D Sec E3		bottom of pit	Map 29
22850	Plain limestone temper	NV	Tr 3D Sec E3		top soil	
22860	Killarney Bay Smoothed	flat lip	Tr 3B Sec F-1	2.1' below datum		Map 32
22868	Killarney Bay Smoothed	flat lip	Tr 3D Sec E2		top soil	
23262	Killarney Bay Smoothed	flat lip	Tr 4C Sec I-1	2.5' below datum	sub-soil gravel lens	
23267	Speigel Tool-Impressed	narrow tool	Tr 4C SecI-2`	2.3' below datum	waterlaid pebbles	
23286	Collarless Cord-Marked	Grit-tempered	Tr 4C Sec I-2	2.0' below datum	in water-laid pebbles	
23306	Killarney Bay Smoothed	plain lip	Tr 4C Sec 6J		disturbed top soil	
23306	Killarney Bay Smoothed	flat lip	Tr 4C		top soil	
23307	Speigel Tool-Impressed	pronged	Tr 4C Sec I-3		pit in topsoil	
23344	Killarney Bay Smoothed	plain lip	Tr 4C Sec I-1	2.6' below datum	in waterlaid strata	
23362	Collarless Cord-Marked	NV	Tr 4C		washed from throw out pile	
23598	Speigel Tool-Iimpressed	NV	Tr 4C Sec I 10		top soil	
28522	Speigel Tool-Impressed	linear pseudo scallop	Test Trench 7			
28526	Toy pot	NV	Test Trench 7		surface	
28550	Killarney Bay Smoothed	lip-impressed				
28550	Speigel Tool-Impressed	square dentate	Tr 4C Sec 6J	1.65' below datum		
28551	Speigel Tool-Impressed	alternate bands	Test Trench 10			Map 63 & 64
28551	Killarney Bay thick	pseudo scallop shell	Test Trench 10			Map 63 & 64
28674	Killarney Bay Smoothed	rolled lip			plowed up	.

Table 11.4 (page 2). Provenience for Killarney Bay typed ceramics.

UMMA#	Type	Variety	Grid Location	Depth	Stratigraphy	Cultural Assn or notes
28991	Killarney Bay thick		Tr 4F		top soil	
29000	Killarney Bay thick		Tr 3F	24" above lake		
29017	Killarney Bay Smoothed	flat lip	Tr 3F		subsoil	
UMMA#	Type	Variety	Grid Location	Depth	Stratigraphy	Cultural Assn or notes
29273	Speigel Tool-Impressed	square dentate	Tr 3F		bottom of pit	
29274	Killarney Bay Smoothed	flat lip	Tr 6-5 Sec 7F	3.4' below datum		
30245	Killarney Bay Thick	plain lip				
30250	Killarney Bay Smoothed	flat lip	Tr 3E Sec D-5		sandy subsoil	
30253	Killarney Bay Smoothed	NV	Tr 3F SecD-4		topsoil	
38251	Killarney Bay Smoothed	rolled lip				
38443	Killarney Bay Smoothed	flat lip	Tr 3E Sec E4	1.8' below datum	in subsoil	
38445	Killarney Bay Smoothed	rolled lip	Tr 3F Sec E-4	1.8' below datum		
38447	Killarney Bay Thick	pseudo scallop shell	Tr 3F Sec E-4	1.8' below datum	top of sub-soil	
38447	Speigel Tool-Impressed	Banked dentate	Tr 3E Sec E-4	1.8' below subsoil		
38447	Killarney Bay thick	pseudo scallop shell	Tr 3E Sec E4	1.8' below surface	in subsoil	
38463	Killarney Bay Smoothed	NV	Tr 3E Sec G-5	23.2' above lake		
38467	Toy pinch pot	NV	Tr 3E Sec G2	24.2' above lake		
38489	Killarney Bay Thick	plain lip			sands below Burial 8	
38897	Killarney Bay Smoothed	Glittery	Tr 4D Sec G-8	1.7' below datum	subsoil	
38900	Speigel Tool-Impressed	Alternate Bands	Tr 4D Sec D-9	0.75' below surface	topsoil	
38915	Killarney Bay Thick	plain lip	Tr 3D Sec G-4		upper subsoil	
38924	Killarney Bay Smoothed	flat lip	Tr 3D Sec G1	4.2' below surface	in water laid gravels	
38933	Killarney Bay Thick	plain lip	Tr 4D Sec G-9 &10		from hearth	
39487	Killarney Bay Smoothed	flat lip			root cellar fill	
39489	Killarney Bay Thick	plain lip			in sands below Burial 8	
39490	Speigel Tool-Impressed	linear stamp Vinette II			below sacrum in Burial 8	Map 167
39661	Killarney Bay Smoothed	NV			over Burial 8 @ pit edge	
39664	Killarney Bay Smoothed	NV	Mound throw-out pile		Final 1952 stripping	

down in the reducing atmosphere of a partially closed fire. The bases stood up into a free oxidizing atmosphere, likely in the draftier portions of a minimally controlled wood fire.

Killarney Bay Smoothed vessels consist of minimally restricted bowls and open jars with conoidal bases, slightly restricted necks, and vertical to slightly outcurved rims. Body sidewalls average 12.5 mm in thickness, and slightly everted rims average 11.8 mm in thickness. The somewhat obtruded rounded and near-beveled lips average 12.8 mm in thickness, and conoidal basal sherds average 16.3 mm in thickness, thinning to 13.6 mm some 20 mm above the apex.

The undecorated type of Killarney Bay Smoothed has four variants, indicated by rim, lip, or surface modifications. Killarney Bay Smoothed variety Flat Lip was represented by at least five and possibly as many as nine different vessels in the UMMAA collections and by one vessel (represented by two sherds) from the Laurentian excavations (Hawkins 2008). Killarney Bay Smoothed variety Lip Impressed was represented by four vessels in the UMMAA collections and two vessels (represented by 12 sherds) from the Laurentian excavations (Hawkins 2008). The rounded lip, out-folded Killarney Bay Smoothed variety Rolled Lip was represented by three vessels in the UMMAA collections (Hawkins 2008). A single vessel in the UMMAA collection consisted of Killarney Bay Smoothed variety Glittery, the surface of which was floated to reveal the sheen of mica flakes from the crushed gneiss and granite temper (Hawkins 2008).

At least two Killarney Bay Smoothed sherds in the UMMAA collection, and a few in the Laurentian University collections, suggest that exterior surfaces had been impressed with some textile or fabric or cord-wrapped paddle. All Killarney Bay Smoothed sherds, including these two, have been smoothed. The final surface finish occasionally reveals striations from wiping or brushing with stiff grasses. Base interiors rarely bear random patterns of like origin. The vessel rims are undecorated, as are the lips of the Killarney Bay Smoothed variety Plain. Killarney Bay Smoothed variety Ticked Lip vessels had the exterior edge of the flattened lip decorated with simple tool impressions, forming a single row of transverse to oblique tool impressions.

Based on subtle frequency shifts in thickness, tempering size and density, and manufacturing expertise, the Killarney Bay Smoothed ceramics grade into the Killarney Bay Thick type. In the literature, this type (Killarney Bay Smoothed) appears to have been subsumed in the previous descriptions of those presumably Early Woodland or earlier Middle Woodland ceramics. Morphologically, the Killarney Bay Smoothed type resembles the early Middle Woodland Shiawassee series from the Schultz and Bussinger sites in the Saginaw Valley (Fischer 1972; Halsey 1976). Temper sources differ, but the ceramics of this type are also similar to the Bay de Noc Plain from Summer Island and the recently redated North Bay I/II, plain and cord-marked ceramics from northern Lake Michigan (Brose 1968; Brose and Hambacher 1999; Mason 1966, 1992). They are rather unlike a smoothed version of the presumably coeval Couture ceramics of southwest Ontario (Spence et al. 1990). In a number of technological aspects (thickness, tempering size and density, and manufacturing expertise—but again, not in their decorative modes or in their absence of interior marking), they approach the early Point Peninsula from the somewhat later Kant and Ault Park sites (Emerson 1955).

Speigel Tool-Impressed series

The third major ceramic type recovered from Killarney Bay was Speigel Tool-Impressed, a type made up of ten relatively thin and carefully banked and linear plain tool- or fingernail-stamped and dentate-stamped decorative variants. Forty-one vessels, represented by more than 180 sherds, were excavated from 47 1-m squares by Laurentian University. Seventeen vessels, represented by 158 sherds, were recovered from the 1939–1953 excavated provenience sets at Killarney Bay. (It is noteworthy that the University of Michigan field crews found no such sherds in the southernmost and lowest stratified beach deposits.) The earliest discussions assigned these decorated Speigel Tool-Impressed ceramics to Vinette II (Ritchie and MacNeish 1949), but since the early 1970s most archaeologists from Ontario have assigned them to a middling geographic and temporal position in their still imprecisely defined Point Peninsula tradition.[3] Archaeologists trained in the more western portions of the Great Lakes drainage tend to relate them to a nonembossed phase (presumably a late phase of the Laurel tradition, Lugenbeal 1976) or what in the McKern Midwestern Taxonomic System would have been called a focus (southern fringe) of the Laurel tradition.[4]

A few sherds' exterior surfaces below the shoulders reveal that some, if not all, were malleated with a cord-wrapped or textile-covered paddle. Subsequent smoothing makes detailed observation of the fabric imprecise and ubiquity of application uncertain. The final surface finish on vessel necks, sometimes above a single horizontal row of tool impressions, was consistently smoothed. The upper 20 to 35 mm of the vessels' rims are decorated with oblique or vertical bands of simple or complex (dentate or pseudo-scallop shell) tool impressions on a smoothed surface, forming a single horizontal field. The vessel lips rarely bear transverse or oblique tool impressions. While bearing minor variations in decorative element and attitude of application, these ceramics are similar enough that they appear to belong to the same Middle Woodland population.

In all, some 338 rim and decorated body sherds comprised the 58 Speigel Tool-Impressed vessels that represent 10 stylistically distinguishable type variants. An additional 47 spalled and eroded sherds from the UMMAA collections can be assigned to this broad type cluster but cannot be assigned to any particular variety (see Tables 11.1, 11.2). The Laurentian University collections include 3,249 pieces of pottery, of which 81 are from unknown contexts. The 3,249 sherds are assigned only to 40-odd vessels because 2,679 are spalled—that is, they were classified as fragmentary, with only one side of the sherd present. Another 393 are undecorated body sherds. While some plain neck and rim/body sherds were incorporated into the few thick-bodied Killarney Bay Smoothed variety Plain vessels, the remaining 40 Speigel Tool-Impressed vessels are represented by the remaining 180 sherds[5].

All vessels of the Speigel Tool-Impressed type are represented by sherds with a fine sandy to silty and relatively compact clay body, although a few sherds were laminar and somewhat friable. No coil breaks were evident, although sherd breakage at horizontal neck/shoulder junctions suggests many of these vessels were built, at least in part, by coiling or the addition of a ring. Sherd hardness ranges from 2.0 to 3.5 on the Mohs scale, with nearly all sherds clustered around 3.0. Sherd colors are buff to salmon on the exterior and many interior upper vessel surfaces, but even these vessel sections tend to display dark cores and occasionally dark firing clouds on vessel surfaces. This suggests that the vessels were fired in a partially or occasionally oxidizing atmosphere, likely in open wood fires that varied from free draft to rather dense and closed throughout the firing process.

Most of the Speigel Tool-Impressed variety Pseudo-scallop Shell, variety Banked Stamp, and variety Linear-stamped sherds were tempered with the crushed quartz, feldspar, and micas of several species, along with some amount of dark olivine or hornblende. As noted for the Killarney Bay Thick sherds, this is a common mineral suite often observed in large glacially deposited granitic cobbles on the mainland to the north and east of the site. There are also numerous small pebbles of such fine-grained granite along the present shore of Wikwimikong Bay on the north shore of Manitoulin Island to the south of the Killarney Bay site (Darrel Long, personal communication 2007). In contrast, the Speigel Tool-Impressed variety Dentate and variety Square Dentate sherds were tempered with a mixture of crushed medium subrounded quartzite beach sands and finely crushed fragments of pinkish quartzite, probably from crushed pebbles of the local Upper Lorrain Formation or from thermally altered Bar River mylonite, accessible in the nearby Cloche Mountains to the west.

It seems likely that the site at which most of the Speigel Tool-Impressed pottery vessels were manufactured lay some short distance from the Killarney Bay site itself. Sparse temper in the less-common Speigel Tool-Impressed varieties consisted of medium to medium-coarse angular crushed fragments of quartzites and granodiorite quartz and plagioclase felspars. A few sherds (but no specific variety) had tempers of darker minerals. Tempering-particle size ranged from 1.0 mm to 6.4 mm, with a mean diameter of 4.6 mm. As Hawkins (2008) determined for the Speigel Tool-Impressed sherds from the Laurentian University excavations, density of temper appears to have been less than 25 percent aplastic by volume.

Speigel Tool-Impressed vessel shapes consist of minimally restricted small jars with a slightly everted to nearly vertical rim having a plain flattened lip, or one slightly rolled to the outside, creating a slightly thickened exterior upper rim area due to the lip-flattening process. All vessels displayed vertical, minimally outcurved rims with a moderately constricted neck and were rather gradually recurved below the shoulder. As reconstructed from the remaining small and short segments of rims, rim diameters appear to have ranged from just over 18.5 cm to slightly less than 30 cm, with a mean diameter around 20 cm (Figures 11.3, 11.4, 11.5). Speigel Tool-Impressed vessel height and overall capacity are unknown. No vessel sections or isolated sherds assigned to this type displayed a basal configuration, whereas the related Laurel and Point Peninsula traditions to which this type belongs generally terminate in a subconoidal

Figure 11.3. Speigel Tool-Impressed rim and neck sherds: var. zoned punctate; var. narrow tool; var. alternate band.

Figure 11.4. Speigel Tool-Impressed rim and neck sherds: var. banked dentate.

Figure 11.5. Speigel Tool-Impressed rim and neck sherds: var. linear pseudo-scallop shell, aka "Vinette"; var. banked dentate; var pronged; var. blurred knot.

base. Body sherd thickness at the shoulder ranged from 4.7 mm to 8.4 mm, with a mean thickness of 6.1 mm. Rim thickness, measured from 1 to 3 cm below the lip, ranged from 4.2 mm to 7.2 mm, with a mean of 5.9 mm.

Clearly, these ceramics are examples of what Brose and Hambacher (1999) most recently assigned to the Northern Tier Middle Woodland Tradition, which spans the continuum from Laurel on the west to Point Peninsula in the east (Brose 1968, 1973; Fitting 1970; Mason 1966, 1991; Spence and Fox 1986; Stoltman 1962, 1973; Wright 1967). We have distinguished ten varieties of the Speigel Tool-Impressed ceramic type on the basis of minor differences in field (the overall pattern of the decoration), orientation (the angle of the pattern on the vessel), implement (shell, stick, fingernail), or technique (the way the implement was applied to the clay) of decorative motif application[6].

Speigel Tool-Impressed variety Linear Pseudo-Scallop-Shell
Speigel Tool-Impressed variety Narrow Tool
Speigel Tool-Impressed variety Square Dentate
Speigel Tool-Impressed variety Alternate Bands
Speigel Tool-Impressed variety Zoned Punctate
Speigel Tool-Impressed variety Linear Stamped Vinette II
Speigel Tool-Impressed variety Dragged Dentate
Speigel Tool-Impressed variety Banked Dentate
Speigel Tool-Impressed variety Pronged
Speigel Tool-Impressed variety Blurred Knot

Lips on all of the Speigel Tool-Impressed Narrow Tool, Banked Dentate, Square Dentate, and Dragged Dentate variety vessels were plain and flattened. Exterior lip decoration on all varieties consisted of multiple parallel horizontal banks of similarly vertical to slightly oblique rows of tool impressions made by a narrow unnotched or variably unnotched tool. The Banked Dentate impressions appear to have been made by emplacing the edge of the notched tool at an angle and then removing it. The notched end of the Square Dentate tool impressions were made by emplacing the tool perpendicular to the surface of the vessel and then removing it. The Dragged Dentate impressions were made by emplacing the tool either at an angle or square to the vessel surface and then dragging it some distance as it was being removed from the clay (see Brose 1973 for a detailed technological replication).

On the Speigel Tool-Impressed Alternate Bands variety there are at least three parallel horizontal banks of dentate tool impressions, between each of which the orientation of the oblique rows alternates from right oblique to left oblique to right oblique (Figure 11.6). As with the other banked stamp varieties of Speigel Tool-Impressed, repetitive

Figure 11.6. Speigel Tool-Impressed var. alternate band (UMMAA 28551).

The final two related varieties, Speigel Tool-Impressed variety Linear Pseudo-Scallop-Shell and Speigel Tool-Impressed variety Linear Stamped Vinette II, differ most from the other varieties of this type, as they do not bear the characteristic Michigan Laurel-like design of broad horizontal fields of vertical banks of oblique simple tool stamping (viz Brose 1968; Janzen 1968b). Rather, they resemble many of the Ontario Point Peninsula vessels, especially those from the Rice Lake region (Emerson 1955; Johnston 1968a). The varieties from the Killarney Bay site are decorated by at least three parallel horizontal rows, each of which consists of a single row of oblique pseudo-scallop shell or dentate tool impressions. When Greenman (1966) called the decorated dentate-stamped body sherd of this variety (which he recovered from Burial 8) "Vinette II," he implied an occupation significantly later than that which he had earlier identified as Adena based on his initial recovery of Killarney Bay Thick ceramics.

right over left banks of oblique dentate stamping are well represented in both Laurel and Point Peninsula assemblages, from western Lake Superior to Green Bay to north central New York State (c.f Banked Stamp Plain Tool, Chevron variety at Summer Island [Brose 1973:Plate IVg]).

One vessel of Speigel Tool-Impressed variety Zoned Punctated shows a single horizontal field of widely spaced (12 to 15 mm) oblique sets of 4.5 mm-wide ovoid to annular punctates bordered by narrow (9.1 mm) trailed lines, analogous to the linear impressed braided-cord vessel from the first century CE Summer Island site (Brose 1973). This decorative field is bounded along the lip and the upper shoulder by a horizontal row of 1.5-mm triangular punctations about 6 mm apart.

The two related varieties, Speigel Tool-Impressed variety Pronged and Speigel Tool-Impressed variety Blurred Knot, replicate the pattern of horizontal fields of oblique banked stamps seen in most of the other vessels of this provisional type. Rather than stamping by a notched or narrow tool edge, however, the respective pattern on these variants is the result of their having been deeply impressed by a bifurcated rounded-point tool or having been shallowly pressed by what appears to have been a simple overhand knot made by a thin cord of twisted zzS cordage, not unlike many of those seen in the site's organic fabrics that were preserved by the copper grave goods they enclosed (B. Brose, Appendix C, this volume).

The Early Late Woodland wares

During the UMMAA excavations, surface and plow-zone recovery yielded a few relatively thin, limestone- and grit-tempered cord-marked rim and body sherds of what may have been five nondescript late collarless vessels (Figure 11.7) and another two very small, minimally chalky pinch pots, often called toy pots. Hawkins (2008) reports Laurentian University crews recovered a number of grit-tempered corded or undecorated sherds from the plow-zone in the habitation area of Killarney Bay, but she was justifiably reluctant to assign these to separate vessels, as many might have been portions of other vessels whose decorated rims might have been counted as one of the indeterminate variety of Speigel-Tool-Impressed vessels. On the larger of these latest (presumably functional) vessels, the absence of collaring or castellations and the absence of decoration made with a cord-wrapped stick or twisted or knotted cord relates them to the earlier Wayne wares of central to northeast Michigan (Fitting 1970) and to the early Mackinac wares from the Juntunen site (McPherron 1967). They also appear similar to seventh-century Princess Point-like ceramics from the Bruce Peninsula (Fox 1990:184ff) or similar ceramics from a presumably late Middle Woodland assemblage at the Goodwin-Gresham site across Lake Huron (Fitting et al. 1969), which also dated to the early

Figure 11.7. Limestone-tempered Late Woodland sherds from various surfaces and plow-disturbed horizons at Killarney Bay.

seventh century CE. They have been reported in most of the sites along the islands forming the southern line of the DeTour Channel from Mackinac to Georgian Bay (Brose and Hambacher 1999).

Other than the very fine rounded sand grains that seem to have been incorporated in all of the clays used at the site, there was no temper in the few sherds of what have been called juvenile or toy pinch pots. There were a few other larger vessels, represented by a very few sherds, which had cord-marked or smoothed-over, fabric-marked bodies and thickened or out-turned notched lips, akin to (but not assignable to) the Bois Blanc or Spring Creek or Couture ceramics of the seventh through the eleventh centuries (Fitting 1978; McPherron 1967; Spence et al. 1990). These ceramics were all recovered from surface or disturbed contexts and in very low frequencies. No significance should be attributed to the fact that all were tempered with a mixture of rather fine particles that varied from almost pure crushed Silurian dolomitic Engadine and/or brecciated Mackinac limestone to orthoclase feldspar and quartzite. These ceramics could have been made almost anywhere in the northern portions of either the Lake Michigan or the Lake Huron basin, as one or more Silurian reef formations rim both those basins. Wikwemikong Island would have been the closest location for both sedimentary rock and quartzite.

There is so little Late Woodland material present on the Killarney Bay site that it would appear those responsible for it performed most of their economic activity, and probably all of their pottery manufacturing, at some location other than the site itself.

Analysis of ceramics from the habitation area

In this section, we characterize the ceramics recovered during the Laurentian excavations in the habitation area and outline the results of petrographic analysis of a small number of these sherds. These observations are followed by a brief comparison of the material recovered by the Laurentian teams at Killarney Bay to ceramics from other Middle Woodland sites in Ontario.

The nature of the Laurentian University ceramic assemblage

Pottery comprises a small but important component of the material recovered in the Laurentian University excavations. Over many years of excavations, students recovered approximately 3,382 pottery fragments with a total mass

Table 11.5. Pottery recovered by the LU teams by portion of the pot represented.

Nature of object	n	Mass (g)
Rim sherd	66	278
Fragmentary rim sherd	12	15
Neck/shoulder sherd	18	85
Body sherd	517	1117
Base of pot	1	14
Fragmentary sherd	2767	1463
Lump of clay	1	4
Total	3382	2977

of 2,977 g. With an average mass of less than 1 g, most of these pieces are too small to analyze. Table 11.5 provides a summary of the pieces, organized by the part of the pot the fragment derives from. Sherds classified as fragmentary are those that possess only an exterior or interior face or neither. Body sherds are those with both interior and exterior walls present—these can be measured for thickness. By count, more than 80 percent of the recovered pottery consists of fragmentary sherds. This sample of pottery may seem substantial, but in reality only a small portion of it is amenable to analysis.

The spatial distribution of pottery fragments is described in Chapter 6. Overall, pottery density is low within the habitation area. It is greatest in the W16 area, where there is a linear north-south spread of artifacts. As is described below, this location corresponds with a slope, and the high concentration may reflect erosion or disposal away from a flatter, more habitable area.

Characteristics of the Laurentian ceramic assemblage

To begin the analysis, we examined the entire assemblage of Laurentian ceramics to establish a minimum set of "analytical vessels." These were determined based on characteristics such as form (particularly of the upper rim); nature of decoration; nature of the tool used in decoration; wall thickness; and temper density. Larger sherds were examined and grouped with like sherds. In a number of instances, refits were established. In other cases, sherds with similar decoration, form, and technical attributes that nevertheless did not mend were grouped together into a single analytical vessel. Most sherds did not possess enough attributes to allow them to be grouped with any other sherds as analytical vessels.

Using this method, we established 44 analytical vessels. A few of these are comprised of many sherds (Vessel 1=38 sherds; Vessel 2=19 sherds), but the vast majority are represented by one or two sherds. In many cases, the sherds are rims or fragmentary rims, but in a number of instances, the decoration of the body and other attributes are sufficiently different to establish a vessel based on a body or neck sherd. The descriptions and proportions presented here are based on these analytical vessels.

The nature of the paste characteristics was determined by examination with a hand lens (6Xs) and comparison to density charts (Prehistoric Ceramic Research Group 1995). Almost all of the vessels appear to have had some inclusions that are interpreted as temper added to the clay, but at least one shows no visible signs of inclusions. All those with inclusions have mineral temper; not a surprising observation, given that other temper types are rare in Ontario. The mineral inclusions were classified as sand if they appeared round and similar sized, and grit if they varied in size and were more angular. Grit temper is much more common than sand temper (Table 11.6), suggesting that potters usually prepared inclusions by breaking up rocks. In general, visual examination suggests that the density of temper is low. Two vessels have a relatively high proportion of temper (very common = about 30 percent), and an additional five have a moderate amount of temper (moderate = 10–15 percent). The majority show estimated densities of temper below 10 percent.

Size characteristics could be determined for only a small portion of the assemblage. Four vessels are complete enough to allow for estimation of the diameter of the mouth, and all are approximately the same size, averaging 20 cm. Lip thickness was measurable for 23 vessels, and wall thickness was measurable for 37 vessels. The distribution of lip thicknesses is shown in Figure 11.8 and is bimodal. One mode centers on 4 mm and the other on 6 mm. The similarity in these values and the low number of sherds involved suggests that little significance should be attributed

Table 11.6. Characteristics of the temper in LU pottery based on analytical vessels.

Nature of temper	n	Density of temper	n
No temper	1	No temper	1
Grit temper	39	Rare inclusions (1 < 3%)	10
Sand temper	1	Sparse inclusions (3 < 10%)	26
Sand and grit	1	Moderate inclusions (10 < 20%)	5
Mineral, indeterminate	2	Very common (25 < 40%)	2
Total	44	Total	44

to the two modes. The distribution of wall thicknesses is shown in Figure 11.9 and has a single mode, at 7 mm. Wall thickness ranges from 3.2 mm to 9.8 mm (Table 11.7). This, together with the variation in density of temper, suggests that not all vessels fulfilled the same functions. This hypothesis is consistent with the findings of Malainey (Appendix A).

The small size of the sherds in the Laurentian University collection makes it impossible to describe an overall vessel form, but a few notes can be made on the general form of sections of the vessels. The form of the upper rim is observable on 24 analytical vessels. The exterior rim profile is evenly divided between straight and concave examples. The interior rim profiles are mainly convex, with a few examples of straight walls and one example of a concave profile. In most cases, rims are convex interiorly and concave exteriorly (n=12), or straight on both the interior and exterior (n=7). Lip form is observable on 24 rims. Five of these are everted, in that the lip appears to be drawn outwards. Lip forms are nearly equally divided between flat (n=12) and round (n=10). The remaining lips are pointed. Neck and shoulder forms were particularly difficult to determine, but in 15 cases the nature of the transition from the upper rim to the body of the vessel was recorded. In most of these cases (n=9), the transition appears to be gradual or the form of the wall is essentially straight. In the remainder of cases, there is a distinct narrowing of the vessel below the upper rim.

We recorded decoration in a number of ways, including its location, the inferred tool used to apply it, the inferred motion, and the motif. Table 11.8 indicates the locations on the vessel where decoration is observed.

The inferred tools used for decoration include those that are well established in Middle Woodland ceramic collections (pseudo-scallop shell, dentate, cord) and those that are simply inferred based on the shape of the impression in the clay. Table 11.9 shows the inferred tools used by location on the vessels. This demonstrates that pseudo-scallop shell is the most commonly used, both when one examines each location on the pot separately and when the overall instances are totaled. Dentate is also an important decorative tool. Other tools are inferred for only a few vessels. It is noteworthy that most of the tools that were used sparingly were used to decorate vessel bodies. It is likely that the unique character of the decoration, including the tool used, resulted in the isolation of these sherds from the rest of the assemblage. Given that breakage of a vessel results in proportionately more body sherds than rim sherds, it is likely that decoration with these tools also occurred on other parts of the vessels, but we simply have not recovered these.

The motions employed for application of decoration are as follows: impression or stamping, drag-stamping, dragging or incising, and smoothing (Table 11.10). The most common of these is stamping, which is found on all parts of the pot that are decorated. Drag-stamping is also common and occurs on all exterior portions of the pot. Dragging or incising and smoothing only occur on necks and bodies and are quite rare. Where these occur, they

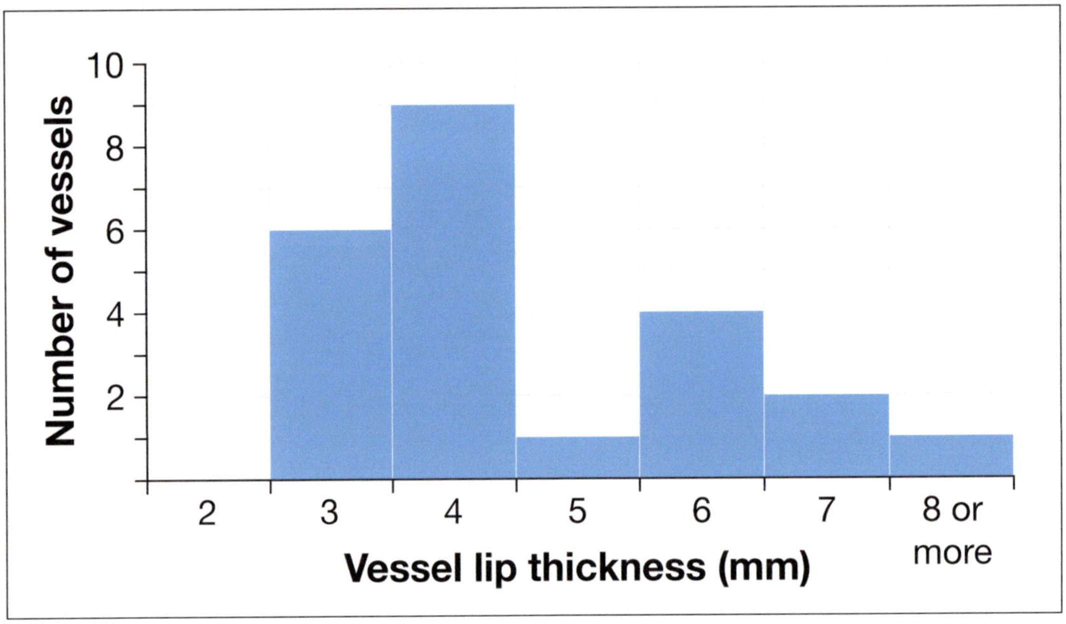

Figure 11.8. Distribution of lip thickness for 23 ceramic vessels in the Laurentian University assemblage.

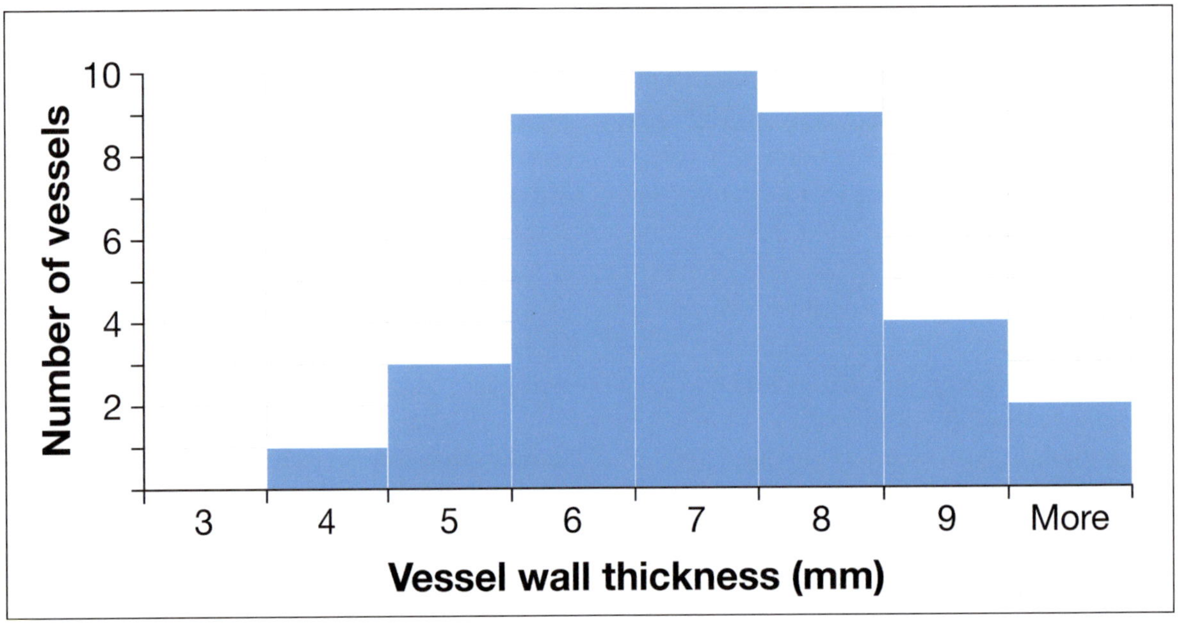

Figure 11.9. Distribution of wall thickness for 37 ceramic vessels in the Laurentian University assemblage.

Table 11.7. Summary metric attributes of the LU ceramics based on analytical vessels.

	Diameter (cm)	Lip thickness (mm)	Wall thickness (mm)
n	4	23	38
Maximum	20	7.2	9.8
Minimum	17	2.2	3.2
Average	19.2	4.1	6.8
Standard deviation	1.5	1.4	1.4

Table 11.8. Locations of decoration on analytical vessels in LU collection.

	Interior rim	Lip	Upper rim	Neck/shoulder	Body
Decoration present	4	5	16	13	20
No decoration	21	18	8	3	0
Not observable	19	21	20	28	24
No decoration was observed on the interior shoulder or body.					

Table 11.9. Inferred tools used for application of decoration by location on vessel.

	Interior rim	Lip	Upper rim	Neck/shoulder	Body	Total number of instances
Pseudo-scallop shell	3	2	11	11	10	37
Dentate	1		4	2	3	10
Cord, Twisted cord					4	4
Wide crescent tool			1	1	1	3
Blunt or rounded tool			1		1	2
Fingernail		2				2
Linear tool		1				1
Pointed tool					1	1
Annular tool					1	1
Tear-drop shaped tool					1	1

Table 11.10. Inferred motions used for application of decoration by location on vessel.

	Interior rim	Lip	Upper rim	Neck/shoulder	Body	Total number of instances
Stamp/impression	4	5	15	10	21	55
Drag-stamp			1	3	9	13
Drag/incised				1	2	3
Smoothing				2	1	3

are found in combination with another decorative motion (e.g., stamping and incising). Potters used both dentate and pseudo-scallop shell tools for stamped decoration and for drag stamped decoration.

It may appear that the ceramic assemblage is diverse, but this is not reflected in the decorative motifs observed (Table 11.11). On the interior rim and lip, the only motifs observed are bands of parallel vertical or oblique lines. A lack of decoration in these areas is most common. On the exterior of the vessel, oblique and vertical lines are also very common. Decoration on the upper rim is also dominated by vertical and oblique lines. More vessels have decoration on the upper rim than lack decoration in this area, but one-third of the sample has undecorated rims. One vessel has a superimposed decoration, with bands of oblique lines overlain by a crossed pattern that extends from the upper rim to the neck and body. Motifs on the neck and body also include rows of vertical or oblique lines, but in this part of the vessel they may be combined with bands of horizontal lines. A few necks are plain. It is impossible to determine the proportion of plain bodies in the collection.

Table 11.12 shows the ceramic types in the Laurentian collection, as proposed by Brose. Although the assignment of specific vessels to particular types may be open to discussion, the overall pattern is clear. The types that are considered to be earlier Middle Woodland (Killarney Bay Thick and Killarney Bay Smoothed) are represented by only a few vessels. The type that is considered later in time (Speigel Tool-Impressed) is represented by the majority of vessels. If the assignment of the above types to different periods in the Middle Woodland is correct, this would support the idea that the habitation area was used more intensively in the later Middle Woodland.

Petrographic analysis of the ceramics from the Laurentian assemblage

Analysis of the ceramics by visual examination suggested that potters may have used different recipes to produce pots of different qualities. The vast majority of pots appear to be modestly tempered with grit produced from local igneous rocks (see Table 11.6). However, a small number have a much higher density of mineral inclusions. To examine the variation in tempering properties, a small sample of sherds was sectioned and subjected to petrographic analysis.

Materials and methods

We selected eleven sherds for analysis. Table 11.13 lists the provenience of these sherds as well as the potential decorative type to which they were assigned. In selecting sherds for analysis, we aimed to include a range of the ceramics present rather than obtain a statistically representative sample of the wares. Specifically, we sought to include pieces with varying amounts and types of temper. In the following discussion, the individual slides analyzed are referred to by sherd number (in Table 11.13) to avoid confusion with the analytical vessels described above.

The sherds were vacuum-impregnated with epoxy and ground to a thickness of about 30 μm by Willard Desjardins in the Department of Earth Science of Laurentian

Table 11.11. Decorative motifs by location on vessel.

	Interior rim	Lip	Upper rim	Neck/shoulder	Body
Plain	21	18	8	3	-
Bands of vertical, right-leaning, or left-leaning lines	4	5	14	5	14
Superimposed			1	1	
Horizontal lines				7	7
Adjoining circles					1

Table 11.12. Proposed types represented in the LU collection.

	Type	Variant	n
Early Middle Woodland	Killarney Bay Thick	Flat lip	2
	Killarney Bay Smoothed	Plain	1
		Thumbnail lip	2
Late Middle Woodland	Speigel Tool-Impressed	Linear PSS	12
		Banked dentate	5
		Square dentate	4
		Blurred knot	4
		Pronged	2
		Vinette II	1
		Punctate	1
		Indeterminate	3
Late Woodland			2
Indeterminate			1
Other	Child's pot		1

Table 11.13. Characteristics of sherds selected for thin sectioning and petrographic analysis.

Slide number	Provenience	Description of sherd	Tentative chronological placement
1	N02W09 3 – 409	Body sherd, plain	Indet. Late Woodland?
2	N04W17 1 – 1293	Plain	Indet. Early Middle Woodland type
3	N08W15 4 – 1350 a	Plain	Indet. Late Woodland?
4	N08W15 4 – 1350 b	Plain	Killarney Bay Thick
5	N08W15 3 - 196	PSS	Speigel Tool-Impressed
6	N06W16 2 – 28	PSS	Speigel Tool-Impressed
7	N02W16 2 – 44	CWS or PSS	Speigel Tool-Impressed
8	N02W16 1 – 92	DST	Speigel Tool-Impressed
9	N08W17 3 – 15	DST	Speigel Tool-Impressed
10	N02W16 1 – 47	PSS	Speigel Tool-Impressed
11	N10W16 1 – 25	FN lip	Speigel Tool-Impressed

Table 11.14. Characteristics of sherds by point counts.

Slide number	Individual point counts			Proportions of total point count				
	Matrix	Temper	Silt	Matrix	Temper	Silt-sized particles	Matrix/silt	Matrix + silt/temper
1	411	177	72	0.62	0.27	0.11	5.7	2.7
2	816	265	139	0.67	0.22	0.11	5.9	3.6
3	1197	485	219	0.63	0.26	0.12	5.5	2.9
4	693	343	146	0.59	0.29	0.12	4.7	2.4
5	205	210	60	0.43	0.44	0.13	3.4	1.3
6	846	79	154	0.78	0.07	0.14	5.5	12.7
7	629	149	94	0.72	0.17	0.11	6.7	4.9
8	670	57	157	0.76	0.06	0.18	4.3	14.5
9	938	196	168	0.72	0.15	0.13	5.6	5.6
10	446	148	100	0.64	0.21	0.14	4.5	3.7
11	685	20	200	0.76	0.02	0.22	3.4	44.3

University. Jordan Mathieu, a geology graduate student, did the mineral identification and characterization using a polarizing microscope. He analyzed the thin sections in two ways.

In a first sweep across the sherd, he undertook point counts (Middleton et al. 1985; Stoltman 1989) using a 0.1-mm count interval. Each point was determined to be one of the following: temper, silt-sized grains, or matrix. Grains identified as temper were those that exceeded 0.0625 mm in any direction. However, as Stoltman points out (1989), such grains may also be natural constituents of sandy clay. Stoltman argues that sand can be distinguished from intentional inclusions based on angularity and mineral composition (1989:149). Mathieu identified the mineralogy of all grains silt-sized or larger. The number of points counted per sherd varies because of the difference in the size of the sherds, but these range from 475 to 1901 (Table 11.14). These data help determine the degree to which the clay matrix contained larger-sized grains (silt and sand-sized) and the proportion of matrix to temper by sherd.

In a second analysis, Mathieu examined individual mineral grains and characterized them by size, angularity, and mineralogy. Angularity was determined by comparison with standard charts (Prehistoric Ceramic Research Group 1995) and the categories used were angular, subangular, subrounded, and rounded. Size categories were as follows: fine (0.0625–0.249 mm), medium (0.25–0.499 mm), coarse (0.5–0.99 mm), very coarse (1–1.99 mm), and gravel (≥ 2 mm). These data are useful in determining if potters sought different types of tempering materials and if there were preferences in terms of processing these tempers. Because of the potential for tempering with sand from local deposits, we did not use Stoltman's (1989) approach to separating temper from sand.

In some cases, a single piece of temper was composed of more than one mineral: these were characterized as "lithic," and in some cases Mathieu was able to identify the type of rock indicated. Voids are a minor element in most cases. These have been counted, and in many cases their sizes are also recorded.

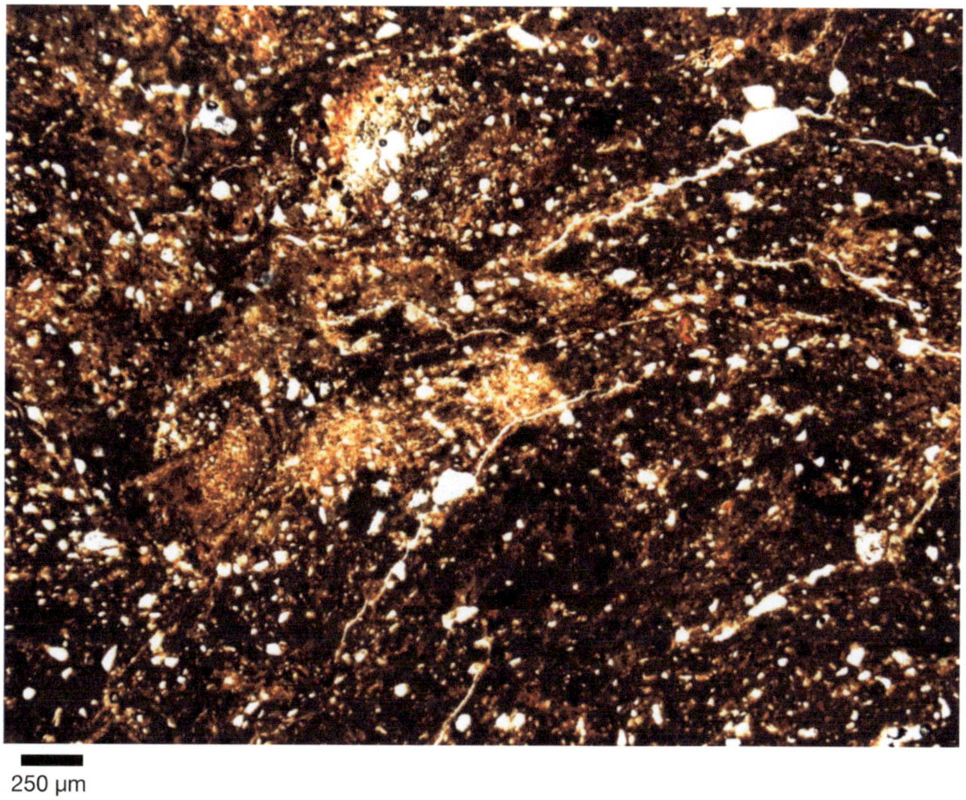

Figure 11.10. Photomicrograph of Sherd 11, with many rounded silt-sized particles and few larger grains. Plane-polarized light, field view 4 mm. Compare with Braun (2010), figure 2 – untempered clay.

The clay-temper mix

This analysis suggests that there are three different groups in terms of proportions of matrix, temper, and silt-sized particles: most sherds have a low amount of temper; one has a very large amount of temper; and a small number have very little to no temper. Table 11.14 shows the number of point counts of temper, silt-sized particles, and matrix. There are at least three possible origins for silt-sized particles in the clay. They may have been naturally present in the clay, they may have been intentional additions, or they may be a combination of the two. If they were intentional inclusions, they could be part of a tempering material that included a wide range of sizes.

To investigate this further, one may consider the number of point counts for matrix versus those for silt-sized particles. If the Killarney Bay potters selected clay from the same location or selected clay with similar properties (both of these being large assumptions), one may expect that there would be little variation in the relationship between counts of silt-sized particles and matrix. Some variation in this relationship is evident: the range is 3.4 to 6.7 (matrix to silt-sized particles). Although some variation occurs in the mineralogy of the larger-grained particles, the vast majority of silt-sized particles are quartz. Further, many of these particles appear rounded (Figure 11.10), as would be expected if the particles were weathered products as opposed to grains fractured recently by humans (Rice 1987:409). For this reason, our working hypothesis at this time is that most of the smaller particles were naturally present in the clay.

To assess the variation in the amount of larger-sized grains in the clay body, we combined the counts for matrix and silt-sized particles. These combined point counts are divided by those for large-sized grains. Three possible groups are evident (see Table 11.14): one sherd (11) with mostly matrix and silt; two sherds (6 and 8) with a lot of matrix and some temper; and the remainder. Stoltman (1989, 1991) asserts that it is not possible to assume that all large-sized grains were intentional inclusions (temper). However, the criteria that he uses to distinguish temper from natural inclusions do not appear to apply to all the sherds in this sample. Instead, we simply distinguish larger-sized inclusions (>0.0625 mm) from smaller ones. It is also possible that potters attempted to obtain a working body with a particular texture, and the source of the larger grains may have been of less concern to them than to contemporary archaeologists.

1. Most sherds have about three to four times as much matrix as large-sized grains, based on point counts. There is some variability within this group, with some having as little as two times and others as much as five. Examples of this group are sherds 1, 2, 7, 9, 10, and 4. (Figure 11.11.)
2. One sherd has an approximately one to one relationship between matrix and large-sized grains. This is sherd 5. (Figure 11.12.)
3. Three sherds have very few mineral inclusions (11 to 34 times the amount of matrix to large-sized grains). The very high values may reflect clay to which no temper was added. Sherd 11 is the best example of this, but sherds 6 and 8 also show vessels with particularly low amounts of inclusions. (See Figure 11.10.)

The nature of the inclusions

The larger-sized mineral inclusions were examined in terms of their mineralogy, size, and angularity.

Table 11.15 and Figure 11.13 show that in all cases, small-sized inclusions are the most numerous. Some variability exists within the group: only 45 percent of the inclusions on sherd 9 are very small, compared with 87–88 percent for sherds 2, 8, and 11. There is an approximately inverse relationship between the number of small-sized particles and the number of medium-sized particles. Sherd 9, for example, has a particularly high proportion of medium-sized grains, while sherds 2, 8, and 11 have a low proportion of such grains. Larger-sized grains are comparatively rare for all analyzed slides.

In a petrographic analysis of pottery from a Uren site in Ontario, Braun (2010:72) found that clastics in untempered clay could be characterized in terms of size, angularity, and mineralogy. Specifically, these grains are less than 0.5 mm in diameter, they are usually rounded to subrounded, and the majority are quartz. In the Killarney Bay sample, if we examine the size of all grains, without taking into account mineralogy, we find that for seven of the eleven sherds, 90 percent or more of the grains are less than 0.5 mm in diameter. If we examine only quartz grains, we find that for all but two sherds, more than 90 percent of the quartz grains are under 0.5 mm. There is considerable variation in the degree to which quartz grains are rounded to subrounded: in some cases, up to 70 percent of grains fit into these two categories. In most cases, however, the proportion is less than 50 percent. Braun (2010) argues that small-sized, rounded to subrounded quartz grains are found in high proportions in untempered clay because of this mineral's resistance to weathering.

There is considerable variability in the degree of angularity of inclusions. We expect that potters created angular grains by breaking rock to prepare temper, while rounded and subrounded inclusions reflect use of temper that is already weathered, such as one would find in sand deposits. Today, sand is available on the shores of Georgian Bay beside the site. While differences in lake levels would have altered the site geography, it is almost certain that sand deposits would have been found near the site at the time of occupation. One sherd (8) has no inclusions determined to be angular. More than 20 percent of inclusions in slide 10 are angular (Figure 11.14). Similarly, slides 5 and 6 have virtually no rounded inclusions, while slides 1 and 2 have more than 70 percent rounded particles (see Figure 11.11). There is no correspondence between the differences in the size of the inclusions and variations in their angularity. Sherds with high amounts of subrounded or rounded inclusions are 1, 2, 4, 5, and 6.

Table 11.16 shows the identification of mineral inclusions, the number of voids, the number of inclusions comprised of two or more minerals (lithic), and the number of inclusions that could not be identified because they were opaque. Quartz is the most common in all except for three sherds (5, 6, and 7). Feldspars were noted in most sherds and in some cases outnumber quartz. The only micaceous mineral noted is biotite, which occurs in small to significant proportions in five sherds. Amphiboles occur in small amounts in about half the sherds and in high amounts in one sherd (8). One heavy mineral, monazite, was observed in two sherds (2 and 3). All of the minerals identified are common mineral inclusions in pottery (Riederer 2004).

Voids are found in eight sherds. Most voids were small (fine) and rounded or subrounded. In some cases, the analyst noted a black halo around the void, which could be the remnant of organic matter that did not completely burn up during firing (Braun 2012; Reedy 2008). The small size of the voids and their roundness suggests that at least some of

Figure 11.11. Photomicrograph of Sherd 1 belonging to group 1 (3 to 4 times as much matrix as temper based on point counts). Plane-polarized light, field view 4 mm. Note also that many of the inclusions are rounded to subrounded.

Figure 11.12. Photomicrograph of sherd 5, belonging to group 2 (one to one ratio of temper to matrix). Plane-polarized light, field view 4 mm.

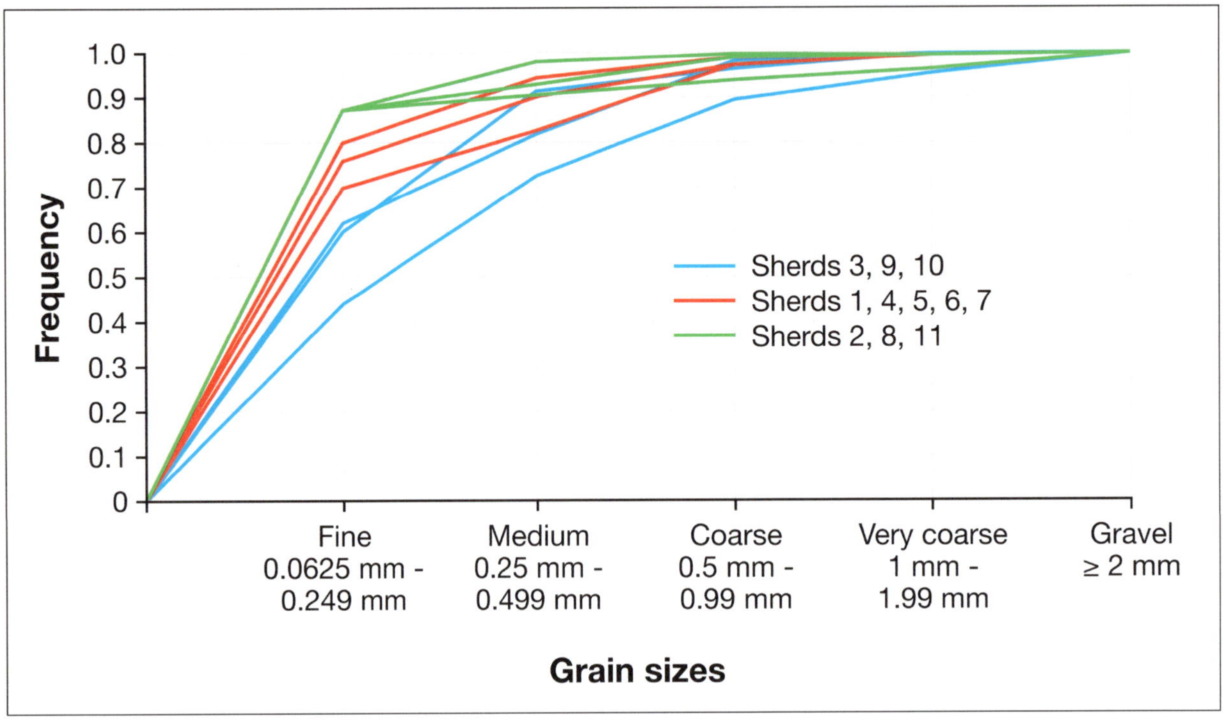

Figure 11.13. Cumulative frequency chart showing the proportions of grains of different sizes. Blue lines = Sherds 3, 9, 10. Red lines = Sherds 1, 4, 5, 6, 7. Green lines = Sherds 2, 8, 11.

Figure 11.14. Photomicrograph of Sherd 10 showing angular and subangular inclusions. Plane-polarized light, field view 4 mm.

Table 11.15. Number of grains by greatest length.

Slide number	Fine (0.0625–0.249 mm)	Medium (0.25 –0.499 mm)	Coarse (0.5–0.99 mm)	Very coarse (1–1.99 mm)	Gravel (≥ 2 mm)	Total
1	55	10	4	3	0	72
2	87	3	4	2	4	100
3	62	19	16	2	0	99
4	58	14	0	3	1	76
5	63	11	15	1	0	90
6	39	6	3	0	0	48
7	58	6	8	0	0	72
8	36	4	1	0	0	41
9	21	13	8	3	2	47
10	29	15	2	2	0	48
11	13	1	1	0	0	15

Table 11.16. Counts of mineral inclusions identified.

	Sherd 1	Sherd 2	Sherd 3	Sherd 4	Sherd 5	Sherd 6	Sherd 7	Sherd 8	Sherd 9	Sherd 10	Sherd 11
Quartz	64	69	53	71	10	8	22	16	30	42	9
Feldspar	2	1	4	1	27	13	33		17		2
Biotite		1	1		9	1	10				
Amphibole		1	2	2		4		25		1	1
Opaque			9								
Monazite	1	1									
Lithic	5	10	17	1						5	
Void		17	13	35	44	22	7			8	3
Total	72	100	99	110	90	48	72	41	47	56	15

Lithics identified are usually granitic. In one case (sherd 10) a few grains of chert were identified.

them may have been naturally occurring organic materials present in the clay, rather than additions intended to alter the properties of the pot.

When the slides are considered in terms of their mineralogy, the following rough groups appear:

1. Sherds dominated by quartz, with 80 percent or more of the grains identified as quartz (1, 2, 4, and 10)
2. Sherds with a high proportion of feldspars (more than 50 percent), with some quartz and biotite (and possibly amphiboles) (slides 5, 6, 7)
3. Sherds with significant amounts of both feldspars and quartz (slides 9 and 11). Slide 3, with a high proportion of grains identified as "lithic," may also fit into this category.
4. A single sherd shows dominance of amphiboles (slide 8).

Braun (2010:72) examined the angularity of minerals of different hardnesses to test the hypothesis that temper added to the clay matrix was prepared by breaking up rocks. In the Killarney Bay sample, softer minerals are represented by biotite and amphiboles. One or both of these minerals were observed in nine of the eleven sherds. While there is some variability in the degree of rounding, in the majority of cases fragments were angular or subangular, suggesting some use of recently broken rock as opposed to weathered sands.

This sample of analyzed sherds is far too small to define ware types for the Middle Woodland occupation at Killarney Bay, but the data can be summarized as follows.

1. One sherd (5) represents a very highly tempered vessel in which the tempering material was composed of feldspars and quartz, and individual grains were mainly subrounded and subangular. This suggests use of local sands derived from granitic rock. This sherd is classified as Speigel Tool-Impressed.
2. Seven sherds had a modest amount of temper. Within this group, there are at least two subgroups based on temper composition.
    - Three sherds (1, 2, and 4) are tempered mainly with quartz and the majority of the inclusions are rounded to subrounded and small in size. This suggests use of a local quartz sand deposit as the source of temper. These sherds are classified as early Middle Woodland types or of indeterminate type (1).
    - Four sherds (3, 7, 9, and 10) have significant amounts of feldspars and quartz and/or identifications as "lithic." One sherd contains more feldspar inclusions than quartz. In all cases, the majority of inclusions are angular to subangular. This suggests breakage of local granitic rock for temper. These sherds are classified as Speigel Tool-Impressed or of indeterminate type (3).
3. Three sherds (6, 8, and 11) had very few inclusions compared with temper. The mineral identification of these inclusions is variable. In one case, amphiboles were dominant, and in a second, there is an approximately equal amount of feldspars and quartz. In both of these cases, the inclusions were angular. In the third case, more feldspar than quartz was noted, and the inclusions were rounded. One of these was classified as a possible child's pot (11), and all are considered to be Speigel Tool-Impressed.

The nature of the inclusions is generally suggestive of the use of local materials. Specifically, the composition of the granite and amphibolites of the Grenville province is consistent with the minerals identified as inclusions in thin section (Card 1978). However, the location of the site and the nature of pottery and other artifact classes clearly indicate that the Killarney Bay inhabitants travelled widely over the landscape of northeast Ontario. We cannot assume that all of the pots recovered from the site were produced onsite. Petrographic analysis has the potential to address this question (cf., Pretola 2002), but this study would need to be much expanded and include a survey of locally available mineral resources and a comparison with the mineralogy of sherds from sites elsewhere in the region. Our very preliminary results could suggest that during the early Middle Woodland, potters tended to select temper from sand deposits, while in the later Middle Woodland, they also produced mineral temper by breaking rocks.

Contextualizing the pottery from the Killarney Bay habitation area

We compared the decorative traits of ceramics from the Laurentian University excavations at Killarney Bay with those from other Middle Woodland sites in the region. The aim is not to classify the site as Saugeen, Laurel, or Point Peninsula, but rather to understand which ceramic assemblages bear the closest resemblance to those from Killarney Bay. This is followed by a brief comparison of the fabric types with those from a Woodland site in Southern Ontario.

Comparison of decorative attributes

Several sites in the southern Georgian Bay area have Middle Woodland components. Baxter, Bressette East, Bressette West, and Bentley (Dodd 1996) are located north of the Severn River in the town of Port Severn. The Kitchikewana site (Mortimer 2012) is located on Beausoleil Island in Georgian Bay, which lies slightly north and west of the Port Severn sites. All of these sites are found at the mouth of the Trent-Severn waterway. To the east, a number of other Middle Woodland sites are found on the same waterway: Jubilee Point, Serpent Mounds, Loucks, Spillsbury Bay, East Sugar Island, Healy Falls, and Log Cabin Point, among others (Curtis 2002, 2004). Killarney Bay lies at the north end of Georgian Bay, near rivers and lakes that connect to the east via the French River, Lake Nipissing, the Mattawa River, and ultimately the Ottawa River. Middle Woodland sites from the Ottawa Valley include Constance Bay (Watson 1972), Sawdust Bay-2 (Daeschel 1981), and BiFw-6 (Miller 2011). In northern Ontario, the best published Middle Woodland sites lie far to the west. We make brief comparisons to Laurel material as summarized by Wright (1967) and Reid and Rajnovich (1991).

Dodd (1996) summarizes the ceramics from the Port Severn sites and compares them with material from northern (Laurel), southeastern (Point Peninsula), and southwestern Ontario (Saugeen). Several sites were examined, but only Baxter has a large enough sample size to allow comparisons (Dodd 1996). The pottery from this site bears similarity to that from sites from southeastern Ontario in the decorative tool employed (pseudo-scallop shell is common) and in the motions used to apply decoration (rocker stamp and drag-stamp are common). The motifs on pottery include those described as "repeated bands of closely spaced obliques applied with short tools." Superposition of trailed motifs is rare at the Port Severn sites, as are crisscross designs. The motifs are considered similar to those observed on pottery from sites in northern Ontario and southeastern Ontario (Dodd 1996). The overall characteristics of the pottery from the Kitchikewana site (Mortimer 2012) are less similar to material from Killarney Bay. Bosses and punctates are found at Kitchikewana but are not in evidence in the Killarney Bay material. Dentate tools are used more frequently than pseudo-scallop shell. In addition to bands of oblique lines, motifs produced by rocker stamping are not uncommon. In terms of similarities, the motifs and tools that are found in small proportion in the Killarney Bay habitation area material also occur in small amounts at Kitchikewana (crescent, annular, cord). Mortimer (2012) sees the use of this multicomponent site as having a duration lasting from circa 250 CE to 1200 CE. This could explain the higher proportion of traits such as dentate stamping and the use of punctuates and bosses.

Curtis (2002, 2004) examined ceramics from a number of Middle Woodland sites in the Rice Lake/Trent River area. Through this analysis, she refined the chronological phasing of the Middle Woodland and provided descriptions of the ceramic attributes for each phase. Ceramics from the Trent phase (ca. 400 BCE) have thin lips (3.7 mm) and are dominated by pseudo-scallop shell decoration. The motifs are bands of obliques, horizontals, and verticals. The Rice Lake phase (ca. 0–600 CE) ceramics are more complex: tools include dentate and cord-wrapped sticks. The motions used to apply decoration are stamping, rocker-stamping, and drag-stamping. The motifs are not specified, except in that Curtis (2002:19) describes them as "ribbon-like bands." The Sandbanks Phase (ca. 700–900 CE) pottery is distinctive for the use of cording and cord-wrapped stick. The uppermost band on the rim may be plain. Punctates and bosses are used as delimiters. The Killarney Bay material bears many similarities to the ceramics described for the Trent and Rice Lake phases from southeastern Ontario.

The material from the Ottawa Valley has not been summarized in a similar fashion, so several studies will serve for comparison. In his work on the material from the BiFw-6 site in the Ottawa area, Miller (2011:113) proposed that both earlier and later Middle Woodland materials are present. The earlier materials he sees as similar to Point Peninsula. As an example of this, he illustrates a rim section with dentate stamping and an everted lip. The motif differs from those seen in the Killarney Bay materials, in that it runs vertically instead of horizontally. The later Middle Woodland, he believes, is distinctive to the Ottawa Valley area. The exact attributes of the later pottery are not outlined, but the illustrated sherd shows the use of pseudo-scallop shell and dentate. The motifs are again different from those seen at Killarney Bay, and the presence of bosses is unparalleled in the Killarney Bay sample. The Sawdust Bay-2 material appears to bear closer resemblance to the Killarney Bay sample. The decorative tool used on the majority of the assemblage is pseudo-scallop shell, followed by dentate (Daechsel 1981). The pottery is not described in terms of motif, but an examination of the illustrations shows that many attributes of the Killarney Bay sample are similar to those from Sawdust Bay-2: the upper rim may be undecorated; the motifs are frequently bands of oblique or vertically stamped lines; these lines may be underlain by horizontal bands. The sample of pottery vessels from Constance Bay is small (Watson 1972). Many of the vessels were decorated with pseudo-scallop shell stamp, but the motifs are different. There is less evidence of bands of oblique lines, and the use of crisscross decoration at Constance Bay is not paralleled in the Killarney Bay sample.

Laurel is estimated to date to between 200 BCE and 1200 CE, and therefore has a longer duration than other Middle Woodland manifestations in Ontario. Wright (1967) proposed a seriation of Laurel sites based on the tools used to produce decoration. Earlier sites had low amounts of dentate stamp and dragged stamp pottery. Through time there is a decrease in the amount of pseudo-scallop shell present. Plain rims occur in reasonably high numbers late in the sequence but are rare to nonexistent at the earlier sites. Ceramics described by Reid and Rajnovich (1991) for the Ballynacree site include high amounts of dentate stamp and punctates and bosses. As described above, pseudo-scallop shell is more common in the Killarney Bay assemblage and there are no sherds with punctates or bosses. Differences between the Laurel material and the Killarney Bay material may pertain to chronology in part.

Comparison of fabric characteristics

It does not appear that any Middle Woodland ceramic materials from Ontario have undergone petrographic analysis. While Stoltman (1989) does take this approach with Early to Middle Woodland material from Wisconsin, there are significant differences in decoration and temper between the Wisconsin and Ontario material.

The petrographic study conducted on material most closely associated with Killarney Bay in space and time is that carried out by Braun (2010, 2012) on material from Antrex, a Uren period site from southern Ontario. The geological context of Antrex is quite different from that of Killarney Bay, lying in an area dominated by limestones and dolostones rather than on the pre-Cambrian shield. Some of the mineral materials used for temper were likely very similar, in that they would be igneous rocks found in glacial tills, on beaches, or in riverbeds. The settlement system of the Antrex people is also likely to be quite different from that of the Killarney Bay people, in that Antrex was a small horticultural village. The manufacturing methods for producing vessels also differed, assuming that the majority of the Killarney Bay material is coil built.

Braun (2012) analyzed a much larger sample than we were able to examine for Killarney Bay, and based on this sample he was able to define fifteen pottery-ware fabrics, which fall into seven broad groups. Three of these groups are defined based on use of light-colored minerals that are rounded to subrounded. Braun (2012:4) suggests these minerals were found in glacial deposits. Three other groups use dark-colored minerals that may give the pot a dark or reflective appearance, particularly when burnished. These tempering materials are angular to subangular. Braun (2012:4) argues that these derive from intentionally fractured rocks with high proportions of mafic minerals.

The Killarney Bay sample appears similar to the Antrex sample in only a few ways. Both samples included small numbers of pots made with untempered clay. In the Antrex example, untempered pots correlated with those described as children's pots. One of the Killarney Bay pots with little temper could be a child's pot (sherd 11), but the other two are decorated in a fashion that suggests a more experienced potter. The use of very low amounts of inclusions may be related to the amount of sand already present in the clay.

The inclusions in the Killarney Bay sample and the Antrex sample are mineral inclusions, and in both cases it would appear that some of these were processed by breaking up local rocks, while in other cases local sands were used as temper. The correlation that Braun finds between the roundness of grains and their mineralogy is not paralleled in the Killarney Bay material. This finding is not surprising, given that 1) it is mainly pipes in the Antrex sample that are tempered with dark-colored mafic minerals, and 2) the size of the sample from Killarney Bay is very small. Braun's (2012) interpretations about the use of different colored tempers in different use-contexts are interesting, and it remains to be seen how widespread such patterns may be.

Summary of the Laurentian assemblage

In summary, the small analyzable sample of ceramics from the Laurentian excavations at Killarney Bay is dominated by variations on the Speigel Tool-Impressed type, as defined in this chapter. The primary tools used in decoration are pseudo-scallop shell and dentate, and decoration is mainly in the form of bands of obliques. In some cases, these are underlain by horizontal bands. These decorative trends appear to most closely resemble those from the Port Severn sites and some of the sites in the Trent-Severn waterway. The lack of punctates and bosses and the relatively low amount of dentate stamping may relate in part to chronological placement, potentially indicating that the use of this part of the Killarney Bay site ended somewhat earlier than use of the Kitchikewana site. The petrographic analysis indicates some variability in the amount and types of temper used and provides no evidence of the use of exotic materials.

Regional and temporal comparisons

Ignoring the potential for historical provenience errors, the Killarney Bay site ceramic assemblage appears to contain at least three Woodland ceramic "wares" (Griffin 1952) or "series" (Fischer 1972). The most plentiful and widely distributed sherds are those assigned to the medium-thick, smoothed, plain lip Killarney Bay Smoothed ceramic type (Figures 11.15, 11.16). These are virtually identical, in all save autochthonous temper, to Mason's (1966, 1969, 1970, 1991) North Bay Plain type. They also resemble the unbossed Bay de Noc Plain ceramics that accompany the Laurel ceramics at the Summer Island site, dated to the first centuries before and in the common era (Brose 1968). Wright has reported similar ceramics from sites along the north shore of Lake Superior (1967) and Janzen (1968b) has described them at the vast assemblage at the Naomikong Point site on the south shore. In southwest Ontario, Johnston (1968a) described Point Peninsula Plain ceramics with outsloping rims and incised flattened lips, and Lee has recovered similar sherds from Sheguiandah (1965), less than 20 km west of the Killarney Bay site.

In terms of the sherd thickness and body, the Killarney Bay Smoothed ceramics seem to be closely related to a number of complexes with still-unresolved relationships (Brose 1968), including North Bay I and II wares from the Door Peninsula of Wisconsin (Mason 1966:75–125, 1967:280–302); the Saugeen Focus (Finlayson 1977; Wright and Anderson 1963); and the Au Sable Series from Michigan (Fitting et al. 1969).

The somewhat thicker sherds of the companion type, Killarney Bay Thick (Figures 11.17, 11.18), appear more similar to the Shiawassee ceramics, dated to the third century BCE, at the Schultz site along the Saginaw River Valley across Lake Huron (Fischer 1972; Halsey 1976). In their morphology, technology, and decorative repertoire, the thick, contorted Killarney Thick ceramics are also akin to the Saugeen Focus ceramics from the Bruce Peninsula Ontario (Wright and Anderson 1963:23–36) and the Au Sable Series from the Goodwin-Gresham site in northeastern Michigan (Fitting et al. 1969).

However, the most prevalent ceramic ware at the site, by number of reconstructed vessels, is the thinner, well fired, and elaborately decorated Speigel Tool-Impressed. With the exception of temper particle size and sherd thickness (factors that are structurally related), the Speigel Tool-Impressed ceramics can clearly be considered as related to the Laurel wares of Minnesota (Stoltman 1962:37–38; Wilford 1950, 1955:133–134), Manitoba (MacNeish 1958:138–154), and western Ontario (Janzen 1968b; Wright 1967). They also resemble the provisionally named Upper Peninsula ceramics from Summer Island and similar ceramics from sites along the north shore of Lake Michigan as far east as the Mackinac Straits (Brose 1968), the Point Peninsula/Vinette II Wares of eastern Ontario and upper New York State (Ritchie and MacNeish 1949:97–106), and sherds from excavations near the Sheguiandah site on Manitoulin Island (Lee 1965), where they are called Point Peninsula (see Ritchie 1949; Ritchie and MacNeish 1949). Wright also illustrates several sherds of Laurel ceramics from the Donaldson site (Wright and Anderson 1963), where they were associated with Saugeen Focus ceramics. Many of these, it had been noted, yielded similar decoration on Saugeen ceramic paste (Wright 1967; Wright and Anderson 1963). Similar sherds have been recovered from Point Peninsula deposits farther south on the Bruce Peninsula at Inverhuron and Swan Lake (Kenyon 1957, 1961) and at the Malcolm site (Dailey and Wright 1955). Just as at the Summer Island site (Brose 1968), there are several problems involved in the comparison of the banked stamp or linear dentate ceramic varieties with material from other sites, as variations in angle of application of the stamp and dentate

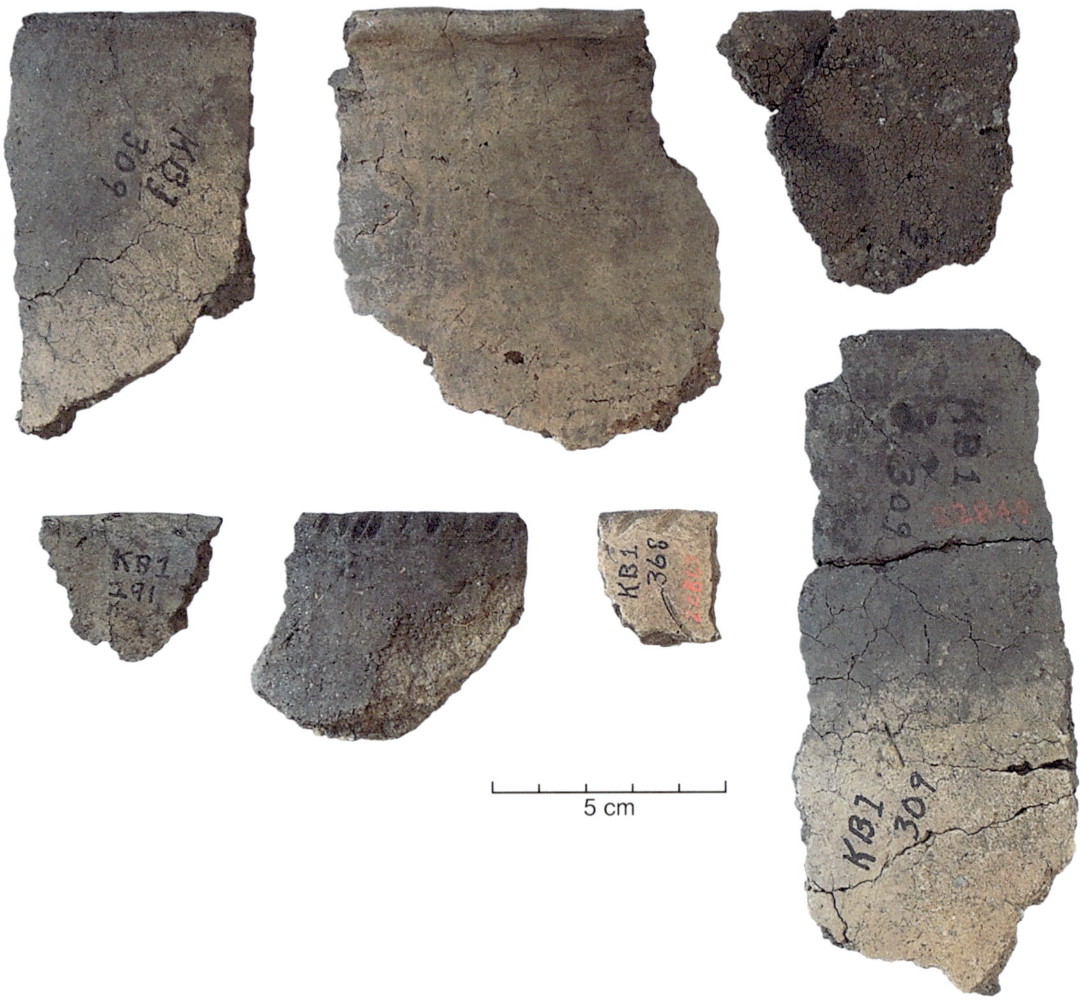

Figure 11.15. Killarney Bay Smoothed. Top row (l-r): KB Smoothed var flat lip, var. rolled lip, encrusted flat lip interior. Bottom row (l-r): KB Smoothed var. glittery interior, var. glittery exterior with impressed lip, var.impressed lip, var. flat lip.

Figure 11.16. Killarney Bay Smoothed rim sherds; encrusted rim interiors.

Figure 11.17. Killarney Bay Thick sherds showing typical spalled interior surfaces.

Figure 11.18. Killarney Bay Thick sherds showing construction ceramic coils and smoothed exterior surfaces.

tool and of its withdrawal from the plastic clay can create quite dissimilar impressions.

The Killarney Bay Thick, Killarney Bay Smoothed, and Speigel Tool-Impressed granite-diorite and/or quartzite-tempered ceramic assemblages from all provenience sets are typologically and technically Middle Woodland. Of some interest is the nearly continuous range of temper density, thickness, and firing control exhibited between some of the better-made, undecorated Killarney Thick sherds and most of the thicker and less well-made Killarney Bay Smoothed sherds. As well, there was a significant degree of overlap between temper density, thickness, and firing control on some of the better-made Killarney Bay Smoothed body sherds and some of the Speigel Tool-Impressed body sherds.

With their focus on one or another of these different types and varieties of ceramics, earlier scholars assigned the whole assemblage to various cultural complexes. There seems little justification for the plethora of descriptions attributing specific sherds to wares intended to represent disparate regional traditions spanning nearly two millennia: Adena and Vinette II (Greenman 1966) or Havana and Point Peninsula (Brown 1964; Fitting and Brose 1971; Spence et al. 1990), Couture or Saugeen and Point Peninsula (Finlayson 1977; Wright 1967), or Laurel and North Bay (Fitting 1970; Mason 1969, 1970, 1991)[7]. In view of the unresolved relationships among these ceramics, and to avoid the confusion occasioned by too-ready assignment to established groups and concomitant forced synthesis (e.g. Finlayson 1977), Brose proposes that the next step will be to look at the different types without assuming that they must belong to any one of those complexes. Indeed, as the distribution and function of each ceramic type is described, the temporal and socio-cultural relationships of these broad ceramic groups as they are manifest at this site must be explored in detail. Only in this manner will it be possible to understand the significance of the site and its exemplary role in the regional ecology of the Middle Woodland period.

Archaeologists have long known that prehistoric ceramics offer far more than stylistic and technological data useful for sociocultural and chronological approximations. To test whether there may have been different uses to which the differing types were put at the Killarney Bay site, 86 out of 602 typologically identifiable sherds were determined to have encrustations (41 out of 225 untyped sherd crumbs also had encrustations[8]). It was expected that the Killarney Bay ceramics contained as much potential to yield new understanding of the cultures that created and/or used them as other recently analyzed Upper Great Lakes ceramic assemblages[9].

Critical radiometric, geophysical, and chemical analyses were proposed for small portions of four encrusted Killarney Bay Thick sherds and two encrusted Killarney Bay Smoothed sherds. These were fragments of larger, better-provenienced and more or less reconstructable ceramic vessels of culturally significant types. Because those sherds appeared likely to yield significant information on prehistoric chronology, cultural ecology, and socioeconomics (the latter issues being particularly murky at present), in 2007 the University of Michigan Museum of Anthropology agreed to their potentially destructive lipid and radiometric analyses (sample for analysis < 0.7 percent). Laurentian University received a grant to cover the cost of analysis and submitted another four sherds: one from an encrusted Killarney Bay Thick sherd, one from an encrusted Killarney Bay Smoothed vessel, and two from encrusted Speigel Tool-Impressed vessels excavated from the habitation area of the site (Hawkins 2008).

The results of Malainey's exhaustive analyses (Appendix A) do seem to indicate that there are functional differences in how some of these ceramics were used at the site. The four Killarney Bay Smoothed vessels (including the borderline case of the aberrantly tempered vessel LU8, which seems to have been made and possibly used offsite) and the two Speigel Tool-Impressed vessels were often used and occasionally reused for cooking both plants, such as wild rice, and fish or scrawny large herbivores, such as winter-starved moose or beaver. One of the four Killarney Bay Thick vessels had been used for cooking conifers alone, and one had cooked conifers with greens and/or berries. The one Killarney Bay Thick vessel that was incorporated into Burial 8 had been used for cooking a large herbivore only, and the other Killarney Bay Thick vessel had cooked plants with fish and/or winter-thinned herbivores.

Exclusive of the Late Woodland and miniature vessels, the plain and stamped granite and quartzite-tempered Killarney Bay ceramic assemblage from all provenience sets is typologically and technically Northern Tier Middle Woodland, representing much of the variability in that overly large taxon. Some of the Killarney Thick variety Plain and variety Pseudo-Scallop Shell ceramics appear similar to Shiawassee wares (Halsey 1976) and are ipso facto similar to Havana wares (Fischer 1972), thus potentially being as early as the fifth century BCE, as are the similar plain-surfaced early Donaldson Saugeen ceramics (Finlayson 1977; Wright and Anderson 1963), which may be as early as ca. 500–600 BCE. Very few of these thicker sherds resemble the thicker Adena Plain as it had been formally described (Dragoo 1963; contra Fitting and Brose 1971; Greenman 1932; Griffin 1942, 1954). At the other extreme of their gross morphology, they do grade into the most plentiful and widely distributed ceramic type at the Killarney Bay site, the Killarney Bay Smoothed, with varieties Plain, Glittery, Rolled Lip, Flat Lip, and Ticked Lip. This medium-thick plain ware is virtually identical in all ways (save its autochthonous temper) to Mason's apparently sequential North Bay I and II types (1966, 1969), which he initially dated between the second and sixth centuries of the common era.

The less common but more variable Speigel Tool-Impressed ceramic types at the site include many decorative varieties represented by only one or two sherds. These are in every way similar to Laurel or Point Peninsula (a/k/a Vinette II) ceramics, which throughout the region are reliably dated between the late second century BCE and the end of the fourth century CE (Brose 1968, 1970a; Brose and Hambacher 1999; Janzen 1968b; Mason 1966, 1969, 1970, 1981; Ritchie 1980; Spence and Fox 1986; Spence et al. 1979; Spence et al. 1990; Wright 1967; Wright and Anderson 1963). These same assemblages occur farther west, as Mason (1991:121) finally acknowledged, claiming that pottery labeled North Bay is in accord with the typical characteristics of that ware, and the one referred to as Laurel is "equivalently assayed" but that "... pots identified as Laurel/North Bay are those already defined as intermediate, choosing between the two names would be arbitrary and would do violence to their overlapping attributes noted for the Summer Island site [Brose 1970: 55–94]." Fortunately, Mason provided descriptions for the overlaps in paste characteristics, metrics, and vessel morphology and decoration. In his latest reworking of the Laurel/North Bay continuum, he presented a radiometric assay for the organic encrustations and thus a chronology for the use of the ceramic vessels themselves (Mason 1991:123–135, 140–146), falling between 35 CE and 270 CE. Both on the basis of ceramic seriation and radiocarbon dating, this is rather early in the Laurel cultural chronology created and applied to sites along the U.S.-Canadian border by others.

James Wright labeled similar ceramics as Laurel when they were recovered from sites along northern Lake Superior (1967) and as Saugeen when recovered from the Bruce Peninsula (Wright and Anderson 1963). Farther east, at Rice Lake, Ontario, Johnston described similar plain ceramics as Point Peninsula (1968a). Thomas Lee (1965:23, Fig. 4, no. 2) did the same for the plain sherds found at the Sheguiandah site, some 20 km from Killarney Bay. This Point Peninsula Plain type, with outslanted rim and flattened lip, is close to the North Bay, Summer Island, and Killarney Bay ceramics. There are also a few anomalously early fourth or fifth century BCE dates from northern Lake Michigan Laurel/North Bay sites that parallel fifth to sixth century BCE dates considered aberrantly early for sites assigned to the Saugeen culture and to Killarney Bay (Brose 1968, 1970a; Brose and Hambacher 1999; Mason 1991:137–139, contra Mason 1970).

Thus at Killarney Bay are found the same combination of ceramic wares and the same presumptive range of dates that characterize the extraordinary variability of ceramic assemblages from the palimpsest-like North Bay and Laurel sites of the northern Lake Michigan and southern Lake Superior regions (Brose and Hambacher 1999; Mason 1981; Wright 1974), the Saugeen sites of Ontario's Bruce Peninsula and lower Severn Sound, 100 km to the south (Finlayson 1977; Wright and Anderson 1963), and even some of the Ontario Point Peninsula sites farther to the southeast (Spence and Fox 1986; Spence et al. 1990).

Decorative motif and typological attributes cannot tell the whole story, however. One must recognize the anthropological importance of discussing the ceramic vessels used by prehistoric peoples rather than focusing on the ceramic sherds studied by archaeologists. The minimal vessel calculations for the Killarney Bay assemblage were hampered by the paucity of large or continuous reconstructable sherd combinations and by the extremely low numbers of sherds recovered from controlled stratigraphic or cultural contexts.

Fortunately, identification of minimal vessels was considerably simplified by one characteristic exhibited by nearly all of these ceramics. With the exception of the single very diagnostic Speigel Tool-Impressed variety Zoned Punctate vessel, all vessels were plain-surfaced below the shoulder. As seems common in many other Laurel-like Middle Woodland assemblages and quite unlike many Saugeen ceramics, these decorated vessels exhibited only a single decorative technique (sometimes repetitive or reflexive) between the exterior lip and an area just above the shoulder. Although angle and pressure of application varied, only a single implement seems to have been employed in the decoration of any one vessel. This is a major characteristic distinguishing the Laurel/North Bay complexes north and west of the Bruce Peninsula from the Point Peninsula complexes (including those mixed with a technologically conservative autochthonous Saugeen tradition on the Bruce peninsula itself) that occur in Ontario and New York sites farther south and east.

The great majority of Laurel and Point Peninsula vessels are hard, well-constructed, constricted-neck storage jars of one size or another, while the majority of North Bay and Saugeen vessels are friable, technically coarse, open to rounded bowls. These differences reflect the functions to which the vessels were put, almost certainly indicating that the sites themselves were distinguished as much by differing demographic, economic, and ritual function as they were by stylistic changes in ceramic decoration across time and space (Brose 1968, 1973).

Within this region, during the two or three centuries before and after the start of the common era, the combination of attributes found on ceramic vessels of both functional classes represents the ancient potters' choice from a suite of traditional design motifs, techniques, implements, and decorative fields to be applied to a number of potential surfaces on ceramic vessels of a particular size and shape (Brose 1970a, 1970b; Brose and Hambacher 1999; Mason 1966, 1969, 1970, 1981). Beyond differences in execution due to any potter's manual dexterity, the way in which these choices among traditional elements were combined, and the sequences in which they were implemented on vessels of limited durability and use, represented the potters' expression of relevant social information within the temporally relevant demographic unit (Brose 1968; Wobst 1977).

Thus the posited ceramic variability not only says something about current archaeological taxonomy, it says something about the prehistoric potters' concepts of site use. Given the very limited number of vessels of all types, the functional restriction of the few Killarney Bay Thick vessels, and the scatter of relatively similar Killarney Bay Smoothed vessels amidst a plethora of Speigel Tool-Impressed varieties of decorative fields, all using the limited set of motifs that characterize the Laurel/Point Peninsula ceramic decorative repertoire, it seems that a fairly large number of related but not sympatric or congruently spaced families visited the site (and each other) for very limited functions, likely of relatively short duration (see Brose 1968). The absence of pollen for wild rice in the back-beach swale sediments is intriguing botanical evidence that argues against that function having anything to do with special, seasonally restricted calorie extraction or processing (McAndrews, personal communication cited in Julig and Long 2010), however important wild rice may have been in the overall Middle Woodland economy of the Upper Great Lakes.

Therefore, one of the significant questions to be addressed at the Killarney Bay site is the degree to which this ceramic variability represents a series of reasonably coeval occupations by a single self-referential ethnic group with a heterogeneous ceramic tradition, or the degree to which the variability represents some alternative combination of diachronic cultural phenomena. Naturally, technology and geology must limit satisfaction with our archaeological definitions for "reasonably coeval," "self-referential ethnic group," or "heterogeneous ceramic tradition" (Brose 2005) and thus mandate inescapable skepticism for any broad anthropological explanations that we may derive. But the bulk of the lithic and copper grave goods represent trans-ecosystem midcontinental Late Archaic/Early Woodland styles, while the ceramics from the Killarney Bay site and the organic containers in which and beside which the grave goods and social persona were buried, are clearly aligned with (if not representative of) regionally widespread but ecologically bounded Middle Woodland complexes (Brose and Hambacher 1999). In this regard, the ceramics from the Killarney Bay site point out our opportunity to study interactions among economic and ritual traditions of differing spatial and temporal scales, whose evolution would set social patterns that characterized the heart of the Great Lakes region until European contact.

Endnotes

1. For decades, scholars have attempted to create an "objective typology" for Woodland ceramics recovered from Great Lakes sites (Brose 2005; Williamson and Watts 1999). Archaeologists have discussed the issue of ceramic attributes or ceramic types as appropriate units of archaeological analysis in Great Lakes assemblages (Finlayson 1977). In differing regions of the Upper Great Lakes, different approaches to ceramic typology often compete (Brose 1968, 1970, 1992, 1996; Brose and Hambacher 1999; Finlayson 1977; Fischer 1972; Fitting et al. 1969; Griffin 1967; Halsey 1976; MacNeish 1952; Mason 1966, 1969; Stoltman 1973; Wright 1967). To a large degree, much of the confusion resulting from these nonconformable approaches to ceramic typology can be traced back to scholars who held quite different concepts of the interaction of material culture and society.

Compounding this situation has been the inappropriate application of nonparametric statistics. The widely imitated method Whallon (1980) advocated has significant problems: Since the attribute first chosen for statistical assemblage division is based on the frequency of that attribute within a site's ceramic assemblage, that same attribute in the unsampled portions of that site's ceramic universe may be only the fifth most frequent or it may not appear at all. So if assemblages from different sites have differing attribute frequencies and thus have differing attribute combination frequencies, the order in which attributes or combinations of attributes will be applied for the division scheme will also differ. Thus, ceramics corresponding to type "X" once discovered or created by this method may later be recognized in other samples from the site or even in samples from different sites, but it is almost certain that type "X" would not have been created and could not be rediscovered in the ceramics samples recovered at different sites if those site samples had yielded differing ceramic attribute frequencies and combinations of attributes (see Brose 1994).

2. Citation of Emerson F. Greenman's journal entries, daily notes, and maps will reference the collected and collated documents in the Bentley Historical Library on the University of Michigan North Campus. The Emerson Frank Greenman Papers cover the period from 1924 to 1972 and consist of 6 linear feet (in 7 boxes): Call number: 851362 Aa 2: in the Bentley Historical Library at 1150 Beal Ave. Ann Arbor, MI 48109-2113.

Greenman's Canadian Site Files series, 1930–1984 (2 linear feet), contains field notes, maps, journals, logs, correspondence, photographs, artifacts lists and other materials related to Greenman's field work in Ontario from the 1930s to 1950s. The series includes significant accumulations of documentation for a number of sites, including Killarney Bay (KB1), George Lake (GL1), Chikanising Creek (CH1) and Point Pelee. The series also includes field journals for work done in Manitoulin from 1939 to 1948.

Box 5 contains the artifact lists for CH1, GL1 and KB1; Correspondence for 1938 (including photos). Two general folders contain artifact lists, field notes and maps from 1939, 1941, 1946-1947, 1948, 1950-1952 and 1953 for Chikanising Creek (CH1). Geological reports for KB1, LC1, CH1 in 1939, and some miscellaneous research papers from 1949-1961 and photographs from 1940-1953. Box 5 also contains much of the Killarney Bay site information including his general notes from 1939-1941 and undated photographs and negatives; artifact lists from 1950-1951; field drawings from the KB1 and CH1 sites in 1941, and general field notes and maps from several sites on the mainland and nearby islands made in 1939, 1940, 1941 and 1942.

Boxes 6 and 7 contain Greenman's journals from 1938 through the 1953 season, along with the Killarney Bay 1 Site students' field notes and Maps from 1944, 46, 47, 48, 49-50, 51-52 and 1953; the Log and field camp expenses from 1940, and lists of maps made from 1939-1950. It also contains several other maps and list of photo for GL1, KB1, MI8, MI9, and CH1, Greenman's general correspondence from Canada for 1930–1932, along with his annual "Report of the Expedition" made to the UMMA Director. There are also two folders of maps.

Box 3 as part of the Research and Miscellaneous [series], largely contains notes on Michigan Native grammar, site locations and mounds, and numerous letters and photographs with details of European Museum Paleolithic collections. There is also a file related to the Great Lakes Research Institute of the mid-1940s.

3. It is important to reiterate that there is nothing unambiguous about the named variants of the three ceramic "types." They are nothing more than the abstraction by modern archaeologists (or art historians) of a number of co-occurring ceramic attributes chosen as having regional or particular historical significance. Their "reality" is a question for metaphysicians but even their interpretive utility is limited by the archaeologist's training, by unique sampling considerations, by the overall size of the site's ceramic assemblage, and by the sample and number of sites the archaeologist decides are comparable. As noted earlier (Brose 1994), a different perception of what are considered regionally significant attributes, or even a different sample from the same site may result in different types and varieties being created or identified from the same assemblage (see Williamson and Watts 1999).

4. The earliest analysis of the Laurel ceramic tradition was that by Richard MacNeish (1957) and, unsurprisingly, was similar to the typological analyses he and William Ritchie had used for coeval New York (and perforce Ontario) Point Peninsula ceramics (Ritchie and MacNeish 1949; MacNeish 1952): they moved from attributes to types by a statistically intuitive (but naïve) method Whallon (1980:20) later called a "monothetic subdivisive clustering algorithm." Because Whallon (1980:12–13) later demonstrated the types Ritchie and MacNeish had "discovered" were not unlike the types he would have discovered from the same assemblage had he relied on Spaulding's analytical methods (1953), he therefore inferred it was the correct method whereby to reveal which attribute associations had been culturally significant types for prehistoric New York societies (though he recognized the system resulted in types which were entirely inappropriate for some ceramic traditions and for some temporal portions of others). Among the many reasons to question the reliance on statistical methods to discover artifact types should be recognition that statistical and cultural significance are seldom identical.

Echoing his earlier focus on attribute analysis for Saugeen and Ontario Laurel ceramics, James Wright (1967; Wright and Anderson 1963), recognized that most previously described ceramic types (including Stoltman's [1962]) were so poorly conceived that any one type would include too much variability in attributes whose temporal and spatial distributions were significant. Yet Wright acknowledged that technical attributes alone were not enough (1980:21) for accurate cultural information.

Nevertheless, because the co-variation of attributes on complete vessels can indicate information exchange at family, work party, and ethnic group levels (Bunzel 1929:49ff; Nelson 1985; Rice 1987; Wobst 1977), a nuanced argument will recognize that some ceramic attributes reflect broad chronological and spatial distributions, thus revealing social interaction and temporal change at a regional level (Brose 1968, 1994; Longacre 1964), while the consistent (albeit ephemeral) association of some ceramic attributes on numerous vessels at some number of relatively coeval sites (that is, types) reflect culturally and temporally bounded social interactions. But because human behavior is largely site-specific, and because taphonomic and geomorphic processes are in part random, there is always some contingency in the attribute correlations observable in any archaeological sample of artifacts recoverable from any single site. This is what worried Ford (1954) when he claimed that slightly varying types, statistically "discovered" at different times or places were merely the reflection of local and ephemeral co-occurences of ceramic attributes which displayed broader and more important distributions in time and space. And for Ford, the important criterion in establishing a given type was to trace cultural interaction through time by choosing ceramic attributes for their broader distributions. This "impasse of non-comparable contingency" can be solved not by statistical computation but rather by adopting the potter's sequential approach to making pots.

Based on ethnographic and ethnoarchaeological accounts (Nelson 1985; Rice 1987; Shephard 1954), and on discussion with modern potters (see Brose 1994 for a detailed explication of this method), regional technology can reveal the order in which those choices were made in every local assemblage. I have argued that these are the appropriate sequential sorting criteria for ceramic typologies. That is, it is possible to identify the manufacturing and decorating steps taken or not taken for functional reasons, or for stylistic reasons, or steps which combine stylistic and functional concerns. It is also possible to identify possible steps or choices that were not made for any reason. This, too, may be of regional typological significance. For both regional ceramic types and occupational ceramic varieties, then, it is important to choose the significant ceramic attributes as these were represented by the potters' choices to implement them in building real vessels, during some real period of time across a functioning cultural region, not merely on their co-occurrences on ceramic vessels from some potentially unrepresentative portion of a single site.

5. In order to assign single sherds to different vessels, Hawkins (2009) compared the sherds and grouped them into a minimal number of vessels. If the decorating tool looked the same, she grouped them together but kept in mind the need to distinguish different vessels by looking at sherd fabric on a microscale. However, she acknowledged that it is possible that different parts of a vessel differed radically and that because of this they may have been assigned to different vessels.

6. Without question, some regional archaeologists (e.g. Finlayson 1977) considered this kind of hair-splitting the *sine qua non* of adequate regional ceramic typology. However, absent any demonstrable broad temporal or geographic significance to the frequencies of these differing but ubiquitous stylistic details (unlike the typological significance of manufacturing sequence steps such as shoulder-encircling punctates or bossing (see Brose 1971, 1994), the value of distinguishing these varieties at the Killarney Bay site likely lies in their potential to explicate intersite relationships.

7. These varying designations appear to depend on the various authors' past familiarity with particular schools of Great Lakes archaeology and the regional taxonomic categories in use by their individual faculty members at the time the authors matriculated. This execrable practice has resulted in a host of improbable implications regarding ethnicity, population movement, and ritual trade.

8. The following sherds were submitted for analyses by Mary Malainey at Brandon University:

- 22674a body sherd Killarney Bay Smoothed variety Plain Lip [KBS pl]. 22674 (KB 153): This sherd fits to 38251, a rim fragment of Killarney Bay Smoothed variety Plain Lip from Trench 4D, Section B10, topsoil. This is one of the more common ceramic types at the site, resembling North Bay II and probably dating the later portion of major occupation between 100 BCE and 300 CE. Sparse tempering is of local granitic grit, although the clays in the paste of many vessels of this type are of unknown sources.
- 30250d neck sherd Killarney Bay Thick var Flat Lip [KBT rl]. 30250 (KB105): This sherd is one of several discontinuous segments of a rim from a moderately sized Killarney Bay Thick var Flat Lip cooking pot, whose coarse and dense temper appears to match the locally derived beach sands. This vessel, reportedly found in the topsoil of Test Trench 2 during the summer of 1939, resembles the early Middle Woodland Shiawassee Wares from the Schultz site and the presumably later early North Bay I ceramics from the northern Lake Michigan basin. Although this is representative of ceramics from Killarney Bay that have been called "Adena," these types, which date to between 250 BCE and 100 CE, seem much more recent than the Adena in the Ohio River valley.
- 38445 neck sherd Killarney Bay Smoothed var Rolled Lip [KBS rl]. 38445 (KB 1266): one of many fragments of a smashed Killarney Bay Smoothed var Rolled Lip vessel recovered from the subsoil in Trench 3F, Section E4 at a depth of -1.8 feet. While provenience suggests a relatively early occupation, the sparse and relatively fine temper might indicate comparability with Mason's (1991) North Bay II and thus date between 100 and 300 CE. Temper is largely local quartzite, while the clay body is of unknown sources.
- 38447 rim sherd Killarney Bay Thick variety Pseudo Scallop Shell Impressed [KBT pss]. 38447 is also from the subsoil in Trench 3F, Section E4 at a depth of -1.8 feet, is an organically encrusted rim fragment of a small, sparsely but coarsely tempered Killarney Bay Thick variety Pseudo Scallop Shell Impressed vessel. In morphology it may represent the earliest ceramic type at the Killarney Bay site, resembling Saugeen ceramics from the Donaldson and Thede "mortuary fishing camps" improbably dated as early as 650 BCE or as late as 600 CE. While AMS dating should eventually refine this imprecision, the lack of any limestone temper in petrographic analyses strongly argues against the earlier suggestion that it may have been imported from the Bruce Peninsula to the south.

- 38933 body sherd Killarney Bay Thick var Plain Lip [KBT pl]. 38933 is one of a series of Killarney Bay Thick var Plain Rim vessels with partially wiped interiors that appear to have been once faintly fabric or cord impressed. This characteristic treatment occurs in the early Point Peninsula Ault Park and Kant sites to the southeast (Emerson 1955) but was also noted among the sixth-century CE Au Sable wares across Lake Huron to the west (Fitting, Brose, Wright, and Dinerstein 1967). Petrographic, AMS dating, and fatty acid analyses were expected to provide new ecological data for the region.
- 38489 rim sherd transitional Killarney Bay Thick var Plain Lip/ Killarney Bay Smoothed var Plain Lip [KBT/KBS pl]. 38489 (KB 225) is a rim sherd with moderate but coarse temper, much of which is nonquartzite. In technology and morphology, it is classified as a Killarney Bay Thick var Plain Rim, but a slightly thinner and less coarsely tempered section of this same vessel may have been as easily classified as a Killarney Bay Smoothed var Plain Rim type. This heavily encrusted cooking pot was recovered during the summer of 1952 from sands beneath the sacrum of the partial Burial 8, as was a rim sherd (39490) of Speigel Tool-Impressed var Linear Dentate [called "Vinette 2" by Greenman]. Burial 8 was accompanied by several large wooden-hafted blades of Wikwemikong [Fossil Hill] chert; strings of local and marine shell and rolled copper beads, and a probable beaver pelt-wrapped copper celt resembling those recovered at the first century CE Hopewell site in central Ohio (Greber and Ruhl 1989).

9. Using gas capillary chromatography, in 2007 Morris and Ballantine (of Alchemia Consultants and Northern Illinois University) identified differing deer, fish, duck, and goose fats, and hickory, sunflower, and other edible oils from encrusted residues on a suite of Havana-like sherds from northern Illinois. At the same time, Dunham (2007) argued that the adoption of early ceramics in the eastern Upper Peninsula of Michigan represented a subsistence response to climatic and ecological change. Applying the technique, he was able to document that this response was reflected in a relative shift from animal fat to edible nut oil residues on fire-cracked rock from aboriginal hearths dating to the Middle and early Late Woodland periods.

Chapter 12

Copper at Killarney Bay

Lisa Marie Anselmi

This chapter presents the analysis of the Killarney Bay native copper artifact assemblage. A large portion of the copper assemblage (n=1,494) was recovered from 1939 to 1952 during a succession of University of Michigan field schools under the direction of Emerson Greenman. That part of the assemblage is presently curated at the University of Michigan Museum of Anthropological Archaeology. It was recovered from a mound at the site that yielded a series of burials containing diagnostic Adena-Middlesex grave goods, including tubular pipes and a slate gorget (Greenman 1966:545). A sample of beaver hide preserved by contact with a copper celt was submitted for radiocarbon dating by Greenman. It yielded a date of 90 BC (M-428; 2040+/-200 uncalibrated; Greenman 1966:545). Prior to formal excavation by Greenman and his crews, the mound had been disturbed by several construction projects, including a sugar shack, a root cellar, and the farming of root crops like potatoes (Greenman 1966:545). Provenience for the copper artifacts from the burial mound is fairly secure and is based on the excavation notes of the field crews.

A second, larger portion of the site's copper assemblage (n=1,829) is curated at the Canadian Museum of History (formerly the Canadian Museum of Civilization) in Hull, Quebec. Accessioned in 1961 by the museum, this material forms part of the Robert Bell collection and is thought to have been collected by Bell at Killarney Bay in the 1870s or 1880s, while Bell was working as a geologist with the Canadian Geological Survey. There is no provenience data beyond the site location for this portion of the collection, and in fact it is unclear if this copper is from the area surrounding the burial mound or from one or more nearby contemporary sites, as the Ontario Database for Archaeological Sites entry for the area suggests (listed under BlHi-1). For this reason, these assemblages will be presented separately within this chapter.

Native copper use in the Eastern Woodlands: Archaic to Middle Woodland

Native copper refers to copper that is found in its native or pure state. This has been documented to be nearly chemically pure copper, with only differences in trace elements to distinguish particular veins or outcrops (see Hancock et al. 1991; Levine 1996; Rapp et al. 1990). Native copper use began during the Late Paleoindian/Early Archaic period (ca. 8000 BC), as evidenced by worked copper recovered in deep stratigraphic contexts in Illinois (Fowler 1959:261, as cited in Halsey 1996:11). Native people mined native copper on a larger scale from the Lake Superior region as early as 6000 BC, during the Middle Archaic Period (Drier and Du Temple 1961; Easby 1966; Fox et al. 1995; Halsey 1996; Levine 1996, 1999; Wayman 1989). Secondary sources of native copper were also available from sites in Labrador and the Appalachian Mountains, in addition to "float" copper—copper that was dispersed across the landscape via glacial advances (Evans 1952; Halsey 1996; Kinkel et al. 1968). Indigenous people worked native copper using both cold-working and annealing techniques, as shown through the detailed analysis of these materials (Leader 1988; Martin 1999; Schroeder and Ruhl 1968; Vernon 1990). Researchers have shown that artifacts were fabricated directly from nuggets of native copper, from laminar plates, or from more complicated combinations of processes such as hammering, flattening, folding, and bending the material into its final form. No evidence for copper smelting or casting has been identified prior to much later contact with Europeans (Smith 1968:242; Vernon 1990). Forms created include socketed projectile/spear points, celts, knives, awls, drills, and beads, among others (Anselmi 2008: plate 1 for illustrative examples; Halsey 1996). Large quantities of artifacts crafted from native copper have been recovered from Late Archaic period sites, attributed to the Old Copper Complex, the Red Ochre Complex, and the Glacial Kame Complex, circa 3000–1000 BC (Martin 1999; Spence 1982). Generally, these artifacts were associated with burials, but they have also been recovered from habitation sites and in caches without human remains (Halsey 1996; Martin 1999).

Early Woodland sites throughout the eastern woodlands have also yielded artifacts crafted from native copper. Artisans of the Adena culture/complex of the Upper Ohio Valley fashioned a number of new types of artifacts, including rectangular gorgets and plates, bracelets, celts, awls, headdresses, foil covering, and beads (Dragoo 1963; Esaery 1986; Halsey 1996). Cultures in contact with the Adena also produced a number of native copper artifacts during this time period (Childs 1994; Halsey 1996; Ritzenthaler and Quimby 1962; Spence and Fox 1986). In Ontario, New York, and southern Quebec, Early Woodland sites are organized into two complexes: Meadowood (ca. 900–400 BC) and Middlesex (ca. 450–0 BC). These are distinguished from previous cultural manifestations by the appearance of pottery (Ferris and Spence 1995:89; Spence and Fox 1986; Spence et al. 1990:125). There are also diagnostic changes in lithic production types: the expanded use of Onondaga chert as a lithic raw material, trapezoidal-shaped stone gorgets, and stylized birdstones (Ferris and Spence 1995; Ritchie 1980; Spence et al. 1990:128–129). Other artifacts recovered on Early Woodland sites include Lamoka-type projectile points, T-shaped drills, fire-making kits with iron pyrite, and copper beads and awls (Ritchie 1980; Spence et al. 1990).

Beginning circa 500 BC, native copper use began to be restricted (Halsey 1996). Curiously, copper is uncommon and marine shell and galena are absent from Ontario Meadowood burial contexts, though it appears that the trading networks through which these materials entered southern Ontario during the Late Archaic were still active (Ferris and Spence 1995:95). The Middlesex complex, known exclusively from mortuary contexts, has been placed in the Early Woodland period due to perceived connections with Adena (Ferris and Spence 1995:96). However, this complex is currently poorly known and may be better understood as transitional to Middle Woodland (Spence et al. 1990). Middlesex mortuary sites often consist of burial mounds that contain exotic materials such as copper, marine shell, and large bifaces crafted from nonlocal cherts (Ferris and Spence 1995:97). Middlesex copper artifacts are extensively reported from relatively few sites; the Boucher site in Vermont is the best known (Heckenberger et al. 1990a, b).

The Middle Woodland Period (c. 300 BC–AD 700) in northeastern North America is characterized by the development of the Hopewell culture in the Ohio River Valley. This culture is associated with burial mounds, earthworks, and effigy mounds, elaborate stamped ceramic vessels, platform and effigy pipes, and an elaborate copper metalworking industry with types including breastplates, headdresses, panpipes, and earspools (Fitting 1978:45). The Hopewell were actively involved in large-scale trading interactions: Exotic goods such as native copper and shark's teeth were imported into the Hopewell heartland from great distances, though it has been recently suggested that some of the copper procurement activities were undertaken by individuals directly (Bernardini and Carr 2005:632). Ohio Hopewell practices appear to have influenced contemporary developments of the same period in New York (labeled Point Peninsula) and in southern Ontario (labeled Couture, Saugeen, and Point Peninsula) (Fitting 1978:47; Ritchie 1980).

During the Middle Woodland period, Hopewell and Point Peninsula metalworkers produced a greater number and a wider variety of native copper artifacts than in the Early Woodland period (Halsey 1996:15). The created artifacts were significantly more complex than earlier forms, and techniques used for the creation of these objects included hammering, cold welding, and repoussé (Halsey 1996; Gadus 1979; Leader 1988; Wayman et al. 1992). There is some debate over whether Hopewell and earlier metalworkers were casting any of the pieces, particularly celts and adzes (see Neiburger 1987a, b, 1991). After detailed examination of the metal artifacts produced at the Hopewell site and their differential interment in nearby burial mounds, Leader (1988) concluded that the metalworkers responsible for the fabrication of these artifacts were specialists. However, due to a limited amount of excavation at the village locations near these burial mounds, no workshops have been identified at the Hopewell site (see Leader 1988:156, 163). Forms produced include elaborate headdresses, earspools, breastplates, panpipe jackets, geometric cutouts, and repoussé plates of birds and fish (Greber and Ruhl 1989; Halsey 1996; Willoughby 1903).

Methods and artifactual summary of the Killarney Bay native copper assemblage

Analysis of the native copper assemblage from the Killarney Bay site employed visual examination techniques under low-power magnification (5 to 20X; following Anselmi 2004, 2008) combined with metric analysis. Metallographic analysis of the materials was not possible due to the destructive nature of the technique itself. Sourcing the raw material using techniques such as instrumental neutron activation analysis or ICP-MS was not undertaken at this time but could be employed in future.

Generally speaking, the artifacts from Killarney Bay are heavily corroded and encrusted with organic adherents such as bark, hide, fur, and cordage. This proved particularly problematic when analyzing the beads recovered from the burials, as many were concreted together in solid masses (see below).

The Robert Bell Collection

A total of 1,829 artifacts were available for examination from the Robert Bell Collection at the Canadian Museum of History. The vast majority are beads (n=1,821); the remaining eight objects are fragments. It is unclear if these fragments were once part of other artifacts from the site or small fragments of sheet that had not been worked into a final form.

Beads are among the most commonly recovered native copper artifacts from all time periods and are known in the Eastern Woodlands from a very broad geographical area (Martin 1999). Their manufacture is fairly consistent through time: A strip or piece of sheet copper is rolled or bent around itself to form a round or cylindrical form with an open center (Martin 1999:233). The method of manufacture is fairly consistent—rolling the material, likely around a mandrel form, with periodic episodes of annealing—but the form and shape of the bead blanks appear to differ between the various bead types.

For this analysis, bead categories were based on manufacturing technique, bead style, and overall size. Due to the presence of heavy corrosion products and the resulting concretion of many of the beads to one another, the metric analysis of the beads was limited, resulting in apparent overlaps in the metric data for some of the resulting categories, such as the width/diameter for medium and large round beads. It should be noted that the average length for these beads is a provisional measure at best, since a large percentage of these beads exhibited severe corrosion and/or were concreted to adjacent beads and were unable to be measured for maximum length. However, the visual examination of these bead types supports their delineation, even when the metric data for characteristics such as overall length cannot be collected.

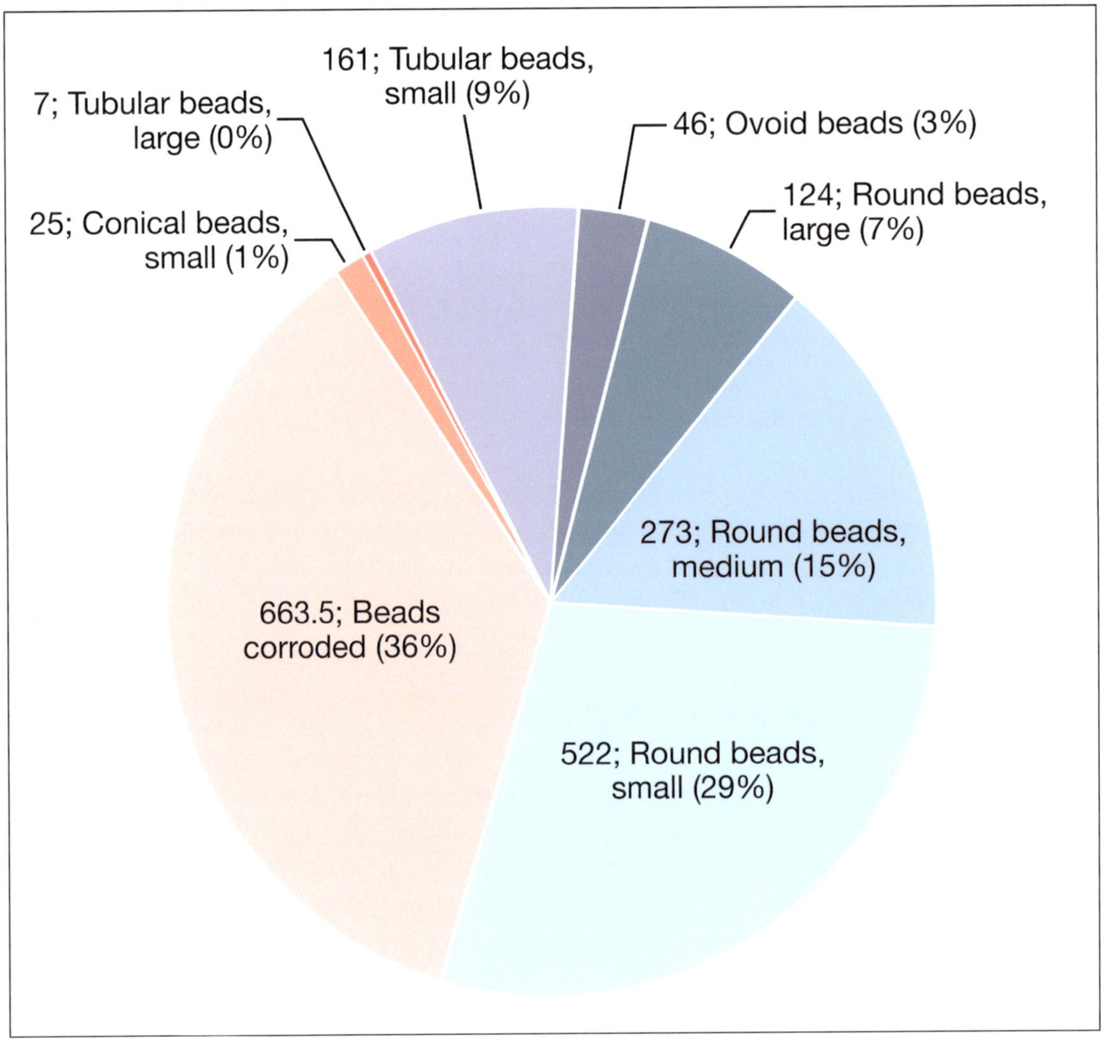

Figure 12.1. Chart showing copper beads from the Robert Bell Collection at the Canadian Museum of History, sorted by type.

Beads form the majority of the copper artifacts in the Robert Bell Collection at the Canadian Museum of History. Many of these are heavily corroded. Organic adherents are common. The Bell collection beads can be categorized into seven types, many of which were also present in the University of Michigan Killarney Bay assemblage. There are small conical-trapezoidal beads, tubular beads (large and small), ovoid beads, and round beads (large, medium, and small) (Figure 12.1).

There are 25 small conical-trapezoidal beads in the collection (Table 12.1, Figures 12.2 and 12.3). The bead preform for this type seems likely to have been a small trapezoidal strip, which was then rolled into final form. These beads appear to have been intentionally nestled together when strung.

There are both large and small tubular beads as well. Seven large tubular beads appear to have been used as accents within necklaces consisting of other bead types—especially medium and large round beads (Figures 12.4, 12.5, and 12.6). Thickness of the metal used to create the beads was not measurable for any of the bead types, due to the corrosion and condition of the beads.

There are also a number of small tubular beads in the Bell collection (see Table 12.1). Many of these beads are strung on leather thongs or cordage with intentional spaces left between the beads (Figure 12.7).

Ovoid beads appear to have been flattened as part of the fabrication process and were likely crafted using bead blanks with a slightly "bulging-center" appearance and tapering ends. Ovoid beads differ from the large, medium,

Table 12.1. Metric data for the Robert Bell Collection, beads.

Bead type	Count	Length: average maximum (mm)	Range of length	Width: average diameter (mm)	Range of width
Conical-trapezoidal, small	25	4.2	4.5–3.7	5.2	5.9–4.8
Tubular, large	7	17.1	23–11.9	7.9	9.1–6.9
Tubular, small	161	5	9.6–3.2	6.1	8.1–4.5
Ovoid	46	5.26	6.6–4.7	7.06	8.4–5.8
Round, large	124	6.2	9.9–4.8	8.6	11.4–6.8
Round, medium	273	5.28	6.2–4.1	6.49	9.0–4.4
Round, small	522	4.1	4.9–3.0	4.5	7.3–3.3

Figures 12.2 (left) and 12.3 (right). Examples of small conical-trapezoidal beads from the Robert Bell Collection, box 2. Photography by L. M. Anselmi ©Canadian Museum of Civilization.

Figure 12.4 (top). Examples of large tubular beads from the Robert Bell Collection, box 3. Figure 12.5 (middle) and Figure 12.6 (bottom). Examples of large tubular and large round beads from the Robert Bell Collection, box 3. Photography for all three figures by L. M. Anselmi ©Canadian Museum of Civilization.

Figure 12.7 (left). Examples of small tubular beads from the Robert Bell Collection, box 3. Figure 12.8 (right). Example of a large round bead from the Robert Bell Collection, box 1, resembling a nugget-like or barrel-shaped bead. Photography for both figures by L. M. Anselmi ©Canadian Museum of Civilization.

and small round beads in the collection from a visual perspective. The round beads are classically rounded or curved in profile. One of the large round beads closely resembles those described elsewhere (Heckenberger 1990a) as nugget-like beads (Figure 12.8).

There is a large quantity of beads (approximately 663.5) that we could not evaluate as to type or subject to metric analysis, due to adhesion of organic materials, general overall corrosion, and overall fragility.

The University of Michigan Killarney Bay copper collection

A total of 1,494 native copper artifacts from ten burials at the Killarney Bay site were available for examination at the University of Michigan's Museum of Anthropological Archaeology (UMMAA) (Table 12.2). This collection comprises the majority of the artifacts recovered from the site during Greenman's excavations, including four intrusive items (three buttons and one fragmented piece of copper-based metal kettle). Unfortunately, this does not include the copper objects (celts, spindles/awls, and beads) reportedly recovered from Burial 1 at the site. Neither the human remains nor the artifacts from Burial 1 are in the UMMAA collections, and it is unclear where they are presently located.

Beads

The Killarney Bay beads at UMMAA can be categorized as one of seven types: conical-trapezoidal beads (large and small), tubular (small), ovoid (small), or round beads (large, medium, and small; Figures 12.9 and 12.10; Table 12.3).

Conical-trapezoidal beads are present in two sizes: large and small. There are 5 large conical-trapezoidal beads (see Table 12.3; Figure 12.11). It appears from the visual examination that the preform or bead blank was in a trapezoidal shape prior to the rolling of the bead itself. There are 17 small conical-trapezoidal beads. One portion of these is still tightly strung together and resembles a nested set of beads or chain links similar to modern tubular chain (Figure 12.12, left). Again, the bead preform seems likely to have been a small trapezoidal strip, which was then rolled into final form.

The third set of beads from the assemblage are small tubular beads manufactured by rolling and bending

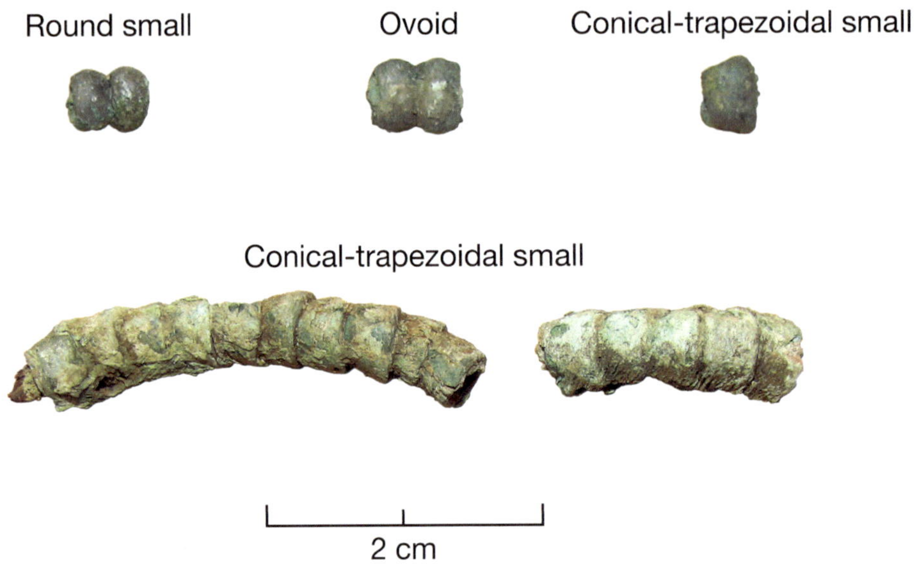

Figure 12.9. Types of Killarney Bay copper beads in the UMMAA collection.

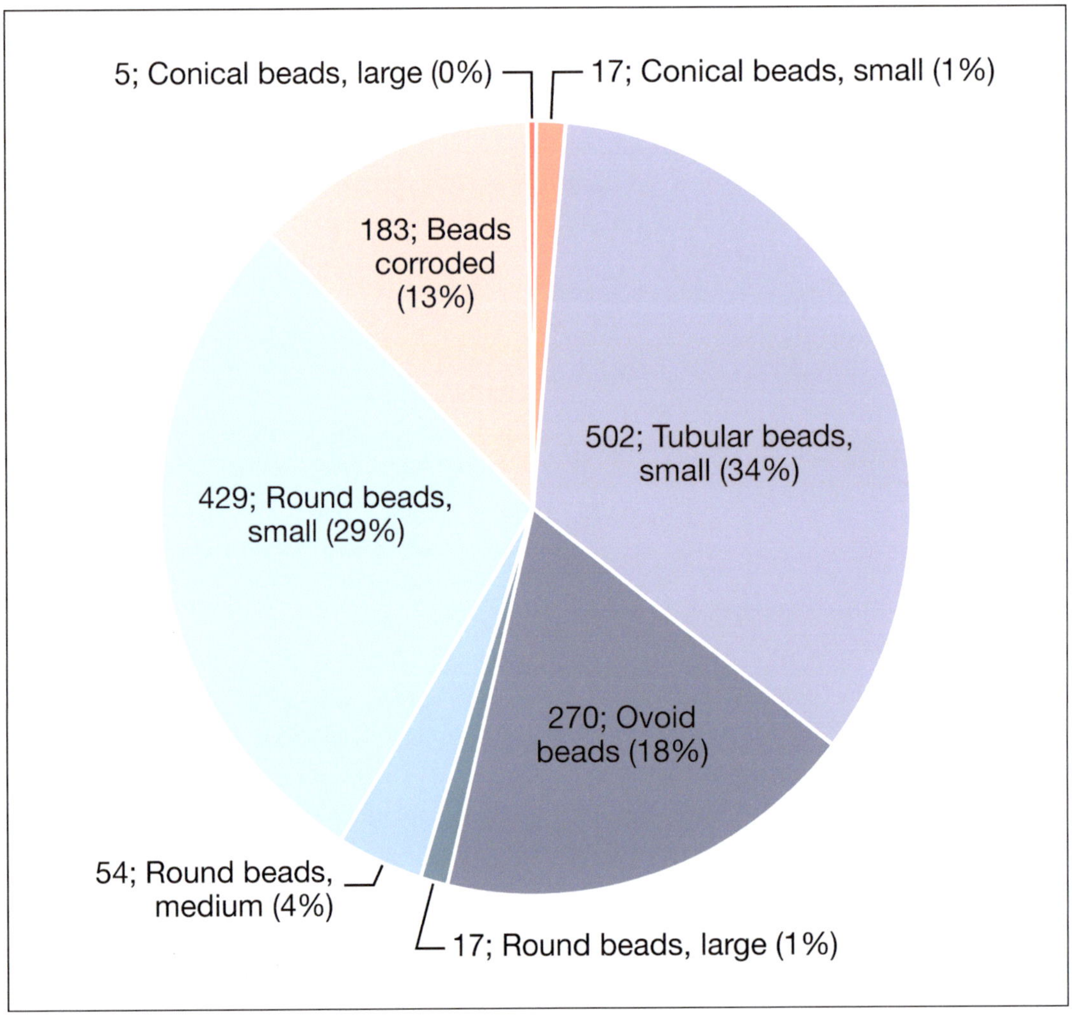

Figure 12.10. Chart showing copper beads from the UMMAA collection, sorted by type.

Table 12.2. Distribution of all copper artifacts, UMMAA Killarney Bay assemblage.

Artifact type	Count	Percentage of assemblage
Awls	4	0.27
Beads	1477	98.86
Celts	6	0.40
Chisel	1	0.07
Sheet	2	0.13
Intrusive	4	0.27
Total	1494	100.00

Table 12.3. Metric data for the UMMAA Killarney Bay copper assemblage, beads.

Bead type	Count	Length: average maximum (mm)	Range of length	Width: average diameter (mm)	Range of width	Average thickness (mm)	Range of thickness
Conical-trapezoidal, large	5	9.9	10.9–8.9	11.3	12.2–6.6	2	2.4–1.7
Conical-trapezoidal, small	17	4.2	X	5.5	X	X	X
Tubular, small	502	4.4	9.2–2.7	5.2	7.3–3.7	1.3	2.0–0.6
Ovoid	270	3.95	5.6–3.2	5.3	6.6–4.1	X	X
Round, large	17	6.5	10.1–4.3	10.2	14.2–8.3	3.1	3.2–2.9
Round, medium	54	5.5	6.1–4.9	6.9	8.8–5.5	X	X
Round, small	429	3.0	3.3–2.9	4.6	5.6–3.8	X	X

Figure 12.11. Examples of two large conical-trapezoidal copper beads, UMMAA 39492; KB-1: 2216. Photograph by L.M. Anselmi with permission of the University of Michigan, Museum of Anthropological Archaeology.

Figure 12.12 (top). Examples of small conical-trapezoidal beads, UMMAA 39689; KB-1: 2358. Figure 12.13 (bottom). Examples of small tubular beads, UMMAA 38511; KB-1: 2144. Both figures photographed by L.M. Anselmi with permission of the University of Michigan, Museum of Anthropological Archaeology.

Figure 12.14 (upper left). Examples of ovoid beads, UMMAA 39497; KB-1: 2240. Figure 12.15 (upper right). Examples of large round beads, UMMAA 38517; KB-1: 2127. Figure 12.16 (lower left). Examples of large round beads with differing cross sections, UMMAA 30286; KB-1: 1171. Figure 12.17 (lower right). Examples of small round beads, UMMAA 39496; KB-1: 2239. These four figures photographed by L.M. Anselmi with permission of the University of Michigan, Museum of Anthropological Archaeology.

small strips of copper sheet around leather thongs. This is described in the literature as being "crimped" around the thong (see Martin 1994, 1999). The beads were predominantly finished by overlapping the copper onto itself (forming an overlapping seam), though there are examples of beads where the copper simply abuts at the seam. There is a series of gaps left between the beads on the thongs, and it is likely that the artisan intentionally produced this distinctive pattern. There are 502 beads of this kind in the assemblage (Figure 12.13).

The beads in the fourth set are small ovoid beads (doughnut-like in cross section). There are 270 beads of this kind in the assemblage (Figure 12.14). These beads appear to have been flattened as part of the fabrication process, resulting in a pronounced central bulge, and were likely crafted using bead blanks with a slightly "bulging-center" appearance and tapering ends.

The last three sets of beads from the assemblage are round beads in three sizes: large, medium, and small. There are 17 large round beads in the assemblage. Of these, 13 are clearly constructed from rolling the sheet over itself with measurable overlap. In cross section, they appear to be oblate spheroids, most closely resembling a doughnut or bulging disc (Figure 12.15). The other four beads exhibit more variable cross section profiles and may be described as nugget-like (Figure 12.16). There are 54 medium round beads in the assemblage. Most appear as smaller versions of the large round beads, with a slight doughnut shape in profile, but 19 have a classically rounded shape in profile. There are 429 small round beads in the assemblage

Figure 12.18. Examples of corroded mass of unidentifiable copper beads, UMMAA 39689; KB-1: 2358. Photograph by L.M. Anselmi with permission of the University of Michigan, Museum of Anthropological Archaeology.

(Figure 12.17). These can also be described as globular or subglobular in form.

There is a large quantity of beads (approximately 183) that we could not evaluate as to type or subject to metric analysis, due to adhesion of organic materials and general overall corrosion (Figure 12.18).

Celts

Celts are commonly recognized as "flat, thin, and tapering [tools], with the working edge perpendicular to the long dimension of the tool" (Martin 1999:235). There are six celts in the Killarney Bay assemblage at the UMMAA. Celts could have been manufactured from nodules of native copper that were formed using cold and/or heated hammering techniques coupled with annealing (Bernardini and Carr 2005; Martin 1999; among others). Items worked in this way display laps, folds, and striations in the metal, and these characteristics are present on the Killarney Bay artifacts. These celts also exhibit pseudomorphs of the textiles/furs in which they were wrapped. This is similar to examples curated at the Hopewell Culture National Historical Park and at the Ohio Historical Society. It has been suggested that some of the Hopewell celts may have been cast (Neiburger 1987a) but this has not been reliably proven (Ehrhardt 2008). The Killarney Bay celts have been analyzed and placed into three size grades (small, medium, and large) based on their weight (following a suggestion from Bernardini and Carr in their 2005 chapter, which argues for the importance of weight for these artifacts). Weights and metric data for the celts are found in Table 12.4.

Table 12.4. Metric data for the UMMAA Killarney Bay celts.

Artifact number	Weight (g)	Maximum length (mm)	Tapering width (mm)	Tapering thickness (mm)
UMMAA 39504 (KB-1: 2258)	150.8	116.3	40.2–9.9	8.1–3.2
UMMAA 39501 (KB-1: 2232)	307.3	195.1	44.9–8.0	9.2–2.8
UMMAA 39503 (KB-1: 2242)	481	192.3	62.8–17.5	11.2–8.3
UMMAA 39688 (KB-1: 2352)	586.6	165.9	57.7–16.9	15.7–6.2
UMMAA 39502 (KB-1: 2241)	652.2	203.2	51.0–12.5	14.6–8.2
UMMAA 38508 (KB-1: 2200)	688.2	199.5	61.2–28.0	13.0–6.8

All six of the celts in the assemblage are flat in cross section. The small celt (UMMAA 39504/ KB-1 2258) is generally well made, though it now exhibits damage at the tapered or poll end (Figures 12.19, 12.20). The medium-sized celt (UMMAA 39501/ KB-1 2232) is heavily encrusted with organics (Figure 12.21). The four large celts weigh, on average, 602 grams and exhibit variable amounts of corrosion and organic adherents (Figures 12.22, 12.23, 12.24, 12.25). Two of these celts bear leather fragments.

Awls

Awls are generally defined as long, narrow tools assumed to function as piercing or perforating implements (Martin 1999:229). There are four awls in the UMMAA Killarney Bay assemblage, initially identified as spindles in Greenman's notes and early catalogs of the material (Figure 12.26). Two of the awls are adhered together, due to heavy corrosion. These are square in cross section and range in length from 181 mm to 192.6 mm. Width measurements are from 11 to 5.8 mm and 9.8 to 4.9 mm respectively, with thickness measurements tapering to an average of 5.5 mm. Manufacturing methods for the awls appear to include the folding and hammering of sheet copper into the final form, as judged by evidence that the surface of the awl was delaminated in one section.

The other two awls were found independent of one another and are rectangular in cross section. One small awl (28.6 grams) was recorded in the artifact catalog as having been inserted into a wooden handle. The handle has become separated from the awl, which is 131.4 mm in length and

Figure 12.19 (top). Example of the small celt, UMMAA 39504; KB-1: 2258.

Figure 12.20 (right). Detail of the small celt showing damage at poll, UMMAA 39504; KB-1: 2258.

Figure 12.21 (below). The medium-sized celt, UMMAA 39501; KB-1: 2232.

Figure 12.22 (bottom). A large sized celt, UMMAA 39503; KB-1: 2242. All four photographs by L.M. Anselmi with permission of the University of Michigan, Museum of Anthropological Archaeology.

Figure 12.23 (top). A large sized celt, UMMAA 39688; KB-1: 2352. Figure 12.24 (middle). A large sized celt, UMMAA 39502; KB-1: 2241. Figure 12.25 (bottom). A large sized celt, UMMAA 38508; KB-1: 2200. All three photographs by L.M. Anselmi with permission of the University of Michigan, Museum of Anthropological Archaeology.

Figure 12.26. Four awls from the UMMAA Killarney Bay assemblage: from top, UMMAA 30284/ KB-1: 1188; UMMAA 39687 a & b/ KB-1: 2351 and UMMAA 39500/KB-1: 2229. Photograph by L.M. Anselmi with permission of the University of Michigan, Museum of Anthropological Archaeology.

Figure 12.27. Two awls from the UMMAA KB-1 assemblage: UMMAA 39687 a & b/ KB-1: 2351, showing apparent delaminating of the surface. Photograph by L.M. Anselmi with permission of the University of Michigan, Museum of Anthropological Archaeology.

Figure 12.28. The chisel from the UMMAA KB-1 assemblage: UMMAA 38509; KB-1: 2201, showing apparent delaminating of the surface. Photograph by L.M. Anselmi with permission of the University of Michigan, Museum of Anthropological Archaeology.

tapers to points at both ends. The last awl weighs 93.8 grams and has a length of 215.5 mm. This awl also yields evidence for a manufacture sequence that included folding sheet copper over itself and then hammering it into place. Evidence for this can be seen in Figure 12.27.

Chisel

There is a single chisel in the assemblage. This identification follows Leader's (1988) definition of chisels as tools that exhibit their widest point at the curved cutting edge, though the chisel from Killarney Bay has marked damage in this area. The tip was somewhat blunted prior to burial, suggesting that this damage occurred to the piece through its use as a chisel (Figure 12.28). The chisel weighs 281.7 grams and is 195.1 mm long. It tapers from 25.2 to 6.8 mm in width and 10.7 to 5.5 mm in thickness. Though also showing heavy corrosion products on its surface, there is evidence for this piece having been ground along its edge.

Sheet fragments

The last two native copper artifacts in the assemblage are two tiny pieces of sheet metal. These weigh 1.1 and 0.6 grams respectively. They range in length from 18.2 to 24.3 mm and in width from 15.1 to 4.9 mm. Both are 0.9 mm thick. It is unclear what function these pieces might have served.

Distribution of the copper artifacts in the burials

Seven of the nine burials curated at the UMMAA contain copper artifacts (Figure 12.29).

Burial 8, identified by Nicodemus (Chapter 9, this volume) as an older adult male interred in a flexed bundle, yielded large quantities of copper artifacts: 631 ovoid and small round beads, 4 celts (2 large, 1 medium, 1 small), and 1 awl. The ovoid and small round beads appear to have been strung together in their existing form with no obvious patterning. The awl was recovered adjacent to the individual's left arm (field notes; Nicodemus, Chapter 9, this volume). One of the celts was wrapped in hide and positioned along the lower left side of the individual's torso (field notes; Nicodemus, Chapter 9, this volume). Two additional celts were positioned near the right shoulder (field notes; Nicodemus, Chapter 9, this volume) and three long bones in this area were covered with the copper beads (field notes; Nicodemus, Chapter 9, this volume). When excavated, the beads were observed as organized into a band of beads, some eleven rows wide (field notes). The fourth celt (small; KB-1:2258) is recorded as recovered from this burial in the museum catalog (and other reports; see Wilmeth 1978) but does not appear in the field notes. Its exact provenience is unclear. This burial also contained the largest amount of copper by weight: 1794.3 grams.

Burial 10 contained numerous copper beads (n=192), including small conical-trapezoidal beads, ovoid, and small round beads. This count significantly under-represents the entire number of beads from this burial, as many are concreted together in a large mass due to corrosion products and organic adherents. Also included with this burial were 2 awls (concreted together) and a large celt. This individual, identified as an adolescent female (Nicodemus, Chapter 9, this volume), is the most complete of the Killarney Bay skeletons and was interred in a tightly flexed position within a basket and then in a hide bag or overlain with a hide (field notes; Nicodemus, Chapter 9, this volume). In addition to the copper artifacts listed above, this individual was reportedly interred with a mass of fused discoidal copper beads (field notes on file). This mass was determined to be a mass of discoidal shell beads, stained green by proximity to copper. Burial 10 contained 897.1 grams of copper.

Burial 6, a young adult male identified by Nicodemus (Chapter 9, this volume), was interred with a strand of tubular copper beads strung on a leather thong. The leather thong is now fragmented, but 383 tubular beads were identified along it.

Burial 2, a young female identified by Nicodemus (Chapter 9, this volume), was interred with 12 small strands of tubular copper beads (n=126) and was reportedly interred clutching two or three large round beads, strung on cord, in her left hand (field notes report three beads but only two appear in the UMMAA collections).

Burial 4, identified as a young child by Nicodemus (Chapter 9, this volume), was interred with two strands of medium round beads (n=54) around his neck.

Burial 3 was the heavily disturbed grave of another young child (Nicodemus, Chapter 9, this volume). This individual was interred with a small fragment of sheet copper and 8 copper beads (6 tubular and 2 large round). The large tubular beads described in the field notes were determined to be copper-stained shell beads.

Burial 7, identified as an infant or young child (Nicodemus, Chapter 9, this volume), was interred with the largest of the large celts (688.2 grams) and the only chisel recovered from the site. These two pieces combined for a weight of 969.9 grams, which is the second highest among the burials.

Burials 5 and 9 did not contain copper artifacts. As mentioned previously, the copper artifacts from Burial 1 are currently unavailable for examination.

Contextualizing the Killarney Bay native copper assemblage

One difficulty in contextualizing the Killarney Bay native copper assemblage is in directly comparing the artifacts recovered from the site to those recovered throughout the Eastern Woodlands. The main impediment is in the variable publication of the assemblages: artifacts are identified at the gross formal level (beads, celts, awls, etc) but are not reported in detail beyond their frequency in site assemblages (for example, see Faulkner 1960; Fogel 1963; Ritzenthaler and Quimby 1962). A comparison of the Killarney Bay assemblage to other site assemblages is most useful for certain types of copper artifacts, including the beads, the celts, and, to a lesser extent, the awls.

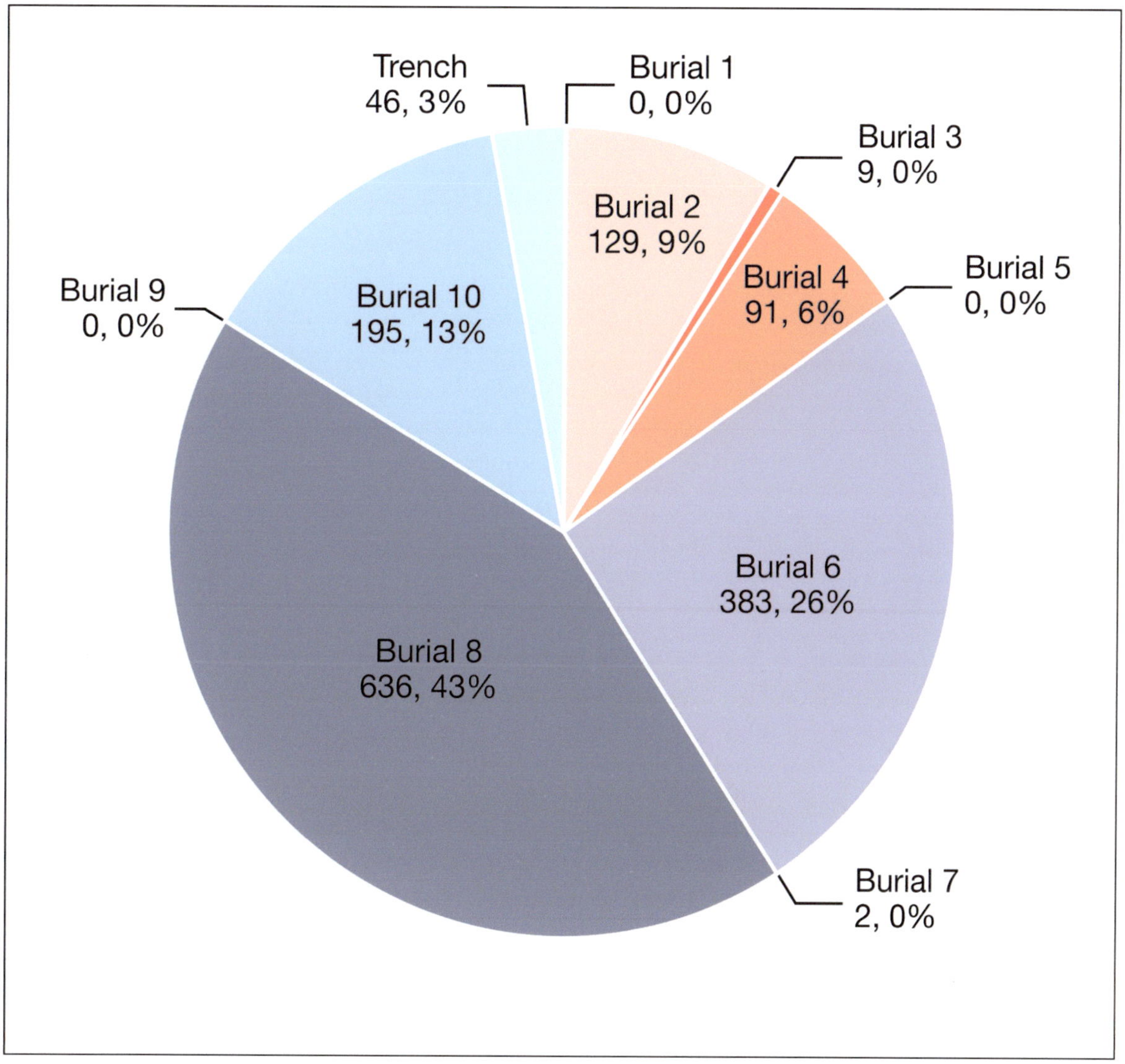

Figure 12.29. Chart showing percentages of copper artifacts found in the Killarney Bay burials, which are curated in the UMMAA collection.

Beads

We can compare the beads from the Killarney Bay assemblage to Adena assemblages such as Cresap Mound (Dragoo 1963) and to Middlesex assemblages such as the well-reported material from the Boucher site in Vermont (Heckenberger et al. 1990a)—a sample of the Boucher material has been subjected to metallographic analysis (Childs 1994). An additional comparison is made to the 20KE20 site in Michigan (Martin 1993, 1994).

Dragoo (1963) reported a single copper gorget/ breastplate, two strips of copper, and 380 beads from eight burial features at Cresap Mound. One of the strips is consistent in size and manufacture with the strips from Killarney Bay (Dragoo 1963:121). Dragoo's description of both metric analysis and method of manufacture of the recovered beads correlates with those found at Killarney Bay, especially regarding the ovoid and small round beads. Dragoo argues that:

> All of the Cresap Mound copper beads were made by rolling a thin, narrow strip of metal. After the desired overlap of a quarter to a half of the circumference was obtained, each bead was smoothed and the rough edges dulled. The beads were then placed with the hole flat and hammered enough to bulge the sides slightly to give it a "barrel-shape." The variation in size and detail indicates that each bead was carefully handcrafted. (Dragoo 1963:122).

Dragoo's description was based primarily on visual examination of the beads from Cresap Mound. He also reports microscopic examination of a small subset of the beads, in an effort to determine if these pieces were annealed during manufacture.

At Boucher, Heckenberger et al. (1990a) report 6,732 native copper artifacts from 43 features at the site. This reflects the presence of copper in approximately one-half of the 84 burials at the site. The majority of the assemblage consists of beads (n=6,729 or 99.95 percent). There are also two nuggets of raw material and a single hafted awl. The hafted awl from Boucher is similar in length to the hafted awl reported from Killarney Bay (Boucher = 125 mm; Killarney Bay = 131.4 mm). Additionally, both are square in cross section and taper to a point. Unfortunately, no comparison can be made of the handles themselves, as the Killarney Bay specimen has become separated from its wooden handle. The two nuggets of raw copper recovered at Boucher do not exhibit signs of modification (Heckenberger et al. 1990a:187).

Based on technological attributes, Heckenberger et al. (1990a:187) sorted the beads from Boucher into three types. Type 1 represents simple rolled beads in sizes ranging from small (<1.5 mm) to large (>12 mm) in length and diameter. Type 2 beads at Boucher are described as rolled tubular beads small in diameter (3.0 to 4. 0 mm) and short to long (<10 mm to >180 mm). The third and final type of bead recovered at Boucher is described as a large nugget bead. Heckenberger et al. (1990a:190–191) report that most beads were strung as necklaces or bracelets, as deduced from their placement in the burials.

Childs' (1994) subsequent metallographic analysis of twelve of the Boucher beads revealed that combinations of hammering, folding, annealing, hot forging, and cold forging were employed in their construction. The earlier beads at the site (based on securely radiocarbon-dated contexts) were shown to be crafted from thicker folded sheet strips with care taken to incorporate any "extra" copper into the finished form (Childs 1994:238). These strips were also noticeably tapered at both ends prior to sequences of rolling/bending and annealing (Childs 1994:238). Childs' (1994) analysis led her to conclude that there was no specific sequence of manufacture steps for the beads.

The final comparison of beads from the Killarney Bay assemblage is with 20KE20, a beadmaker's cache site from northern Michigan (Martin 1993, 1994). Martin (1994) describes the cache as having 43 awls, 300+ beads, a single crescent knife, copper strips (n=1000+), and raw nuggets. Of particular note is the uniformity in the size of the strips: they have average lengths of 7.5 mm and widths of 2.5 mm (Martin 1994:52). "The sides of the blanks appear to have a slight central bulge, and the ends, which will eventually abut or overlap, are tapered slightly" (Martin 1994:52). According to Martin, these blanks would appear to represent finished beads of between 1.5 and 2.5 mm in length.

Celts/Adzes/Chisels and Awls

Comparing the celts/adzes/chisels and awls from the Killarney Bay assemblage is complicated by the variable publication of the specifics of these kinds of artifacts.

In order to attempt the most meaningful comparison possible, we examined celts/adzes/chisels from the Hopewell Mound City group (n=3; curated at Hopewell Culture National Historic Park, Chillicothe, Ohio) and

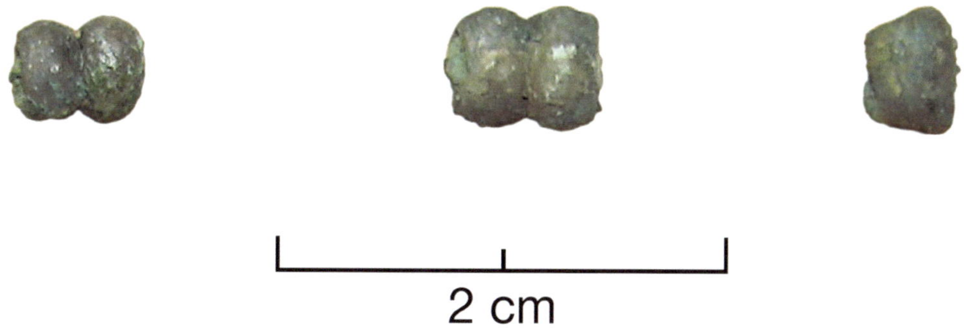

Figure 12.30 (top). Left to right: Small round, ovoid, and small conical-trapezoidal beads from Killarney Bay: UMMAA 39496; KB-1: 2239.

Figure 12.31 (left). Large celt, "poll end" with damage: UMMAA 39503; KB-1: 2242.

Both photographs by L.M. Anselmi with permission of the University of Michigan, Museum of Anthropological Archaeology.

the Bell, Reeves, and Williams collections (n=3, n=2, n=4, respectively; all curated at the Canadian Museum of History).

Additionally, we relied on full descriptions from the Ohio Historical Society online catalog of nine celts/adzes/chisels from the Hopewell site, seven from Seip Mound, three from Edwin Harness Mound, one from Fortney Mound, one from Esch Mound, and one from Truman Mills Mound. Published reports were available for celts from several Hopewell mound and Point Peninsula sites throughout Ohio, New York, and Ontario, including: Hopewell Mound (Greber and Ruhl 1989), Seip Mound (Mills 1909), Bluff Point (a Point Peninsula site, Carpenter 1950), Wheatland (a Point Peninsula site, Carpenter 1950), Squackie Hill (a Point Peninsula site, Ritchie 1938), and Sugar Island (a Point Peninsula site, Johnston 1968a). From Bernardini and Carr (2005: Appendix 17.1) we took a final source of metric data for a large number of Hopewell celts, including those from Newark (n=1), Rochhold (n=1), Esch (n=2), Hopewell (n=62), Fortney (n=1), Liberty (n=2), and Seip (n=18) mound sites.

One difficulty with a comparison of artifacts of this type is with the labels that the artifacts now carry. The terms celt, adze, and even chisel have been used uncritically to describe these pieces since the earliest recorded discoveries in the 1800s. Martin (1999:235) includes the terms wedge, gouge, and axe within this category as well. She defines the group as including "implements that vary widely in shape, function, and size. The basic form of the tool is flat, thin, and tapering, with the working edge perpendicular to the long dimension of the tool" (1999:235). The Killarney Bay assemblage as described above includes 6 celts (of various sizes) and a chisel, where the chisel is narrower in width than any of the celts. A distinguishing feature of all the celts from Killarney Bay is their flat profile, as opposed to a plano-convex shape seen in some of the celts/adzes from a number of the Ohio Hopewell sites (such as the Hopewell, Seip, and Edwin Harness mounds). A total of 15 out of the 46 celts/adzes/chisels for which full descriptions were available carried this profile (approximately 33 percent). Metric data for the celts/adzes/chisels is variable. Average weight for an artifact of this type is approximately 752 grams, with a range of between 30 and 17,270 grams. If the outliers are removed (i.e., 5 celts: 1 from Seip and 4 from Hopewell) this average falls to 421 grams, with a range between 30 and 2,000 grams. The Killarney Bay celts and chisel, by comparison, have an average weight of 449 grams.

In terms of overall form, the Killarney Bay celts are remarkably similar to many of those examined at the other locations, including those recovered from Ohio Hopewell sites and from New York and Ontario. They are flat in profile with flaring bits and tapering polls (see Figures 12.19–12.25). An overall average for maximum length of the celts is 136.9 mm, with a range of 599 to 50.8 mm; an average maximum width is 63.45 mm, with a range of 124 to 24.13 mm; and an average maximum thickness is 11.06 mm, with a range of 18.6 to 5.6 mm. The Killarney Bay artifacts yield metric characteristics similar to these averages.

For the awls, comparative material was drawn from direct examination of awls in the Mound City Group (n=1, curated at Hopewell Culture National Historic Park, Chillicothe, Ohio) and the Williams collection (n=4, curated at the Canadian Museum of History). Descriptions were taken for 4 awls from Seip Mound (Mills 1909) and for the 43 awls recovered at 20KE20 in Michigan (Martin 1994). Metric data and descriptions for an additional 13 awls from Hopewell Mound (n=8), Seip Mound (n=4), and Edwin Harness Mound (n=1) were taken from the Ohio Historical Society online catalog.

The Killarney Bay awls (or spindles, as Greenman referred to them) are fairly consistent with awls from other Middle Woodland sites throughout the region. They are generally square to rectangular in cross section, with tapering, pointed ends (see Figures 12.26 and 12.27). This is very similar to the awl from the Mound City group's Mica Grave (mound 13), awls from the Hopewell and Seip Mound sites, the Williams collection (from a grave site in Prince Edward County, Ontario), and the 20KE20 site in Michigan. Some examples do appear almost rounded in cross section, and several examples yield evidence for the ends having been twisted during the manufacturing process. Average overall weight for an awl is 61.52 grams, with a range of 132 to <1 grams. Average length is 133.65 mm, with a range of 305 to 35 mm. Average width is 7.96 mm, with a range of 13.2 to 3.2 mm. The four Killarney Bay awls have similar averages for weight, width, and thickness, but they are somewhat longer, with an average length of 180.87 mm.

Discussion and preliminary conclusions

The Killarney Bay native copper assemblage, including the Robert Bell collection, includes beads, celts, awls, a chisel, and small fragments of sheet material. Though present in high numbers on sites throughout the Eastern Woodlands, beads are often not as diagnostic as one would like, due to their long and widespread use and the relatively stable methods of manufacture used in their creation (Martin 1999). At Killarney Bay, beads form the largest artifact category among the native copper artifacts. By count, they make up 98.86 percent of the Killarney Bay copper assemblage curated at UMMAA and 99.56 percent of the Robert Bell collection.

The conical-trapezoidal beads are the most distinctive of those recovered at Killarney Bay. There are reports of large conical beads from other sites and collections (see West 1929 for one example), but the small conical beads and the interesting nested arrangement of the small strands in the Killarney Bay assemblage appear to be distinctive (see Figures 12.3 and 12.13).

Tubular beads at Killarney Bay are markedly smaller than Type II beads at Boucher and elsewhere. In the UMMAA assemblage, these small beads have an average maximum length of 4.38 mm. The large tubular beads from the Bell collection have an average maximum length of 17.1 mm. Both of these results are notably different than the largest of these beads at Boucher, which have a maximum length in excess of 180 mm. The Killarney Bay tubular beads do appear to have been formed or crimped around leather thongs, as they are at many other sites, including 20KE20.

The last categories identified in the Killarney Bay assemblage—ovoid and round beads—resemble Type 1 beads as described at the Boucher site and 20KE20 and on many other sites throughout the Eastern Woodlands. Though they appear distinct to this researcher, they may not have to their original manufacturers/users (Figure 12.30). The ovoid and small round beads are found strung on the same strands. Any patterning that may have existed originally has been lost.

The celts, awls, and chisel from the assemblage are also types commonly reported from sites throughout the region. Of interest is the possible wear damage on the blade of the chisel. Also interesting is the upturned end of one of the large celts, which could have been deformed during manufacture or during use (Figure 12.31). The celts, awls, and chisel forms are consistent with Middle Woodland copper forms from other sites.

In terms of the distribution of the artifacts, Burial 8 is by far the richest in terms of absolute number of copper artifacts (n=638) and weight of copper artifacts included in the burial (1.7943 kg). Clearly the copper had significance on a ritual or religious level for the people who constructed the burial mound at Killarney Bay, and likely on an economic level as well. It has been suggested that the people at Killarney Bay were a group of southern migrants (i.e., Adena) who moved north to this location (Spence et al. 1990:142). It is possible that the location was attractive as a position along a hypothesized access route to the Lake Superior native copper outcrops (Brose and Hambacher 1998). These people may have served as middlemen in a down-the-line exchange of this material. However, there is no evidence in the native copper assemblage to suggest that any of the individuals buried with native copper artifacts were metalworkers themselves.

Acknowledgements

I would like to thank Pat Julig, David Brose, and Alicia Hawkins for inviting me to participate in the re-analysis of the Killarney Bay assemblage; the session at the 2009 Canadian Archaeological Association meetings on the site and this volume; John O'Shea and Karen O'Brien for access to the Killarney Bay assemblage at the University of Michigan Museum of Anthropological Archaeology; Amy Nicodemus and Alice Wright for sharing their analysis of the Killarney Bay skeletal material; Kathleen Brady, curator at Hopewell Culture National Historical Park, for access to the Mound City collections; and Jean-Luc Pilon and Stacey Girling-Christie for access to the Robert Bell and other collections at the Canadian Museum of History.

Chapter 13

Botanical and Faunal Remains

Amy Nicodemus and J. Amadeaus Scott

The Killarney Bay site, located on the north shore of Georgian Bay in Ontario, Canada, contains an early Middle Woodland burial complex dating to approximately 330 BC to AD 210. The botanical and faunal remains presented in this study derive primarily from Emerson Greenman's excavations of the principal mound in 1939–1952. A small sample of animal bone from Robert Bell's excavations in the 1870s is also included. The Killarney Bay assemblage is not large, but it is nonetheless important, as a wide range of objects were recovered, including animal bone, hides, basketry, cordage, bark sheets, and hafting. Such excellent preservation is a rare occurrence in this region, where acidic forest soils normally destroy these materials. In this case, copper salts from grave goods preserved a variety of organic artifacts within the burials. Additionally, extreme burning and the presence of alkaline ash preserved botanical and faunal remains within the mound fill, deriving directly or indirectly from hearths and other thermal features.

The Killarney Bay organic collection allows burial activities to be detailed to a degree seldom achieved for Upper Great Lakes cultures of this antiquity. Animal bone and plant remains from hearths, pits, and general mound fill document the types of foods that residents consumed and the wood they used for cooking during site visitation and funerary events. This material also indicates the season of site use and patterns of resource exploitation within the local environment. Perhaps most importantly, the organic grave goods illustrate dimensions of mortuary programs rarely encountered and contribute to a greater understanding of both Middle Woodland funerary practices and material culture.

Methodology

Animal bone was identified to taxon as specifically as possible. In many cases, bone could only be assigned to size categories within taxonomic classes, particularly for mammals (Appendix 13.1). Element, portion, side, and age were documented, as well as taphonomic condition, including both pre- and postdepositional alteration. No bones were complete enough to take standardized measurements (von den Driesch 1976). Number of identified specimens (NISP) quantification was used, given the small sample size, high level of fragmentation, and often ambiguous temporal/stratigraphic relationships. Bone identification was aided by comparative skeletal collections from the University of Michigan's Museum of Anthropological Archaeology (UMMAA) Zooarchaeology Range and the Museum of Zoology (UMMZ) Bird and Herpetology divisions.

Many of the Killarney Bay animal pelts are preserved sufficiently to identify species using macroscopic and low-magnification microscopic techniques. Color, texture, density, length, and shape of the outer guard and fine underhair were assessed for each specimen. These variables were compared against UMMZ Mammal Division pelt samples from fur-bearing species of the Georgian Bay region.

Archaeobotanical materials include basketry, cordage, bark sheeting, hafting, charcoal, and a nut fragment. These were identified using low-magnification microscopy. Analysis was aided by manuals (Core et al. 1979; Harrar 1964; Hoadley 1990; Hosie 1979) and comparative materials provided by the UMMAA Ethnobotany Range and the Great Lakes Range. Samples were counted and, if possible, weighed. Basketry, hafting, and some fibers were not weighed, due to their fragility. Materials equal to or larger than 0.5 cm^2 were analyzed in detail, excepting two very large charcoal samples, from which only fragments greater than 1 cm^2 were considered. Samples that included soil were screened with a 0.5-cm geological sieve and residues were retained for future analysis. Basketry and cordage descriptions follow terminology from Adovasio (1977) and Hurley (1979), respectively.

Original field catalog numbers (KB1-X) were used in the text for both faunal and botanical specimens. Where available, UMMAA catalog numbers were provided in the chapter appendices.

Results

Animal bone

The Killarney Bay mound excavations produced 172 animal bone fragments from the Bell and Greenman excavations (Table 13.1, Figure 13.1, Appendix 13.2). The bulk of the sample, which derives from mound fill and nonburial features, is calcined and highly fragmented, as is typical for this region. The topsoil and burials produced a number of unburned bones. Animal bone was collected opportunistically, and no screening or flotation took place.

Topsoil

The topsoil mound layer contained a mix of prehistoric and historic/modern material, including 21 animal bone fragments. Unlike material from other nonburial mound contexts, little of the topsoil bone is calcined. Given soil acidity, this well-preserved unburned bone is likely of relatively recent origin, a conclusion supported by the presence of domesticates, frequency of whitetail deer, and modern butchery marks.

The topsoil fauna is diverse. Sixteen mammalian bones are present, representing at least five species. The most common animal is whitetail deer (*Odocoileus virginianus*) and it is likely that most, if not all, of the indeterminate large mammal (Class IV) fragments also are this taxon (rather than woodland caribou, *Rangifer tarandus*, which has been locally extirpated). There are at least two juvenile deer around two years old present, based on fusion state and size of the distal tibiae. One weathered mandible fragment was severed from the cranium with a heavy modern metal implement. Snowshoe hare (*Lepus americanus*) and domestic pig (*Sus scrofa domesticus*) are the only other mammals identified to species. Several medium mammal bones are also present, including a rib fragment that likely belongs to one of the smaller carnivores in this group (e.g., fox, otter, or raccoon). The very large mammal bone is an unfused lumbar vertebra fragment belonging to a larger ungulate like moose, elk, cattle, or horse. There are three bird species represented by a single humerus each: Canada goose (*Branta canadensis*), domestic goose (*Anser anser domesticus*), and an indeterminate duck (Anatinae). There are also two fish vertebrae: one from a northern pike (*Esox*

Table 13.1. Killarney Bay animal bone by context.

Common name	Scientific name	Bell Collection	Topsoil	Subsoil	Hearths	Pits	Burials	Prehistoric total*	Site total
Moose	cf. *Alces alces*	2						2	2
Whitetail deer	*Odocoileus virginianus*		2						2
	cf. *Odocoileus virginianus*		3						3
Woodland caribou	*Rangifer tarandus caribou*	1						1	1
Caribou/deer	*Rangifer/Odocoileus*		2		7			7	9
	cf. *Rangifer/ Odocoileus*				13			13	13
Domestic pig	*Sus scrofa domesticus*		1						1
Beaver	cf. *Castor canadensis*						1	1	1
Snowshoe hare	*Lepus americanus*	1	1					1	2
	cf. *Lepus americanus*				1			1	1
Carnivore	Carnivora		1	1				1	2
Very large mammal	Mammalia Class V		1						1
Large mammal	Mammalia Class IV		4	7		1	2	10	14
Medium mammal	Mammalia Class III		1	1	15			16	17
Mammal (indet)	Mammalia			4	73			77	77
Total mammal		**4**	**16**	**13**	**109**	**1**	**3**	**130**	**146**
Blanding's turtle	*Emydoidea blandingi*			1				1	1
Snapping turtle	cf. *Chelydra serpintina*			1				1	1
Turtle (indet)	Testudines			1	2	10	1	14	14
Total reptile				**3**	**2**	**10**	**1**	**16**	**16**
Canada goose	*Branta canadensis*		1						1
Domestic goose	cf. *Anser anser domesticus*		1						1
Mallard	*Anas platyrhynchos*	1							1
Duck (indet)	Anatinae	1	1				1	1	3
Total bird		**2**	**3**				**1**	**1**	**6**
Lake sturgeon	*Acipenser fulvescens*			1				1	1
Pike/muskellunge	*Esox* spp.		1						1
Sucker	Catostomidae		1						1
Total fish			**2**	**1**				**1**	**3**
Grand total		**6**	**21**	**17**	**111**	**11**	**5**	**148**	**171**

*Excludes unburned Bell Collection fauna

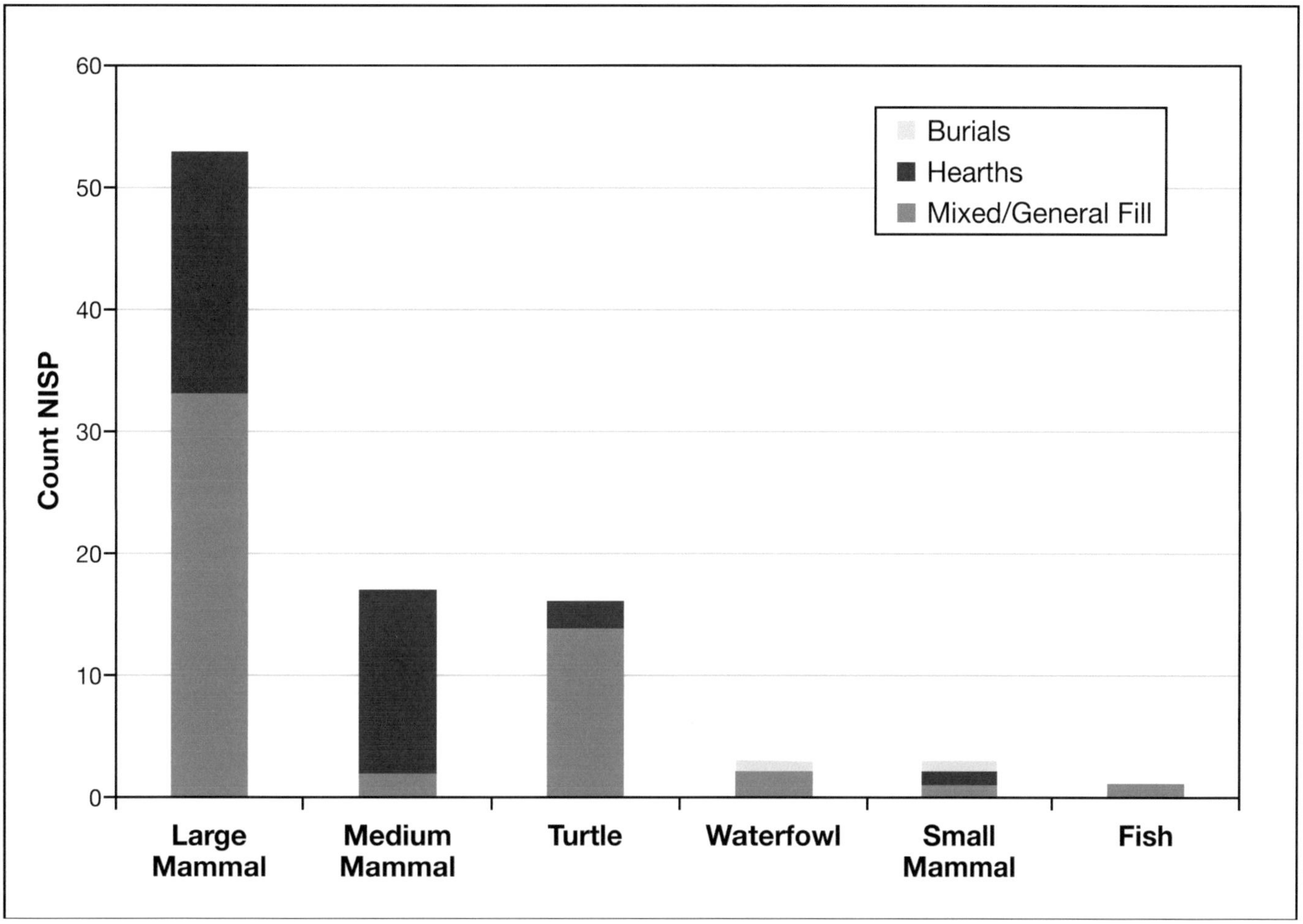

Figure 13.1. Animal bone composition by taxon and context (excluding topsoil).

lucius) or muskellunge (*E. masquinongy*) and the other from a member of the sucker family (Catostomidae). Both are large individuals.

Unfortunately, the topsoil assemblage is a mix of historic and prehistoric material. While some of the animal bone is clearly historic, any prehistoric fauna cannot be reliably separated. This material is not included in further analysis.

Subsoil

Seventeen animal bones were recovered from "subsoil" mound fill layers, all calcined and highly fragmented, few of which could be identified to species. Most of these are mammalian, predominately from a larger species such as woodland caribou. Woodland caribou and whitetail deer bones are difficult to separate, particularly in highly fragmented samples such as this one. Woodland caribou would have been the dominant species of the two prehistorically, as deer have only recently expanded their ranges into much of Ontario with the spread of agriculture and other modern forest disturbances (Eder 2002). While the indeterminate elements are assumed to be from this taxon, it cannot be completely excluded that deer may have been present in small numbers as well.

At least one of the medium mammal bones is a likely carnivore.

Three turtle bones are present, including a Blanding's turtle (*Emydoidea blandingi*) carapace fragment and a long bone fragment from a large species like snapping turtle (cf. *Chelydra serpintina*). There is also a dermal plate fragment from a lake sturgeon (*Acipenser fulvescens*), which is the only fish bone from a secure prehistoric context.

Thermal features

Three contexts associated with hearths in Trench 4D produced calcined animal bone. The Section G9 hearth contained a large collection of highly fragmented material (107 pieces), the majority of which could only be separated into general vertebrate classes. However, seven caribou/deer bones were identified, including vertebra, femur, and tooth enamel fragments. Eleven large mammal shaft fragments may also be caribou. There are fourteen medium mammal shaft fragments and a single small mammal vertebra fragment, consistent with snowshoe hare. The only nonmammalian bones are two indeterminate turtle shell fragments: one from the carapace and one from the plastron.

The other thermal features are "streamers" of burned material associated with nearby hearths. The Section C9 streamer, related to the C10 hearth, contained three large mammal long bone shaft fragments—again, probably caribou. The other streamer, in Sections D8–9, only had two very small bone fragments: one medium mammal rib and an indeterminate mammalian bone fragment. No fish, reptile, or bird bone was found in either of these features.

Pits

Two nonburial pit features within the mound deposits contained animal bone. While these were both artifact-rich, they produced few faunal remains (eleven fragments). The bones are calcined and highly fragmented, like the hearth and fill material. A pit in Trench 4D, Section B9, contained a single caribou/deer epiphysis fragment. The second pit lay adjacent to Burial 2 and is associated with fire-cracked rock and a charcoal-rich hearth. It contains ten indeterminate turtle carapace fragments, probably from a single shell.

Burials

Three graves contained animal bone, including the only unburned prehistoric material. Their preservation is no doubt related to the copper artifacts within the burials. Burial 8 (adult male) produced two unburned animal bones: a large rodent incisor and a duck tibiotarsus, found in association with copper-preserved animal hide. The highly fragmented incisor is within the size class of beaver (*Castor canadensis*) or porcupine (*Erethizon dorsatum*). Given the frequency of beaver incisor objects at Middle Woodland sites elsewhere, it is more likely from this species. The duck tibiotarsus, the only prehistoric bird bone, is also fragmented and cannot be more specifically identified.

The remaining bones are all small calcined fragments and unlikely to have been grave goods. Burial 3, which is disturbed, contained a calcined carapace fragment from an indeterminate turtle species. In Burial 9, a large mammal bone fragment (clearly faunal) was mixed in with the human cremations. These isolated finds probably originate from general mound fill. A calcined shaft fragment from Burial 8 appears to be human and likely derives from Burial 9.

Bell Collection

A small collection of animal bone (six pieces) was stored with cremated human remains from Bell's excavations. Unfortunately, this material has no contextual information, and it is unclear if these originated from burials or elsewhere. Several well-preserved elements are unburned and show no obvious traces of copper staining. These include a mallard (*Anas platyrhynchos*) humerus and an indeterminate duck tibiotarsus shaft. These may derive from more recent contexts (e.g., topsoil) or from burials. The remaining bones are calcined and resemble other prehistoric material from Killarney Bay. This includes fragments from moose (cf. *Alces alces*), juvenile caribou, and snowshoe hare. Because of the uncertain origin of the Bell collection, this material is kept separate or omitted in further analyses.

Animal hides

Nearly all of the Killarney Bay burials contain portions of animal hide preserved by copper grave goods (Table 13.2, Appendix 13.3). It is sometimes difficult to determine each specimen's original form with certainty, but it is clear that these leather and fur fragments are variously remnants of garments, burial wrappings, bags, and bead thongs. Six burials contain furred pelts with hair in a sufficient state of preservation for taxon attribution. All of the identifiable pelts are beaver, except for a single winter deer hide, although excavation notes suggested the presence of additional hairy deerskins.

The leather fragments, lacking fur, are not identifiable to taxon. Most of these derive from lots with beaver pelts, and many may be fragments separated from the fur. Others are likely to be cervid, particularly the bag/garment fragments and leather thongs from copper and shell bead necklaces.

Table 13.2. Animal hide artifacts from Killarney Bay burials.

Burial	Leather sheet*	Leather bead thong	Leather/sinew lashing	Beaver pelt	Cervid hide	Comments
2	X	X		?		possible garment
3	X	X				
4	X	X		X		
5	X			X		
6	X	X				leather sheet over bundle
7		X		X		pelt bag? hair wrapped with leather thong
8	X	X	X	X		leather knot, pelt bag?
10	X		X	?	X	decorated leather bag

X = present, ? = tentative identification
*includes possible clothing fragments and bags

Traces of leather and/or sinew lashing are also present on several hafted bifaces. This analysis is restricted to materials collected by Emerson Greenman and now housed at UMMAA. Additional fur and leather fragments are in the Bell collection at the Canadian Museum of History, including cordage made of hair.

Burial 2 (young adult female)

A number of leather pieces and beaver fur were collected from a possible garment with fiber thongs, preserved by copper bead strands and a copper awl near the neck and chest. One end of this awl was also wrapped in leather and associated with a wood fragment, possibly a handle. The leather wrapping may be remnants of a bag.

Burial 3 (child)

Although this burial was disturbed, a number of small possible leather fragments were recovered from contexts within it containing human remains. Greenman notes that some of the human bone appeared to have "leather wrapping placed around the bones" (1950:17). This material is highly fragmented, and it is possible that at least some of these are pieces of human skin, given the amount of preserved tissue encasing articulated skeletal elements.

Burial 4 (child)

Two copper bead strands preserved several organic objects, including the leather necklace thong and several leather and beaver fur fragments that overlay the body (Figure 13.2a). It is unclear whether the leather is part of the beaver pelt or from a separate cervid hide.

Burial 5 (child)

Three copper beads found above the burial had a piece of leather adhering to them. Additional copper-stained leather and beaver pelt fragments were collected from around the cranium/dentition.

Burial 6 (young adult male)

A basket containing the human remains has copper beads sewn around its rim, which preserved numerous plant fiber and hide objects. Leather thongs are present within many of the bead strands. A leather sheet was placed over the entire bundle, overlain with birch bark. Many fragments of this hide are preserved, including pieces adhering to the basketry and the copper beads themselves.

Burial 7 (infant)

Remnants of fur and leather were recovered under the body, in association with a copper celt and chisel placed beneath the individual's right shoulder. Several beaver pelt fragments also were collected from the head and neck area, just west of the copper items. These appear to be pieces of a "skin bag" (Greenman 1950:31) sewn with shell beads, which contained grave goods. It is uncertain whether all the pelt fragments ultimately originate from the bag(s) or if another pelt lined the bottom of the burial pit. There is also a loosely twisted strand of hair wrapped with a leather thong (Z-twist). It was not possible to examine this hair in detail, so it is not known whether it is human or faunal.

Burial 8 (adult male)

This burial produced the largest collection of hide remnants. Apart from thongs and lashing, all of the "leather" in the present collection is beaver pelt fragments. The copper spindle and bead strands around the right arm preserved many beaver fur pieces. Greenman (1952:4) mentions the presence of leather between these beads and the body in the field—perhaps they are clothing remnants. The celts all appeared to be wrapped in several folds of furred hide when excavated (Figure 13.2b). Importantly, where complete enough to discern, the beaver pelts encasing the celts have the leather facing inwards on both sides, suggesting that the artifacts may have been placed within bags, as seen in Burials 6, 10, and possibly 2. The small leather knot (Figure 13.2c) associated with celts KB1-2241 and 2242 (on the individual's right shoulder with hand resting on top) may be the tie for such a pouch (like that found in Burial 10) or for a single large hide bag in which the body was placed, as proposed in the field notes. Larger hide sheets are not present in the current assemblage, but they may have been present as well. Excavators documented a "thickness of deer skin with its hair of about ½ inch underlying the whole deposit" (Greenman 1952:5). Three of the stone bifaces with the above copper artifacts were hafted. Two of the hafts (KB1-2233 and 2236) appear to have traces of degraded leather and/or sinew lashing.

Burial 10 (young adult female)

Burial 10 contains a large amount of leather but little beaver fur. A copper celt was placed inside a leather bag (with leather thong tie), situated on the individual's abdomen. This bag preserves incised decoration and wrapped leather tassels (Figure 13.2d). Two copper awls were placed on this bag, and the leather associated with these artifacts may originate from the celt pouch. Additional leather fragments, either fragments of bags or garments, were collected from "various places" within the burials (Greenman 1953:10). Cordage found adhering to some of this leather (near the copper beads around the right wrist) may be fringe decoration or a very loosely woven net bag. The excavators encountered an area associated with the artifact cluster on the right shoulder that may have been the remains of a highly degraded leather bag—it contained cache blades and two tubular pipes. The awls and celt also preserved several pieces of fur and basketry fragments, the latter of which contained a second set of cache blades. One of these stone bifaces (KB1-2331) was hafted, and the shaft showed possible traces of lashing. Several strands of copper beads wrapped around the individual's right wrist had hairy cervid hide—probably caribou—adhering to them. These are the only clear remnants of nonbeaver furred pelts in the current assemblage.

Archaeobotanicals

The Killarney Bay archaeobotanical assemblage, containing more than 600 analyzed fragments, derives from a range of contexts, including burials, pits, thermal features, subsoil mound fill, gravels, and "old surfaces" (Table 13.3, Appendix 13.4). The majority of botanical remains are charred and derive directly or indirectly from hearths and other thermal features. However, a diverse collection of basketry, cordage, bark, wood, and other organic artifacts were preserved in the burials by nearby copper grave goods. These rare items have the potential to reveal much about craft production, including weaving and hafting techniques, as well as the significance of these materials within Middle Woodland mortuary programs. The charred material offers insight into season of site occupation, fuel choices, and—

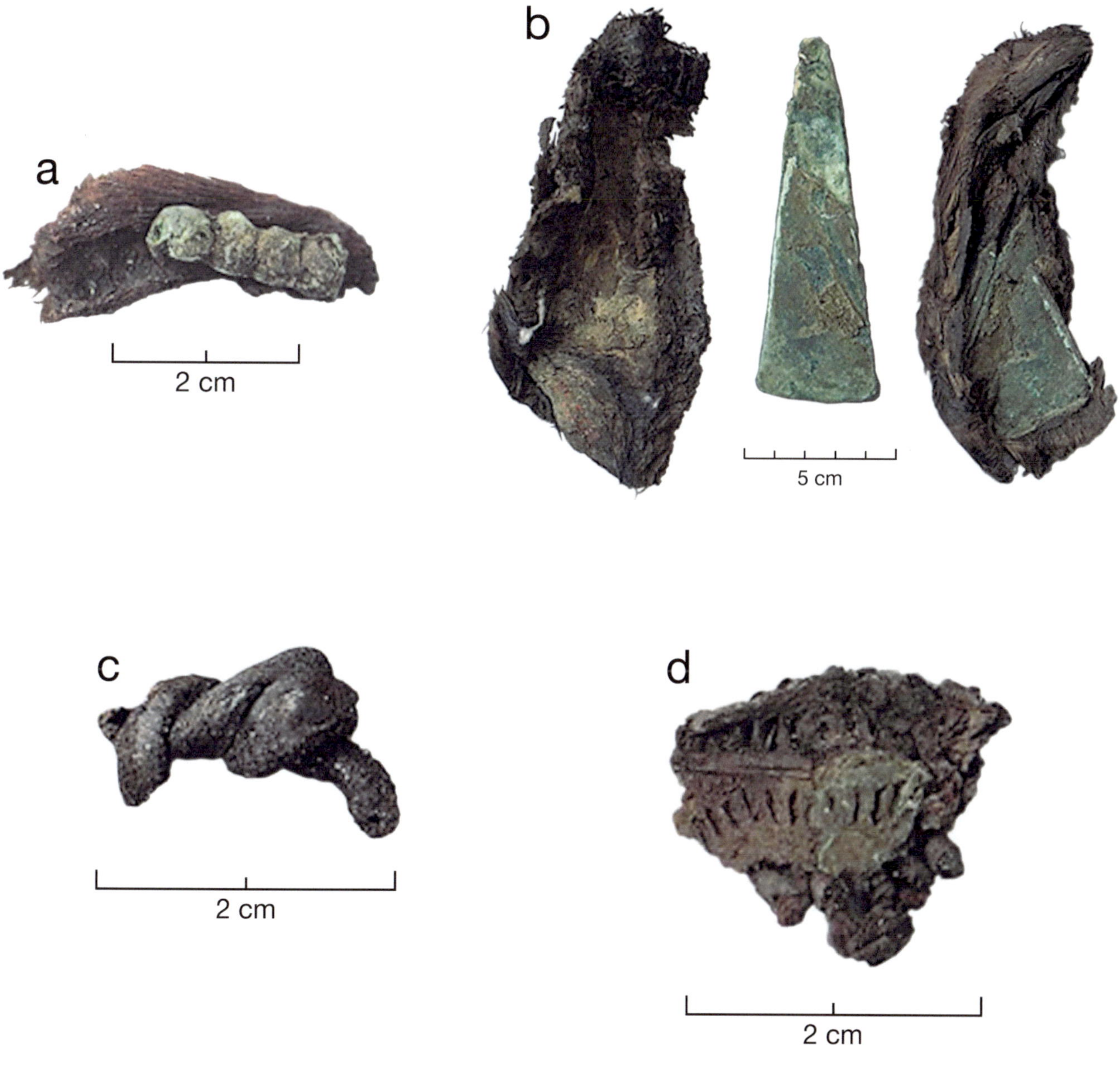

Figure 13.2, a-d. Fur and leather artifacts from burials at Killarney Bay. a. Burial 4 beads with beaver fur and ochre (KB1-2118); b. Burial 8 celt with possible beaver pelt bag (KB1-2258); c. Burial 8 leather knot associated with celts and leather bag (KB1-2242); d. Burial 10 decorated leather bag (KB1-3252).

Table 13.3. Killarney Bay archaeobotanicals by context.

Context	Charcoal	Nut	Sheet bark	Basketry	Cordage	Hafting	Pipe residue	Unburned wood	Comments
Subsoil (mound fill)	X	X							
Old surfaces	X								
Gravels								X	intrusive roots/twigs?
Pits	X								
Hearths	X								
Burial 2			X		X				cordage garment decoration?
Burial 3	X		X						
Burial 5	X		X						
Burial 6			X	X					
Burial 8	X					X			
Burial 9	X								
Burial 10	X			X	X	X	X	X	cordage garment/ bag decoration? and modern branch

through correlation with pollen cores—further establishes the types of trees growing (and exploited) in the site's catchment. This study only includes artifacts from the Greenman excavations curated at UMMAA.

Subsoil

Only one sample was specifically described in field notes as being collected from the subsoil mound fill (KB1-217): a single black ash (*Fraxinus nigra*) charcoal fragment. This was listed as originating "deeper than hearth" in Trench 4D, Section C10. However, there are additional charcoal samples from trench excavations that do not have specific contextual information. These likely originate from general mound fill as well. Seven large northern red oak (*Quercus rubra*) fragments were recovered from Trench 2 (KB1-63). In Trench 3D, another red oak sample is present (five pieces), along with a possible white cedar (cf. *Thuja occidentalis*) bark fragment (KB1-389). Red oak charcoal (ten pieces) also was present in Trench 4D, along with one fragment of eastern white pine (*Pinus strobus*) (KB1-1419). The last wood charcoal sample, from Trench 4F, includes fifteen willow (*Salix* spp.), three black ash, and five indeterminate fragments (KB1-794). A single charred beaked hazelnut (*Corylus cortuna*) was also collected from mound fill in Trench 3D, Section E1 (KB1-331).

Old surface

This context is described in field notes as either a living surface or a buried soil horizon. The single charcoal sample (KB1-759) contains only one species, represented by seven fragments of black ash.

Gravel

Sample KB1-1059 contains twenty-seven indeterminate unburned wood and small root and/or twig fragments that are similar in structure to sassafras (*Sassafras albidum).* Sassafras is not indigenous to the Killarney Bay region, but it is found elsewhere in southern Ontario (Hosie 1979) and thrives in disturbed areas. Because these specimens are not burned or associated with copper grave goods, this sample is likely to be modern and intrusive.

Pits

Two charcoal samples derive from pit features, one of which was dug into the gravel field and the other within Trench 3D (presumably within the subsoil mound fill). The gravel pit sample (KB1-1244) is relatively large, containing thirty-three charcoal fragments from several species. These include sixteen white cedar fragments, six pieces of probable silver maple (*Acer* cf. *saccharinum*), one willow (*Salix* spp.), and ten unidentifiable fragments. The Trench 3D pit has five fragments of willow (KB1-391).

Thermal features

Four hearths produced charcoal samples: one in Trench 3F ("old surface"), two in Trench 4D (subsoil, perhaps associated with each other), and another in Trench 4E ("water laid land"). The Trench 3F hearth contained a mix of species: seven black ash, three willow, and three unidentifiable fragments associated with fire-cracked rock (KB1-808). The first sample from Trench 4D (KB1-237) includes five willow and two unidentifiable fragments. The second Trench 4D hearth (KB1-1465) produced a large sample with ten willow, six indeterminate maple (*Acer* spp.), five black ash, three Eastern white pine, and eight indeterminate charcoal fragments. The Trench 4E hearth includes thirty-five pieces from one species: black ash (KB1-1481). Field notes for this sample describe the hearth as a "kiln."

Burials

All of the noncremation burials housed at UMMAA preserved portions of organic grave goods, including basketry, cordage, wooden hafts, and bark sheets. Charcoal from the burial fill is likely to be incidental for all but the cremations (Burial 9).

Burial 2 (young adult female) has two samples of unburned botanicals. There are fourteen well-preserved white cedar bark fragments from a sheet that overlaid the burial (KB1-1186). There are also many fragments of a possible garment (KB1-1183), which has approximately six preserved strands of 2-ply cordage (Z-spun strands, S-twist cords) adhering to leather and fur. These may have been ties or tassel/fringe decoration for the garment or part of a net bag (Figure 13.3). The fine fibers are likely bast from an herbaceous plant.

Burial 3 (child) produced bark and charcoal. Three white birch (*Betula papyrifera*) bark fragments (KB1-2042) derive from a sheet that likely covered this disturbed burial originally. A single unidentifiable vitrified charcoal fragment may not be associated (KB1-2041).

Burial 5 (child) contained a white birch bark fragment (KB1-2125), probably from a sheet overlying the burial. There was also a large amount of charcoal in the grave fill, including forty-two black ash, one willow, and two indeterminate fragments (KB1-2131).

Burial 6 (young adult male) includes basketry and two types of bark sheeting. Bark sample KB1-2197 is composed of seventy-two fairly large and well-preserved eastern hemlock (*Tsuga canadensis)* bark fragments. Bark sample KB1-2147 is highly fragmented, containing ninety-two small pieces of white birch bark and three eastern hemlock fragments that probably originate from the first sample. Additional hemlock and birch bark were collected with leather sheeting (KB1-2146). According to field notes, the birch bark covered the entire burial. Under this was a sheet of leather, and then hemlock bark, over the bundle.

The body and cache blades were placed within a basket made of loosely woven white cedar bark strips. Three portions of this basket are preserved (KB1-2148, 2153, 2196), showing several weaving techniques. The basket is a combination of plaiting and twining (Figure 13.4a): the former is simple plaiting with two elements per set and the latter is open simple twining with S-twist wefts. There is leather and copper bead residue in the area where the plaiting merges with the twined portion. There are also several braided elements that are probably portions of the handle (Figure 13.4b). Two braided elements are woven together into angled plaiting where the handle presumably joins the selvage. This area is also wrapped with loose 2-ply, S-twist cordage and has traces of copper and leather.

Burial 8 (adult male) held hafting and charcoal. Three large bifaces placed on the individual's chest included preserved fragments of hafting (Figure 13.5a–c). KB1-2233 and KB1-2236 have shafts made of ash splints (white ash, *Fraxinus americana,* for the latter), which were simply split to hold the biface base. KB1-2233 also has thin wooden strips of softwood (probably cedar) folded around the

Figure 13.3. Burial 2 cordage adhering to possible leather garment near the neck area (KB1-1183).

notching and base of the biface as part of the lashing, as well as traces of leather/sinew. The interior of the split shaft shows traces of an organic residue—possibly an adhesive. The KB1-2236 haft also has evidence of leather or sinew lashing and there is an impression where a wooden splint may have been present. There is a hole drilled into the base of the shaft. The KB1-2245 haft differs from the others. The shaft is a more formally shaped beech (*Fagus grandifolia*) branch with the base cut to a point. The other end has a carved notch for the biface. There is a thin white ash splint strip around the notching. There are no visible traces of other organic lashing or adhesives.

The first charcoal sample (KB1-2250), comprised of three willow and one unidentified fragment, was found under celt KB1-2242 on the individual's chest. Charcoal sample KB1-2254 contains seven black ash fragments, also from the chest area, and sample KB1-2256 includes sixty-eight black ash fragments.

Burial 9 (adult male and adolescent) contains five white pine charcoal fragments from the northern edge of the cremation pit (KB1-2307). These may be remnants of the fuel wood used in the funeral pyre (not yet located) that were collected with the human remains.

Burial 10 (young adult female) produced the largest collection of botanical remains, represented by eight samples of bark, basketry, cordage, hafting, pipe residue, wood charcoal, and unburned wood. One basketry fragment (KB1-2326) is preserved, adhering to fur with heavy

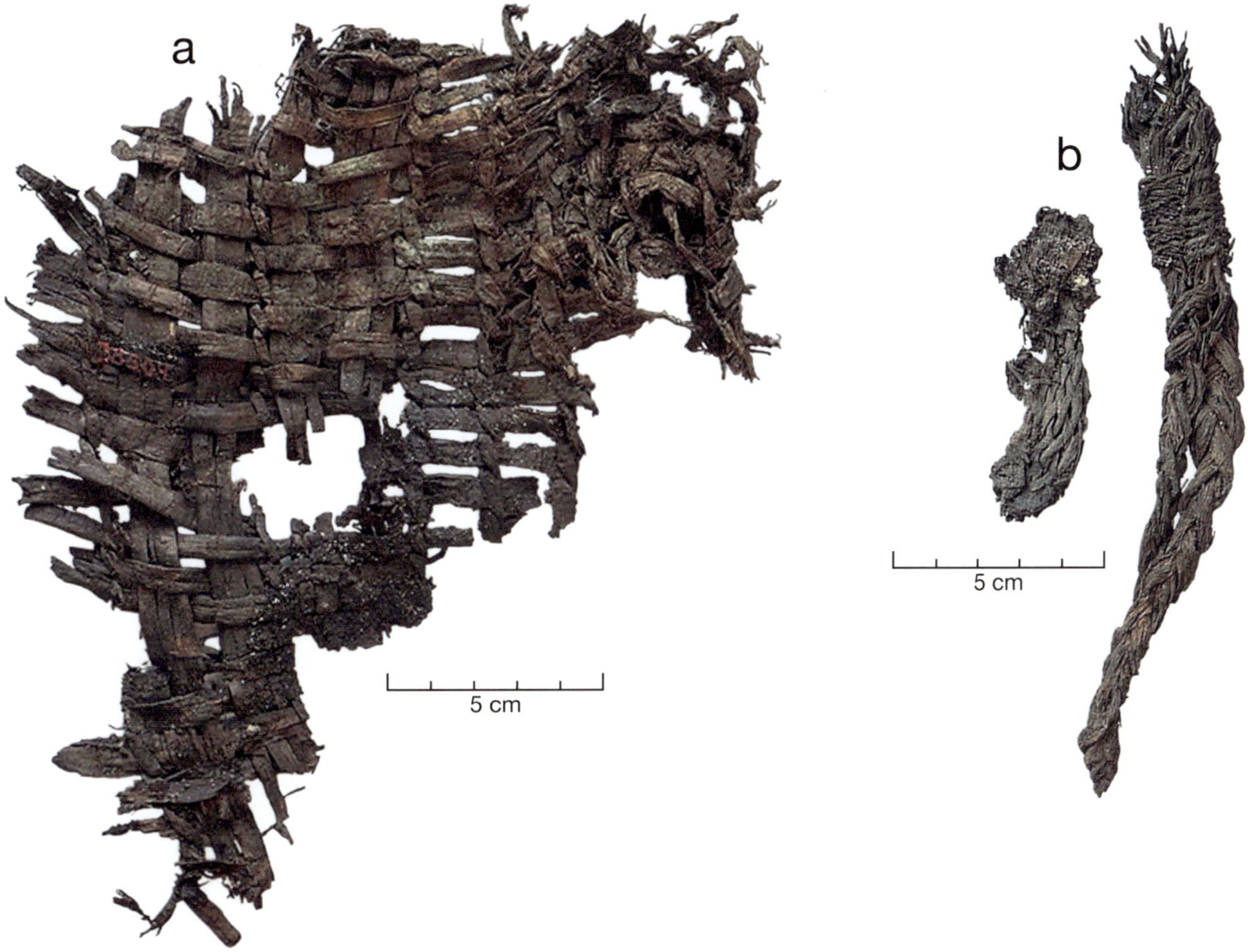

Figure 13.4, a-b. Basketry from Burial 6. a. Plaited and twined basketry containing bundle burial (KB1-2196); b. Braided elements from basket handle/selvage (KB1-2153).

preservative. This was described in field notes as a possible "net bag" containing the cache blades. It shows an unusual simple plaited weave with two different elements: thicker cedar bark fiber strips and opposing loose S-twist cordage of indeterminate material (Figure 13.6a). There is one element per set. The KB1-2327 cordage is also adhering to leather with copper staining from beads around the right wrist. It is a mass of 2-ply cordage (Z-spun strands, S-twist cords) of a relatively fine fiber, probably an herbaceous bast (Figure 13.6b). These cords are arranged in parallel but do not appear to be interwoven with one another in this sample. There is a general resemblance to the cordage from Burial 2, and these cords may likewise be some form of tassel or fringe decoration from a garment or, alternatively, from a separate, very loosely woven net bag.

There are also four fragments of white birch bark (KB1-2364), as seen in Burials 3, 5, and 6. A single hafted biface on top of the cache blades was placed near the right shoulder (see Figure 13.5). It is similar in form and manufacture to the ash hafts KB1-2233 and KB1-2236 from Burial 8. There are traces of both leather/sinew lashing and possible adhesive. No wooden lashing was present. The two stone pipes (KB1-2321, KB1-2323) from the artifact cache near the right shoulder produced charcoal and other indeterminate burned organic materials (KB1-2322 and KB1-2325 respectively), none of which was of sufficient size or preservation for taxon identification. Charcoal sample KB1-2327, recovered from the cache area with basketry, includes a single piece of charred black ash. Additional charcoal from KB1-2362, from near the lower

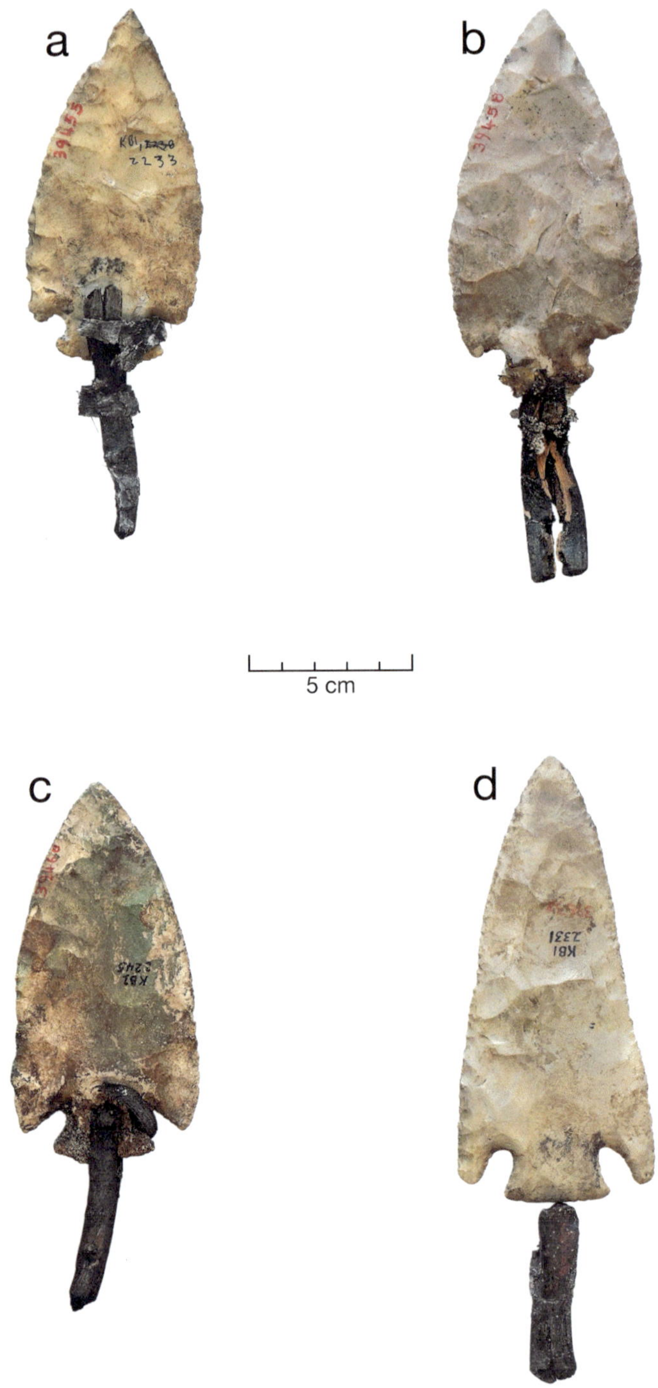

Figure 13.5, a-d. Examples of hafting from Killarney Bay. a. Burial 8 (KB1-2233); b. Burial 8 (KB1-2236); c. Burial 8 (KB1-2245); d. Burial 10 (KB1-2331).

right arm, consists of sixteen white cedar, one white pine, and six indeterminate fragments. KB1-2303 produced thirty pieces of black ash. The unburned wood (KB1-2360) is a substantial branch fragment that appears to be modern and intrusive and therefore was not analyzed.

Discussion

Local environment

The Killarney Bay site, located on the north shore of Lake Huron, lies within the Great Lakes-St. Lawrence Forest Region. This ecological zone is a mix of conifer and broadleaf forest, acting as a transition between northern boreal and southern deciduous forests. Modern vegetation studies and pollen cores produce a large-scale view of the regional environment, showing a forest dominated by pines, hemlock, and birch with other boreal (e.g., fir, spruce) and southern species (e.g., ash, maple, oak, beech) intermixed (Anderson 2002; Friedman et al. 2001; Hosie 1979; Liu 1990; Morton and Venn 1984; Webb 1974).

At a smaller scale, the immediate environment surrounding Killarney mounds in the Middle Woodland can be reconstructed through past lake level estimation and sediment/pollen cores, in combination with direct evidence provided by archaeological plant and animal materials. Julig and Long (Chapter 2, this volume) have shown that 2,000 years ago, the site was located on a narrow beach point—a possible portage—on a former near-shore island in northern Georgian Bay. While forests would have covered much of the rockier and higher elevated areas, there would have been considerable swamps in the low, wet margins of the embayment behind the beach.

The flora and faunal remains from the mound fill and nonburial features support this description. Despite the great diversity in tree species within the Great Lakes-St. Lawrence Forest Region, the majority of the charcoal (90 percent) derives from taxa endemic to swampy habitats, such as black ash, willow, white cedar, and silver maple (Table 13.4). Eastern white pine and red oak, characteristic of mixed forests on rocky outcrops, comprise the remaining sample (Morton and Venn 1984).

The faunal assemblage also shows a variety of species inhabiting forest and wetland environments (see Table

Figure 13.6, a-b. Basketry from Burial 10. a. A "net bag" containing cache blades, adhering to fur and leather (KB1-2326); b. Cordage mass with bead impressions from wrist area (KB1-2327).

13.1, Figure 13.1). Medium-sized cervids, most likely woodland caribou, are the most abundant taxa. Caribou favor coniferous forests. Snowshoe hare also is a forest species. Moose occupy wetlands and northern forests, and beavers are common to freshwater environments. The nonmammalian species are all aquatic, including duck, sturgeon, and turtles. Both snapping and Blanding's turtles prefer water with muddy bottoms and abundant vegetation, making them more common inhabitants of marshy shores and interior lakes (Cook 1984; Froom 1976).

This particular botanical and faunal assemblage suggests a significant wetland environment around the mounds. The wood charcoal composition indicates the presence of mixed forest swamp with wet soils that favor species like black ash, cedar, white birch, and willow. Where the ground was permanently flooded, swamps dominated by silver maple would have developed, with significant quantities of black ash (Morton and Venn 1984). These and other wetland environments along the Georgian Bay shore and interior waters provided rich habitat for moose, beaver, waterfowl, turtles, and fish. In more elevated, rocky areas near the site, an open forest of white pine, red oak, and red maple would have been typical. This supported important forest animals like woodland caribou, snowshoe hare, and various carnivores.

Seasonality

The Killarney Bay faunal and botanical remains from nonburial contexts can help to identify season(s) of site use. Unfortunately, few of the prehistoric animal bones retain traditional markers of seasonality, particularly ageable elements of young animals. The only informative specimen is an unfused moose pelvis fragment from the Bell collection, which, if prehistoric, indicates a summer or

Table 13.4. Killarney Bay wood charcoal frequency and primary taxon habitats.

Taxon	Common name	Count	Habitat	Comments*
Fraxinus nigra	Black ash	206	swamp	Common in swampy woodland and forest and on shores
Salix spp.	Willow	43	swamp	Common along water edges and swamps
Thuja occidentalis	White cedar	32	swamp	Abundant everywhere, especially swamps and wet forests
Quercus rubra	Red oak	22	forest	Common in deciduous/mixed forests, characteristic of quartzite/granite outcrops
Acer saccharinum	Soft maple	12	swamp	Dominant in swamp forest and swampy shores of inland lakes
Pinus strobus	White pine	10	forest	Common on elevated ground, dominant on Precambrian Shield outcrops
Total		325		

*Habitat information from Morton and Venn (1984)

early fall occupation. The presence of temporally restricted species provides more information. The majority of animal bone is from mammals that are present throughout the year, but the nonmammalian taxa are only available in warmer months. All turtles in the northern Georgian Bay area hibernate. The duck bone from Burial 8, if not a curated item, may also suggest warm-weather site visitation. Very few ducks overwinter in the Killarney area, and those that do inhabit ice-free areas of large lakes, which are difficult to access and of limited extent around Georgian Bay in deep winter (Bezener 2000). Overwintering species include long-tailed duck, common golden eye, and red-breasted and common mergansers, all of which are frequently found in archaeological assemblages in the Great Lakes region (Sadler and Savage 2003). Lake sturgeon are present in larger bodies of water year round, but they are typically deep-water bottom feeders (Page and Burr 1991), being more vulnerable to harpooning during their early summer spawning as they move to shallower waters.

The only seasonally restricted plant specimen is a charred beaked hazelnut shell, which is available in August and September (Yarnell 1964). However, cedar and birch bark are easiest to remove from live trees when sap is flowing during the summer, particularly in June (Densmore 1928; Geniusz 2009). Unfortunately, it is not known whether the burial bark sheets were collected around the time of interment or not.

This range of plant and animal remains suggests that the mounds were utilized during warmer months, perhaps from summer into the early fall. This period of occupation has also been suggested for the adjacent habitation area, where the artifact assemblage is consistent with hide processing (Julig et al., Chapter 8, this volume). Winter visitation cannot be ruled out, but there are no species in the assemblage that are available exclusively during winter months. If regional subsistence-settlement patterns apply to mortuary site use, small dispersed winter camps would be more likely found further inland (Finlayson 1977; Mason 1981; Spence et al. 1990; Wright 1995).

Site subsistence and mortuary feasting

Funerary rites typically include some form of food consumption events by the participants. The Killarney Bay organic remains from primary mound features provide valuable information about such feasting or other food-related rituals associated with Middle Woodland burial activities. Materials from mound fill and secondary, nonburial deposits provide a more general view of subsistence practices at the site. Although the present assemblage is limited by small sample size and nonsystematic collection strategies, it nonetheless provides a basic picture of plant and animal exploitation during occupation, including the targeted species and food preparation practices.

As at most northern Great Lakes sites with acidic soils, the animal bone is predominately small calcined fragments (Dawson 1974; Wright 1967, 1995). Taken as a whole, the Killarney Bay faunal remains are dominated by mammals, which comprise 88 percent of the assemblage (see Table 13.1, Figure 13.1). Medium-sized cervids like woodland caribou are the most common species present. Medium-sized mammals are also well represented, but unfortunately, few of these are identifiable to taxon. At least some of these are from smaller carnivores, but it is possible that beaver is represented as well, given the abundance of their fur in burials and their often high frequency at other sites in the region (Arthurs 1986; Dawson 1981; Finlayson 1977; Inksetter 2000; Wright 1967, 1995). Moose and snowshoe hare are present in small numbers. These species are all regularly found, albeit in varying quantities, at other northern Great Lakes sites (Arthurs 1986; Dawson 1974, 1976, 1981; Finlayson 1977; Inksetter 2000; Meyer 1983; Reid and Rajnovich 1991; Wright 1967, 1995).

Mammalian body part representation is similar across mound contexts. The vast majority of bones come from limbs (Figure 13.7). Elements from the head and extremities are strongly underrepresented, suggesting primary butchery took place elsewhere and only the meatiest portions were consumed on/near the mound. This pattern may in part reflect density-mediated attrition and recovery techniques. However, the near absence of robust dental elements supports offsite butchery practices.

Most of the nonmammalian bones are turtle, which are relatively common but low-frequency finds from Middle Woodland sites within the limits of their ecological ranges (Cook 1984; Mason 1981; Sadler and Savage 2003; Spence et al. 1990). Snapping and Blanding's turtles are among the most frequent turtle species utilized at Great Lakes sites (Adler 1968).

Turtles are used both for food and as a raw material for shell objects like containers and rattles. Engraved containers have been found at Michigan Hopewell sites to the south, including Norton Mounds and Schultz (Flanders 1965; Halsey 1966). However, these objects are rare or absent in more northern sites. Note that nearly all of these shell bowls are from Blanding's turtle and only bowls from this species are engraved. Additional bowls from common box turtles (*Terrapene carolina*) were found at Norton Mounds. Turtle shell bowls were exchanged regionally. At Killarney Bay, it is likely that the turtles were caught locally and eaten, given the presence of long bones and their association with hearths, but it cannot be ruled out that some of the turtle shell fragments may have originally derived from containers.

Birds and fish are rare in the mound deposits, especially when compared against the topsoil material. This may be related to site taphonomy. Bird bones are not uncommon at habitation sites where preservation is good, although they generally make up only a small percentage of the faunal assemblage. A notable exception is the McClusky site, where bird bones comprise 48 percent of the small assemblage—predominantly waterfowl (Dawson 1974). All of the Killarney Bay bird remains are waterfowl: two loon, thirteen duck, and five goose/swan species. Waterfowl are by far the most abundant birds recovered from Woodland occupations in the Great Lakes region. At least 20 species have been found at Ontario sites (Sadler and Savage 2003). In northern sites, common loons are the most frequently encountered taxon. Ground birds are also important food birds. Grouses are variably present at sites in their respective ranges, and to the south, wild turkey is prevalent (Sadler and Savage 2003).

As for fish at Killarney Bay, there is only a single lake sturgeon cranial bone. Fishing was central to a number of larger spring aggregation sites, such as Summer Island (Brose 1970a), Wyoming Rapids (Kenyon and Fox 1983), and Donaldson (Finlayson 1977; Wright and Anderson 1963). All these sites were located in areas with significant fish spawning runs, particularly for suckers, pickerel, and sturgeon. Indeed, the characteristic toggle-head harpoon of the northern Middle Woodland cultures may be specifically linked to taking sturgeon (Janzen 1968b). However, the very low number of fish remains, especially from larger species (even taking into account differential preservation and recovery bias), along with the lack of fishing gear, argues against Killarney Bay being a specialized, early-season, fish-procurement site.

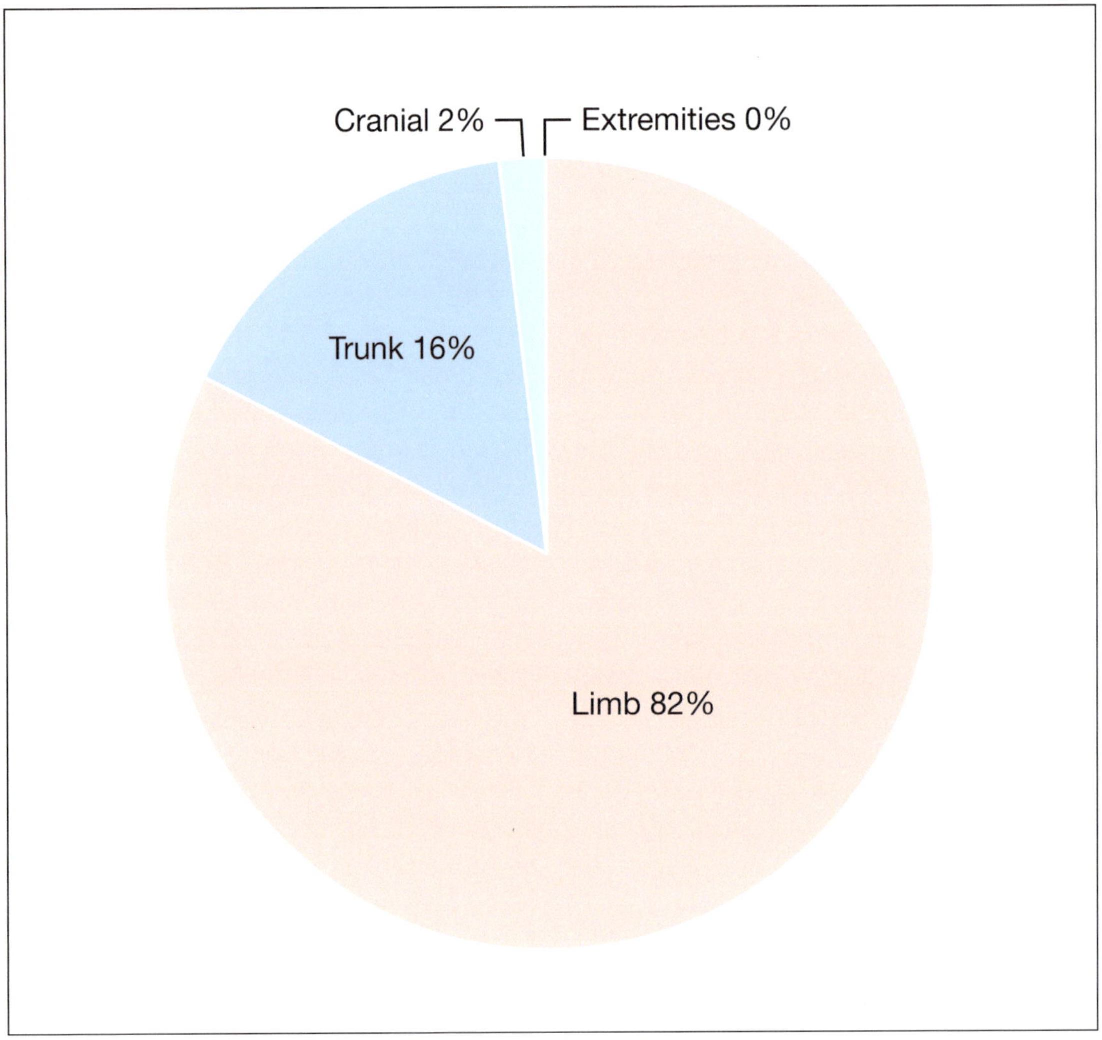

Figure 13.7. Mammal bone body part representation (prehistoric, nonburial).

Overall, the Killarney Bay fauna suggests that a generalized hunting-fishing-collecting system was employed. Inhabitants exploited a range of species available in mixed forest, wetland, and Great Lakes ecozones, but focused on medium to large mammals, particularly cervids. The system resembles that of a number of other Great Lakes Woodland sites with mixed but mammal-dominated procurement strategies, such as Heron Bay (Wright 1967), McCluskey (Dawson 1974), Inverhuron-Lucas (Finlayson 1977), Burley (Jury and Jury 1952), and Vandenbygaard (Hamalainen 1975). These sites have been interpreted as summer or fall occupations, based on the relative abundance of larger game and/or range of plant species. This lends support to the other faunal and botanical evidence for summer to early fall site use at Killarney Bay.

Consumption

There may be differences in meat consumption between mortuary and habitation areas at Killarney Bay. Unfortunately, there is some ambiguity as to chronological and contextual placement of some mound features and deposits (Julig and Long, Chapter 6, this volume). The fauna from mound fill may largely originate from general site occupation debris that was incorporated during mound construction, a portion of which appears to be contemporary with the later burials. It appears that the adjacent early Middle Woodland habitation area was used as part of a seasonal round that was focused on craft production, particularly for banded slate gorget production and possibly hide working as well (Julig et al., Chapter 8, this volume). Material from hearths and other thermal features within the mound itself, often situated above graves, is more likely to be directly linked to mortuary activities. Some of these features may be related to sweat lodges, crematory pits, or other ritual fires, as seen at sites like Ault Park (Wright 1995), Indian River (Ritchie 1953b), or Cameron's Point (Spence and Harper 1968), but at least a portion of these—particularly those with abundant faunal remains—seem to have been used primarily for ritual food preparation and/or burnt animal offerings.

Hearths within the mound itself produced the majority of animal bone from the site and contain a more restricted range of species than in other contexts. Nearly all hearth remains are mammalian (98 percent): mostly cervids and indeterminate medium-sized mammals. In the fill and pits, despite the smaller sample size, there is a wider range of taxa present. Nonmammalian species are more abundant, and medium-sized mammals are underrepresented. It is possible that the large amount of turtle bone in a pit above Burial 2 is part of a ritual deposit.

The reason for differences in species composition between contexts is unclear, particularly since the origin for the mound fill debris is not secure. If the fauna from the mound fill and associated hearths does represent funerary/ritual debris, it suggests that a narrow selection of animals was used in mortuary events (excluding grave goods), and this selection focused primarily on mammals. The near-exclusive recovery of mammals in mound hearths may in part reflect seasonal resource use, as described above. But it may also be related to mortuary or other community feasting activities, in which large-bodied animals and high-quality meat would be favored. Seeman (1979a) has found this pattern to characterize Middle Woodland mortuary sites to the south.

Little can be said about plant consumption, given the lack of systematic collection strategies and flotation. A single beaked hazelnut shell fragment, recovered from general mound fill, is the only remnant. It is probable that a range of species was exploited, including other nuts, seeds, and berries, as recovered from Great Lakes Middle Woodland sites like Donaldson (Finlayson 1977), Thede (Finlayson 1977), Schultz (Yarnell 1964), Dawson Creek (Jackson 1983), and Couture (Spence and Fox 1986). These sites are located further southeast in regions with more deciduous nut-bearing trees, and the plant remains include black walnut, hickory, beechnut, butternut, acorn, raspberry, elderberry, fire cherry, and dogwood.

It is not known whether wild rice (*Zizania palustris*) was utilized at Killarney Bay. The lack of wild rice pollen in the core samples (Julig and Long, Chapter 2, this volume) and extant macrobotanical collection argues against its harvesting at this site. However, the environmental reconstruction indicates the presence of potentially suitable habitats, and researchers have previously suggested that some of the stone-lined pits and fire-cracked rock debris may be related to rice parching (Julig et al., Chapter 8, this volume). Further, the relatively high caries rate compared to typical hunter-gatherers suggests significant carbohydrate consumption (Nicodemus, Chapter 9, this volume).

The charcoal remains demonstrate that locally abundant swampland trees were the primary fuel source (see Table 13.4). This wood was probably collected from nearby stands. There was a preferential selection for hardwoods, which burn longer and hotter than softwoods. Black ash is the most frequent fuel wood used, which may be related to its relatively light density and quick-drying nature (Arno 2001b). Anecdotally, the phrase "ash wood wet or ash wood dry, a king will warm his slippers by" refers to the ability of this wood to burn while still green. Contemporary Anishinaabe black ash basket making practice can result in leftover wood and bark, which may be utilized for secondary purposes such as fuel (Bolen 2020). Similar past industries may correlate with the prevalence of black ash charcoal. Also of note is the near-exclusive presence of white pine charcoal with the Burial 9 cremation, which is probably remains from the funeral pyre. This species was also used for the cremations at Serpent Mounds (Johnston 1968b).

Grave goods

The organic grave goods are perhaps the most important portion of the botanical and faunal assemblage, as they provide insight into how these rarely recovered items were used in Middle Woodland funerary programs (see Tables 13.1–13.3). The zooarchaeological grave goods include various leather objects (garments, sheets, bags, lashing, and bead thongs), beaver furs, deer hides, a beaver incisor, and possibly a duck tibiotarsus. Beaver pelts are present in most of the burials. Some of these appear to have been sewn into bags containing copper artifacts, as in Burials 7 and 8, and sometimes were adorned with shell beads. Beaver fur also may have been used for clothing—for example, as fur trim for the possible Burial 2 garment. Unfortunately, the other pelts are too fragmentary to reconstruct their original form.

Leather was used in many of the same ways as were the beaver pelts. Leather artifact bags were recovered from Burial 10 and perhaps Burial 2. The Burial 10 copper celt bag is embellished with incisions/pointelle decorations and tassels. Some of the sheet leather fragments may have been burial wrappings and others garment remnants. This is particularly noted for Burials 2 and 10 (both young adult females), which are associated with possible cordage ties and/or tassel/fringe decoration, or, alternatively, net bags. In other cases, the hides were laid over or under the body, as in Burial 6, where a leather sheet covered the basket containing the remains. A hairy winter deer hide was placed in Burial 10, and Burial 8 may have rested on hairy deerskin as well. Rawhide, along with bast cordage, was used for copper and shell bead strands as well as bag/garment ties. Sinew and/or leather were used as haft lashing.

The large rodent (probable beaver) incisor from Burial 8 currently represents the only bone tool in the Killarney collection. Rodent incisors are common at Middle Woodland sites throughout the region, both in mortuary and domestic contexts. Beaver incisor engravers, either singly (within mandibles/maxillae) or as antler-hafted tools, have been recovered from numerous Saugeen, Point Peninsula, Laurel, and Michigan Hopewell burials (Griffin et al. 1970; Mason 1981; Spence et al. 1990; Wright 1967; Wright and Anderson 1963). While far less common, porcupine incisors have been recovered from Saugeen graves (Spence et al. 1990). The Killarney Bay incisor was likely a loose tooth, as there is no trace of bone, antler, or any hafting material associated with it. Given its poor state of preservation, it is unclear whether it was ground or shows use wear. Notably, there is no evidence of other worked mammal bone, antler, or tooth objects in the Killarney assemblage, despite their frequency and variety at other Middle Woodland sites, particularly in burials to the south (Spence et al. 1990). It is possible, however, that other animal bone artifacts were deposited in these graves away from copper and therefore not preserved.

As mentioned previously, the burned turtle shell from the pit above Burial 2 may also have had ritual significance. The duck tibiotarsus, also from Burial 8, is more ambiguous in its context. Bird bones are not uncommon grave goods in this period. Some of these are tools, such as turkey bone awls, which are frequently found at sites within the range of this species' distribution (Flanders and Cleland 1964; Sadler and Savage 2003). However, many bird bones appear to be ceremonial items. These tend to be cranial elements, wings, or talons from ritually important species—especially birds of prey, but also loons at more northern sites (Flanders and Cleland 1964; Griffin et al. 1970; Johnston 1968b; Sadler and Savage 2003; Spence et al. 1990). Given its taxon and element, it is possible that the duck bone at Killarney Bay is food debris incidentally preserved in the burial rather than a more symbolic item.

The archaeobotanical grave goods include sheet bark, basketry, cordage, and biface hafting. These objects derive from a limited number of species (white cedar, hemlock, white ash, beech, white birch), indicating that specific raw materials were being chosen for craft manufacture and/or use in burial treatment, at least in part reflecting the physical properties of these taxa. This is underscored by the near absence of these particular species in the charcoal assemblage, suggesting that they may not have been abundant immediately around the site (although present in the greater Killarney area) and/or were not viewed as ideal fuel woods, perhaps because of their utility in craft making.

Sheet bark without significant cultural modification was used as a burial covering in the majority of interments, often in conjunction with leather or pelts. White birch bark was used most frequently, placed over Burials 3, 5, and 6. Burial 6 also included hemlock, while white cedar was used in Burial 2. All of these species have bark that is easily removed in large pieces and, at least for birch and cedar, was commonly used in domestic craft production both archaeologically and historically. Although the barks of these trees have physical properties amenable for working, this does not exclude the species from having symbolic importance as well, as documented ethnographically among Anishinaabe groups (Densmore 1928; Geniusz 2009).

Fiber perishables were present in four graves. In Burial 6, the burial basket was loosely woven and embellished with copper beads. It shows a combination of plaiting and S-twist twining with braided elements for the handle. In Burial 10, the basket was a container for cache blades; leather and fur bags were used in this manner in other burials. This basketry was also adhering to leather and fur, which may have been used as a lining, as found at the Boucher site (Heckenberger et al. 1996). Plaiting used opposing cedar bark and S-twist cordage elements. The Killarney Bay basketry/woven bags were made of white cedar bark fiber, either in strips or loosely spun, or with finer bast cordage. White cedar is frequently used for basketry and cordage among Great Lakes and northeastern groups (Densmore 1928; Geniusz 2009; Gordon 1990; Ritzenthaler and Ritzenthaler 1983) and was likely a common tree in the wet forests surrounding the site. It is not clear whether the baskets were woven specifically for mortuary use or taken from a domestic context. However, the bundle burial basket was possibly special purpose, given its copper bead decoration.

Burials 2 and 10, both young adult females, contained masses of 2-ply cordage (S-twist, Z-spun) that may have been parts of net bags or tassel or fringe embellishment for garments. If garment elements, these decorations were located around the neck and along the sleeve, respectively. All of the cordage was spun from relatively fine bast fibers, probably from herbaceous plants like Indian hemp/dogbane (Apocynaceae), nettle (Urticaceae), or milkweed (Asclepiadaceae), which were commonly used throughout eastern North America for fiber production (Densmore 1928; Gordon 1990; Heckenberger et al. 1996; Jakes et al. 1994; McMullen 1990; Ritzenthaler and Ritzenthaler 1983; Whitford 1941). Taxonomic identification of processed archaeological fibers is difficult without aid of more intensive analytical techniques, including scanning electron microscopy, infrared microspectroscopy, and energy dispersive X-ray microanalysis (Jakes et al. 1994). It should be noted that all of the cordage and twined baskets at Killarney Bay are S-twist.

While a comprehensive analysis of these fiber industries is beyond the scope of this discussion, further study would be beneficial. There has been little work on prehistoric textiles in the Upper Great Lakes region (Hamilton et al. 1996). However, basketry and cordage manufacturing techniques, from weave classes to cordage spin, have been used successfully in neighboring regions to better define burial practices, social groups, and patterns of interaction (Carr and Maslowski 1995; Church 1984; Heckenberger et al. 1996; Maslowski 1996; Petersen 1996b; Thompson and Jakes 2005).

Hafting was preserved with three bifaces in Burial 8 and one biface in Burial 10. Ash (including white ash) and beech were used for the shafts, with the former being crafted from splints rather than a full worked branch. Strips of an indeterminate ash species and a softwood (probably cedar) were used in the lashing, in combination with sinew/leather and sometimes adhesive. Despite the relatively elaborate lashing, the haft shafts are both very thin and short in comparison to the large bifaces, and it is unlikely that these would have been functional as utilitarian objects. One of the small shafts, KB1-2236, appears to have a hole drilled into its distal end (where the shaft has now split), perhaps for suspension. The materials and techniques used in these mortuary items may reflect general hafting methods, including wood selection. For example, white ash and beech woods are ideal shaft woods. Beech is strong and hard and has good shock-absorbing abilities (Kline 2001). White ash is strong and flexible, dries quickly, and holds its shape well after drying (Arno 2001a), making it suitable for the construction of items like snowshoe frames and sleds (Densmore 1928). Ash wood, especially black ash, is also commonly used for making splints, including splint baskets, as it splits readily along its annual rings (Gordon 1990; McMullen 1990; Ritzenthaler and Ritzenthaler 1983). This may account for its use both as splint shafts and as lashing strips. White ash has greater density and strength than black ash, making it preferable for shaft construction over locally abundant black ash (Hosie 1979).

Fur, hide, bark, textiles, and other organic remains, typically preserved by copper artifacts in graves, have been found occasionally throughout the Great Lakes region. The inclusion of such items dates back at least to the Middle or Late Archaic, as evidenced by the Feeheley site in Michigan, with bark-lined bundle burials with basketry and/or skin bags (Yarnell 1964). Another similarity between Killarney Bay and Feeheley is the dominance of ash in charcoal recovered from both sites, as well as the presence of oak and pine as fuel choices. Lake levels were higher at both sites during this time period, suggesting a swampier environment in which ash would have been readily available. A comparison of the botanical assemblages from both sites could help to support the cultural significance of these mortuary practices.

Textile and/or animal hide items also have been found at the Early/Middle Woodland sites of Arrowhead Drive (where grave goods were placed within a skin bag that appeared to be made from a scrotum from a large mammal, like moose) (McPherron 1967), Serpent Mounds (Johnston 1968b), Long Sault Island (Ritchie and Dragoo 1960),

Muskalonge Lake (Ritchie 1955), Boucher (Heckenberger et al. 1996), McKinstry Mound 2 (Webster 1973), and Morrison's Island II (Spence and Fox 1986). Donaldson Cemetery II also showed organic residues associated with several of the burials (Finlayson 1977). Birch bark containers used in mound construction have been found at the Laurel mortuary sites of MacGillivray (Dawson 1980) and Armstrong Mounds (Kenyon 1971).

Conclusion

The Killarney Bay mounds produced a wealth of botanical and faunal remains, including animal bone, hides, basketry, cordage, and hafting. Most of these materials are rarely preserved in this region. They allow a more nuanced look into Upper Great Lakes mortuary practices, as well as details about site use and craft production. Animal bone and charred botanicals from nonburial contexts suggest that a typical mixed forest of the Great Lakes-St. Lawrence region existed in the area, with swampy wetlands near the site. Fuel wood was collected from local stands with a preference for hardwoods, especially black ash. Despite the availability of aquatic resources, large mammals, particularly cervids, were the targeted species. Primary butchery of these animals appears to have taken place away from the mortuary area, with only the meatiest portions, primarily limbs, being consumed near the mound and during funerary activities. Seasonal indicators suggest that the mounds were visited during the summer and into early fall, although other seasons of site use cannot be excluded. A summer-early fall occupation may account for the focus on larger mammals, along with food preferences for mortuary events.

Copper grave goods preserved a wealth of organic artifacts. Many of the burials contained fragments of beaver pelt and/or leather garments, bags, and burial coverings, with evidence of decoration on personal articles. White cedar, hemlock, and white birch bark were also used to cover graves. Twined and/or plaited cedar bark basketry was found in two burials, used to hold cache blades and a burial bundle. All of the twining and cordage is S-twist. Four mortuary bifaces were hafted, showing relatively elaborate techniques used on apparently nonutilitarian objects. Only a single bone tool was present—a probable beaver incisor engraver. A duck leg bone and a burned turtle shell may have been ritual offerings.

Acknowledgements

The authors would like to thank David Brose, Patrick Julig (Laurentian University), and John O'Shea (University of Michigan) for inviting us to analyze the plant and animal remains from the Killarney Bay mounds. We would also like to thank the following people for allowing access to comparative materials: Stephen Hinshaw and Philip Myers (UMMZ Mammal Division), Gregory Schneider (UMMZ Herpetology Division), Janet Hinshaw (UMMZ Bird Division), as well as Karen O'Brien Dively, Amanda Logan, and Laura Motta (UMMAA Archaeobotany Range and UMMAA Great Lakes Range). Study of the Bell Collection material was facilitated by Jean-Luc Pilon, Janet Young, and Stacey Girling from the Canadian Museum of History. Participation in the CAA 2009 conference, where the preliminary data was presented, was made possible by travel grants from the University of Michigan Rackham Graduate School.

Appendix 13.1. Size classes for mammals in the greater Killarney Bay region.

Size class	Taxon	Common name	Weight (kg)[†]	Comments
Class V (very large): >100 kg	*Alces alces*	Moose	230-540	
	Cervus elaphus	Elk	180-500	extirpated (now reintroduced)
	Ursus americana	Black bear	40-270	
Class IV (large): 25-100 kg	*Rangifer tarandus caribou*	Woodland caribou	90-110	extirpated
	Odocoileus virginianus	Whitetail deer	30-115	less common in the past, only isolated populations
	Puma convolor	Cougar	30-90	extirpated
	Canis lupus	Gray wolf	25-80	
Class III (medium): 5-25 kg	*Castor canadensis*	Beaver	16-30	
	Canis latrans	Coyote	10-22	expanded greatly since lowered wolf populations in modern times
	Lynx canadensis	Lynx	7-18	
	Gulo gulo	Wolverine	7-16	unclear past distribution in ON, may not be present in Georgian Bay
	Lynx rufus	Bobcat	7-13	
	Procyon lotor	Raccoon	5-14	
	Lontra canadensis	River otter	5-11	
	Erethizon dorsatum	Porcupine	3.5-18	
	Vulpes fulva	Red fox	3.5-6.8	
Class II (small): 1-5 kg	*Martes pennanti*	Fisher	2-5.5	
	Mephitis mephitis	Striped skunk	1.9-4.2	
	Marmota monax	Woodchuck	1.8-5.4	
	Lepus americanus	Snowshoe hare	1-1.5	
	Ondatra zibethica	Muskrat	0.8-1.6	
	Mustela vison	Mink	0.6-1.4	
	Martes americana	Pine marten	0.5-1.2	
Class I (very small): <1 kg	*Sciurus carolinensis*	Eastern gray squirrel	0.4-0.7	
	Tamiascurus hudsonicus	Red squirrel	0.1-0.3	
	Mustela frenata	Long-tailed weasel	0.09-0.4	
	Glaucomys sabrinus	Northen flying squirrel	0.08-0.2	
	Mustela ermina	Short-tailed weasel	0.05-0.1	
	Mustela nivalis	Least weasel	0.03-0.08	

*Excludes insectivores, bats and rodents <.1 kg.

[†] Species weights and distribution from Eder (2002)

Appendix 13.2 (page 1). Killarney Bay animal bone inventory.

KB1 #	Tr	Sec	Feature	Layer	Other context	Taxon	Element	Portion	Side	N	Age	Alteration	Notes
1068	3E	D4		topsoil	"shoulder of mound"	*cf. Odocoileus virginianus*	femur	proximal epiphysis	R	1	U		
1060	3F	D5		topsoil		*cf. Odocoileus virginianus*	tibia	distal shaft	R	1	U		
756				topsoil		*Odocoileus virginianus*	femur	proximal shaft	L	1	U		2 pieces
765				topsoil		*Odocoileus virginianus*	mandible	condyle	R	1		weathered, chopped	modern butchery marks
857				topsoil		*cf. Odocoileus virginianus*	tibia	distal epiphysis and shaft	L	1	Fsg		large, robust individual, probably male
870				topsoil		*Rangifer/Odocoileus*	lumbar vertebra	articular facet and centrum fragment		1	U	calcined	2 pieces
878				topsoil		*Rangifer/Odocoileus*	cranium	occipital condyle fragment		1		calcined	
642	4C	H9		topsoil		*Sus scrofa domesticus*	MT IV	proximal epiphysis and shaft	R	1	U		
765				topsoil		*Lepus americanus*	femur	proximal epiphysis and shaft	R	1	F		
791				topsoil		Mammalia Class V	lumbar vertebra	centrum fragment		1	U	calcined	cf. L5 vertebra, probably large ungulate (elk/moose/cattle/horse)
604	4C	J1		topsoil	depth .5', map 48	Mammalia Class IV	longbone	shaft fragment		1			
605	4C	J1		topsoil		Mammalia Class IV	longbone	shaft fragment		1			NOT worked as suggested in notes
765				topsoil		Mammalia Class IV	NID	fragment		1			
847				topsoil		Mammalia Class IV	longbone	shaft fragment		1			
765				topsoil		Mammalia Class III	longbone	shaft fragment		1			
803				topsoil		Mammalia Class III	rib	fragment		1			medium carnviore?
765				topsoil		*Branta canadensis*	humerus	proximal shaft	R	1			
847				topsoil		*cf. Anser anser domesticus*	humerus	proximal shaft	R	1			
765				topsoil		Anatinae	humerus	proximal half	L	1			
765				topsoil		*Esox spp.*	vertebra	centrum		1			*Esox lucius* or *E. masquinongy*
765				topsoil		Catostomidae	vertebra	centrum		1			*Catostomus/Moxotoma spp.*
246	4D	D8		subsoil		Mammalia Class IV	longbone	shaft fragment		3		calcined	1 bone in 6 pieces
1268	3E	F1		subsoil	2.3' b.s.	Mammalia Class IV	longbone	shaft fragment		1		calcined	
2204	3E	H1		subsoil	under burial 7	Mammalia Class IV	longbone	shaft fragment		1		calcined	
1371	3D	G4		subsoil		Mammalia Class IV	longbone	shaft fragment		1		calcined	
1371	3D	G4		subsoil		Mammalia Class IV	rib	fragment		1		calcined	
341	3D	E2		subsoil		Mammalia Class III	longbone	shaft fragment		1		calcined	medium carnviore?
341	3D	E2		subsoil		Mammalia Class III	NID	fragment		1		calcined	
246	4D	D8		subsoil		Mammalia	NID	fragment		2		calcined	
1268	3E	F1		subsoil	2.3' b.s.	Mammalia	NID	fragment		2		calcined	
1268	3E	F1		subsoil	2.3' b.s.	*cf. Chelydra serpintina*	longbone	shaft fragment		1		calcined	
1194	3E	E2		subsoil	sandy subsoil under burial 2	*Emydoidea blandingi*	carapace	margin 7-9		1		calcined	
1194	3E	E2		subsoil	sandy subsoil under burial 2	Testudines	shell	fragment		1		calcined	
1268	3E	F1		subsoil	2.3' b.s.	*Acipenser fulvescens*	dermal plate	fragment		1		calcined	
233	4D	C9	"streamer"	subsoil	"streamer"/burned area from C10 hearth	*cf. Rangifer/Odocoileus*	longbone	shaft fragment		3		calcined	class IV mammal
250	4D	D8-9	"streamer"	subsoil		Mammalia Class III	rib	fragment		1		calcined	
250	4D	D8-9	"streamer"	subsoil		Mammalia	longbone	shaft fragment		1		calcined	
1466	4D	G9	hearth			*Rangifer/Odocoileus*	tooth	enamel fragment		1		calcined	premolar/molar fragment
1466	4D	G9	hearth			*Rangifer/Odocoileus*	vertebra	articular facet		2		calcined	
1466	4D	G9	hearth			*Rangifer/Odocoileus*	vertebra	neural arch fragment		1		calcined	
1466	4D	G9	hearth			*Rangifer/Odocoileus*	femur	distal epiphysis fragment		3		calcined	may be same bone
1466	4D	G9	hearth			*cf. Rangifer/Odocoileus*	longbone	shaft fragment		11		calcined	class IV mammal

Appendix 13.2 (page 2). Killarney Bay animal bone inventory.

KB1 #	Tr	Sec	Feature	Layer	Other context	Taxon	Element	Portion	Side	N	Age	Alteration	Notes
1466	4D	G9	hearth			Mammalia Class III	longbone	shaft fragment		11		calcined	
1466	4D	G9	hearth			Mammalia Class III	longbone	epiphysis fragment		3		calcined	
1466	4D	G9	hearth			*cf. Lepus americanus*	lumbar vertebra	neural arch fragment		1		calcined	class II mammal, hare sized
1466	4D	G9	hearth			Mammalia	NID	fragment		72		calcined	
1466	4D	G9	hearth			Testudines	plastron	fragment		1		calcined	
1466	4D	G9	hearth			Testudines	carapace	fragment		1		calcined	
160	4D	B9	pit			Large Mammal	longbone	epiphysis fragment		1		calcined	
1154	3E	E2	pit	topsoil	"pit over Burial 2", SW corner of section	Testudines	carapace	fragment		8		calcined	
1154	3E	E2	pit	topsoil	"pit over Burial 2", SW corner of section	Testudines	carapace	margin fragment		2		calcined	
2041			Burial 3		disturbed, with cranium, axial skeleton, elv. 26'	Testudines	plastron	fragment		1		calcined	
2222			Burial 8			*cf. Castor canadensis*	incisor	fragment		1			highly fragmented and degraded
2222			Burial 8			Mammalia Class IV	longbone	shaft fragment		1		calcined	in 7 pieces (highly fragmented), may be human femur, possibly disturbed from Burial 9
2222			Burial 8			Anatidae	tibiotarsus	shaft fragment	L	1			
2306			Burial 9		with human cremations	Mammalia Class IV	NID	fragment		1		calcined	unusual bone fragment, may or may not be human
					Bell collection, CMCC	*cf. Alces alces*	pelvis	pubis	L	1	U	calcined	class 5 mammal, probably moose
					Bell collection, CMCC	*cf. Alces alces*	rib	body		1		calcined, weathered	class 5 mammal, probably moose
					Bell collection, CMCC	*Rangifer tarandus*	femur	distal epophysis	L	1	U	calcnined	
					Bell collection, CMCC	*Lepus americanus*	scapula	glenoid/body fragment	L	1	F	calcined	
					Bell collection, CMCC	*Anas platyrhynchos*	humerus	near complete	R	1			may be modern? possibly burned?
					Bell collection, CMCC	Anatidae	tibiotarsus	shaft fragment		1			may be modern?

Note: Age indicated by epiphyseal fusion statuses. U = unfused, F = fully fused, Fsg = in the process of fusing

Appendix 13.3. Killarney Bay animal hide inventory.

Burial	KB1 #	UMMA #	Object	Body placement	Associated artifacts	Comments
2	1171	30286	Leather thong	L wrist	copper bead bracelet	
2	1176	30287	Leather thong	(NW corner burial)	copper beads	
2	1178	30292	Leather thong	under skull	copper necklace	
2	1178	30292	Leather sheet	under skull	copper necklace	adhering to bead strands
2	1182	30287	Leather thong	L neck, chest	copper necklace	
2	1183	30293	Beaver pelt?	neck, chest	cordage, basketry, [human rib], {copper beads 1176, 1178, 1182, awl 1188}	possible beaver pelt with "leather covering" over body, adhering to basketry, heavily encrusted with consolidant
2	1183	30293	Leather sheet	neck, chest	cordage, basketry, [human rib], {copper beads 1176, 1178, 1182, awl 1188}	"leather covering" under copper/shell bead necklaces, laying over body (and awl 1188)
2	1187	30307	Leather sheet	chest	{awl 1188}	leather wrapping end of awl 1188
3	2041	38479	Leather sheet?	neck, chest	human remains, {copper beads 2038, 2040, sheet copper 2031}	disturbed
3	2042	38480	Leather sheet?	neck, chest	human remains, {copper beads 2038, 2040, sheet copper 2031}	disturbed
3	2038, 2040	38480	Leather thong	neck, chest	copper beads 2038, 2040	disturbed
4	2118	38515	Beaver pelt	neck, chest	copper bead necklace with leather thong, leather, [ochre]	
4	2118	38515	Leather thong	neck, chest	copper bead necklace with leather thong, leather, [ochre, beaver pelt]	
4	2118	38515	Leather sheet	neck, chest	copper bead necklace with leather thong, leather, [ochre, beaver pelt]	
5	2075/ 2127	38514	Leather sheet	above burial	(3/6) copper beads?	found above burial, may not be associated?
5	2124	38495	Beaver pelt	skull	[ochre]	cataloged as "leather"
6	2143	38496	Leather sheet	SE of bundle	{copper beads 2136, 2138?}	
6	2144/5	38511	Leather thong	encircling bundle	copper beads with leather thong	with KB1 2136-2138 beads sewn around edge of basketry
6	2144/5	38511	Leather sheet	encircling bundle	copper beads with leather thong	with KB1 2136-2138 beads sewn around edge of basketry, part of 2146 adhering to beads
6	2146	38497	Leather sheet	encircling bundle	{copper beads 2136-2138, 2144-2145}	leather sheet overlying burial with copper bead impressions
6	2153	38503	Leather sheet	S edge bundle	basketry	fragment adhering to basketry
7	2199	38489	Beaver pelt	skull, neck	human remains, {celt 2200, chisel 2201}	
7	2203	38498	Beaver pelt	skull, neck, hand?	{celt 2200}	2 pieces with celt impresstion, catalogued as "leather bag"
7	2209	38506	Beaver pelt	shoulder?	cordage	
7	2210	38499	Beaver pelt	"area x," R shoulder	{celt 2200, chisel 2201}	"5 pieces fur and matting"
7	2211	38491	Beaver pelt	"area x," R scapula	human remains, {celt 2200, chisel 2201}	part of 2210 pelt
8	2222	39505	Beaver pelt	neck? L chest, arm	{awl 2229, carbon samples 2220, 2221}	"probably deer"
8	2231	39506	Leather sheet	neck? L chest, arm	{awl 2229}	"1 oval piece of rawride or leather" "south point of spindle"
8	2232	39501	Beaver pelt	leg, chest?	celt	"embedded in hair," "in wrapping of deer skin," "upper end leg bone"
8	2233	38445	Leather/sinew	R shoulder	hafted biface	degraded lashing on haft
8	2236	39458	Leather/sinew	R shoulder	hafted biface	degraded lashing on haft
8	2242	39503	Leather thong	R shoulder	celt	leather knot
8	2244	39512	Beaver pelt	R femur	human remains	
8	2252	39507	Leather sheet	R femur		"1 piece leather, from bottom"
8	2253	39518	Beaver pelt	R scapula	human remains, {celts 2241, 2242}	
8	2255	39508	Beaver pelt	R shoulder	{celts 2241, 2242}	"1 box beaver hair associated with 2 copper celts"
8	2257	39520	Beaver pelt	lumbar vertebrae	human remains	
8	2258	39504	Beaver pelt	L shoulder?	celt	"embedded in hair," possible hide bag
8	2239, 2240	39496	Leather thong	R arm?	copper beads	
8	2281	39499	Leather thong	R shoulder	copper stained shell beads	
8	2281	39499	Beaver pelt	R shoulder	copper stained shell beads	
10	2326	39684	Beaver pelt?	torso	[basketry fragments embedded in fur, ochre], {awls 2351, celt 2352}	"1 piece fabric," "north end of 2 spindles, 1 celt," encrusted in heavy consolidant, not deer, probably beaver
10	2327	39685	Winter deer pelt?	R lower arm, hand	{copper bead bracelet 2358}	"1 piece fabric," "lay over copper beads," probably same as material adhering to 2358 copper beads
10	2331	39637	Leather/sinew	R shoulder	hafted biface	degraded lashing on haft
10	2351	39688	Leather sheet	torso	2 awls	
10	2352	39687	Leather sheet	torso	celt	"celt with remains of leather," leather is decorated (incised) and has tassles (leather strips from the sheet wrapped with dark, shiny material?), bag fragment
10	2358		Winter cervid pelt	R lower arm, hand	copper bead bracelet	coarse winter cervid hide with fur, fragments adhering to beads, likely caribou?
10	2364	39686	Leather sheet	torso	{awls 2351, celt 2352}	"fragments of leather garments or bags from various places"

[X]=not listed in catalog for lot, {X}=associated with artifact in different lot, "X"=from field/catalog notes

Appendix 13.4 (page 1). Killarney Bay archaeobotanical inventory.

Context	Location	KB1#	UMMA#	Object	Taxon	Common Name	N	Comments
subsoil	Tr. 4D Sec. C10	217		charcoal	*Fraxinus nigra*	Black ash	1	white residue on surface
subsoil?	Tr. 2	63	22527	charcoal	cf. *Quercus rubra*	Northern red oak	7	may be *Fraxinus nigra?*
subsoil?	Tr. 3D Sec. E1	331		nut	*Corylus cortuna*	Beaked hazelnut	1	charred
subsoil?	Tr. 3D	389		charcoal	*Quercus rubra*	Northern red oak	5	
subsoil?	Tr. 3D	389		charcoal	indeterminate		1	may be conifer bark
subsoil?	Tr. 4F	794		charcoal	*Salix* spp.	Willow	15	
subsoil?	Tr. 4F	794		charcoal	*Fraxinus nigra*	Black ash	3	
subsoil?	Tr. 4F	794		charcoal	indeterminate		5	
subsoil?	Tr. 4D	1419		charcoal	*Quercus rubra*	Northern red oak	10	
subsoil?	Tr. 4D	1419		charcoal	*Pinus strobus*	Eastern white pine	1	
old surface		759		charcoal	*Fraxinus nigra*	Black ash	7	
gravel		1059	30312	wood	indeterminate		27	small roots/twigs, likely modern/intrusive. cf. *Sassafras albidum*
pit	Tr. 3D	391		charcoal	*Salix* spp.	Willow	5	may be *Populus* spp.?
pit	gravel	1244	30231	charcoal	cf. *Thuja occidentalis*	Northern white cedar	16	
pit	gravel	1244	30231	charcoal	*Acer* cf. *saccharinum*	Silver maple	6	
pit	gravel	1244	30231	charcoal	*Salix* spp.	Willow	1	
pit	gravel	1244	30231	charcoal	indeterminate		10	
hearth	Tr. 4D subsoil	237		charcoal	*Salix* spp.	Willow	5	
hearth	Tr. 4D subsoil	237		charcoal	indeterminate		2	cf. *Fraxinus nigra?*
hearth	Tr. 4D subsoil	1465		charcoal	*Salix* spp.	Willow	10	
hearth	Tr. 4D subsoil	1465		charcoal	*Acer* spp.	Maple	6	
hearth	Tr. 4D subsoil	1465		charcoal	*Fraxinus nigra*	Black ash	5	
hearth	Tr. 4D subsoil	1465		charcoal	*Pinus strobus*	Eastern white pine	3	
hearth	Tr. 4D subsoil	1465		charcoal	indeterminate		8	one vitrified
hearth	Tr. 3F old surface	808		charcoal	*Fraxinus nigra*	Black ash	7	
hearth	Tr. 3F old surface	808		charcoal	*Salix* spp.	Willow	3	
hearth	Tr. 3F old surface	808		charcoal	indeterminate		3	
hearth	Tr. 4E water laid	1481		charcoal	*Fraxinus nigra*	Black ash	35	noted as "kiln"
Burial 2		1186	30313	bark	*Thuja occidentalis*	Northern white cedar	14	
Burial 2		1183	30293	cordage	indeterminate			~6 strands of 2-ply cordage, fine fibers, adhering to leather/fur, tassels/fringe (part of garment)?
Burial 3		2042	38480	bark	*Betula papyrifera*	White birch	3	
Burial 3		2041	38479	charcoal	indeterminate		1	vitrified branch
Burial 5		2125	38500	bark	*Betula papyrifera*	White birch	1	
Burial 5		2131	38507	charcoal	*Fraxinus nigra*	Black ash	42	
Burial 5		2131	38507	charcoal	*Salix* spp.	Willow	1	
Burial 5		2131	38507	charcoal	indeterminate		2	cf. *Fraxinus* spp.?
Burial 6		2197	38505	bark	*Tsuga canadensis*	Eastern hemlock	92	primary lot, well preserved

Appendix 13.4 (page 2). Killarney Bay archaeobotanical inventory.

Context	Location	KB1#	UMMA#	Object	Taxon	Common Name	N	Comments
Burial 6		2146	38497	bark	*Tsuga canadensis*	Eastern hemlock	8	mixed in with leather lot
Burial 6		2147	38501	bark	*Tsuga canadensis*	Eastern hemlock	1	mixed in with birch bark lot
Burial 6		2147	38501	bark	*Betula papyrifera*	White birch	72	primary lot
Burial 6		2146	38497	bark	*Betula papyrifera*	White birch	3	mixed in with leather lot
Burial 6		2196	38504	basketry	*Thuja occidentalis*	Northern white cedar		cedar bark fiber strips, fragments with two weaving styles: plaiting and twining, copper bead/leather residue
Burial 6		2153	38503	basketry	*Thuja occidentalis*	Northern white cedar		cedar bark fiber strips, braided fragments (handle/selvage) and twined fragments
Burial 6		2148	38502	basketry	*Thuja occidentalis*	Northern white cedar		small fragments of braided and plaited elements (see other lots)
Burial 8		2233	38455	hafting	*Fraxinus* spp.	Ash	1	splint shaft
Burial 8		2233	38455	hafting	cf. *Thuja occidentalis*	Northern white cedar	1	thin lashing strips of softwood, likely cedar
Burial 8		2236	39458	hafting	cf. *Fraxinus americana*	White ash	1	splint shaft
Burial 8		2245	39460	hafting	*Fagus grandifolia*	Beech	1	carved shaft
Burial 8		2245	39460	hafting	*Fraxinus americana*	Ash	1	thin splint lashing strips
Burial 8		2250	39517	charcoal	*Salix* spp.	Willow	3	one is vitrified
Burial 8		2250	39517	charcoal	indeterminate		1	may be *Fraxinus nigra?*
Burial 8		2254	39519	charcoal	*Fraxinus nigra*	Black ash	7	
Burial 8		2256	39509	charcoal	*Fraxinus nigra*	Black ash	68	
Burial 9		2307		charcoal	*Pinus strobus*	Eastern white pine	5	
Burial 10		2326	39684	basketry	*Thuja occidentalis*	Northern white cedar		unusual simple plaited weave with 2 different elements: cedar bark strips and loose S-twist cordage, adhering to fur with heavy preservative
Burial 10		2327	39670	cordage	indeterminate			mass of numerous parallel (not inter-woven) 2-ply cordage, tassels or fringe? embedded in leather
Burial 10		2322		pipe residue	indeterminate			
Burial 10		2325		pipe residue	indeterminate			
Burial 10		2331	39637	hafting	*Fraxinus* spp.	Ash	1	splint shaft
Burial 10		2360	39683	wood			1	not identified--modern branch
Burial 10		2303		charcoal	*Fraxinus nigra*	Black ash	30	burial 10?
Burial 10		2327	39670	charcoal	*Fraxinus nigra*	Black ash	1	2 pieces
Burial 10		2362	39681	charcoal	cf. *Thuja occidentalis*	Northern white cedar	16	
Burial 10		2362	39681	charcoal	*Pinus strobus*	Eastern white pine	1	3 pieces
Burial 10		2362	39681	charcoal	indeterminate		6	

Part IV

Conclusions

Chapter 14

The Killarney Bay Site in Context

John O'Shea

The previous chapters have described the history and results of multiple investigations at the Killarney Bay site. It is clear from this history that the site represented very different things to different investigators, ranging from an early New World occupation to an important funerary site with potential links to the Meadowood, Adena, and Hopewell complexes. It is also clear that the dazzling array of exotic materials interred with the dead was, and continues to be, a source of fascination for archaeologists. It is left to this brief final discussion to put the site, its finds, and its funerary rites back into their cultural and temporal context. To do this, I will draw on the results from the preceding chapters to address a series of fundamental questions:

1) when was the site occupied?
2) what was the nature of its cultural use?
3) what was the nature of the burial complex?
4) how did the site fit into the larger regional context of the Upper Great Lakes and beyond?

The question of when the site was occupied entails both a question of chronology, as in over what period of time, and also seasonality: during what season or seasons of the year were inhabitants there? For the question of chronology, the new ^{14}C dates, along with the new analyses of the material culture, allow us to provide a reasonably sure answer. From the calibrated and modeled radiocarbon dates, the site appears to have been used over a span of about 500 years, from about 335 BC to AD 210. While the site was not continuously occupied over this period, the episodes of use appear evenly spaced across the time span. During this time, people periodically reoccupied the site and created new burials. There is no obvious hiatus in site use nor burial construction, and there is nothing in the material evidence to suggest any abrupt change in the cultural tradition of the people using the location. Two caveats should be added to this statement. The first is that other interments were placed in the immediate vicinity and in the general locality, and that our estimate of interment frequency is limited to those burials recovered in the small area examined by Greenman. The second caveat is that the dated range of occupation and burial does not necessarily reflect the full span of time over which the site was used. For example, a scattering of Late Woodland sherds, representing visits to the site well into the twelfth and thirteenth century, are also present.

While the evidence for dating the site is reasonably clear, the data for determining the season or seasons of use is less so. The physical setting of the site would not be conducive to occupation during the winter months but would have been an appealing place for hunter-gather-fisher subsistence during the spring and autumn (Chapter 2). The relatively limited faunal evidence recovered from the site (Chapter 13) likewise is suggestive of a warmer weather occupation, perhaps from summer into the early autumn. The harvest of wild rice would also fall within this late summer–early autumn window. Wild rice, however, remains something of a wild card in the Killarney Bay subsistence system. It was an important harvested resource among the historic inhabitants of the Upper Great Lakes, and is argued to be a major component in the region's Middle Woodland diet, yet no physical evidence of wild rice was recovered from the site, nor was wild rice pollen identified in the core sample taken near the site (Chapter 2).

While the site locality was attractive for hunter-gatherer use, it is not associated with any extraordinarily rich or seasonally available resource that might serve as a magnet for occupation, as might be found at the site of an anadromous fish run. As such, the long duration of site occupation and cyclical reuse was likely due to factors relating to its social significance rather than to its local resource base.

One significant social use of the site was for the burial of the dead, although it remains unresolved whether the burial area was composed of intentionally constructed mounds or simply natural features that the ancient inhabitants made opportunistic use of. Given the presence of burials and the rough correspondence in time to the mound building associated with Adena/Hopewell, it is easy to imagine why it would be assumed that the mounds were intentionally constructed.

Julig and Long, in their review of the sedimentology of the site (Chapter 2), argue that the sediments are not consistent with naturally occurring aeolean deposits and note that the site is comprised mainly of beach sands. However, they also point out that this does not mean that the mounds were intentionally constructed, and they suggest the possibility that the mounds were an incidental result of human activity, including burial, on top of the beach ridge. Likewise, Brose (Chapter 7) in his stratigraphic assessment of the burials, notes layers of seemingly clean deposit overlying and separating groups of graves. Given its location proximate to the lakeshore, and the overall topography of the site, it seems quite possible that the observed ridges were created via a combination of windblown sand and the deposition of near shore lacustrine materials during periodic rises in lake level and storm surge events. Deposits of this kind are ubiquitous around the shore of modern Lake Huron and there is no reason to believe similar depositional processes were not occurring in the past.

The absence of any clear structure underlying the dune feature or enclosing the burials further supports the idea that the feature was not a planned construction. This is not to imply that it was not enhanced by use, nor does it mean that the ancient people did not recognize the location as a burial locality, but simply that it most probably was an enhanced natural feature rather than an intentionally planned and built mound.

A similar conclusion is reached when the layout of features in the burial area is considered. Most of the discussions have focused on the distribution of the burials; the ten documented graves and the additional ones that were unearthed in the Bell excavation and subsequent cellar construction (see Chapters 5, 6, and 7). Greenman's plan of the burials (Figure 14.1) suggests that the graves are clustered near the highest point of the mound or ridge. There is also the suggestion of some micro-grouping of the graves into clusters (Figure 14.2). Taking the nine mapped grave locations and clustering them simply by spatial separation produces three clusters: a western cluster (Burials 2, 4, and 5), a central cluster (Burials 3, 6, and 7), and an eastern cluster (Burials 8, 9, and 10). Each of these clusters has at least one ^{14}C date. These dates reinforce Brose's comment that the sequence (and location) of the burials is not a reliable guide for their internal chronology. As Figure 14.2 indicates, the eastern cluster produced a middling date, the central cluster produced the earliest date, and the western cluster produced a middling date and the latest date (this cluster also contained Burial 9, which Brose speculated might be the initial interment created at the site). For now it is sufficient to note that they are all located in a restricted

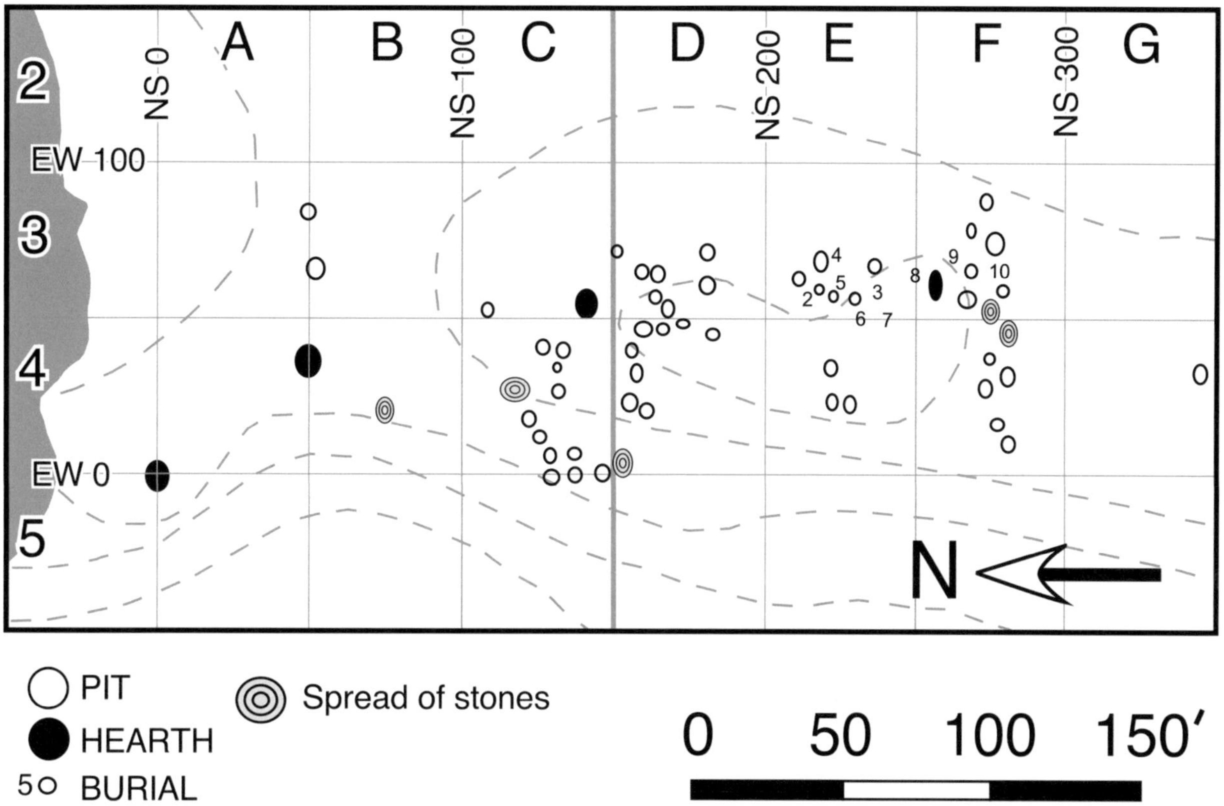

Figure 14.1. Greenman's plan of the burials at Killarney Bay.

portion of the landform, but with no obvious chronological trend to their location or spacing.

The same clustering is not observed, however, among the other mapped features. Pits are scattered across the higher ground in no particular relationship to the burials, although at right angles to the run of the ridge, while the stone clusters and hearths are distributed along the long axis of the landform, again with no particularly association with the burials. The hearth features, in particular, show an approximately even spacing along the ridge. These are not distributions that suggest a central focus on the burials or a potential mound. The clear and even spacing of the hearths and stone piles contrast with the normal expectation for a site that is continually reoccupied by hunter-gatherers, in which the deposits would tend to "smear" into a palimpsest of features and middens. The fact that the hearths, in particular, are evenly spaced might suggest a structured and marked character to the site, with or without a formally constructed mound. The problem with this interpretation is that there are only four observed hearths within the excavated area. If inhabitants had constructed these at even time intervals over the use span of the site, they would have built one roughly every century. A more plausible explanation is that they represent one or a small number of occupational events, which occurred over a relatively short span of time. If this interpretation is correct, it might imply that the occupation associated with the hearths had either no relationship to the burials or that they were only associated with a single interment event.

The discussion of the physical setting and use of the burial area leads naturally to questions about who was buried at the site and what the location represented within the ancient network of regional movement and settlement. Based on the osteological analyses from Chapter 9, the remains of at least 17 individuals were recorded from the various excavations, although this may not represent the total number of individual interred at the site or in the vicinity. Looking at the age and sex breakdown of the burial

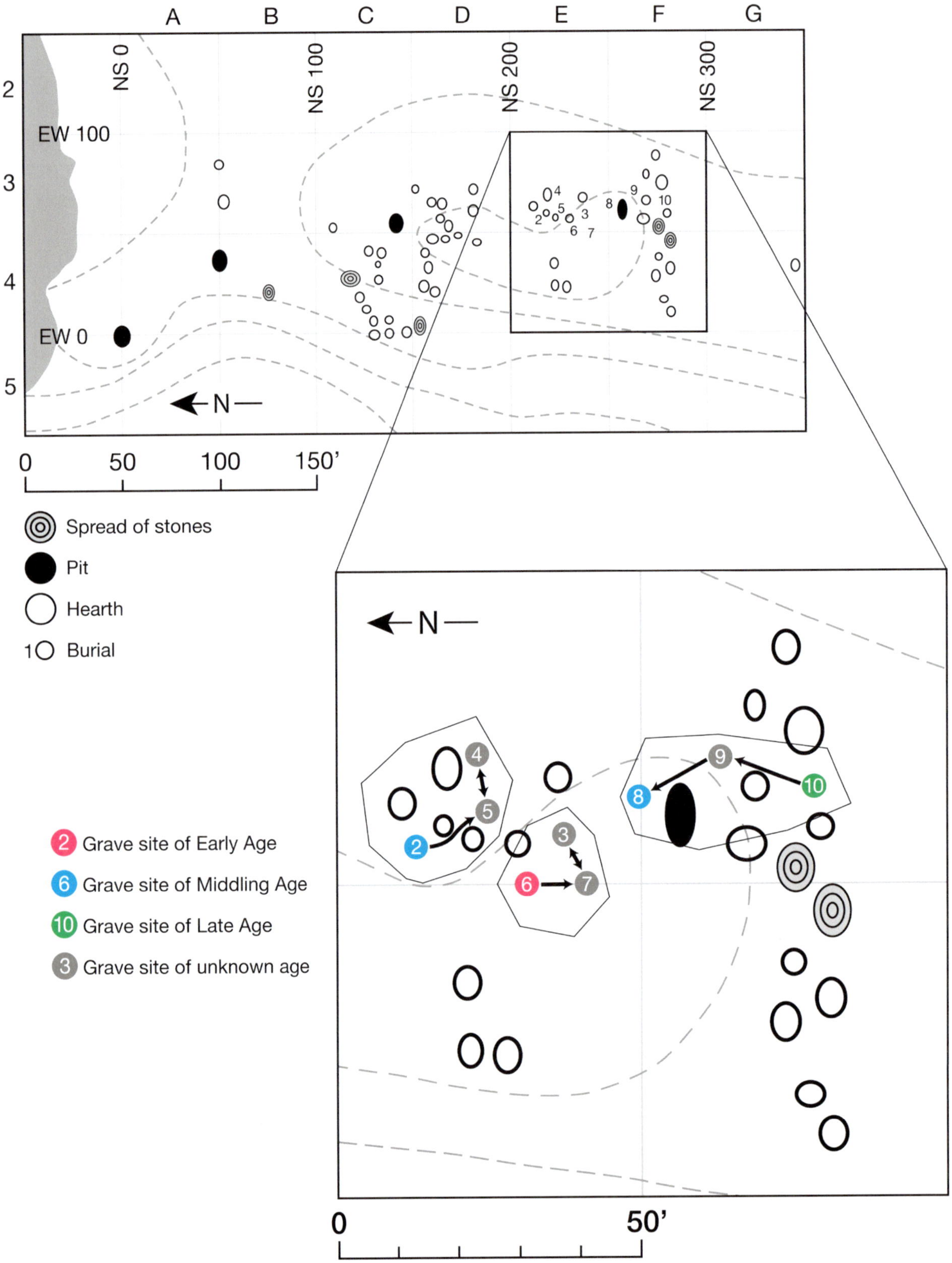

Figure 14.2. The nine mapped burials as three clusters: a western cluster (Burials 2, 4, and 5), a central cluster (Burials 3, 6, and 7), and an eastern cluster (Burials 8, 9, and 10).

population, it is readily apparent that it does not represent the burial site for the entire band that utilized the site, nor do the individuals present represent a "natural" death population. That is, this is not a representative sample of normal mortality. Most notably, compared to a natural death population, infants are substantially underrepresented, and children and adolescents/young adults are overrepresented (Acsádi and Nemeskéri 1970; Coale and Demeny 1966). As such, the individuals interred at the site represent a specifically selected subset of the dead that were brought to the site for interment.

The underrepresentation of infants is not surprising. Not only are the fragile bones of infants the least likely to preserve, infants often must reach a certain age of viability before they are treated as fully social persons. The proportionately high number of older children and adolescent/young adults *is* surprising, since these ages normally exhibit the lowest levels of mortality. In essence, these individuals are people who should not be dying, and equally, they are the individuals whose loss would have the greatest impact on the reproduction and continuity of the social group. As such, one possible reason why these individuals were accorded special funerary treatment is that they were the people that the society could least afford to lose. As such, their deaths represented moments of particular social dislocation for the community. Yet for the estimated 500-year span of site use there should still be more than the one death per generation represented at the site.

The sense that these individuals were special or unique is supported by the fact that some of the individuals (and even possibly all) had died elsewhere and were transported to the Killarney Bay site for burial. Of the adolescent/young adults from Greenman's excavation, three are young women. One is a cremation interred with an older adult male; both of these were transported to the site for burial. The other two are represented as a flexed and an extended inhumation. There is also a slightly older young adult male who appears to have died and been disarticulated elsewhere and was then transported to the site in a basket. Whether the mounds are intentional creations or a natural accretion resulting from site use and occupation, it does appear that the location itself held some particular significance that warranted the transport of these special individuals to the site for interment (Table 14.1).

In this regard, it must also be noted that for most, if not all, of the burials, the exotic goods placed with the dead were likely not their own personal possessions nor items they had required during their lifetimes. Rather, the grave accompaniments were acquired and placed with the dead by others as part of the funerary rite. These goods may have been placed by relatives, or they may have been collected among all those attending the burial at the site. As most of these accompaniments were exotic and not part of the routine material culture assemblage, this latter option would be consistent with the use of the site as a node where materials were collected and transferred in the long-distance exchange networks (see below).

Another unusual characteristic of the burial site is the amount of variation seen in the treatment of the dead. The minimum common treatment appears to be burial at the site, the covering of the remains in a wrapping of bark or fur, and the placement of stone bifaces and copper ornaments with the dead. Red ochre was common, but not universal—it appears in roughly half of the burials. The elaboration of these treatments includes variation in the number and variety of grave accompaniments, posture, orientation, and interment type (primary, secondary, cremation). These variable treatments might have reflected the specific life and death circumstances of the individuals interred, or they might be attributable to a range of other factors. One possibility is that the variations represent different groups conducting the individual burials; another possibility is that normative practices varied over time (as favored by Brose in Chapter 7); and a third is that the variations represent a relatively individualistic and personalized approach to burial that was not highly conventionalized within the society.

While any of these possibilities (or combination of possibilities) might account for the observed variation, the lack of a highly prescriptive approach to burial norms fits well with the other observations about the site and with contemporary sites in the region, where all of these burial types, along with the placement of secondary bundled burials in caves and crevasses, are commonly found. The fact that burials at Killarney Bay are in some sense "out of the ordinary" and that the remains were seemingly processed elsewhere and transported by the community for an undetermined amount of time prior to burial, lends additional strength to the possibility that treatments were highly individualized.

A well-established principle of funerary archaeology is that the existence of specialized and bounded disposal areas is associated with corporate groups asserting claim to

Table 14.1. Burials excavated by Greenman's team at the Killarney Bay site.

Burial number	Sex	Age	Treatment
1		Child/juvenile	Flexed inhumation?
2	Female	Young adult	Extended inhumation
3		5-6 years	Flexed inhumation
4		6 years	Flexed inhumation
5		Child	Disturbed
6	Male	20-30 years	Secondary burial in basket
7		2-4 years	Secondary burial
9a	Female?	14-18 years	Secondary cremation with old adult male
10	Female	16-22 years	Flexed inhumation

a scarce or valued resource (cf. Goldstein 1981; Saxe 1970). Does the Killarney Bay occurrence represent a bounded cemetery (disposal area) used exclusively for the interment of the dead? Here the answer is ambiguous. While there might be intentionally constructed or augmented mounds, many other activities occurred at or in the immediate vicinity of the burials. Greenman believed these must have represented ritual activities related to the dead (Chapter 7), but given the span of time over which the features appear to have accumulated and their general lack of association with the burials, this may not be the case. There are numerous instances among hunter-gatherer populations where substantial numbers of burials were placed within an actively accreting midden or living area (e.g. at Indian Knoll: Rothschild 1979; Webb 1974). At Killarney Bay, the area designated as relating to habitation is immediately adjacent to the burial area (Chapter 6), while clusters of rock and fire-cracked rock, and the series of evenly spaced hearths, are all suggestive of occupational activities overlapping on the area of the recovered burials. It does appear that the material debris in the burial area is somewhat different in kind from the assemblages recovered from the habitation area of the site, and as such may specifically related to the burial rites, but we do not, at present, have the chronological or seasonal resolution to assess this possibility.

In any event, it seems unlikely that the site represented a bounded location used exclusively for the disposal of the dead. If not a bounded cemetery, what might the site represent? One possibility is that the site, as a whole, represented a gathering place to which a band, or multiple bands, returned on some cyclical basis. Yet, given the absence of a densely available seasonal subsistence resource, the size and duration of the gathering would have been limited. The funerary aspect of the site would, like a bounded cemetery, serve the function of asserting rights or claims to the locality and may have figured in ceremonial activities that occurred when bands came together at the locality. A somewhat similar use of the dead at social aggregation sites is known from the Late Woodland period in northern Lower Michigan, where pairs of circular enclosure sites typically incorporated a small number of mound burials to mark the locality (cf. Howey and O'Shea 2006).

Killarney Bay is well suited to serve as a meeting place. It is located on the northern shore of Lake Huron, sheltered from the open waters of the lake by Manitoulin Island and the small embayment. The Killarney region represents the transition from the protected "Inner Passage" down from the Sault to the open wind and waves of Lake Huron. As such it is a location where any down-lake canoeist would stop to wait for clear weather, or where an up-lake bound canoe might pull in after battling Georgian Bay: it provides a natural meeting place. It also would have been easily accessible by water from the inland rivers that empty into the lake in this vicinity. On a broader scale, the site is located along the east-west corridor of the earlier Meadowood exchange system and at the northern end of the Adena/Hopewell systems to the south. Inhabitants of the site would have been particularly well situated to exploit and control the movement of Lake Superior copper into both of these networks. In addition to this, research in the habitation area of the site suggests occupants were engaged in the manufacture of slate gorgets, as well as the relatively intense processing of pelts and hides (Chapter 8).

This potential role in the larger Midwestern exchange networks may help to explain the array of exotic artifacts that served as grave accompaniments—particularly the numerous elaborate bifaces fashioned from southern cherts and marine shell beads. By contrast, the richness of copper artifacts may be more apparent to archaeologists than real to the inhabitants, as they would have represented a nearby good that was being exchanged outward into the broader Adena/Hopewell world. The Killarney Bay locality could have served as a kind of depot or concentration point where exotic materials like northern cherts, copper, and pelts were accumulated and prepared for trade eastward or southward. It is tempting to view these activities through the lens of the rendezvous of the fur trade era, but this would be inaccurate. These exchanges would have been less mercantile and would have been deeply embedded in the other ritual activities, including burial, which occurred during these brief gatherings. Nevertheless, the degree to which these local hunter-gatherers were integrated into continent-wide networks is remarkable.

Yet even as we contemplate the exchange of exotic goods and linkages over great distances, there is nothing in the record to suggest that the site was more than a temporary stop, briefly occupied, by small groups of hunter-fisher-gatherers. Killarney was a significant place and one to which, on exceptional occasions, people brought the remains of exceptional individuals to be interred. The dispersed bands may have come together here to participate in these rites and to assemble diverse exotic materials for exchange. And although the rituals and activities did not last long, they were faithfully repeated over hundreds of years.

Appendices

Appendix A
Analysis of Lipid Residues

Mary E. Malainey

Ten sherds from Middle Woodland vessels recovered from the Killarney Bay site were submitted for lipid residue analysis in 2009. Exterior surfaces were ground off to remove any contaminants, samples were crushed, and absorbed lipid residues were extracted with organic solvents. Ancient lipid residues were analyzed using gas chromatography (GC), high-temperature gas chromatography (HT-GC), and high-temperature gas chromatography with mass spectrometry (HT-GC/MS). Residues were identified on the basis of fatty acid decomposition patterns of experimental residues and lipid distribution patterns, and through the presence of biomarkers. In this chapter we outline general procedures for the identification of archaeological residues and present the analytical methodology and results of the analysis of Killarney Bay residues.

The identification of archaeological residues

Lipids are a broad category of compounds that are insoluble in water. Those of archaeological interest include fatty acids, triacylglycerols, sterols, waxes, and terpenes. Over the last five decades, different instrumental techniques have been used to obtain information about archaeological lipid residues. The most commonly employed involve component separation with gas chromatography: gas chromatography with a flame ionization detector (GC) and gas chromatography with mass spectrometry (GC/MS). Ancient residues can be characterized on the basis of relative fatty acid composition and the presence of biomarkers. Fatty acid composition provides a general characterization: the origin of a residue cannot be proven, but potential sources can be eliminated. Biomarkers can clarify the source of the residue as either animal or plant. In some cases, the residue contains specific biomarkers that provide solid evidence or unequivocal proof of its origin.

Identification of fatty acids

Fatty acids are the major constituents of fats and oils (lipids) and occur in nature as triglycerides, consisting of three fatty acids attached to a glycerol molecule by ester-linkages. The shorthand convention for designating fatty acids, Cx:yωz, contains three components. The "Cx" refers to a fatty acid with a carbon chain length of x number of atoms. The "y" represents the number of double bonds or points of unsaturation, and the "ωz" indicates the location of the most distal double bond on the carbon chain, i.e., closest to the methyl end. Thus, the fatty acid expressed as C18:1ω9 refers to a mono-unsaturated isomer with a chain length of 18 carbon atoms with a single double bond located nine carbons from the methyl end of the chain. Similarly, the shorthand designation, C16:0 refers to a saturated fatty acid with a chain length of 16 carbons.

Their insolubility in water and relative abundance compared to other classes of lipids, such as sterols and waxes, make fatty acids suitable for residue analysis. Since employed by Condamin et al. (1976), gas chromatography has been used extensively to analyze the fatty acid component of absorbed archaeological residues. The composition of uncooked plants and animals provides important baseline information, but it is not possible to directly compare modern uncooked plants and animals with highly degraded archaeological residues. Unsaturated fatty acids, which are found widely in fish and plants, decompose more readily than saturated fatty acids, sterols, or waxes. In the course of decomposition, simple addition reactions might occur at points of unsaturation (Solomons 1980) or peroxidation might lead to the formation of a variety of volatile and nonvolatile products that continue to degrade (Frankel 1991). Peroxidation occurs most readily in fatty acids with more than one point of unsaturation.

Attempts have been made to identify archaeological residues using criteria that discriminate different types of uncooked foods (Loy 1994; Marchbanks 1989; Skibo 1992). The major drawback of the distinguishing ratios proposed by Marchbanks (1989), Skibo (1992), and Loy (1994) is that they have never been empirically tested. The proposed ratios are based on criteria that discriminate food classes on the basis of their original fatty acid composition. The resistance of these criteria to the effects of decompositional changes has not been demonstrated. Rather, Skibo (1992) found his fatty acid ratio criteria could not be used to identify highly decomposed archaeological samples.

In order to identify a fatty acid ratio unaffected by degradation processes, Patrick et al. (1985) simulated the long-term decomposition of one sample and monitored the resulting changes. An experimental cooking residue of seal was prepared and degraded in order to identify a stable fatty acid ratio. Patrick et al. (1985) found that the ratio of two C18:1 isomers, oleic and vaccenic, did not change with decomposition. This fatty acid ratio was then used to identify an archaeological vessel residue as seal. While the initial fatty acid composition of uncooked foods must be known, Patrick et al. (1985) showed that the effects of thermal degradation and oxidative decomposition over long periods of time on the fatty acids must be understood in order to identify an archaeological cooking residue.

Development of the identification criteria

As the first stage in developing the identification criteria used herein, the fatty acid compositions of more than 130 uncooked native food plants and animals were determined using gas chromatography. These foods were exploited by those who inhabited Western Canada and parts of the Upper Midwest and Northern Plains states prior to European contact (Malainey 1997; Malainey et al. 1999a). When the fatty acid compositions of modern food plants and animals were subject to cluster and principal component analyses, the resultant groupings generally corresponded to divisions that exist in nature (Table A.1). Clear differences in the fatty acid composition of large mammal fat, large herbivore meat, fish, plant roots, greens, and berries/seeds/nuts were detected, but the fatty acid composition of meat from medium-sized mammals, such as beavers and muskrats, resembles berries/seeds/nuts.

Samples in cluster A, the large mammal and fish cluster, had elevated levels of C16:0 and C18:1 (Table A.1). Divisions within this cluster stemmed from the very

Table A.1. Summary of average fatty acid compositions of modern food groups generated by hierarchical cluster analysis.

Cluster		A						B					C		
Subcluster type	**I**	**II**	**III**	**IV**	**V**	**VI**	**VII**	**VIII**	**IX**	**X**	**XI**	**XII**	**XIII**	**XIV**	**XV**
	Mammal, fat and marrow	Large herbivore meat	Fish	Fish	Berries and nuts	Mixed	Seeds and berries	Roots	Seeds	Mixed	Greens	Berries	Roots	Greens	Roots
C16:0	19.9	19.39	16.07	14.1	3.75	12.06	7.48	19.98	7.52	10.33	18.71	3.47	22.68	24.19	18.71
C18:0	7.06	20.35	3.87	2.78	1.47	2.36	2.58	2.59	3.55	2.43	2.48	1.34	3.15	3.66	5.94
C18:1	56.77	35.79	18.28	31.96	51.14	35.29	29.12	6.55	10.02	15.62	5.03	14.95	12.12	4.05	3.34
C18:2	7.01	8.93	2.91	4.04	41.44	35.83	54.69	48.74	64.14	39.24	18.82	29.08	26.24	16.15	15.61
C18:3	0.68	2.61	4.39	3.83	1.05	3.66	1.51	7.24	5.49	19.77	35.08	39.75	9.64	17.88	3.42
VLCS	0.16	0.32	0.23	0.15	0.76	4.46	2.98	8.5	5.19	3.73	6.77	9.1	15.32	18.68	43.36
VLCU	0.77	4.29	39.92	24.11	0.25	2.7	1.0	2.23	0.99	2.65	1.13	0.95	2.06	0.72	1.1

VLCS = Very Long Chain (C20, C22, and C24) Saturated Fatty Acids
VLCU = Very Long Chain (C20, C22, and C24) Unsaturated Fatty Acids

Table A.2. Criteria for the identification of archaeological residues based on the decomposition patterns of experimental cooking residues prepared in pottery vessels.

Identification	Medium chain	C18:0	C18:1 isomers
Large herbivore	$\leq 15\%$	$\geq 27.5\%$	$\leq 15\%$
Large herbivore with plant or bone marrow	low	$\geq 25\%$	$15\% \leq X \leq 25\%$
Plant with large herbivore	$\geq 15\%$	$\geq 25\%$	no data
Beaver	low	low	$\geq 25\%$
Fish or corn	low	$\leq 25\%$	$15\% \leq X \leq 27.5\%$
Fish or corn with plant	$\geq 15\%$	$\leq 25\%$	$15\% \leq X \leq 27.5\%$
Plant (except corn)	$\geq 10\%$	$\leq 27.5\%$	$\leq 15\%$

high level of C18:1 isomers in fat, high levels of C18:0 in bison and deer meat, and high levels of very long-chain unsaturated fatty acids (VLCU) in fish. Differences in the fatty acid composition of plant roots, greens, and berries/seeds/nuts reflect the amounts of C18:2 and C18:3ω3 present. The berry, seed, nut, and small mammal meat samples appearing in cluster B have very high levels of C18:2, ranging from 35 percent to 64 percent (Table A.1). Samples in subclusters V, VI, and VII have levels of C18:1 isomers from 29 percent to 51 percent, as well. Plant roots, plant greens, and some berries appear in cluster C. All cluster C samples have moderately high levels of C18:2; levels of C16:0 are also elevated except for the berries in subcluster XII. Higher levels of C18:3ω3 and/or very long-chain saturated fatty acids (VLCS) are also common, except in the roots, which form subcluster XV.

Secondly, the effects of cooking and degradation over time on fatty acid compositions were examined. Originally, 19 modern residues of plants and animals from the Northern Plains, adjacent parkland, and southern boreal forest were prepared by cooking samples of meats, fish, and plants, alone or combined, in replica vessels over an open fire (Malainey 1997; Malainey et al. 1999b). After four days at room temperature, the vessels were broken and a set of sherds analysed to determine changes after short-term decomposition. A second set of sherds remained at room temperature for 80 days and was then placed in an oven at 75°C for a period of 30 days in order to simulate the processes of long-term decomposition. The relative percentages were calculated on the basis of the ten fatty acids (C12:0, C14:0, C15:0, C16:0, C16:1, C17:0, C18:0, C18:1ω9, C18:1ω11, and C18:2) that regularly appeared in precontact-period vessel residues from Western Canada. Observed changes in fatty acid composition of the experimental cooking residues enabled the development of a method for identifying the archaeological residues (Table A.2).

Differences in the levels of medium-chain fatty acids (C12:0, C14:0, and C15:0) and C18:0 and C18:1 isomers effectively distinguished degraded experimental cooking residues with respect to the foods used to prepare them (Malainey 1997; Malainey et al. 1999b). Higher levels of medium-chain fatty acids, combined with low levels of C18:0 and C18:1 isomers, were detected in the decomposed experimental residues of plants, such as roots, greens, and most berries. High levels of C18:0 indicated the presence of large herbivores. Moderate levels of C18:1 isomers, with low levels of C18:0, indicated the presence of either fish or foods similar in composition to corn. High levels of C18:1 isomers with low levels of C18:0 were found in residues of beaver or foods of similar fatty acid composition. The criteria for identifying six types of residues were established experimentally. The seventh type—plant with large herbivore—was inferred (Table A.2). These criteria were applied to residues extracted from more than 200 pottery cooking vessels from 18 Western Canadian sites (Malainey 1997; Malainey et al. 1999c, 2001b). The identifications were found to be consistent with the evidence from faunal and tool assemblages for each site.

Work has continued towards understanding the decomposition patterns of various foods and food combinations (Malainey et al. 2000a, b, c, 2001a; Quigg et al. 2001). The collection of modern foods has expanded to include plants from the Southern Plains and adjacent regions. Experimental residues of many of these plants, alone or in combination with deer meat, have been prepared by boiling foods in clay cylinders or using sandstone for either stone boiling (Quigg et al. 2000) or as a griddle. In order to accelerate the processes of oxidative degradation that naturally occur at a slow rate with the passage of time, the rock or clay tile containing the experimental residue was placed in an oven at 75°C. After either 30 or 68 days, residues were extracted and analysed using gas chromatography. The results of these decomposition studies enabled refinement of the identification criteria (Malainey 2007a).

Using lipid distribution and biomarkers to identify archaeological residues

Archaeological scientists working in the United Kingdom have had tremendous success using high-temperature gas chromatography (HT-GC) and gas chromatography with mass spectrometry (HT-GC/MS) to identify biomarkers. High-temperature gas chromatography is used to separate and assess a wide range of lipid components, including fatty acids, long-chain alcohols and hydrocarbons, sterols, waxes, terpenoids, and triacylglycerols (Evershed et al. 2001). The molecular structure of separated components is elucidated by mass spectrometry (Evershed 2000).

Triacylglycerols, diacylglycerols, and sterols can be used to distinguish animal-derived residues from plant-derived residues. Animal-derived residues contain cholesterol and significant levels of both triacylglycerols. Plant-derived residues are indicated by plant sterols such as β-sitosterol, stigmasterol, and campesterol, and only traces of triacylglycerols (Dudd and Evershed 1998; Evershed 1993; Evershed et al. 1997a). Barnard et al. (2007), however, have recently suggested that microorganisms living off residues can introduce β-sitosterol into residues resulting from the preparation of animal products. Waxes, which are long-chain fatty acids and long-chain alcohols that form protective coatings on skin, fur, feathers, leaves, and fruit, also resist decay. Evershed et al. (1991) found epicuticular leaf waxes from plants of the genus *Brassica* in vessel residues from a Late Saxon/Medieval settlement. Cooking experiments later confirmed the utility of nonacosane, nonacosan-15-one, and nonacosan-15-ol to indicate the preparation of leafy vegetables, such as turnip or cabbage (Charters et al. 1997). Reber et al. (2004) recently suggested *n*-dotriacontanol could serve as an effective biomarker for maize in vessel residues from sites located in midwestern and eastern North America. Beeswax can be identified by the presence and distribution of n-alkanes with carbon chains 23 to 33 atoms in length and palmitic acid wax esters with chains between 40 and 52 carbons in length (Evershed et al. 1997b; Heron et al. 1994).

Terpenoid compounds, or terpenes, are long-chain alkenes that occur in the tars and pitches of higher plants. The use of GC and GC/MS to detect the diterpenoid, dehydroabietic acid, from conifer products in archaeological residues extends over a span of almost 40 years (Heron and Pollard 1988; Shackley 1982). Lupeol, α- and β-amyrin, and their derivatives indicate the presence of plant materials (Regert 2007). Eerkens (2002) used the predominance of the diterpenoid Δ–8(9)-isopimaric acid in a vessel residue from the western Great Basin to argue it contained piñon resins. Other analytical techniques have also been used to identify terpenoid compounds. Sauter et al. (1987) detected the triterpenoid betulin in Iron Age tar using both ^{1}H and ^{13}C nuclear magnetic resonance spectroscopy (NMR), confirming the tar was produced from birch.

Methodology

Lipid preservation is enhanced by protection from, or minimizing exposure to, oxygen, heat, water, and sunlight (Frankel 1991). For this reason, lipids absorbed into the matrix tend to be better preserved than lipids occurring on the surface of an artifact. Lipids absorbed into pores are also less vulnerable to postdepositional contamination than lipids on the surface. While Charters et al. (1993 and 1997) suggest rim sherds of boiling pots should be targeted for residue analysis, it is important to note that the area of fat accumulation extends over the entire upper third of

Table A.3. List of Killarney Bay 1/Speigel pottery samples.

Lab no.	Catalog no.	Typology	Provenience	Sample size (g)
9LU 1	39489	Killarney Bay thick var. plain rim	KB1/2251 from B8	6.331
9LU 2	38933	Killarney Bay thick var. plain rim	KB1	8.645
9LU 3	30250	Killarney Bay thick, var. flat lip	KB1/105 test trench 2	6.597
9LU 4	38445	Killarney Bay smooth var. rolled lip	KB1 1266 trench 3	4.838
9LU 5	38447	Killarney Bay thick var. pseudo-scallop shell impressed	KB1 trench 3	5.704
9LU 6	22674	Killarney Bay smooth var. plain lip	KB1/153 trench 4D	4.346
9LU 7	247	(LU vessel 3) fingernail impressed lip	N10W13 layer 4	5.194
9LU 8	293	(LU vessel 2) shell temper Killarney Bay thick, var. plain lip	N01E05 layer 2	5.052
9LU 9	1424	pseudo-scallop shell neck	N33W20 layer 4	4.397
9LU 10	5	(LU vessel 1) Speigel tool impressed	N8W15 layer 3	7.362

these vessels. Cooking vessels are not filled to capacity, and evaporative loss reduces water levels during boiling, so sherds from the neck or shoulder area are also suitable and may be more easily obtained than rim sherds. In this study, both rim and neck sherds were selected for lipid residue analysis. Descriptions of the potsherds analyzed are presented in Table A.3.

The extraction and analysis of lipid residues is a multistep process, which is presented in detail below. In lay terms, after removal of the exterior surfaces, the sample is crushed and the powder is agitated with a mixture of chloroform and methanol, which are nonpolar solvents that dissolve lipids. After washing to remove water-soluble contaminants, the extraction solution separates into two layers. Evaporation is used to recover the lipid residue from the chloroform layer. In order to make the lipids more suitable for analysis by gas chromatography, portions of the extract are treated with chemicals that convert them into slightly different compounds. This process is called derivatization. Gas chromatography uses differences in boiling point (volatility) and degree of interaction with the chemical coating on the interior of the GC column to separate complex mixtures into their constituent compounds. An ancient lipid residue is separated into its constituent fatty acids, triacylglycerols, sterols, waxes, and/or terpenes. When a separated component emerges from the column during GC analysis, a flame ionization detector records the time lapsed since the sample was injected (retention time) and its concentration. Identifications are based on comparisons with known lipid standards run under identical conditions. When coupled with a mass spectrometer for GC/MS analysis, components emerging from the column are fragmented through impact with an electron beam and the resulting ions are sorted according to their mass-to-charge ratios. Component identification is made by comparing its fragmentation pattern (i.e., its spectra) to those in a computerized database of known compounds.

Experimental details

Possible contaminants were removed by grinding off the exterior surfaces with a Dremel tool fitted with a silicon carbide bit. Immediately thereafter, the sample was crushed with a hammer mortar and pestle and the powder transferred to an Erlenmeyer flask. Lipids were extracted using a variation of the method developed by Folch et al. (1957). The powdered sample was mixed with a 2:1

mixture, by volume, of chloroform and methanol (2 × 25 mL) using ultrasonication (2 × 10 min). Solids were removed by filtering the solvent mixture into a separatory funnel. The lipid/solvent filtrate was washed with 13.3 mL of ultrapure water. Once separation into two phases was complete, the lower chloroform-lipid phase was transferred to a round-bottomed flask and the chloroform removed by rotary evaporation. Any remaining water was removed by evaporation with 2-propanol (1.5 mL), and 1.5 mL of chloroform-methanol (2:1, v/v) was used to transfer the dry total lipid extract to a screw-top glass vial with a Teflon®-lined cap. The sample was flushed with nitrogen and stored in a -20°C freezer.

Preparation of FAMES

A 400 μL aliquot of the total lipid extract solution was placed in a screw-top test tube and dried in a heating block under nitrogen. Fatty acid methyl esters (FAMES) were prepared by treating the dry lipid with 5 mL of 0.5 N anhydrous hydrochloric acid in methanol (68°C; 60 minutes). Fatty acids that occur in the sample as di- or triglycerides are detached from the glycerol molecule and converted to methyl esters. After cooling to room temperature, 3.4 mL of ultrapure water was added. FAMES were recovered with petroleum ether (2.5 mL) and transferred to a vial. The solvent was removed by heat under a gentle stream of nitrogen; the FAMES were dissolved in 75 μL of *iso*-octane, then transferred to a GC vial with a conical glass insert.

Preparation of TMS derivatives

A 100 μL aliquot of the total lipid extract solution was placed in a screw-top vial and dried under nitrogen. Trimethylsilyl (TMS) derivatives were prepared by treating the lipid with 70 μL of *N,O*-bis(trimethylsilyl)trifluoroacetamide (BSTFA) containing 1 percent trimethylchlorosilane by volume (70°C; 30 minutes).

Solvents and chemicals were checked for purity by running a sample blank. Traces of contamination were subtracted from sample chromatograms. The relative percentage composition was calculated by dividing the integrated peak area of each fatty acid by the total area of fatty acids present in the sample.

The step in the extraction procedure where the chloroform, methanol, and lipid mixture is washed with water is standard procedure for the extraction of lipids from modern samples. Although Evershed et al. (1990) suggest this is not required for archaeological samples, it is performed to remove impurities so that clearer chromatograms could be obtained in the region where very long-chain fatty acids (C20:0, C20:1, C22:0, and C24:0) occur. It was anticipated that the detection and accurate assessment of these fatty acids could be instrumental in separating residues of animal origin from those of plant (Malainey et al. 2000a, b, c, 2001a).

In order to identify the residue on the basis of fatty acid composition, the relative percentage composition was determined first with respect to all fatty acids present in the sample (including very long-chain fatty acids) (see Table A.3) and secondly with respect to the ten fatty acids utilized in the development of the identification criteria (C12:0, C14:0, C15:0, C16:0, C16:1, C17:0, C18:0, C18:1ω9, C18:1ω11, and C18:2) (not shown). The second step is necessary for the application of the identification criteria presented in Table A.2. It must be understood that the identifications given do not necessarily mean that those particular foods were actually prepared, because different foods of similar fatty acid composition and lipid content would produce similar residues. It is possible only to say that the material of origin for the residue was similar in composition to the food(s) indicated. HT-GC and HT-GC/MS are used to further clarify the identifications.

Gas chromatography analysis parameters

The GC analysis was performed on a Varian 3800 gas chromatograph fitted with a flame ionization detector connected to a personal computer. Samples were separated using a DB-23 fused silica capillary column (30 m × 0.25 mm I.D.; J&W Scientific, Folsom, California). An autosampler injected a 1-3 μL sample using a split/splitless injection system. Hydrogen was used as the carrier gas with a column flow of 1.0 mL/min. Column temperature was held at 80°C for 1 minute, and then increased to 140°C at a rate of 20 °C per minute. It was then programmed from 140 to 230°C at 4°C per minute. The upper temperature was held for 17 minutes. Chromatogram peaks were integrated using Varian MS Workstation software and identified through comparisons with external qualitative standards (NuCheck Prep, Elysian, Minnesota).

High-temperature gas chromatography and gas chromatography with mass spectrometry

Both HT-GC and HT GC-MS analyses were performed on a Varian 3800 gas chromatograph fitted with both a flame ionization detector and Varian 4000 mass spectrometer connected to a personal computer. For HT-GC analysis, the sample was injected onto a DB-1ht fused silica capillary column (15 m × 0.32 mm I.D.; Agilent J&W, Santa Clara, California) connected to the flame ionization detector, using hydrogen as the carrier gas. For HT-GC/MS analysis, samples were injected onto a VF-5ht fused silica capillary column (30 m × 0.25 mm I.D.; Varian, Palo Alto, California) connected to the mass spectrometer, using helium as the carrier gas. For both analyses, the column temperature was held at 50°C for 2 minutes, and then increased to 350°C at a rate of 10°C per minute. The Varian 4000 mass spectrometer was operated in electron-impact ionization mode scanning from m/z 50-700. Chromatogram peaks and MS spectra were processed using Varian MS Workstation software and identified through comparisons with external qualitative standards (Sigma Aldrich, St. Louis, Missouri and NuCheck Prep, Elysian, Minnesota), reference samples, and the National Institute of Standards and Technology (NIST) database.

Results of archaeological data analysis

The lipid compositions of residues extracted from 9 of the 10 samples are presented in Tables A.4, A.5, A.6, and A.7. The term Area represents the area under the chromatographic peak of a given fatty acid, as calculated by the Varian MS Workstation software minus the solvent blank. The term Rel% represents the relative percentage of the fatty acid with respect to the total fatty acids in the sample.

Residues containing mainly (or only) large herbivore products

Residue 9LU 1 is characterized by elevated levels of C18:0 (31.12 percent), and the sterol biomarker cholesterol was detected with HT-GC/MS. As noted previously, elevated levels of C18:0 occur in residues produced from large herbivore meat from animals such as moose, deer, and bison. Based on the low levels of C18:1 isomers (less than 6 percent), the large herbivore meat was quite lean. A moderate level of medium-chain fatty acids occurs in the residue (8 percent), which could suggest traces of plant material. The presence of the cholesterol confirms the identification of animal products, but plant sterols were not detected. Other foods, such as javelina meat and the seed oils of certain tropical plants, are known to produce residues with high levels of C18:0, but they are not likely to be the source of Middle Woodland vessel residues from northern Ontario.

Residues containing (somewhat) fatty animal products

The level of C18:1 isomers in residue 9LU 9 is 25.50 percent, which falls on the border between medium fat content and moderate-high fat content foods. The level of medium-chain saturated fatty acids is low, indicating the absence of plants with low fat content. The level of C18:0 in the residue is 23.91 percent, which suggests animal products are present, but probably not from large herbivores (moose, deer, or bison). The animal sterol cholesterol was also present in the residue. The fatty meat of medium-sized mammals, such as beaver, is known to produce residues of moderate-high fat content. A variety of animal foods are known to produce medium fat content residues (Malainey 2007a): the most relevant ones include fish and fat-depleted elk.

Residues containing medium fat content animal products and low fat content plants

The composition of residue 9LU 5 is characterized by high levels of medium-chain saturated fatty acids and somewhat elevated levels of C18:0 and C18:1 isomers. When only the ten fatty acids used to develop the criteria are considered, it clearly falls in the original category *Fish or corn with plant*. As above, the high level of medium-chain saturated fatty acids strongly suggests the presence of low fat content plants, even though no plant sterols were detected. A variety of animal foods are known to produce medium fat content residues: the most relevant are fish and fat-depleted elk.

Residues containing lean animal products and low fat content plants

The compositions of residues 9LU 7 and 9LU 8 are very similar, and both have levels of medium-chain saturated

Table A.4. Fatty acid composition and identification of residues.

	9LU1		9LU3		9LU5		9LU7		9LU8		9LU9	
Fatty acid	Area	Rel%	Area	Rel%	Area	Rel%	Area	Rel%	Area	Rel%	Area	Rel%
C12:0	35181	1.22	26774	4.94	31771	4.17	177863	5.94	156451	8.54	87831	0.42
C14:0	114974	4.00	29543	5.45	57065	7.48	276645	9.24	121245	6.62	456189	2.20
C14:1	11224	0.39	15863	2.93	8807	1.15	0	0.00	0	0.00	260393	1.26
C15:0	81027	2.82	30604	5.65	34888	4.57	89445	2.99	44899	2.45	383363	1.85
C16:0	1396215	48.52	149220	27.53	307239	40.28	1275856	42.63	772710	42.20	8112195	39.12
C16:1	1698	0.06	12501	2.31	8797	1.15	27705	0.93	20035	1.09	15113	0.07
C17:0	88351	3.07	18986	3.50	29857	3.91	70951	2.37	54455	2.97	687881	3.32
C17:1	14880	0.52	12391	2.29	11783	1.54	23990	0.80	11911	0.65	0	0.00
C18:0	895483	31.12	57973	10.70	117519	15.41	697968	23.32	366425	20.01	4959223	23.91
C18:1s	164339	5.71	132577	24.46	108369	14.21	252180	8.43	194278	10.61	5288704	25.50
C18:2	9599	0.33	4702	0.87	10056	1.32	19134	0.64	23027	1.26	53843	0.26
C18:3ω3	0	0.00	19294	3.56	4179	0.55	0	0.00	18472	1.01	0	0.00
C20:0	23763	0.83	2108	0.39	2766	0.36	12506	0.42	18135	0.99	192565	0.93
C20:1	6516	0.23	12060	2.23	10669	1.40	37900	1.27	18341	1.00	63934	0.31
C24:0	23991	0.83	0	0.00	12634	1.66	22312	0.75	0	0.00	99686	0.48
C24:1	10595	0.37	17379	3.21	6362	0.83	8527	0.28	10529	0.58	76015	0.37
Total	2877836	100.00	541975	100.00	762761	100.00	2992982	100.00	1830913	100.00	20736935	100.00
Biomarker(s)	Cholesterol		TMS esters of dehydroabietic acid and 7-oxodehydroabietic acid		Cholesterol		Cholesterol		Cholesterol		Cholesterol	
Identification	Large herbivore		A combination of low, medium, and moderate high fat content plants, including conifer products		A combination of low fat content plants and medium fat content animal products		Lean animal flesh and low fat content plants		Lean animal flesh and low fat content plant		Borderline moderate-high (beaver) and medium (fish/ fat-depleted elk) animal flesh	

Note: Residue 9LU 2 contained TMS esters of dehydroabietic acid and 7-oxodehydroabietic acid, indicating the presence of conifer products.

fatty acids of about 18 percent. This strongly suggests the presence of low fat content plants, even though no plant sterols were detected. Plant foods known to produce low fat content residues include roots, greens, certain berries, and starchy seeds. The levels of C18:0 in the residue range between 20.01 percent and 23.32 percent, which suggests animal products are present, but probably do not originate from large herbivores (moose, deer, or bison). Based on the low levels of C18:1 isomers, the animal flesh is quite lean. If rabbit or other small mammal bones are present in the faunal assemblage, they may be the source.

Residues containing only plant products

Residue 9LU 3 is characterized by a C18:1 isomer level that falls on the border between medium fat content and moderate-high fat content foods—24.46 percent. The presence of low fat content foods is indicated by relatively high levels of medium-chain saturated fatty acids C12:0, C14:0, and C15:0. No plant or animal sterols were detected, but the low level of C18:0 suggests only foods of plant origin. The TMS esters of dehydroabietic acid and 7-oxodehydroabietic acid were detected by HT-GC/MS and indicate the presence of conifer products. Plants known to produce moderate-high fat content residues are seeds, such as Texas ebony seeds. Plant foods known to produce medium fat content residues include corn, cholla, and mesquite beans, but the biomarker for corn, n-dotriacontanol, was not detected. Seeds from locally available plants, such as cattails and bulrushes, or seed oils from the pits of certain berries, such as pincherries and chokecherries, are possible sources, but this must be confirmed through the preparation of experimental residues. Plant food known to produce low fat content residues include roots, greens, certain berries, and starchy seeds.

The remaining sample, residue 9LU 2, was virtually devoid of fatty acids, but two biomarkers associated with conifer products—the TMS esters of dehydroabietic acid and 7-oxodehydroabietic acid—were detected by HT-GC/MS. As noted above, these biomarkers were also detected in residue 9LU 3.

Samples with apparent C16:0 contamination

Three residues—9LU 4, 9LU 6, and 9LU 10—have very large C16:0 peaks. This fatty acid appears in all archaeological food residues, but the amounts in these residues are larger than expected. The occurrence of similarly high levels of C16:0 occurred in several pottery residues extracted from a site in Arizona: it was suggested that the extra amount of C16:0 relates to a substance applied to the pots as a sealant (Malainey 2007b). It appears that these three Killarney Bay pottery residues also contain fatty acids from both the former vessel contents and a contaminant with high levels of C16:0. Because the extraction technique targets absorbed residues, if a substance such as a sealant was applied to a new vessel, that substance would dominate the pot residues and essentially contaminate ancient food residues. If only the contaminating material was retained in the vessel fabric, one would expect the extracted residues to be identical. However, differences exist between the fatty acid composition of Killarney Bay vessel residues, and they likely relate to vessel function.

In order to assess the former vessel contents, it was necessary to reconstruct the possible food residue by subtracting the C16:0 contamination. As mentioned previously, C16:0 appears in all foods and archaeological food residues. The mean and standard deviation of C16:0 levels in 600 archaeological residues previously identified as food was determined and found to be 31 ± 9 percent. The average in Killarney Bay residues is higher. To reconstruct the most likely fatty acid composition of possible archaeological food residue, the relative fatty acid composition was recalculated with C16:0 at the mean (31 percent), at one standard deviation above the mean (40 percent), and at one standard deviation below the mean (22 percent). The fatty acid compositions of the original residues, the recalculations, and the identifications at each of these levels of C16:0 was then determined (Tables A.5, A.6, and A.7). Given that the average level of C16:0 in other residues from this site is 40.04 percent, the identification made at C16:0 = 40 percent would be the most probable.

Residues likely to contain large herbivore products and low fat content plants

The identification of residue 9LU 6, based on uncorrected values, is somewhat ambiguous in that cholesterol is present but the level of C18:0 is quite low (Table A.5). Reducing C16:0 levels dramatically increased the levels of medium-chain fatty acids and C18:0. The recalculation produces the unequivocal identification of large herbivore flesh and low fat content plants.

Table A.5. Calculation of the relative fatty acid composition of residue 9LU 6, with an average level (31%) of C16:0, as well as one standard deviation above (40%) and below (22%) the average C16:0 level.

	Unaltered		C16:0 = 31%	C16:0 = 40%	C16:0 = 22%
Fatty acid	**Area**	**Rel%**	**Rel%**	**Rel%**	**Rel%**
C12:0	21967	1.56	2.81	2.44	3.17
C14:0	54450	3.86	6.96	6.05	7.87
C14:1	0	0.00	0.00	0.00	0.00
C15:0	47935	3.40	6.13	5.33	6.93
C16:0	870580	61.73	31.00	40.00	22.00
C16:1	438	0.03	0.06	0.05	0.06
C17:0	53439	3.79	6.83	5.94	7.72
C17:1	9012	0.64	1.15	1.00	1.30
C18:0	262392	18.60	33.54	29.16	37.91
C18:1s	38439	2.73	4.91	4.27	5.55
C18:2	7289	0.52	0.93	0.81	1.05
C18:3ω3	3316	0.24	0.42	0.37	0.48
C20:0	7837	0.56	1.00	0.87	1.13
C20:1	10924	0.77	1.40	1.21	1.58
C24:0	14890	1.06	1.90	1.65	2.15
C24:1	7503	0.53	0.96	0.83	1.08
Total	1410411	100.00	100.00	100.00	100.00
Biomarker(s)	Cholesterol		Cholesterol	Cholesterol	Cholesterol
Identification	Low fat content plant and lean animal?		Large herbivore and low fat content plant	Large herbivore and low fat content plant	Large herbivore and low fat content plant

Table A.6. Calculation of the relative fatty acid composition of residue 9LU 10, with an average level (31%) of C16:0, as well as one standard deviation above (40%) and below (22%) the average C16:0 level.

	Unaltered		**C16:0 = 31%**	**C16:0 = 40%**	**C16:0 = 22%**
Fatty acid	**Area**	**Rel%**	**Rel%**	**Rel%**	**Rel%**
C12:0	537869	5.85	10.23	8.90	11.56
C14:0	360478	3.92	6.86	5.96	7.75
C14:1	219356	2.38	4.17	3.63	4.72
C15:0	213420	2.32	4.06	3.53	4.59
C16:0	5570205	60.56	31.00	40.00	22.00
C16:1	75773	0.82	1.44	1.25	1.63
C17:0	249275	2.71	4.74	4.12	5.36
C17:1	25197	0.27	0.48	0.42	0.54
C18:0	1345288	14.63	25.59	22.25	28.92
C18:1s	377856	4.11	7.19	6.25	8.12
C18:2	58925	0.64	1.12	0.97	1.27
C18:3ω3	13591	0.15	0.26	0.22	0.29
C20:0	62382	0.68	1.19	1.03	1.34
C20:1	28868	0.31	0.55	0.48	0.62
C24:0	37954	0.41	0.72	0.63	0.82
C24:1	21309	0.23	0.41	0.35	0.46
Total	9197746	100.00	100.00	100.00	100.00
Biomarker	Cholesterol		Cholesterol	Cholesterol	Cholesterol
Identification	Low fat content plant and lean animal?		Lean animal flesh and low fat content plant	Lean animal flesh and low fat content plant	Large herbivore flesh and low fat content plant

Table A.7. Calculation of the relative fatty acid composition of residue 9LU 4, with an average level (31%) of C16:0, as well as one standard deviation above (40%) and below (22%) the average C16:0 level.

	Unaltered		C16:0 = 31%	C16:0 = 40%	C16:0 = 22%
Fatty acid	**Area**	**Rel%**	**Rel%**	**Rel%**	**Rel%**
C12:0	24929	0.81	2.05	1.78	2.32
C14:0	80655	2.61	6.64	5.77	7.50
C14:1	9652	0.31	0.79	0.69	0.90
C15:0	80521	2.60	6.62	5.76	7.49
C16:0	2254643	72.89	31.00	40.00	22.00
C16:1	6157	0.20	0.51	0.44	0.57
C17:0	92844	3.00	7.64	6.64	8.64
C17:1	11146	0.36	0.92	0.80	1.04
C18:0	317251	10.26	26.10	22.70	29.51
C18:1s	120054	3.88	9.88	8.59	11.17
C18:2	18884	0.61	1.55	1.35	1.76
C18:3ω3	2337	0.08	0.19	0.17	0.22
C20:0	28927	0.94	2.38	2.07	2.69
C20:1	9560	0.31	0.79	0.68	0.89
C24:0	33247	1.07	2.74	2.38	3.09
C24:1	2493	0.08	0.21	0.18	0.23
Total	3093300	100.00	100.00	100.00	100.00
Biomarker	Not present		Not present	Not present	Not present
Identification	Unknown		Lean animal flesh and low fat content plant	Lean animal flesh and low fat content plant	Large herbivore flesh and low fat content plant

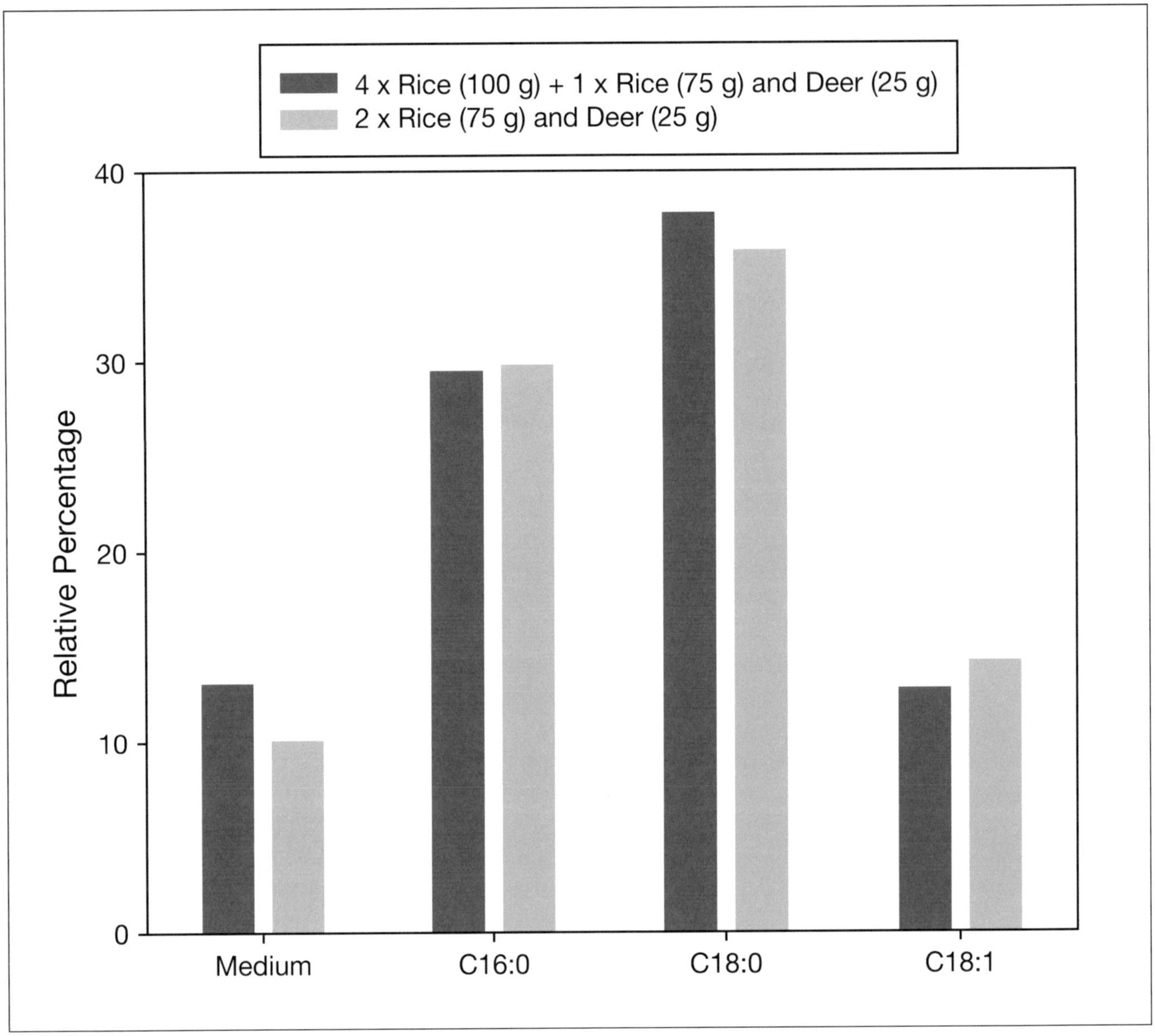

Figure A.1. The relative fatty acid composition of residues produced by different combinations of wild rice and deer meat after two months of oven storage at 75°C.

Residues likely to contain lean animal or large herbivore products and low fat content plants

The identification of 9LU 10 based on uncorrected levels of fatty acids is somewhat unclear, in that cholesterol is present but the level of C18:0 is very low; the presence of low fat content plants is indicated (Table A.6). Reducing the level of C16:0 in residue 9LU 10 alters its composition so that it strongly resembles residues 9LU 7 and 9LU 8. These residues have high levels of medium-chain saturated fatty acids, which strongly suggested the presence of low fat content plants. Once again, plant foods known to produce low fat content residues include roots, greens, certain berries, and starchy seeds. The levels of C18:0 in the residue at C16:0 = 31 percent and C16:0 = 40 percent are between 22.2 percent and 25.6 percent, which suggests animal products are present, but not from large herbivores (moose, deer, or bison). Based on the low levels of C18:1 isomers, the animal flesh is quite lean. If rabbit bones are present in the faunal assemblage, they may be the source.

At C16:0 = 22 percent, the C18:0 level reaches the level of large herbivores, but this is the least probable identification.

Residues possibly containing lean animal or large herbivore products and low fat content plants

Without alteration, the level of C16:0 in residue 9LU 4 is almost 73 percent, making it the most heavily contaminated residue (Table A.7). Reducing the level of the fatty acid alters its composition so that it resembles residues 9LU 10, 9LU 7, and 9LU 8, described above. High levels of medium-chain saturated fatty acids strongly suggest the presence of low fat content plants. The levels of C18:0 in the residue at C16:0 = 31 percent and C16:0 = 40 percent are between 22.7 percent and 26.1 percent, which suggests animal products are present, but not from large herbivores (moose, deer, or bison). At C16:0 = 22 percent, the C18:0 level reaches that of large herbivores. The absence of cholesterol means the presence of animal products cannot be confirmed.

Experimental residues

Experimental residues were prepared by boiling wild rice and deer flesh in fired clay cylinders placed inside 2 L beakers, using electric hot plates as the heat source. The first residue was produced by boiling 100 g of wild rice in a fired clay cylinder on four separate occasions and cooking 75 g of wild rice and 25 g of deer flesh once. Another experimental cooking residue was prepared by boiling 75 g of wild rice and 25 g of deer flesh in a fired clay cylinder on two separate occasions. Each cooking episode lasted about two hours and the fired clay cylinder was dried completely between each event. Tiles cut from the fired clay cylinder were stored in an oven at 75°C for a period of two months to simulate the effects of long-term oxidative degradation (Malainey 1997; Malainey et al. 1999b). Residues were extracted from the clay tiles and analyzed using the procedures outlined above.

The relative fatty acid compositions of the two degraded residues were found to be almost identical (Figure A.1). In both cases, the level of C18:0 ranged between 35 percent and 38 percent. Medium-chain saturated fatty acids and C18:1 isomers both occurred at levels between 10 percent and 15 percent. With further degradation of unsaturated fatty acids, the relative level of saturated fatty acids would increase slightly. These results clearly show that wild rice could be the source of elevated levels of medium-chain fatty acids in archaeological vessel residues from the Killarney Bay site.

Conclusions

Lipid residue analysis shows that the compositions of vessel residues are variable. Specific Killarney Bay vessels appear to have been used to prepare specific food or nonfood products. Low fat content plant products are common in the vessel residues examined. Elevated levels of medium-chain saturated fatty acids occur in 8 of the 10 residues. Residues produced in replication experiments and stored in a 75°C oven to simulate the effects of long-term decomposition suggest that wild rice is a possible source.

Animal products are common in the vessel residues. The animal sterol cholesterol was detected in 7 of the 10 vessel residues. Differing levels of C18:0 suggest that more than one type of animal was exploited. In addition to large herbivore flesh, the lean meat of other animals and fish was also prepared in the vessels. Conifer products were detected in two residues, 9LU 2 and 9LU 3, which could indicate the former site inhabitants prepared spruce tea in these vessels (Patrick Julig and David Brose, personal communication 2009). The presence of dehydroabietic acid and 7-oxodehydroabietic acid in residue 9LU 2, combined with the absence of fatty acids, sterols, or other lipids, could indicate the sole purpose of the vessel was the preparation of spruce tea.

Acknowledgements

Timothy Figol and Mary Malainey performed residue analysis at the Brandon University archaeological lipid residue analysis laboratory. Results were presented in a paper titled Analysis of Lipid Residues from Speigel/Killarney Bay 1 Middle Woodland Pottery, at the Canadian Archaeological Association 40th Annual Meeting, in Thunder Bay, Ontario, in May 2009. Funding for this research was provided by Laurentian University, the Canada Research Chair program, the Canada Foundation for Innovation New Opportunities Fund and CRC Infrastructure Fund, the Brandon University Research Committee, and the University of Manitoba-SSHRC grant program.

Appendix B
Shell Beads

Colin Quinn

As personal adornment items, the shell beads at Killarney Bay likely played a role in the social, economic, and ritual organization of the community. Shell beads were valuable objects that were worn, displayed, and exchanged; they were used in multiple and complex ways; and they were often circulated across vast distances, between cultures, for long periods of time (Trubitt 2003). Adornment items are often associated with information exchange, and their association with mortuary contexts adds another layer of significance for archaeologists. Beads can be linked to social identities (Carey 1998; O'Hear 1998; Sciama 1998; Trubitt 2003). By wearing certain types and quantities of beads in particular patterns, individuals are able to convey information about political prowess, socioeconomic standing, gender, age, occupation, kin group, cultural group, wealth, status, and religious identity in a clear and simple manner that otherwise would be impossible to visually display (Dublin 1987, 1999; Vanhaeren 2005; Vanhaeren and d'Errico 2006; Wright and Garrard 2003). Adornment items have also been used in studies of economic systems, including trade and exchange (Allen et al. 1997; Brose 1994a; Galm 1994; Quinn 2006; Stiner 1999). Shell beads are a key class of material culture throughout the Woodland period in Ontario (Ferris and Spence 1995) and were a key item in prehistoric exchange networks throughout eastern North America (Brose 1994a; Ritchie 1937; Yerkes 1983). Situating the shell beads within the site of Killarney Bay can provide insight into past ritual systems, economic organization, and social information exchange.

About the collections

A variety of shell beads were found at Killarney Bay. Shell beads from Killarney Bay are curated at the University of Michigan Museum of Anthropological Archaeology (UMMAA) and the Canadian Museum of History (CMH). The UMMAA collection has associated field notes, photographs, and provenience information, while the materials curated at the CMH have no field documentation.

The UMMAA collection contains 178 shell beads and the CMH collection contains 968 shell beads (for a total of 1146 shell beads from the site). All of the UMMAA beads were analyzed for metrics, morphology, genus/species, drilling evidence, evidence of stringing, archaeological context, and initial typological assessment. All of the CMH beads were analyzed for morphology, genus/species, drilling evidence, evidence of stringing, and initial typological assessment. Given the quantity of shell beads at the CMH and limited time with the collections, metrics were recorded for only a sample of the beads (a total of 75).

Metric analysis of the beads will come from a sample of beads drawn from both the UMMAA and CMH collections. The patterns are not significantly changed when the CMH collections are omitted from morphological analysis and they are included here to increase the robusticity of analysis. Because contextual information is lacking from the CMH collection, the contextual analyses will only include shell beads curated at the UMMAA.

Species in the Killarney Bay assemblage

The difficulties of identifying the sources of freshwater and marine shell found in archaeological contexts have generated an extensive literature (cf. Claassen 1998). All such analyses must initially depend on secure species identification, which is no small problem when different species within broadly distributed genera are only occasionally identifiable by variations in shell form or color. In archaeological contexts, there are added problems when shell form or color is distorted by human modification or taphonomic processes. As such, the species identifications presented here should be considered both preliminary and coarse. More detailed scientific analyses are needed to accurately identify the species and source of all of the shells in the Killarney Bay assemblage.

Within this assemblage, there are several broadly distinguishable species represented. Two of the species have undergone minimal human modification to turn them into beads. First, there are tusk shell beads, which are commonly identified as *Dentalium*. It is possible that these shells are one of any of the various *Dentalium* sp., or the nearly indistinguishable species of *Antalis occidentalis* and *Antalis antillaris*, which are found in the waters of the Atlantic Ocean (from the north and the St. Lawrence Seaway and off the coast of New England to the south and the Gulf of Mexico) (Brunel et al. 1998; Kraeuter 2009; Stimpson 1851) .

The other species of shell that has undergone minimal modification is the spiral shell bead commonly identified as *Marginella*. Shells from the family Marginellidae, including the common Atlantic marginella (*Prunum apicinum*) (Menke 1828), are found in intertidal waters in the Gulf of Mexico and along the Atlantic Coast of the United States as far north as North Carolina (Da Silva et al. 2011; Felder and Earle 2009).

The rest of the shell beads at Killarney Bay have undergone significant human modification that makes identification of species more difficult. The shell bead production process can remove diagnostic visual markers of species. These beads are common throughout the Eastern Woodland prehistoric deposits and may be made from the collumella of marine conch or marine whelks such as *Busycon* sp. (Brose et al. 1985; Winters 1968).

One major avenue of investigating the nature of Middle Woodland social relationships relies on accurately assessing the geographic connections for exotic goods. Because *Marginella*, *Dentalium*, and *Busycon* are among the most widely occurring marine gastropods, it is nearly impossible to identify specific geographic source locations based on visual inspection of the shells alone. Additional chemical analyses may be able to elucidate this issue (see Claassen and Sigmann 1993). Nevertheless, the species represented in the shell bead assemblage are evidence of long-distance exchange. Nonlocal marine shell would have been procured through trade networks.

Typology

There are four different types of shell beads at Killarney Bay (Table B.1). Within the literature on the prehistoric Eastern Woodland, there are typologies based on raw material and shape that have limited integration and quantified justification. In order to adequately characterize the variation and patterns within the Killarney Bay assemblage, a typological analysis was conducted in order to identify morphological types. This morphological typology links species identification and shape descriptions that have been previously employed into a coherent framework.

Table B.1. The shell bead typology and summary data from the Killarney Bay assemblage.

	Qualitative description		Quantitative description (in mm)			Total		
Type	Shape	Species	Mean length (std. deviation)	Mean width (std. deviation)	Mean perforation diameter (std. deviation)	UMMAA	CMH	with metrics
Type 1	Tubular bead	Conch/ Whelk	5.54 (1.86)	10.88 (0.82)	4.33 (0.66)	26	194	48
Type 2	Disc bead	Conch/ Whelk	1.85 (0.45)	7.11 (0.67)	3.19 (0.44)	107	774	79
Type 3	Dentalium (narrow tusk shaped) bead	Dentalium	13.07 (5.20)	3.59 (0.34)	na	16	0	12
Type 4	Marginella bead	Marginella	9.22 (0.76)	6.22 (0.47)	na	29	0	22

For this analysis, several metric measurements were recorded for the beads (Figure B.1). The measurements were taken according to the way in which they would have been strung, worn, and seen. Length is the distance along the string. Width is the thickness of the bead perpendicular to the length and string axis. In some cases (for noncircular beads), an additional thickness measure of height was recorded. The maximum perforation diameters were also recorded.

Different species will produce shells of varying morphology. The initial shell morphology will significantly restrict the morphology of beads that they are modified to produce. As such, the first step in the analysis is to determine the species or genus of each bead. In the Killarney Bay collection, *Marginella* spp., *Dentalium* spp., and *Busycon* spp. are represented.

For some shells, their morphology allows for more manipulation by humans into a range of bead shapes and sizes. As such, the second contributing factor to shell morphology is intentional manufacture by humans. In the Killarney Bay assemblage, the *Busycon* shells show the most intensive human modification.

Together, the parent shell shape and human modification will produce beads with different morphologies. The distribution of the shell beads at Killarney Bay, plotted by length and width, produces morphological clusters that can be seen in Figure B.2. Within this plot, four clusters of beads can be identified. The different clusters represent at least three different shell species (*Dentalium* spp., *Marginella* spp., and *Busycon* spp.), and intentional human manufacture of beads of different morphological clusters from one species (likely *Busycon* spp.). These clusters are the four different types of beads at Killarney Bay (see Table B.2).

Type 1 beads are short and tubular-shaped, although their length can vary to the point that some of these beads range from disc-shaped to almost cylindrical (Figure B.3). Type 2 beads, which are disc beads, are smaller and much more standardized than Type 1 beads (Figure B.4). Type 3 beads, because they are made from *Dentalium*, are thin and tusk-shaped (Figure B.5). Type 3 beads vary in length due to snapping and cutting into segments, but their width is much more standard (and smaller than all other types of beads). Type 4 beads retain the shape of the *Marginella*

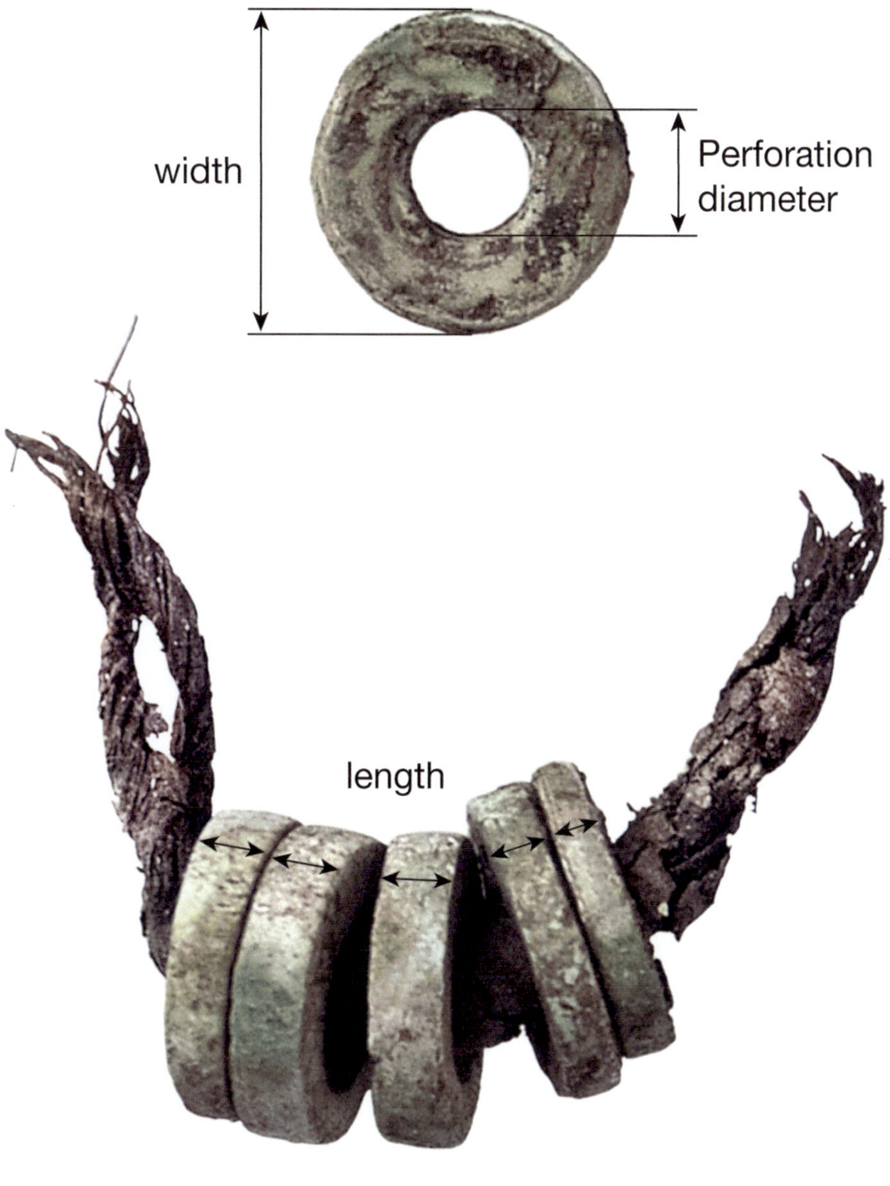

Figure B.1. Schematic showing the location and orientation of measurements taken on the Killarney Bay 1 bead assemblage, including length, width, and perforation diameter.

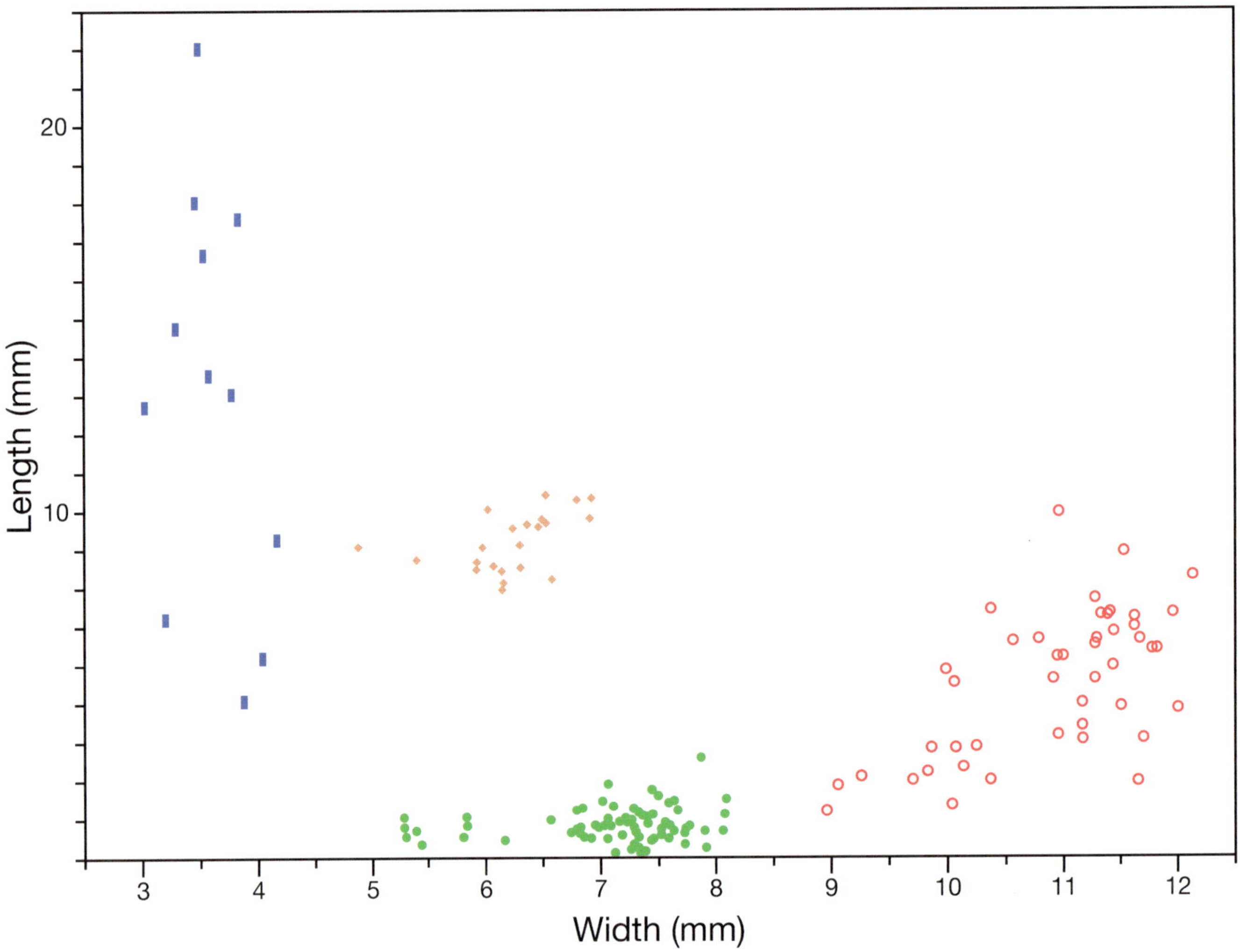

Figure B.2. Shell bead morphology and typology at Killarney Bay. There are four different shapes of shell beads in the assemblage: Type 1 beads (red circles) are tubular beads; Type 2 beads (green dots) are disc beads; Type 3 beads are *Dentalium* beads (blue rectangles); and Type 4 beads are *Marginella* beads (orange diamonds). The two human manufactured shapes show distinct distributions reflecting human intention (Types 1 and 2), though Type 1 has a much larger variance in shape than Type 2 beads. Type 3 and Type 4 are limited by the morphological shape of the species shell, though Type 3 beads have a wider distribution due to intentional and unintentional snapping and cutting.

Table B.2. Shell beads by burial at Killarney Bay.

Burial	Age	Sex	Type 1	Type 2	Type 3	Type 4	Total
1	Child	Unknown	0	0	0	0	0
2	Adult	Female	0	102	0	0	102
3	Child	Unknown	2	0	0	0	2
4	Adult	Male	0	0	0	0	0
5	Unknown	Unknown	0	0	0	0	0
6	Adult	Male	0	(1?)	0	0	(1?)
7	Infant	Unknown	0	0	16	27	43
8	Adult	Male	17	4	0	0	21
9	Adolescent and adult	Unknown	0	0	0	0	0
10	Adolescent	Female	0	(cluster)	0	0	0

Figure B.3. Type 1 (tubular) beads.

Figure B.4. Type 2 (disc) beads.

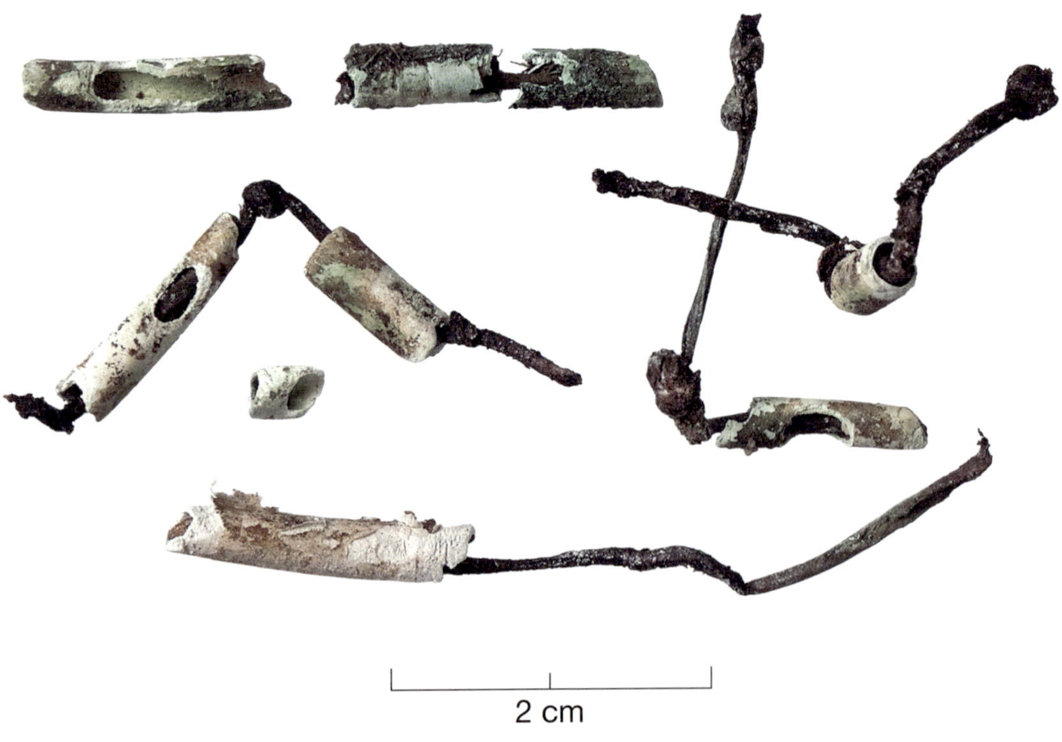

Figure B.5. Type 3 (*Dentalium*) beads.

Figure B.6. Photograph of Type 4 (Marginella) beads.

shells they are made from (Figure B.6). As a result, Type 4 beads do not vary much in terms of size or morphology.

Bead Production

The different species of shell underwent different types of modification to turn them into beads. The *Dentalium* shells were easily turned into beads because of their naturally hollow centers. The *Dentalium* shells at Killarney Bay show some evidence of snapping the shell into segments for the beads, although some of this snapping may be associated with postproduction taphonomic processes. The *Marginella* shells at Killarney Bay had sawed-off ends that created perforations for stringing. The *Busycon* beads were cut, ground, biconically drilled, and then polished. All of the beads in the Killarney Bay assemblage were finished beads.

Stringing of Beads

The shell beads were strung together using a leather cord (Figure B.7). There are preserved leather cords in the collection, and some of the bead are still strung together. Field photographs from the excavation also suggest that a majority, if not all, of the beads were strung at the time of deposition. The lengths of some of the preserved pieces (particularly in the CMH collection) suggest that they were likely necklaces, though it is possible that they were worn and placed on other areas of the body as well.

Multiple lines of evidence suggest that the different morphological types identified in the collection were never mixed on the strings. First, all of the preserved strands all have only one type of bead on them. Second, field descriptions suggest associations even when the material is not currently preserved. For example, field notes state

Figure B.7. Type 2 disc beads with leather cord still in place.

that the Type 3 beads from Burial 7 were strung together with a knot between them. Unfortunately, the leather cord articulating the beads from Burial 7 was not preserved. Third, the perforations on the beads—particularly Type 1 and Type 2 shell beads, which were intentionally drilled—suggest they were manufactured for leather cords of different thicknesses. An initial examination of all Type 1 and Type 2 beads suggests that the perforation size is not normally distributed (Figure B.8a). Additionally, the distribution appears to have two modes. When separated by morphological type, the two modes strongly correspond with the two different bead types, each of which has a normally distributed perforation size within their own type (Figures B.8b and B.8c). This further supports the suggestion that these bead types are not only identifiable for archaeologists, but that they were intentionally manufactured by people in the past. As such, they likely indexed different types of socially, economically, and ritually significant information for the people at Killarney Bay.

Contextual Analysis

The shell beads at Killarney Bay were buried as grave goods. Mortuary treatments are conscious and intentional decisions made by the living (O'Shea 1996:10). Mortuary rituals are not passive snapshots of identities or the social relationships among the living. The funerary process and associated rituals are social contexts in which the natures of social relationships are reified, unmade, or reorganized. Funerary events are venues for performance, and as spectacles and public events have distinct political implications (Inomata and Coben 2006). As such, within the contextual analysis of the beads at Killarney Bay, we must be cognizant of the specific formation processes of the mortuary record. There are very few shell beads at the site, but some of the initial patterning in deposition suggests that those beads that are there may hold the key to important social information about the inhabitants.

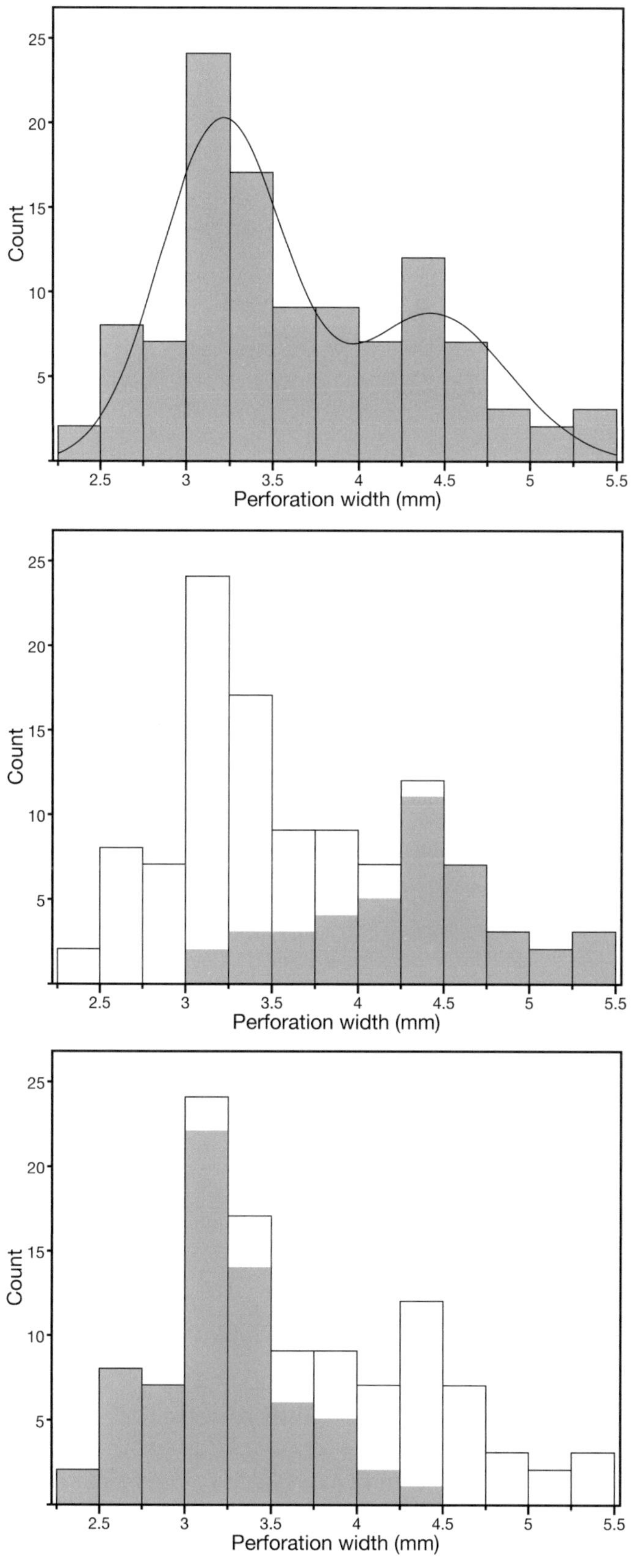

Figure B.8. Distributions of perforation diameter for Type 1 and Type 2 beads. The two types have normal but overlapping distributions. The two different modes suggest intentional manufacture for two different size leather cords.

a (top). Type 1 and 2 beads by perforation width with a best fit line for the mixture of two normal distributions.
b (middle). Type 1 beads by perforation width (highlighted in gray).
c (bottom). Type 2 beads by perforation width (highlighted in gray).

Among the UMMAA collections, 168 of the 178 shell beads came from known mortuary contexts. The rest were found in surface contexts and likely were from disturbed graves. (The CMH beads were omitted from this analysis because they lack detailed contextual information.) One bead was tentatively associated with Burial 6 in field notes because it came from the topsoil near the burial. This bead may or may not be associated with Burial 6.

The distribution of shell beads by type in the burials at Killarney Bay can be found in Table B.2. Shell beads were found in five of the ten burials at the site (50 percent). Burial 2, an adult female, was interred with 102 Type 2 beads. Burial 3, a child, was interred with 2 Type 1 beads. Burial 7, an infant, was interred with 16 Type 3 and 27 Type 4 beads. Burial 8, an adult male, was buried with 17 Type 1 and 4 Type 2 shell beads. Burial 10, an adolescent female, contained a cluster of Type 2 beads that has been cemented by nearby copper objects. Type 1 beads were found in Burial 8 and Burial 3. Type 2 beads were found in Burial 2, Burial 8, and Burial 10 (all adults or adolescents, mostly associated with females). Type 3 and Type 4 beads were only found in Burial 7.

The bead types are unequally distributed in burials. Additionally, the distribution pattern of shell beads can be compared with the distribution of copper beads (see Anselmi, Chapter 12, this volume). Burial 8 is rich in both Type 1 and copper beads, and Burial 2 and Burial 10 have a mix of copper and shell beads. Burials 4 and 6, both adult males, have significant quantities of copper beads, but no directly associated shell beads. Burial 7, an infant buried with the only *Dentalium* and *Marginella* beads at the site, did not contain copper beads. This unequal distribution indicates that the types identified through morphological analysis are chronologically or socially meaningful. The different bead types may contain information about the buried individual and the group of people who buried them.

With only five burials having shell beads, and with only a small quantity of burials, the data are not robust enough to allow us to draw more conclusions from the initial patterns. For example, Type 3 and Type 4 beads were only found in the infant burial and not in any of the adult burials. It is impossible to determine if Type 3 and Type 4 beads are associated with any specific identity or social role, such as an age class, based on a singular case. Additionally, chronological variation between burials may have had an impact on the presence or abundance of certain types of shell beads. Exchange systems, social obligations, and ritual fashions are all dynamic and can shift very rapidly. Together, the patterns of shell bead distribution at this site are suggestive of an important role played by shell beads in the construction, marking, and maintenance of social identities within a ritual context, even if the specific information associated with different types of beads remains unknown.

Discussion

In sum, the shell beads from Killarney Bay are evidence of long-distance exchange networks, material representation of social identities, and variable mortuary practices. The marine shells used to make the beads (and possibly the finished beads themselves) were acquired through long-distance exchange systems. Even as part of this larger economic system, the production types and stringing of beads suggests that beads played an important role in adornment and materialization of social identities. The burial of shell beads in mortuary contexts, and especially the restriction of shell beads and shell bead types to certain burials, also suggests that shell beads played a key role within the mortuary ritual activities.

Appendix C

Textiles

Barbara Brose

The following artifact analysis took place in the Great Lakes Range of the University of Michigan Museum of Anthropological Archaeology from 2008 to 2010. Although the Killarney Bay field notes describe some organic artifacts that were affixed to skeletal and human remains, these materials are not included in this analysis. That is because many of the organic artifacts associated with biological and physical anthropological materials were curated in a separate facility, out of respect for Indigenous peoples, and those materials were not made accessible for this study.

Woven fiber artifacts were reported in four of the ten burials at Killarney Bay. As described in the field notes, the fibers in Burial 2 are "leather-wrapped fiber thongs or lengths [of] woven cordage" (Figure C.1), and those in Burial 7 are "knot-spaced, double-twisted and sheathed fiber thongs" (catalog number UMMAA 38506). The notes also refer to fiber artifacts in Burial 10 (Figures C.2–C.5): [1] objects "apparently in baskets or woven string bags;" [2] "... another string bag;" and [3] "...a leather or repoussé leather or rawhide bag or fabric with babiche ties." The field notes also report a basket in Burial 6.

The Burial 6 basket

The largest fiber remnant preserved in the Killarney Bay collections is this fiber basket—or more probably, bag—from Burial 6 (Figure C.6). It was preserved as a result of copper salts. Powdery fragments of the basket might provide a sample large enough for testing (thus avoiding destructive analysis of the rest of the artifact). At the time of this study, however, there had been no scientific analysis of the fiber. It appeared to be inner bark; possibly eastern white cedar (*Thuja occidentalis L.*) or another of the arboreal species that would have been readily available. In *Ojibwa Crafts*, Carrie Lyford specifically refers to cedar bark bags and notes that at the time of her writing (1943:86), "A cedar bark bag... continues to be used as one of the containers for storing wild rice, one of the most valuable of the native foods."

Earlier, Frances Densmore (1929:157) documented the use of "the inner bark of the cedar, basswood, and slippery elm" for manufacturing bags. The dimensions of the basket/ bag fragment discovered at Killarney Bay are 11.4 cm x

Figure C.1. Fibers from Burial 2, described in field notes as "leather-wrapped fiber thongs or lengths of woven cordage." Catalog number UMMAA 30293.

8.5 cm. There is no remaining selvedge. (Selvedge is an edge, woven so that it does not ravel or fray. In this artifact, no selvedge technique—such as a sewn edge, or warps looping back into the textile, or wefts looped around a terminal warp—is evident.) Photographs taken at the time of discovery show only the underside of the basket, weave patterns evident in disintegrating particles, and staining that appears to indicate the general outline of the original and intact basket. While a photograph of the bag's entire contents is not available, the record shows that they included "one long bone, skull and mandible fragments and part of the pelvis lying on top of some 38 'grayish blue' flint cache blades." A field photograph shows the cache blades in situ (see Figure 7.10, this volume; see also Chapter 9 for details on Burial 6).

Placement of cache blades

A simple experiment with a small collection of unprovenienced Late Archaic and Early Woodland stemmed and corner notched projectile points and 6" x 6" bags clearly demonstrated the relationship of the points' orientation to the position of the Burial 6 bag.

Starting with a cloth bag, the points were tipped in randomly and then observed to determine how they settled to the bottom. The process was repeated several times with the same results, and then the points were placed in a clear plastic bag to see if they settled in the same manner for visual documentation. They did. The photograph showing the cache blades found with the bag at the Killarney Bay

Figures C.2 (left) and C.3. Front and back of fiber artifacts from Burial 10, described as remnants of woven string bags or baskets. Catalog number UMMAA 39670.

site shows that they were parallel to the bag's warp rather than perpendicular, as the experiment demonstrated should be expected. From this, it was clear that the bag was held sideways at the time it was deposited. Given the weight and orientation of the bag's contents, one can safely assume that the placement of the bag in the burial was not at all casual. Lyford (1943:77) points out that "A well-made bag would last a hundred years or more." This reference to the useful life of a basket, the relatively sharp edges of the numerous blades in the Killarney Bay basket, and the obvious care with which it was placed, require one to consider the issue of its possible antiquity at the time it was deposited.

Function and style

In addition to fiber analysis and the orientation of the points, we considered the weaver's intent and the function of the weaving technique. Lyford's (1943:77) comments also refer to design: "The construction of bags demanded a peculiar skill. The techniques necessarily varied with the materials used and with the different workers." These skilled makers would have been aware that what appears to be a purely decorative feature is often a matter of function.

Densmore (1929:158) provides a more specific example of how design and function are related in her comparison of a bag for storing rice and a bag intended for boiling and extracting gum.

Figure C.4 (above). Another fiber artifact from Burial 10. Catalog number UMMAA 39684.

Figure C.5 (left). Field notes for Burial 10 also describe a "leather or repousse leather or rawhide bag." Catalog number UMMAA 39688.

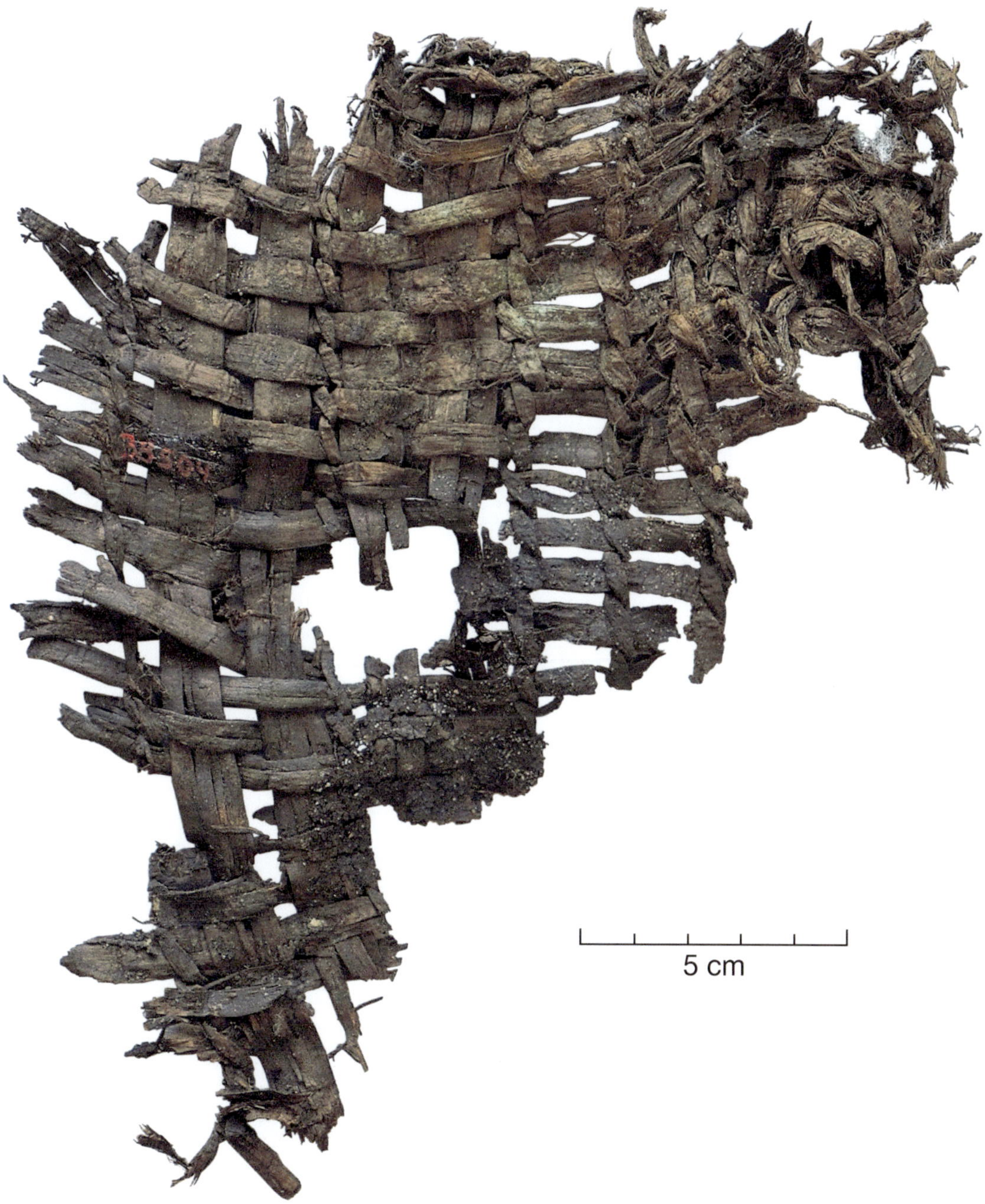

Figure C.6. This is the largest fiber remnant from Killarney Bay: part of a basket or bag, apparently made from inner bark, possibly eastern white cedar. It was preserved in Burial 6 by its proximity to copper. Catalog number UMMAA 38504.

Table C.1. Warp and weft in the fiber basket remnant from Burial 6.

	Warp	cm		Weft	cm	Twist
1	warp	0.5	A	twining weft	0.5	S
2	warp	0.5	B	space	1.0	
3	warp	0.5	C	twining weft	0.5	S
4	warp	0.5	D	space	1.3	
5	warp	0.5	E	twining weft	0.5	S
6	warp	0.6	F	flat weft	1.4	
7	warp	0.5	G	flat weft	1.4	
8	warp	0.8	H	twining weft	0.3	S
9	warp	0.5	I	flat weft	1.0	
10	warp	0.5	J	flat weft	1.4	
11	warp	0.6	K	twining weft	0.3	S
12	warp	0.5		NA	NA	

Patterns in the basket

Fortunately, the fragment of contiguous parts of the Burial 6 bag is large enough to indicate (some) intended pattern features and construction. The largest contiguous fragment of the basket contains 12 rows of warp and 11 rows of weft (Table C.1). As the warps are clearly only fragments, individual warp lengths were not measured. Nine of the twelve warps measure 0.5 cm across, two are 0.6 cm across, and one is 0.8 cm across. The ease (spacing) between warps is consistent and ranges up to 0.3 cm. Inconsistencies are just as likely to be the result of stretching and distortion in situ and/or in unsupported storage containers as they are likely to be the result of the basketmaker's technique. The basketmaker has employed variations in technique, size, and spacing in the weft to create a pattern. The combination of loose open weave with secure twining leads one to infer that the basket was intended to be flexible and sturdy. This is consistent with the actual weight of its contents: 3.5 pounds in cache blades alone. The weft pattern evident in the fragment is as follows: twined fiber 0.5 cm; space 1.0 cm; twined fiber 0.5 cm; wide space 1.3 cm; twined fiber 0.5 cm; wide flat fiber 1.4 cm; wide flat fiber 1.4 cm; twined fiber 0.3 cm; wide flat fiber 1.0 cm; wide flat fiber 1.4 cm; and twined fiber 0.3 cm. What Adovasio (1977:20) calls the "stitch slant" of all twined fibers is an "S slant." Lyford's (1943:78) description of the construction of a basswood fiber bag illustrates a common technique.

> ...strips of untwisted fiber about one-eighth of an inch or more in width which were to serve as a warp were hung over a suspended rod so that they were equally long on both sides of the rod. Before being put on the rod a pair of weft

threads of twisted basswood fiber running at right angles to the warp was carried across the untwisted warp threads on top of the rod. One weft passed behind, and the other in front of a warp or group of warps, then they were give a half turn and carried on to the next warp or group of warps and given a half twist between each, all the way across the rod. Another pair of wefts was then carried across the warps at a distance of about one inch below the rod, over and under each warp each warp or group of warps, with a half turn between each, in the same way that they had been carried across the rod. The second pair of wefts passes all the way round the warps on both sides of the rod. Additional rows of weft threads are woven into the warp at regular intervals.

Textile fragments at Killarney Bay

In addition to the larger sections of twined fabrics from Burial 6 and apparently also from Burial 10, there were a number of short segments of twisted cord and leather thong from Burial 4, on which copper beads had been or were still strung (Figures C.7–C.9; see also Chapter 12, this volume). There was also at least one 3-ply plaited or braided fragment (Burial 6, UMMAA 38502), which may have been a knot at the end of a longer segment.

The four undamaged segments of leather ("babiche" or "rawhide") thongs that could be measured were between 5.2 and 7.6 cm in length (mean = 6.7). The cross sections were rectangular and were approximately 3.5 by 2.5 mm.

Of the eighteen fragmented segments of cordage and/or basketry recovered at Killarney Bay, three are associated with Burial 6 (Figures C.10–C.12). One of these appears to be a fragment of the Burial 6 basket/bag described above. It seems likely to be made of the bark of eastern white cedar: its appearance is that of cedar, and the bark of eastern white cedar was widely used. It is stylistically similar in the proportion of the warp and weft, and in the distinctive spacing of the twining wefts. The two other fragments from this burial cannot be so easily defined as part of the basket. They are of similar material, but rather than being woven, each represents a distinctly different form of braiding. A pair of braided tassels, about 18 cm long and tapering from 2 cm wide to 1 cm, are formed from a bundle of small fibers, loosely braided into small braids and wrapped by a tightly woven fiber band from which the tassels emerge. The tops of the bundled fibers are frayed, and the bottom ends of thc tassels are missing. The fragility of these fibers made it difficult to examine them thoroughly. However, under magnification it appeared that 18 tiny strands of fiber had been braided into 6 strands, which were then incorporated into the 3-plait braided tassels.

The third fiber fragment in Burial 6 displays a more complex braiding technique, familiar to modern fiber workers as a lanyard braid (http://www.youtube.com/watch?v=UT6u-uetGNY, accessed July 29, 2021). Lanyard braids commonly use from 4 to 16 plaits. Brose (1970b:73–76) discusses the few recorded examples of braided-cord-impressed motifs on ceramic vessels in *The Archaeology of Summer Island*. His schematic "reconstruction of a braided cord" and the photograph (Plate XI, "k") show a simple 4-plait lanyard braid.

Textile remains from other sites

In previous chapters, the Killarney Bay site has been identified as an early Middle Woodland site. Other archaeological sites from this period provide examples of textiles for comparison.

Hopewell textiles

The coarseness and weave of Killarney Bay textiles is similar to the few samples found in Ohio village contexts. Woven material from the Hopewell burial mounds, however, is consistently finer than either (David Brose, personal communication).

In her study of variability among 120 charred or copper-salts-preserved fabrics from three of the classic Ohio Hopewell Mounds (200 BCE–300 CE), Church (1984) correlates differences in technique and style to measures of social status. Omitting nearly 60 small or unprovenienced fragments, and ignoring the "wattle work" twined basketry, Church concentrated her measurements and descriptions on woven fabrics. She proposed that these represented sumptuary clothing (Church 1984:5–8). Church identified three or four major styles of fabric construction represented in varying frequencies in each of the different Hopewell mounds, but noted the predominance (half or more) of the spaced alternate-weft pair twining pattern. The spaced alternate-weft pair twining fragments recovered from the few Hopewell habitation sites then known were coarser in size and compactness than those in the mounds—a fact documented

Figures C.7, C.8, and C.9 (above). In Burial 4, there were several short pieces of twisted cord and leather thong with copper beads. Catalog number UMMAA 38515.

Figure C.10 (opposite page). A fiber fragment from Burial 6, possibly from the basket or bag shown in Figure C.6. Catalog number UMMAA 38503.

Figures C.11 and C.12. Fragments of braided tassels from Burial 6. Catalog number UMMAA 38503.

by Volney Jones (1936) 35 years earlier. Church assumed that the finer samples were more valuable to their makers, as their construction required a greater investment of time. She assumed that the finer textiles were a mark of higher status, but they might easily have been tied to other factors.

In addition, Church's assumption that fabric was associated with copper—previously identified as a marker of status (c.f. Greber 1976)—overlooked the fact that copper created an unusual geothermal environment for the preservation of organic remains. Looking beyond Church's assumptions, one might want to also consider the functionality of the finer weave—in other words, did the finer weave serve a particular use?

Textiles at the Boucher site

At the Boucher site, along the Missiquoi River near Lake Champlain, between the eighth and first centuries BCE, another unusual copper-salt-enriched environment preserved 99 examples of twined basketry, bags, burial shrouds, and fragments of uncertain function. In addition, there were 56 fragments of twisted cordage on which copper beads were strung (Heckenberger et al. 1996: Table 3.1). Most of the 43 flexed and 17 multiple cremation burials of all ages were accompanied by rolled, tapered copper beads similar to those at Killarney Bay (Chapter 12). The points recovered at Boucher resembled early Adena types, similar to those found at Killarney Bay, and some were chipped of Midwestern chert (Heckenberger et al. 1996:52).

Almost all of the fabrics at Boucher—Adovasio and Heckenberger use the terms fabric and textile interchangeably (ibid. p. 57)—incorporated twining of some sort. Eighty-four percent of the twining was simple open twining with single and (rarely) paired Z- or S-twisted 2-row wefts and S- or Z- twisted cord-wrapped warps, both about 1 mm in diameter. Some textile fragments included 3-ply braided or plaited elements. Most of the relatively thin and tightly twisted 2-ply Z-spun S-twist cords were made of milkweed or Indian hemp, while the majority of textile wefts and warps were basswood bast (ibid. p 56, Table 3.2, 3.3).

Nearly all bags were made with open and diagonal twining, with two rows of paired wefts and warps. On the other hand, shrouds, which are assumed to be clothing, tended to be open simple twining. These were wrapped with strands of copper beads, around individuals wearing long hide shirts. Some small bags (ca. 15 cm x 20 cm) appeared to have hide linings. One of these (Feature #41) contained several large Lake Superior copper nuggets, while another (on the chest of a female burial) contained the mollusk shells and the bones of a small mammal, possibly representing a medicine bag (Heckenberger et al. 1996:65–69).

The Late Riverside Cemetery site

The investigators noted how very similar the Boucher site textiles were to those from other sites in the Upper Great Lakes (Petersen 1996a), especially the spun and twisted cordage and textile fragments from the partially looted Old Copper and/or Red Ochre and early Middle Woodland burials at the Late Riverside Cemetery site. This site, located where the Menominee River empties into Green Bay, is in the northwest Lake Michigan drainage basin (c.f. King 1978). As at Boucher, Riverside Cemetery site radiocarbon dates suggest episodic reuse of burial grounds from the early tenth through the late third centuries BCE. During the latter years of use, a large block of obsidian from Obsidian Cliff on the upper Yellowstone River was carried to the site (Brose and Hambacher 1999:173; Robertson et al. 1999), surely another indication of the ceremonial and sacred importance of this location.

Conclusion

Only at Killarney Bay do we discover the opportunity to match the functional nature of the textile (volume and load-bearing capacity) with its careful placement in the burial. That is, the textile from Burial 6 indicates that the inhabitants of Killarney Bay were involved in the practical questions of physics as well as those of status and decoration.

The Burial 6 textile was sturdy enough to carry the weight of the 38 flint cache blades, plus a long bone and skull and mandible fragments. We know that it was deliberately placed in the burial so that all of the blades were aligned with the bag's warp and all the tips were pointed.

Analysis of this textile reminds us that elements that appear to be merely ornamental are often in fact functional.

Appendix D
ICP-MS Analysis of Artifacts

Balz Kamber and Darrel G. F. Long

Inductively coupled plasma mass spectroscopy (ICP-MS) analysis provides an effective means of characterizing the trace and rare earth (REE) element distribution patterns in many samples of archaeological interest, including chert (Kamber 2009; Kato et al. 2002; Kunimaru et al. 1988; Milne et al. 2009; Nadar et al. 2006; Olofsson and Rodushkin 2011; Segal et al. 2005; Speakman and Neff 2005). It has a distinct advantage over XRF analysis in requiring only a few micrograms of powdered or chipped material, hence allowing minimum destruction of rare artifacts. In addition, the method provides high-precision data at low detection limits for a much wider array of elements than XRF (e.g. Kamber 2009). The main limitation of chemical investigation of artifacts is that it relies on the existence or development of a library of geological reference data to be fully effective. It is also relatively expensive compared to conventional XRF analysis.

Chert is a particularly suitable material to analyze by ICP-MS because its main constituent (SiO_2) is vaporised upon chemical digestion with hydrofluoric acid. Therefore, digested chert is very low in residual salts, which allows for ICP-MS analysis at low apparent dilution factors (see Baldwin et al. 2011 for a full discussion of this analytical peculiarity). The net result is that trace elements at single digit parts per billion (ppb) concentrations in chert can still be analyzed with high (1–2 percent) precision. The data presented in this study were obtained with the same analytical protocol as reported in Baldwin et al. (2011).

Visual analyses of material from the Killarney Bay site indicate that the main geological source for chert used in artifact production is the Fossil Hill Formation (including Collingwood, Wiki, and Detour varieties), which makes up 88 percent of the curated collection by number and 89 percent by weight (see Chapter 10, this volume). Artifacts made from Hudson Bay Lowlands cherts (HBL), including material from the Ordovician Bad Cache Rapids Formation, the Silurian Severn River Formation, and the Devonian Stooping River Formation, make up 12 percent of the curated material by number and 10 percent by weight. Small quantities of more exotic, southern Ontario cherts have also been tentatively identified, including material possibly made from the Amabel, Bobcaygeon, Onondaga, Gull River, Lockport, and Kettle Point formations, which would have been available to the south in the area now forming the Bruce Peninsula (Figure D.1) and around the margins of the Michigan basin. Visual examination suggests that only 0.02

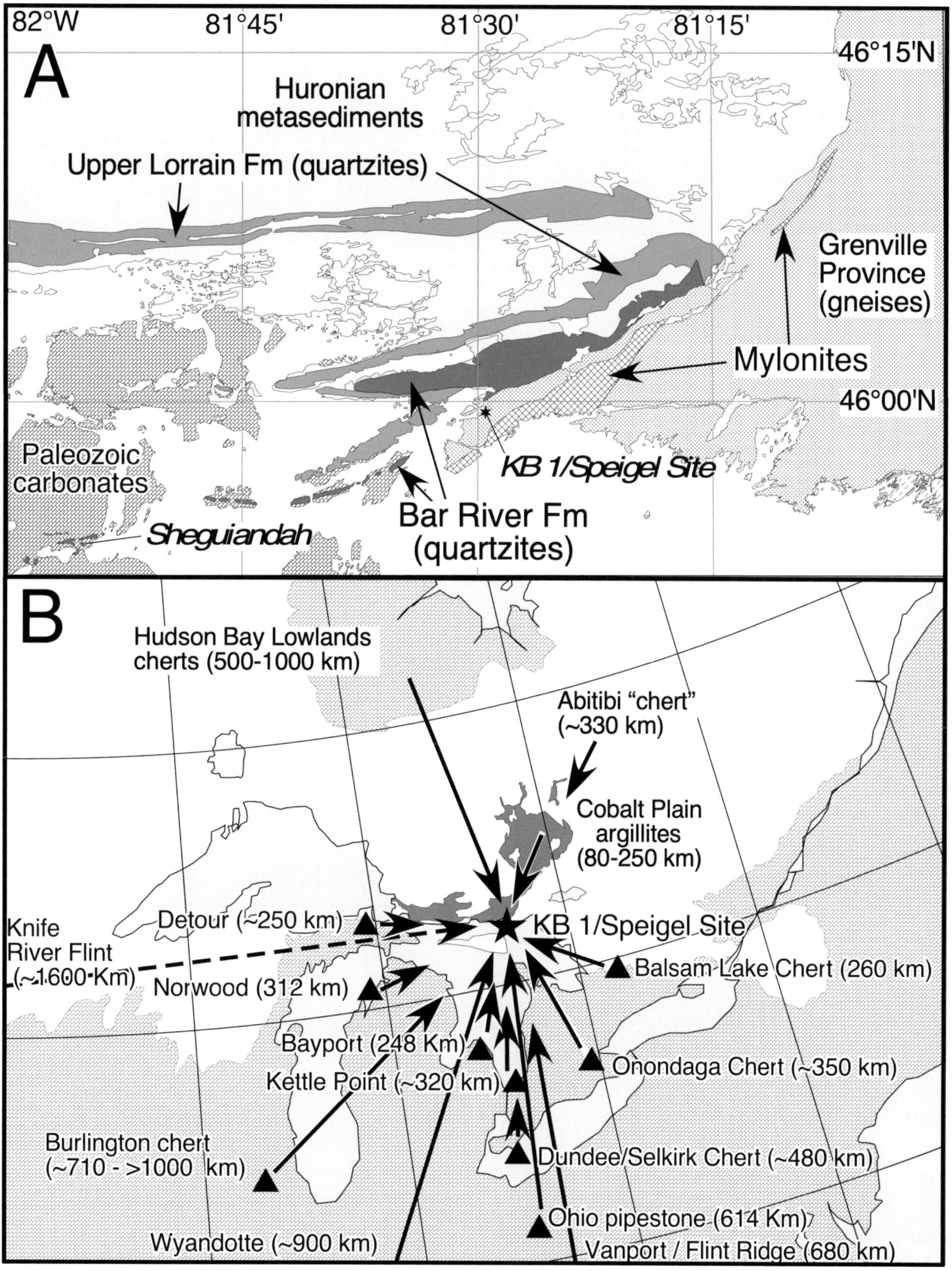

Figure D.1. Potential chert and lithic sources: A = Local, B = Regional.

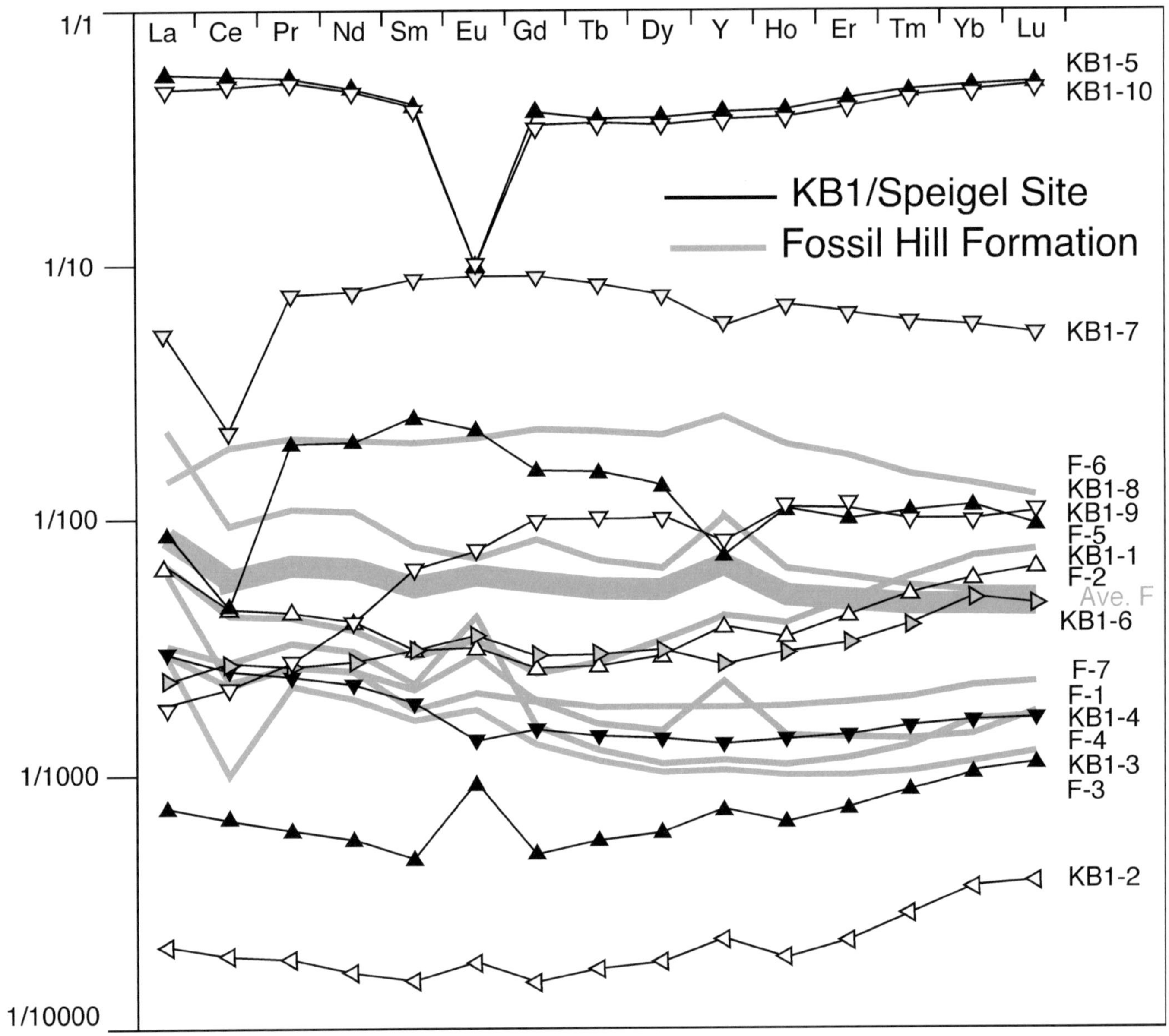

Figure D.2. Plots of selected artifacts from the KB-1/Speigel Site (black) compared with material from the Fossil Hill Formation, normalized to shale standard MuQ (Kamber et al. 2005).

percent of the artifacts fall into this category (0.05 percent by weight). Knife River Flint, which may have been traded over a wide area, was represented by only one sample in the curated collection (0.01 percent by number and weight). So-called "Gordon Lake chert" (a silicified Paleoproterozoic mudstone) made up 0.5 percent of the collection by number and 0.25 percent by weight.

In this study, solution-based ICP-MS analysis of ten representative artifacts from the Killarney Bay site, including a broad range of colors, is compared with three suites of geological samples. The geological samples are: six samples from the Fossil Hill Formation (Figure D.2); eight samples of HBL chert (Figure D.3); and seven samples of Knife River Flint (Figure D.4). No samples of Gordon Lake "chert" or other Great Lakes cherts were examined. Data for a total of 45 elements is reported and discussed in three separate sections. In the first section, straight visual comparison of the rare earth element (REE and Y) patterns is

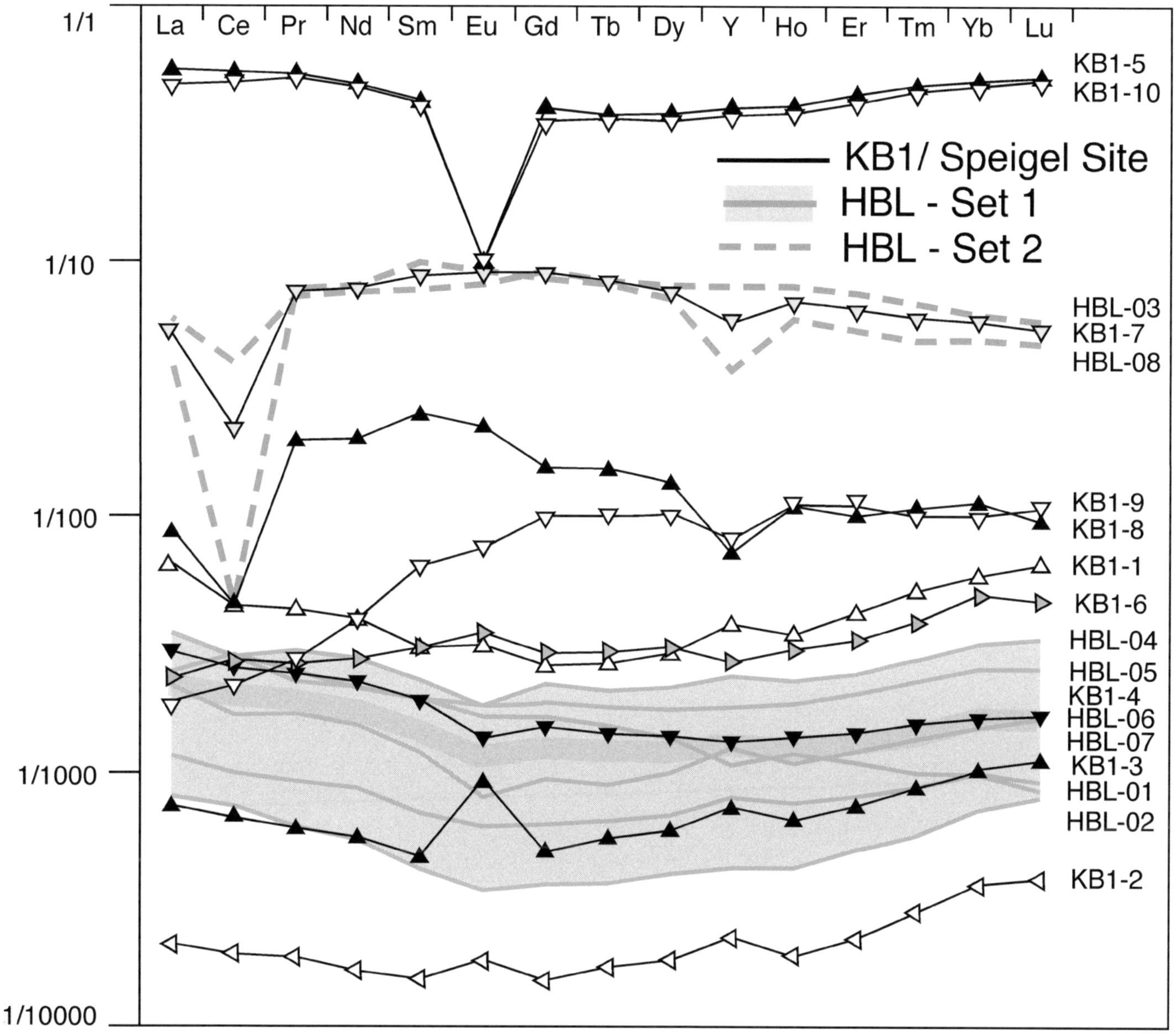

Figure D.3. Plots of selected artifacts from the KB-1/Speigel Site (black) compared with two groups of Hudson Bay Lowland material, normalized to shale standard MuQ (Kamber et al. 2005). Note that all of the larger group (dark gray) plots have a pronounced sag, with depletion of middle REEs, and that the two samples with higher REE concentrations (HBL-03 and 08 – in light gray with dashes) have slight LREE enrichment, with pronounced Ce and Y anomalies.

used to identify the most obvious and best matches between artifacts and geological samples. In the second section, the comparison is quantified using REE ratios. Finally, the comparison of ratios is expanded to further diagnostic trace elements.

In a first step, the REE+Y data are presented here normalized to the average composition of typical upper continental crust, represented by the Mud of Queensland (MuQ) composite alluvial sediment that was analyzed with the same analytical protocol (Kamber et al. 2005). As the trace element chemistry of chert largely mimics that of the associated water mass (Shields and Webb 2004), with minor modification from included terrigenous material, and diagenetic changes (Baldwin et al. 2011; Johannesson et al. 2006; Kamber and Webb 2007; Murray et al. 1991, 1992), the REE+Y diagrams can be used to visually characterize individual chert sources. Three diagrams were produced in which the artifact REE patterns were

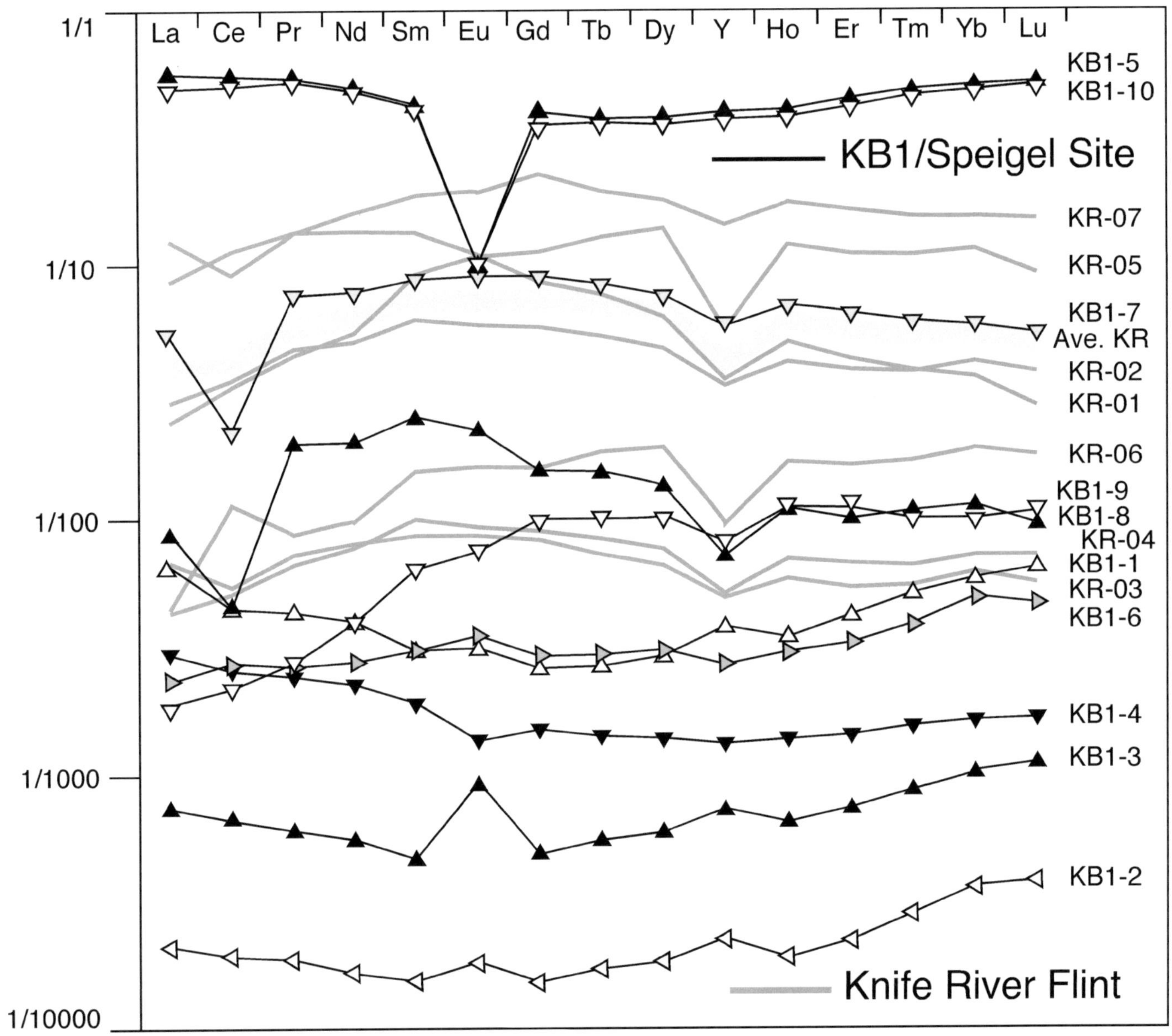

Figure D.4. Plots of selected artifacts from the KB-1/Speigel Site (black) compared with Knife River Flint material, normalized to shale standard MuQ (Kamber et al. 2005). Average REE concentrations in the KRF material are higher than most of the HBL material and have an upward bowed profile, indicative of postdepositional modification.

superimposed over the three geological suites (Figures D.2, D.3, and D.4).

By comparison with typical open marine cherts, the REE+Y patterns for Fossil Hill samples (Figure D.2) are more enriched in the LREE (light rare earth element), resulting in a relatively flat overall average pattern (thick gray line in Figure D.2). They have both minor positive and negative yttrium (Y) anomalies, and minor negative cerium (Ce) anomalies. These features are typical for chert deposited in an oxygenated but restricted marine basin. Of the artifacts, KB1-1 and KB1-6 have marked LREE enrichment, with profiles that closely match sample F-5 (from Manitoulin Island). Their patterns are so similar that this source is closely indicated by REE+Y evidence alone.

Sample KB1-4 has a spectrum that resembles Fossil Hill samples F1, F3, F4, and F7 in many aspects, but also matches many features of Hudson Bay Lowlands sample HBL-02 (Figure D.3), which has a matching slightly negative Eu anomaly. Sample KB1-2 has a similar spectrum, with much lower overall concentration of REEs, so although it could be argued that it was worked from a more silica rich variety of Fossil Hill material, it is more likely (as is KB1-4) to be a variant of the larger group of HBL material, having a closer total REE content, and a middle REE (MREE) deficiency (marked by a downward sag), closely matching sample HBL-02 (Figure D.3).

Geological samples from the Hudson Bay Lowland collections fall into two distinct groups (Figure D.3). The first (larger group), including samples HBL-1 to 2 and 4 to 7, is characterized by flat to concave patterns (MREE depletion), with very low total REE concentrations and no marked Ce or Y anomalies. The second group (HBL-3 and 8) has flat REE patterns, with much higher total REE concentrations than both the first group and all of the Fossil Hill Samples. In addition, they have marked negative Ce and Y anomalies. Sample KB1-8 closely resembles samples HBL-5 and 8 in both form and total REE concentration, and so is considered to match the smaller group of HBL samples. Sample KB1-3 has a profile and REE concentrations falling into the larger group of HBL material (Figure D.3).

Geological samples from the Knife River Flint typically have concentrations of REEs that are an order of magnitude higher than the average for Fossil Hill Material (Figure D.4). The average curve has a flat to slightly positive bowed pattern (suggesting some MREE enrichment), with minor HREE enrichment. The spectra typically exhibit pronounced negative Y and, to a lesser extent, Ce anomalies. Sample KB1-9 has a similar profile to KR-06, but with a slightly lower REE concentration. Sample KB1-7 closely matches the average curve for Knife River Flint but has a more pronounced negative Ce anomaly, suggesting that it is better correlated with the smaller HBL population.

Samples KB1-5 and KB1-10 are unlike any of the three analyzed sets of geological chert. The high concentration of REE elements and the generally flat pattern suggests that these may be silicified mudstones rather than chert. A strong negative Eu anomaly, as seen in these curves, is typical of mudstones derived from deeply weathered crustal sources (Nyakairu and Koeberl 2001; Taylor and McLennan 1985). This material may be from the so-called Gordon Lake "cherts." These are very fine-grained quartz-lutites (siliceous mudstones) from the Proterozoic Huronian Supergroup. They are abundant locally to the northwest of the Killarney Bay site (Figure D.1-A) in strata between the Bar River and Lorrain Formations.

Johannesson et al. (2006) have suggested that a number of REE element ratios (Ce/Ce*; Pr/Pr*; Gd/Gd*; Eu/Eu*; La/Yb; Pr/Yb; Gd/Yb; Y/Ho) can be useful for distinguishing chert types. Average Ce/Ce*, Pr/Pr*, and Gd/Gd* ratios are typically not diagnostic of any of the chert sources examined, due to substantial overlap (Table D.1, Figure D.5).

Average Ce/Ce* is 0.70 (range 0.38–1.09) in the Fossil Hill material, 0.89 (range 0.70–1.71) for Knife River Flints, and 0.90 (range 0.08–1.22) for the larger group of HBL cherts. The two HBL chert samples with marked negative Ce and Eu anomalies do have a distinct ratio of 0.35 (range 0.08–0.60) that distinguishes them from the other geological sources documented. Artifacts KB1-1 and KB1-6, identified above as having a probable source in the Fossil Hill Formation, have Ce/Ce* ratios of 0.82 and 1.10, which fall well within the documented range for the formation. Artifacts KB1-2, KB1-3, and KB1-4 have Ce/Ce* values of 0.97, 0.98, and 0.96, which are all close to the average for the larger group of HBL samples. Samples KB1-7 and KB1-8 have Ce/Ce* ratios of 0.86 and 0.30. The latter is consistent with a source in the smaller of the two HBL assemblages. The values for KB1-7 overlap with values obtained from the Fossil Hill, Knife River, and the larger HBL assemblages. The Ce/Ce* value (0.96) for sample KB1-9 (0.96) falls within the range of all the chert

Table D.1. Key geochemical shale-normalized ratios for geological and archaeological samples.

Sample	Ce/Ce*	Pr/Pr*	Gd/Gd*	Eu/Eu*	La/Yb	Pr/Yb	Nd/Yb	Gd/Yb	Y/Ho
GEOLOGICAL SAMPLES									
Fossil Hill Formation									
FH-1	0.504	1.086	1.164	1.128	4.452	1.798	1.735	1.310	1.640
FH-2	0.557	1.097	1.150	0.862	4.357	2.117	2.059	1.600	1.617
FH-3	0.379	1.485	1.004	1.222	2.685	1.959	1.758	1.151	1.041
FH-4	0.838	1.147	0.989	2.175	1.976	2.031	1.863	0.957	1.077
FH-5	0.761	1.064	0.881	1.214	0.947	0.584	0.516	0.346	1.090
FH-6	1.093	1.052	1.059	0.985	1.021	1.515	1.495	1.647	1.294
FH-7	0.762	1.138	0.985	1.438	1.355	1.206	1.143	0.868	1.001
Hudson Bay Lowlands chert									
HBL-1	1.220	0.909	0.983	0.906	2.501	2.337	2.190	1.682	0.898
HBL-2	1.046	0.951	0.962	0.870	1.145	0.859	0.758	0.514	1.004
HBL-3	0.600	1.257	1.114	0.971	0.987	1.180	1.227	1.501	1.015
HBL-4	0.896	1.050	1.001	0.798	1.094	0.933	0.869	0.680	1.075
HBL-5	0.912	1.054	0.948	0.855	1.329	1.159	1.064	0.735	0.975
HBL-6	0.846	1.076	0.950	0.735	1.451	1.146	1.031	0.623	1.205
HBL-7	0.901	1.037	0.958	0.902	1.229	0.975	0.886	0.659	1.043
HBL-8	0.077	1.841	0.993	0.998	0.825	1.541	1.583	1.718	0.625
Knife River flint									
KR-1	1.031	1.096	0.896	0.995	2.406	3.766	3.694	2.371	0.711
KR-2	0.935	1.088	1.014	0.986	0.694	1.133	1.228	1.370	0.815
KR-3	0.776	1.091	1.057	1.042	1.082	1.180	1.285	1.312	0.830
KR-4	0.932	1.045	1.018	0.999	0.586	0.938	1.084	1.221	0.734
KR-5	0.988	1.021	0.972	1.034	0.212	0.396	0.476	1.007	0.465
KR-6	1.711	0.829	0.913	1.044	0.232	0.461	0.520	0.836	0.561
KR-7	0.701	1.084	1.155	0.950	0.799	0.884	1.040	1.444	0.815
ARCHAEOLOGICAL SAMPLES									
KB-1	0.815	1.029	0.928	1.073	1.131	0.737	0.671	0.438	1.111
KB-2	0.974	1.032	0.926	1.232	0.587	0.519	0.468	0.420	1.203
KB-3	0.982	1.003	0.921	1.922	0.712	0.587	0.532	0.468	1.119
KB-4	0.962	1.024	0.957	0.810	1.778	1.541	1.414	0.921	0.962
KB-5	1.001	1.033	0.982	0.250	1.120	1.069	0.974	0.771	1.008
KB-6	1.100	0.960	0.954	1.167	0.472	0.533	0.558	0.586	0.893
KB-7	0.859	1.037	0.875	1.015	0.578	0.421	0.383	0.392	1.118
KB-8	0.303	1.633	0.836	1.111	0.779	1.741	1.751	1.369	0.650
KB-9	0.956	0.859	1.129	0.934	0.186	0.258	0.389	0.967	0.689
KB-10	0.999	1.056	0.961	0.242	1.009	1.047	0.956	0.733	0.988

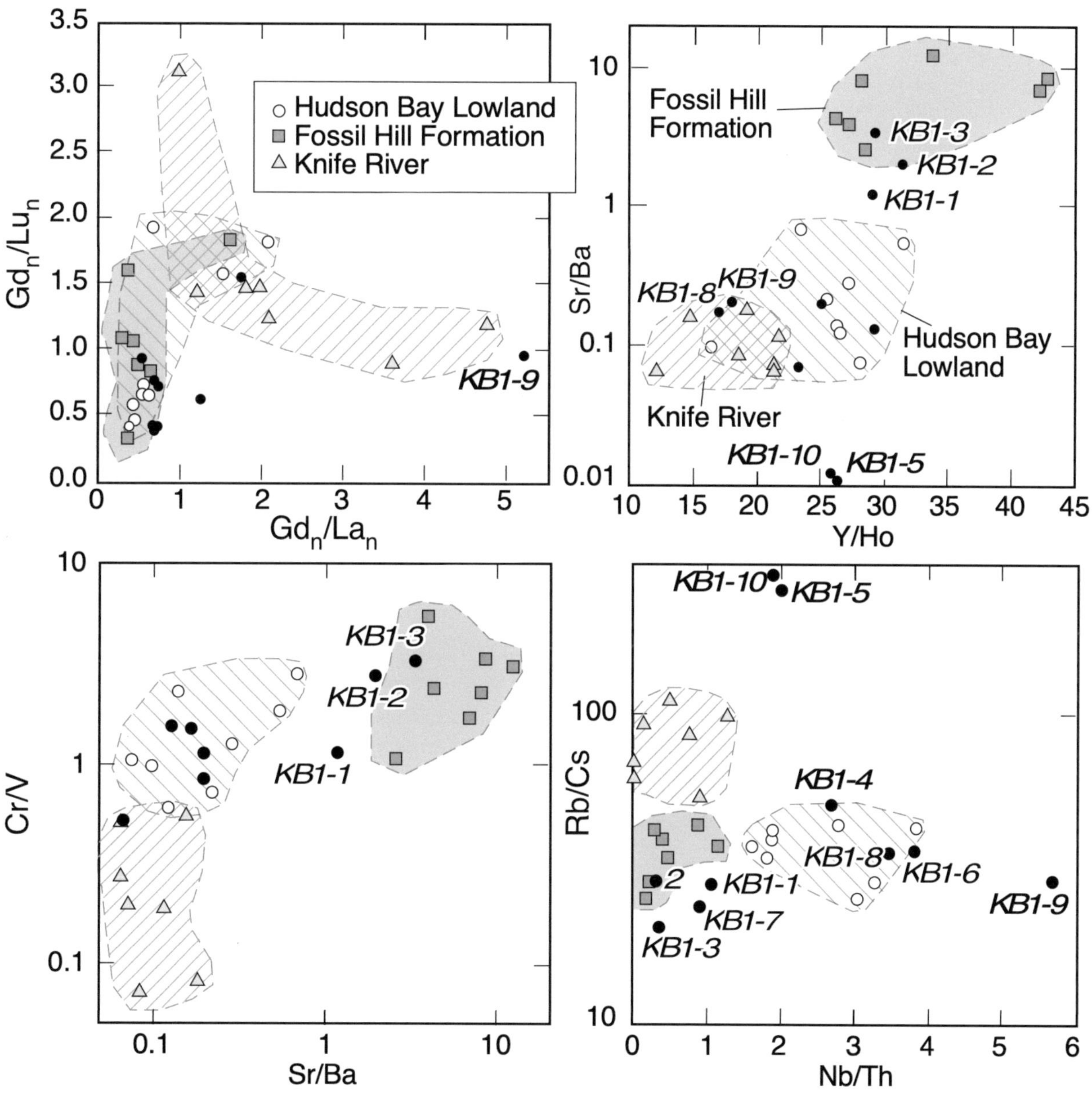

Figure D.5. Cross-plots of selected elements that may be useful for distinguishing local artifact sources.

Table D.2. Potential chert sources based on REE+Y data.

Sample	Closest pattern	Best geochemical match
KB-1	F-5	Fossil Hill Formation
KB-2	HBL-02	Hudson Bay Lowlands (large set)
KB-3	HBL-01, HBL-02	Hudson Bay Lowlands (large set)
KB-4	HBL-04	Hudson Bay Lowlands (large set)
KB-5	None	Gordon Lake "chert"
KB-6	F-5	Fossil Hill Formation
KB-7	HBL-05, HBL-08	Hudson Bay Lowlands (small set)
KB-8	HBL-05, HBL-08	Hudson Bay Lowlands (small set)
KB-9	KR-06	Knife River Flint
KB-10	None	Gordon Lake "chert"

groups examined, except for the smaller of the two HBL groups, so it is not especially diagnostic.

Eu/Eu* values can be used to confirm identification of material derived from the larger group of HBL material (average = 0.879, range 0.735–0.998). The three samples identified as part of the larger HBL group have values starting from within this range (0.81 to somewhat higher). Eu/Eu* ratios of other groups are not diagnostic.

Y/Ho ratios may be useful for identifying samples of Knife River flint (average = 0.69, range 0.46–0.83). Values for the Fossil Hill material average 1.31 (range 1.00–1.64). The larger group of HBL material has an average value of 1.03 (range 0.90–1.21), and the smaller group has an average of 0.82 (range 0.63–1.02). The one sample tentatively identified as potentially being made of Knife River material (KB1-9) has a Y/Ho ratio that is the same as the average for that source and is outside of the range of the other chert sources.

Conclusions

The analysis of ten artifacts from the Killarney Bay site confirms the presence of two artifacts sourced from the Fossil Hill Formation, five from two distinct populations of HBL chert, and one from Knife River material (Table D.2). It is also hypothesized that two samples were derived from chert look-alikes from the Gordon Lake Formation, although, as no bedrock samples were analyzed, this is not proven. There is a clear difference in the proportion of artifact sources from that predicted by the visual analysis (see Chapter 10, this volume). This may be due to selection of cherts for a range of colors rather than for representative abundance. The identification of two samples of Gordon Lake "chert" (siltstone) indicate that optical analysis alone may not be sufficient to identify this material. ICP-MS analysis does provide a viable method for characterization of the curated artifacts, but the results would be improved by analyzing a greater number of artifacts and a broader range of potential source materials.

Appendix E

Pollen Stratigraphy of MTO Swamp, Killarney, Ontario

Patrick Julig and John H. McAndrews

This project was designed by Patrick Julig; he supplied sediment samples, together with a stratigraphic diagram, and funded the pollen analysis. Charlie Turton counted the pollen and made insightful comments. Jock McAndrews organized the analysis, produced the graphics, and wrote the interpretive report.

Although deposition was not continuous, the 170 cm thick deposit shows the four regional pollen zones and thus spans the last 12,000 years. There was no pollen of wild rice (*Zizania*).

Introduction

Wild rice (*Zizania*) is an aquatic grass (Poaceae) with edible seeds that, although important in aboriginal cuisine, produce virtually no fossils. In contrast, the distinctive pollen, with a relatively large diameter (28-38 μm) and psilate surface (McAndrews et al. 1973), may be super-abundant in lake sediment (McAndrews 1969). Stratigraphic pollen analysis shows that in some places wild rice grew adjacent to archaeological sites of Woodland (McAndrews 1969; Lee et al. 2004) and Archaic periods (McAndrews 1984; Yu and McAndrews 1994), implying that these prehistoric peoples harvested the wild rice.

The Ministry of Transportation of Ontario (MTO) Swamp borders the Killarney Bay site, a Middle Woodland archaeological site whose function is speculative. The swamp (which was a flooded bay during the occupation of the Killarney Bay site) may have supported wild rice, an attractive seasonal food. The objective was to generally analyze fossil pollen for a chronology and in particular to search for pollen of wild rice.

Methods

Eighteen samples were submitted from 45 59.480N, 81 29.359W. Each sample was dispersed in warm dilute KOH and then sieved to obtain the 250 to 15-μm size fraction,

Fawn Lake

fawn.pol October 29, 2008, Zicheng Yu, analyst   Ontario, 45.42N, 79.38W

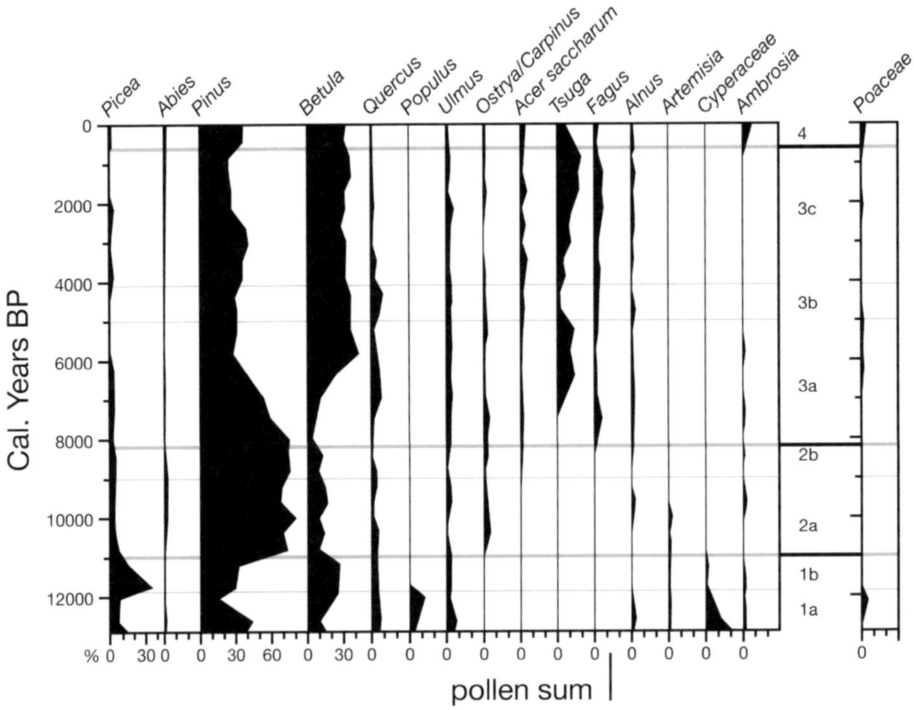

MTO Swamp Killarney ON

mtoswamp.pol June 16, 2010. C.L. Turton, analyst.

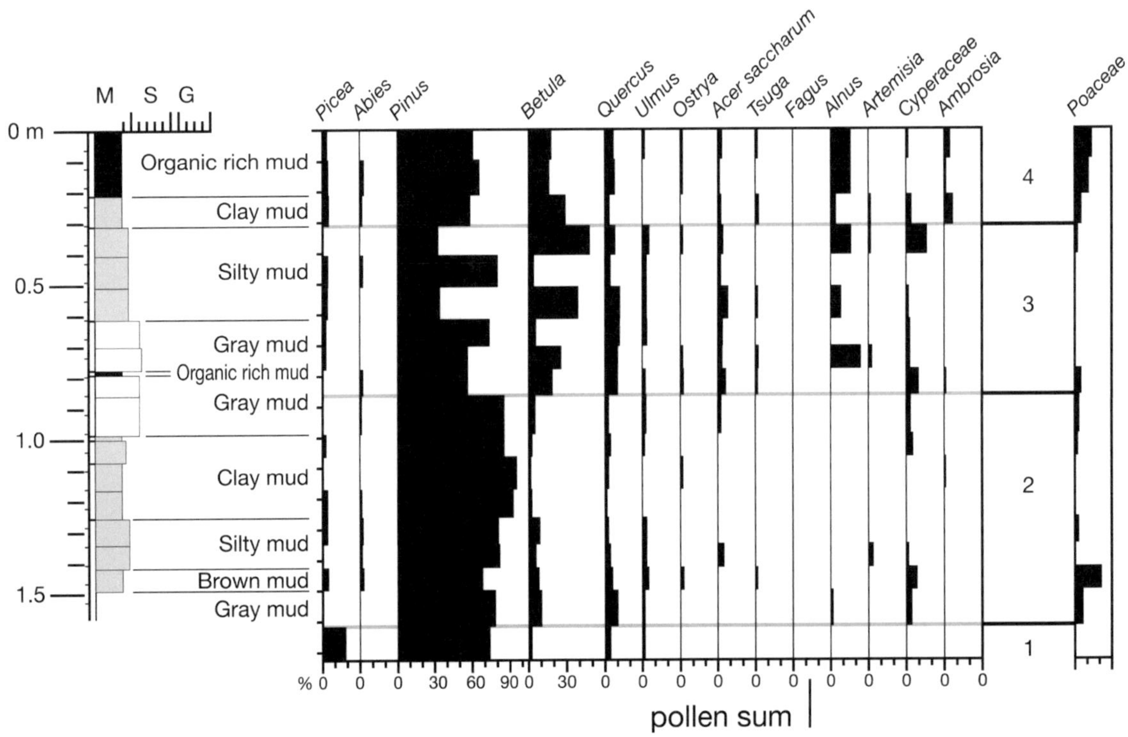

stained with safraine and mounted on microscope slides with glycerin. One-hundred tree pollen was counted, together with herb pollen and pteridophyte spores. In the one sample (142–150 cm) with a peak of grass pollen, the diameters of 50 individual grass pollen were measured to the nearest micrometer on an enlarged monitor image.

Results

There were four lithological units in the 170 cm thick section that bottomed at 170 cm. Gray sand at 170–150 cm and 100–60 cm (Figure E.1a) perhaps represents Lake Algonquin and Lake Nipissing with the intervening and overlying clay, silt and mud deposited in an isolated basin.

As expected, pine dominated the well-preserved pollen flora. The four regional pollen zones (Figure E.1a) correlate with the diagram from Fawn Lake (Figure E.1b) but the subzones cannot be distinguished. There may be a hiatus between zones 2 and 3. Three radiocarbon dates anchor the Fawn Lake calibrated-year chronology.

The small Poaceae (grass) peak in Figure E.1a at 142–150 cm has a size distribution (Figure E.2) too small to be wild rice.

Discussion

We were surprised that all four pollen zones were represented by sediment. We were disappointed that there was no wild rice.

Conclusion

It is likely that the MTO Swamp never supported wild rice.

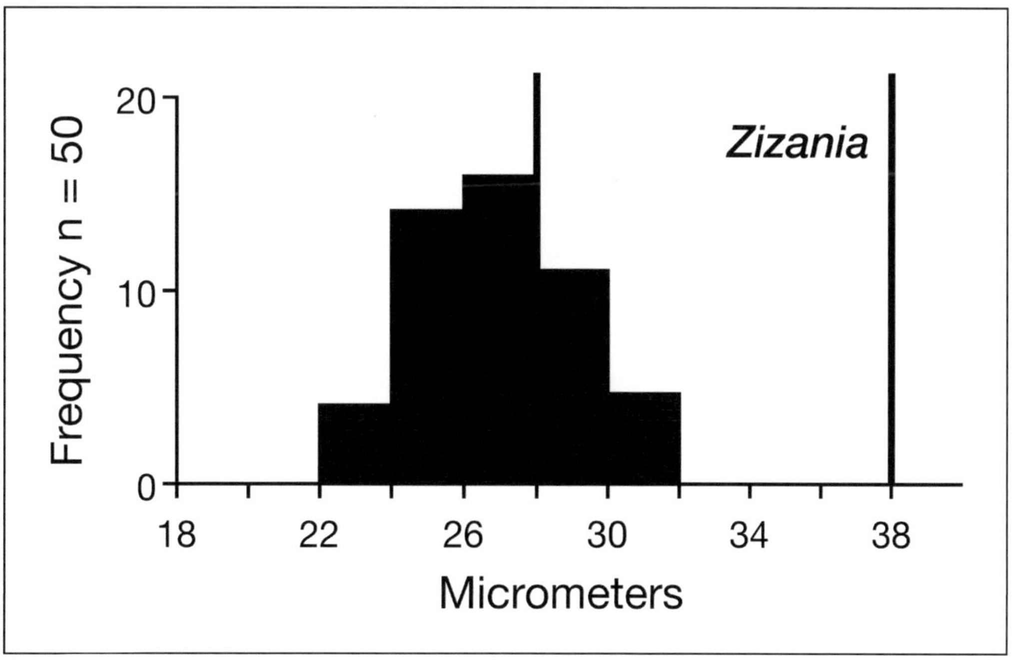

Figure E.1 (opposite page). Diagram showing results of pollen analysis from a swamp in close proximity to Killarney Bay. No evidence of wild rice (*Zizania palustrus*) was identified. *a* (top). Main pollen diagram from Fawn Lake. For detail, see the North American Pollen Database. *b* (bottom). Lithology and main pollen stratigraphy for MTO Swamp.

Figure E.2 (above). Size distribution for 50 Poaceae pollen from MTO Swamp level 142–150. The vertical lines represent *Zizania* 903% size distribution.

Appendix F

A Summary of the Schlegel Site Report

Kristin Thor

2008

The Schlegel site (BfGw-6) is a Middle Woodland site on southeastern Georgian Bay that consists of a collection excavated by the landowners in 1962. The Schlegel site lies approximately 10 m above the present average Lake Huron water level (176 meters asl) on a small peninsula in the community of Honey Harbor. Radiometric dating places the site between 55 BC and AD 125. At the time of habitation, the higher waters of Georgian Bay would have flooded the marsh area to the south and created an island of the peninsula, making it an ideal campsite, habitation, or mortuary location protected from the open waters of Georgian Bay.

The site appears to be the burial of one or possibly two individuals, and possibly a habitation component based on chert debitage. Although the only human remains recovered was a single human molar, various artifacts and exotic cherts interpreted as grave goods from the Adena/Middlesex mortuary complex burial were uncovered. This includes the presence of red ochre and artifacts such as copper beads, numerous bifaces made from exotic raw materials, cache blades, ground argillite ornaments, an argillite gorget preform, and three blocked-end tubes. Exotics included cherts from Ohio, Illinois, and Michigan and quartzite from central Québec.

Few Middle Woodland sites with Adena-like assemblages have been identified this far north in the Great Lakes region, and the verification of the date of this site extends our knowledge of the range of the Adena-like influence in northeast Lake Huron. The artifact assemblage bears a very close resemblance to that found at the Killarney Bay site. Other finds along the Hwy 69 corridor in the Honey Harbor area show Middle Woodland use for habitations and the manufacture of ground stone Gowganda argillite artifacts like gorgets, likely destined for trade to southern sites (Dodd 1996:1).

Site background and excavation

Prior to excavations, the Schlegel site surface area had produced much chert debitage in sandy beach deposits, and a few artifacts, such as one biface and a diamond-shaped, black polished stone ornament. A prominent sand mound 1.8 m in height and 6 to 9 m in diameter was recorded (Schlegel 1970:1). This was originally believed to be a beach deposit. During house building and leveling of the sand mound, a large boulder was uncovered beneath the mound. The owners assumed that the "mound" was a natural ancient beach and sand dune deposit around the large boulder (Schlegel 1970:2). However, in retrospect, this mound may have been a mortuary feature or burial mound such as that found at Killarney Bay (Julig and Long, Chapter 2, this volume). Although they were not professional archaeologists, the Schlegel family used good field methods, including screening the sand through 1/8-inch mesh and keeping accurate records of the excavation. They also curated the collection carefully for about four decades, until it was analyzed by the author, Kristin Thor.

The site contained three artifact concentrations, approximately 2 m apart, interpreted as representing two mortuary areas and a campfire/habitation area (Areas 1-3, Figure F.1). Investigators found Area 1 when digging a refuse pit in 1961, and excavations revealed an area stained with red ochre, 10 chert bifaces, pieces of a broken clay tube pipe, a stone "skinning tool" or adze, and 5 or 6 copper beads approximately 60 cm below the surface (Figures F.2 and F.3). The tubular pipe pieces mend to form approximately 80% of the original tube. The subsequent 1962 excavations produced a second cluster of artifacts (Area 2). Area 2 contained the remains of a fringed hide pouch, a small leather pouch, a large oval quartzite biface, a large mass of copper, copper beads, two argillite ornaments, and two more clay tube pipes, one of which was intact (Figures F.4, F.5, and F.6). The native copper in the pouch remnants produced copper sulfates, which acted as a preservative for the hide. The immediate surrounding area contained numerous chert bifaces and copper beads. The Schlegels believed that all of these items may have at one time been the contents of the pouch, and over time, as the pouch disintegrated, the smaller artifacts became scattered in the immediate area.

Additional excavation trenches nearby exposed several firepit areas (stained features), and one area (Area 3) containing charcoal and chert debitage and a human tooth, which appears to be either a lower right or upper left molar. The artifacts were within 10 cm of the surface in an area approximately 1.8 m in diameter. The excavators did not find any formed tools in the hearth areas, but it is possible that the discarded chert debitage may have contained small unidentified utilized flakes or thumbnail scrapers. No ceramics were recovered in the excavations.

Subsequent to the excavation, James V. Wright visited the site and viewed the artifacts in the collection. His field notes, which are on file at the Museum of Civilization in Gatineau, Québec, comment on the similarity of the Schlegel artifacts to the burial artifacts found at Killarney Bay (Wright 1968). The Schlegel family curated the artifact collection for the next four decades with no additional analysis (Figure F.7). In 2006, the author analyzed the collection for an undergraduate thesis at Laurentian University (Thor 2006), under the supervision of Patrick Julig.

Lithic artifact analysis

Initial identifications of the biface raw materials were through visual inspection by Jack Holland (Holland Lithics Lab in Buffalo), Patrick Julig, Jeff Bursey, and Bill Fox, and by reference to geological samples at Laurentian University for distant and exotic cherts and quartzite.

The existing lithic assemblage consists of 46 items, including points, bifaces, triangular cache blades, scrapers, a gorget preform, ground stone ornaments, and an adze. Most (> 90%) are bifaces. Measurement parameters for the chipped lithics follow the methods of Callahan (1979) and Julig (1994) in identification of the biface stage of production. The excavation originally uncovered a large amount of chipping debitage, which the owners considered unimportant and unfortunately eventually discarded. The debitage ranged in size from very small flakes up to pieces 10 cm in length. A photograph of the debitage in the Schlegel's report is all that remains and is estimated at about 300 items, so it is certain that lithic manufacture and maintenance occurred at the site.

The percentages of the raw materials of the lithic tools by number include Fossil Hill chert (28 percent) and Kettle Point chert (22 percent), which account for 50 percent of the lithics by number. By weight, Burlington chert (36 percent) and Gowganda argillite (14 percent) account for 50 percent of the lithic material due to a large gorget preform, a large biface, and an adze. Janusas (1984:85) reports that Kettle Point chert reached its maximum occurrence in assemblages during the Early Woodland Period in Ontario, averaging 23

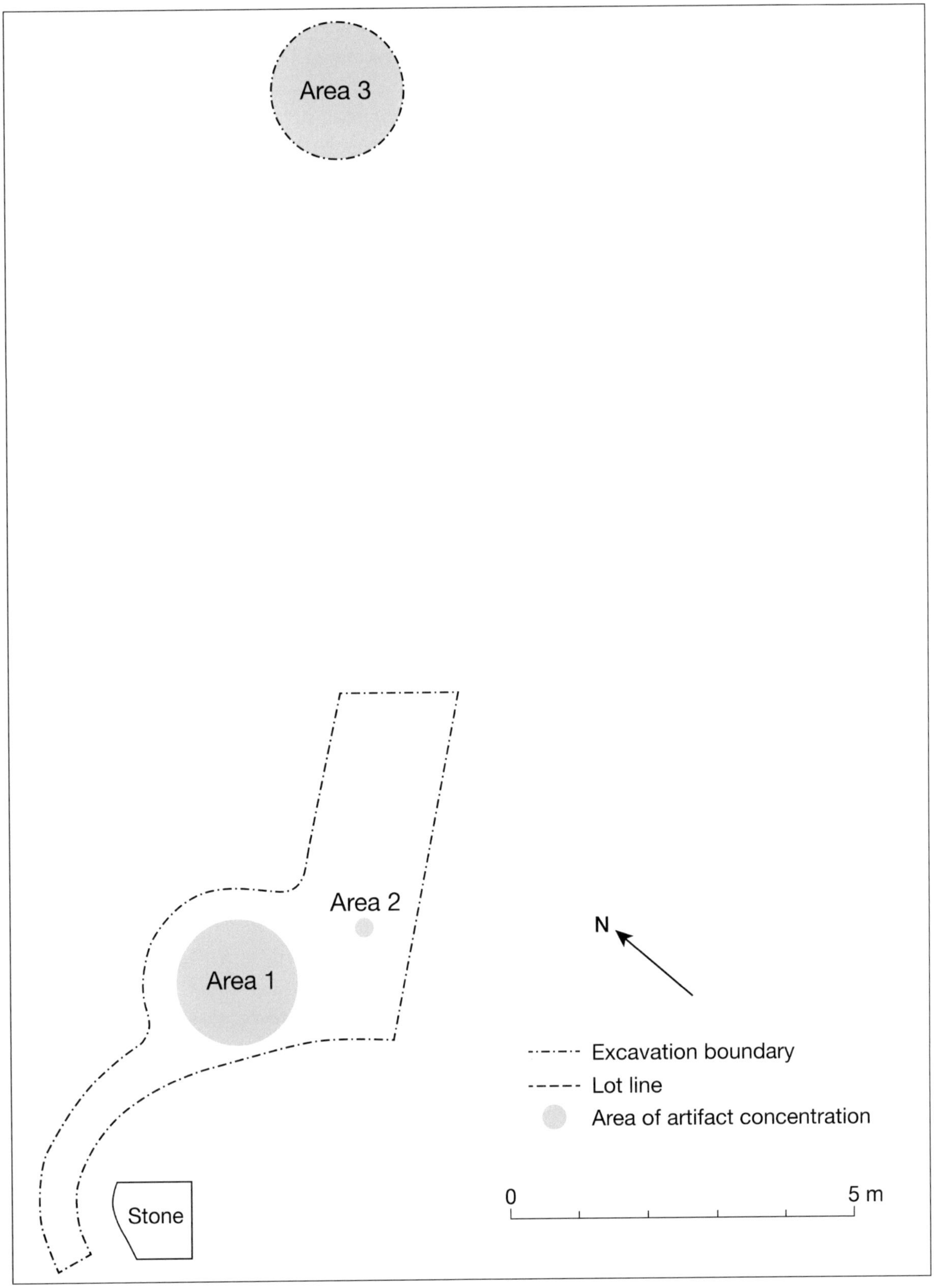

Figure F.1. Excavation map of the Schlegel site (Schlegel 1970).

Figure F.2. Preliminary finds from Area 1 (refuse pit): chert bifaces, adze or skinning tool, and a pipestone tube. Photograph by Kristin Thor.

percent of the total. At 22 percent, the Schlegel site fits the model quite nicely.

A significant feature of Middle Woodland Period mortuary complex sites is the presence of exotic raw materials, indicating the existence of long-distance trade patterns (Spence et al. 1990:139). Relatively local materials include quartz, mudstone, argillite, Fossil Hill chert, and Kettle Point chert, all found within 200 km of the site. Some artifacts were made of materials from more distant sources (greater than 200 km), including Bayport, Detour, and Onondaga cherts. Exotic raw materials such as Flint Ridge, Burlington, and Wyandotte (also known as Indiana hornstone) cherts originated in Ohio, Indiana, Illinois, and Iowa. Mistassini quartzite came from central Quebec. The procurement of these materials would have likely been part of extensive trade routes and patterns. Although local materials account for the bulk of the assemblage by both number and mass, exotic materials also account for a significant portion, representing 17 percent by number and 47 percent by mass. Three large exotic bifaces explain the high representation of exotics by mass. It is important to note that the Ohio pipestone blocked end tube pipes discussed later are not included here, but are also made from exotic lithic material.

Bifaces and preforms

Various biface forms comprise the bulk of the Schlegel assemblage, including 5 chert side-notched convex-based points and 2 triangular cache blades made from Flint Ridge and Onondaga chert, and various other biface forms and preforms. Most bifaces were found in Area 2. A large burnt corner-notched Onondaga point was found on the

Figure F.3. Preliminary finds from Area 1 (refuse pit): chert bifaces. Photograph by Kristin Thor.

property prior to the excavation and thus lacks provenience information. This specimen and a cache blade in Area 2 are the only two burnt items in the entire assemblage.

Area 1 Bifaces

Biface preforms include one of very distant Burlington chert showing evidence of use wear and residue deposits on the larger rounded end. An ovoid biface of Fossil Hill chert also had evidence of use wear. Eight additional bifaces were identified in Area 1, of which #35 and #39 have edge abrasions that may suggest they have been used as scrapers.

Area 2 Bifaces

Artifact #36, a beautifully crafted large oval biface, is one of the most unusual items of the lithic assemblage. Jack Holland (personal communication 2000) suggests that it was made from Mistassini quartzite from central Quebec. Comparison to a sample of Mistassini quartzite in the Laurentian Archaeology lab shows great resemblance, although Ramah quartzite from Labrador and Diana are also other possibilities. Both of the alternative suggestions originate in northern Labrador. Ramah chert artifacts from the Early Woodland period have been found in the Gatineau region along the Ottawa River system (Pilon 2000). The quartzite is fine grained and a dark gray color, changing to a brownish gray near the thinner edges. Patches on both surfaces are ochre and copper stained. The biface is oval in shape, with one end slightly pointed. An examination of the edges revealed dark staining, some dark residue, and micro chipping along most edges, suggesting that the artifact had been used.

Twenty-three additional bifaces were identified in Area 2, of which #32 and #33 have edge abrasions that may suggest they have also been used as scrapers. Raw materials for these bifaces included Kettle Point, Fossil Hill, Bayport, Burlington, Onondaga, and Detour chert. Several of the specimens displayed evidence of use wear. The raw materials came from relatively local sources such as Fossil Hill, sources at a moderate distance such as Kettle Point, and more distance sources from a very wide area of northeastern North America.

Additional specimens lacking provenience include a thick bifacially worked piece of exotic distant Burlington chert with a mean edge production angle of 60°, width to thickness ratio of 2.6, and rough flaking, suggesting it is an early stage biface preform. There is evidence of some use wear on the lateral edges near the more pointed end. Although the exact provenience of this biface is unknown, it was recovered during the 1962 excavations, which included trenches east and west of Area 2 and around Area 1. This find suggests that some "cache bifaces" may have been transported in an unfinished early stage of production and possibly used as tools.

Residues and edge wear on bifaces

All artifacts were examined under low-power binocular magnification (40x) for residues and use-wear patterns. Residue was present on 42 percent of the bifaces. Organic artifacts such as cordage and beaver fur are discussed later (and ^{14}C dating), but due to copper beads and copper sulfates there was enhanced organic preservation. All the objects exhibit signs of use wear based on low-power edge examination, including those without visible residue.

Analysis found that all of the presumed Stage 2 and 3 preforms appeared to be used as tools. This does not preclude them from functioning as manufactured preforms to be worked into points at a later date. Many of these fit the hand quite nicely as knives and have a preferred edge of use. Edge angles of production for Stage 2 and 3 bifaces tended to be slightly sharper than the ranges established for the corresponding stage of production based on width to thickness ratios as set out by Callahan (1979). The fact that Stage 2 and 3 bifaces were being used as knives might provide an explanation, as they are more easily used if they are slightly thicker in the body but still possess a thin sharp edge for cutting. However, if they were planned as mortuary items, this may be different from regular biface stage reduction processes. The residues may in future studies provide additional ^{14}C dates for the assemblage and possibly tool functional use and subsistence information.

Ground stone industry

Similar to other regional Middle Woodland sites, ground stone tools, ornaments, and specialized artifacts such as pipes are present at Schlegel. Some were manufactured locally or onsite and some were imported from a distance. Functional tools include an adze of silicified Precambrian Gowganda formation mudstone (D. Long, personal communication 2009). The adze underside is highly polished and flat, the top is rounded, the sides were ground to a rough trapezoidal cross-section, and it has a very sharp bit edge. The degree of polish on the poll end indicates that this is likely a handheld woodworking tool and not hafted.

Two ground stone pendants or pins from Area 2 are made from banded argillite, a material from the Gowganda Formation widely found in secondary deposits throughout this region of Ontario. They are tapered and beveled, and the flat sides are polished with a crosshatched pattern. One is drilled at the center of the wide end. The hole tapers in size to the center on both sides, with a diameter at the midpoint of about 5.0 mm. There are striations along the sides of the hole parallel to the edge, indicating a circular drilling action.

Both pendants are a dark greenish gray, with surfaces that are slightly ochre stained in places. The dark areas appear to be the result of residue, as there are areas where the dark discoloration is only present in the grinding scar lines. The drilled hole may indicate that this ornament was worn as a pendant, although there is no exceptional wear on the edges of the hole. It could also have functioned as a pin or toggle for clothes or a bag latch. It is very similar to those from Killarney Bay site. A second specimen is not drilled on the wide end, indicating that it not a pendant. It is difficult to ascertain the use of this item. Approximately one-third of the way from the point, the edges are much more rounded, possibly suggesting wear from rubbing due to use as a toggle of some sort or as a pin in a "cup and pin" game. It could also have served as an awl for soft materials or for separating fibers during basket weaving or net making. At the Killarney Bay site basketry is present, as well as similar awls and pendants. Ground stone gorgets are common on Middle Woodland sites and were manufactured on sites

Figure F.4. Excavations in 1962 uncovered Area 2 at the Schlegel site. Among the artifacts were pipestone tubes, copper beads, a quartzite biface, and argillite ornaments. Photograph by Kristin Thor.

Figure F.5. Beaver hide cordage from the Area 2 excavations. Photograph by Kristin Thor.

such as Killarney Bay. A preform in the Schlegel collection is made of banded Gowganda argillite and roughly formed in a "bowtie shape" but lacks provenience. The preform has a twist, which may have made it unsuitable for further finishing as a gorget by grinding.

Tubular pipes

The other major ground stone artifact class at Schlegel collection was made up of three blocked end tubes (pipes): two from Area 2 and one and large broken tube from Area 1. The greenish raw material was visually identified by Jack Holland as Ohio pipestone (personal communication 2000). Ohio pipestone is a silica-based rock and a member of the argillite family. These tubes are commonly called "blocked end" pipes, as there is a significant inner constriction close to the smaller end, which then widens again to the end of the tube. It has been reported that the centers of tube pipes were removed by circular drilling (Gehlbach 1994), showing striations perpendicular to the length of the tube. In all three Schlegel pipes, the tubes exhibited lengthwise striations running the full length of the interior surface, possibly widening a small drilled hole with lengthwise rasping. Low-power microscopy did not reveal any evidence of residue from use, so the use of the tubes is uncertain. Similar tubes from other Middle Woodland sites show evidence of being smoking pipes (Spence et al. 1990:138). It has also been suggested that a shaman may have used such tubes for ritual medicinal practices. The outside surfaces of the tubes are polished and are medium olive gray in color with slight ochre staining.

Two of the tubes were broken. It appears that one (shorter tube) may have originally been longer and then, when partially broken, may have had the broken edges polished to allow for continued use. Considering these tubes are made from "exotic" materials, repair for reuse seems a plausible option.

Organic remains: cordage and hide

The Schlegel collection contains fragments of a beaver hide pouch, cordage of beaver hair, and a portion of a small

Figure F.6. Beaver hide pouch fragments from the Area 2 excavations. Photograph by Kristin Thor.

leather pouch, all of which have been preserved by the copper that was contained within them (Wright 1968). They are all from Area 2. A collection of smaller (cache) bifaces found in close association may have originally been contained within the larger hide pouch (Schlegel 1970:4). Five beaver hide fragments with the fur intact form part of a fringed hide pouch. The cordage, which appears to be a fringe for the pouch, consists of a matted mass of approximately 17 cords. The construction of the cordage is a 4-ply twist—also known as a compound 2-ply twist (Hamilton et al. 1996:123)—and is made entirely of beaver hairs. The matted mass of cordage reveals that the cords alternate between a "Z" and "S" twist, as defined by Emery (1994:11).

The smaller leather pouch is stained green by the copper found within and measures approximately 5 cm in length along the sewn edge and 3 cm wide at the widest section. A running stitch of multi-ply "Z" twist fiber secures the raw edges of the pouch together. Preservation of organic material (including beaver fur) by copper was also found at the Killarney Bay site.

Copper artifacts

The collection includes a mass of native copper and 722 copper beads found in Area 2 in close association with the hide and leather pouches. Area 1 contained 5 or 6 copper beads, but these were lost and are not included in the existing artifacts (Schlegel 1970:3). The beads were situated close together in a small area and many were in small strings of 2 or 3 (W. Schlegel, personal communication 2010). It is likely that larger strings existed and the excavation digging damaged them. The mass of copper weighs 140.5 g and is composed of many small fragments. The copper is likely from the Lake Superior region, although no chemical analysis was performed.

Analysis of the copper bead collection was based on general morphology (and followed Anselmi, Chapter 12, this volume), identifying the beads as either tubular, round, ovoid or conical-trapezoidal, in both small and medium sizes based on the diameter measurement of the bead. Small bead diameters are within the range of 3 to 4 mm, and medium bead diameters measure approximately 5 to 7 mm. Several beads were too fragmentary for classification and are categorized as indeterminate. The beads were generally manufactured by rolling a cold- hammered thin strip of copper known as a bead blank around a form (Anselmi, Chapter 12, this volume; Ellis et al. 1990:89). The bead blank strip may be overlapped or butted and is often tapered and thinned at both ends (Anselmi, Chapter 12, this volume). Both types are present in the Schlegel bead collection.

Tubular beads are cylindrical in shape with squared edges. Ovoid beads are doughnut-like in shape with slightly flattened sides, resulting in a bulging ridge in the center of the circumference of the bead. Round beads are very similar to ovoid beads, but the sides present a more rounded shape and lack the obvious center ridge around the circumference. Conical trapezoidal beads are wider at one end than the other, resulting in a bell shape.

Medium beads total 688 and comprise 95 percent of the total bead collection, with the remaining 34 beads, or 5 percent, being small in size. Ovoid beads are the predominate form and account for approximately 76 percent of the total, with tubular representing 15 percent and round beads 8 percent. All three forms are present in both small and medium sizes. There is only 1 conical-trapezoidal bead and 2 that are indeterminate in form. Many of the copper fragments are partially worked and flattened, perhaps indicating that they are part of a bead maker's kit. The presence of such fragments has been interpreted as evidence for copper working localities at other sites (Martin 1999:172).

Date of the Schlegel site and comparison to other adjacent sites

The ^{14}C date of a beaver hide pouch sample from the Schlegel site by the IsoTrace Laboratory in Toronto (2005) is between 55 BC and AD 125 (calibrated), based on a confidence of 95.5 percent (1970 ± 50 BP uncalibrated). The calibrated dates suggest that the Schlegel site falls into the Middlesex complex of the Early Woodland Period (500 BC–0 BC) or the Point Peninsula complex of the Middle Woodland Period (200 BC–AD 900).

The Schlegel site bears a striking resemblance to three other Middle Woodland sites in that area of central and northeastern Ontario: Baxter, Bressette, and Killarney Bay. Distinctive artifacts include argillite gorget preforms (production/manufacturing), argillite "whetstones" or ornaments, exotic Ohio blocked-end tube pipes, copper beads and bead manufacture, red ochre, and cache bifaces with distant exotics. Blocked-end tubes and red ochre are generally only associated with burials sites. The Schlegel artifacts are most like those from the burial components of Killarney Bay, including the presence of beaver hide. The significant difference between these two sites is the complete lack of end scrapers at the Schlegel site and the large quantity recovered from Killarney Bay. However, Killarney Bay has both habitation and mortuary components. The uniface part of the Schlegel assemblage may also have been discarded along with the debitage. No ceramics were recovered at Schlegel, but it is possible that the site was only partly excavated.

Killarney Bay site and Schlegel are obviously very similar; the artifact assemblages at nearby Baxter and Bressette also show close similarities. These sites are in southern Georgian Bay, and they were surveyed and excavated in 1996 as part of the Highway 69 Corridor expansion (Dodd 1996:1; Lennox et al. 1994:38). Both are classified as Middle Woodland, and Baxter also has an Archaic component (Dodd 1996:1). The sites lie immediately west of Hwy 69, less than 10 km from the Schlegel site. Bressette is identified as a small camp dating between 300 BC and AD 700 (Dodd 1996:32). A wide variety of cherts are present at the site, including Detour (Michigan), Bayport, Kettle Point, Huronia, and Collingwood (Dodd 1996:50). At 24 percent of the total for tools, the more distant Detour chert appears to be the preferred material for tool manufacture (Dodd 1996:36). Dodd also found a ground argillite "whetstone" at the Bressette site. Baxter has an Early Archaic component, identified by the presence of a single bifurcated point (Dodd 1996:65), but the major component of the site dates between 100 BC and AD 200, based on pottery and the presence of argillite gorget and whetstone preforms, typical in Middlesex and Early Point Peninsula sites (Dodd 1996:112). The high incidence of argillite preforms indicates that these items were likely

Figure F.7. The entire artifact collection from the Schlegel site. Photograph by Kristin Thor.

being manufactured onsite, possibly similar to Killarney Bay (Buchanan 1990:118; Dodd 1996:97). Of the 12 points recovered, 10 are side-notched. Detour was the preferred chert of manufacture for points (Dodd 1996:92). Exotic cherts at Baxter include Detour, Wyandotte, Bayport, Norwood, and Burlington (Dodd 1996:16).

Interpretations and conclusions

The Schlegel site was used between 55 BC and AD 125, at which time it was situated on an island due to the higher water levels of Georgian Bay (Larsen 1985:67), similar to the Killarney Bay site. The forests were generally white pine, hemlock, birch, and beech (Dodd 1996:20). In addition to a mortuary location and a likely small burial mound, the site functioned as a short term camp; there was evidence of tool manufacture in the form of a significant amount of chert debitage and firepits in several locations. Although the Schlegels found no postmolds or other evidence of dwellings, it is unclear if they were looking for such features or if they would recognize them if found. Excavation concentrated on the mound area, and the entire site was not excavated.

At Killarney Bay, the habitation portion of the site is situated slightly downslope from the mortuary mounds and closer to the water (Julig and Long, Chapter 2, this volume). If a similar pattern existed at the Schlegel site, the habitation area could possibly be closer to the shore near the firepit area or along the shore on the slightly lower areas to the northwest. The occupants of the site were involved in long-distance trade, as exotic cherts account for a significant portion of the raw materials of the assemblage. These materials came from as far away as central Ohio, Michigan, Illinois, and central Quebec in trade patterns described by Taché (2011b:41) as part of the Meadowood Interaction Sphere. Copper from the Lake Superior region was also procured through trade (Ellis et al. 1990:89).

The Schlegels found no signs of bones, but the acidic nature of the soil due to the predominance of pine could easily result in the destruction of bones over the 2,000-year time frame. The only human remains found was a single molar, but this was in association with an old firepit, debitage, and possible hammerstones, and not the burial artifacts. The large number of copper beads and the exquisite oval biface may indicate that this person was of significant status. Copper was considered a valued item with spiritual connections and the ability to bring good fortune (Martin 1999:204). The small pouch of copper scraps in Area 2 could also suggest that the person was a craftsperson, or it may simply be a ritual item (Martin 1999:191). Although investigators originally thought that the presence of the tubes suggested that the person was a shaman, tubes are often found in burials of this time period and do not signify the person's occupation. Two of the Killarney Bay tubes were recovered from Burial 10, that of an adolescent female (Nicodemus, Chapter 9, this volume). James V. Wright reports on a different site near Honey Harbor, near a large stone, which was the burial of a child, and which also contained a blocked-end tube of Ohio pipestone and other Adena traits (Wright 1999:667). He does not identify the site, other than to state it was found during his fieldwork. No further reference or details could be found in his notes at the Museum of Civilization.

The Schlegel artifacts were found in two clusters approximately 1.8 m apart. The first cluster contained one tube, a skinning tool, 3 bifacial scrapers, 7 bifaces, and 5 or 6 copper beads. It is interesting to note that no points were found at this location. It is possible that the site contains two or more burials, perhaps that of a male and a female. Area 1, with bifacial scrapers and no points, may be the burial of a female. Area 2, with the large number of beads, argillite items, two tubes, bifaces, cache blades, and finished biface points, may be the burial of a male. However, the presence of two blocked-end tubes in this area may not support that theory. Artifacts at the Boucher mortuary site indicated that there was a clear distinction between male and female burial items, and blocked-end tubes were never included in male burials (Taché 2011b:69). There is no significant difference in the chert raw materials between the two areas, as both contain local and the more exotic distant cherts.

The Schlegel site leaves us with unanswered questions. Is this truly a mortuary site or several caches of mortuary items? How large is the habitation area associated with the mortuary artifact area? There are important similarities with the mortuary complex of Killarney Bay: an island location, similar dating, the presence of a small mound, possible multiple burials, and similar mortuary artifact assemblages. In addition, bead making and gorget making is evident on these sites.

Acknowledgements

I would like to thank the following individuals: Pat Julig, for all his guidance and assistance during my initial research and analysis of the Schlegel site; Jack Holland, Jeff Bursey, Darrel Long, and William Fox for assistance with lithic raw material identification; Jean-Luc Pilon and Stacey Girling-Christie for access to James V. Wright's field notes and collections at the Canadian Museum of Civilization; and Bill Allen for kindling my interest in researching the Schlegel artifacts and introducing me to the people who would later be so influential in that task. My greatest thanks go to my parents, Iven L. and Winnifred Schlegel, for including the entire family in the excavation process, keeping such meticulous records of the excavation, and preserving the artifacts with such care.

Appendix G
Summaries of Select Killarney Bay Field Entries

David Brose

The following descriptions of Killarney Bay features are based on the "maps" or drawings and the accompanying notes in the journals kept by the students each year during the field seasons led by Emerson Greenman. Following the field season, Greenman edited these in a frequently hand-corrected typescript. These were then restudied by Greenman in the summer of 1955 in preparation for constructing a master feature map. Unfortunately, no such map could be found in 2006. The manuscript in his hand bears this statement: "These maps supercede [sic] the large ones of pits hearths and baths. These are all checked with the large ones showing the same detail and the large one is corrected to conform [?]." Ceramic type/variety attributions were added following inspection in late 2011, based on the descriptions reported in Chapter 11 of this volume.

Brief feature descriptions

Pit from topsoil – 4C I9:

A depression in the bottom of topsoil sands 5 feet across in vertical face. Upper part adjoining bottom of topsoil is dark gray with eroded rock. Lower part is observed simply by being drier and looser than the surrounding subsoil.

Early description (1940) of a deep pit which yielded the conical base of a KB Smooth vessel:

Tr 4C Sect H2: V-shaped in vertical face. 2.7′ across at top which is 2.4′ blow laminated pebbly stratified sand… as if water-filled. In subsoil there is a pot-base (KB1-69) at west edge of this pit and in drawing of this face.

Description of a buried early hearth:

Tr 3D Sec C1 FN 29 (1940) Map 25. A deposit of fire-cracked stones, the topmost at .4′ below bottom of topsoil, with subsoil intervening. The stones lie on black sand containing charcoal. The hearth is U-shaped about 3′ across and 1′ wide [thick ?]. No pottery or anything else in it.

Unusual examples of intersecting storage pits from different periods of occupation:

TR4C Sec GH/1-2. "This is two overlapping pits, one between E 5-9, the other between E 9-12. The former is stratified, coming down from the topsoil to a depth of 1.9′ below the surface, and 3.4′ wide in vertical face. Lens of yellow sand, then medium gray sand at bottom. The other pit is filled with undifferentiated black sands."

An early, water-washed hearth, called a "Spread of stones" in Trench 4A. See FN8 extending into Tr 4B Sec A8 and A9. Poorly described but clearly resting on water-laid sand at a depth of 2.4′ below surface.

A possible cremation pit encountered within or near the mound:

TR 3D Sec F2-3 FN37-38. Pit comes down from topsoil and contains a blade of chert [KB1-361], 8 fire-cracked rocks, about 100 chips of quartzite and a block of cherty quartzite [???] at depth in pit of 2.4′ below the surface.

Another early (possibly rice parching?) pit:

TR4C Sec I2 Map 46, 1941 Horizontal FN 13, 14. Pit is 3.3′ long, 2.5′ wide, greatest depth 1.6′. Top 0.7′ below topsoil. 1 sherd, 105 flakes quartzite, 1 piece of crude blade [KB1-473]. In a pocket of the pit NS 141.8–142.6, E7.7′ – 8.2′ there were about 80–100 chert and quartzite flakes [KB1 528] and portions of 35 chert blades [KB1 529], along with a dozen sherds [KB1 527] of a nondescript Killarney Bay paste.

Early description from 1946 testing:

TR3D Sec D3: NS 167.5, E615 to E64 FN33. 1.5′ below surface. Sherd KB1-283. Possibly piece of pipe. Several quartzite chips, no fire-cracked rock.

An example of redacting earlier interpretation:

TR 3D Sec E2 FN 35 Map 30 ML. Center of pit E 55.6, depth 1.2′ below surface. 1.9′ wide in vertical face. These are at 175 on the map shown as 1 pit on the map M, L, bottom of which is 4.4′ below surface. In FN 35 it says this pit becomes 2 pits at NS 170.5, one in Sec E3 of Tr #D and the other in Sec E2, 1 sherd 1.25′ below surface comp .35 a streamer of the E side in the pit is mentioned. Sherd KB1-340 on map, sherds KB1-301, 310 in FN 35. Also KB1-312, 298 on FN 36. In secE3 at NS 170.3 the pit is 1.8′ deep and 3.2′ wide E-W. At 171 the pit is 2.4′ deep and nearly 4′ wide where it merges into the topsoil. Sherds in bottom of pit are KB1-309 also with about 200 chips of quartzite, slate, scatters all through the pit. None saved.

Description of a possible cremation hearth or spread of stones found in 1946:

Tr 3C Sec I1, I2 5′ north of NS 145, E60 FN3 1946. Areas of darkened soil and abundance of fire-cracked stone. A small pit about 1.5′ wide in vertical face is at NS 145 E 53 and is apparently part of this spread of stones. It is saucer-shaped, 0.5′ thick, beginning at bottom of topsoil and described on Map 59 as burnt earth. Field Notes say a red tinge to the sand beneath the stone.

A small hearth encountered in a test near small cabins in 1946:

Tr 6M[?] Sec J1 FN 6 (1946). Map 61. Drawing shows saucer-shaped depression 3′ diameter, 0.5′ deep at rim of TT but deeper than this below rim. This is in front of the little cabins, Negative 7236. Extends into subsoil 1 foot.

A late intrusive pit described in TR 3F Sec G continued FN 21, 22:

Outlines not described. Contents 1 end scraper (KB1 825), 1 quartzite flake; 1 half end-scraper. In topsoil, 1 sherd, 1 slate artifact, 1 piece worked flint and sherds (KB1-832) in subsoil around this pit.

A washed-over very early hearth in Tr 4D Sec D 10 "Streamer hearth" FN 39:

Black sand and charcoal with fire-cracked stones. 2.1′ wide in vertical face, 0.7′ thick. Top of pit 1′ below bottom of topsoil with subsoil in between.

A late pit seen coming down from topsoil, found in 1948:

TR 4F Sec 6 FN 23, Map 91B: Pear-shaped area on the horizontal 5′ NS/3.6′ E-W at widest part from topsoil.

Charcoal and fire-cracked rock 2.3′ deep. Flint flakes and end scrapers.

A deep and old hearth encountered in Tr 3E Sec E2 FN 14,15- 1949. Maps 120, 125: (Neg.# 7295):

Measured at 2.3′ diameter, consisting of 16 fire-cracked rocks enclosing a black stained area within a semi-circle. The black stain being 0.15′ thick of charcoal and containing 1 small quartzite flake. See Map 120. This hearth was under a pit coming down from the topsoil but not reaching the surface of this hearth.

A 1949 pit yielding charcoal sample:

TR 4E Sec F6 FN 37; FN seq sect E7. Dip of topsoil, base of dip 2′ east of NS 225, E23. Sherd of Killarney Bay Thick variety Plain [KB1-1109].

A refilled pit seen in 1949:

Tr 3E, Sec E3, Fn 33 1949 Map 125; footnotes it was along Section E2 toward the eastern side. Much charcoal. 3′ deep below surface and with 10 fire-cracked rocks at the bottom but no signs of fired earth.

A possible burial pit potted by Bell [?] found in 1951 near center of mound:

TR 4D Sec G9 FN 9,10 Map 148. 1.45′ deep below surface 1.3′ wide. Pit has rounded corners, a flat bottom, and perpendicular sides. It contained considerable amount of bone, charcoal, sherds, quartzite and flint chips; 2 large slate pieces and 6 fire-cracked rocks. One bone had a green stain on it and there was a Speigel Tool-Impressed variety indeterminate sherd [KB1-1464] and a single piece of charcoal [KB1-1111] at a depth of 2.6′ below the surface.

Another pit possibly yielding the 1951 radiocarbon sample:

TR 3D Sec G4 FN 8: 2.9′ wide, .5′ deep in subsoil and upper topsoil. Killarney Bay Smoothed var flat lip sherds [KB1-1405] in an area .7 x .65′ at NS 181.35, E67.35. Contents: charcoal, red ochre, KB1-1406, flint KB1-1388.

A probable emptied cremation pit seen in 1951 mound area work:

TR 3D Sec G3 FNS 1951. This is a continuation of the hearth shown on Map 33 from 1940. This will be recorded only on the 1940 map. The 1951 notes say it is a thick black soil reaching a depth of 2 feet. Red and white chips with small fire-cracked rocks and many granite chips. The 1940 note says bell-bottomed of is [?] in subsoil at least 2.8′ wide, 0.5′ thick. There is a complex of strata hard to interpret.

A "Spread of stones" or probable hearth:

Seen in Tr 4D Sec A5 at a depth of 0.5′ below base of topsoil, containing fire-cracked stones 18′ wide [?], topmost stone at elevation of 23.1′ and bottom-most stone was 1.1′ below that, 1 flint chip was recovered.

A pit revealing the difficulty of working near the root cellar in in the rainy summer of 1952:

Tr 3E Sec J5 FN6 1952. Field Notes say I5 Charcoal piece in pit at 4′ south of NS 240 E71. Pit is 4.5′ in diameter, but "This is the old and new root-cellar area and doubtful."

A section of burned floor at the front edge of where excavation would cut into the mound the following summer:

Tr 4F Sec F7 FN 26–28 1948 Maps 93, 98: "The whole eastern quarter of this section, from area beginning just below topsoil to a depth of about 2.7′ below surface is indicative of much fire activity. The area is reddened, filled with large pieces of charcoal and much fire-cracked rock. No definite hearth outlines show up and rocks are in no order. Contiguous with topsoil Map 93 has a good vertical ---- [?] at depth of pit 3.3′ below rim."

Bibliography

Abbott, D. H, L. H. Burkle, P. Biscayne, D. Berger, and J. Cole-Dai.
2010. *Unusual Calcium Carbonate, GlassLike Shards, and Low Latitude Diatoms in the GISP2 Ice Core What Are They Telling Us?* Abstract #C13B-0561; American Geophysical Union; AS Bibliographic Code; 2010 AGUFM.C13B0561A. The SAO/NASA Astrophysics Data System, Harvard-Smithsonian Center for Astrophysics. Accessed 25 December 2013.

Abel, T.J., D.M. Stothers, and J.M. Koralewski
2001. The Williams Mortuary Complex: A Transitional Archaic Regional Interaction Center in Northwestern Ohio. In *Archaic Transitions in Ohio & Kentucky Prehistory*, edited by O. Prufer, S. Pedde, and R. Meindl, pp. 290–327. The Kent State University Press.

Ackerman, R.E. and L.A. Ackerman
1973. Ethnoarcheological Interpretations of Territoriality and Land Use in Southwestern Alaska. *Ethnohistory* 20(4):315–334.

Adler, K.
1968. Turtles from Archaeological Sites in the Great Lakes Region. *Michigan Archaeologist* 14:147–163.

Adovasio, J.M.
1977. *Basketry Technology: A Guide to Identification and Analysis*. Aldine Manuals on Archaeology, Chicago.

Albert, D.A.
1995. Regional landscape ecosystems of Michigan, Minnesota and Wisconsin: a working map and classification. General Technical Report NC-178. U.S. Dept. of Agriculture, Forest Service, North Central Forest Experiment Station. St. Paul, MN.

Aldenderfer, M.S.
1993. Ritual, Hierarchy, and Change in Foraging Societies. *Journal of Anthropological Archaeology* 12(1):1–40.

Allen, P.M.
1980. The Augustine Mound and Oxbow Site: A Study of Possible Cultural Connections. Manuscript on file. Archaeology, New Brunswick Department of Tourism, Recreation, and Heritage, Fredericton, New Brunswick.

Allen, J., S. Holdaway, and R. Fullagar
1997. Identifying Specialisation, Production and Exchange in the Archaeological Record: The Case of Shell Bead

Manufacture on Motupore Island, Papua. *Archaeology in Oceania* 32:13–38.

Allen, W.A.
2002. Wa-nant-git-che-ang: Canoe Route to Lake Huron through Southern Algonquian. *Ontario Archaeology* 73:38–68.

Alvard, M.S. and L. Kuznar
2001. Deferred Harvests: The Transition from Hunting to Animal Husbandry. *American Anthropologist* 103(2):295–311.

Ami, H.M.
1927. Memorial of Robert Bell. *Geological Society of America Bulletin* 38:18–34.

Anderson, D.G.
1999. Climate and Culture Change in Prehistoric and Early Historic Eastern North America. Paper prepared for presentation in the Carnegie Lectures in Global Environmental Change series, Carnegie Museum of Natural History, Pittsburgh, Pennsylvania, September 1999. Revised October 1999.

Anderson, J.E.
1963. Osteology of the Donaldson Site. In *The Donaldson Site*, edited by J.V. Wright and J.E. Anderson, pp. 95–113. Bulletin 184. National Museum of Canada, Ottawa.

1968. *The Serpent Mounds Site: Physical Anthropology*. Royal Ontario Museum, Art and Archaeology Division, Occasional Paper 11.

Anderson, T.W.
2002. Pollen stratigraphy and vegetation history, Sheguiandah archaeological site. In *The Sheguiandah Site: Archaeological, Geological and Paleobotanical Studies at a Paleoindian Site on Manitoulin Island, Ontario*, edited by P. Julig, pp. 179–194. Canadian Museum of Civilization, Hull, Quebec.

Anderton, J.B., S.B. Dunham, and M.C. Branstner.
1996. 1995 Cultural Resource Surveys: Hiawatha National Forest. U.S. Department of Agriculture, Forest Service, Hiawatha National Forest, Escanaba, Michigan. Great Lakes Research Associates, Inc., Williamston, MI.

Andrefsky, W.
1994. Raw-material Availability and the Organization of Technology. *American Antiquity* 59(1):21–34.

2005. *Lithics: Macroscopic Approaches to Analysis*. Cambridge University Press, Cambridge.

Angel, M.
2002. *Preserving the Sacred : Historical Perspectives on the Ojibwa Midewiwin*. University of Manitoba Press, Winnipeg.

Annual Reports of Geological Survey of Canada, Explorations and Surveys, 1876–1877:209. https://doi.org/10.4095/297014

Anselmi, L.M.
2004. *New Materials, Old Ideas: Native Use of European-Introduced Metals in the Northeast.* Doctoral dissertation, University of Toronto.

2008. *Native Peoples Use of Copper-Based Metals in NE North America: Contact Period Interactions.* VDM Verlag, Saarbrucken.

Arno, J.
2001a. *Fraxinus americana.* In *A Guide to Useful Woods of the World*, edited by J.H. Flynn and C.D. Holder, pp. 242–243. Forest Products Society, Madison, WI.

2001b. *Fraxinus nigra.* In *A Guide to Useful Woods of the World*, edited by J.H. Flynn and C.D. Holder, pp. 246–247. Forest Products Society, Madison, WI.

Arnold, D.E.
1985. *Ceramic Theory and Cultural Process*. Cambridge University Press, Cambridge.

Arnold, J.E., editor
1996. *Emergent Complexity: The Evolution of Intermediate Societies*. International Monographs in Prehistory, Ann Arbor.

Arthurs, D.
1986. *Archaeological Investigations of the Long Sault Site (Manitou Mounds)*. Ontario Ministry of Citizenship and Culture, Heritage Branch, Northwestern Region, Conservation Archaeology Report No. 7. Kenora, Ontario.

Arzigian, C.
2000. Middle Woodland and Oneota contexts for wild rice exploitation in southwestern Wisconsin. *Midcontinental Journal of Archaeology* 25(2):245–268.

Acsádi, G. and J. Nemeskéri
1970. *History of Human Life Span and Mortality*. Budapest, Akadémiai Kiadó.

Aufderheide, A.C. and C. Rodriguez-Martin
1998. *The Cambridge Encyclopedia of Human Paleopathology*. Cambridge University Press, Cambridge.

Ayer, J.A., J.E. Chartrand, N.F. Trowell, and A.Wilson
2010. *Geological compilation of the Maple Mountain area, Abitibi Greenstone Belt*. Ontario Geological Survey, Preliminary Map P.3620, scale 1: 100 000.

Baby, R. and C. Snow
1957. *The Adena People*. Columbus: The Ohio State Museum.

Baedke, S.J., T.A. Thompson, J.W. Johnston, and D.A. Wilcox
2004. Reconstructing paleo lake levels from relict shorelines along the Upper Great Lakes. *Aquatic Ecosystems and Heath and Management* 7(4):435–449.

Baker, F.C., J.B. Griffin, R.G. Morgan, G.K. Neumann, and J.L. Taylor
1941. *Contributions to the Archaeology of the Illinois Valley*. Transactions of the American Philosophical Society, New Series, Vol. 32, Pt. 1. American Philosophical Society, Philadelphia.

Baldwin, G.J., P.C. Thurston, and B.S. Kamber
2011. High-precision rare earth element, nickel, and chromium chemistry of chert microbands pre-screened with in-situ analysis. *Chemical Geology* 285:133–143.

Barker, A.W.
1999. Chiefdoms and the Economics of Perversity. Unpublished PhD dissertation in anthropology, University of Michigan, Ann Arbor.

Barnard, H., A.N. Dooley, and K.F. Faull
2007. Chapter 5: An Introduction to Archaeological Lipid Analysis by GC/MS. In *Theory and Practice of Archaeological Residue Analysis*, edited by H. Barnard and J.W. Eerkens, pp.42–60. British Archaeological Reports International Series 1650. Oxford, UK.

Barnett, P.J.
1992. Quaternary geology of Ontario. In *Geology of Ontario: Ontario Geological Survey, Special Volume 4(2)*, edited by P.C. Thurston, H.R. Williams, R.H. Sutcliffe and G.M. Stott, pp. 1011–1088. Ministry of Northern Development and Mines.

2002. Quaternary geology, stratigraphy and sedimentology of the Sheguiandah site. In P. J. Julig (editor), *The Sheguiandah Site: Archaeological, Geological and Paleobotanical Studies at a Paleoindian Site on Manitoulin Island, Ontario*. Mercury Series, Archaeological Survey of Canada, Paper 161, Canadian Museum of Civilization, Hull, Quebec.

Barondess, D.A.
1994. An Analysis of the Human Skeletal Remains from the Fayette Cliffs Site, Delta County, Michigan. Office of the State Archaeologist. Unpublished report.

Barth, F.
1967. On the Study of Social Change. *American Anthropologist* 69(6):661–669.

Bayliss, A. and C. Bronk Ramsey
2004. Pragmatic Bayesians: a Decade of Integrating Radiocarbon Dates into Chronological Models. In *Tools for Constructing Chronologies: Crossing Disciplinary Boundaries*, edited by C.E. Buck and A. R. Millard, pp. 25–41. Vol. 177. Springer Verlag, London.

Beauthier, J.-P., P. Lefevre, M. Meunier, R. Orban, C. Polet, J.-P. Werquin and G. Quatrehomme
2010. Palatine Sutures as Age Indicator: A Controlled Study in the Elderly. *Journal of Forensic Sciences* 55(1):153–158.

Bell, R.
1876. *Letters between Robert and Agnes Bell 1876*. Library and Archives Canada. R7346-6-5-E, Vol. 4, File No. 15.

1896. Report on the geology of the French River sheet, Ontario. Annual Report of the Geological Survey, Canada, Vol 6.

Benchley, E., D.J. Marcucci, Cheong-Yip Yuen, and K.L. Griffin
1988. Final Report of Archaeological Investigation and Data Recovery at the Trout Point 1 Site, Alger County, Michigan. University of Wisconsin-Milwaukee Archaeological Research Laboratory, Report of Investigations 89.

Bender, B.
1985. Prehistoric Developments in the American Midcontinent and in Brittany, Northwest France. In *Prehistoric Hunter-Gatherers: The Emergence of Cultural Complexity*, edited by T.D. Price and J.A. Brown, pp. 205–227. Academic Press, New York.

1993. Introduction: Landscape-Meaning and Action. In *Landscape Politics and Perspectives*, edited by B. Bender, pp. 1–18. Berg, Oxford.

Benn, D.W.
1980. Hadfields Cave: A Perspective on Late Woodland Culture in Northeastern Iowa. Report No. 13. Office of the State Archaeologist, University of Iowa, Iowa City.

Bernardini, W. and C. Carr
2005. Hopewellian Copper Celts from Eastern North America. In *Gathering Hopewell: Society, Ritual and Ritual Interaction*, edited by C. Carr and D.T. Case, pp. 624–647. Kluwer Academic/ Plenum Publishing, New York.

Bernardini, W.
2004. Hopewell Geometric Earthworks: A Case Study in the Referential and Experiential Meaning of Monuments. *Journal of Anthropological Archaeology* 23(3):331–356.

Bertulli, M.M.
1981. Mississagi, River with Many Mouths: An Analysis

of the Archaeological Occupation of the Mississagi River Delta, Algoma, Ontario. Archaeological Survey of Laurentian University. Report No 9. Sudbury, Ontario.

Bertulli, M.M. and L. Kilpatrick
1977. The Renard Site, Fox Island, Mississagi Delta: A Preliminary Report on a Terminal Woodland Site in Algoma. Archaeological Survey of Laurentian University. Report No 3. Sudbury, Ontario.

Bettarel, R.L. and S. Harrison
1962. An Early Ossuary in Michigan. *The Michigan Archaeologist* 8(4):37–42.

Beukens, R.P., L.A. Pavlish, RGV. Hancock, R.M Farquhar, G.C. Wilson, P.J. Julig and W. Ross
1992. Radiocarbon Dating of Copper-Preserved Organics, *Radiocarbon* 34:890–892.

Bezener, A.
2000. *Birds of Ontario*. Lone Pine, Edmonton.

Bianchi, T.H.
1974. Description and Analysis of the Prehistoric Ceramic Materials Recovered on the Winter Site. Unpublished master's thesis, Department of Anthropology, Western Michigan University, Kalamazoo.

Binford, L.R.
1963. The Pomranky Site: A Late Archaic Burial Station. In *Miscellaneous Studies in Typology and Classification*, by A. Montet-White, L.R. Binford, and M. Papworth. Anthropological Papers of the University of Michigan Museum of Anthropology, No. 19. Ann Arbor.

1979. Organization and Formation Processes: Looking at Curated Technologies. *Journal of Anthropological Research* 35(3):255–273.

1980. Willow smoke and dog's tails: hunter gatherer settlement systems and archaeological site formation. *American Antiquity* 45(1):4–20.

Binford, L.R. and G.I. Quimby
1963. Indian Sites and Chipped Stone Materials in the Northern Lake Michigan Area. *Fieldiana* 36:277–307.

Birnbaum, M.
2009. Home sweet home: Middle Woodland structures for the Richter Site (47DR80), Washington Island, Wisconsin. *The Wisconsin Archeologist* 90(1&2).

Blackbird, A.J.
1887. History of the Ottawa and Chippewa Indians of Michigan. The Ypsilantian job printing house, Ypsilanti, MI.

Blatt, S.H., B. Redmond, V. Cassman, and P.W. Sciulli
2011. Dirty Teeth and Ancient Trade: Evidence of Cotton Fibres in Human Dental Calculus from Late Woodland, Ohio. *International Journal of Osteoarchaeology* 21(6):669–678.

Bloch, M.
1971. *Placing the Dead: Tombs, Ancestral Villages and Kinship Organization in Madagascar*. Seminar Press, New York and London.

Bolen, A.
2020. A Silent Killer: Black Ash Basket Makers are Battling a Voracious Beetle to Keep Their Heritage Alive. *National Museum of the American Indian.* Spring 2020. 21(1).

Bourque, B.J.
1994. Evidence for Prehistoric Exchange on the Maritime Peninsula. In *Prehistoric Exchange Systems in North America*, edited by J. Ericson and T. Baugh, pp. 23–46. Plenum Press, New York.

Bowen, J.E.
1989. The Late Prehistory of Northwestern Ohio: Part I. Late Archaic-Early Woodland. Unpublished dissertation review draft for PhD in anthropology. Ohio State University, Columbus.

Boyle, D.
1887. Annual Archaeological Report for Ontario, Toronto.

1888. Annual Report of the Canadian Institute, Session 1886-87, Being Part of Appendix to the Report of the Minister of Education, Ontario 1887. Toronto.

1889. Annual Report of the Canadian Institute, Session 1887-8, Being Part of Appendix L to the Report of the Minister of Education, Ontario 1888. Toronto.

1902. Annual Archaeological Report 1901, Being Part of Appendix to the Report of the Minister of Education Ontario. Toronto.

Bradley, R.
2000. *An Archaeology of Natural Places*. Routledge, London.

Branstner, C.N.
1996. Archaeological Investigations at the Cloudman Site (20CH6): A Multicomponent Native American Occupation on Drummond Island, Michigan, 1992 and 1994 Excavations. Report on file at the Consortium for Archaeological Research, Michigan State University, East Lansing.

Branstner, C.N. and C.E. Cleland
1994. A Laurel High? Paper presented at the Consortium for Archaeological Research Symposium, Michigan State University, East Lansing.

Brashler, J.
1981. *Early Late Woodland Boundaries and Interaction: Indian Ceramics of Southern Lower Michigan*. Anthropological Series, Vol. 3, No. 3, Publications of the Museum, Michigan State University, East Lansing.

Brashler, J.G. and E.B. Garland
1993. The Zemaitis Site (20OT68): A Stratigraphic Woodland Occupation on the Grand River in Michigan. Paper presented at the 38th annual Midwest Archaeological Conference.

Brashler, J., M. Hambacher, T. Martin, K. Parker and J. Robertson
2006. Middle Woodland Occupations in the Grand River Basin of Michigan, in *Recreating Hopewell*, edited by D. Charles and J. Buikstra, pp. 261–284. University Presses of Florida, Gainesville.

Braun, D.P.
1987. Coevolution of Sedentism, Pottery Technology, and Horticulture in the Central Midwest, 200 B.C. – A.D. 600. In *Emergent Horticultural Economies of the Eastern Woodlands*, edited by W. Keegan, pp. 153–181. Occasional Paper 7. Center for Archaeological Investigations, Southern Illinois University, Carbondale.

Braun, D. and S. Plog
1982. Evolution of "Tribal" Social Networks: Theory and Prehistoric North American Evidence. *American Antiquity* 47(3):504–525.

Braun, G.V.
2010. Technological choices: ceramic manufacture and use at the Antrex site (AjGv-38). *Ontario Archaeology* 89/90:69–96.

2012. Petrography as a technique for investigating Iroquoian ceramic production and smoking rituals. *Journal of Archaeological Science* 39(1):1–10.

Braun, K. and E. Loftus
1998. Advertising's misinformation effect. *Applied Cognitive Psychology* 12:569–591.

Bridges, P.S.
1994. Vertebral Arthritis and Physical Activities in the Prehistoric Southeastern United States. *American Journal of Physical Anthropology* 93(1):83–93.

Brizinski, M.J.
1975. River Channels and Beach Ridges: An Archaeological Survey of the Mississagi Delta, Algoma. Archaeological Survey of Laurentian University. Report No 2. Sudbury, Ontario.

1977. The Semiwite Lake Site: A Woodland Site North of Elliot Lake, Algoma. Archaeological Survey of Laurentian University. Report No. 4. Sudbury, Ontario.

Brizinski, M. and H. Savage
1983. Dog Sacrifices Among the Algonkian Indians: An Example from the Frank Bay Site. *Ontario Archaeology* 39:33–40.

Bronk Ramsey, C.
2009. Bayesian analysis of radiocarbon dates. *Radiocarbon* 51(1):337–360.

2020. OxCal 4.4, https://c14.arch.ox.ac.uk/OxCal/OxCal.html

Brose, D.S.
1968. The Archaeology of Summer Island: Changing Settlement systems in Northern Lake Michigan. Unpublished PhD dissertation in anthropology, University of Michigan, Ann Arbor.

1970a. *The Archaeology of Summer Island: Changing Settlement Systems in Northern Lake Michigan*. Anthropological Papers of the University of Michigan Museum of Anthropology, No. 41. Ann Arbor.

1970b. *The Summer Island Site: A Study of Prehistoric Cultural Ecology and Social Organization in the Northern Lake Michigan Area*. Cleveland: Case Western Reserve University Studies in Anthropology 1.

1971. The Direct Historic Approach to Michigan Archaeology. *Ethnohistory* 18(1):52–63.

1973. Development of Archaeology in Northeastern America. In *The Development of North American Archaeology*, edited by J. Fitting, pp. 116–139. Anchor Press, Garden City, NY.

1978. Late Prehistory of the Upper Great Lakes. In *Handbook of North American Indians, Vol. 15: The Northeast*, edited by B.G. Trigger, pp. 569–582. W. Sturtevant, general editor. Smithsonian Institution, Washington, DC.

1979. Introduction; A Speculative Model of the Role of Exchange in the Prehistory of the Eastern Woodlands. In *Hopewell Archaeology: The Chillicothe Conference*, edited by D. Brose and N. Greber, pp. 1–8. Midcontinental Journal of Archaeology Special Papers 3. Kent: Kent State University Press.

1985. The Woodland Period. In *Ancient Art of the American Woodland Indians*, edited by D.S. Brose, J.A. Brown, and D.W. Penney, pp. 43–92. Harry N. Abrams Inc., New York.

1990. Toward a Model of Exchange Values for the Eastern Woodlands. *Midcontinental Journal of Archaeology* 15(1):100–136.

1991. Protecting the Past from a Museum. In *Protecting the Past: Readings in Archaeological Resource Protection*, edited by G.Smith and J.Erenhard, pp. 187–191. Telford Press, New York.

1992. Changing Paradigms in the Explanation of Southeastern Prehistory. In *The Development of Southeastern Archaeology*, edited by J. Johnson, pp. 1–17. University of Alabama Press, Tuscaloosa.

1994a. Trade and Exchange in the Midwestern United States. In *Prehistoric Exchange Systems in North America*, edited by J.Erikson and T. Baugh, pp. 215–240. Plenum Press, New York.

1994b. *The South Park Site and the Late Prehistoric Whittlesey Tradition of Northeast Ohio.* Monographs in World Archaeology 20. Madison: The Prehistory Press.

2001a. Introduction to Eastern North America at the Dawn of European Colonization. In *Societies in Eclipse: The Archaeology of the Eastern Woodland Indians A.D. 1400–1700*, edited by D. Brose, W. Cowan, and R. Mainfort, Jr., pp. 1–8. Smithsonian Institution Press, Washington, DC.

2001b. Penumbral Protohistory on Lake Erie's South Shore. In *Societies in Eclipse: Archaeology of the Eastern Woodland Indians, A.D. 1400–1700*, edited by D. Brose, W. Cowan, and R. Mainfort, Jr. Smithsonian Institution Press, Washington, DC.

2002. Museum Paradigms and the History of Southeastern Archaeology. In *Histories of Southeastern Archaeology*, edited by S. Tushingham, J. Hill, and C. McNutt, pp. 13–25. University of Alabama Press, Tuscaloosa.

2005. Taxonomic Homogeneity and Cultural Divergence in the Mid-continent. In *Woodland Period Systematics in the Middle Ohio Valley*, edited by D. Applegate and R. Mainfort, pp. 168–177. University of Alabama Press, Tuscaloosa.

2006. *Appraisal of the Andrew Johnson Patterson Collection of Mounted Ornithological Specimens owned by Mr. John Young of Maiden, North Carolina: Report to the Curator of Birds in the Department of Biological Sciences, Smithsonian Institution, National Museum of Natural History, Washington, DC*. Imprints from the Past, West Bloomfield.

2008. Ancient and Historic Period Archaeology in the Midwest. In *Archaeology in America: An Encyclopedia*, Volume 2, edited by F. McManamon, L. Cordell, K. Lightfoot, and G. Milner, pp. 9–21. Greenwood Press, Westport.

2016. The Dunn's Farm Site; 20LU22: A Late Middle Woodland Event in Northwest Michigan. Kalamazoo: Imprints from the Past, accessed at Academia.edu.

Brose, D., J.A. Brown, and D.W. Penney
1985. *Ancient Art of the American Woodland Indians*. Harry N. Abrams, Inc., New York.

Brose, D.S. and N. Greber, editors
1979. *Hopewell Archaeology: The Chillicothe Conference*. Midcontinental Journal of Archaeology Special Papers 3. Kent State University Press.

Brose, D. and M. Hambacher
1998. Draft chapter of *The Middle Woodland in Northern Michigan.* Manuscript on file at University of Michigan Museum of Anthropological Archaeology, Ann Arbor.

1999. The Middle Woodland in Northern Michigan. In *Retrieving Michigan's Buried Past: The Archaeology of the Great Lake State*, edited by J. Halsey, pp. 173–192. The Cranbrook Institute of Science, Bloomfield Hills, MI.

Brown, J.A.
1964. The Northeastern Extension of the Havana Tradition. *Illinois State Museum Scientific Papers* 12(4):107–122. Springfield.

Brown, J.A., editor
1971. *Approaches to the Social Dimensions of Mortuary Practices*. Memoir No. 25. Society for American Archaeology: Washington, DC.

Brown, J.A.
1997. The Archaeology of Ancient Religion in the Eastern Woodlands. *Annual Review of Anthropology* 26:465–485.

2004. Mound City and Issues in the Developmental History of Hopewell Culture in the Ross County Area of Southern Ohio. In *Aboriginal Ritual and Economy in the Eastern Woodlands,* edited by A.-M. Cantwell, L.A. Conrad, and J.E. Reyman, pp. 147–168. Illinois State Museum, Springfield.

2006. Where's the Power in Mound Building? An Eastern Woodland Perspective. In *Leadership and Polity in Mississippian Society*, edited by B.M. Butler and P.D. Welch, pp. 197–213. Center for Archaeological Investigations. Southern Illinois University, Carbondale.

Brown J.A., R.A. Kerber, and H.D. Winters
1990. Trade and the evolution of exchange relations at the beginning of the Mississippian period. In *The Mississippian Emergence*, edited by B.D. Smith, pp. 251–280. Smithsonian Institution Press, Washington, DC.

Brunel, P., L. Bossé and G. Lamarche
1998. *Catalogue of the Marine Invertebrates of the Estuary and Gulf of St. Lawrence.* Canadian Special Publication of Fisheries and Aquatic Sciences 126. NRC Research Press, Ottawa.

Brunton, F.R., E. Turner, and D. Armstrong
2009. *A guide to the Paleozoic geology and fossils of Manitoulin Island and northern Bruce Peninsula, Ontario, Canada.* Geological Association of Canada, Paleontology Section, Canadian Paleontology Conference, Field Trip Guidebook No. 14.

Buchanan, K.T.
1979a. An Archaeological Survey of Lake of the Sudbury Area and a Site Near Lake of the Mountains. Archaeological Survey of Laurentian University. Report No 6. Sudbury, Ontario.

1979b. A Walk in the Woods: The Archaeological Component of the Environmental Assessment-Road Benefit Study from Killarney to Whitefish Falls. Archaeological Survey of Laurentian University. Report No 7. Sudbury, Ontario.

1981. To Walk a Crooked Mile, The Archaeological Assessment of the Proposed Highway 637 Realignment and the Excavation of the Tyson Site. Archaeological Survey of Laurentian University. Report No 10. Sudbury, Ontario.

1990. The Speigel (BlHl-1) Survey 1982. Archaeological Survey of Laurentian University, Report No. 16, Sudbury, Ontario.

1992. The 1991 Speigel Site Excavation. Archaeological Survey of Laurentian University, Report No. 19, Sudbury, Ontario.

1995a. The 1993 Speigel Site Excavation. Archaeological Survey of Laurentian University, Report No. 21, Sudbury, Ontario.

1995b. The 1994 Speigel Site Excavation. Archaeological Survey of Laurentian University, Report No. 22, Sudbury, Ontario.

1996. The 1995 Speigel Site Excavation. Archaeological Survey of Laurentian University, Report No. 23, Sudbury, Ontario.

1997. The 1996 Speigel Site Excavation. Archaeological Survey of Laurentian University, Report No. 24, Sudbury, Ontario.

1998. The 1997 Speigel Site Excavation. Archaeological Survey of Laurentian University, Report No. 25, Sudbury, Ontario.

1999. The 1998 Speigel Site Excavation. Archaeological Survey of Laurentian University, Report No. 31, Sudbury, Ontario.

2000. The 1999 Speigel Site Excavation and Field School. Archaeological Survey of Laurentian University, Report No. 32, Sudbury, Ontario.

2001. The 2000 Speigel Site Excavation and Field School. Archaeological Survey of Laurentian University, Report No. 35, Sudbury, Ontario.

2002. The 2001 Speigel Site Excavation and Field School. Laurentian University Archaeological Survey, Report No. 36, Sudbury, Ontario.

Buckmaster, M.M. and J.R. Paquette
1988. The Gorto Site: Preliminary Report on a Late Paleo-Indian Site in Marquette County, Michigan. *The Wisconsin Archeologist* 69:101–124.

Buikstra, J. and D. Charles
1999. Centering the Ancestors: Cemeteries, Mounds, and Sacred Landscapes of the Ancient North American Midcontinent. In *Archaeologies of Landscape : Contemporary Perspectives*, edited by W. Ashmore and A.B. Knapp, pp. 201–228. Blackwell Publishers, Malden.

Buikstra, J.E. and D.H. Ubelaker, editors
1994. *Standards for Data Collection from Human Skeletal Remains*. Arkansas Archaeological Survey Research Series No. 44. Fayetteville, Arkansas.

Bunzel, R.
1929. *The Pueblo Potter*. Columbia University Contributions to Anthropology No 8. New York.

Byers, A.M.
2005. *The Ohio Hopewell Episode: Paradigm Lost and Paradigm Gained.* The University of Akron Press, Akron, Ohio.

Caldwell, J.R.
1958. *Trend and Tradition in the Prehistory of the Eastern United States.* Illinois State Museum Scientific Papers, Vol. 10. Memoirs of the American Anthropological Association, No. 88.

1964. Interaction Spheres in Prehistory. In *Hopewellian Studies*, edited by J.R. Caldwell and R.L. Hall, pp. 133–143. Scientific Papers 12(6). Illinois State Museum, Springfield.

Callahan, E.
1979. Basics of Biface Knapping in the Eastern Fluted Point Tradition. *Archaeology of Eastern North America* 7(1):1–180.

Cantin, M.
2008. Provenience, Description, and Archaeological Use of Selected Chert Types of Indiana. Indiana State University Anthropology Laboratory Technical Report No. 05-01.Terre Haute.

Card, K.
1978. *Geology of the Sudbury–Manitoulin area*. Ontario Geological Survey, Report 166.

Card, K.D., W.H. McIlwaine, and H.D. Meyn
1973. Geology of the Maple Mountain Area, Districts of Tlmiskaming. Nipiissing, and Sudbury. Ontario Division of Mines, Ministry of Natural Resources, Toronto. Geological Report 106.

Carey, M.
1998. Gender in African Beadwork. In *Beads and Bead Makers: Gender, Material Culture and Meaning*, edited by L. D. Sciama and J.B. Eicher. Berg, Oxford.

Carpenter, E.
1950. Five Sites of the Intermediate Period. *American Antiquity* 15(4):298–314.

Carr, C. and D.T. Case, editors
2005. *Gathering Hopewell: Society, Ritual and Ritual Interaction*. New York: Kluwer/Plenum Publishers.

Carr, C. and R.E. Maslowski
1995. Cordage and Fabrics: Relating Form, Technology, and Social Processes. In *Style, Society, and Person: Archaeological and Ethnological Perspectives*, edited by C. Carr and J. Neitzel. Plenum Press, New York.

Carr, C. and D.T. Case.
2006. The Gathering of Hopewell. In *Gathering Hopewell: Society, Ritual, and Ritual Interaction*, edited by C. Carr and D.T. Case, pp. 19–50. Springer Science+Business Media, Inc., New York.

Chang, K.C.
1962. *Settlement Archaeology*. National Press, Palo Alto, CA.

Chapdelaine, C. and E. Graillon, editors
2020. Kruger 2: un site du Paléoindien récent à Brompton. PALÉO-QUÉBEC 39. Recherches amérindiennes au Québec. Montreal.

Charles, D. and J. Buikstra
2002. Siting, Sighting and Citing the Dead. In *The Space and Place of Death*, edited by H. Silverman and D. Small. Archaeological Papers of the American Anthropological Association, Vol. 11. American Anthropological Association, Arlington, VA.

Charters, S., R.P. Evershed, L.J. Goad, P.W. Blinkhorn, and V. Denham
1993. Quantification and Distribution of Lipid in Archaeological Ceramics: Implications for Sampling Potsherds for Organic Residue Analysis and the Classification of Vessel Use. *Archaeometry* 35(2):211–223.

Charters, S., R.P. Evershed, A. Quye, P.W. Blinkhorn, and V. Denham
1997. Simulation Experiments for Determining the Use of Ancient Pottery Vessels: The Behaviour of Epicuticular Leaf Wax during Boiling of a Leafy Vegetable. *Journal of Archaeological Science* 24:1–7.

Childs, S.T.
1994. Native Copper Technology and Society in Eastern North America. In *Archaeometry of Pre-Columbian Sites and Artifacts*, edited by D.A. Scott and P. Meyers, pp. 229–253. Proceedings of a symposium organized by the UCLA Institute of Archaeology and the Getty Conservation Institute, Los Angeles.

Christie, J.J., editor and contributor
2009. *Landscapes of Origin in the Americas: Creation Narratives Linking Ancient Places and Present Communities*. The University of Alabama Press, Tuscaloosa.

Church, F.
1984. Textiles as Markers of Ohio Hopewell Social Identities. *Midcontinental Journal of Archaeology* 9(1):1–25.

Claassen, C.
1998. *Shells*. Cambridge University Press, Cambridge.

Claassen, C. and S. Sigmann
1993. Sourcing Busycon Artifacts of the Eastern United States. *American Antiquity* 58(2):333–347.

Clark, C.P.
1995. Archaeological Survey and Testing Isle Royal National Park 1987–1990 Seasons. Midwest Archaeological Center Occasional Studies in Anthropology No. 32. National Park Service, Lincoln, NE.

Clay, R.B.
1983. Pottery and graveside ritual in Kentucky Adena. *Midcontinental Journal of Archaeology* 8(1):109–126.

1986. Adena Ritual Spaces. In *Early Woodland Archaeology*, edited by K.B. Farnsworth and T.E. Emerson, pp. 881–895. Center for American Archaeology, Kampsville, IL.

1991. Adena ritual development: an organizational type in a temporal perspective. In *The Human Landscape in Kentucky's Past,* edited by C. Stout and C.K. Hensley, pp. 30–39. The Kentucky Heritage Council, Frankfort.

1998. The Essential Features of Adena Ritual and Their Implications. *Southeastern Archaeology* 17(1):1–21.

Clayton, L., W.B. Bickley, and W.J. Stone Jr
1970. Knife River Flint. *Plains Anthropologist* 15:282–290.

Cleland, C.E.
1966. *The Prehistoric Animal Ecology and Ethnozoology of the Upper Great Lakes Region*. Anthropological Papers of the University of Michigan Museum of Anthropology, No. 29. Ann Arbor.

1982. The Inland Shore Fishery of the Northern Great Lakes: Its Development and Importance in Prehistory. *American Antiquity* 47(4):761–784.

1984. Review of *Great Lakes Archaeology*, by Ronald Mason, and *Archaic Hunters and Gatherers in the American Midwest*, by James L. Phillips and James A. Brown. *American Anthropologist* 86:1011–1013.

1992. *Rites of Conquest: The History and Culture of Michigan's Native Americans*. University of Michigan Press, Ann Arbor.

Clermont, N.
1990. Le Sylvivole Inférieur au Québec. Recherches Amérindiennes au Québec XX(1):5–17.

Coale, A.J. and P. Demeny
1966. *Regional Model Life Tables and Stable Population*. Princeton University Press, Princeton, NJ.

Cobb, C.R.
2003. Mississippian Chiefdoms: How Complex? *Annual Review of Anthropology*. 32:63–84.

Collins, M. B., B. Ellis and C. Dodt-Ellis
1990. *Excavations at the Camp Pearl Wheat Site (41KR243): An Early Archaic Campsite on Town Creek, Kerr County, Texas*. Studies in Archaeology 6. Texas Archaeological Research Laboratory, The University of Texas at Austin.

Condamin, J., F. Formenti, M.O. Metais, M. Michel, and P. Blond
1976. The Application of Gas Chromatography to the Tracing of Oil in Ancient Amphorae. *Archaeometry* 18(2):195–201.

Coniglio, M. P. Karrow, and P. Russell
2006. *Manitoulin Rocks! – Rocks, fossils and landforms of Manitoulin Island*. Earth Sciences Museum (University of Waterloo) and Geological Association of Canada.

Conolly, J.
2018. Hunter-gatherer Mobility, Territoriality, and Placemaking in the Kawartha Lakes Region, Ontario. *Canadian Journal of Archaeology* 42(2):1–28.

Converse, R.N.
1979. *The Glacial Kame Indians*. The Archaeological Society of Ohio, Columbus.

Conway, T.
1979. Heartland of the Ojibway. In *Collected Archaeological Papers*. Archaeological Research Report 13, edited by D. Melvin, pp. 1–28. Historical Planning and Research Branch, Ontario Ministry of Culture and Recreation. Toronto.

1980. Point aux Pins Archaeology: Woodland and Historic Components. Archaeological Research Report 13, pp. 29–64. Historical Planning and Research Branch, Ontario Ministry of Culture and Recreation. Toronto.

1981. *Archaeology in Northeast Ontario: Searching for our Past*. Historical Planning and Research Branch, Ontario Ministry of Culture and Recreation. Toronto.

1989a. An Early Historic Woodland Caribou Kill Site and Seasonal Fishing Camp of the Ottawa (Odawa) on Manitoulin Island. Draft document on Shawana Site, BkHk-1, Ontario Ministry of Citizenship and Culture.

1989b. Scotia Lake Pictograph Site: Shamanic Rock Art in Northeastern Ontario. *Man in the Northeast* 37:1–24.

Conway, T. and J. Conway
1989. An Ethno-Archaeological Study of Algonkian Rock Art in Northeastern Ontario, Canada. *Ontario Archaeology* 49(3): 34–59.

Cook, F.R.
1984. *Introduction to Canadian Amphibians and Reptiles*. National Museum of Canada, Ottawa.

Coon, M.
2009. Variations in Ohio Hopewell Political Economies. *American Antiquity* 74(1):49–76.

Core, H.A., W.A. Core, and A.C. Day
1979. *Wood Structure and Identification*. Syracuse University Press, Syracuse, NY.

Cowan, C.W.
1977. Excavations at the Haystack Rockshelters, Powell County, Kentucky. Unpublished PhD dissertation in anthropology. University of Michigan, Ann Arbor.

1978. The Prehistoric Use and Distribution of Maygrass in Eastern North America: Cultural and Phytogeographical Implications. *Names: Journal of the American Name Society* 67:263–288.

Crane, H.R.
1956. University of Michigan Radiocarbon Dates I. *Science* 124(3224):664–672.

Crane, H.R. and J.B. Griffin
1958. University of Michigan Radiocarbon Dates II. *Science* 127(3306):1098–1105.

1959. University of Michigan Radiocarbon Dates IV. *Radiocarbon* 1:173–198.

1966. University of Michigan Radiocarbon Dates XI. *Radiocarbon* 8:256–285.

Curtis, J.E.
2002. A Revised Temporal Framework for Middle Woodland Ceramics in South-central Ontario. *Ontario Archaeology* 73: 15–28.

2004. Processes of Cultural Change: Ceramics and Interaction Across the Middle to Late Woodland Transition in South-central Ontario. Unpublished PhD dissertation, Department of Anthropology, University of Toronto.

Da Silva, C.M., B. Landau, and R. La Perna
2011. Biogeography of Iberian Atlantic Neogene Marginelliform Gastropods (Marginellidae, Cystiscidae): Global Change and Transatlantic Colonization. *Journal of Paeolontology* 85(6):1052–1066.

Daechsel, H.J.
1981. Sawdust Bay-2: The Identification of a Middle Woodland Site in the Ottawa Valley. Unpublished master's thesis. McMaster University, Department of Anthropology.

Dailey, R.C. and J.V. Wright
1955. The Malcolm Site. *Transactions of the Royal Canadian Institute* 31(1):24–68. Toronto.

Davis, S.A.
1991. Excavations at Whites Lake, 1987. In *Archaeology in Nova Scotia 1987 and 1988*, edited by S.A. Davis, C. Lindsay, R. Ogilvie, and B. Preston, pp. 57–67. Curatorial Report, Vol. 69. Nova Scotia Museum, Halifax, Nova Scotia.

Dawson, K.C.A.
1974. *The McCluskey Site*. Archaeological Survey of Canada 25. National Museums of Canada, Ottawa.

1976. *Algonkian of Lake Nipigon: An Archaeological Survey*. Archaeological Survey of Canada 48. National Museums of Canada, Ottawa.

1980. The MacGillivray Site: a Laurel tradition site in northwestern Ontario. *Ontario Archaeology* 34:45–68.

1981. The Wabinosh River site and the Laurel Tradition in northwestern Ontario. *Ontario Archaeological Society* 36:3–46.

Deal, M.
2001. Early Woodland: Northeastern Middlesex Tradition. Lecture Notes Week Seven: Anthropology 3291 (www.ucs.mun.ca/~mdeal/Anth3291/notes7.htm).

Debicki, R.L.
1982. Geology and Scenary, Killarney Provincial Park Area, Ontario Geological Survey Guidebook No. 6.

Deetz, J.
1965. *The Dynamics of Stylistic Change in Arikara Ceramics*. University of Illinois Press, Urbana.

de Lamorandière, P.R.
1922. At Killarney 300 years ago. *Sudbury News*.

Deller, D.B.
1976. The Heaman Site: A Preliminary Report on a Paleo-Indian Site in Middlesex County, Ontario. *Ontario Archaeology* 27:13–28.

Deller, D.B., C.J. Ellis, and M. Franklin
2018. The Rogers Site: An Early Paleoindian Site in the Niagara Peninsula Region of Ontario. *Archaeology of Eastern North America* 46:103–134.

Demers, P.A.
1991. Report on the St. Mary's River Archaeological Survey: Archaeological Reconnaissance and Limited Testing on the Lower St. Mary's River, Chippewa County, Michigan. Report submitted to the Michigan Bureau of History, Project No. S90-281. Lansing.

Densmore, F.
1928. The Use of Plants by the Chippewa Indians. *Bureau of American Ethnology* 44:275–397.

1929. *Chippewa Customs. Bulletin of the Bureau of American Ethnology 86.* U.S. Government Printing Office, Washington, DC.

Derry, M.E.
2007. *Georgian Bay Jewel: The Killarney Story*. Poplar Lane Press, Caledon, Ontario, Canada.

Devereux, H.E.
1982. A Brief Survey of the Killarney Bay 1 (Speigel) Site, District of Manitoulin, Ontario. Archaeological Survey of Laurentian University, Report No. 11, Sudbury, Ontario.

Dietler, M. and B. Hayden, editors
2001. *Feasts: Archaeological and Ethnographic Perspectives on Food, Politics, and Power*. Smithsonian Institution Press, Washington, DC.

Dodd, C.
1996. *An Archaeological Assessment of Highway 69 and Excavation of the Baxter, Bentley and Bressette Sites in Georgian Bay Township, Ontario.* Manuscript on file at Ontario Ministry of Transport, Toronto.

Donaldson, W.S. and S. Wortner
1995. The Hind Site and the Glacial Kame Burial Complex in Ontario. *Ontario Archaeology* 95:5–95.

Dore, W.G.
1969. *Wild Rice*. Canada Department of Agriculture, Publication 1393, Ottawa, Ontario.

Dragoo, D.W.
1963. *Mounds for the dead: an analysis of the Adena Culture*. Annals of the Carnegie Museum, Volume 37. Pittsburg.

1964. The development of Adena culture and its role in the formation of Ohio Hopewell. In *Hopewellian Studies*, edited by J.R. Caldwell and R.L. Hall, pp. 2–34. Scientific Papers 12(6). Illinois State Museum, Springfield.

1976. Adena and The Eastern Burial Cult. *Archaeology of Eastern North America* 4:1–9.

Drier, R. and O. Du Temple
1961. *Prehistoric Copper Mining in the Lake Superior Region: A Collection of Reference Articles*. Privately published, Michigan.

Dublin, L.S.
1987. *The History of Beads, From 30,000 B.C. to the Present*. Thames and Hudson, London.

1999. *North American Indian Jewelry and Adornment, From Prehistory to the Present*. Harry N. Abrams Inc., New York.

Dudd, S.N. and R.P. Evershed
1998. Direct demonstration of milk as an element of archaeological economies. *Science* 282: 1478–1481.

Dunham, S.B.
2000. Cache Pits: Ethnohistory, Archaeology, and the Continuity of Tradition. In *Interpretations of Native North American Life: Material Contributions to Ethnohistory*, edited by M. Nassaney and E.S. Johnson, pp. 225–260. University of Florida Press, Gainesville.

Dyke, A.S.
2002. An outline of North American deglaciation with emphasis on central and northern Canada. In *Quaternary Glaciations – extent and chronology*, edited by J. Ehlers and P.L. Gibbard, pp. 373–424. Elsevier B.V.

Dyke, A.S., D. Giroux, and L. Robertson
2004. *Paleovegetation maps of Northern North America, 18 000 to 1 000 BP*. Geological Survey of Canada, Open File 4682.

Easby Jr., D.
1966. Early Metallurgy in the New World. *Scientific American* 214:72–81.

Edelman, M.
1996. *From Art to Politics: How Artistic Creations Shape Political Conceptions*. University of Chicago Press.

Eder, T.
2002. *Mammals of Ontario*. Lone Pine, Edmonton.

Eerkens, J.W.
2002. The Preservation and Identification of Pinon Resins by GC-MS in Pottery from the Western Great Basin. *Archaeometry* 44(1):95–105.

Ehrhardt, K.
2008. Copper Working Technologies, Contexts of Use, and Social Complexity in the Eastern Woodlands of Native North America. Paper presented at the Society of American Archaeology meeting, Vancouver, British Columbia, Canada.

Eley, B. and P. Von Bitter
1989. *Cherts of Southern Ontario*. Royal Ontario Museum. Toronto.

Ellis, C.J.
2000. *An Early Paleo-Indian Site Near Parkhill, Ontario*. Canadian Museum of Civilization, Mercury Series Paper No. 159. Ottawa.

Ellis, C. J. and N. Ferris, editors
1990. *The Archaeology of Southern Ontario to A.D. 1650*. Occasional Publications of the London Chapter, Ontario Archaeological Society No. 5, London, Ontario.

Ellis, C.J., I. Kenyon, and M. Spence
1990. The Archaic. In *The Archaeology of Southern Ontario to AD 1650*, edited by C.J. Ellis and N. Ferris, pp. 65–124. Occasional Publication of the London Chapter, Ontario Archaeological Society No. 5, London, Ontario.

Ellis, C.J., J. Keron, J. Menzies, S. Monckton, and A. Stewart
2015. For Immediate Occupancy: Cozy 3000 Year Old Heritage Winter House with River View Near Lake Huron: Apply to Terminal Archaic Realty. In *Building the Past: Studies of Prehistoric Wooden Post Architecture in the Ohio Valley-Great Lakes*, edited by B.G. Redmond and R.A. Genheimer, pp. 29–62. University Presses of Florida, Gainesville.

Emerson, J.N.
1955. The Kant Site: A Point Peninsula Manifestation in Renfrew County, Ontario. *Transactions of the Royal Canadian Institute* 31(1):3–66.

Emerson, T.E., K.B. Farnsworth, S.U. Wisseman, and R.E. Hughes
2013. The Allure of the Exotic: Reexamining the Use of Local and Distant Pipestone Quarries in Ohio Hopewell Pipe Caches. *American Antiquity* 78(1):48–67.

Emerson T.E, D. McElrath, and A. Fortier, editors
2000. *Late Woodland Societies: Tradition and Transformation Across the Midcontinent*. University of Nebraska Press, Lincoln.

Emery, I.
1994. *The Primary Structure of Fabrics: an Illustrated Classification*. The Textile Museum, Washington, DC.

Ensor, B.
2011. Kinship Theory in Archaeology: From Critiques to the Study of Transformations. *American Antiquity* 76(2):203–228.

Esarey, D.
1986. Red Ocher Mound Building and Marion Phase Association: A Fulton County, Illinois Perspective. In *Early Woodland Archaeology*, edited by K.B. Farnsworth and T.E. Emerson, pp. 231–243. Volume 2. Center for American Archaeology, Kampsville, IL.

Eschman, D.F. and P.F. Karrow
1985. Huron basin glacial lakes: a review. In *Quaternary Evolution of the Great Lakes,* edited by P.F.Karrow and P.E. Calkin, pp. 79–93. Geological Association of Canada, Special Paper, Vol. 30.

Evans, E.L.
1952. Native Copper Discoveries in the Seal Lake Area, Labrador. *Proceedings of the Geological Association of Canada* 5:111–116.

Evans, A.A., Y.B. Wolframm, R.E. Donahue, and W.A. Lovis
2007. A pilot study of "black chert" sourcing and implications for assessing hunter-gatherer mobility strategies in Northern England. *Journal of Archaeological Science* 34(12):2161–2169.

Evershed, R.P.
1993. Biomolecular Archaeology and Lipids. *World Archaeology* 25(1):74–93.

2000. Biomolecular Analysis by Organic Mass Spectrometry. In *Modern Analytical Methods in Art and Archaeology*, edited by E. Ciliberto and G. Spoto, pp. 177–239. Volume 155, Chemical Analysis. John Wiley & Sons, New York.

Evershed, R.P., S.N. Dudd, M.J. Lockheart, and S. Jim
2001. Lipids in Archaeology. In *Handbook of Archaeological Sciences*, edited by D.R. Brothwell and A.M. Pollard, pp. 331–349. John Wiley & Sons, New York.

Evershed, R.P., C. Heron, and L.J. Goad
1990. Analysis of Organic Residues of Archaeological Origin by High Temperature Gas Chromatography and Gas Chromatography-Mass Spectroscopy. *Analyst* 115:1339–1342.

1991. Epicuticular Wax Components Preserved in Potsherds as Chemical Indicators of Leafy Vegetables in Ancient Diets. *Antiquity* 65:540–544.

Evershed, R.P., H.R. Mottram, S.N. Dudd, S. Charters, A.W. Stott, G.J. Lawrence, A.M. Gibson, A. Conner, P.W. Blinkhorn, and V. Reeves
1997a. New Criteria for the Identification of Animal Fats in Archaeological Pottery. *Naturwissenschaften* 84:402–406.

Evershed, R.P., S.J. Vaugh, S.N. Dudd, and J.S. Soles
1997b. Fuel for Thought? Beeswax in Lamps and Conical Cups from Late Minoan Crete. *Antiquity* 71:979–985.

Farnsworth, K.B., T.E. Berres, R.E. Hughes, and D.M. Moore
2004. Illinois platform pipes and Hopewellian exchange: a mineralogical study of archaeological remains. In *Aboriginal ritual and economy in the Eastern Woodlands: Essays in*

memory of Howard Dalton Winters, edited by A.-M. Cantwell, L.A. Conrad, and J.E. Reyman, Illinois State Museum, Scientific Papers, Vol. X.

Farnsworth, K., T.E. Emerson, R.E. Hughes, S.U. Wisseman, and M. Hynes
2005. Tremper Mound, Hopewell Catlinite, and PIMA Technology. *Midcontinental Journal of Archaeology* 30(2):189–216.

Faulkner, C.
1960. The Red Ochre Culture: An Early Burial Complex in Northern Indiana. *The Wisconsin Archeologist* 41(2):35–49.

Felder, D.L. and S.A. Earle
2009. *Gulf of Mexico Origin, Waters, and Biota: Biodiversity*. Texas A&M University-Corpus Cristi Press, Corpus Cristi.

Ferris, N.
2009. *The Archaeology of Native-Lived Colonialism: Challenging History in the Great Lakes*. University of Arizona Press, Tucson.

Ferris, N. and M.W. Spence
1995. The Woodland Traditions in Southern Ontario. *Revista de Arqueología Americana* 9:83–138.

Finlayson, W.D.
1977. *The Saugeen Culture: a Middle Woodland Manifestation in Southwestern Ontario*. National Museum of Man, Archaeological Survey of Canada, Mercury Series No. 61. Ottawa.

Fischer, W.
1972. Ceramic Complexes from the Schultz Site. In *The Schultz Site at Green Point: A Stratified Occupation Area in the Saginaw Valley of Michigan*, edited by J. Fitting. Memoirs of the University of Michigan Museum of Anthropology, No. 4. Ann Arbor.

Fischer, A. and J. Heinemeier
2003. Freshwater reservoir effect in ^{14}C dates of food residue on pottery. *Radiocarbon* 45(3):449–66.

Fitting, J.E.
1964. Ceramic Relationships of Four Late Woodland sites in Northern Ohio. *The Wisconsin Archeologist* 45(4):160–175.

1965. *Late Woodland Cultures of Southeastern Michigan*. Anthropological Papers of the Museum of Anthropology, University of Michigan, No. 24. Ann Arbor.

1966. Archaeological Investigations of the Carolinian-Canadian Edge Area in Michigan. *Michigan Archaeologist* 12(4):143–149.

1970. *The Archaeology of Michigan: A Guide to the Prehistory of the Great Lakes Region*. Natural History Press, New York.

1972. *The Schultz Site at Green Point, A Stratified Occupation Area in the Saginaw Valley of Michigan.* Memoirs of the University of Michigan Museum of Anthropology, No.4. Ann Arbor.

1974. The Nelson Site (SIS-34). *Michigan Archaeologist* 20:121–138.

1975. *The Archaeology of Michigan: A Guide to the Prehistory of the Great Lakes Region*. 2nd ed. Cranbrook Institute of Science, Bloomfield Hills, MI.

1978. Regional Cultural Development, 300 BC to AD 1000. In *Handbook of North American Indians, Vol. 15: The Northeast*, edited by B.G. Trigger, pp. 44–57. W. Sturtevant, general editor. Smithsonian Institution, Washington, DC.

1979. Middle Woodland Cultural Development in the Straits of Mackinac Region: Beyond the Hopewell Frontier. In *Hopewell Archaeology: The Chillicothe Conference*, edited by D. Brose and N. Greber, pp. 109–112. Midcontinental Journal of Archaeology Special Papers 3. Kent State University Press.

n.d. The Gyftakis and McGreggor Sites: Middle Woodland Occupations from St. Ignace. Unpublished manuscript on file, Michigan Historical Center, Lansing.

Fitting, J.E. and D.S. Brose
1971. The Northern Periphery of Adena. In *Adena, The Seeking of an Identity*, edited by B.J. Schwartz, pp. 29–55. Ball State University Press, Muncie.

Fitting, J.E., D.S. Brose, H.T. Wright, and J.A. Dinerstein
1969. The Goodwin-Gresham Site, 20IS8, Iosco County, Michigan. *The Wisconsin Archeologist* 50(3):125–183.

Fitting, J.E. and C.E. Cleland
1969. Late Prehistoric Settlement Patterns in the Upper Great Lakes. *Ethnohistory* 16(4):289–302.

Fitting, J.E. and K.A. Cushman
1974. The Sposito Site. *The Michigan Archaeologist* 20: 171–194.

Fitting, J.E. and J.R. Halsey
1966. Rim Diameter and Vessel Size in Wayne Ware Vessels. *The Wisconsin Archeologist* 47(4):208–211.

Fitting, J.E. and R. Zurel
1976. The Detroit and St. Clair River Area. In *Late Prehistory of the Lake Erie Basin, A Symposium*, edited by D.S. Brose, pp. 214–250. Papers of the Museum of Natural History, Cleveland.

Flanders, R.E.
1965. Engraved Turtle Shells from the Norton Mounds near Grand Rapids, Michigan. *Papers of the Michigan Academy of Science, Arts, and Letters* 50:361–364.

Flanders, R.E. and C. Cleland
1964. The Use of Animal Remains in Hopewell Burial Mounds, Kent County, Michigan. *The Jack-Pine Warbler* 42:302–309.

Fogel, I.
1963. The Dispersal of Copper Artifacts in the Late Archaic Period of Prehistoric North America. *The Wisconsin Archeologist* 44(3):129–180.

Folch, J., M. Lees, and G.H. Sloane-Stanley
1957. A simple method for the isolation and purification of lipid extracts from brain tissue. *Journal of Biological Chemistry* 191:833.

Ford, J.A.
1954. The Type Concept Revisited. *American Anthropologist* 56:42–54.

Ford, R.I.
1977. Evolutionary ecology and the evolution of human ecosystems: a case study from the midwestern USA. In *The Explanation of Prehistoric Change,* edited by J.N. Hill, pp. 153–184. University of New Mexico Press, Albuquerque.

Ford, R.I., editor
1985. *Prehistoric Food Production in North America.* Anthropological Papers of the University of Michigan Museum of Anthropology, No. 75. Ann Arbor.

Ford, R.I. and D.S. Brose
1975a. Wild Rice Utilization and Late Archaic Ceremonial Patterns in Northern Michigan. *The Wisconsin Archeologist* 55(1):17–19.

1975b. Prehistoric Wild Rice from the Dunn Farm Site, Leelanau County, Michigan. *The Wisconsin Archeologist* 56(9–15).

Fowler, M. and R. Hall
1978. Late Prehistory of the Illinois Area. In *Handbook of North American Indians, Vol. 15: The Northeast*, edited by B.G. Trigger, pp. 560–568. W. Sturtevant, general editor. Smithsonian Institution, Washington, DC.

Fox, W.A.
1975. The Palaeo-Indian Lakehead Complex. In *Canadian Archaeological Association – Collected Papers March 1975*, pp. 29–53. Research Report 6, Ontario Ministry of Natural Resources. Historical Sites Branch, Toronto.

1980. Miskwo Sinnee Munnidominug. *Archaeology of Eastern North America* 8:88–98.

1990. The Odawa. In *The Archaeology of Southern Ontario to A.D. 1650*, edited by C.J. Ellis and N. Ferris. Occasional Publications of the London Chapter, OAS Number 5.

1992. The Serpent's Copper Scales. *Kewa: Newsletter of the London Chapter, Ontario Archaeological Society*. 92-3:3–13.

2004. Islands of Creation, Islands of Rebirth. *The Bulletin: Journal of the New York State Archaeological Association* 120:47–57.

2008. Reciprocal Symbols: A Review of Ontario Iroquois Archaeological Evidence Relating to Long-Distance Contacts. *Northeast Anthropology* 75/76:1–22.

2009. Ontario Cherts Revisited. In *Painting With A Broad Brush. Papers in Honour of James Valliere Wright*, edited by D.L. Keenlyside and J.-L. Pilon, pp. 339–354. Mercury Series Archaeology Paper 170. Canadian Museum of Civilization. Gatineau.

2010. Exotic Giants. *Arch Notes: The Newsletter of the Ontario Archaeological Society* 15(5):5–12.

Fox, W.A., B. Deller, and C. Ellis
2015. Chert Sources and Utilization in the Southern Huron Basin during the Early Holocene. In *Caribou Hunting in the Upper Great Lakes: Archaeological, Ethnographic, and Paleoenvironmental Perspectives*, pp. 67–72. Memoirs of the University of Michigan Museum of Anthropology, No. 57. Ann Arbor.

Fox, W.A. and C. Garrad
2004. Hurons in an Algonquian Land. In *An Archaeological Generation: A Festschrift for Dr. Martha A. Latta*, edited by M. Kapches and P. Reed, pp. 121–134. *Ontario Archaeology* 77/78.

Fox, W.A., J-L. Pilon, and C. Crann
2016. Sunken Vessels. *Arch Notes: The Newsletter of the Ontario Archaeological Society* 21(3):5–7.

Fox, W. and M. Spence
1990. The Early and Middle Complexes of Southern Ontario.In *The Archaeology of Southern Ontario to A.D. 1650*, edited by C.J. Ellis and N. Ferris. Occasional Publication of the London Chapter, Ontario Archaeological Society, Number 5.

Fox, W., R. Hancock, and L. Pavlish
1995. Where East Met West: The New Copper Culture. *The Wisconsin Archeologist* 76(3-4):269–293.

Frankel, E.N.
1991. Recent Advances in Lipid Oxidation. *Journal of the Science of Food and Agriculture* 54:465–511.

Frarey, M.J.
1977. *Geology of the Huronian belt between Sault Ste. Marie and Blind River, Ontario*. Geological Survey of Canada, Memoir 383.

Fraser, J.
2005. The "Green Man" from Killarney Bay. On file at the Canadian Museum of Civilization, Archaeology and History Division, Ottawa.

Friedman, S.K., P.B. Reich and L.E. Frelich
2001. Multiple Scale Composition and Spatial Distribution Patterns of the North-Eastern Minnesota Presettlement Forest. *Journal of Ecology* 89:538–554.

Froom, B.
1976. *The Turtles of Canada*. McClelland and Stewart, Toronto.

Gadus, E.F.
1979. The Harness Copper Plate. *Ohio Archaeologist* 29(3):27–29.

Galm, J.
1994. Prehistoric Trade and Exchange in the Interior Plateau of Northwestern North America. In *Prehistoric Exchange Systems in North America*, edited by T.G. Baugh and J.E. Ericson. Plenum, New York.

Garland, E.B.
1986. Early Woodland Occupations in Michigan: A Lower Saint Joseph Perspective. In *Early Woodland Archaeology*, edited by K.B. Farnsworth and T.E. Emerson, pp. 47–83. Volume 2. Center for American Archaeology, Kampsville, IL.

Garland, E.B., editor
1990. *Late Archaic and Early Woodland Adaptation in the Lower St. Joseph River Valley, Berrien Co. Michigan: The US-31 Berrien County Freeway Project.* Michigan Cultural Resource Investigation Series 2. Lansing.

Garland, E.B. and S.G. Beld
1999. The Early Woodland: Ceramics, Domesticated Plants, and Burial Mounds Foretell the Shape of the Future. In *Retrieving Michigan's Buried Past: The Archaeology of the Great Lakes State,* edited by J.R. Halsey, pp. 125–146. Cranbrook Institute of Science, Bloomfield Hills, MI.

Garte, E.
1984. *Circle of Life: Cultural Continuity in Ojibwe Crafts.* Duluth: Exhibition Catalogue of the Depot St. Louis County Heritage and Arts Center.

Geniusz, W.M.
2009. *Our Knowledge Is Not Primitive: Decolonizing Botanical Anishinaabe Teachings*. Syracuse University Press, Syracuse.

Gehlbach, D.R.
1994. Flared Mouthpiece Adena Tube Pipes: A Rare Diagnostic Art Form. *Ohio Archaeologist* 44(4):31. https://kb.osu.edu/bitstream/handle/1811/55915/OHIO_ARCHAEOLOGIST_44_4_FALL_1994.pdf?sequence=1. Accessed August 2021.

Gifford, S.M.
1948. A Brief Summary of Three Years Digging on the Orwell Site. *The Bulletin of the Fort Ticonderoga Museum* 8(1):25–28.

Gilbert, B.M.
1990. *Mammalian Osteology*. Missouri Archaeological Society Inc., Columbia, Missouri.

Gilmore, M.R.
1933. *Some Chippewa Uses of Plants*. University of Michigan Press, Ann Arbor.

Glascock, M.D.
2004. Neutron activation analysis of chert artifacts from a Hopewell mound. *Journal of Radioanalytical and Nuclear Chemistry* 262(1):97–102.

Goldstein, L.
1981. One-dimensional archaeology and multi-dimensional people: spatial organization and mortuary analysis. In *The Archaeology of Death*, edited by R. Chapman, L. Kinnes, and K. Randsborg, pp. 53–69. University Press, Cambridge.

Gordon, D.L.
2013. A Lake Through Time: Archaeological And Palaeo-Environmental Investigations at Lake Temagami, 1985–1994. *Ontario Archaeology* 93:52–158.

Gordon, J.
1990. Micmac Indian Basketry. In *The Art of Native American Basketry: A Living Legacy*, edited by F.W. Porter III, pp. 17–44. Greenwood Press, New York.

Gramly, R.M.
1977. Deerskins and Hunting Territories: Competition for a Scarce Resource of the Northeastern Woodlands. *American Antiquity* 42(4):601–605.

Granger, J.E., Jr.
1978. *Meadowood Phase Settlement Pattern in the Niagara Frontier Region of Western New York State.* Anthropological Papers of the University of Michigan Museum of Anthropology No. 65. Ann Arbor.

Greber, N.

1976. *Within Ohio Hopewell*. Unpublished PhD dissertation in anthropology. Case Western Reserve University. Cleveland.

1979. A Comparative Study of Site Morphology and Burial Patterns at Edwin Harness Mound and Seip Mounds 1 and 2. In *Hopewell Archaeology*, edited by D.S. Brose and N. Greber, pp. 27–38. Kent State University Press, Kent.

2005. Adena and Hopewell in the Middle Ohio Valley: To Be or Not To Be? In *Woodland Period systematics in the Middle Ohio Valley*, edited by D. Applegate and R.C. Mainfort, pp. 19–39. University of Alabama Press, Tuscaloosa.

Greber, N. and K. Ruhl

1989. *The Hopewell Site: A Contemporary Analysis Based on the Work of Charles C. Willoughby*. Investigations in American Archaeology. Westview Press, Boulder. Revised and reprinted by Eastern National, 2000.

Greenman, E.F.

1926. Report on Michigan Archaeology, Discussion and Comment. *American Anthropologist* [N.S.] 28:311–313.

1927. The Earthwork Inclosures of Michigan. Unpublished PhD dissertation. University of Michigan, Ann Arbor.

1932. Excavation of the Coon Mound and Analysis of the Adena Culture. *Ohio State Archaeological and Historical Quarterly* 41(3):369–523.

1935a. Excavation of the Reeve Village Site. *Ohio State Archaeological and Historical Quarterly* 44(1):2–64.

1935b. Seven Prehistoric Sites in Northern Ohio. *Ohio State Archaeological and Historical Quarterly*. 44(2):220–237.

1937a. Two Prehistoric Village Sites Near Cleveland Ohio. *Ohio State Archaeological and Historical Quarterly* 46(4):305–366.

1937b. *The Younge Site: An Archaeological Record from Michigan*. Occasional Contributions from the University of Michigan Museum of Anthropology, No. 6. Ann Arbor.

1937c. A Porcelain Baton. *American Antiquity* 2(3):204–205.

1938. Hopewellian Traits in Florida. *American Antiquity* 4:327–333.

1938–1953. Field notes from the KB1 site (Killarney Bay). University of Michigan Museum of Anthropological Archaeology archives.

1939a. Cultural Relationships of Archaeological Sites in the Upper Great Lakes Region. *Papers of the Michigan Academy of Science, Arts and Letters* 24:1–10.

1939b. *Guide to Serpent Mound*. Ohio State Archaeological and Historical Society.

1939c. *The Wolf and Furton Sites, Macomb County, Michigan*. Occasional Contributions from the University of Michigan Museum of Anthropology, No. 8.

1940. Prehistoric Sites in Ontario. *Man* 40:100.

1943a. The Archaeology and Geology of Two Early Sites near Killarney, Ontario. *Papers of the Michigan Academy of Sciences, Arts and Letters* 28:505–531.

1943b. An Early Industry on a Raised Beach near Killarney, Ontario. *American Antiquity* 8(3):260–265.

1945. The Hopewellian in the Detroit-Windsor Area. *Papers* of the *Michigan Academy of Science, Arts and Letters* 30:457–464.

1948. The Killarney Sequence and its Old World Connections. *Papers of the Michigan Academy of Sciences, Arts and Letters* 32:313–319.

1949–1953. Field Notes. University of Michigan Museum of Anthropological Archaeology archives.

1950. Killarney Bay 1, Folder #9 Diagrams. Unpublished field notes. Photocopies on file at Laurentian University Anthropology Department. Sudbury, Ontario.

1951. *Old Birch Island Cemetery and the Early Historic Trade Route Georgian Bay, Ontario*. Occasional Contributions from the University of Michigan Museum of Anthropology, No. 11. Ann Arbor.

1953. Killarney Bay 1, Folder #22. Unpublished field notes. Photocopies on file at Laurentian University Anthropology Department. Sudbury, Ontario.

1955. Field Notes. University of Michigan Museum of Anthropological Archaeology archives.

1957. The Riviere au Vase Site. *The Michigan Archaeologist*. 3:9–11.

1959–1960. Field Notes. University of Michigan Museum of Anthropological Archaeology archives.

1961. *The Indians of Michigan*. Lansing: The Michigan Historical Commission.

1963. The Upper Paleolithic and the New World with CA Comment. *Current Anthropology* 4(1)41–91.

1966. Chronology of Sites at Killarney, Canada. *American Antiquity* 31(4):540–551.

Greenman, E.F. and G.M. Stanley
1941. Two Post-Nipissing Sites near Killarney, Ontario. *American Antiquity* 6(4):305–313.

Griffin, J.B.
1942. Adena Pottery. *American Antiquity* 7(4):344–358.

1943. *The Fort Ancient Aspect*. Anthropological Papers of the University of Michigan Museum of Anthropology, No. 28. Ann Arbor.

1946. Cultural Change and Continuity in Eastern United States Archaeology. In *Man in Northeastern North America*, edited by Fredrick Johnson, pp. 37–95. Papers of the Robert S. Peabody Foundation for Archaeology, Vol 3., Andover.

1952. Culture Periods in Eastern United States Archeology. In *Archeology of the Eastern United States*, edited by J.B. Griffin, pp. 352–336. University of Chicago Press, Chicago.

1954. The Ceramic Affiliation of the Ohio Valley Adena Culture. In *The Adena People*, edited by W. Webb and C. Snow, pp. 220–246. University of Kentucky Reports in Anthropology and Archaeology, Lexington.

1964. The Northeast Woodlands Area. In *Prehistoric Man in the New World*, edited by J.D. Jennings and E. Norbeck, pp. 223–258. University of Chicago Press, Chicago.

1967. Eastern North American Archaeology: A Summary. *Science* 156:175–191.

1974. Emerson F. Greenman. 1895–1973. *American Antiquity* 39(2):271–273.

Griffin, J.B., R.E. Flanders, and P.F. Titterington
1970. *The Burial Complexes of the Knight and Norton Mounds in Illinois and Michigan*. Memoirs of the University of Michigan Museum of Anthropology, No. 2. Ann Arbor.

Guindon, F.
2009. Iroquoian Pottery at Lake Abitibi: A Case Study of the Relationship Between Hurons and Algonkians on the Canadian Shield. *Canadian Journal of Archaeology* 33:65–91.

Guthe, C.
1939. The Basic Needs of American Archaeology. *Science* 90:528–530.

Halsey, J.R.
1966. Additional Hopewell Engraved Turtle Shells from Michigan. *Papers of the Michigan Academy of Science, Arts, and Letters* 51:389–398.

1976. *The Bussinger Site: A Multicomponent Site in the Saginaw Valley of Michigan, with a Review of Early Late Woodland Mortuary Complexes in the Northeastern Woodlands*. Unpublished PhD dissertation in anthropology. The University of North Carolina, Chapel Hill.

1996. Without Forge or Crucible: Aboriginal Native American Use of Metals and Metallic Ores in the Eastern Woodlands. *The Michigan Archaeologist* 42(1):1–58.

2013. Introduction: After Hopewell: The Jack's Reef Horizon and its Place in the Early Late Woodland Mortuary and Settlement Patterns in Northeastern North America. *Archaeology of Eastern North America* 41:1–4.

Halsey, J.R. and J.G. Brashler
2013. More than Grave Lots? The Jack's Reef Horizon in Michigan. *Archaeology of Eastern North America* 41:145–192.

Hamalainen, P.
1975. Faunal Analysis of Two Middle Woodland Sites in Southern Ontario. In *Canadian Archaeological Association Collected Papers--March 1975*, pp. 54–56. Historical Sites Branch Research Report.

Hambacher, M.
1992. The Skegmog Point Site: Continuing Studies in the Cultural Dynamics of the Carolinian-Canadian Transition Zone. Unpublished PhD dissertation in anthropology. Michigan State University, East Lansing.

Hamilton, N.D., J.B. Petersen, and A.L. McPherron
1996. Fiber Industries from the Upper Great Lakes: A Late Woodland Case Study from the Juntunen Site. In *A Most Indispensable Art: Native Fiber Industries from Eastern North America*, edited by J.B. Petersen, pp. 120–143. University of Tennessee Press, Knoxville.

Hamilton, S.
2013. A World Apart? Ontario's Canadian Shield. Chapter 5 in *Before Ontario: the Archaeology of a Province*, edited by M.K. Munson and S.M. Jamieson. McGill-Queen's University Press, Montreal.

Hancock, R.G.V., L.A. Pavlish, R.M. Farquhar, R. Salloum, W.A. Fox, and G.C. Wilson
1991. Distinguishing European Trade Copper and Northeastern North American Native Copper. *Archaeometry* 53(1):69–86.

Hanks, C.
1988. *The Foxie Otter Site.* Anthropological Papers of the University of Michigan Museum of Anthropology, No. 79. Ann Arbor.

Harpending, H.C. and H. Davis
1977. Some Implications for Hunter-gatherer Ecology Derived from the Spatial Structure of Resources. *World Archaeology* 8(3):275–286.

Harrar, E.S.
1964. *Hough's Encyclopedia of American Woods.* Robert Speller and Sons, New York.

Hart, J.P. and W.A. Lovis
2007. A Multi-regional Analysis of AMS and Radiometric Dates from Carbonized Food Residues. *Midcontinental Journal of Archaeology* 32(2):201–261.

2014. A Re-Evaluation of the Reliability of AMS Dates on Pottery Food Residues from the Late Prehistoric Central Plains of North America: Comment on Roper (2013). *Radiocarbon* 56(1):341–353. DOI:10.2458/56.16898.

Hart, J.P., W. Lovis, and A. Katzenberg
2021. Early Maize in Northeastern North America: A Comment on Emerson and Colleagues. *American Antiquity* 86(2):425–427.

Hawkins, A.
2008. Making Pots for Different Uses? A Consideration of Technological Variation in a Middle Woodland Assemblage from Georgian Bay, Ontario. Presented at the Annual Meeting of the Canadian Archaeological Association, Peterborough, Ontario.

Hayes, C.F.
1963. A Point Peninsula Burial. *Bulletin of the Rochester Museum Arts and Sciences* 36(1):6–7.

Heckenberger, M., J. Petersen, and L. Basa
1990a. Early Woodland Period Ritual Use of Personal Adornment at the Boucher Site. *Annals of Carnegie Museum* 59(3):173–217.

Heckenberger, M.J., J.B. Peterson, L.A. Basa, E.R. Cowie, A.E. Spiess, and R.E. Stuckenrath
1990b. Early Woodland Period Mortuary Ceremonialism in the Far Northeast: A View from the Boucher Cemetery. *Archaeology of Eastern North America* 18:109–144.

Heckenberger, M.J., J.B. Petersen, F.B. King, and L.A. Basa
1996. Fiber Industries from the Boucher Site: An Early Woodland Cemetery in Northwestern Vermont. In *A Most Indispensable Art: Native Fiber Industries from Eastern North America*, edited by J.B. Petersen, pp. 50–72. University of Tennessee Press, Knoxville.

Heidenreich, C.
1987. The Iroquois Disruptions, 1660–1666, Plate 37. In *Historical Atlas of Canada,* edited by R.C. Harris, University of Toronto Press, Toronto.

1988. An Analysis of the 17th Century Map "Nouvelle France." *Cartographica* 25(3):67–111.

1990. History of the St. Lawrence-Great Lakes Area to A.D. 1650. In *The Archaeology of Southern Ontario to A.D. 1650*, edited by C.J. Ellis and N. Ferris. Occasional Publications of the London Chapter, Ontario Archaeological Society, London, Ontario.

Henry, E.R.
2013. Review of *Sacred Games, Death and Renewal in the Ancient Eastern Woodlands: The Ohio Hopewell system of Cult Sodality Heterarchies* by Martin Byers. *Southeastern Archaeology* 32(2):285–287.

Herbert, J.
2009. *Woodland Potters and Archaeological Ceramics of the North Carolina Coast.* University of Alabama Press, Tuscaloosa.

Heron, C., N. Nemcek, K.M. Bonfield, J. Dixon, and B.S. Ottaway
1994. The Chemistry of Neolithic Beeswax. *Naturwissenschaften* 81:266–269.

Heron, C. and A.M. Pollard
1988. The Analysis of Natural Resinous Materials from Roman Amphoras. In *Science and Archaeology Glasgow 1987. Proceedings of a Conference on the Application of Scientific Techniques to Archaeology, Glasgow, 1987*, edited by E.A. Slater and J.O. Tate, pp. 429–447. BAR British Series 196 (ii), Oxford.

Hill, M.
2012. Tracing Social Interaction: Perspectives in Archaic Copper Exchange from the Upper Great Lakes. *American Antiquity.* 77(2):279–292.

Hoadley, R.B.
1990. *Identifying Wood: Accurate Results with Simple Tools.* Taunton Press, Newtown, CT.

Holland, J.D.
2005. Types and varieties of archaeologically relevant Ohio chert. *Ohio Archaeologist* 55:20–22.

2008a. Illinois Chert Types. *Illinois Antiquity* 43(1):3–17.

2008b. Indiana Chert Types. *Illinois Antiquity* 43(1):18–26.

Holman, M.B.
1984. Pine River Ware: Evidence for In Situ Development of the Late Woodland in the Straits of Mackinac Region. *The Wisconsin Archeologist* 65:32–48.

Holmes, W.H.
1884. Prehistoric Textile Art of the Eastern United States. *Thirteenth Annual Report of the Bureau of Ethnology for the Years 1891–1892.* Smithsonian Institution, Washington, DC.

Hosie, R.C.
1979. *Native Trees of Canada*. Fitzhenry and Whiteside, Ottawa.

Howey, M.
2012. *Mound Builders and Monument Makers of the Northern Great Lakes, 1200–1600*. University of Oklahoma Press, Norman.

Howey, M.C.L. and J.M. O'Shea
2006. Bear's Journey and the Study of Ritual in Archaeology. *American Antiquity* 71(2):261–282.

Hruska, R.
1967. The Riverside Site: A Late Archaic Manifestation in Michigan. *The Wisconsin Archeologist* 48(3):145–260.

Hurley, W.M.
1979. *Prehistoric Cordage: Identification of Impressions on Pottery*. Aldine Manuals on Archeology 3. Taraxacum, Washington, DC.

Inksetter, L.
2000. Laurel et Blackduck: L'Apport du Site Roger Marois. *Archéologiques* 14:11–23.

Inomata, T. and L.S. Coben
2006. Overture: An Invitation to the Archaeological Theater. In *Archaeology of Performance: Theaters of Power, Community, and Politics*, edited by T. Inomata and L.S. Coben, pp. 11–44. AltaMira Press, Lanham.

Iso Trace Laboratories
2005 Results of Carbon-14 Dating of Schlegel Site. Toronto.

Ivakhiv, A.J.
2001. *Claiming Sacred Ground: Pilgrims and Politics at Glastonbury and Sedona*. University of Indiana Press, Bloomington.

Jackson, L.J.
1983. New Evidence for Early Woodland Seasonal Adaptation from Southern Ontario, Canada. *American Antiquity* 51:389–401.

Jakes, K.A., L.R. Sibley, and R. Yerkes
1994. A Comparative Collection for the Study of Fibres Used in Prehistoric Textiles from Eastern North America. *Journal of Archaeological Science* 21:641–650.

James, G.W.
1903. *Indian Basketry and How to Make Baskets*. 3rd edition. Privately printed by the author, Pasadena, CA.

Janusas, S.E.
1984. *A Petrological Analysis of Kettle Point Chert and Its Spatial and Temporal Distribution in Regional Prehistory.* Archaeological Survey of Canada, Paper No. 128. National Museum of Canada, Ottawa.

Janusas, S.E., S.M. Blasco, S. McClellan, and J. Lusted
2004. Prehistoric Drainage and Archaeological Implications Across the Submerged Niagara Escarpment North of Tobermory, Ontario. In *The Late Palaeo-Indian Great Lakes Geological and Archaeological Investigations of Late Pleistocene and Early Holocene Environments*, edited by L. Jackson and A. Hinshelwood, pp. 303–314. Canadian Museum of Civilization. Mercury Series Archaeology, Paper 165.

Janzen, D.E.
1968a. Excavations and Survey at Burnt Bluff in 1965. In *The Prehistory of the Burnt Bluff Area*, edited by J.E. Fitting. Anthropological Papers of the University of Michigan Museum of Anthropology, No. 34. Ann Arbor.

1968b. *The Naomikong Point Site and the Dimensions of Laurel in the Lake Superior Region*. Anthropological Papers of the University of Michigan Museum of Anthropology, No. 36. Ann Arbor.

Jebens, H., editor
2004. *Cargo, Cult, and Culture Critique*. University of Hawai'i Press, Honolulu.

Jodry, M.A.
2005. Envisioning Water Transport Technology in Late Pleistocene America. In *Paleoamerican Origins Beyond Clovis*, edited by R. Bonnichsen, B. Lepper, D. Stanford, and M. Waters, pp. 133–160. A Peopling of the Americas Publication, Center for the Study of the First Americans, Texas A&M University.

Johannesson, K.H., D.L. Hawkins, Jr., and A. Cortés
2006. Do Archean chemical sediments record ancient seawater

rare earth element patterns? *Geochimica et Cosmochimica Acta* 70: 871–890.

Johnston, R.B.
1958a. The Findings after Two Years of Work at Serpent Mounds Site, Rice Lake, Ontario. *Proceedings of the Indiana Academy of Science* 67:96–97.

1958b. The Serpent Mounds Site, 1957. Royal Ontario Museum, *Bulletin of the Division of Art and Archaeology* 27:3–7.

1960. More Findings at the Serpent Mounds Site, Rice Lake, Ontario. *Proceedings of the Indiana Academy of Science* 69:73–77.

1968a. *Archaeology of Rice Lake, Ontario*. Anthropological Papers 19, National Museum of Canada, Ottawa.

1968b. *The Archaeology of the Serpent Mounds Site*. Royal Ontario Museum, Art and Archaeology Division, Occasional Paper 10. Toronto.

Jones, V.
1936. Some Chippewa and Ottawa Uses of Sweet Grass. *Papers of the Michigan Academy of Science, Arts and Letters, Vol. 21*. Ann Arbor.

1946. Notes on the manufacture of cedar-bark mats by the Chippewa Indians. *Papers of the Michigan Academy of Science, Arts and Letters, Vol. 32*. Ann Arbor.

Julig, P.J.
1982. Human Use of the Albany River from Pre-Ceramic Times to the Late Eighteenth Century. Unpublished master's thesis, York University.

1988. Prehistoric site survey in the Western James Bay Lowlands, Northern Ontario. In *Boreal Forest and Subarctic Archaeology*, edited by C.S. Reid, pp. 121–145. Occasional Publications of the London Chapter, Ontario Archaeological Society Inc., No. 6.

1994. *The Cummins Site Complex and Paleoindian Occupations in the Northwestern Lake Superior Region*. Ontario Archaeological Reports 2, Ontario Heritage Foundation, University of Toronto Press.

2004. The 2002 Speigel Site Field School Excavation. Archaeological Survey of Laurentian University. Report No. 41, Sudbury, Ontario.

Julig, P.J., editor
2002. *The Sheguiandah Site: Archaeological, Geological and Paleobotanical Studies at a Paleoindian Site on Manitoulin Island, Ontario*. Mercury Series, Archaeological Survey of Canada, Paper 161, Canadian Museum of Civilization, Hull, Quebec.

Julig, P.J. and G. Beaton
2015a. Archaeology of the Late Paleoindian/Early Archaic in the Lake Huron Region, with New Data from the Sheguiandah Site. In *Caribou Hunting in the Upper Great Lakes: Archaeological, Ethnographic, and Paleoenvironmental Perspectives*, edited by E. Sonnenburg, A.K. Lemke, and J.M. O'Shea, pp. 53–68. Memoirs of the University of Michigan Museum of Anthropology, No. 57. Ann Arbor.

2015b. Stage 1 and 2 Archaeological Assessment of the Speigel Property, Killarney, Ontario. Assessment P100-0033-2015, submitted to Ontario Ministry of Tourism, Culture and Sport, Toronto, Ontario.

Julig, P., A. Hawkins, and D.G.F. Long
2009. Sourcing of Chert Artifacts from the Killarney Bay 1/Speigel Site, Killarney, Ontario. Paper presented at the 75th Annual Meeting of the Eastern States Archaeological Federation. November 2008, Lockport, NY.

Julig, P.J. and D.G.F. Long
2006. Quarrying Behavior and Facies Selection of Bar River Formation Quartzite at the Sheguiandah Paleo-Indian Site. Paper presented at 71st Annual Meeting of the Society for American Archaeology, San Juan, Puerto Rico.

2010. Why did Paleo-Indians select the Sheguiandah Site: An evaluation of quarrying and quartzite material selection based on petrographic analysis of core artifacts. In *Ancient Mines and Quarries: A Trans-Atlantic Perspective*, edited by M. Brewer-LaPorta, A. Burke, and D. Fields, pp. 97–108. Oxbow Books, Oxford, UK.

2013. Spanish River Lithic Cache, Sudbury Region of Ontario. Special Publication on Archaeology of Northeastern Ontario, edited by A. Hawkins and W. Fox. *Ontario Archaeology* 93:32–51.

Julig, P.J., D.G.F. Long, and R.G.V. Hancock
1998. Cathodoluminescence and Petrographic Techniques for Positive Identification of Quartz-rich Lithic Artifacts from Late Paleoindian Sites in the Great Lakes Region, *The Wisconsin Archaeologist* 79(1):68–88.

Julig, P.J., L.A. Pavlish, C. Clark and R.G.V. Hancock
1992. Chemical Characterization and Sourcing of Upper Great Lakes Cherts by INAA. *Ontario Archaeology* 54:7–50.

Julig, P.J., L.A. Pavlish, and R.G.V. Hancock
1989. Late Paleoindian Lithic Technological Organization in the Northwest Lake Superior Region, Canada. In *Eastern Lithic Resource Use*, edited by C.J. Ellis and J.C. Lothrop, pp. 293–322. Westview Press, Boulder, Colorado.

1991. INAA provenance studies of lithic materials from the western Great Lakes region of North America. In *Archaeometry '90*, edited by E. Pernicka and A.W. Gunther, pp. 435–444. Proceedings of the 27th International Symposium on Archaeometry, Birkhauser Verlag Basel, Heidelberg, Germany.

Julig, P.J., H. Pitawanakwat, C.G. Peltier
2006. *Archaeological Survey of Point Grondine and Collins Inlet: Report on 2005 and 2006 Field Season.* Report submitted to the Wikwemikong Heritage Organization, Wikwemikong Unceded Indian Reserve #26.

Julig, P.J., P.L. Storck, and W.C. Mahaney
1991. Re-investigations at Sheguiandah: The Application of a Geoarchaeological Approach. Paper presented at Great Lakes Archaeology and Paleoecology Symposium, Quaternary Sciences Institute, University of Waterloo.

Jury, W. and E.M.M. Jury
1952. *The Burley Site.* Museums Board of the University of Western Ontario, London, Ontario.

Justice, N.D.
1987. *Stone Age Spear and Arrow Points of the Midcontinental and Eastern United States, A Modern Survey and Reference.* Indiana University Press, Bloomington.

Kagelmacher, M.L.
2001. *Ohio Cherts of Archaeological Interest: A Macroscopic and Petrographic Examination and Comparison.* Kent State University.

Kamber, B.S.
2009. Geochemical fingerprinting: 40 years of analytical development and real world applications. *Applied Geochemistry* 24(6):1074–1086.

Kamber, B.S., A. Greig, and K.D. Collerson
2005. A new estimate for the composition of weathered young upper continental crust from alluvial sediments, Queensland, Australia. *Geochimica et Cosmochimica Acta* 69(4):1041–1058.

Kamber, B.S. and G.E. Webb
2007. Transition metal abundances in microbial carbonate: a pilot study based on in situ LA-ICP-MS analysis. *Geobiology* 5:375–389.

Kan, M.
2005. 'U' to Return Burial Remains to Tribe. *The Michigan Daily News*, March 18. University of Michigan, Ann Arbor.

Kaplan, M.
1995. *Neither Cargo nor Cult: Ritual Politics and the Colonial Imagination in Fiji.* Duke University Press, Durham.

Kato, Y., K. Nakao, and Y. Isozaki
2002. Geochemistry of Late Permian to Early Triassic pelagic cherts from southwest Japan: implications for an oceanic redox change. *Chemical Geology* 182:15–34.

Kenyon, W.A.
1957. *The Inverhuron Site: Bruce County, Ontario.* Royal Ontario Museum of Anthropology and Archaeology Occasional Paper 1. University of Toronto.

1961. *The Swan Lake Site.* Royal Ontario Museum of Anthropology and Archaeology Occasional Paper 3. University of Toronto.

1971. The Armstrong Mound on Rainy River, Ontario. *Canadian Historic Sites: Occasional Papers in Archaeology and History 3*, pp. 65–84. National Historic Sites Service, Department of Indian Affairs and Northern Development, Ontario, Canada.

1975. The Quetico Report. In *Voices from the Rapids: An Underwater Search for Fur Trade Artifacts 1960–73*, edited by R. Wheeler, pp. 45–54. Minnesota Historical Archaeology Series No. 3, Minnesota Historical Society, St. Paul.

Kenyon, W.A. and N.S. Cameron
1960. *The Brock Street Burial.* Royal Ontario Museum, Art and Archaeology Division, Occasional Paper 3:39–55.

Kenyon, I. and W.A. Fox
1983. The Wyoming Rapids Saugeen Component:1983 Investigations. *Kewa* 83(7):2–19.

Kerrich, R., A. Polart, and Q. Xie
2008. Geochemical systematics of 2.7 Ga Kinojevis Group (Abitibi), and Manitouwadge and Winston Lake (Wawa) Fe-rich basalt-rhyolite associations: backarc rift oceanic crust. *Lithos* 101:1–23.

Killan, G.
1988. *The Canadian Encyclopedia.* Volume 1, p. 264. Hurtig Publishers, Edmonton, Canada.

King, F.B.
1978. Analytical Methods and Prehistoric Textiles. *American Antiquity* 43(1):89–98.

Kingsley, R.G.
1981. Hopewell Middle Woodland Settlement Systems and Cultural Dynamics in Southern Michigan. *Midcontinental Journal of Archaeology* 6:131–178.

1984. An Analysis of Mortuary Practices at the Norton Mounds Site. *The Wisconsin Archeologist* 65:99–115.

1990. Rethinking Hopewell Ceramic Typology in Michigan. In *Pilot of the Grand: Papers in Tribute to Richard E. Flanders*, edited by T.J. Martin and C.E. Cleland. *The Michigan Archaeologist* 36(3-4):211–231.

1999. The Middle Woodland Period in Southern Michigan. In *Retrieving Michigan's Buried Past: The Archaeology of the Great Lakes State,* edited by J. R. Halsey, pp.148–172. Bulletin No. 64, Cranbrook Institute of Science, Bloomfield Hills, MI.

Kinietz, W.V.
1940. *The Indians of the Western Great Lakes, 1615–1760.* Occassional Contributions of the University of Michigan Museum of Anthropology, No. 10. Ann Arbor.

Kinkel, A.J., S. Feitler, and R. Hobbs
1968. Copper and Sulfur. In *Mineral Resources of the Appalachian Region*, pp. 377–385. Professional Paper No. 580, U.S. Geological Survey. DOI: 10.3133/pp580.

Kline, M.
2001. *Fagus grandifolia.* In *A Guide to Useful Woods of the World*, edited by J.H. Flynn and C.D. Holder, pp. 238–239. Forest Products Society, Madison, WI.

Knapp, A.M.
1993. Preventative Conservation Recommendations for Organic Objects. *Preservation of Museum Collections Conserv-O-Gram Number 1/3.* The National Park Service Curatorial Services Division, Washington DC.

Koldenhoff, B.H. and K.B. Farnsworth
2018. From Tubes to Platforms: Transformations in Early Smoking Pipes and Ancient Rituals. In *Archaeology and Ancient Religion in the American Midcontinent.*, edited by B. Koldenhoff and T. Pauketat, pp. 29–80. University of Alabama Press, Tuscalosa.

Kraeuter, J.N.
2009. Scaphopoda (Mollusca) of the Gulf of Mexico. In *Gulf of Mexico: Origins, Waters, and Biota*, edited by D.L. Felder and D.K. Camp, pp. 745–749. Texas A&M Press, College Station.

Krakker, J.
1983. *Late Woodland Mortuary Complexes of the Great Lakes Regions of Southeastern Michigan.* Unpublished PhD dissertation in anthropology, University of Michigan, Ann Arbor.

1997. Biface Caches, Exchange, and Regulatory Systems in the Prehistoric Great Lakes Region. *Midcontinental Journal of Archaeology* 22(1):1–41.

1999. Late Woodland Settlement Patterns, Population, and Social Organization Viewed from Southern Michigan. In *Retrieving Michigan's Buried Past : The Archaeology of the Great Lakes State*, edited by J.R. Halsey and M.D. Stafford, pp. 228–243. Cranbrook Institute of Science, Bloomfield Hills, MI.

Kritsch-Armstrong, I.D.
1982. A technological analysis of the Jessup lithic workshop site. M.Sc. thesis, Department of Anthropology, McMaster University, Hamilton, Ontario.

Kuhn, S.L.
1992. On planning and curated technologies in the Middle Paleolithic. *Journal of Anthropological Research* 48:185–214.

Kunimaru, T., H. Shimizu, K. Takahashi, and S. Yubuki
1988. Differences in geochemical features between Permian and Triassic cherts from the Southern Chichibu terrane, southwest Japan: REE abundances, major element compositions and Sr isotopic ratios. *Sedimentary Geology* 119:195–217.

Larsen, C.E.
1985. Lake Level, Uplift and Outlet Incision, the Nippising and Algoma Great Lakes. In *Quaternary Evolution of the Great Lakes,* edited by P.F. Kerrow and P.E. Calkin, pp. 63–77. Special Paper 30. Geological Association of Canada, St. John's.

Larsen, C.E.
1987. *Geological history of glacial Lake Algonquin and the Upper Great Lakes*. U.S. Geological Survey, Bulletin 1801.

Leader, J.M.
1988. *Technological continuities and specialization in prehistoric metalwork in the eastern United States.* PhD dissertation, University of Florida.

Lee, G.-A, A.M. Davis, D.G. Smith, and J.H. McAndrews
2004. Identifying fossil wild rice (*Zizania*) pollen from Cootes Paradise, Ontario: a new approach using scanning electron microscopy. *Journal of Archaeological Science* 31:411–421.

Lee, R.E.
2013. Projectile Points and Refitted Artifacts at the Sheguiandah Site: Their Position and Meaning. *Ontario Archaeology* 93: 6–31.

Lee, T.E.
1954a. The First Sheguiandah Expedition, Manitoulin Island, Ontario. *American Antiquity* 20:101–111.

1954b. The Discovery and Exploration of the Ancient Sheguiandah Site, Manitoulin Island. *Inland Seas* 10(3) 155–162.

1955. The Second Sheguiandah Expedition, Manitoulin Island, Ontario. *American Antiquity* 21:63–71.

1957. The Sheguiandah Site, *Canadian Field Archaeologist.*

1965. A Point Peninsula site, Manitoulin Island, Lake Huron. *Bulletin of the Massachusetts Archaeological Society*. 26(2):19–29. Attleboro, Mass.

Lemke, A. and J. O'Shea
2019. The End of an Era? Early Holocene Paleoindian Caribou Hunting in a Great Lakes Glacial Refugium. In *People and Culture in Ice Age Americas: New Dimensions in Paleoamerican Archaeology*, edited by R. Suárez and C.F. Ardelean, pp. 156–171. University of Utah Press, Salt Lake City.

Lennox, P.A., C. Dodd, and P. Timmins
1994. Ministry of Transportation Archaeological Investigations in the Southwest Region. *Annual Archaeological Report, Ontario (*New Series) 5:38–41. Ontario Heritage Foundation, Toronto.

Lepper, B.T., K.L. Leone, K.A. Jakes, L.L. Pansing, and W.H. Pickard
2014. Radiocarbon Dates on Textile and Bark Samples from the Central Grave of the Adena Mound 33RO1, Chillicothe, Ohio. *Midcontinental Journal of Archaeology* 39:1–21.

Levine, M.A.
1996. *Native Copper, Hunter-Gatherers, and Northeastern Prehistory.* PhD dissertation, University of Massachusetts Amherst.

1999. Native Copper in the Northeast: An Overview of Potential Sources Available to Indigenous Peoples. In *The Archaeological Northeast*, edited by M.A. Levine, K.E. Sassaman, and M. S. Nassaney, pp. 183–199. Native Peoples of the Americas, L. Weinstein, general editor. Bergin and Garvey, Westport, CT.

Lewis, C.F.M, S.M. Blasco, and P.L. Gareau
2005. Glacial isostatic adjustment of the Laurentian Great Lakes basin: using the empirical record of strandline deformation for reconstruction of early Holocene paleo-lakes and discovery of a hydrologically closed phase. *Géographie physique et Quaternaire* 59(2-3):187–210.

Lewis, C.F.M., C.W. Heil Jr., J.B. Hubeny, J.W. King, T.C. Moore Jr., and D.K. Rea
2007. The Stanley unconformity in Lake Huron basin: Evidence for a climate driven closed lowstand about 7900 ^{14}C BP, with similar implications for the Chippewa lowstand in Lake Michigan basin. *Journal of Paleolimnology* 37(3): 435–452.

Li, B.P., A. Greig, J.X. Zhao, K.D. Collerson, K.S. Quan, Y.H. Meng, and Z.L. Ma
2005. ICP-MS trace element analysis of Song dynasty porcelains from Ding, Jiexiu and Guantai kilns, north China. *Journal of Archaeological Science* 32(2):251–259.

Li, B.-P., J.-X Zhao, K.D. Collerson, and A. Greig
2003. Application of ICP-MS trace element analysis in study of ancient Chinese ceramics. *Chinese Science Bulletin* 48: 1219–1224.

Libby, W.F., E.C. Anderson, and J.R. Arnold
1949. Age determination by radiocarbon content: world-wide assay of natural radiocarbon. *Science* 109(2827):227–228.

Liu, K.-B.
1990. Holocene Paleoecology of the Boreal Forest and Great Lakes-St. Lawrence Forest in Northern Ontario. *Ecological Monographs* 60:179–212.

Long, D.G.F.
2004. The tectonostatigraphic evolution of the Huronian basement and the subsequent basin fill: geological constraints on impact models of the Sudbury Event. *Precambrian Geology*, 129(3-4):203–223.

Long, D.G.F., P.J. Julig, and R.G.V. Hancock
2002. Characterization of Sheguiandah quartzite and other potential sources of quartzarenite artifacts in the Great Lakes region. In *The Sheguiandah Site: archaeological, geological and paleobotanical studies at a Paleoindian site on Manitoulin Island, Ontario*, edited by P.J. Julig, pp. 265–295. Mercury Series, Archaeological Survey of Canada Paper 161.

Long, D.G.F., B. Silveira, and P. Julig
2001. Chert analysis by infrared spectroscopy. Proceedings of the Canadian Archaeological Association. CD-ROM.

Long, D.G.F., and A.C. Colvine
1986. Geology of Huronian strata in part of the northwestern Cobalt Plain, including Sheard, Ogilvie, Amyot, Browning, Hodggets, Unwin, Lamoman and Leask townships, and parts of North Williams, Dufferin, Stull, Valin and Marshay Townships. Districts of Timiskaming and Sudbury. Ontario Geological Survey, Map P.3048, scale 1: 50 000.

Longacre, W.A.
1970. *Archaeology as Anthropology: A Case Study*. University of Arizona Press, Tucson.

1972. *Reconstructing Prehistoric Pueblo Societies*. University of New Mexico Press, Albuquerque.

Lopinot, N.H.
1987. Archaeobotany. In *Archaeology in the Mississippi River Floodplain at Sand Run Slough, Iowa*, edited by D.W. Benn, pp. 203–225. CAR-690. Center for Archaeological Research, Southwest Missouri State University, Springfield.

Loring, S.
1985. Boundary Maintenance, Mortuary Ceremonialism and Resource Control in the Early Woodland: Three Cemetery Sites in Vermont. *Archaeology of Eastern North America* 13:93–112.

Lovejoy, C.O.
1985. Dental wear in the Libben population: Its functional pattern and role in the determination of adult skeletal age at death. *American Journal of Physical Anthropology* 68:47–56.

Lovis, W.A., R.E. Donahue, and M. Holman
2005. Long-Distance Logistic Mobility as an Organizing Principle Among Northern Hunter-Gatherers: A Great Lakes Holocene System-Settlement System. *American Antiquity* 70:669–693.

Lovis, W.A. and R.I. MacDonald
1999. Archaeological Implications of Great Lakes Paleoecology at the Regional Scale. In *Taming the Taxonomy*, edited by R. F. Williamson and C. M. Watts, pp. 125–150. Eastendbooks, Toronto.

Lovis, W. and J. O'Shea
1993. Reconsideration of Archaeological Research Design in Michigan. *Michigan Archaeologist* 39(3):107–126.

Lovis, W.A. and J. Robertson
1989. Rethinking the Archaic Chronology of the Saginaw Valley, Michigan. *Midcontinental Journal of Archaeology* 14(2):226–260.

Loy, T.
1994. Residue Analysis of Artifacts and Burned Rock from the Mustang Branch and Barton Sites (41HY209 and 41HY202). In *Archaic and Late Prehistoric Human Ecology in the Middle Onion Creek Valley, Hays County, Texas. Volume 2: Topical Studies*, edited by R.A. Ricklis and M.B. Collins, pp. 607–627. Studies in Archeology 19, Texas Archaeological Research Laboratory, The University of Texas at Austin.

Luedtke, B.E.
1978. Chert sources and trace element analysis. *American Antiquity* 43:413–423.

1979. The identification of sources of chert artifacts. *American Antiquity* 44(4):744–757.

Lugenbeal, E.
1976. The Archaeology of the Smith Site: A Study of the Ceramics and Culture History of Minnesota Laurel and Black Duck. PhD dissertation in anthropology. University of Wisconsin, Madison.

1978. The Blackduck ceramics of the Smith Site (21kc3) and their implications for the history of Blackduck ceramics and culture in Northern Minnesota. *Midcontinental Journal of Archaeology* 3(1):45–68.

Lyford, C.
1943. *Ojibwa Crafts (Chippewa).* Branch of Education, Bureau of Indian Affairs, Department of the Interior, Washington, DC.

Lynott, M., editor
2009. *In the Footprints of Squier and Davis: Archaeological Fieldwork in Ross County, Ohio.* Midwest Archaeological Center Special Report No. 5. National Park Service, Lincoln, NE.

MacDonald, B.H.
1995. Searching for Gold: Reconstructing a Private Library - The Case of Dr. Robert Bell. *Canadian Bulletin of Medical History* 12:385–410.

MacDonald, B., W. Fox, L. Dubreuil, J. Beddard, and A. Pidruczny
2018. Iron Oxide Geochemistry in the Great Lakes Region (North America): Implications for Ochre Provenance Studies. *Journal of Archaeological Science Reports* 19:476–490.

MacDowell, M., editor
1999. *Gatherings: Great Lakes Basket and Box Makers.* Nokomis Learning Center and the Michigan State University Museum. Okemos and East Lansing, MI.

MacLeod, D.
1973. *Annual Review: Archaeology 72–73*. Research Report 1. Historical Sites Branch. Ontario Ministry of Natural Resources. Toronto.

MacNeish, R.
1958. *An Introduction to the Archaeology of Southeast Manitoba*. Bulletin 157. Anthropological Series No. 4. National Museum of Canada, Ottawa.

Mainville, A., and M.R. Craymer
2005. Present-day tilting of the Great Lakes region based on water level gauges. *Geological Society of America Bulletin* 117(7-8):1070–1080.

Malainey, M.E.
1997. The Reconstruction and Testing of Subsistence and Settlement Strategies for the Plains, Parkland and Southern boreal forest. Unpublished PhD thesis, University of Manitoba.

2007a. Chapter 7: Fatty Acid Analysis of Archaeological Residues: Procedures and Possibilities. In *Theory and Practice of Archaeological Residue Analysis*, edited by H. Barnard and J.W. Eerkens, pp.77–89. British Archaeological Reports International Series 1650. Oxford, UK.

2007b. Analysis of the Fatty Acid Compositions of Archaeological Pottery Residues from U.S. 60 Superior to Florence Junction Project Sites. Report prepared for Statistical Research Inc., Tucson.

Malainey, M.E., K.L. Malisza, R. Przybylski, and G. Monks
2001a. The Key to Identifying Archaeological Fatty Acid Residues. Paper presented at the 34th Annual Meeting of the Canadian Archaeological Association, Banff, Alberta.

Malainey, M.E., R. Przybylski, and G. Monks
2000a. The identification of archaeological residues using gas chromatography and applications to archaeological problems in Canada, United States and Africa. Paper presented at The 11th Annual Workshops in Archaeometry, State University of New York at Buffalo.

2000b. Refining and testing the criteria for identifying archaeological lipid residues using gas chromatography. Paper presented at the 33rd Annual Meeting of the Canadian Archaeological Association, Ottawa.

2000c. Developing a General Method for Identifying Archaeological Lipid Residues on the Basis of Fatty Acid Composition. Paper presented at the Joint Midwest Archaeological & Plains Anthropological Conference, Minneapolis, MN.

Malainey, M.E., R. Przybylski, and B. L. Sherriff
1999a. The Fatty Acid Composition of Native Food Plants and Animals of Western Canada. *Journal of Archaeological Science* 26:83–94.

1999b. The Effects of Thermal and Oxidative Decomposition on the Fatty Acid Composition of Food Plants and Animals of Western Canada: Implications for the Identification of archaeological vessel residues. *Journal of Archaeological Science* 26:95–103.

1999c. Identifying the former contents of Late Precontact Period pottery vessels from Western Canada using gas chromatography. *Journal of Archaeological Science* 26(4): 425–438.

2001b. One Person's Food: How and Why Fish Avoidance May Affect the Settlement and Subsistence Patterns of Hunter-Gatherers. *American Antiquity* 66(1):141–161.

Mandrak, N.E. and E.J. Crossman
1992. *A Checklist of Ontario Freshwater Fishes*. Royal Ontario Museum, Toronto, Ontario.

Manitowabi, D. and P. Julig
2010. 37th Annual Symposium of the Ontario Archaeological Society, Killarney, Ontario: Friend or Foe? A Dialogue on the Aboriginal-Archaeological Relationship I, II.

Mann, R.W., R.L. Jantz, W.M. Bass, and P.S. Willey
1991. Maxillary Suture Obliteration: A Visual Method for Estimating Skeletal Age. *Journal of Forensic Sciences* 36(3):781–791.

Marchbanks, M.L.
1989. Lipid Analysis in Archaeology: An Initial Study of Ceramics and Subsistence at the George C. Davis Site. Unpublished master's thesis, The University of Texas at Austin.

Marchbanks, M.L. and J.M. Quigg
1990. Appendix G: Organic Residue and Phytolith Analysis. In *Phase II Investigations at Prehistoric and Rock Art Sites, Justiceburg Reservoir, Garza and Kent Counties, Texas, Volume II*, by D.K. Boyd, J.T. Abbott, W.A. Bryan, C.M. Garvey, S.A. Garvey, and R.C. Fields. pp. 496–519. Reports of Investigations No. 71. Prewitt and Associates, Inc, Austin.

Marlow, G.
1999. Year One: Radiocarbon Dating and American Archaeology, 1947–1948. *American Antiquity* 64(1):9–32.

Martin, S.R.
1985. Models of Change in the Woodland Settlement of the Northern Great Lakes Region. PhD dissertation, Michigan State University.

1989. A Reconsideration of Aboriginal Fishing Strategies in the Northern Great Lakes Region. *American Antiquity* 54(3):594–604.

1993. 20KE20: Excavations at a Prehistoric Copper Workshop. *The Michigan Archaeologist* 39(3-4):127–193.

1994. A Possible Bead Maker's Kit from America's Lake Superior Copper District. *Beads: Journal of the Society of Bead Researchers* 6:49–60.

1999. *Wonderful Power: the story of ancient copper working in the Lake Superior Basin.* Wayne State University Press, Detroit.

Martin, T.J.
1980. Animal remains from the Winter Site, A Middle Woodland Occupation in Delta County, Michigan. *The Wisconsin Archeologist* 61(1):91–99.

Maslowski, R.E.
1996. Cordage Twist and Ethnicity. In *A Most Indispensable Art: Native Fiber Industries from Eastern North America*, edited by J.B. Petersen, pp. 88–99. University of Tennessee Press, Knoxville.

Mason, R.J.
1966. *Two Stratified Sites on the Door Peninsula of Wisconsin* Anthropological Papers of the University of Michigan Museum of Anthropology, No. 26. Ann Arbor.

1967. The North Bay Component at the Porte des Morts Site, Door County, Wisconsin. *The Wisconsin Archeologist* 48(4):267–345.

1969. Laurel and North Bay: Diffusional Networks in the Upper Great Lakes. *American Antiquity* 34(3):295–302.

1970. Hopewell, Middle Woodland, and the Laurel Culture: A Problem in Archaeological Classification. *American Anthropologist* 72(4):802–815.

1981. *Great Lakes Archaeology*. Academic Press, New York.

1991. Rock Island and the Laurel Cultural Frontier in Northern Lake Michigan. *Midcontinental Journal of Archaeology* 16(1):118–155.

1992. Compilation of Door Peninsula Radiocarbon Dates. *The Wisconsin Archeologist* 73(3-4):111–117.

2007. *Inconstant Companions: Archaeology and North American Indian Oral Traditions.* University of Alabama Press, Tuscaloosa.

Matson, F.
1951. Ceramic Technology as an Aid to Cultural Interpretation: Techniques and Problems. In *Essays in Archaeological Methods*, edited by J.B. Griffin, pp. 102–127. Anthropological Papers of the University of Michigan Museum of Anthropology, No.8. Ann Arbor.

McAndrews, J.H.
1969. Paleobotany of a wild rice lake in Minnesota. *Canadian Journal of Botany* 47:1671–1679.

1984. Late Quaternary vegetation history of Rice Lake, Ontario, and the McIntyre archaeological site. *Archaeological Survey of Canada Paper* 26:161–189.

McAndrews, J.H., A.A. Berti and G. Norris
1973. *Key to the Quaternary pollen and spores of the Great Lakes Region.* Royal Ontario Museum Life Sciences Miscellaneous Publication.

McCarthy, F. and J. McAndrews
2012. Early Holocene drought in the Laurentian Great Lakes basin caused hydrologic closure of Georgian Bay. *Journal of Paleolimnology* 47:411–428.

McCarthy, F., J. McAndrews, and E. Papangelakis
2015. Paleoenvironmental Context for Early Holocene Caribou Migration on the Alpena-Amberley Ridge. In *Caribou Hunting in the Upper Great Lakes: Archaeological, Ethnographic, and Paleoenvironmental Perspectives*, edited by E. Sonnenburg, A. Lemke, and J. O'Shea, pp. 13–30. Memoirs of the University of Michigan Museum of Anthropology, No. 57. Ann Arbor.

McGhee, R. and J.A. Tuck
1975. An Archaic Sequence in the Strait of Belle Isle, Labrador. National Museum of Man, Archaeological Survey of Canada, Mercury Series 34.

McManamon, F., A. Cordell, K. Lightfoot, and G. Milner, editors
2009. *Archaeology in America: An Encyclopedia*. Greenwood Press, Westport, London.

McMullen, A.
1990. Many Motives: Change in Northeastern Native Basket Making. In *The Art of Narive American Basketry: A Living Legacy*, edited by F.W. Porter, pp. 45–78. Greenwood Press, New York.

McPherron, A.L.
1967. *The Juntunen Site and the Late Woodland Prehistory of the Upper Great Lakes Area.* Anthropological Papers of the University of Michigan Museum of Anthropology, No. 30. Ann Arbor.

Meehan, A.
2008. Spatial Analysis of Fire Cracked Rock (FCR) at the Speigel Site (BlHj-1). Honours thesis for bachelor's in anthropology, Anthropology Department, Laurentian University, Sudbury, Canada.

Menke, K.T.
1828. Synopsis methodica molluscorum generum omnium et specierum eorum, quae in Museo Menkeana adservantur: cum synonymia critica et novarum specierum diagnosibus. *G. Uslar, Pyrimonti*: 91.

Meyer, D.
1983. Saskatchewan Laurel: An Overview. *Saskatchewan Archaeology* 4:3–24.

Middleton, A.P., I.C. Freestone, and M.N. Leese
1985. Textural Analysis of Ceramic Thin Sections: Evaluation of Grain Sampling Procedures. *Archaeometry* 27(1):64–74. https://doi.org/10.1111/j.1475-4754.1985.tb00348.x

Miller, A.
2011. Le site BiFw-6, au carrefour des influences culturelles: Nouveau regard sur le Sylvicole moyen de la vallée de l'Outaouais. *Archéologiques* 24:103–114.

Mills, W.C.
1909. Explorations of the Seip Mound. *Ohio Archaeological and Historical and Historical Quarterly* 25:262–398.

1922. Exploration of the Mound City Group. *Ohio Archaeological and Historical Society Quarterly*. 31:422–584.

Milne, S.B., A. Hamilton, and M. Fayek
2001. Combining Visual and Geochemical Analyses to Source Chert on Southern Baffin Island, Arctic Canada. *Geoarchaeology* 24(4):429–449.

Milner, C.M.
1998. Ceramic Style, Social Differentiation, and Resource Uncertainty in the Late Prehistoric Upper Great Lakes. PhD dissertation, University of Michigan.

Milner, C.M. and J.M. O'Shea
1998. The Socioeconomic role of Late Woodland Enclosures in Northern Lower Michigan. In *Ancient Earthen Enclosures of the Eastern Woodlands*, edited by R.C. Mainfort and L.P. Sullivan, pp. 181–201. University Press of Florida, Gainesville.

Miner, H.
1936. The importance of textiles in the archaeology of the Eastern United States. *American Antiquity* 1:181–192.

Mitchell, B.M.
1963. Occurrence of Overall Corded Pottery in the Upper Ottawa Valley, Canada. *American Antiquity* 29(1):114–115.

Molto, J.E.
1979. *Saugeen Osteology: The Evidence of the Second Cemetery at the Donaldson Site*. Bulletin 14. Museum of Indian Archaeology at the University of Western Ontario, London, Ontario.

1983. *Biological Relationships of Southern Ontario Woodland Peoples: The Evidence of Discontinuous Cranial Morphology*. Mercury Series. National Museum of Man, Ottawa.

Molyneaux, B.
1983. *The Study of Prehistoric Sacred Places: Evidence from Lower Manitou Lake.* Archaeology Paper 2. Royal Ontario Museum, Toronto.

Monaghan, G. and W. Lovis
2005. *Modeling Archaeological Site Burial in Southern Michigan: A Geoarchaeological Synthesis*. Michigan State University Environmental Research Series, Vol. 1.

Moorehead, W.K.
1922. *A Report on the Archaeology of Maine*. Andover Press, Andover, MA.

Morgan, R.
1952. Ohio Archaeology. In *Archaeology of the Eastern United States*, edited by J.B. Griffin. University of Chicago Press, Chicago.

Morrill, R.L.
1970. The Shape of Diffusion in Time and Space. *Economic Geography* 46 (2). Reissued in 1973 as Warner Modular Reprint 440:1–10.

Morrow, C.A., J.M. Elam, and M.D. Glascock
1992. The use of blue-grey chert in Midwestern prehistory. *Midcontinental Journal of Archaeology* 17(2):166–197.

Morrow, J.E.
1995. Clovis projectile point manufacture: a perspective from the Ready/Lincoln Hills site 11JY46, Jersey County, Illinois. *Midcontinental Journal of Archaeology* 20(2).

Morse, D.
1963. *The Steuben Village and Mounds: A Multi-Component Late Hopewell Site in Illinois*. Anthropological Papers of the University of Michigan Museum of Anthropology, No. 30. Ann Arbor.

Mortimer, B.J.
2012. Whose Pot Is This? Analysis of Middle to Late Woodland Ceramics from the Kitchikewana Site, Georgian Bay Islands National Park of Canada. Unpublished master's thesis, Department of Anthropology, Trent University, Peterborough, Ontario.

Morton, J.K. and J.M. Venn
1984. *The Flora of Manitoulin Island and the Adjacent Islands of Lake Huron, Georgian Bay and the North Channel*. 2nd ed. University of Waterloo Biology Series, No. 40. Waterloo, Ontario. (Reprinted 2000, 3rd ed.)

Mullet, A.N.
2009. Paleoindian mobility ranges predicted by the distribution

of projectile points made of Upper Mercer and Flint Ridge flint. Master's thesis, Kent State University, Ohio.

Munsell Color Company, Inc.
1954. Munsell Soil Color Charts, 1954 edition. Baltimore.

Munson, P.J., P. Parmalee, and R. Yarnell
1971. Subsistence Ecology of Scovill, a Terminal Middle Woodland Village. *American Antiquity* 36(4):410–431.

Murray, R.W., M.R. Buchholtz ten Brink, D.C. Gerlach, G.P. Russ, III, and D.L. Jones
1991. Rare earth, major and trace elements in chert from the Franciscan Complex and Monterey Group, California: Assessing REE sources to fine-grained marine sediments. *Geochimica et Cosmochimica Acta* 55:1875–1895.

Murray, R.W., D.L. Jones, and M.R. Buchholtz ten Brink
1992. Diagenetic formation of bedded chert: Evidence from chemistry of the chert-shale couplet. *Geology* 20:271–274.

Myers, T.P.
1976. Defended Territories and No-man's Lands. *American Anthropologist* 78(2):354–356.

Nadar, F.H., A-F.M. Abdel-Rahman, and A.T. Haidar
2006. Petrographic and chemical traits of Cenomanian platform carbonates (central Lebanon): implications for depositional environments. *Cretaceous Research* 27:689–706.

Nassaney, M.S. and K.E. Sassaman, editors
1995. *Native American Interactions: Multiscalar Analyses and Interpretations in the Eastern Woodlands*. University of Tennessee Press, Knoxville.

Neiburger, E.J.
1987a. Did Midwest Precolumbian Indians Cast Metal? *Central States Archaeological Journal* 34(2):60–74.

1987b. Isotope Radiography of the Largest Prehistoric Copper Celt. *North American Archaeologist* 10(1):55–61.

1991. Melted Copper from the Archaic Midwest. *North American Archaeologist* 12(4):351–360.

Nelson, B., editor
1985. *Decoding Prehistoric Ceramics*. Southern Illinois University Press, Carbondale.

Nelson, M.
1991. The study of technological organization. *Archaeological Method and Theory* 3:57–100.

Nolan, K.C., M.A. Hill, M.F. Seeman, E. Olson, E. Butcher, S. Chavali, N. Hillard, and L. Dussubieux
2016. Scale and Community in Hopewell Networks (SCHoN): Summary of Preliminary Results. Paper presented at Hopewell Research in the Twenty-first Century: Ohio and Beyond, May 13 and 14, 2016, Chillicothe, Ohio.

Norder, J.W.
2003. Marking Place and Creating Space in Northern Algonquian Landscapes: The Rock-art of the Lake of the Woods Region, Ontario. Unpublished PhD dissertation in anthropology, University of Michigan.

Nyakairu, G.W.K. and C. Koeberl
2001. Mineralogical and chemical composition and distribution of rare earth elements in clay-rich sediments from central Uganda. *Geochemical Journal* 35:13–28.

O'Brien, M.J. and R.L. Lyman
2001. *Setting the Agenda for American Archaeology: The National Research Council Conferences of 1929, 1932, and 1935*. Classics of Southeastern Archaeology. University of Alabama Press, Tuscaloosa.

O'Hear, A.
1998. Lantana Beads: Gender Issues in their Production and Use. In *Beads and Bead Makers: Gender, Material Culture and Meaning,* edited by L.D. Sciama and J.B. Eicher. Berg, Oxford.

Olofsson, A., and I. Rodushkin
2011. Provenancing flint artefacts with ICP–MS using REE signatures and Pb isotopes as discriminants: preliminary results of a case study from northern Sweden. *Archaeometry* 53:1142–1170.

O'Shea, J.M.
1996. *Villagers of the Maros: Portrait of an Early Bronze Age Society*. Plenum Press, New York.

O'Shea, J., A. Lemke, B. Nash, E. Sonnenburg, J. Ferguson, A. Nyers, and D. Riebe
2021. Central Oregon obsidian from a submerged early Holocene archaeological site beneath Lake Huron. *PLOS One* 16(5): e0250840. DOI: 10.1371/journal.pone.0250840.

Otto, M. and B. Redmond, editors
2008. *Transitions: Archaic and Early Woodland Research in the Ohio Country.* Ohio University Press, Athens.

Ozker, D.
1982. *An Early Woodland Community at the Schultz Site 20SA2 in the Saginaw Valley and the Nature of the Early Woodland Adaptation in the Great Lakes Region.* Anthropological Papers

of the University of Michigan Museum of Anthropology, No. 70. Ann Arbor.

Pacheco, P., editor
1996. *View From the Core: A Synthesis of Ohio Hopewell Archaeology*. Ohio Archaeological Council, Columbus.

Page, L.M. and B.M. Burr
1991. *Freshwater Fishes*. Houghton Mifflin, New York.

Parsons, J.R.
1972. Archaeological Settlement Patterns. *Annual Review of Anthropology* 1:127–150.

Patrick, M., A.J. de Konig and A.B. Smith
1985. Gas Liquid Chromatographic Analysis of Fatty Acids in Food Residues from Ceramics Found in the Southwestern Cape, South Africa. *Archaeometry* 27(2):231–236.

Patterson, D.K.
1984. *A Diachronic Study of Dental Paleopathology and Attritional Status of Prehistoric Ontario Pre-Iroquois and Iroquois Populations*. Mercury Series. National Museum of Man, Ottawa.

Pauketat, T.R.
2001. *The Archaeology of Traditions: Agency and History Before and After Columbus.* University of Florida Press, Tallahassee.

Peebles, C.S. and S. Kus
1977. Some archaeological correlates of ranked societies. *American Antiquity* 42:421–448.

Penney, D.W.
1985. The Archaic Period. In *Ancient Art of the American Woodland Indians*, edited by D.S. Brose, J.A. Brown, and D.W. Penney, pp. 15–42. Harry N. Abrams Inc., New York.

Perkins, G.H.
1873. On an Ancient Burial Ground in Swanton, Vermont. Proceedings of the American Association for the Advancement of Science, Report of the 22nd Annual Meeting, pp. 76–100.

Perry, J.B.
1868. On the Swanton Site. *Proceedings of the Boston Society of Natural History* 17:219–222.

Petersen, J.B.
1996a. Introduction. In *A Most indispensable Art: Native Fiber Industries from Eastern North America,* edited by J.B. Petersen, pp. 6–24. University of Tennessee Press, Knoxville.

1996b. Fiber Industries from Northern New England: Ethnicity and Technological Traditions during the Woodland Period. In *A Most Indispensable Art: Native Fiber Industries from Eastern North America*, edited by J.B. Petersen, pp. 100–119. University of Tennessee Press, Knoxville.

Peterson, R.L.
1966. *The Mammals of Eastern Canada.* Oxford University Press, Toronto, Ontario.

Pfeiffer, S.
1977. *The Skeletal Biology of Archaic Populations of the Great Lakes Region*. National Museums of Canada, Ottawa.

1978a. Report of Skeletal Material from the Liahn II Site. In *Report of Excavations of the Early Woodland Liahn II Site (AcHo-2) and Test Excavations at the Peterkin Site (AcHo-9), Mitchell's Bay, Ontario*, edited by R.F. Williamson, pp. 138–146. Research Report Vol. 8. Museum of Indian Archaeology at the University of Western Ontario, London, Ontario.

1978b. Report of Skeletal Material from the Peterkin Site. In *Report of Excavations of the Early Woodland Liahn II Site (AcHo-2) and Test Excavations at the Peterkin Site (AcHo-9), Mitchell's Bay, Ontario*, edited by R.F. Williamson, pp. 147–162. Research Report Vol. 8. Museum of Indian Archaeology at the University of Western Ontario, London, Ontario.

1979. Archaic Population Affinities as Determined by Analysis of Cranial Morphology. *Ontario Archaeology* 32:35–41.

Phillips, P., J.A. Ford, and J.B. Griffin
1951. *Archaeological Survey of the Lower Mississippi Alluvial Valley, 1940–1947*. Papers of the Peabody Museum of American Archaeology and Ethnology, Vol. 25. Harvard University, Cambridge, MA.

Pilon, J-L.
2000. *Ramah Quartzite Bifaces from the Mouth of the Gatineau River.* Report for the Ottawa Chapter of the Ontario Archaeology Society. http://www.ottawaoas.ca/Chapters/chapters.htm. Date accessed: July 29, 2021.

Pilon, J-L. and W.A. Fox
2015. St. Charles or Dovetail Points in Eastern Ontario. *Arch Notes: Newsletter of the Ontario Archaeological Society* 20 (1):5–9.

Pitawanakwat, H., C. Peltier, and P. Julig
2004. Archaeological Survey of Point Grondine Reserve #3. Licence Report to the Ontario Ministry of Tourism, Culture and Sport.

Pleger, T.C.
2000. Old Copper and Red Ocher Social Complexity. *Midcontinental Journal of Archaeology* 25(2):169–190.

Pollock, J.W.
1975. Algonquian Culture Development and Archaeological Sequences in Northeastern Ontario. *Canadian Archaeological Association Bulletin* 7:1–53.

1976. *The Culture History of the Kirkland Lake District, Northeastern Ontario*. Mercury Series. Archaeological Survey of Canada, Paper 54. National Museum of Man.

1984. A technological analysis of Lake Abitibi bifaces. PhD thesis, Department of Anthropology, University of Alberta, Edmonton, Alberta.

Pollock, J.W., D.R. Ball, and D.G. MacLeod
1977. *Northern Ontario Fur Trade Posts Archaeological Survey – 1975*. Data Box Research Manuscript Series. Historical Planning and Research Branch, Ontario Ministry of Culture and Recreation. Toronto.

Pompeani, D.P., B. Steinman, M. Abbott, K. Pompeani, W. Reardon, S. DePasqual, and R. Mueller
2021. On the Timing of the Old Copper Complex in North America: A Comparison of Radiocarbon Dates from Different Archaeological Contexts. *Radiocarbon* 63(2):513–531.

Poulin, J.
2014. Analysis of Archaeological Residues in Four Ceramic Vessels for Canadian Museum of History, Gatineau, Quebec. Conservation Science Division, Report No. CSD 5207, CCI 127406. Canadian Conservation Institute Report. Ottawa.

Prahl, E.J., D.S. Brose, and D.M. Stothers
1976. Prehistoric Developments in the Western Basin. In *Late Prehistory of the Lake Erie Drainage Basin: A 1972 Symposium, Revised*, edited by D. Brose, pp. 251–281. Scientific Papers, Museum of Natural History, Cleveland.

Prehistoric Ceramics Research Group. 1995. *The study of later prehistoric pottery: general policies and guidelines for analysis and publication*. Prehistoric Ceramics Research Group, London.

Prentice, G.
1983. Cottage industries: concepts and implications. *Midcontinental Journal of Archaeology* 8:17–48.

Pretola, J.P.
2002. An Optical Mineralogy Approach to Northeastern Ceramic Diversity. In *Lasting Impression: Coastal, Lithic, and Ceramic Research in New England Archaeology*, edited by J.E. Kerber, pp. 179–205. Praeger, Westport.

Prufer, O.
1964. The Hopewell Cult. *Scientific American* 62:90–102.

Quigg, J.M., C. Lintz, S. Smith, and S. Wilcox
2000. *The Lino Site: A Stratified Late Archaic Campsite in a Terrace of the San Idelfonzo Creek, Webb County, Southern Texas*. Technical Report No. 23765, TRC Mariah Associates Inc., Austin. Texas Department of Transportation, Environmental Affairs Division, Archaeological Studies Program Report 20, Austin.

Quigg, J.M., M.E. Malainey, R. Przybylski, and G. Monks
2001. No bones about it: using lipid analysis of burned rock and groundstone residues to examine Late Archaic subsistence practices in South Texas. *Plains Anthropologist* 46(177):283–303.

Quinn, C.P.
2006. Exotics, Exchange, and Elites: Exploring Mechanisms of Movement of Prestige Goods in the Interior Northwest. *Journal of Northwest Anthropology* 41:207–224.

Ramsden, P.
1975. *Rocky Ridge: A Stratified Archaic Site near Inverhuron, Ontario*. Ministry of Culture and Recreation, Historical Planning and Research Branch, Research Report 7. Toronto.

Rapp Jr., G., E. Henrickson, and J. Allert
1990. Native copper sources of artifact copper in pre-Columbian North America. In *Archaeological Geology of North America*, edited by N.P. Lasca and J. Donahue, pp. 479–498. Centennial Special Vol. 4. The Geological Society of America.

Reber, E.A., S.N. Dudd, N.J. van der Merwe, and R.P. Evershed
2004. Direct detection of maize in pottery residue via compound specific stable carbon isotope analysis. *Antiquity* 78: 682–691.

Redmond, B.G., B.J. Ruby, and J.Burks, editors
2019. *Encountering Hopewell in the Twenty-First Century, Ohio and Beyond. Volume 1: Monuments and Ceremony*. University of Akron Press, Akron.

2020. *Encountering Hopewell in the Twenty-First Century, Ohio and Beyond. Volume 2: Settlements, Foodways, and Interaction*. University of Akron Press, Akron.

Reedy, C.L.
2008. *Thin-section petrography of stone and ceramic cultural materials*. Archetype Publications, London.

Regert, M.
2007. Chapter 6: Elucidating Pottery Function using a Multi-step Analytical Methodology combining Infrared Spectroscopy, Chromatographic Procedures and Mass Spectrometry. In *Theory and Practice of Archaeological Residue Analysis*,

edited by H. Barnard and J.W. Eerkens, pp.61–76. British Archaeological Reports International Series 1650. Oxford, UK.

Reid, C.S. and G. Rajnovich
1991. Laurel: A reevaluation of the spatial, social and temporal paradigms. *Canadian Journal of Archaeology* 15:193–234.

Rice, P.
1987. *Pottery Analysis: A Sourcebook*. University of Chicago Press.

Riederer, J.
2004. Thin Section Microscopy Applied to the Study of Archaeological Ceramics. *Hyperfine Interactions* 154:143–158.

Ritchie, W.A.
1937. Culture Influences from Ohio in New York Archaeology. *American Antiquity* 2(3):182–194.

1938. Certain Recently Explored New York Mounds and Their Probably Relation to the Hopewell Culture. *Researches and Transactions of the New York State Archeological Association* 8(3):103–142.

1944. *The Pre-Iroquoian Occupations of New York State*. Rochester Museum of Arts and Sciences, Memoir 1. Rochester.

1949. *An Archaeological Survey of the Trent Waterway of Ontario, Canada, and its Significance for New York Prehistory*. Rochester Museum of Arts and Sciences, Research Records No. 9. Rochester.

1953a. Point Peninsula Ceremonialism in the Light of Recent Discoveries in New York. *Eastern States Archaeological Federation* 11:7–8.

1953b. New Finds Relating to the Early Point Peninsula Burial Complex. *Eastern States Archaeological Federation* 12:8.

1955. *Recent Discoveries Suggesting an Early Woodland Burial Cult in the Northeast*. New York State Museum and Science Service Circular 40. The University of the State of New York, Albany.

1965. The Archaic in New York. *New York State Archaeological Association Bulletin* 52:2–12.

1980. *The Archaeology of New York State*. Harbor Hill Books, Harrison, NY.

Ritchie, W.A. and D.W. Dragoo
1959. The eastern dispersal of Adena. *American Antiquity* 25:43–50.

1960. *The Eastern Dispersal of Adena*. New York State Museum and Science Service Bulletin 379. The University of the State of New York, Albany.

Ritchie, W.A. and R.E. Funk
1973. *Aboriginal Settlement Patterns in the Northeast*. New York State Museum and Science Service Memoir 20. The University of the State of New York, Albany.

Ritchie, W.A. and R.S. MacNeish
1949. The Pre-Iroquoian Pottery of New York State. *American Antiquity* 15(2):97–124.

Ritzenthaler, R., editor
1957. The Old Copper Culture of Wisconsin. *The Wisconsin Archeologist* 38(4):185–329.

Ritzenthaler, R.E. and G.I. Quimby
1962. The Red Ocher Culture of the Upper Great Lakes and Adjacent Areas. Chicago Natural History Museum. *Fieldiana: Anthropology* 36(11):243–275.

Ritzenthaler, R.E. and P. Ritzenthaler
1983. *The Woodland Indians of the Western Great Lakes*. Natural History Press, Garden City, NY.

Robertson, D.A.
2001. Mourning, Curing, Feasting or Industry? The Interpretation of the Quinte and Perch Lake Mounds. *Ontario Archaeology* 72:38–63.

Robertson, D.A. and R.F. Williamson, editors
1992. Archaeological Master plan for the Township of Howland Ojibways of Sucker Creek Sheguiandah First Nation Manitoulin, Ontario. Archaeological Services Inc. (ASI). Toronto, Ontario.

Robertson, J.A. and K.D. Card
1972. *Geology and scenery north shore of Lake Huron region*. Ontario Division of Mines, Geological Guide Book 4.

Robertson, J., W. Lovis, and J. Halsey
1999. The Late Archaic: Hunters and Gatherers in an Uncertain Environment. In *Retrieving Michigan's Buried Past: The Archaeology of the Great Lakes State*, edited by J.R. Halsey. The Cranbrook Institute of Science, Bloomfield Hills, MI.

Robinson, J.H.
1904. *Readings in European History*. Volumes I and II. Ginn & Company, Boston.

Rogers, E.S. and E. Leacock
1981. Montagnais-Naskapi. In *Handbook of North American*

Indians, Vol. 6, edited by J. Helm, pp. 169–189. W. Sturtevant, general editor. Smithsonian Institution, Washington, DC.

Rogers, T.L.
2005. Determining the Sex of Human Remains through Cranial Morphology. *Journal of Forensic Sciences* 50(3):1–8.

Romain, W.F.
2015. *An Archaeology of the Sacred: Adena-Hopewell Astronomy and Landscape Archaeology*. Ancient Earthworks Project, Olmsted Township, Ohio.

Roper, D.C.
2013. Evaluating the Reliability of AMS Dates on Food Residue on Pottery from the Late Prehistoric Central Plains of North America. *Radiocarbon* 55(1):151–162. DOI: 10.2458/azu_js_rc.v55i1.16115

Ross, I.B.
1935. Remains of an Ancient People Found in Vermont. *The Vermonter* 40(12):227–228.

Rothschild, N.A.
1979. Mortuary Behavior and Social Organization at Indian Knoll and Dickson Mounds. *American Antiquity* 44(4): 658–675.

Rowe, J.S.
1972. *Forest Regions of Canada*. Department of the Environment. Canadian Forestry Service Publication No. 1300, Ottawa.

Sadler, D.C. and H.G. Savage
2003. *Birds from the Ground: The Record of Archaeology in Ontario*. Occasional Papers in Anthropology 15. Department of Anthropology, University of Trent, Peterborough, Ontario.

Sahlins, M.D.
1961. The Segmentary Lineage: An Organization of Predatory Expansion. *American Anthropologist* 63(2):322–345.

Sahlins, M.D. and E.R. Service, editors
1960. *Evolution and Culture*. University of Michigan Press, Ann Arbor.

Sauter, F., E.W.H. Hayek, W. Moche, and U. Jordis
1987. Betulin aus archäologischem Schwelteer. *Z. für Naturforsch* 42c (11–12):1151–1152.

Saxe, A.
1970. Social Dimensions of Mortuary Practices. PhD dissertation, University of Michigan.

Scheuer, L. and S. Black
2004. *The Juvenile Skeleton*. Elsevier, London.

Schlegel, I.
1970. Notes on the 1962 Excavation of the Schlegel Site. Unpublished.

Schroeder, D. and K. Ruhl
1968. Metallurgical Characteristics of North American Prehistoric Copper Work. *American Antiquity* 33(2):162–169.

Schulting, R., C. Bronk Ramsey, V. Bazaliiskii, and A. Weber
2015. Highly Variable Freshwater Reservoir Offsets found along the Upper Lena Watershed, Cis-Baikal, Southeast Siberia. *Radiocarbon* 57(4):581–593.

Sciama, L.D.
1998. Gender in the Making, Trading and Uses of Beads: An Introductory Essay. In *Beads and Bead Makers: Gender, Material Culture and Meaning*, edited by L.D. Sciama and J.B. Eicher. Berg, Oxford.

Scott, W.B. and E.J. Crossman
1973. *Freshwater Fishes of Canada.* Fisheries Research Board of Canada, Bulletin 184, Ottawa, Ontario.

Seeman, M.F.
1979a. Feasting with the Dead: Ohio Hopewell Charnal House Ritual as a Context for Redistribution. In *Hopewell Archaeology*, edited by D.S. Brose and N. Greber, pp. 39–46. Kent State University Press, Kent, Ohio.

1979b. *The Hopewell Interaction Sphere: The Evidence for Interregional Trade and Structural Complexity*. Prehistory Research Series 5(2). Indiana Historical Society.

1986. Adena "houses" and their implications for Early Woodland Settlement Models in the Ohio Valley. In *Early Woodland Archaeology*, edited by K.B. Farnsworth and T. Emerson, pp. 564–580. Center for American Archaeology, Kampsville, IL.

1991. When Words Aren't Enough: Hopewell Symbolism and the Use of Symbols at the GE. Mound. In *Native American Interactions: Multiscalar Analyses and Interpretations in the Eastern Woodlands,* edited by M.S. Nassaney and K.E. Sassaman, pp. 122–144. University of Tennessee Press, Knoxville.

2020. Twenty-First Century Hopewell. In *Encountering Hopewell in the Twenty-First Century, Ohio and Beyond. Volume 2: Settlements, Foodways, and Interaction.*, edited by B.G. Redmond, B.J. Ruby, and J.Burks. University of Akron Press, Akron.

Segal, I., N. Taacov, V. Zbenovich, and E. Barzilay
2005. Geochemical characterization of cherts and flint artifacts

from the Modi'in area. *Israeli Journal of Earth Science* 54: 229–236.

Service, E.R.
1962. *Primitive Social Organization: An Evolutionary Perspective*. Random House, New York.

Shackley, M.
1982. Gas Chromatographic Identification of a Resinous Deposit from a 6th Century Storage Jar and Its Possible Identification. *Journal of Archaeological Science* 9:305–306.

Shetrone, H.C.
1930. *The Mound-Builders: A Reconstruction of the Life of a Prehistoric American Race, Through Exploration and Interpretation of Their Earth Mounds, Their Burials, and Their Cultural Remains*. D. Appleton & Co., New York.

Shetrone, H.C. and E.F. Greenman
1931. Explorations of the Seip Group of Prehistoric Earthworks. *Ohio Archaeological and Historical Quarterly* 40:342–509.

Shields, G.A. and G.E. Webb
2004. Has the REE composition of seawater changed over geological time? *Chemical Geology* 204:103–107.

Skibo, J.M.
1992. *Pottery Function: A Use-Alteration Perspective*. Plenum Press, New York.

Smith, B.D.
1992. *Rivers of Change: Essays on Early Agriculture in Eastern North America*. Eliot Werner Publications, Clinton Corners, NY.

Smith, C.S.
1968. Metallographic Study of Early Artifacts Made from Native Copper. *Actes du XI Congres International d'Histoire de Sciences* VI:237–252.

Smith, E.E.
1990. Paleoindian economy and settlement patterns in the Wyandotte chert source area, unglaciated south-central Indiana. In *Research in Economic Anthropology: Early Paleoindian economies of eastern North America*, edited by K.B. Tankersley and B.L. Isaac, pp. 217–258. JAI Press, Inc., London.

Smith, N.M.
1965. The Saunders Group and subsequent Muldraugh Formation (Mississippian) in Indiana. *Indiana Geological Survey Report of Progress* 29.

Solomons, T.W.G.
1980. *Organic Chemistry*. John Wiley & Sons, Toronto.

Sonnenburg, E., A.K. Lemke, and J.M. O'Shea, editors
2015. *Caribou Hunting in the Upper Great Lakes: Archaeological, Ethnographic, and Paleoenvironmental Perspectives*. Memoirs of the University of Michigan Museum of Anthropology, No. 57. Ann Arbor.

Spaulding, A.C.
1952. The origin of Adena culture of the Ohio Valley. *Southwestern Journal of Anthropology* 8:260–268.

Speakman, R.J. and H. Neff
2005. *Laser ablation ICP–MS in archaeological research*, University of New Mexico Press, Albuquerque.

Spence, M.W.
1967. *A Middle Woodland Burial Complex in the St. Lawrence Valley*. Anthropology Papers 14. National Museum of Canada, Ottawa.

1982. The Social Context of Production and Exchange. In *Contexts for Prehistoric Exchange*, edited by J. Ericson and T. Earle, pp. 173–197. Academic Press, New York.

1986. Band Structure and Interaction in Early Southern Ontario. *Canadian Review of Physical Anthropology* 5(1):83–95.

Spence, M.W., W.D. Findlayson, and R.Pihl
1979. Hopewellian Influences on Middle Woodland Cultures in Southern Ontario. In *Hopewell Archaeology: The Chillicothe Conference*, edited by D.S. Brose and N. Greber, pp 115–121. Midcontinental Journal of Archaeology Special Papers 3. Kent State University Press.

Spence, M.W. and W.A. Fox
1979. The Bruce Boyd Site and Early Woodland in Ontario. Paper presented at the Canadian Archeological Association meeting, Vancouver.

1986. The Early Woodland Occupations of Southern Ontario. In *Early Woodland Archaeology*, edited by K.B. Farnsworth and T.E. Emerson, pp. 4–46. Volume 2. Center for American Archaeology, Kampsville, IL.

Spence, M.W. and J.R. Harper
1968. *The Cameron's Point Site*. Royal Ontario Museum, Art and Archaeology Division, Occasional Paper 12. University of Toronto.

Spence, M.W., R. Pihl, and J.E. Molto
1984. Hunter-Gatherer Social Group Identification: A Case Study from the Middle Woodland Southern Ontario. In

Exploring the Limits: Frontiers and Boundaries in Prehistory, edited by S. DeAtley and F. Findlow, pp. 117–142. British Archaeological Reports, International Series 223, Oxford.

Spence, M.W., R. Pihl, and C. Murphy
1990. Cultural Complexes of the Early and Middle Woodland Periods. In *The Archaeology of Southern Ontario to AD 1650*, edited by C.J. Ellis and N. Ferris, pp. 125–170. Occasional publication of the London Chapter of the Ontario Archaeological Society, Vol. 5. Ontario Archaeological Society, London, Ontario.

Squire, E.G. and E.H. Davis
1848. *Ancient Monuments of the Mississippi Valley*. Smithsonian Institution Contributions to Knowledge No 1.

Stafford, M.
1998. Norwood Revisited: A Preliminary Investigation of a Northern Michigan Chert Source. *The Michigan Archaeologist* 44(2):88–100.

Steckley, J.L.
1990. The Early Map "Nouvelle France": A Linguistic Analysis. *Ontario Archaeology* 51:17–29.

Stimpson, W.
1851. On Several New Species of Shells from the Northern Coast of New England. *Proceedings of the Boston Society of Natural History* 4:113–114.

Stiner, M.
1999. Trends in Paleolithic Mollusc Exploitation at Riparo Mochi (Balzi Rossi, Italy): Food and Ornaments from the Aurignacian Through Epigravettian. *Antiquity* 73:735–754.

Stoltman, J.B.
1962. A Proposed Method for Systematizing the Modal Analysis of Pottery and its Application to the Laurel Focus. Unpublished master's thesis, University of Minnesota, Minneapolis.

1973. *The Laurel Culture in Minnesota*. Minnesota Historic Archaeology Series 8. Minnesota Historical Society, St. Paul.

1978. Temporal Models in Prehistoric Archaeology from Eastern North America [with CA Comments and Replies] *Current Anthropology* 19(4):703–746.

1989. A Quantitative Approach to the Petrographic Analysis of Ceramic Thin Sections. *American Antiquity* 54(1):147–160.

1991. Ceramic Petrography as a Technique for Documenting Cultural Interaction: An Example from the Upper Mississippi Valley. *American Antiquity* 56(1):103–120. DOI: 10.2307/280976.

Storck, P.L.
1974. Two Probable Shield Archaic Sites in Killarney Provincial Park, Ontario. *Ontario Archaeology* 21:3–36.

1997. *The Fisher Site: Archaeological, Geological and Paleobotanical Studies at an Early Paleo-Indian Site in Southern Ontario, Canada*. Memoirs of the University of Michigan Museum of Anthropology, No. 30. Ann Arbor.

Stothers, D.M.
1974. The East Sugar Island Burial Mound. *Pennsylvania Archaeologist* 44:20–25.

Stothers, D.M. and T.J. Abel
1993. Archaeological Reflections on the Late Archaic and Early Woodland Time Periods in the Western Lake Erie Basin. *Archaeology of Eastern North America.* 21:25–110.

2008. Early Woodland Prehistory (1000 B.C. – A.D. 1) in the Western Lake Erie Drainage Basin. In *Transitions: Archaic and Early Woodland Research in the Ohio Country.*, edited by M.P. Otto and B.G. Redmond, pp. 79–116. Ohio University Press, Athens.

Struever, S.
1963. The Hopewell Interaction Sphere in Riverine-Western Great Lakes Culture History. In *Hopewellian Studies*, edited by J.R. Caldwell and R.L. Hall, pp. 85–106. Scientific Papers 12(6). Illinois State Museum, Springfield.

1965. Middle Woodland Culture History in the Great Lakes Riverine Area. *American Antiquity* 31(2):211.

Struever, S. and G.L. Houart
1972. An Analysis of the Hopewell Interaction Sphere. In *Social Exchange and Interaction*, edited by E.N. Wilmsen, pp. 47–80. Anthropological Papers of the University of Michigan Museum of Anthropology, No. 46. Ann Arbor.

Sullivan, A.P. and K.C. Rozen
1985. Debitage Analysis and Archaeological Interpretation. *American Antiquity* 50(4):755–779.

Sundick, R.I.
1978. Skeletal Material. Submitted to draft manuscript.

Taché, K.
2011a. *Structure and Regional Diversity of the Meadowood Interaction Sphere*. Memoirs of the University of Michigan Museum of Anthropology, No. 48. Ann Arbor.

2011b. New Perspectives on Meadowood Trade Items. *American Antiquity* 76(1):41–79.

Taché, K. and J. Hart
2013. Chronometric Hygiene of Radiocarbon Databases for Early Durable Cooking Vessel Technologies in Northeastern North America. *American Antiquity* 78(2):359–372.

Taylor, S.R. and S.H. McLennan
1985. *The Continental Crust: Its Composition and Evolution*. Blackwell, Oxford.

Telford, P.G. and G.A. Tarrant
1975. Paleozoic geology of Dunnville area, southern Ontario; Ontario Division of Mines, Preliminary Map P.988, scale 1:50 000.

Thompson, A.J. and K.A. Jakes
2005. Textile Evidence for Ohio Hopewell Burial Practices. *Southeastern Archaeology* 24:137–141.

Thor, K.
2006. *The Schlegel Site Report (BfGw-6)*. Unpublished undergraduate thesis. Laurentian University, Sudbury, Canada.

Torbenson, M., A. Aufderheide, and E. Johnson
1992. Punctured Human Bones of the Laurel Culture from Smith Mound Four, Minnesota. *American Antiquity* 57(3):506–514.

Torbenson, M., O. Langsjoen, and A. Aufderheide
1994. Laurel Culture Human Remains from Smith Mounds Three and Four. *Plains Anthropology* 39(150):429–444.

Trigger, B.G.
1990. Monumental Architecture: A Thermodynamic Explanation of Symbolic Behaviour. *World Archaeology* 22(2):119–132.

Trotter, M.
1970. Estimation of Stature from Intact Long Limb Bones. In *Personal Identification in Mass Disasters*, edited by T. D. Stewart, pp. 71–83. National Museum of Natural History, Washington, DC.

Trubitt, M.B.D.
2000. Mound building and prestige goods exchange: changing strategies in the Cahokia chiefdom. *American Antiquity*. 65:669–690.

2003. The Production and Exchange of Marine Shell Prestige Goods. *Journal of Archaeological Research* 11(3):243–277.

Turnbull, C.J.
1976. The Augustine site: a mound in the Maritimes. *Archaeology of Eastern North America* 4:50–62.

1986. *The McKinlay Collection: Another Middlesex Tradition Component from Red Bank, Northumberland County, New Brunswick*. Manuscripts in Archaeology. Department of Tourism, Recreation, and Heritage, Fredericton, New Brunswick.

Tyyska, A.E. and J.A. Burns
1973. *Archaeology from North Bay to Mattawa*. Research Report 2. Historical Sites Branch, Ontario Ministry of Natural Resources. Toronto.

Vanhaeren, M.
2005. Speaking with Beads: The Evolutionary Significance of Bead Making and Use. In *From Tools to Symbols, From Early Hominids to Modern Humans*, edited by F. d'Errico and L. Backwell. Wits University Press, Johannesburg.

Vanhaeren, M. and F. d'Errico
2006. Aurignacian Ethno-linguistic Geography of Europe Revealed by Personal Ornaments. *Journal of Archaeological Science* 33:1105–1128.

Varney, T.
1994. Report on the Osteological Analysis of Skeletal Material from the Hind Site. Manuscript on file. Ontario Heritage Museum, Toronto.

Varney, T. and S. Pfeiffer
1995. The People of the Hind Site. *Ontario Archaeology* 59:96–108.

Vennum, T.
1988. *Wild Rice and the Ojibway People*. Minnesota Historical Society, St. Paul.

Vernon, W.
1990. New archaeometallurgical perspectives on the Old Copper industry of North America. In *Archaeological Geology of North America*, Vol. 4., edited by N.P. Lasca and J. Donahue, pp. 499–512. Geological Society of America.

Versaggi, N.M.
1999. Regional Diversity within the Early Woodland of the Northeast. *Northeast Anthropology* 57:45–56.

Von Bitter, P.H. and B. Eley
1984. Balsam Lake Chert from the upper member of the Middle Ordovician Bobcaygeon Formation of Southern Ontario. *Canadian Journal of Archaeology* 8(2):135–148.

von den Driesch, A.
1976. *A Guide to the Measurement of Animal Bones from Archaeological Sites*. Peabody Museum Publications, Cambridge, MA.

Waiser, W.A.
2000. *Robert Bell (1841–1917)*. Dictionary of Canadian Biography Online, Volume XIV. University of Toronto/ Université Laval.

Walthall, J.A.
1981. *Galena and Aboriginal Trade in Eastern North America.* Scientific Papers 17. Illinois State Museum, Springfield.

Walthall, J.A. and E. Benchley
1987. The River L'Abbe Mission: A French Colonial Church for the Cahokia Illini on Monks Mound. *Studies in Illinois Archaeology No. 2*. Illinois Historic Preservation Agency, Springfield.

Watson, G.D.
1972. A Woodland Indian site at Constance Bay, Ontario. *Ontario Archaeology* 18:1–24.

Wayman, M.
1989. Native Copper: Humanity's introduction to metallurgy? In *All that glitters: Readings in Historical Metallurgy*, edited by M. Wayman, pp. 3–6. Friesen and Sons, Manitoba.

Wayman, M.L., J.C.H. King, and P.T. Craddock
1992. Analysis of the Copper Artifacts in the 'Squier and Davis' Collection, Museum of Mankind. In *Aspects of Early North American Metallurgy*, edited by M.L. Wayman, J.C.H. King, and P.T. Craddock, pp. 95–144. Occasional Paper No 79. Departments of Scientific Research and Ethnography, British Museum, London.

Webb, T.
1974. Corresponding Patterns of Pollen and Vegetation in Lower Michigan: A Comparison of Quantitative Data. *Ecology* 55:17–28.

Webb, W.S.
1942. The C and O mounds at Paintsville, sites Jo2 and Jo9, Johnson County, Kentucky. *University of Kentucky Reports in Anthropology and Archaeology* 5(2):341–349.

1974. *Indian Knoll*. University of Tennessee Press, Knoxville.

Webb, W.S. and R.S. Baby
1957. *The Adena People - No. 2.* Ohio Historical Society and Ohio State University Press, Columbus.

Webb, W.S. and C.E. Snow
1945. *The Adena People.* Reports in Anthropology and Archaeology Vol. 6. University of Kentucky, Lexington.

Webster, D.
1973. Nonceramic Artifacts from Laurel Culture Sites Excavated Prior to 1961. *Minnesota Prehistoric Archaeology Series* 8:94–111.

West, G.
(1929) 1970. *Copper: Its Mining and Use by the Aborigines of the Lake Superior Region*. Greenwood, Westport, CT.

Weston, J.L.
(1920) 1957. *From Ritual to Romance.* Cambridge University Press, Cambridge. (Reprinted by Dover Books, New York.)

Whallon, R.
1980. On the Monothetic Nature of "Traditional" Pottery Types: A Contribution from the Analysis of Owasco and Iroquoian Ceramics. Proceedings of the 1979 Iroquois Pottery Conference Rochester Museum and Science Center Research Records 13:9–20.

Whitford, A.C.
1941. Textile Fibers Used in Eastern Aboriginal North America. *Anthropological Papers of the Museum of Natural History* 38:5–21.

Wiessner, P.
1983. Style and Social Information in Kalahari San Projectile Points. *American Antiquity* 48(2):253–276.

Wilford, L.A.
1950. The Prehistoric Indians of Minnesota: Some Mounds of the Rainy River Aspect. *Minnesota History* 3(3):161–171.

1955. A Revised Classification of the Prehistoric Cultures of Minnesota. *American Antiquity* 21(2):130–142.

Wilkinson, R.G.
1971. *Prehistoric Biological Relationships in the Great Lakes Region.* Anthropological Papers of the University of Michigan Museum of Anthropology, No. 43. Ann Arbor.

Willey, G.R. and P. Phillips
1958. *Method and Theory in American Archaeology.* University of Chicago Press, Chicago.

Willey, G. and J. Sabloff
1980. *A History of American Archaeology.* W.H. Freeman Publishers, New York.

William, H.B., E. Atherton, T.C. Buschbach, C. Collinson, J.C. Frye, M.E. Hopkins, J.A. Lineback and J.A. Simon
1975. *Handbook of Illinois stratigraphy*. Illinois State Geological Survey, Bulletin 95.

Willoughby, C.C.
1903. Primitive Metal Working. *American Anthropologist* 5:55–57.

1935. *Antiquities of the New England Indians*. Peabody Museum of American Archaeology and Ethnology, Cambridge, MA.

Wilmeth, R.
1978. *Canadian Archaeological Radiocarbon Dates*. University of Ottawa Press, Mercury Series # 77. National Museum of Man.

Wilson, D.
1890. Trade and Commerce in the Stone Age. Proceedings and Transactions of the Royal Society Canada 1989. Section II: 59–87. Dawson Brothers, Montreal.

Wilson, J.A.
1990. The Boresma Site: A Middle Woodland Basecamp in the Thames River Valley. Master's thesis, Department of Anthropology, McMaster University, Hamilton.

Wintemberg, W.J.
1928. *Artifacts from Ancient Graves and Mounds in Ontario*. Proceedings and Transactions (Series 3) 22:175–206. Royal Society of Canada, Ottawa.

Winters, H.D.
1968. Value Systems and Trade Cycles of the Late Archaic in the Midwest. In *New Perspectives in Archaeology*, edited by S.R. and L.R. Binford, pp. 175–221. Aldine Publishing: Chicago.

Wisseman, S., D. Moore, R. Hughes, M. Hynes, and T. Emerson. 2002. Mineralogical Approaches to Sourcing Pipes and Figurines from the Eastern Woodlands, U.S.A. *Geoarchaeology: An International Journal* 17(7):689–715.

Wobst, H.M.
1977. Stylistic Behavior and Information Exchange. In *For the Director: Research Essays in Honor of James B. Griffin*, edited by C.E. Cleland, pp. 317–342. Anthropological Papers of the University of Michigan Museum of Anthropology, No. 61. Ann Arbor.

Wright, J.V.
1967. *The Laurel Tradition and the Middle Woodland Period*. Anthropological Series 79. Bulletin 217. National Museum of Canada, Ottawa.

1968. Field Notes:1968, Ontario: Lake Attiwapiskat, Donaldson, Knechtel, Georgian Bay, W. Quebec. Transcript. Ms. 1659, Vol. 1. On file, Canadian Museum of Civilization. Hull, Quebec.

1972a. *The Knechtel I Site, Bruce County, Ontario*. Mercury Series No. 4, National Museum of Man. Ottawa.

1972b. *Ontario Prehistory: An Eleven-Thousand-Year Archaeological Outline.* National Museum of Canada, National Museum of Man, Ottawa.

1974. Archaeological Taxonomy: Apples and Oranges. *Bulletin of the Canadian Archaeological Association* 6:206–209.

1987. Prehistoric Trade: spread of the Adena Burial cult. In *Historical Atlas of Canada, Volume 1 (From the Beginning to 1800)*, edited by R.C. Harris. Plate 14. University of Toronto Press, Toronto.

1995. *A History of the Native People of Canada: Volume I (10,000 to 1,000 B.C.)*. Mercury Series, Archaeological Survey of Canada. Canadian Museum of Civilization, Hull, Quebec.

1999. *A History of the Native People of Canada: Volume II (1,000 B.C. – A.D. 500)*. Mercury Series, Archaeological Survey of Canada. Canadian Museum of History, Quebec, Ottawa.

Wright, J.V. and J.E. Anderson
1963. *The Donaldson Site*. Bulletin 184. National Museum of Canada, Ottawa.

Wright, K. and A. Garrard
2003. Social Identities and the Expansion of Stone Bead-Making in Neolithic Western Asia: New Evidence from Jordan. *Antiquity* 77:267–284.

Yarnell, R.A.
1964. *Aboriginal Relationships Between Culture and Plant Life in the Upper Great Lakes Region*. Anthropological Papers of the University of Michigan Museum of Anthropology, No. 23. Ann Arbor.

Yerkes, R.W.
1983. Microwear, Microdrills, and Mississippian Craft Specialization. *American Antiquity* 48(3):499–518.

2002. Hopewell Tribes: A Study of Middle Woodland Social Organization in the Ohio Valley. In *The Archaeology of Tribal Societies*, edited by W.A. Parkinson, pp. 227–245. International Monographs in Prehistory, Ann Arbor.

Young, G.M., D.G.F. Long, C.M. Fedo, and H.W. Nesbitt
2001. Paleoproterozoic Huronian basin: product of a Wilson cycle punctuated by glaciations and a meteorite impact. *Sedimentary Geology* 141-142:233–254.

Yu, Z. and J.H. McAndrews
1994. Holocene water levels at Rice Lake, Ontario, Canada: sediment, pollen and plant macrofossil evidence. *The Holocene* 4:141–152.